# Large-Scale Systems

NORTH-HOLLAND SERIES IN
# SYSTEM SCIENCE
# AND ENGINEERING
Andrew P. Sage, *Editor*

# Large-Scale Systems
## Modeling and Control

Series Volume 9

## Mohammad Jamshidi

Department of Electrical and Computer Engineering
The University of New Mexico, Albuquerque

**NORTH-HOLLAND**
New York · Amsterdam · Oxford

Elsevier Science Publishing Co., Inc.
52 Vanderbilt Avenue, New York, New York 10017

Sole distributors outside the United States and Canada:

Elsevier Science Publishers B.V.
P.O. Box 211, 1000 AE Amsterdam, The Netherlands

Library of Congress Cataloging in Publication Data

Jamshidi, Mohammad.
    Large-scale systems.
    (North-Holland series in system science and engineering; 9)

    Includes bibliographies and indexes.
    1. Large scale systems. I. Title. II. Series.
QA402.J34   1983        003        82-8158
ISBN 0-444-00706-7              AACR2

Manufactured in the United States of America

*To three*
*who meant the most in my life*
*My Mother*
*My Wife Jila*
*My Brother Ahmad*

# Contents

# Preface

Many real-life problems facing nations of the world are brought forth by present-day technology and by societal and environmental processes which are highly complex, "large" in dimension, and stochastic in nature. The notion of "large-scale" is a subjective one in that one may ask: How large is *large*? Many viewpoints have been presented on this issue. One viewpoint has been that a system is considered large in scale if it can be decoupled or partitioned into a number of interconnected subsystems for either computational or practical reasons. Another viewpoint considers "large-scale systems" to be simply those whose dimensions are so large that conventional techniques of modeling, analysis, control design, and optimization fail to give reasonable solutions with reasonable computational efforts.

Needless to say, many real problems are considered to be "large-scale" by nature and not by choice. In my opinion, two important attributes of large-scale systems are (i) they often represent complex, real-life systems and (ii) their hierarchical (multilevel) and decentralized information structures depict systems dealing with societal, business, and management organizations, the economy, the environment, data networks, electric power, transportation, aerospace (including space structures), water resources, and, last but not least, energy. As a result of these important properties and potential applications, several researchers have paid a great deal of attention to various facets of large-scale systems such as modeling, model reduction, control, stability, controllability, observability, optimization, and stabilization. These concepts have been applied to various problems and have helped with the creation of different notions of systems analysis, design, control, and optimization. Topics such as hierarchical control, decentralized control, estimation and filtering, model reduction, robust control, perturbation, and decomposition methods have appeared in leading control and system journals.

The topic of "large-scale systems" has been the subject of a few full-scale national and international conferences, including two IFAC Conferences on Large-Scale Systems (Udine, Italy, in 1976 and Toulouse, France, in 1980). An international symposium on large-scale systems sponsored by IEEE was held in Virginia Beach, Virginia, in October 1982. The subject has been partially treated at many national conferences, such as the annual IEEE Conference on Decisions and Control (CDC), the Joint Automatic Control Conference (JACC), and the American Control Conference (ACC). Relatively few books, however, have been published on the topic in any complete and extended detail. Noteworthy exceptions to this are *Dynamical Hierarchical Control* by M. G. Singh (North-Holland, 1977 and 1980), *Methodologies for Large-Scale Systems* by A. P. Sage (McGraw-Hill, 1977), *Large-Scale Dynamic Systems — Stability and Structure* by D. D. Šiljak (Elsevier North-Holland, 1978) and *Decentralised Control* by M. G. Singh (North-Holland, 1981). Perhaps a most encouraging outcome is the publication of the new journal *Large Scale Systems — Theory and Application* by North-Holland Publishing Company in 1980. Unfortunately, the book by A. P. Sage is one of very few books on large-scale systems written with the intention of actually communicating with instructors and students. This is probably justifiable, since many topics in large-scale systems theory are newly developed, and the subject matter has not found its way into the formal graduate education in system engineering. In fact, the Department of Electrical and Computer Engineering at the University of New Mexico is one of the few departments to offer a formal course in this area.

The purpose of this book is to present a balanced treatment of the large-scale systems by featuring past, present, and potential trends of the subject. An attempt is made to introduce the fundamental and more-or-less settled issues on the subject. The general theme throughout the book is algorithmic. Most of the theoretical concepts are stated with proofs, followed by an algorithm showing how to use the results. One or more numerical examples then illustrate the theoretical concept. A great majority of the numerical examples in the book were solved on an HP-9845 computer using BASIC, and several programs and subroutines were developed for that purpose. Because most problems of the book (denoted by a "C" in the problem sections) require the use of a computer, the interested reader may write directly to the author for a copy of the source programs at a nominal cost. A notable exception is Chapter 6, where more research-oriented topics are presented.

The book will address two main issues: (1) modeling and model decomposition and (2) fundamental concepts in optimum, near-optimum control, and systems properties such as stability, controllability, observability, pole assignment, and hierarchical and decentralized control. The detailed plan of the book is depicted on page xv.

Chapter 1 presents an introduction to large-scale systems, important classes such as hierarchical or multilevel control systems, and decentralized

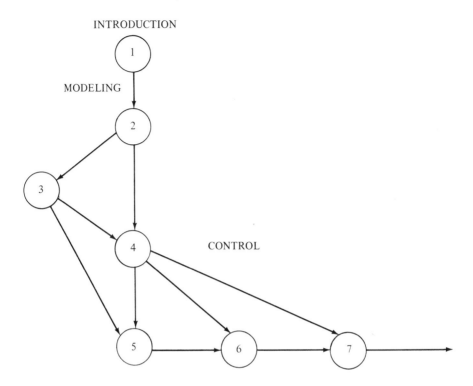

control systems are presented. Portions of this chapter, as well as other chapters, were inspired by the Special Issue on Large-Scale Systems of the *IEEE Transactions on Automatic Control* (April 1978), brought about by the fine efforts of Mike Athans, Nil Sandell and their colleagues. The majority of the models and control strategies is devoted to large-scale linear time-invariant continuous-time systems. However, several exceptions presented throughout deal with large-scale time-varying, nonlinear, time-delay, and discrete-time systems.

Models and model reduction of large-scale systems are treated in Chapters 2 and 3. Time-domain modeling schemes, such as aggregation, perturbation, and descriptive variable approaches, are discussed in Chapter 2. The survey of aggregation and perturbation methods presented here relies on the results of M. Aoki, E. J. Davison, P. V. Kokotović, R. E. Larson, D. L. Luenberger, W. R. Perkins, and many others. Model reductions of single-input–single-output and multiinput–multioutput systems in the frequency domain are given in Chapter 3. Several methods of model reduction are overviewed and accompanied with many numerical examples. The results of C. F. Chen, B. Friedland, T. C. Hsia, S. S. Lamba, A.S. Rao, A. S. S. R. Reddy, V. Seshadri, Y. Shamash, and L. S. Shieh, among many others, have been considered here.

Chapters 4 through 6 are concerned with control, analysis, design, and optimization of large-scale systems. Hierarchical control is taken up in

Chapter 4. Both the open- and closed-loop hierarchical control systems in continuous and discrete forms are treated. The material in this chapter is based on the works of A. P. Sage, M. G. Singh, A. Titli, and many others. In Chapter 5, decentralized control constitutes the main theme. Decentralized stabilization, the decentralized robust servomechanism problem, sequentially stable controllers and stochastic decentralized control are treated. This chapter relies heavily on the pioneer works of E. J. Davison, D. D. Šiljak, and others. Chapter 6 is concerned with the application of optimal control theory to large-scale linear, nonlinear, and time-delay systems. A number of near-optimum control schemes have been developed using, in part, the model reduction techniques of Chapters 2 and 3, hierarchical and decentralized control of Chapters 4 and 5, and such methods as parameter sensitivity, parameter imbedding, and linearization. A detailed discussion on the degradation of optimal performance index in each case is presented. The discussion concentrates, in part, on the results of M. Aoki, J. B. Cruz, Jr., E. J. Davison, P. V. Kokotović, M. G. Singh, and others.

The structural properties (stability, controllability, and observability) of large-scale systems are considered in Chapter 7. Both the Lyapunov and Input–Output stability approaches have been treated on an equal basis. In addition, the related notion of "connective" stability is introduced, and a comparative discussion on the main stability approaches is given. The controllability and observability of composite systems, including their relation with system connectability and structural controllability, are given. A substantial amount of material on stability stems from the results of pioneers in the field such as M. Araki, F. N. Bailey, L. T. Grujić, A. N. Michel, D. D. Šiljak, and others. Discussions on controllability and observability rely on the results of E. J. Davison, J. B. Pearson, B. Porter, and H. H. Rosenbrock, among others.

The instructor or the reader can use this book in several possible ways. Chapters 1, 2, 3, 5, and 7 may be used for analysis and control of large-scale systems. Optimization of large-scale systems can be treated by studying Chapters 1, 2, and 4, while their optimal control can be studied in Chapters 1, 2, 4, 5, and 6. Structural properties and modeling of large-scale systems are concentrated in Chapters 1 through 5 and 7. The book can be used as a text for a second-year course in optimal control of large-scale systems, optimization of large systems, or simply for studying special topics in large-scale systems. The manuscript has been used as the text for a second-year graduate course on large-scale systems at the Department of Electrical and Computer Engineering of the University of New Mexico. This book may also be of use to graduate students in electrical, system, and control engineering, as well as to qualified economics and business students. The book may also appeal to researchers in the field, since most topics treated present an up-to-date survey with references in each chapter.

The author is indebted to many people for their various contributions. Foremost, I would like to thank **Joe Cruz**, **Petar Kokotović**, and **Bill Perkins** (University of Illinois at Champaign-Urbana), who have been instrumental in my education in control and systems engineering. I would also like to thank **Peter Dorato** (Chairman of EECE Department at the University of New Mexico), and **Lotfi Zadeh** (University of California, Berkeley), who have always inspired me and have always been helpful in my career formation. I am especially grateful to the many researchers and workers in large-scale systems, without whose work this book could not have become a reality. In particular, I am indebted to **Ted Davison** (University of Toronto), **Drago Šiljak** (University of Santa Clara), **Madan Singh** (University of Manchester Institute of Technology), and **Andy Sage** (University of Virginia at Charlottesville), whose works on large-scale systems have been instrumental here. I am indebted to Andy Sage in yet another capacity, as the editor of Elsevier's System Science and Engineering Series, for which this book has been written, for his review of the manuscript.

I have been fortunate to have the benefit of cooperation of many co-researchers. Among them, I would like to thank Manu Malek-Zavarei (Bell Laboratories) and Ümit Özgüner (Ohio State University). This book, as a project, was motivated by the chairman of my department, Peter Dorato, who first suggested the establishment of a new course on the subject. For that I am thankful, and I appreciate his continuous encouragements. The encouragement and help from my colleague Shlomo Karni and former colleague Mehdi Etezadi (Arizona Public Service Company) are also appreciated. The use of the computer facilities at the University of New Mexico, especially the HP-9845 computers, and the assistance of their supervisor, my colleague Ruben Kelly, are especially appreciated. I am very thankful to Louise Calabro Schreiber, Elsevier's Senior Desk Editor, for her many valuable suggestions.

I am particularly indebted to many of my present and former students, especially Emil Kadlec (Sandia National Laboratories, Albuquerque, NM), Ching-An Lin (University of California, Berkeley), and Richard Owen (University of New Mexico) for two of the computer simulations in Chapter 4 and one in Chapter 6, and patience in the classroom. Last but not least the typing and editorial assistance of many who helped prepare the manuscript are appreciated. In particular, I would like to thank my own editorial assistant, Gladys Ericksen, for her excellent typing and patience with all the revisions and alterations of the manuscript. I would also like to thank Marilyn Smiel, Joan Lillie, and Mirium Arnold for their additional fine typing work.

M. Jamshidi

*May 10, 1982*
*Albuquerque, New Mexico*

# Large-Scale Systems

# Chapter 1
# Introduction to Large-Scale Systems

## 1.1 Historical Background

A great number of today's problems are brought about by present-day technology and societal and environmental processes which are highly complex, "large" in dimension, and stochastic by nature. The notion of "large-scale" is a very subjective one in that one may ask: How large is *large*? There has been no accepted definition for what constitutes a "large-scale system." Many viewpoints have been presented on this issue. One viewpoint has been that a system is considered large-scale if it can be decoupled or partitioned into a number of interconnected subsystems or "small-scale" systems for either computational or practical reasons (Ho and Mitter, 1976). Another viewpoint is that a system is large-scale when its dimensions are so large that conventional techniques of modeling, analysis, control, design, and computation fail to give reasonable solutions with reasonable computational efforts. In other words, a system is large when it requires more than one controller (Mahmoud, 1977).

Since the early 1950s, when classical control theory was being established, engineers have devised several procedures, both within the classical and modern control contexts, which analyze or design a given system. These procedures can be summarized as follows:

1. Modeling procedures which consist of differential equations, input–output transfer functions, and state-space formulations.
2. Behavioral procedures of systems such as controllability, observability, and stability tests, and application of such criteria as Routh–Hurwitz, Nyquist, Lyapunov's second method, etc.
3. Control procedures such as series compensation, pole placement, optimal control, etc.

The underlying assumption for all such control and system procedures has been "centrality" (Sandell et al., 1978), i.e., all the calculations based upon system information (be it a priori or sensor information) and the information itself are localized at a given center, very often a geographical position.

A notable characteristic of most large-scale systems is that centrality fails to hold due to either the lack of centralized computing capability or centralized information. Needless to say, many real problems are considered large-scale by nature and not by choice. The important points regarding large-scale systems are that they often model real-life systems and that their hierarchical (multilevel) and decentralized structures depict systems dealing with society, business, management, the economy, the environment, energy, data networks, power networks, space structures, transportation, aerospace, water resources, ecology, and flexible manufacturing networks, to name a few. These systems are often separated geographically, and their treatment requires consideration of not only economic costs, as is common in central-ized systems, but also such important issues as reliability of communication links, value of information, etc. It is for the decentralized and hierarchical control properties and potential applications that many researchers throughout the world have devoted a great deal of effort to large-scale systems in recent years.

## 1.2 Hierarchical Structures

One of the earlier attempts in dealing with large-scale systems was to "decompose" a given system into a number of subsystems for computa-tional efficiency and design simplification. The idea of "decomposition" was first treated theoretically in mathematical programming by Dantzig and Wolfe (1960) by treating large linear programming problems possessing special structures. The coefficient matrices of such large linear programs often have relatively few nonzero elements, i.e., they are sparse matrices. There are two basic approaches for dealing with such problems: "coupled" and "decoupled." The coupled approach keeps the problem's structure intact and takes advantage of the structure to perform efficient computa-tions. The "compact basis triangularization" and "generalized upper bound-ing" are two such efficient methods (Ho and Mitter, 1976). The "decoupled" approach divides the original system into a number of subsystems involving certain values of parameters. Each subsystem is solved independently for a fixed value of the so-called decoupling parameter, whose value is subse-quently adjusted by a coordinator in an appropriate fashion so that the subsystems resolve their problems and the solution to the original system is obtained.

Perhaps the most active group in axiomatizing the decoupled approach has been Mesarovic, Lefkowitz, and their colleagues at the Case Western

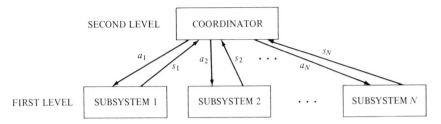

**Figure 1.1** Schematic of a two-level hierarchical system

Reserve University, who have termed it the "multilevel" or "hierarchical" approach (Mesarovic et al., 1970). Consider a two-level system shown in Figure 1.1. At the first level, $N$ subsystems of the original large-scale system are shown. At the second level a coordinator receives the local solutions of the $N$ subsystems, $s_i$, $i = 1, 2, \ldots, N$, and then provides a new set of "interaction" parameters, $a_i$, $i = 1, 2, \ldots, N$. The goal of the coordinator is to arrange the activities of the subsystems to provide a feasible solution to the overall system.

The success of the hierarchical multilevel approach has been primarily in social systems (Mayne, 1976) and water resources systems (Haimes, 1977). The multilevel structure, according to Mesarovic et al. (1970), has five advantages: (i) the decomposition of systems with fixed designs at one level and coordination at another is often the only alternative available; (ii) systems are commonly described only on a stratified basis; (iii) available decision units have limited capabilities, hence the problem is formulated in a multilayer hierarchy of subproblems; (iv) the overall system resources are better utilized through this structure; and (v) there will be an increase in system reliability and flexibility. There has been some disagreement among system and control specialists regarding these points. For example, Varaiya (1972) has mentioned that the first three advantages are a matter of opinion, and there is no evidence in justifying the other two. One shortcoming of most multilevel structures is that they are inherently open-loop structures, although closed-loop structures have been proposed (Singh 1980). Detailed discussion on the hierarchical (multilevel) method will be given in Chapter 4.

## 1.3 Decentralized Control

Most large-scale systems are characterized by a great multiplicity of measured outputs and inputs. For example, an electric power system has several control substations, each being responsible for the operation of a portion of the overall system. This situation arising in a control system design is often referred to as *decentralization*. The designer for such systems determines a structure for control which assigns system inputs to a given set of local

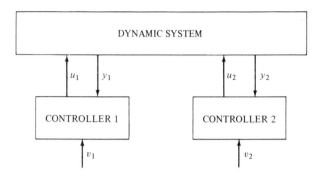

**Figure 1.2** A two-controller decentralized system

controllers (stations), which observe only local system outputs. In other words, this approach, called *decentralized control*, attempts to avoid difficulties in data gathering, storage requirements, computer program debuggings, and geographical separation of system components. Figure 1.2 shows a two-controller decentralized system. The basic characteristic of any decentralized system is that the transfer of information from one group of sensors or actuators to others is quite restricted. For example, in the system of Figure 1.2, only the output $y_1$ and external input $v_1$ are used to find the control $u_1$, and likewise the control $u_2$ is obtained through only the output $y_2$ and external input $v_2$.

The determination of control signals $u_1$ and $u_2$ based on the output signals $y_1$ and $y_2$, respectively, is nothing but two independent output feedback problems which can be used for stabilization or pole placement purposes. It is therefore clear that the decentralized control scheme is of feedback form, indicating that this method is very useful for large-scale linear systems. This is a clear distinction from the hierarchical control scheme, which was mainly intended to be an open-loop structure. Further discussion of decentralized control and its applications for stabilization, robust controllers, etc., will be considered in Chapters 5 and 6.

In this and the previous two sections the concept of a large-scale system and two basic hierarchical and decentralized control structures were briefly introduced. Although there is no universal definition of a large-scale system, it is commonly accepted that such systems possess the following characteristics (Ho and Mitter, 1976):

1. Large-scale systems are often controlled by more than one controller or decision maker involving "decentralized" computations.
2. The controllers have different but correlated "information" available to them, possible at different times.
3. Large-scale systems can also be controlled by local controllers at one level whose control actions are being coordinated at another level in a "hierarchical" (multilevel) structure.

4. Large-scale systems are usually represented by imprecise "aggregate" models.
5. Controllers may operate in a group as a "team" or in a "conflicting" manner with single- or multiple-objective or even conflicting-objective functions.
6. Large-scale systems may be satisfactorily optimized by means of sub-optimal or near-optimum controls, sometimes termed a "satisfying" strategy.

## 1.4 Scope

Since the subject of large-scale systems is rather new, and since the literature is still growing, it is difficult and pointless to attempt to cite every reference. On the other hand, if we were to confine the discussion to one or two subtopics and use only immediate references, it would hardly reflect the importance of the subject. In this text an attempt is made to consider primarily modeling and control of large-scale systems. Other important topics, such as stability, controllability, and observability, are discussed briefly. Most of our discussions are focused on large-scale linear, continuous-time, stationary, and deterministic systems. However, other classes of systems, such as discrete-time, time-delay, nonlinear, and stochastic large-scale systems, are also considered. Among control strategies, the main focus has been on hierarchical (multilevel) and decentralized controls. On the modeling side, aggregation and perturbation (regular and singular) are among the primary topics discussed. Other topics such as identification and estimation as well as large-scale systems control and modeling schemes, such as the Stackelberg approach (Cruz, 1978), component connection model (Saeks and DeCarlo, 1981), multilayer and multiechelon structures, and Nash games, are either considered very briefly or have not been discussed. The emphasis has been on the use of the subject matter in the classroom for students of large-scale systems in a simple and understandable language. Most important theorems are proved, and many easily implementable algorithms support the theory and ample numerical examples demonstrate their use.

## Problems

**1.1.** Develop a multilevel (hierarchical) structure for a business organization with a board of directors, a chairman of the board, a president, three vice presidents (marketing–sales, research, technology), etc.

**1.2.** Explain whether the concept of "centrality" holds for each of the following systems. State your reasons in a sentence.
   **a.** An autopilot aircraft control system.
   **b.** A three-synchronous machine power system.
   **c.** A computer system involving a host computer and five terminals.

**Problem 1.2.** (*continued*)

    **d.** A home heating system.

    **e.** A radar control system.

**1.3.** The allocation of water resources in any state is commonly the responsibility of the state engineers' office which checks for overall system feasibility by overseeing municipalities and conservancy districts, which work independently and report their programs to the state engineers' office. Consider a two-municipality and three-district state and draw a block diagram representing the water resources system.

## References

Cruz, J. B., Jr. 1978. Leader-follower strategies for multilevel systems. *IEEE Trans. Aut. Cont.* AC-23:244–255.

Dantzig, G., and Wolfe, P. 1960. Decomposition principle for linear programs. *Oper. Res.* 8:101–111.

Haimes, Y. Y. 1977. *Hierarchical Analysis of Water Resources Systems*. McGraw-Hill, New York.

Ho, Y. C., and Mitter, S. K., eds. 1976. *Directions in Large-Scale Systems*, pp. v–x. Plenum, New York.

Mahmoud, M. S. 1977. Multilevel systems control and applications: A survey. *IEEE Trans. Sys. Man. Cyb.* SMC-7:125–143.

Mayne, D. Q. 1976. Decentralized control of large-scale systems, in Y. C. Ho and S. K. Mitter, eds., *Directions in Large Scale Systems*, pp. 17–23. Plenum, New York.

Mesarovic, M. D.; Macko, D.; and Takahara, Y. 1970. *Theory of Hierarchical Multilevel Systems*. Academic Press, New York.

Saeks, R., and DeCarlo, R. A. 1981. *Interconnected Dynamical Systems*. Marcel Dekker, New York.

Sandell, N. R., Jr.; Varaiya, P.; Athans, M.; and Safonov, M. G. 1978. Survey of decentralized control methods for large-scale systems, *IEEE Trans. Aut. Cont.* AC-23:108–128 (special issue on large-scale systems).

Singh, M. G., 1980. *Dynamical Hierarchical Control*, rev. ed. North Holland, Amsterdam, The Netherlands.

Varaiya, P. 1972. Book Review of Mesarovic et al., Theory of hierarchical multi-level systems. *IEEE Trans. Aut. Cont.* AC-17:280–281.

# Chapter 2
# Large-Scale Systems Modeling:
## Time Domain

## 2.1 Introduction

Scientists and engineers are often confronted with the analysis, design, and synthesis of real-life problems. The first step in such studies is the development of a "mathematical model" which can be a substitute for the real problem.

In any modeling task, two often conflicting factors prevail—"simplicity" and "accuracy." On one hand, if a system model is oversimplified, presumably for computational effectiveness, incorrect conclusions may be drawn from it in representing an actual system. On the other hand, a highly detailed model would lead to a great deal of unnecessary complications and should a feasible solution be attainable, the extent of resulting details may become so vast that further investigations on the system behavior would become impossible with questionable practical values (Sage, 1977; Šiljak, 1978). Clearly a mechanism by which a compromise can be made between a complex, more accurate model and a simple, less accurate model is needed. Such a mechanism is not a simple undertaking. The key to a valid modeling philosophy is to set forth the following outline (Brogan, 1974):

1. The *purpose* of the model must be clearly defined; no single model can be appropriate for all purposes.
2. The *system*'s *boundary* separating the system and the outside world must be defined.
3. A *structural relationship* among different system components which would best represent desired or observed effects must be defined.
4. Based on the physical structure of the model, a set of *system variables* of interest must be defined. If a quantity of important significance cannot be labeled, step (3) must be modified accordingly.

5. Mathematical descriptions of each system component, sometimes called *elemental equations*, should be written down.

6. After the mathematical description of each system component is complete, they are related through a set of physical laws of *conservation* (or *continuity*) and *compatibility*, such as Newton's, Kirchhoff's, or D'Alembert's.

7. Elemental, continuity, and compatibility equations should be *manipulated*, and the mathematical *format* of the *model* should be *finalized*.

8. The last step to a successful modeling is the analysis of the model and its comparison with real situations.

Should there be any significant discrepancies, steps 1–8 must be reexamined and modified accordingly.

The above steps for a system model development emphasize the fact that a great deal of experience is needed for a sound compromise between accuracy and simplicity. The common practice has been to work with simple and less accurate models. There are two different motivations for this practice: (i) the reduction of computational burden for system simulation, analysis, and design; and (ii) the simplification of control structures resulting from a simplified model. It should be emphasized that these motivations are distinct in the sense that one does not necessarily imply the other. This distinction has been demonstrated by Gelb (1974) for the reduced-order Kalman filter design. It has been shown that the determination of a Kalman filter's error covariance matrix requires the solution of $n^2$ equations, $n$ being the system order. The error covariance matrix for a reduced-order model of $l$th dimension would require the solution of $(n + l)^2$ equations instead. This example leads one to conclude that simplified structure and computational reduction are two separate issues in system modeling which are not necessarily compatible (Sandell et al., 1978).

Thus far we have outlined the necessary steps for a system model with "centralized" structure and have indicated that "reduced computation" and "simplified structures" are two characteristics every system analyst would wish to attribute to models he or she would be dealing with. These desirable properties are of even more concern for the decentralized control of large-scale systems, introduced briefly in Chapter 1. This concern may very well be more subjective for large-scale systems than regular systems, mainly due to the fact that the state of the art in large-scale systems calls for more desirable structures.

Until recently there have been only two schemes for modeling large-scale systems, and they have been around for quite sometime—"aggregation" and "perturbation." These schemes have been carried on from economic theory and mathematics, respectively, to systems modeling, analysis, and control. Other large-scale systems structures and strategies, such as the hierarchical (Mesarovic et al., 1970), decentralized control (Sandell et al.,

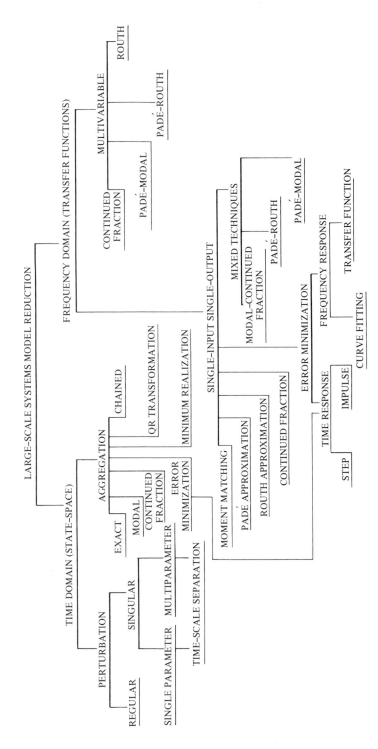

**Figure 2.1** Large-scale systems model reduction methods.

1978), and Stackelberg (leader-follower) approaches (Cruz 1976), are not considered modeling schemes for the sake of discussion here. They are treated as system control strategies in Chapters 4 and 5.

An aggregate model of a system is described by a "coarser" set of state variables. The underlying reason for aggregating a system model is to be able to retain the key qualitative properties of the system, such as stability, which is viewed by Šiljak (1978) as a natural process through the second method of Lyapunov. In other words, the stability of a system described by several state variables is entirely represented by a single variable—the Lyapunov function.

The other scheme for large-scale systems modeling has been perturbation, which is based on ignoring certain interactions of the dynamic or structural nature in a system. Here again the benefits received from reduced computations must not be at the expense of key system properties. Although both perturbation and aggregation schemes tend to provide reduction in computations and perhaps simplification in structure, there has been no hard evidence that they are the most desirable for large-scale systems.

A recent effort along these lines is perhaps the *descriptive variable* scheme for large-scale systems modeling due to Larson, Luenberger and their associates (Luenberger, 1977, 1978; Stengel et al., 1979). The fundamental issue in this modeling philosophy is that the accuracy of a given large-scale system model is most likely preserved if the system is represented by the actual physical or economical *variables* which *describe* the operation of the system; hence the name "descriptive variable."

This chapter is devoted to detailed examinations of "aggregation," "perturbation," and an introduction to "descriptive variable" methods viewed as modeling alternatives for large-scale systems. Portions of this chapter and next are based on a recent survey by the author (Jamshidi, 1982). Figure 2.1 provides a summary of all time-domain (Chapter 2) and frequency-domain (Chapter 3) methods of large-scale systems model simplification schemes.

## 2.2  Aggregation Methods

Aggregation has long been a technique for analyzing static economic models. The treatment of aggregation in modern time is probably due to Malinvaud (1956), whose formulation is shown in Figure 2.2a (Aoki, 1978). In this diagram, $\mathcal{X}$, $\mathcal{Y}$, $\mathcal{Z}$, and $\mathcal{V}$ are topological (or vector) spaces, $f$ represents a linear continuous map between the exogeneous variable $x \in \mathcal{X}$ and endogenous variable $y \in \mathcal{Y}$. The aggregation procedures $h: \mathcal{X} \to \mathcal{Z}$, and $g: \mathcal{Y} \to \mathcal{V}$, lead to aggregated variables $z \in \mathcal{Z}$ and $v \in \mathcal{V}$. The map $k: \mathcal{Z} \to \mathcal{V}$, is to represent a simplified or an aggregated model. The aggregation is said to be "perfect" when $k$ is chosen such that the relation

$$gf(x) = kh(x) \tag{2.2.1}$$

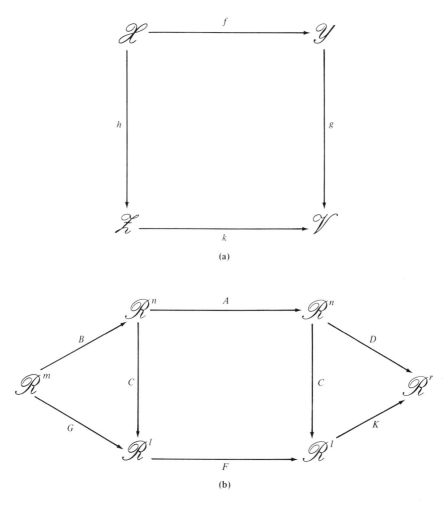

**Figure 2.2** A pictorial representation of aggregation (**a**) a static system, and (**b**) a dynamic linear system.

holds for all $x \in \mathcal{X}$. The notion of perfect aggregation is an idealization at best, and in practice it is approximated through two alternative procedures according to econometricians (Chipman, 1976). These are (i) to impose some restrictions on $f$, $g$, and $h$ while leaving $\mathcal{X}$ unrestricted and (ii) to require (2.2.1) to hold on $\mathcal{X}_o$ some subset of $\mathcal{X}$.

In this section, aggregation of large-scale linear time-invariant systems is introduced and it is shown that it is not merely a model reduction scheme but, more importantly, a conceptual basis for other approximation techniques, including the modal aggregation (Davison, 1966, 1968) which retains the dominant modes of the original system.

## 2.2.1 Exact and Modal Aggregation

The procedures of aggregation can be similarly applied to a large-scale linear time-invariant system; i.e., consider, a linear controllable system

$$\dot{x}(t) = Ax(t) + Bu(t), \quad x(0) = x_o \qquad (2.2.2a)$$

$$y(t) = Dx(t) \qquad (2.2.2b)$$

where $x(t)$, $u(t)$, and $y(t)$ are $n \times 1$, $m \times 1$, and $r \times 1$ state, control, and output vectors, respectively, $A$, $B$, and $D$ are $n \times n$, $n \times m$, and $r \times n$ matrices. It is desired to describe the time behavior of

$$z(t) = Cx(t), \quad z(0) = z_o = Cx_o \qquad (2.2.3)$$

where $C$ is an $l \times n$ $(l < n)$ constant aggregation matrix and $l \times 1$ vector $z$ is called the aggregation of $x$. On the other hand, assuming that $x$ is available and starting from $z_o = Cx_o$, it is desired to maintain the relation (2.2.3). Without loss of generality, it is assumed that $\text{rank}(C) = l$. Then the aggregated system is described by

$$\dot{z}(t) = Fz(t) + Gu(t), \quad z(0) = z_o \qquad (2.2.4a)$$

$$\hat{y}(t) = Kz(t) \qquad (2.2.4b)$$

where the pair $(F, G)$ satisfy the following, so-called *dynamic exactness* (perfect aggregation) conditions:

$$FC = CA \qquad (2.2.5)$$

$$G = CB \qquad (2.2.6a)$$

$$KC \cong D \qquad (2.2.6b)$$

The aggregation of the dynamic system (2.2.2) is illustrated in Figure 2.2b. The vector $\hat{y}$ is an $r \times 1$ approximate output. It is noted that (2.2.5)–(2.2.6) can not hold simultaneously if $l < n$ and (2.2.2) is assumed to be irreducible, hence the condition (2.2.6b) is an approximation (Hickin and Sinha, 1980).

If an error vector is defined as $e(t) = z(t) - Cx(t)$, then its dynamic behavior is given by $\dot{e}(t) = Fe(t) + (FC - CA)x(t) + (G - CB)u(t)$, which reduces to $\dot{e}(t) = Fe(t)$ if conditions (2.2.5)–(2.2.6a) hold. Hence, if $e(0) = 0$, then $e(t) = 0$ for all $t \geqslant 0$. Should $e(0) \neq 0$ but $F$ be a stable matrix, then $\lim_{t \to \infty} e(t) = 0$; i.e., dynamic exactness condition (2.2.5)–(2.2.6a) is asymptotically satisfied.

In order to determine the aggregation matrices $(F, G)$, two procedures can be followed. The first results from Penrose solvability condition (Penrose, 1955); i.e.

$$F = CAC^T(CC^T)^{-1} \qquad (2.2.7)$$

Thus, once matrix $C$ is known the aggregated matrix $F$ is obtained by (2.2.7) and the aggregated control matrix $G$ is determined from (2.2.6a). The analysis of identities (2.2.5)–(2.2.7) gives some insight in the choice of the "aggregation matrix" $C$. Aoki (1968, 1971) has shown that the analysis of

(2.2.5) will lead to a description of the aggregated state vector $z(t)$, which is a linear combination of certain modes of $x(t)$. It must be noted, however, that aggregated matrix $F$ is obtained from (2.2.7) only if the conditions (2.2.5)–(2.2.6) are satisfied. Under these circumstances, the eigenvalues of $F$ constitute a subset of eigenvalues of $A$. As mentioned earlier for the static models of econometrics, the dynamic exactness (perfect aggregation) is an idealized situation. The use of (2.2.7), as in Michailesco and Siret (1980), is an approximation which in fact minimizes the square of the norm $\|FC - CA\|$ unless a consistency relation

$$CAC^+C = CA \qquad (2.2.8)$$

is satisfied. In (2.2.8), the matrix $C^+ \triangleq C^T(CC^T)^{-1}$ is the generalized inverse of $C$.

The linear system aggregation procedure described thusfar requires the knowledge of all eigenvalues of $A$. This requirement would make the method rather impractical for large-scale systems. A second approach which does not require the knowledge of the eigenvalues of $A$ has also been proposed by Aoki (1968). Consider the controllability matrix:*

$$W_A \triangleq \left[ B, AB, \ldots, A^{n-1}B \right] \qquad (2.2.9)$$

and a modified controllability matrix of (2.2.4),

$$W_F \triangleq \left[ G, FG, \ldots, F^{n-1}G \right] \qquad (2.2.10)$$

it can be seen from (2.2.5)–(2.2.6b) that these matrices are related by

$$W_F = CW_A \qquad (2.2.11)$$

Thus using the generalized (pseudo-) inverse, matrix $C$ can be obtained by

$$C = W_F W_A^+ = W_F W_A^T \left( W_A W_A^T \right)^{-1} \qquad (2.2.12)$$

since by initial controllability assumption rank $(W_A) = n$. Therefore, if $F$ is specified, say $F = \text{diag}(\lambda_1, \lambda_2, \ldots, \lambda_l)$, and $G$ is chosen to make (2.2.4) completely controllable, i.e. rank$(W_F) = l$, then $C$ is obtained by (2.2.12). It is noted here that this procedure would, in effect, forego the dynamic exactness conditions (2.2.5)–(2.2.6). Before it is demonstrated that the modal (dominate pole) aggregation (Davison, 1966, 1968; Chidambara, 1969) is a special case of the above, a numerical example is presented.

**Example 2.2.1.** Consider a third-order unaggregated system described by

$$\dot{x} = \begin{bmatrix} -0.1 & 1 & 2 \\ 1 & -4 & 0 \\ 2 & 0 & -6 \end{bmatrix} x + \begin{bmatrix} 1 \\ 1 \\ 1 \end{bmatrix} u. \qquad (2.2.13)$$

It is desired to find a second-order aggregated model for this system.

_____

*For a discussion on controllability, see Chapter 7.

SOLUTION: This example is solved using the two methods described above. The first solution is obtained by the use of the eigenvalues of $A$ in (2.2.13), which are $\lambda\{A\} = \{-0.70862, -6.6482, -4.1604\}$. From the relative magnitudes of $\lambda_i\{A\}$, it is clear that the first mode is the slowest of all three. A possible choice for aggregation matrix $C$ can be

$$C = \begin{bmatrix} 1 & 0 & 0 \\ 0 & 0.5 & 0.5 \end{bmatrix} \tag{2.2.14}$$

which implies that the first aggregated state is chosen to be approximately the slowest mode while an average of the two faster modes constitutes the second aggregated state. From (2.2.7) and (2.2.6a), the aggregated model becomes

$$\dot{z}(t) = Fz(t) + Gu(t) = \begin{bmatrix} -0.1 & 3 \\ 1.5 & -5 \end{bmatrix} z(t) + \begin{bmatrix} 1 \\ 1 \end{bmatrix} u(t) \tag{2.2.15}$$

It is clear from (2.2.13)–(2.2.15) that for this choice of aggregation matrix, the condition (2.2.5) for dynamic exactness is not satisfied. The resulting aggregated system, as mentioned earlier, is at best an approximation. The resulting error vector $e(t)$ satisfies

$$\dot{e}(t) = Fe(t) + \begin{bmatrix} 0 & 0.5 & -0.5 \\ 0 & -0.5 & 0.5 \end{bmatrix} x(t) \tag{2.2.16}$$

An alternative choice of $C$,

$$C = \begin{bmatrix} 1 & 0 & 0 \\ 0 & 1 & 0 \end{bmatrix} \tag{2.2.17}$$

results in an aggregated system

$$\dot{z}(t) = \begin{bmatrix} -0.1 & 1 \\ 1 & -4 \end{bmatrix} z(t) + \begin{bmatrix} 1 \\ 1 \end{bmatrix} u(t) \tag{2.2.18}$$

with an error system

$$\dot{e}(t) = Fe(t) + \begin{bmatrix} 0 & 0 & -2 \\ 0 & 0 & 0 \end{bmatrix} x(t) \tag{2.2.19}$$

This latter choice of aggregation matrix provided better results as evident from (2.2.19). However, this case is not exact either. In later discussions it will be demonstrated how dynamic exactness can be achieved. In some problems $F$ may even turn out to be a null matrix regardless of what $C$ one may try.

The second solution is obtained by evaluating controllability matrices. Following the discussions made earlier, let $F = \text{diag}(-0.70862, -4.1604)$, then by trial and error a $G = (1\ 1)^T$ column vector can be found so that the pair $(F, G)$ is controllable. The controllability matrix $W_A$ and matrix $W_F$ defined by (2.2.9)–(2.2.10) are given,

$$W_A = \begin{bmatrix} 1 & 2.9 & -11.29 \\ 1 & -3 & 14.9 \\ 1 & -4 & 29.8 \end{bmatrix}, \quad W_F = \begin{bmatrix} 1 & -0.70862 & 0.502 \\ 1 & -4.1604 & 17.309 \end{bmatrix} \tag{2.2.20}$$

and hence a possible aggregation matrix is obtained from (2.2.12),

$$C = \begin{bmatrix} 0.32 & 1.08 & -0.4 \\ -0.24 & 1.5 & -0.26 \end{bmatrix} \qquad (2.2.21)$$

This scheme leads to dynamically unexact aggregation also. In fact, its approximate nature is somewhat more difficult to estimate than the first procedure.

We next turn to two modal aggregation schemes due to Davison (1966, 1968) and Chidambara (1969) and demonstrate that they are a special case of aggregation due to Aoki (1968, 1971, 1978).

Consider the system (2.2.2) and let the aggregated (reduced) model be (2.2.4). Then the aggregated matrix pair $(F, G)$ is given by

$$F = M_l P \Lambda P^T M_l^{-1} \qquad (2.2.22)$$

$$G = M_l P M^{-1} B \qquad (2.2.23)$$

where $M$ is the modal matrix of (2.2.2) consisting of the eigenvectors of $A$ arranged in ascending* order of the $\text{Re}[\lambda_i\{A\}]$, $M_l$ is an $l \times l$ matrix which includes the $l$ dominant eigenvectors of $A$ corresponding to the retained modes of the original system, and

$$P: \begin{bmatrix} I_l & \vline & 0 \end{bmatrix} \qquad (2.2.24)$$

is an $l \times n$ transformation matrix. Modal matrix $M$ can be represented by

$$M = l \left\{ \begin{bmatrix} \overbrace{M_l}^{l} & \vline & M_{12} \\ \hline M_{21} & \vline & M_{22} \end{bmatrix} \right\} n \qquad (2.2.25)$$

$$\underbrace{\phantom{MMMMMMMM}}_{n}$$

The aggregation matrix $C$ in $z = Cx$ is given by (Lamba and Rao, 1978),

$$C = M_l P M^{-1} \qquad (2.2.26)$$

It is noted that this scheme works for the case where $A$ has complex or repeated eigenvalues as well. Under those conditions the columns of $M$ can be real and imaginary parts of the complex eigenvectors or generalized eigenvectors in addition to regular eigenvectors (see Problem 2.6).

**Example 2.2.2.** Consider a third-order system

$$\dot{x}(t) = \begin{bmatrix} 0.5 & 0.5 & 0 \\ 0 & 1 & 0 \\ 0.833 & -2.1667 & -0.333 \end{bmatrix} x(t) + \begin{bmatrix} 1 \\ 1 \\ 2 \end{bmatrix} u(t). \quad (2.2.27)$$

It is desired to find a reduced-order model.

_____

*The ordering can also be in accordance to any number of the eigenvalues which are to be retained.

SOLUTION: This example will be solved by using both the modal aggregation described by (2.2.22)–(2.2.23) and the aggregation under dynamic
exactness conditions (2.2.5)–(2.2.7).

a. *Modal*. The eigenvalues of $A$ are

$$\lambda\{A\} = \{0.5, 1, -0.333\} \qquad (2.2.28)$$

which indicates that the system is unstable. The resulting aggregated
model based on (2.2.22)–(2.2.23) is given by

$$\dot{z}(t) = \begin{bmatrix} 0.5 & 0.5 \\ 0 & 1 \end{bmatrix} z(t) + \begin{bmatrix} 1 \\ 1 \end{bmatrix} u(t) \qquad (2.2.29)$$

which has retained the two eigenvalues with positive real parts. It is
noted that the aggregated system is also unstable.

b. *Exact*. This solution is demonstrated by three different choices of
matrix $C$ and each time the dynamic exactness is checked. First,
consider

$$C^1 = \begin{bmatrix} 1 & 0 & 0 \\ 0 & 0.5 & 0.5 \end{bmatrix} \qquad (2.2.30)$$

which by virtue of (2.2.7) and (2.2.6a) leads to

$$\dot{z}^1(t) = \begin{bmatrix} 0.5 & 0.5 \\ 0.416 & -0.75 \end{bmatrix} z^1(t) + \begin{bmatrix} 1 \\ 1.5 \end{bmatrix} u(t) \qquad (2.2.31)$$

This aggregation leads to an error system equation,

$$\dot{e}^1(t) = F^1 e^1(t) + \begin{bmatrix} 0 & -0.25 & 0.25 \\ 0 & 0.208 & -0.208 \end{bmatrix} x(t) \qquad (2.2.32)$$

which indicates that this choice of $C$ is far from a perfect aggregation.
Next, a second $C$ matrix,

$$C^2 = \begin{bmatrix} 0 & 1 & 0.5 \\ 0.5 & 0 & 0.5 \end{bmatrix} \qquad (2.2.33)$$

is tried and results in the following aggregated and error systems:

$$\dot{z}^2(t) = \begin{bmatrix} 1 & 0 \\ -0.8335 & 0.5 \end{bmatrix} z^2(t) + \begin{bmatrix} 1 \\ 1.5 \end{bmatrix} u(t) \qquad (2.2.34)$$

and

$$\dot{e}^2(t) = F^2 e^2(t) + \begin{bmatrix} 0 & 0 & 0 \\ 0.417 & 0 & 0.417 \end{bmatrix} x(t) \qquad (2.2.35)$$

The second choice of $C$ matrix, although still not exact, has resulted in
a reduced-order model closer to perfect aggregation as is evident from
(2.2.35) as compared to (2.2.32). The third choice of $C$ matrix is

$$C^3 = \begin{bmatrix} 1 & 0 & 0 \\ 0 & 1 & 0 \end{bmatrix} \qquad (2.2.36)$$

which provides the following aggregated and error systems:

$$\dot{z}^3(t) = \begin{bmatrix} 0.5 & 0.5 \\ 0 & 1 \end{bmatrix} z^3(t) + \begin{bmatrix} 1 \\ 1 \end{bmatrix} u(t) \tag{2.2.37}$$

$$\dot{e}^3(t) = F^3 e^3(t) + \begin{bmatrix} 0 & 0 & 0 \\ 0 & 0 & 0 \end{bmatrix} x(t) \tag{2.2.38}$$

This choice of aggregation matrix has resulted in a perfect aggregation in which the dynamic exactness conditions (2.2.5)–(2.2.6a) are satisfied. Comparison of this third aggregated system (2.2.37) and the aggregated system through modal aggregation given by (2.2.29) reveals that the two aggregated systems are identical. This implies that the modal approach is in fact a special case of the exact one, as expected.

Next, let us discuss another modal aggregation, originally due to Chidambara (1969) but also presented by Rao and Lamba (1974). Let the large-scale linear time-invariant system (2.2.2a) be rewritten as

$$\dot{x}(t) = \begin{bmatrix} \dot{z}(t) \\ \dot{x}_2(t) \end{bmatrix} = \begin{bmatrix} A_1 & A_{12} \\ A_{21} & A_2 \end{bmatrix} \begin{bmatrix} z(t) \\ x_2(t) \end{bmatrix} + \begin{bmatrix} B_1 \\ B_2 \end{bmatrix} u(t) \tag{2.2.39}$$

where $z$ is the aggregated state. System (2.2.39) can be reduced to its modal form,

$$\begin{bmatrix} \dot{w}(t) \\ \dot{v}_2(t) \end{bmatrix} = \begin{bmatrix} \Lambda_1 & 0 \\ 0 & \Lambda_2 \end{bmatrix} \begin{bmatrix} w(t) \\ v_2(t) \end{bmatrix} + \begin{bmatrix} \Gamma_1 \\ \Gamma_2 \end{bmatrix} u(t) \tag{2.2.40}$$

where $w$ is the vector of retained dominant (aggregated) variables,

$$x = Mv = M\begin{bmatrix} w & | & v_2 \end{bmatrix}^T, \quad \Lambda = \text{Block-diag}\,(\Lambda_1, \Lambda_2) = M^{-1}AM$$

and

$$\Gamma = \begin{bmatrix} \Gamma_1 & | & \Gamma_2 \end{bmatrix}^T = M^{-1}B$$

and $M$ is the modal matrix corresponding to matrix $A$. For simplicity, it is assumed that all the eigenvalues of $A$ are real and distinct. The approach can be similarly extended for complex and/or repeated eigenvalues (see Problem 2.7). Referring back to systems (2.2.39)–(2.2.40), it is desired to retain $l(l < n)$ dominant modes (vector $w$) of (2.2.40), i.e.,

$$\dot{w}(t) = P\Lambda P^T w(t) + P\Gamma u(t) \tag{2.2.41}$$

where $P$ is given by (2.2.24) and $w = Pv$. In (2.2.40) let the dimension of $\Lambda_1$ be $l \times l$ and take the Laplace transform of the $v_2$-equation to yield

$$V_2(s) = (sI - \Lambda_2)^{-1} \Gamma_2 U(s) \tag{2.2.42}$$

If only the DC transmission between $u(t)$ and $v_2(t)$ is of interest, and since $\Lambda_2$ represents nondominant (fast) modes, (2.2.42) can be approximated by

$$v_2(t) \cong -\Lambda_2^{-1} \Gamma_2 u(t) \triangleq Lu(t) \tag{2.2.43}$$

The partitioned forms of $x$ and $v$ lead to

$$\begin{bmatrix} z \\ x_2 \end{bmatrix} = \begin{bmatrix} M_1 & M_{12} \\ M_{21} & M_2 \end{bmatrix} \cdot \begin{bmatrix} w \\ v_2 \end{bmatrix} \qquad (2.2.44)$$

or

$$z = M_1 w + M_{12} v_2, \quad x_2 = M_{21} w + M_2 v_2 \qquad (2.2.45)$$

Solving for $w$ in the first equation of (2.2.45) and substituting it in the second while using (2.2.43) leads to

$$x_2 = M_{21} M_1^{-1} z + \left( M_2 + M_{21} M_1^{-1} M_{12} \right) Lu \triangleq Nz + Eu \qquad (2.2.46)$$

Eliminating $x_2$ in the $\dot{z}$-equation (2.2.39) by virtue of (2.2.46) leads to the aggregated model

$$\dot{z}(t) = Fz(t) + Gu(t) \qquad (2.2.47)$$

where $F \triangleq A_1 + A_{12} N$ and $G \triangleq B_1 + A_{12} E$. This is the desired aggregated model. The following example illustrates it.

**Example 2.2.3.** Consider a fourth-order system

$$\dot{x} = \begin{bmatrix} 0 & 1 & 0 & 0 \\ 0 & 0 & 1 & 0 \\ 0 & 0 & 0 & 1 \\ -0.6 & -9.22 & -33.32 & -11.3 \end{bmatrix} x + \begin{bmatrix} 0 \\ 1 \\ 0 \\ 1 \end{bmatrix} u \qquad (2.2.48)$$

It is desired to find an aggregated system for it.
SOLUTION: The eigenvalues of $A$ are $-0.1$, $-0.2$, $-5.0$, and $-6.0$, which indicates that the first two eigenvalues are dominant and hence a second-order reduced model will be sought. The modal matrix whose columns are ordered in ascending order of eigenvalues real parts is

$$M = \begin{bmatrix} 1 & 1 & 1 & 1 \\ -0.1 & -0.2 & -5 & -6 \\ 0.01 & 0.04 & 25 & 36 \\ -0.001 & -0.008 & -125 & -216 \end{bmatrix} \qquad (2.2.49)$$

and diagonal matrix $\Lambda = \text{diag}\{-0.1, -0.2, -5, -6\}$ and modal input matrix $\Gamma^T = (11.48, -11.5, 0.12, -0.074)$. The aggregated matrices are

$$F = \begin{bmatrix} 0 & 1 \\ -0.02 & -0.3 \end{bmatrix}, \quad G = \begin{bmatrix} 0 \\ 1.144 \end{bmatrix} \qquad (2.2.50)$$

which results in a set of retained eigenvalues $\lambda\{F\} = \{-0.1, -0.2\}$ corresponding to the dominant ones of (2.2.48). This example was also solved using the first modal aggregation and the results were identical.

Before we leave our initial discussions on aggregation, it is useful to see the correlation between the exact and modal aggregations. Let $\xi$ be the right eigenvector of $A$ corresponding to eigenvalue $\lambda$, i.e., $A\xi = \lambda\xi$. Premultiplying both sides of this equality by $C$ leads to

$$CA\xi = \lambda C\xi \qquad (2.2.51)$$

Now denoting $\gamma = C\xi$ and remembering the condition (2.2.5), (2.2.51) can be rewritten as

$$FC\xi = F\gamma = \lambda\gamma \qquad (2.2.52)$$

which indicates that $\gamma$ is a right eigenvector of matrix $F$ under perfect aggregation condition, provided that $C\xi \neq 0$. Therefore $F$ inherits a set of eigenvalues $\{\lambda_1, \lambda_2, \ldots, \lambda_l\}$ of $A$ corresponding to those eigenvectors of $A$ with $C\xi \neq 0$. Now let the left eigenvectors of $A$, i.e., the set of all row vectors $\nu_i$ such that $\nu_i A = \lambda_i \nu_i$, be the rows of the aggregation matrix, i.e.,

$$C = \begin{bmatrix} \nu_1 \\ -- \\ \nu_2 \\ -- \\ \vdots \\ -- \\ \nu_l \end{bmatrix} \qquad (2.2.53)$$

Then the aggregated system (2.2.4) using (2.2.7) reduces to

$$\dot{z} = \Lambda_l z + Gu \qquad (2.2.54)$$

when $\Lambda_l = \text{diag}(\lambda_1, \lambda_2, \ldots, \lambda_l)$ and $G = CB$. Moreover, it is easy to see that this aggregation does satisfy the dynamic exactness condition (2.2.5). Assume that the modal representation of (2.2.2a) is $\dot{q} = \Lambda q + \Gamma u$ with $\Lambda = M^{-1}AM = \text{Block-diag}\{\Lambda_1, \Lambda_2\}\Gamma = M^{-1}B = \begin{bmatrix} \Gamma_1^T & | & \Gamma_2^T \end{bmatrix}^T$. Thus, the modal representation of the reduced model is $\dot{q}_l = \Lambda_l q_l + \Gamma_l u$ or $q_l = [I_l : 0]M^{-1}x = C_o x$, hence the aggregation Equation (2.2.3) is redefined by $z = Cx = Mq_l = MC_o x$ or $C = MC_o$. Note that to compute $C_o$ it is not necessary to obtain $M^{-1}$. The $l$ rows of $C_o$ are the eigenvectors of $A^T$ associated with the $l$ retained eigenvalues.

The above development indicates that if the aggregation matrix is properly chosen, one can use exact aggregation to retain the dominant modes of the system, i.e., modal aggregation. This explains the correlation between exact and modal aggregation as demonstrated in Example 2.2.2 and further in Problem 2.5.

## 2.2.2 Aggregation by Continued Fraction

One of the more popular methods for large-scale systems order reduction has been the "continued fraction" technique first introduced by Chen and Shieh (1968) and extended by many others. The original technique is based on a Taylor series expansion of the system's closed-loop transfer function about $s = 0$. This technique is treated in Chapter 3 (Section 3.5). Our objective here is to use the continued fraction technique to obtain a reduced-order model for large single-input single-output linear time-invariant systems which falls under the concept of aggregation. Consider

$$\dot{x} = Ax + Bu \qquad (2.2.55a)$$

$$y = C_n x \qquad (2.2.55b)$$

where, without loss of generality, the matrix $A$ is assumed to be in companion form (Lamba and Rao, 1978)

$$A = \begin{bmatrix} 0 & 1 & 0 & & \cdots & 0 \\ 0 & 0 & 1 & & \cdots & 0 \\ \vdots & \vdots & \vdots & & \cdots & \\ 0 & 0 & 0 & 0 & \cdots & 1 \\ -a_{11} & -a_{12} & -a_{13} & -a_{14} & \cdots & -a_{1n} \end{bmatrix} \qquad (2.2.56a)$$

and

$$B^T = \begin{bmatrix} 0 & 0 & \cdots & 0 & 1 \end{bmatrix}, \quad C_n = \begin{bmatrix} a_{21} & a_{22} & \cdots & a_{2n} \end{bmatrix}$$
$$(2.2.56b)$$

Chen and Shieh (1969) have shown that the unaggregated system (2.2.55) can be aggregated through a transformation matrix $P$, corresponding to its continued fraction expansion, i.e.,

$$\dot{q} = Hq + Ku \qquad (2.2.57a)$$
$$v = C_q q \qquad (2.2.57b)$$

where the transformed vector $q$ is

$$q = Px \qquad (2.2.58)$$

Matrix $P$ is obtained through the modified Routh–Hurwitz array,

$$\begin{array}{|ccccccccc}
a_{11} & a_{12} & a_{13} & a_{14} & a_{15} & \cdots & a_{1n} & 1 \\
a_{21} & a_{22} & a_{23} & a_{24} & \vdots & \cdots & a_{2n} & 0 \\
a_{31} & a_{32} & a_{33} & & \vdots & \cdots & 1 & \\
a_{41} & a_{42} & & & \vdots & \cdots & 0 & \\
a_{51} & \vdots & & & & & & \\
\vdots & \vdots & & & & & & \\
\vdots & & & & & & & \\
a_{2n-1,1} & 1 & & & & & & \\
a_{2n,1} & 0 & & & & & & \\
1 & & & & & & &
\end{array} \qquad (2.2.59)$$

whose first two rows are extracted from the $n$th row of $A$ and elements of output vector $C_n$ in (2.2.56). The remaining rows are calculated from the common Routh–Hurwitz iterative formula. The matrix $P$ is then extracted from (2.2.59) as

$$P = \begin{bmatrix} a_{31} & a_{32} & a_{33} & \cdots & & 1 \\ 0 & a_{51} & a_{52} & \cdots & & 1 \\ 0 & 0 & a_{71} & \cdots & & 1 \\ \vdots & & & & \vdots & \\ 0 & 0 & 0 & \cdots & a_{2n-1,1} & 1 \\ 0 & 0 & 0 & \cdots & 0 & 1 \end{bmatrix} \qquad (2.2.60)$$

A comparison of (2.2.55) and (2.2.58) implies that

$$\dot{q} = PAP^{-1}q + PBu \qquad (2.2.61)$$

which indicates that matrices $H$ and $K$ in (2.2.57a) are

$$H = PAP^{-1}, \quad K = PB \qquad (2.2.62)$$

The continued fraction expansion simplification of (2.2.55) from $n$th to $l$th order corresponds to retaining the first $l$ variables of $q$ in (2.2.57a). Let the first $l$ elements of $q$ be called $z$; then it is clear that

$$z = Rq, \quad R = \begin{bmatrix} I_l & \vdots & 0 \end{bmatrix} \qquad (2.2.63)$$

where $I_l$ is an $l$-dimensional identity matrix. Using (2.2.63), (2.2.57a) becomes

$$\dot{z} = RHq + RKu \qquad (2.2.64)$$

which, when compared to the desired aggregated system state equation

$$\dot{z} = Fz + Gu \qquad (2.2.65)$$

leads to

$$FR = RH, \quad G = RK = RPB \qquad (2.2.66)$$

A comparison of (2.2.58) and (2.2.63) implies

$$z = RPx = Cx \qquad (2.2.67)$$

where $C$ is the $l \times n$ "aggregation" matrix. A relation involving the aggregated system output matrix $C_l$ from the corresponding equation $w = C_l z$ can be obtained by equating $y = w$, which yields

$$C_n = C_l C \qquad (2.2.68)$$

Now by using the pseudo-inverse (generalized inverse) of matrices $R$ and $C$ in (2.2.66) and (2.2.69), the aggregated system matrices are

$$F = RHR^+ = RHR^T(RR^T)^{-1} = RPAP^{-1}R^T(RR^T)^{-1} \qquad (2.2.69)$$

$$C_l = C_n C^+ = C_n C^T(CC^T)^{-1}, \quad G = RPB \qquad (2.2.70)$$

with the aggregation matrix expressed by

$$C = RP \tag{2.2.71}$$

The proposed method is very convenient for computational purposes and its effectiveness is examined by an example.

**Example 2.2.4.** Consider a fourth-order system in companion form

$$\dot{x} = \begin{bmatrix} 0 & 1 & 0 & 0 \\ 0 & 0 & 1 & 0 \\ 0 & 0 & 0 & 1 \\ -120 & -180 & -102 & -18 \end{bmatrix} x + \begin{bmatrix} 0 \\ 0 \\ 0 \\ 1 \end{bmatrix} u \tag{2.2.72a}$$

$$y = \begin{bmatrix} 120 & 90.0 & 24.8 & 1.4 \end{bmatrix} x \tag{2.2.72b}$$

which corresponds to a single-output case of an example treated by Hutton and Friedland (1975). It is desired to find a second-order aggregated system.

SOLUTION: The transformation matrix $P$ based on the Routh–Hurwitz array is

$$P = \begin{bmatrix} 90 & 77.2 & 16.6 & 1 \\ 0 & 95.76 & 17.07 & 1 \\ 0 & 0 & 13.2 & 1 \\ 0 & 0 & 0 & 1 \end{bmatrix} \tag{2.2.73}$$

and with $R = [I_2 : 0]$, the aggregated system and aggregation matrices are

$$F = \begin{bmatrix} -1.34 & 0.13506 \\ -1.34 & -0.80479 \end{bmatrix}, \quad G = \begin{bmatrix} 1 \\ 1 \end{bmatrix} \tag{2.2.74}$$

$$C_I = \begin{bmatrix} 13.35 & -1.274 \end{bmatrix}, \quad C = \begin{bmatrix} 90 & 77.2 & 16.6 & 1 \\ 0 & 95.76 & 17.07 & 1 \end{bmatrix} \tag{2.2.75}$$

The resulting aggregated system was simulated on the digital computer for a unit step input with almost indistinguishable responses, as shown in Figure 2.3. In fact, reasonably good results were obtained for many other examples, some of which are discussed in the problems section of this chapter.

A few comments regarding this aggregation method and those in Section 2.2.1 are due. The method as discussed here is only an aggregation of the state and not the output vector, as pointed out by Michailesco and Siret (1980), and, hence, the matrix $C$ in (2.2.71) is at best an "approximate aggregation matrix." Although the necessary conditions (2.2.66) for exact aggregation are satisfied, they are guaranteed if and only if the eigenvalues spectrum of $F$ are contained in that of $H$ (Gantmacher, 1966), i.e., $\sigma(F) \in \sigma(H)$. The use of a pseudo-inverse to solve for $F$ in (2.2.69)–(2.2.70) is again an approximation which minimizes the square of the norm $\|FR\text{-}RH\|$ unless a similar consistency relation $(RHR^+)R = RH$ is satisfied. Thus the aggregated state $z$ in (2.2.67) is an approximation, $z \cong RPx$. This last deduction is, of course, not too surprising because of the nature of continued fraction

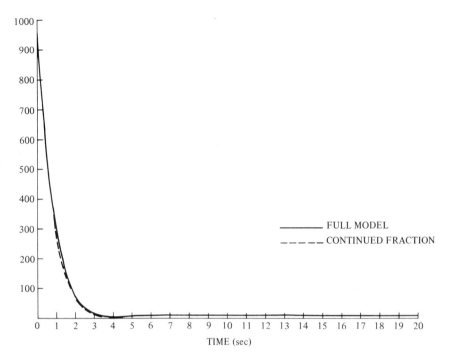

FULL MODEL

CONTINUED FRACTION

TIME (sec)

**Figure 2.3** Time responses for Example 2.2.4 using continued fraction aggregation method.

and Padé approximants (Chapter 3, Section 3.3), which do not retain the full model's eigenvalues. Furthermore, it is worth noting that the above approximate relation for $z$ can be obtained by other schemes when $l$ state variables are retained and the remaining $(n - l)$ are discarded, such as Routh approximation (Hutton and Friedland, 1975) (Chapter 3, Section 3.4) or "chained aggregation" through the generalized Hessenberg transformation (Tse et al., 1977), to be discussed next. Finally, it is noted that exact aggregation can be most useful when a particular objective or application is in mind (Bertrand et al., 1977; Aoki, 1978). This point will be brought up in the next section again.

### 2.2.3 Chained Aggregation

One of the more recent approaches in aggregating large-scale linear time-invariant systems is "chained aggregation", developed by Perkins and his colleagues (Tse et al., 1977; Tse, 1978). Based on the unaggregated large-scale system's information structure, the system is described through a "chain" of "aggregations" by a "Generalized Hessenberg Representation" (GHR). The procedure would allow one to discard the weakly observable part of the system. Consider a large-scale linear time-invariant system

$$\dot{x} = Ax + Bu \qquad (2.2.76)$$

$$y = C_1 x \qquad (2.2.77)$$

where dimensions of $x$ and $y$ are $n$ and $r_1$, respectively, and without any loss of generality it is assumed that $\text{rank}(C_1) = r_1$ and furthermore suppose that through an ordering of the states, $C_1$ can be represented by

$$C_1 = \begin{bmatrix} C_{11} & \vdots & C_{12} \end{bmatrix}, \quad \det C_{11} \neq 0 \qquad (2.2.78)$$

Let us define a nonsingular transformation matrix

$$T_1 = \begin{bmatrix} C_{11} & \vdots & C_{12} \\ \hline 0 & \vdots & I_{n-r_1} \end{bmatrix} \qquad (2.2.79)$$

which would transform (2.2.76) to

$$\dot{z} = \begin{bmatrix} \dot{z}_1 \\ \hline \dot{z}_2 \end{bmatrix} = \begin{bmatrix} F_{11} & \vdots & \tilde{F}_{12} \\ \hline \tilde{F}_{21} & \vdots & \tilde{F}_{22} \end{bmatrix} \begin{bmatrix} z_1 \\ \hline z_2 \end{bmatrix} + \begin{bmatrix} G_1 \\ \hline \tilde{G}_2 \end{bmatrix} u \qquad (2.2.80)$$

If the system (2.2.76) is "completely aggregable" (Tse, 1978), i.e., the "dynamic exactness" conditions (2.2.5)–(2.2.6) are satisfied, then $\tilde{F}_{12} = 0$. The upper partition of (2.2.80), i.e.,

$$\dot{z}_1 = F_{11} z_1 + \tilde{F}_{12} z_2 + G_1 u \qquad (2.2.81)$$

is termed the "aggregated subsystem" of (2.2.80), and the second partition,

$$\dot{z}_2 = \tilde{F}_{21} z_1 + \tilde{F}_{22} z_2 + \tilde{G}_2 u \qquad (2.2.82)$$

is called "residual subsystem" of (2.2.80). If $\tilde{F}_{12} = 0$, the strict "aggregation" condition (see Equation (2.2.5))

$$C_1 A = F_{11} C_1 \qquad (2.2.83)$$

holds and the large-scale system can be presented by two tandem subsystems, shown in Figure 2.4. However, if $\tilde{F}_{12} \neq 0$, as it is in general, it may be possible to find an aggregate model by enlarging the output vector. This process would begin by finding a matrix $\tilde{C}_1$ of maximum rank $\rho < n - r_1$ so

**Figure 2.4** Tandem position of aggregated and residual subsystems under perfect aggregation.

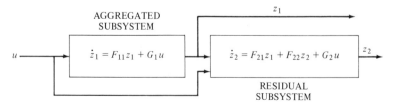

that (2.2.76) is completely aggregable with respect to

$$C = \begin{bmatrix} C_1 \\ \tilde{C}_1 \end{bmatrix} \tag{2.2.84}$$

In order to find the aggregable subsystem with $\tilde{C}_1$, the procedure follows by considering $v_2 = \tilde{F}_{12} z_2$ as the output of the residual subsystem in (2.2.82) and obtaining an aggregation of this subsystem with respect to $v_2$. It is noted that since $\tilde{F}_{12}$ has a dimension of $r_1 \times n_2 (n_2 = n - r_1)$, it does not have a full rank in general. However, there exists a nonsingular matrix $E_2$ such that

$$E_2 v_2 = E_2 \tilde{F}_{12} z_2 = \begin{bmatrix} C_2 \\ 0 \end{bmatrix} z_2 \tag{2.2.85}$$

which extracts linearly independent components of $v_2$. In (2.2.85) matrix $C_2$ has a dimension of $r_2 \times n_2$, $r_2 \le r_1$. Tse (1978) notes that $E_2$ is obtained by the product of matrices of the type found in Gaussian elimination. Now let us define $y_2 = C_2 z_2$, which can be used to find an expression for $v_2$ from (2.2.85), i.e.,

$$v_2 = E_2^{-1} \begin{bmatrix} C_2 \\ 0 \end{bmatrix} z_2 = E_2^{-1} \begin{bmatrix} I \\ 0 \end{bmatrix} y_2 \triangleq F_{12} y_2 \tag{2.2.86}$$

Denoting $z_1 = x^1$, then the residual subsystem (2.2.82) can be rewritten as

$$\dot{z}_2 = \tilde{F}_{21} x^1 + \tilde{F}_{22} z_2 + \tilde{G}_2 u \tag{2.2.87a}$$

$$y_2 = C_2 z_2 \tag{2.2.87b}$$

Recalling the initial ordering of states for the original system as indicated by (2.2.78), one can now proceed with chained aggregation for the residual subsystem (2.2.87) and partition $C_2$,

$$C_2 = \begin{bmatrix} C_{22} & | & C_{23} \end{bmatrix}, \quad \det C_{22} \ne 0 \tag{2.2.88}$$

and determine an $n_2 \times n_2$ nonsingular transformation matrix $D_2$,

$$D_2 = \begin{bmatrix} C_{22} & | & C_{23} \\ -- & | & -- \\ 0 & | & I_{n_2 - r_2} \end{bmatrix} \tag{2.2.89}$$

Once again applying (2.2.89) to (2.2.87a) and repeating the two aggregation steps similar to (2.2.79)–(2.2.82), i.e., by letting

$$D_2 x^2 = \begin{bmatrix} x^2 \\ -- \\ z_3 \end{bmatrix} \tag{2.2.90}$$

then the new aggregated set of subsystems becomes

$$\dot{x}^1 = F_{11} x^1 + F_{12} x^2 + G_1 u \tag{2.2.91a}$$

$$\dot{x}^2 = F_{21} x^1 + F_{22} x^2 + \tilde{F}_{23} z_3 + G_2 u \tag{2.2.91b}$$

$$\dot{z}_3 = \tilde{F}_{31} x^1 + \tilde{F}_{32} x^2 + \tilde{F}_{33} z_3 + \tilde{G}_3 u \tag{2.2.91c}$$

At this point if $\tilde{F}_{23} = 0$, then the chained aggregation process halts, and if not, then the new residual subsystem (2.2.91c) is aggregated with respect to a new output $v_3 = \tilde{F}_{23}z_3$. This chain of aggregation would terminate in $1 \leqslant k \leqslant n_2 = n - r_1$ iterations—a finite number. The final format of the transformed system state matrix after a chain of $k$ aggregations will be of the form

$$
F = \begin{bmatrix}
F_{11} & F_{12} & 0 & \cdots & & & & 0 \\
F_{21} & F_{22} & F_{23} & 0 & \cdots & & & 0 \\
\vdots & \vdots & \vdots & & & & & \\
F_{j1} & F_{j2} & & F_{jj} & F_{j,j+1} & 0 & 0 & \\
\vdots & \vdots & & & & & & \\
F_{k-1,1} & F_{k-1,2} & & & & & F_{k-1,k} \\
F_{k,1} & F_{k,2} & \cdots & & & & F_{k,k}
\end{bmatrix} \qquad (2.2.92)
$$

Control and output matrices will be

$$
G^T = \begin{bmatrix} G_1 G_2 \cdots G_j \cdots G_k \end{bmatrix}, \quad D = \begin{bmatrix} I_{r_1} 0 \cdots 0 \end{bmatrix} \qquad (2.2.93)
$$

where the submatrices $F_{ii}$ have $r_i \times r_i$ dimensions, $r_i \geqslant r_{i+1}$, $n = r_1 + r_2 + \cdots + r_k$ and $I_{r_1}$ is an identity matrix of order $r_1$.

Before the chained aggregation is illustrated by an example, it is worth making a few more remarks on possible interpretation of the aggregation procedure. The GHR $F$ matrix in (2.2.92) is a generalization of block matrices in the lower Hessenberg forms which are commonly used in numerical transformations of matrices, such as the QR algorithm (Householder, 1964; Wilkinson, 1965). A possible interpretation of chained aggregation is a string of similarity transformations (Tse, 1978)

$$
T_j = \begin{bmatrix}
I_1 & & & & \\
& I_2 & & 0 & \\
& & I_{j-1} & \\
0 & & & D_j
\end{bmatrix} \qquad (2.2.94)
$$

on the original system for $j = 2, 3, \ldots, k - 1$, with $D_j$ defined by

$$
D_j = \begin{bmatrix} C_{jj} & C_{j,j+1} \\ 0 & I_{nj} \end{bmatrix}, \quad n_j = n - \sum_{i=1}^{j} r_i \qquad (2.2.95)
$$

$$
P = T_{k-1}T_{k-2}T_{k-3}\cdots T_2 T_1 \qquad (2.2.96)
$$

Matrix $P$ would be of lower block triangular form. However, should it be necessary to permute states of the residual subsystems at intermediate steps to make sure matrices $C_{ii}$ are nonsingular, $P$ would no longer be a lower block-triangular and would be given by

$$P = T_{k-1}H_{k-1}T_{k-2}H_{k-2}\cdots T_1 H_1 \qquad (2.2.97)$$

where $H_i$, $i = 1, 2, \ldots, k-1$ are the state permutation matrices.

**Example 2.2.5.** Consider a sixth-order system

$$\dot{x} = \begin{bmatrix} -0.42 & -0.2 & -0.008 & 0 & 0.95 & 10^{-5} \\ 1 & -0.053 & -3\times 10^{-4} & 10^{-4} & 3.5\times 10^{-4} & 0 \\ 0 & 0 & 0 & 1 & 0 & 0 \\ 0 & 0 & -688 & -5.9 & 0 & 0 \\ 0 & 0 & 0 & 0 & 0 & 1 \\ 0 & 0 & 0 & 0 & -4880 & -18.5 \end{bmatrix} x$$

$$+ \begin{bmatrix} -9.15 \\ -5.2\times 10^{-2} \\ 10^{-2} \\ 899 \\ 10^{-3} \\ -488.5 \end{bmatrix} u \qquad (2.2.98)$$

$$y = \begin{bmatrix} 1 & 0 & 0 & 8.85\times 10^{-4} & 0 & -9.82\times 10^{-3} \\ 0 & 1 & 0 & 0 & 0 & 0 \end{bmatrix} x$$

which is a modified form of a flexible booster problem considered by Medanić et al. (1979). It is desired to find an aggregated model of order $l < 6$ through chained aggregation.

SOLUTION: The chained aggregation procedure begins by examining the $C_1$ matrix in (2.2.98), which is already of the form (2.2.78) with $C_{11} = I_2$. A transformation matrix $T_1$

$$T_1 = \begin{bmatrix} 1 & 0 & | & 0 & 8.85\times 10^{-4} & 0 & -9.82\times 10^{-3} \\ 0 & 1 & | & 0 & 0 & 0 & 0 \\ \hline & 0 & | & & & I_4 & \end{bmatrix}$$
$$(2.2.99)$$

results in the following submatrices $F_{jj}$, $F_{j,j+1}$, $F_{j-1,j}$, etc.

$$F_{11} = \begin{bmatrix} -0.42 & -0.2 \\ 1 & -0.053 \end{bmatrix},$$

$$\tilde{F}_{12} = \begin{bmatrix} -0.617 & -4.85\times 10^{-3} & 48 & 0.177 \\ -3.0\times 10^{-4} & -7.85\times 10^{-4} & 3.5\times 10^{-4} & -0.053 \end{bmatrix}$$

$$\tilde{F}_{21} = \begin{bmatrix} 0 & 0 \\ 0 & 0 \\ 0 & 0 \\ 0 & 0 \end{bmatrix}, \quad \tilde{F}_{22} = \begin{bmatrix} 0 & 1 & 0 & 0 \\ -688 & -5.9 & 0 & 0 \\ 0 & 0 & 0 & 1 \\ 0 & 0 & -4880 & -18.5 \end{bmatrix}$$
$$(2.2.100)$$

and

$$G_1 = \begin{bmatrix} -3.557 \\ -0.952 \end{bmatrix}, \quad \tilde{G}_2^T = \begin{bmatrix} 0.01 & 899 & 10^{-3} & -488.5 \end{bmatrix}$$

It is noted that $\tilde{F}_{12}$ has a full rank, but $\tilde{F}_{12} \neq 0$, and hence an aggregation is performed on the fourth-order residual subsystem defined by (2.2.82), matrices $\tilde{F}_{21}$, $\tilde{F}_{22}$ and $\tilde{G}_2$ by (2.2.100), and choosing $v_2 = \tilde{F}_{12} z_2$ as the output, we can take $E_2 = I_2$ in (2.2.85). The equivalent GHR in partial form for this system after rounding is given by

$$F = \begin{bmatrix} -0.42 & -0.2 & -0.62 & -0.005 & 0 & 0 \\ 1 & -0.053 & 0 & 0 & 0 & 0 \\ 0 & 0 & 0 & 1 & 0 & 0 \\ 0 & 0 & -688 & -5.9 & 0 & 0 \\ 0 & 0 & 0 & 0 & 0 & 1 \\ 0 & 0 & 0 & 0 & -4880 & -18.5 \end{bmatrix}$$

$$G^T = \begin{bmatrix} -3.557 & -0.052 & 0.01 & 899 & 0 & -488.5 \end{bmatrix} \qquad (2.2.101)$$

$$D = \begin{bmatrix} 1 & 0 & 0 & 0 & 0 \\ 0 & 1 & 0 & 0 & 0 \end{bmatrix}$$

Based on this partial GHR form, two aggregated models of second and fourth order may be extracted by neglecting $F_{12}$

$$\dot{z}^2 = \begin{bmatrix} -0.42 & -0.2 \\ 1 & -0.053 \end{bmatrix} z^2 + \begin{bmatrix} -3.56 \\ -0.052 \end{bmatrix} u \qquad (2.2.102)$$

$$v^2 = \begin{bmatrix} 1 & 0 \\ 0 & 1 \end{bmatrix} z^2 \qquad (2.2.103)$$

and

$$\dot{z}^4 = \begin{bmatrix} -0.42 & -0.2 & -0.62 & -0.005 \\ 1 & -0.053 & 0 & 0 \\ 0 & 0 & 0 & 1 \\ 0 & 0 & -688 & -5.9 \end{bmatrix} z^4 + \begin{bmatrix} -3.56 \\ -0.052 \\ 0.01 \\ 899 \end{bmatrix} u$$

$$\qquad (2.2.104)$$

$$v^4 = \begin{bmatrix} 1 & 0 & 0 & 0 \\ 0 & 1 & 0 & 0 \end{bmatrix} z^4 \qquad (2.2.105)$$

Figure 2.5 shows the time response of the first output for a unit step input. The results indicate that although the chained aggregation was carried out for only two steps, the aggregated models are fairly good approximations of the full model.

Some final remarks must be made regarding the final form of the GHR matrix $F$ in (2.2.92). In some applications the inspection of the off-diagonal blocks $F_{j, j+1}$, $j = 1, 2, \ldots, k-1$, may not indicate what the exact decomposition of the system into an aggregated and residual subsystem should be.

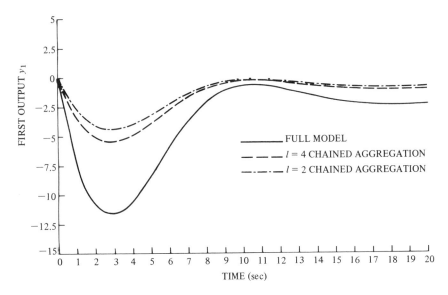

**Figure 2.5** Time responses for Example 2.2.5 using chained aggregation.

When this is the case, Tse and colleagues (1977, 1978) suggest that a new GHR matrix can be obtained by using a modified QR algorithm, called QL by Francis (1961). Tse (1978) has demonstrated that a significant improvement on the time responses of reduced models can be obtained through this modified QR algorithm.

Before leaving the topic of chained aggregation, it is noted that the application of the original QR algorithm for decomposition of linear time-invariant systems has already been proposed by Drenick (1975). Drenick utilized the QR transformation and a sequence of transformations like (2.2.94) and (2.2.96) to resolve modal responses of a linear time-invariant system. No computational test of his approach has been presented however.

Before we turn to the other important approach for large-scale systems modeling, i.e., "perturbation," a few comments on the works of authors in regard to aggregation through another method based on error minimization are due. One of the earliest attempts in aggregating linear time-invariant systems via this criterion is due to Meier and Luenberger (1967), who have synthesized reduced-order transfer functions for SISO systems by a minimization of the mean-square error between outputs of full and aggregated systems. The necessary conditions for this minimization process, similar to another one by Wilson (1970), lead to a set of nonlinear equations for pole-zero locations for aggregated system transfer functions. These equations are solved by an iterative scheme such as the Newton or Gradient scheme. Another approach, due to Anderson (1967), fits the output data from a large-scale discrete-time system to a reduced order model. Still another effort is due to Sinha and Berezani (1971), who use a "pattern-search algorithm" to minimize the sum of output error norms at different time instances raised to a prespecified power. Galiana (1973) extended the fitting methods of Anderson (1967) to multivariable systems. The criterion is a weighted quadratic error, and the necessary conditions are nonlinear matrix equations which are solved by iterative methods.

A possible formulation of these schemes is to obtain the matrices $(F, G, D)$ of

$$\dot{z}(t) = Fz(t) + Gu(t) \qquad\qquad (2.2.106\text{a})$$

$$\hat{y}(t) = Dz(t) \qquad\qquad (2.2.106\text{b})$$

by minimizing a quadratic function of the reduction error

$$e(t) = y(t) - \hat{y}(t)$$

i.e.,

$$J = \int_{0}^{\alpha} e^{T}(t) Q e(t)\, dt \qquad\qquad (2.2.107)$$

where $Q$ is an $r \times r$ symmetric positive-definite matrix (Mahmoud and Singh, 1981). Although all the error minimizations are technically sound, the extraction of an aggregated model requires the solution of a set of rather complicated nonlinear matrix equations which cannot always be used for large-scale systems.

Further readings on this topic may be obtained from Wilson (1974), Wilson and Mishra (1979a, b), Siret et al. (1977b), Riggs and Edgar (1974), Edgar (1975), Hirzinger and Kreisselmeier (1975), Nagarajian (1971), Mishra and Wilson (1980), Mahmoud and Singh (1981), as well as Section 3.6 of Chapter 3. Discussion and comments on the aggregation methods are given in Section 2.5.


## 2.3 Perturbation Methods

The basic concept behind perturbation methods is the approximation of a system's structure through neglecting certain interactions within the model which leads to lower order. From a large-scale system modeling point of view, perturbation methods can be considered as approximate aggregation techniques.

There are two basic classes of perturbations applicable for large-scale systems modeling purposes: "weakly coupled" models and "strongly coupled" models. This classification is not universally accepted, but a great number of authors have adapted it; others refer to them as nonsingular and singular perturbations.

## 2.3.1 Weakly Coupled Models

In many industrial control systems certain dynamic interactions are neglected to reduce computational burdens for system analysis, design, or both. Examples of such practice are in chemical process control and space guidance (Kokotović, 1972), where different subsystems are designed for flow, pressure, and temperature control in an otherwise coupled process or for each axis of a three-axis attitude control system. However, the computational advantages obtained by neglecting weakly coupled subsystems are offset by a loss in overall system performance. In this section the weakly coupled models for large-scale linear systems are introduced. Nonlinear large-scale systems are considered, in part, in Chapter 6, where near-optimum control of these systems is discussed. Consider the following large-scale system split into $k$ linear subsystems,

$$
\begin{bmatrix} \dot{x}_1 \\ \dot{x}_2 \\ \vdots \\ \dot{x}_k \end{bmatrix} = \begin{bmatrix} A_1 & \varepsilon A_{12} & \cdots & \varepsilon A_{1k} \\ \varepsilon A_{21} & A_2 & \varepsilon A_{23} & \varepsilon A_{2k} \\ \vdots & & & \vdots \\ & & & \varepsilon A_{k-1,k} \end{bmatrix} \cdot \begin{bmatrix} x_1 \\ x_2 \\ \vdots \\ x_k \end{bmatrix}
$$

$$
+ \begin{bmatrix} B_1 & \varepsilon B_{12} \cdots & \\ \varepsilon B_{21} & B_2 & \\ \vdots & & \vdots \\ & & B_k \end{bmatrix} \begin{bmatrix} u_1 \\ u_2 \\ \vdots \\ u_k \end{bmatrix} \tag{2.3.1}
$$

where $\varepsilon$ is a small positive coupling parameter, $x_i$ and $u_i$ are $i$th subsystem state and control vectors, respectively, and all $A$ and $B$ matrices are assumed to be constant. A special case of (2.3.1), when $k = 2$, has been called the "$\varepsilon$-coupled" system by Kokotović et al. (1969, 1972), i.e.,

$$
\begin{bmatrix} \dot{x}_1 \\ \dot{x}_2 \end{bmatrix} = \begin{bmatrix} A_1 & \varepsilon A_{12} \\ \varepsilon A_{21} & A_2 \end{bmatrix} \begin{bmatrix} x_1 \\ x_2 \end{bmatrix} + \begin{bmatrix} B_1 & \varepsilon B_{12} \\ \varepsilon B_{21} & B_2 \end{bmatrix} \begin{bmatrix} u_1 \\ u_2 \end{bmatrix} \tag{2.3.2}
$$

It is clear that when $\varepsilon = 0$, the above system decouples into two subsystems,

$$
\dot{\hat{x}}_1 = A_1 \hat{x}_1 + B_1 \hat{u}_1
$$

$$
\dot{\hat{x}}_2 = A_2 \hat{x}_2 + B_2 \hat{u}_2 \tag{2.3.3}
$$

which correspond to two approximate aggregated models (Sandell et al., 1978), one for each subsystem. In this way the computation associated with simulation, design, etc., will be reduced drastically, especially for large-scale system order $n$ and $k$ larger than two subsystems. In view of the decentralized structure of large-scale systems briefly introduced in Chapter 1, these

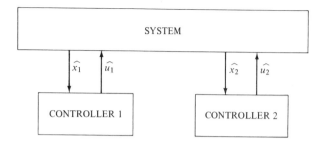

**Figure 2.6** A decentralized control structure for two weakly coupled subsystems.

two subsystems can be designed separately in a decentralized fashion shown in Figure 2.6.

**Example 2.3.1.** In this example a 17th-order linear system representing a simplified model of a three-stand cold rolling mill considered by Jamshidi (1972) is considered. See Figure 2.7. The corresponding state equation is

$$\dot{x}(t) = A(r)x(t) + B(r)u(t) \qquad (2.3.4)$$

where $r$ is pay-off (winding) reel radius considered to be a slow-varying parameter. It is desired to decouple the system.

SOLUTION: The details of this system will be given in Chapter 6; however, for the sake of present example, the $A(r)$ and $B(r)$ matrices are given below for a $3 \times 3$ partitioned form. The first six variables represent the dominant modes of the winding reel (coiler); the next six variables describe the dominant modes of the three-stands; and the last five variables belong to the pay-off reel (decoiler) subsystems. In the formulation shown most,

**Figure 2.7** An $N$-stand cold rolling mill.

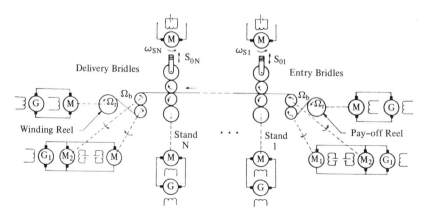

off-diagonal submatrices are highly sparse. The $A(r)$ and $B(r)$ matrices for the three-stand cold rooling mill are shown in (2.35a)–(2.35b), pp. 34–35.

The research regarding weakly coupled systems has taken two main lines. The first line is to set $\varepsilon = 0$ in (2.3.2) and try to find a quantitative measure of the resulting approximation when in fact $\varepsilon \neq 0$ in actual condition. Bailey and Ramapriyan (1973) have provided conditions which would give an estimation on the loss in the optimal performance in a linear state regulator formulation of (2.3.2). Furthermore, they have presented conditions for a criterion of weak coupling, a task similar to that of Milne (1965), whose results will be presented here. The loss of optimal performance for various large-scale systems control laws is discussed in Chapter 6. In Chapter 4, a formal treatment of the effects of subsystems interactions (i.e., $\varepsilon \neq 0$) on the overall performance under the context of hierarchical control will be presented. Pérez-Arriaga et al. (1980, 1981) have proposed a so-called "selective modal analysis" procedure for the separation of "relevant" (not necessarily slow) and "less relevant" (not necessarily fast) parts of the system. Although they have presented a separation criterion based on a "participation factor" and an algorithm to implement it, relatively little computational results and widespread applications of their procedure are available at this time.

Consider a coupled $A$ matrix as presented in (2.3.2) and assume that $A_1$, $A_{12}$, $A_{21}$, and $A_2$ are $n_1 \times n_1$, $n_1 \times n_2$, $n_2 \times n_1$, and $n_2 \times n_2$, respectively, with $n = n_1 + n_2$ being the order of the original large-scale coupled system. Furthermore, let

$$\lambda_i\{A_1\} = \left\{\hat{\lambda}_1, \hat{\lambda}_2, \ldots, \hat{\lambda}_{n_1}\right\}, \quad i = 1, 2, \ldots, n_1$$

$$\lambda_j\{A_2\} = \left\{\hat{\lambda}_{n_1+1}, \ldots, \hat{\lambda}_n\right\}, \quad j = n_1 + 1, \ldots, n \qquad (2.3.6)$$

$$\lambda_k\{A\} = \{\lambda_1, \lambda_2, \ldots, \lambda_n\}, \quad k = 1, 2, \ldots, n$$

be the eigenvalues of diagonal submatrices $A_1$, $A_2$ and matrix $A$. Let us postulate that the moduli of the eigenvalues of $A_1$ and $A_2$ are widely separated from each other (Milne, 1965). Without any loss of generality one can take $|\lambda_i\{A_1\}| \ll |\lambda_j\{A_2\}|$. Let the eigenvalues of $A_1$ be on or inside a circle with radius $r = \max|\lambda_i\{A_1\}|$, $i = 1, 2, \ldots, n_1$ and the eigenvalues of $A_2$ be on or outside a circle with radius $R = \min|\lambda_j\{A_2\}|$, $j = n_1 + 1, n_1 + 2, \ldots, n$, as shown in Figure 2.8. If the following conditions are satisfied, then the system is said to be weakly coupled (Aoki, 1971):

$$(r/R) \ll 1 \qquad (2.3.7a)$$

$$(n_1 \varepsilon_{12} \varepsilon_{21})/R^2 \ll 1 \qquad (2.3.7b)$$

where $\varepsilon_{12} = \max|(A_{12})_{i,j}|$ and $\varepsilon_{21} = \max|(A_{21})_{k,l}|$ for $i, j = 1, 2, \ldots, n_1$ and $k, l = 1, 2, \ldots, n_2$. The term $(r/R)$ is called the "separation ratio", $\varepsilon_{12}$ and $\varepsilon_{21}$ represent the maximum of the moduli of the elements of $A_{12}$ and $A_{21}$ submatrices, respectively.

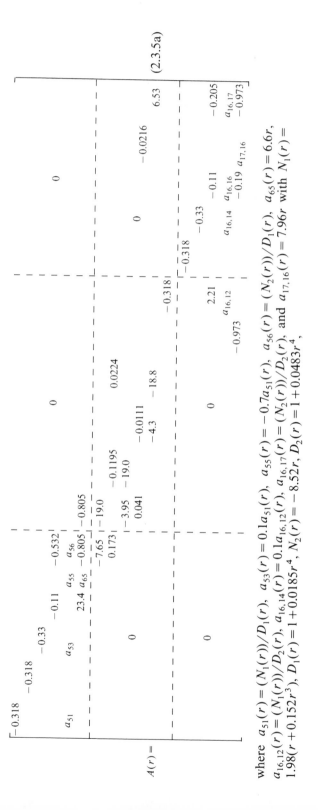

$$A(r) =$$

(2.3.5a)

where $a_{51}(r) = (N_1(r))/D_1(r)$, $a_{53}(r) = 0.1a_{51}(r)$, $a_{55}(r) = -0.7a_{51}(r)$, $a_{56}(r) = (N_2(r))/D_1(r)$, $a_{65}(r) = 6.6r$, $a_{16,12}(r) = (N_1(r))/D_2(r)$, $a_{16,14}(r) = 0.1a_{16,12}(r)$, $a_{16,17}(r) = (N_2(r))/D_2(r)$, and $a_{17,16}(r) = 7.96r$ with $N_1(r) = 1.98(r + 0.152r^3)$, $D_1(r) = 1 + 0.0185r^4$, $N_2(r) = -8.52r$, $D_2(r) = 1 + 0.0483r^4$,

35

and

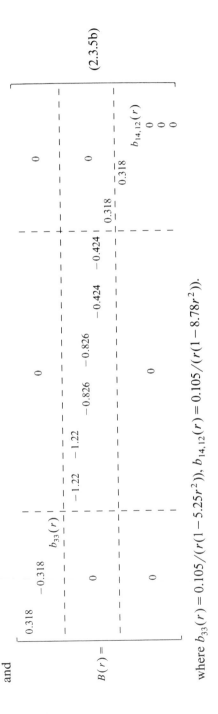

$$B(r) = \begin{bmatrix} 0.318 & -0.318 & & & & 0 & & 0 \\ & b_{33}(r) & & & & & & \\ & & -1.22 & -1.22 & & & & \\ 0 & & -0.826 & -0.826 & & & 0 & \\ & & & & -0.424 & -0.424 & & \\ & & & & & 0.318 & 0.318 & \\ 0 & & & & & & & b_{14,12}(r) \\ & & & & & & & 0 \\ & & & & & & & 0 \\ & & & & & & & 0 \end{bmatrix} \quad (2.3.5b)$$

where $b_{33}(r) = 0.105/(r(1 - 5.25r^2))$, $b_{14,12}(r) = 0.105/(r(1 - 8.78r^2))$.

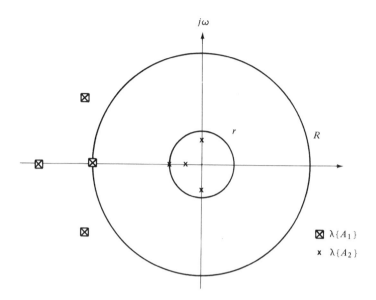

**Figure 2.8** Relative locations of the eigenvalue of $A_1$ and $A_2$ submatrices in a weakly coupled system.

**Example 2.3.2.** Consider a sixth-order system

$$\dot{x} = \begin{bmatrix} 0 & 1 & 0 & 0 & 0 & 0 \\ 0 & 0 & 1 & 0.2 & 0.05 & 0 \\ -400 & -170 & -23 & 0.05 & -0.02 & 0 \\ 0 & -0.01 & -0.02 & 0 & 1 & 0 \\ 0 & 0.01 & -0.015 & 0 & 0 & 1 \\ 0 & 0 & 0 & -0.04 & -0.53 & -1 \end{bmatrix} \quad (2.3.8)$$

We wish to check whether it is weakly coupled.

SOLUTION: The eigenvalues of $A$ are $-9.94$, $-8.08$, $-4.97$, $-0.0816$, $-0.7924$, and $-0.52$, indicating that the first three are much farther away from the $j\omega$-axis than the last three which can be considered as dominant. For two $3 \times 3$ diagonal submatrices, it can be seen that the submatrices $A_1$ and $A_2$ are both in companion forms with the following eigenvalues:

$$\lambda_i\{A_1\} = \{-5, -10, -8\}, \quad \lambda_j\{A_2\} = \{-0.1, -0.8, -0.5\} \quad (2.3.9)$$

implying that $r = 0.8$, $R = 5$, and $(r/R) = 0.16$, which is much smaller than 1; hence condition (2.3.7a) holds. The values of $\varepsilon_{12}$ and $\varepsilon_{21}$ are 0.2 and 0.02, respectively, and the quantity $(n_1 \varepsilon_{12} \varepsilon_{21})/R^2 = 0.00048 \ll 1$. Therefore, it is concluded that system (2.3.8) is weakly coupled.

The second line of research regarding weakly coupled systems has been to exploit such a system in an algorithmic fashion to find an approximate optimal feedback gain through a MacLaurin's series expansion of the accompanying Riccati matrix in the coupling parameter $\varepsilon$. It has been shown that retaining $k$ terms of the Riccati matrix expansion would give an approximation of order $2k$ to the optimal cost (Kokotović et al., 1969). In Chapter 6 this approximate solution of the Riccati matrix will be used for near-optimum design of large-scale systems. The remainder of this section is devoted to strong coupling of large-scale systems.

### 2.3.2 Strongly Coupled Models

Strongly coupled systems are those whose variables have widely distinct speeds. The models of such systems are based on the concept of "singular perturbation", which differs from the regular perturbation (weakly coupled systems) in that perturbation is to the left of the system's state equation, i.e., a small parameter multiplying the time derivative of the state vector. In practice many systems, most of them large in dimension, possess fast changing variables displaying a singularly perturbed characteristic. A few examples were given before; others like power systems the frequency and voltage transients vary from a few seconds in generator regulators, shaft stored energy, and speed governor motion, to several minutes in prime mover motion, stored thermal energy, and load voltage regulators (Kokotović, 1979). Similar time scale properties prevail in many other practical systems and processes, such as industrial control systems, e.g., cold rolling mills as in Figure 2.7 (Jamshidi, 1974); biochemical processes (Heineken et al., 1967); nuclear reactors (Kelley and Edelbaum, 1970); aircraft and rocket systems (Asatani et al., 1971; Ardema, 1974); and chemical diffusion reactions (Cohen, 1974). In fact, some of the "order reduction" techniques which are discussed in the next chapter can be explained in terms of singular perturbation (Kokotović et al., 1976).

Consider a singularly perturbed system described by

$$\dot{x}(t) = A_1 x(t) + A_{12} z(t) + B_1 u(t), \quad x(t_0) = x_0 \qquad (2.3.10)$$

$$\varepsilon \dot{z}(t) = A_{21} x(t) + A_2 z(t) + B_2 u(t), \quad z(t_0) = z_0 \qquad (2.3.11)$$

If $A_2$ is nonsingular, as $\varepsilon \to 0$, (2.3.10) and (2.3.11) become

$$\dot{\hat{x}}(t) = \left( A_1 - A_{12} A_2^{-1} A_{21} \right) \hat{x} + \left( B_1 - A_{12} A_2^{-1} B_2 \right) \hat{u} \qquad (2.3.12)$$

$$\hat{z}(t) = - A_2^{-1} A_{21} \hat{x} - A_2^{-1} B_2 \hat{u} \qquad (2.3.13)$$

Equation (2.3.12) is an approximate aggregated model for (2.3.10)–(2.3.11), which in effect means that the $n$ eigenvalues of the original system are approximated by the $l$ eigenvalues of $(A_1 - A_{12} A_2^{-1} A_{21})$ matrix in (2.3.12). This observation follows the same line of argument when discussing conditions for weakly coupled systems considered by Milne (1965), Aoki (1971, 1978), and Bailey and Ramapriyan (1973). The following example illustrates a singularly perturbed system.

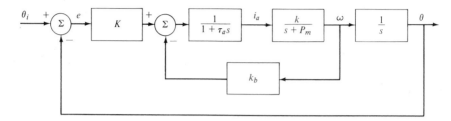

**Figure 2.9** A position control servosystem.

**Example 2.3.3.** Consider a classical third-order position control servosystem shown in block diagram form in Figure 2.9. Find its corresponding state-space model.

SOLUTION: This system has three states, $x_1 = \theta$, $x_2 = \dot{\theta} = \omega$, and $x_3 = i_a$. The corresponding time-domain equations for this system can be written by inspection,

$$\dot{\theta} = \omega, \quad \dot{\omega} + P_m\omega = ki_a, \quad \tau_a di_a/dt + i_a = Ke - k_b\omega,$$
$$e = \theta_i - \theta \tag{2.3.14}$$

where $\theta$ = angular position, $\dot{\theta} = \omega$ = angular velocity, $k$ = motor time constant, $P_m$ = motor pole (reciprocal of time constant), $i_a$ = armature current, $\tau_a = L_a/R_a$ is the armature circuit time constant, $k_b$ = back emf constant, $K$ = amplifier gain, and $\theta_i$ = input position. Letting $u = \theta_i$ and the defined states, the three state equations from (2.3.14) are

$$\dot{x}_1 = \dot{\theta} = \omega = x_2$$
$$\dot{x}_2 = \dot{\omega} = kx_3 - P_mx_2 \tag{2.3.15}$$
$$\tau_a\dot{x}_3 = Ku - Kx_1 - k_bx_2 - x_3$$

It is known that the armature circuit inductance $L_a$ is of the order of a few millihenries, while the armature resistance is of the order of a few ohms. Thus the armature current varies much faster than mechanical variables such as motor speed and position. If we let $\varepsilon = \tau_a$ and $z = x_3$, then (2.3.15) will become

$$\dot{x} = \begin{bmatrix} 0 & 1 \\ 0 & -P_m \end{bmatrix} x + \begin{bmatrix} 0 \\ k \end{bmatrix} z \triangleq A_1 x + A_{12} z \tag{2.3.16}$$
$$\varepsilon\dot{z} = [-K - k_b]x - z + Ku \triangleq A_{21}x + A_2 z + B_2 u$$

which is in a singularly perturbed form. Therefore the usual assumption of ignoring the armature circuit dynamic in a DC motor is in fact a singular perturbation of the original third-order system to a second-order reduced model:

$$\dot{\hat{x}} = \left( A_1 - A_{12}A_2^{-1}A_{21} \right)\hat{x} - A_{12}A_2^{-1}B_2 u \tag{2.3.17}$$
$$\hat{z} = -A_2^{-1}\left( A_{21}\hat{x} + B_2 u \right) \tag{2.3.18}$$

## 2.3.2.a Boundary Layer Correction

It is noted that in going from (2.3.10)–(2.3.11) to (2.3.12) the initial condition $z_o$ of $z(t)$ is lost and the values of $\hat{z}(t_o)$ and $z(t_o) = z_o$ are in general different; the difference is termed a left-side "boundary layer", which corresponds to the fast transients of (2.3.10)–(2.3.11) (Kokotović et al., 1976; Hadlock et al., 1970). To investigate this phenomenon, which in effect explains under what conditions $\hat{x}$ and $\hat{z}$ approximate $x$ and $z$, let $u$ be zero in (2.3.10)–(2.3.11) and let the error between $z$ and $\hat{z}$ be defined by

$$\eta(t) = z(t) - \hat{z}(t) = z(t) + A_2^{-1}A_{21}\hat{x}(t) \qquad (2.3.19)$$

and choose a matrix $E_1(\varepsilon)$ so that when

$$\eta(t) = z(t) + A_2^{-1}A_{21}x(t) + \varepsilon E_1(\varepsilon)x(t) \qquad (2.3.20)$$

is substituted in (2.3.10) and (2.3.11) with $u = 0$, the error vector $\eta$ and slow state $x$ are separated as

$$\dot{x}(t) = \left( A_1 - A_{12}A_2^{-1}A_{21} + \varepsilon E_2 \right)x(t) + A_{12}\eta(t) \qquad (2.3.21)$$

$$\varepsilon\dot{\eta}(t) = \left( A_2 + \varepsilon E_3 \right)\eta(t) \qquad (2.3.22)$$

It can be shown that there exists an $\varepsilon^*$ such that $E_i = E_i(\varepsilon)$, $i = 1,2,3$, is bounded over $[0, \varepsilon^*]$. As $\varepsilon \to 0$, the eigenvalues of (2.3.22) would tend to infinity very much like $\lambda\{A_2/\varepsilon\}$ would. Now a new time variable $\tau$, called "stretched time-scale," is defined:

$$\tau = (t - t_o)/\varepsilon \qquad (2.3.23)$$

where $\tau = 0$ at $t = t_o$ and $dt = \varepsilon d\tau$. For a change of $t$ to $\tau$, the system (2.3.22) will become

$$d\eta(\tau)/d\tau = (A_2 + \varepsilon E_3)\eta(\tau) \qquad (2.3.24)$$

which continuously depends on $\varepsilon$, and at $\varepsilon = 0$ it becomes

$$d\eta(\tau)/d\tau = A_2\eta(\tau) \qquad (2.3.25)$$

with initial condition

$$\eta(0) = z(t_o) - \hat{z}(t_o) \qquad (2.3.26)$$

The Equations (2.3.25) and (2.3.26) constitute the so-called boundary layer correction for $z(t) = \hat{z}(t) + \eta((t - t_o)/\varepsilon)$. From the above formulation, it can be shown that the "slow" and "fast" states $x(t)$ and $z(t)$ are

$$x(t) = \hat{x}(t) + 0(\varepsilon) \qquad (2.3.27)$$

$$z(t) = \hat{z}(t) + \eta(\tau) + 0(\varepsilon) \qquad (2.3.28)$$

where $0(\varepsilon)$ is a "large-0"-order of $\varepsilon$ and is defined as a function whose norm is less than $k\varepsilon$, with $k$ being a constant (Kokotović et al., 1976). It is noted that the boundary layer correction is only significant for the first short seconds away from $t_o$ and reduces to zero after $t = t_1$ seconds as an exponential decay in $\tau = (t - t_o)/\varepsilon$. Figure 2.10 shows the boundary layer phenomenon for the fast state $z(t)$.

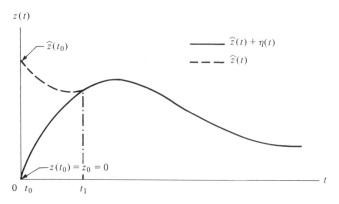

**Figure 2.10** The boundary layer correction for fast state $z(t)$.

### 2.3.2.b Time-Scale Separation

Systems which possess multi-time scales often have distinct clusters of eigenvalues (Avramović, 1979; Kokotović, 1979; Kokotović et al., 1980). It is commonly beneficial to show that linked with this system property there is a distinct possibility of decoupling the system into subsystems, i.e.,"slow" and "fast." One usual scheme for showing this coupling has been decomposition. In fact, the initial model reduction due to Davison (1966, 1968) discussed earlier makes use of this property to separate the slowest subsystem. The main shortcoming of that method is the need to compute the entire set of eigenvalues and eigenvectors. Here an iterative scheme based on a successive weakening of the coupling between slow and fast subsystems is presented. A computational algorithm as well as a numerical example illustrates the separation procedure.

Consider a linear unforced system in singularly perturbed form:

$$\dot{x} = Ax + Ez, \quad x(t_o) = x_o \tag{2.3.29}$$

$$\varepsilon\dot{z} = Cx + Fz, \quad z(t_o) = z_o \tag{2.3.30}$$

where matrix $F$ is assumed to be nonsingular. It was deduced already that when $\varepsilon = 0$, corresponding to a "quasi-steady-state" (qss), the actual $x$ and $z$ differ from qss values $\hat{x}$ and $\hat{z}$ mainly in their fast portions of response. We will now follow this notion in accordance with a report by Kokotović et al. (1980) to develop an iterative procedure for the separation of time scales. Let $\eta_1(t)$ be

$$\eta_1(t) = z - \hat{z} = z + F^{-1}Cx \tag{2.3.31}$$

which transforms (2.3.29)–(2.3.30) into the following set of equations, similar to (2.3.21)–(2.3.22):

$$\dot{x} = A_1 x + E\eta_1 \tag{2.3.32}$$

$$\varepsilon\dot{\eta}_1 = C_1 x + F_1\eta_1 \tag{2.3.33}$$

where

$$A_1 \triangleq A - EF^{-1}C, \quad C_1 \triangleq \varepsilon F^{-1}CA_1 \triangleq \varepsilon B_1, \quad F_1 \triangleq F + \varepsilon F^{-1}CE \tag{2.3.34}$$

The Equations (2.3.32)–(2.3.33) are in a linear time-invariant singularly perturbed form, as in the unforced case of (2.3.10)–(2.3.11). However, the important difference is that in the latter case, as is evident from (2.3.34), slow state $x$ has a weaker presence in (2.3.33). In a similar fashion, for $\varepsilon = 0$ in (2.3.32)–(2.3.33), the qss of $\eta_1$ is obtained from

$$0 = C_1\hat{x} + F_1\hat{\eta}_1 \tag{2.3.35}$$

which is $\hat{\eta}_1 = -F_1^{-1}C_1\hat{x}$. Now introducing $\eta_2$,

$$\eta_2 = \eta_1 - \hat{\eta}_1 = \eta_1 + F_1^{-1}C_1\hat{x} \tag{2.3.36}$$

to represent the error due to letting $\varepsilon \to 0$, $\eta_1$ can be eliminated from (2.3.32)–(2.3.33) in a similar fashion using (2.3.36) to yield

$$\dot{x} = A_2 x + E\eta_2 \tag{2.3.37}$$

$$\varepsilon\dot{\eta} = C_2 x + F_2\eta_2 \tag{2.3.38}$$

where

$$A_2 \triangleq A_1 - EF_1^{-1}C_1, \quad C_2 \triangleq \varepsilon F_1^{-1}C_1 A_2, \quad F_2 \triangleq F_1 + \varepsilon F_1^{-1}C_1 E \tag{2.3.39}$$

Note that (2.3.37)–(2.3.38) is again singularly perturbed with $x$ now having an even weaker presence in (2.3.38) as is evident from (2.3.39) and (2.3.34), where

$$C_2 = \varepsilon^2 F_1^{-1}B_1 A_2 \triangleq \varepsilon^2 B_2 \tag{2.3.40}$$

In a similar fashion, after the $i$th step (2.3.37)–(2.3.38) become

$$\dot{x} = A_i x + E\eta_i \tag{2.3.41}$$

$$\varepsilon\dot{\eta}_i = C_i x + F_i\eta_i \tag{2.3.42}$$

where, similar to (2.3.39),

$$A_i \triangleq A_{i-1} - EF_{i-1}^{-1}C_{i-1}, \quad A_o = A \tag{2.3.43a}$$

$$C_i \triangleq \varepsilon F_{i-1}^{-1}C_{i-1}A_i \triangleq \varepsilon^i B_i, \quad C_o = C \tag{2.3.43b}$$

$$F_i = F_{i-1} + \varepsilon F_{i-1}^{-1}C_{i-1}E, \quad F_o = F \tag{2.3.43c}$$

where $C_i$ is reduced to an order $0(\varepsilon^i)$, as is evident from (2.3.43b). A combination of (2.3.31), (2.3.36), and

$$\eta_i = \eta_{i-1} + F_{i-1}^{-1}C_{i-1}\hat{x} \tag{2.3.44}$$

reveals that

$$\sum_{k=1}^{i} (\eta_k - \eta_{k-1}) = \eta_i - z = \sum_{k=1}^{i} \left(F_{k-1}^{-1}C_{k-1}\right)\hat{x} \tag{2.3.45}$$

which indicates that the slow state $x$ remains the same, while the new fast state $\eta_i$ has identical meaning with $z$ (Kokotović et al., 1980). As the iteration $i$ approaches infinity $A_\infty = A - EF^{-1}C + 0(\varepsilon)$ and $F_\infty = F + 0(\varepsilon)$. It is noted that even after the $i$th iteration, the fast state $\eta_i$ still influences $x$, as shown by (2.3.41). Now if $\eta_i$ is solved by (2.3.42) and substituted in (2.3.41),

$$\dot{x} - \varepsilon EF_i^{-1}\dot{\eta}_i = \left(A_i - EF_i^{-1}C_i\right)x \triangleq A_{i+1}x \tag{2.3.46}$$

it is seen that

$$\zeta_1 = x - \varepsilon EF_i^{-1}\eta_i \tag{2.3.47}$$

is the slow part of $x$. Following this observation, the slow subsystem (2.3.41) becomes

$$\dot{\zeta}_1 = A_{i1}\zeta_1 + \varepsilon A_{i1}EF_i^{-1}\eta_i \triangleq A_{i1}\zeta_1 + E_{i1}\eta_i \tag{2.3.48}$$

Note that $E_{i1}$ is $0(\varepsilon)$, which means that the influence of the fast state $\eta_i$ in the slow system has been reduced. In general,

$$\dot{\zeta}_j = A_{ij}\zeta_j + E_{ij}\eta_i, \quad \zeta_j(0) = \zeta_j^o \tag{2.3.49}$$

$$\varepsilon\dot{\eta}_i = C_i\zeta_j + F_{ij}\eta_i, \quad \eta_i(0) = \eta_i^o \tag{2.3.50}$$

where

$$A_{ij+1} = A_{ij} - E_{ij}F_{ij}^{-1}C_i, \quad A_{io} = A_i \tag{2.3.51a}$$

$$E_{ij+1} = \varepsilon A_{ij+1}E_{ij}F_{ij}^{-1}, \quad E_{io} = E \tag{2.3.51b}$$

$$F_{ij+1} = F_{ij} + \varepsilon C_i E_{ij}F_{ij}^{-1}, \quad F_{io} = F \tag{2.3.51c}$$

which completes the iterative separation of slow and fast modes. Using previous discussions on weakly coupled systems conditions and above development, the following algorithm summarizes the separation of time-scales:

**Algorithm 2.1.** Separation of Time Scales

   *Step 1:* Set $i = j = 0$ and start with $A_i = A, C_i = C, E$ and $F_i = F$ in (2.3.29)–(2.3.30).

   *Step 2:* Evaluate $A_{i+1}, C_{i+1}$, and $F_{i+1}$ from (2.3.43). Set $i = i + 1$.

   *Step 3:* Use $A_{ij}, E_{ij}, F_{ij}$, and (2.3.51) to compute $A_{ij+1}, E_{ij+1}$, and $F_{ij+1}$. Set $j = j + 1$.

*Step 4:* Check for conditions for weakly coupled systems outlined by (2.3.7):

$$f_1 = (r/R) \ll 1, \quad f_2 = n_f \delta_{sf} \delta_{fs}/R^2 \ll 1 \quad (2.3.52a)$$

where

$$r = \max_k |\gamma_k\{A_{ij}\}|, \quad R = \min_k |\gamma_k\{F_{ij}\}| \quad (2.3.52b)$$

$$\delta_{sf} = \max_{l,k} |\{E_{ij}\}_{l,k}|, \quad \delta_{fs} = \max_{l,k} |\{C_i/\varepsilon\}_{l,k}| \quad (2.3.52c)$$

*Step 5:* If conditions (2.3.52) are satisfied, stop. Otherwise go to Step 2.

In above algorithm $\delta_{sf}$ and $\delta_{fs}$ are the maximum moduli of elements in the interaction matrices between slow-fast and fast-slow subsystems, respectively, and $n_f$ is the order of the fast subsystem. Kokotović et al. (1980) have reported excellent results in applying one iteration of (2.3.43) and one of (2.3.51) for a seventh-order model of a single machine-infinite bus system, which is considered in detail here to illustrate the method.

**Example 2.3.4.** Consider the following unforced system:

$$\dot{x} = \begin{bmatrix} -0.58 & 0 & 0 & -0.269 & 0 & 0.2 & 0 \\ 0 & -1 & 0 & 0 & 0 & 1.0 & 0 \\ 0 & 0 & -5 & 2.12 & 0 & 0 & 0 \\ 0 & 0 & 0 & 0 & 377 & 0 & 0 \\ -0.141 & 0 & 0.141 & -0.2 & -0.28 & 0 & 0 \\ 0 & 0 & 0 & 0 & 0 & 0.0838 & 2 \\ -173 & 66.7 & -116 & 40.9 & 0 & -66.7 & -16.7 \end{bmatrix} x$$

$$(2.3.53)$$

which represents a single-machine infinite bus (Calović, 1971). The above method is required to separate its time scales.

SOLUTION: The system's eigenvalues are found to be $0.362 \pm j0.556$, $-0.858 \pm j8.38$, $-3.94$, $-8.55 \pm j8.2$, indicating that two slow and five fast states are present. The system in its present form has the following coupling factors, defined by (2.3.52): $r = \max|\lambda_i\{A_1\}| = 1$, $R = \min|\lambda_j\{A_2\}| = 3.7225$, $\delta_{sf} = 1$, $\delta_{fs} = 173$, and $n_f = 5$; hence $f_1 = r/R = 0.2686$, $f_2 = 62.4$, which indicates that the slow and fast subsystems are highly coupled. The iterative time scale decoupling Algorithm 2.1 was simulated on a digital computer and the factor $f_1$ was reduced to 0.16825, while $f_2$ decreased to 0.00108 in three iterations. Figure 2.11 shows the weakening between the two subsystems. The system $A$ matrix after three iterations is shown in (2.3.54) which indicates that (2.3.53) can be reduced to (2.3.55)–(2.3.56).

$$
\tilde{A} =
\left[
\begin{array}{cc:ccccc}
-0.754 & 0.202 & 3.37\times10^{-3} & -2.77\times10^{-2} & 2.67\times10^{-5} & 2.97\times10^{-5} & -2.44\times10^{-6} \\
-2.315 & 3.5\times10^{-2} & 1.05\times10^{-2} & -6.42\times10^{-4} & 0.104 & 9.74\times10^{-5} & -1.46\times10^{-5} \\
\hdashline
6.84\times10^{-3} & 3.68\times10^{-4} & -5.01 & 2.005 & -0.611 & 0.083 & -2.7\times10^{-4} \\
1.45\times10^{-3} & 4.6\times10^{-5} & -0.026 & -0.272 & 375.53 & 0.196 & -6.24\times10^{-4} \\
-5.66\times10^{-5} & -2.24\times10^{-6} & 0.141 & -0.199 & -0.28 & 9.98\times10^{-7} & 2.64\times10^{-7} \\
-9.1\times10^{-3} & -3.08\times10^{-3} & 0.231 & -0.67 & 1.564 & -0.496 & 1.992 \\
-3.25\times10^{-2} & 1.84\times10^{-2} & -116.0 & 40.93 & -0.066 & -66.67 & -16.69
\end{array}
\right]
\tag{2.3.54}
$$

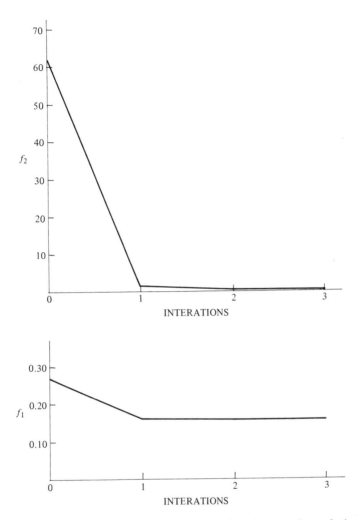

**Figure 2.11** Coupling factors $f_i$, $i = 1, 2$, versus iteration number of time-scale separation of Algorithm 2.1.

$$\text{Slow: } \dot{\zeta}_3 = \begin{bmatrix} -0.754 & 0.202 \\ -2.315 & 0.035 \end{bmatrix} \zeta_3 \qquad (2.3.55)$$

$$\text{Fast: } \varepsilon \dot{\eta}_3 = \begin{bmatrix} -5.01 & 2.005 & -0.611 & 0.083 & 0 \\ -0.026 & -0.272 & 375.53 & 0.196 & 0 \\ 0.141 & -0.199 & -0.28 & 0 & 0 \\ 0.231 & -0.67 & 1.564 & -0.496 & 1.992 \\ -116 & 40.93 & 0.066 & -66.67 & -16.69 \end{bmatrix} \eta_3$$

$$(2.3.56)$$

Note that the iterative time-scale separation has been applied for $A, E, C$, and $F$. This implies that the actual value of parameter $\varepsilon$ does not have to be explicitly specified in order for the method to converge (Kokotović et al., 1980). The method was successfully applied to several other examples, some of which appear as problems at the end of this chapter.

Another iterative time-scale separation scheme, due to Avramović (1979) and Phillips (1979), makes use of a basis for the dominant eigenspace (Stewart, 1976). Due to space limitations, this scheme could not be considered here, but it too is very straightforward and computationally effective.

### 2.3.2.c Multimodeling

A recent effort along the lines of singular perturbation has been the concept of multimodeling introduced by Khalil and Kokotović (1978, 1979a, b, c). The basic idea is to describe a large-scale system by a set of strongly coupled slow and weakly coupled fast subsystems in which each decision maker has a chance to use different simplified models of the same system. A prime example of this concept is a multiarea power system in which each area (subsystem) uses a detailed model of its own area and simplified "equivalent" models for the other areas. In view of this primary information structure for each decision maker, the classical "single" parameter perturbation is extended to the case of "multiparameter" singular perturbation.

Consider a multiparameter singularly perturbed system,

$$\dot{x} = A_o x + \sum_{j=1}^{N} A_{oj} z_j + \sum_{j=1}^{N} B_{oj} u_j, \quad x(0) = x_o \qquad (2.3.57)$$

$$\varepsilon_i \dot{z}_i = A_{io} x + A_{ii} z_i + \sum_{j \neq i} \varepsilon_{ij} A_{ij} z_j + B_{ii} u_i, \quad z_i(0) = z_{io} \qquad (2.3.58)$$

where $x, z_i, u_i$ are $n_o$-, $n_i$-, and $m_i$-dimensional slow state, fast state, and control vectors, respectively, for $i = 1, 2, \ldots, N$. The small positive parameters $\varepsilon_i$ can represent different physical "parasitic" quantities in different subsystems, such as small time-constants, i.e., $\varepsilon_i = c_i T_i$; high amplifier gains, i.e., $\varepsilon_j = c_j / K_j$; and small masses, i.e., $\varepsilon_l = c_l m_l$, where $c_i, c_j$, and $c_l$ are constant factors, and $T_i, K_j$, and $m_l$ are $i$th subsystem "time constant," $j$th subsystem "gain," and $l$th subsystem "mass," i.e., plant, parameters. The parameters $\varepsilon_{ij}, k \neq i$, represent weak coupling between different subsystems. To avoid nested single parameter perturbations in which $z_{i+1}$ is faster than $z_i$, $i = 1, 2, \ldots, N$ the following additional assumption is made:

$$\overline{m}_{ij} \leqslant \varepsilon_i / \varepsilon_j \leqslant \overline{M}_{ij}, \quad j = 1, 2, \ldots, N \qquad (2.3.59)$$

which, in effect, means that the ratios of $\varepsilon_1, \ldots, \varepsilon_N$ are bounded. This is a distinction from all previously treated singularly perturbed systems

(Kokotović et al., 1976) in which all "parasitic" parameters are related to the same parameter.

Let us consider the system (2.3.57)–(2.3.58) again and assume that the $k$th subsystem decision maker neglects the fast dynamics of all other subsystems (i.e., $\varepsilon_j = 0$, $j \neq k$) and its own weak coupling (i.e., $\varepsilon_{ij} = 0$); then we have

$$\dot{x}_k = A_o x_k + \sum_{j=1}^{N} A_{oj} z_j + \sum_{j=1}^{N} B_{oj} u_j \qquad (2.3.60)$$

$$\varepsilon_k \dot{z}_k = A_{ko} x_k + A_{kk} z_k + B_{kk} u_k \qquad (2.3.61)$$

$$0 = A_{io} x_k + A_{ii} z_i + B_{ii} u_i \qquad (2.3.62)$$

with $i \neq k$, $i = 1, 2, \ldots, N$. If $A_{ii}$ are nonsingular, $z_i$ can be solved for from (2.3.62)

$$z_i = - A_{ii}^{-1} (A_{io} x_k + B_{ii} u_i), \quad i \neq k, \quad i = 1, \ldots, N \qquad (2.3.63)$$

and substituted into (2.3.60) and (2.3.61) to give

$$\dot{x}_k = A_k x_k + A_{ok} z_k + B_{ok} u_k + \sum_{j \neq k} B_{kj} u_k \qquad (2.3.64)$$

$$\varepsilon_k \dot{z}_k = A_{ok} x_k + A_{kk} z_k + B_{kk} u_k \qquad (2.3.65)$$

where

$$A_k = A_o - \sum_{j \neq k} A_{oj} A_{jj}^{-1} A_{jo}, \quad B_{kj} = B_{oj} - A_{oj} A_{jj}^{-1} B_{jj} \qquad (2.3.66)$$

The model thus formulated by (2.3.64)–(2.3.65) is the $k$th subsystem. Under this formulation a feedback regulator design has been shown to be stabilizing and near-optimal (Khalil and Kokotović, 1979b). A sufficiency condition called "block D-stability" has been derived (Khalil and Kokotović, 1979a) for testing multiparameter boundary layers. The multimodeling procedure has been applied to decentralized design in Khalil and Kokotović (1979c).

## 2.4 Descriptive Variable Approach

One area in which research is needed is in the development of new structures and techniques for modeling large-scale systems. One such effort is the recent work on a modeling philosophy in which system variables describe the system operation while preserving structure; it is known as the "descriptive variable method" (Stengel et al., 1979; Luenberger, 1977, 1978).

## 2.4.1 Descriptor Variable System

Consider a set of dynamic relations representing a system in discrete-form:

$$g_o(x(0), x(1), u(0)) = 0$$
$$g_1(x(1), x(2), u(1)) = 0$$

$$\vdots \qquad\qquad (2.4.1)$$

$$g_{N-1}(x(N-1), x(N), u(N-1)) = 0$$

$x(k)$ is an $n$-dimensional descriptor vector for each $k = 0, 1, 2, \ldots, N$

$u(k)$ is an $m$-dimensional input vector for each $k = 0, 1, 2, \ldots, N-1$

$g_k(\cdot)$ is an $n$-dimensional vector function for $k = 0, 1, 2, \ldots, N-1$

The above set of relations is said to be in "descriptor form." A special case of (2.4.1) is a linear set of dynamic equations in vector notation:

$$E_{k+1}x(k+1) = A_k x(k) + B_k u(k) \qquad (2.4.2)$$

for $k = 0, 1, 2, \ldots, N-1$, where $E_k$ and $A_k$ are $n \times n$ matrices and $B_k$ is an $n \times m$ matrix for each $k$. The linear descriptor system model (2.4.2) will be reduced to a familiar case when the matrix $E_{k+1} = I_n$, $n \times n$ identity matrix,

$$x(k+1) = A_k x(k) + B_k u(k) \qquad (2.4.3)$$

which is the linear discrete-time system.

The descriptive variables $x(k)$ represent natural interpretations and have natural meanings for a given system. In a Newtonian system, positions, velocities, and accelerations are considered as descriptive variables; so are prices and quantities of commodities in an economic system.

The descriptive variable model of a system given by (2.4.2) can be seen as a general description of a large-scale system consisting of a number of interconnected subsystems. Consider the $i$th subsystem state equation

$$x_i(k+1) = A_i x_i(k) + B_i v_i(k) \qquad (2.4.4)$$
$$z_i(k) = C_i x_i(k) + D_i v_i(k) \qquad (2.4.5)$$

where $x_i(k)$, $v_i(k)$, and $z_i(k)$ are state, input, and output vectors of the $i$th subsystem, respectively. The subsystems can be combined to form the composite system equations

$$x(k+1) = Ax(k) + Bv(k) \qquad (2.4.6)$$
$$z(k) = Cx(k) + Dv(k) \qquad (2.4.7)$$

The relations between subsystem variables and overall system input $v(t)$ and output $y(t)$ may be defined as

$$v(k) = Lz(k) + Mu(k) + Ny(k) \qquad (2.4.8)$$
$$y(k) = Pz(k) + Qu(k) + Rv(k) \qquad (2.4.9)$$

The system equations (2.4.6) and (2.4.7) can be seen to be special cases of (2.4.2), with the descriptor vector equal to $(x(k), v(k), z(k), y(k))$.

The singularly perturbed model of large-scale system discussed in the previous section can also be seen to lead to a set of equations similar to (2.3.10)–(2.3.11). Consider the following discrete-time singularly perturbed system:

$$x_1(k+1) = A_{11}x_1(k) + A_{12}x_2(k) + B_1u(k) \qquad (2.4.10)$$

$$\varepsilon x_2(k+1) = A_{21}x_1(k) + A_{22}x_2(k) + B_2u(k) \qquad (2.4.11)$$

where $x_1(k)$ and $x_2(k)$ are slow and fast subsystem state vectors, respectively, $u(k)$ is the input vector, and $\varepsilon$ is a small coupling parameter. When $\varepsilon = 0$, (2.4.10) and (2.4.11) will be reduced to

$$E_1 x(k+1) = A_1 x(k) + B_1 u(k) \qquad (2.4.12)$$

$$E_2 x(k+1) = A_2 x(k) + B_2 u(k) \qquad (2.4.13)$$

where

$$E_1 \triangleq \left[\begin{array}{c|c} I & 0 \\ \hline 0 & 0 \end{array}\right], \quad E_2 \triangleq \left[\begin{array}{c|c} 0 & 0 \\ \hline 0 & 0 \end{array}\right]$$

$$A_1 = \left[A_{11} \mid A_{12}\right], \quad A_2 = \left[A_{21} \mid A_{22}\right] \qquad (2.4.14)$$

It is therefore clear that the singularly perturbed system model ($\varepsilon = 0$) in (2.4.10)–(2.4.11) is a special case of a descriptor variable system (2.4.2), as indicated by (2.4.12)–(2.4.13).

**Example 2.4.1.** A fundamental model in economic analysis due to W. W. Leontief, called the dynamic Leontief model, is given by Luenberger (1977):

$$x(k) = Ax(k) + B[x(k+1) - x(k)] + d(k) \qquad (2.4.15)$$

where $x(k)$ is the $n$-dimensional production vector of $n$ sectors, $A$ is an $n \times n$ input–output (or production) matrix, $B$ is an $n \times n$ capital coefficient (or stock) matrix, and $d(k)$ is an $n$-dimensional demand vector. Find a descriptive variable reformulation of the Leontief's model.

SOLUTION: The term $Ax(k)$ in (2.4.15) is the fraction of the production required as input for the current production. The second term $B[x(k+1) - x(k)]$ of (2.4.15) is the amount for capacity expansion (Stengel et al., 1979), while the third term $d(k)$ is, as mentioned, the amount of production going for final consumption or demand. The capital coefficient matrix $B$ has commonly very few nonzero elements, since only a few sectors contribute to capital expansion; hence, $B$ is singular. A possible treatment of Leontief's model is by the descriptive variable approach. Rewriting equation (2.4.15),

$$\begin{aligned} Bx(k+1) &= x(k) - Ax(k) + Bx(k) - d(k) \\ &= (I - A + B)x(k) - d(k) \end{aligned} \qquad (2.4.16)$$

which is of the descriptive form (2.4.2).

### 2.4.2 Solvability and Conditionability

The linear time-varying descriptor system (2.4.2) can be rewritten in the following block matrix form,

$$
\begin{bmatrix}
-A_o & E_1 & & & & \\
0 & -A_1 & E_2 & & & \\
& & & \ddots & & \\
& & & \ddots & & \\
& & & & E_{N-1} & 0 \\
& & & 0 & -A_{N-1} & E_N
\end{bmatrix}
\begin{bmatrix}
x(0) \\
x(1) \\
\vdots \\
\vdots \\
x(N-1) \\
x(N)
\end{bmatrix}
=
\begin{bmatrix}
u(0) \\
u(1) \\
\vdots \\
\vdots \\
u(N-2) \\
u(N-1)
\end{bmatrix}
$$

$$(2.4.17)$$

where each $A_k$ and $E_k$ is an $n \times n$ matrix, $x(k)$ is the descriptive variable vector, and $u(k)$ is the control vector. It is noted from (2.4.17) that there are $N+1$ unknown $x(k)$ vectors or $n(N+1)$ scalar unknowns, while there are only $nN$ equations. Thus there is an excess of $n$ unknowns in (2.4.17). Therefore, one may expect that there is not one but a family of $n$ linearly independent solutions (Luenberger, 1977). The notion of "solvability" is introduced to find the condition for a solution of (2.4.17). Before this condition can be given, let us denote the $Nx(N+1)$ block coefficient matrix in (2.4.17) by $P(0, N)$. This matrix can also be thought of having a dimension of $nN$ by $n(N+1)$. Consider the following two definitions due to Stengel et al. (1979).

**Definition 2.4.1.** A linear time-varying descriptive system whose model is given by (2.4.17) is said to be "solvable" if its coefficient matrix $P(0, N)$ has rank $nN$, i.e., full rank.

As indicated above, the linear descriptive system (2.4.17) may have more than one solution; hence, any solution may not be unique. An additional definition is necessary to define a unique solution. This would lead one to another notion called "conditionability," which is defined shortly. Let us delete the first and the last $n$ columns of the coefficient matrix $P(0, N)$ in (2.4.17) and denote it by $Q(0, N)$:

$$
Q(0, N) =
\begin{bmatrix}
E_1 & & & & \\
-A_1 & E_2 & & & \\
& -A_2 & & & \\
& & \ddots & & \\
& & & \ddots & \\
& & & & E_{N-1} \\
& & & & -A_{N-1}
\end{bmatrix}
$$

$$(2.4.18)$$

which has an $nN \times n(N-1)$ dimension and is termed as the "condition matrix."

**Definition 2.4.2.** A linear time-varying descriptive system whose model is given by (2.4.17) is said to be "conditionable" if the condition matrix $Q(0, N)$ has full rank, i.e., $nN - n$.

It is noted that the conditionability is equivalent to the case in which two separate solutions of (2.4.17) differ only in at least one boundary descriptive vector. Conditionability may also be viewed as a condition specifying a unique solution in terms of boundary points. Luenberger (1977) mentions that in fact both "conditionability and solvability of the whole implies conditionability and solvability of a subset."

**Example 2.4.2.** Consider a linear descriptive variable system

$$
\begin{bmatrix} -A_o & E_1 & 0 \\ 0 & -A_1 & E_2 \end{bmatrix} \begin{bmatrix} x(0) \\ x(1) \\ x(2) \end{bmatrix} = \begin{bmatrix} u(0) \\ u(1) \end{bmatrix}
\tag{2.4.19}
$$

where

$$
A_o = \begin{bmatrix} 1 & 0 \\ 1 & 1 \end{bmatrix}, \quad A_1 = \begin{bmatrix} 1 & 1 \\ 0 & 1 \end{bmatrix}, \quad E_1 = \begin{bmatrix} 0 & 1 \\ -1 & 0 \end{bmatrix}, \quad E_2 = \begin{bmatrix} 1 & 1 \\ 1 & 0 \end{bmatrix}
\tag{2.4.20}
$$

Find out whether this system is solvable and/or conditionable.

SOLUTION: For this example, $n = 2$ and $N = 2$; hence, the $4 \times 6$-dimensional descriptive system's coefficient matrix $P(0,2)$ in (2.4.19) is given by

$$
P(0,2) = \begin{bmatrix} -1 & 0 & 0 & 1 & 0 & 0 \\ -1 & -1 & -1 & 0 & 0 & 0 \\ 0 & 0 & -1 & -1 & 1 & 1 \\ 0 & 0 & 0 & -1 & 1 & 0 \end{bmatrix}
\tag{2.4.21}
$$

which has a full rank equal to $nN = 4$; hence, the system (2.4.19) is solvable. The condition matrix $Q(0,2)$ is, on the other hand, $4 \times 2$ dimensional and is obtained by eliminating the first and the last two columns of $P(0,2)$ in (2.4.21):

$$
Q(0,2) = \begin{bmatrix} 0 & 1 \\ -1 & 0 \\ -1 & -1 \\ 0 & -1 \end{bmatrix}
\tag{2.4.22}
$$

which has a rank 2 and hence is conditionable.

### 2.4.3 Time Invariance

A more convenient and simpler case of a descriptive variable system is when $E_{k+1}$ and $A_k$ matrices in (2.4.2) are time-invariant, i.e.,

$$Ex(k+1) = Ax(k) + Bu(k), \quad k = 1,2,\ldots,N-1 \qquad (2.4.23)$$

It is expected that the time-invariant descriptive variable system would have stronger results concerning structure than the more general case. In fact, some definite properties of normal linear discrete systems, such as polynomial methods, can be exploited for linear time-invariance descriptive systems. From an effective point of view, systems described by (2.4.23) should be well-behaved and represent real situations as accurately as possible. Luenberger (1978) indicates that it is often desired to have a procedure for converting the system to be solvable and possess favorable structural properties. This procedure is termed the shuffle algorithm (Luenberger, 1978; Stengel et al., 1979).

The solvability and conditionability of time-invariant descriptor system (2.4.23) is checked by satisfying the rank conditions given above for every value of $N$. A new property of this system is that it is solvable if and only if it is conditionable. A relatively simpler criterion for checking both conditionability and solvability is obtained by utilizing a polynomial matrix defined by $P(s) = [A - sE]$. This criterion is stated as follows: a time-invariant linear descriptive system (2.4.23) is solvable (and conditionable) if and only if the determinant, $\det P(s) = |A - sE|$, does not identically vanish (Luenberger, 1978). This criterion has been presented as a theorem in (Stengel et al., 1979) and (Luenberger, 1978), and a proof has been given by using polynomial matrices "equivalents."

**Example 2.4.3.** Consider a time-invariant linear descriptor system with the following matrices:

$$E = \begin{bmatrix} 1 & 0 & 0 \\ 0 & 1 & 0 \\ 0 & 1 & 0 \end{bmatrix}, \quad A = \begin{bmatrix} 0 & 0 & 1 \\ 1 & 0 & 0 \\ 0 & 1 & 1 \end{bmatrix} \qquad (2.4.24)$$

Check its solvability and conditionability.

SOLUTION: If $E$ is nonsingular, then the system would be solvable; but here $E$ is singular. The polynomial matrix $P(s) = [A - sE]$ is

$$P(s) = \begin{bmatrix} -s & 0 & 1 \\ 1 & -s & 0 \\ 0 & 1-s & 1 \end{bmatrix} \qquad (2.4.25)$$

whose determinant is $\det P(s) = s^2 - s + 1 \neq 0$. Thus the system (2.4.24) is both conditionable and solvable by the criterion.

Luenberger (1978) has applied some of the system theory concepts by introducing canonical structure for descriptive variable systems using matrix pencil $[A - sE]$. The canonical structure is achieved by a change of variable, which makes it inconvenient from a computational viewpoint. The following algorithm is subsequently suggested to acquire computational efficiency and does not require a change of variable.

### 2.4.4 Shuffle Algorithm

Consider the following $n \times 2n$ array:

$$\left[ E \mid A \right] \tag{2.4.26}$$

If $E$ is nonsingular, then the system is solvable and the algorithm is terminated. Otherwise, through row operations the array (2.4.26) is transformed into the following form:

$$\begin{bmatrix} M & \mid & A_1 \\ \hline 0 & \mid & A_2 \end{bmatrix} \tag{2.4.27}$$

where $M$ is a matrix of full rank with dimension of $n_M \times n$, $n_M < n$; matrices $A_1$ and $A_2$ represent a partition on the second side of the array after the row transformations. The dimensions of $A_1$ and $M$ would clearly be the same. The next step is to "shuffle" the array (2.4.27) to obtain

$$\begin{bmatrix} M & \mid & A_1 \\ \hline A_2 & \mid & 0 \end{bmatrix} \tag{2.4.28}$$

If the $n \times n$ matrix to the left of the array in (2.4.28) is nonsingular, then the algorithm would terminate and the system is solvable. If not, the algorithm continues in such a way to obtain null rows in the left, as in (2.4.27), and again make a shuffle back to the form in (2.4.28). This algorithm may terminate in two different ways: when the $n \times n$ matrix $[M^T \mid A_2^T]^T$ of (2.4.28) is nonsingular or when a complete $2n$-dimensional row becomes identically zero, indicating that the system is not solvable. It has been pointed out that the algorithm would terminate one way or the other in $n$ steps or less (Stengel et al., 1979).

**Example 2.4.4.** For a time-invariant descriptive system with $E$ and $A$ matrices,

$$[E \quad A] = \begin{bmatrix} 1 & 0 & 1 & \mid & 0 & 0 & 1 \\ 0 & 0 & 1 & \mid & 0 & 1 & 0 \\ 0 & 0 & 1 & \mid & 0 & 0 & 1 \end{bmatrix} \tag{2.4.29}$$

Apply the shuffle algorithm to check for solvability.

SOLUTION: Since matrix $E$ is singular, the shuffle algorithm is applied to check for solvability. A row operation on (2.4.29) (row 3 − row 2) would give

$$\left[\begin{array}{ccc|ccc} 1 & 0 & 0 & 0 & 0 & 1 \\ 0 & 0 & 1 & 0 & 1 & 0 \\ \hline 0 & 0 & 0 & 0 & -1 & 1 \end{array}\right] \tag{2.4.30}$$

which gives

$$M = \begin{bmatrix} 1 & 0 & 0 \\ 0 & 0 & 1 \end{bmatrix}, \quad A_1 = \begin{bmatrix} 0 & 0 & 1 \\ 0 & 1 & 0 \end{bmatrix}, \quad A_2 = \begin{bmatrix} 0 & -1 & 1 \end{bmatrix}$$

A shuffle of (2.4.30) would give

$$\begin{bmatrix} 1 & 0 & 0 & 0 & 0 & 1 \\ 0 & 0 & 1 & 0 & 1 & 0 \\ 0 & -1 & 1 & 0 & 0 & 0 \end{bmatrix} \tag{2.4.31}$$

At this point the $3 \times 3$-dimensional left matrix in (2.4.31) is nonsingular; hence, the system is solvable.

It is noted that in the shuffle algorithm discussed above the $B$ matrix did not appear, mainly because the solvability does not depend on $B$. However, a general shuffle algorithm is suggested by Luenberger (1978) which performs on the array

$$\left[ E \mid A \mid B \right]$$

The above discussion on the "descriptor variable" system was introduced to make a point that new modeling efforts are necessary for treating large-scale systems more effectively. The formulation of descriptor variable systems falls quite naturally within the context of systems theory and matrix pencils. The shuffle algorithm is a major contribution in checking system solvability and a recursive form which does not change the variable. The descriptor variable systems approach, as promising as it seems, is only an initial step for more efficient large-scale system modeling.

## 2.5 Discussion and Conclusions

In this chapter three main topics concerning modeling and model reduction of large-scale systems represented in time domain—"aggregation," "perturbation," and "descriptor variable" approaches—were considered.

The aggregation of a large-scale system refers simply to a model which uses a "coarses" set of variables. There are two situations in which an aggregated model may be most desirable: when the aggregate state $z(t)$ is of immediate interest, and when $z(t)$ is of concern to the extent that it approximates the actual physical variables. In the first situation, the aggregated model (2.2.4) can be obtained provided that the aggregation conditions (2.2.5)–(2.2.6) are met. It is cautioned here that when an aggregate state $z(t)$ is used for feedback purposes, the unretained modes of the system can be excited by the feedback actuating signals, resulting in instability in the system. The second situation is much more difficult. One important issue is the accuracy of the approximation, which depends on the particular aggregation technique, system inputs, and outputs. For example, if an aggregation scheme tends to neglect fast modes and feedback signals from the aggregated outputs tend to excite such modes, clearly another aggregation technique should be adapted.

In short, the most fundamental question that one can ask is how should one aggregate a system? The answer to this question depends on the very *objectives* of the aggregation procedure. Sandell et al. (1978) raise this issue and mention that an aggregated model with order $l < n$ ($n$ being the original system order) may be appropriate for control purposes but not for estimation, prediction, or more complicated problems such as stochastic control, which involves estimation and control problems combined. Most of the aggregation methods overviewed in this chapter were concerned with reduction of order being based on retaining the dominant modes. The methods of Davison (1966, 1968) and Chidambara (1969) all depend on the eignevalue-eigenvector calculations. Along the same line is the method considered by Anderson (1967) for the reduction of large discrete-time systems. Another notion which has been considered by some authors (Aoki, 1978) is "disaggregation." As the name indicates, disaggregation is the opposite of aggregation; i.e., it is said that vector $z(t)$ is disaggregated into vector $x(t)$ by proper inverse maps (see Figure 2.2). In other words, aggregation and disaggregation can be considered as the basis for constructing approximation techniques in control and estimation of large-scale systems. Further comments on the use of aggregation in control are given in Chapter 6. The interested reader should see Aoki's work (Aoki, 1978). Other schemes, such as continued fraction technique (Chen and Shieh, 1968, 1969; Lamba and Rao, 1978), are concerned with reduction based on certain properties of system matrices and series expansions. The aggregation procedure based on continued fractions has the tendency of providing unstable models emphasizing the point made earlier regarding the excitation of unretained modes. There are two aggregation procedures with definite objectives: one in which a measure of deviation error between the original and reduced-order models outputs is minimized (Wilson, 1970; Sinha and Berezani, 1971); and a second, the chained aggregation method (Tse et al., 1977; Tse, 1978; Medanic et al., 1979), which emphasizes the information structure (output measurements) which is considered as a generalization of the early aggregation method of Aoki (1968, 1971). Chained aggregation is in fact an important step toward determining a systematic procedure for aggregation of large-scale systems. This effort is in line with the theoretical needs for large-scale systems aggregation which may be summarized here. The system aggregation must incorporate not only the order of reduction and important properties such as stability, but it should also include a measure of system performance; a measure of system response; the output measurements and available sensors; and the input disturbances of the system.

It must be mentioned that the discussion of aggregation given in Section 2.2 was devoted solely to time-domain models, but these methods coincide with the frequency-domain model reduction methods of the next chapter. Therefore, further discussion of on time-domain and comparison with frequency-domain methods is presented in Section 3.10.

The second important topic discussed in this chapter was "perturbation," which refers to cases in which some system dynamic interactions are ignored. This concept leads to two related issues of "weakly" and "strongly" coupled systems. The common ground between them is the fact that most large-scale systems have clusters of closed-loop poles (or eigenvalues) which contribute to a system dynamics which is influenced by more than one time scale. The main problem with "strongly coupled" or "singularly perturbed" systems, as discussed in Section 2.3, is that large-scale systems models hardly come in a convenient fashion, with a small parameter multiplying the derivatives of certain variables (Sandell et al., 1978). Thus the main obstacles are that, first, the system's eigenvalues must be ordered and, second, the slow and fast variables should somehow be separated. Fortunately, substantial efforts have been made along both lines. Through matrix iterative techniques such as "double QR," one can first change the system matrix into a "quasi-triangular" form, where the eigenvalues appear on the main diagonal, and then through similarity transformations by unitary matrices the eigenvalues are ordered (Kwatny and Bhatt, 1979; EISPAK, 1973; Wilkinson, 1965; Householder, 1964). Separation of time scales has also been achieved rather elegantly by Kokotović and his associates (1979, 1980), with one powerful iterative algorithm presented in this chapter. There are still some rather important issues remaining in the application of singular perturbation for large-scale system modeling. One such issue is the extension of singular perturbation to discrete-time systems. Many large-scale systems, especially in economics, transportation, energy, resources management, and the like, are best described in discrete time. Pérez-Arriaga et al. (1980) indicate that their "selective modal analysis" encompasses singular perturbation, a claim which must be carefully considered in future research efforts.

An opinion which is shared by many authors regarding large-scale systems has been the need for new methodologies for modeling (Sandell et al. 1978) which would not necessarily stem from "centralized" systems models such as state-space representation (Sections 2.2 and 2.3) or frequency-domain transfer function description (Chapter 3). This need is apparent not only in modeling but also in areas such as control, estimation, and filtering. One of the recent efforts along these lines is the "descriptor variable" representation of large-scale systems (Stengel et al., 1979; Luenberger, 1977, 1978) in which the system structure is preserved by describing the system by its actual physical variables, which seems to be the opposite modeling philosophy of aggregation or perturbation. However, for control and optimization purposes, the natural separation and decomposition of subsystems (e.g., power plants in a power pool) are exploited and a chain structure is assumed for them. A new optimization technique, called *spatial dynamic programming*, is proposed (Stengel et al., 1979) which depends on an effective sequencing of subsystems and the identification of their interaction parameters. For a detailed discussion on continuous-time descriptor systems and their solvability, characterization, numerical analysis, singular perturbations, use in circuit analysis, and applications to power systems, see Manke (1979).

Another recent approach for the modeling of large-scale systems is the component connection model (CCM) due to Saeks and DeCarlo (1979, 1981). CCM for a linear system consists of a set of two vector matrix equations which describe component dynamics and component interconnections separately. Interconnections are linear algebraic and are accounted for by conservation laws such as Kirchhoff's voltage and current laws. The use of CCM within the context of model reduction has been considered by Wasynczak and DeCarlo (1981). Here the reduction occurs on the component level as opposed to the composite system level. The main result here is the establishment of a link between singular perturbation as a model reduction technique and the CCM-based component level reduction scheme. This link is basically as follows: under certain conditions, performing a reduction on the component level and then forming a reduced composite system model is equivalent to forming a composite system–state model and then reducing it in accordance to a singularly perturbed formulation as described by (2.3.10)–(2.3.13). The approach seems very promising, but as a result of a lack of space it cannot be treated in greater detail here.

## Problems

**2.1.** For a system

$$(A, B) = \left( \begin{bmatrix} -1 & 0.5 & 1 \\ 2 & -10 & 0 \\ 1 & 0 & -20 \end{bmatrix}, \begin{bmatrix} 1 \\ 1 \\ 1 \end{bmatrix} \right)$$

find a second-order aggregated model using the two approaches discussed in Example 2.2.1. Are these dynamically exact?

**2.2.** A third-order system is described by

$$\dot{x} = \begin{bmatrix} -1.25 & 0.02 & 0 \\ -0.5 & -0.1 & -1 \\ -1 & -0.5 & -0.08 \end{bmatrix} x + \begin{bmatrix} 1 \\ 0 \\ 1 \end{bmatrix} u$$

Find an aggregated model using the model scheme of Davison (1966) described in Section 2.2.1.

**2.3.** Repeat Problem 2.2 using the modal scheme of Chidambara (1969).

**2.4.** A second-order system is given by

$$\dot{x} = \begin{bmatrix} -1 & 0 \\ 1 & -10 \end{bmatrix} x + \begin{bmatrix} 1 \\ 1 \end{bmatrix} u.$$

Find an aggregation matrix which would provide a dynamically exact aggregation. Repeat for both the dominant and nondominant eigenvalues of the system.

**2.5.** Show that aggregation matrix $C$ described by Equation (2.2.53) provides perfect aggregation.

**2.6.** Suppose that a $4 \times 4$ $A$ matrix has $\lambda\{A\} = \{a, a, b \pm jc\}$; then it is known (Fortman and Hitz, 1977) that its modal matrix is

$$M = \begin{bmatrix} \xi_1 & | & \nu_1 & | & \upsilon_1 & | & w_1 \end{bmatrix},$$

where $\xi_1$ is a right eigenvector, $\nu_1$ is a generalized eigenvector, and $u_{1,3} = \upsilon_1 \pm jw_1$ is a pair of complex conjugate eigenvectors. Using this, extend the modal aggregation of Davison (1966) for repeated and complex eigenvalues-eigenvectors.

**2.7.** Repeat Problem 2.6 for the method of Chidambara (1969).

**2.8.** Use modal aggregation methods to find a second-order reduced model for

$$\dot{x} = \begin{bmatrix} 0 & 1 & 0 & 0 \\ 0 & 0 & 1 & 0 \\ 0 & 0 & 0 & 1 \\ -400 & -460 & -262 & -32 \end{bmatrix} x + \begin{bmatrix} 1 \\ 0 \\ 1 \\ 1 \end{bmatrix} u$$

**2.9.** Repeat Problem 2.8 for

$$(A, B) = \left( \begin{bmatrix} 0 & 1 & 0 \\ 0 & 0 & 1 \\ -20 & -22 & -12 \end{bmatrix}, \begin{bmatrix} 1 \\ 1 \\ 1 \end{bmatrix} \right)$$

**C2.10.*** A system is described by

$$(A,B) = \left( \begin{bmatrix} -2 & -1 & -0.5 & -0.1 & -0.05 \\ 0.5 & -1 & 0.2 & -4 & 0.8 \\ 1 & -0.1 & -0.25 & 0 & -1 \\ 0 & 1 & -0.1 & -0.1 & 0 \\ 1 & -1 & -1 & 0.5 & -5 \end{bmatrix}, \begin{bmatrix} 1 \\ 0 \\ 1 \\ 1 \\ 1 \end{bmatrix} \right)$$

Using a computer routine for eigenvalue-eigenvector evaluations, find an aggregated model using the modal method of Davidson (1966).

**2.11.** Consider a fourth-order system

$$\dot{x} = \begin{bmatrix} 0 & 1 & 0 & 0 \\ 0 & 0 & 1 & 0 \\ 0 & 0 & 0 & 1 \\ -0.5 & -1 & -10 & -3 \end{bmatrix} x + \begin{bmatrix} 0 \\ 0 \\ 0 \\ 1 \end{bmatrix} u, \; y = \begin{bmatrix} 1 & 1 & 2 & 2 \end{bmatrix} x$$

Find a reduced-order model for the system using the continued fraction method of Section 2.2.2.

**2.12.** Repeat Problem 2.11 for the system of Problem 2.8 using an output equation $y = \begin{bmatrix} 1 & 2 & 3 & 4 \end{bmatrix} x$.

**C2.13.** For the system of Problem C2.10, let the output be defined by

$$y = \begin{bmatrix} 1 & 0 & 0 & 0.05 & -0.01 \\ 0 & 1 & 0.01 & 0 & 0 \end{bmatrix} x$$

Find a chained aggregated model for the system.

**2.14.** Is the system

$$(A,B,C) = \left( \begin{bmatrix} 0 & 1 & 0 \\ 0 & 0 & 1 \\ -0.5 & -5.6 & -6.1 \end{bmatrix}, \begin{bmatrix} 0 \\ 0 \\ 1 \end{bmatrix}, \begin{bmatrix} 1 & 0 & 1 \end{bmatrix} \right)$$

weakly coupled?

**2.15.** For a system

$$(A,B,C) = \left( \begin{bmatrix} 0 & 1 & 0 \\ 0 & 0 & 1 \\ -1 & -a & -b \end{bmatrix}, \begin{bmatrix} 1 \\ 0 \\ 1 \end{bmatrix}, \begin{bmatrix} 1 & 0 & 1 \end{bmatrix} \right)$$

find the region(s) in the $(b-a)$ plane such that the system is weakly coupled.

---

*Problems with a letter "C" denote computer problems.

**C2.16.** Consider an eighth-order unforced system

$$\dot{x} = \begin{bmatrix}
-0.5 & 0 & 0 & -0.2 & 0.1 & 0.2 & 0 & 0.1 \\
0 & -1 & 0 & 0.1 & 0 & 1 & 0 & 0 \\
0.1 & 0 & -2 & 0 & 0 & 0 & 1 & 0 \\
0.05 & 0 & 0 & -20 & -1 & 0 & 0 & 0 \\
-0.15 & 1 & 0 & 1 & 30 & 1 & 0 & 0 \\
0 & 0 & 0.15 & -0.2 & -0.3 & -1 & 0 & 0 \\
-15 & 0 & 0 & 1 & 0 & 0 & 0.08 & 2 \\
-80 & 60 & -10 & 0 & -50 & 0 & 6 & -15
\end{bmatrix} x$$

Use Algorithm 2.1 and your favorite computer program to separate the time scales.

**C2.17.** Use an appropriate computer program to check whether the system

$$\dot{x} = \begin{bmatrix}
-0.21054 & -0.10526 & -0.007378 & 0 & 0.0706 & 0 \\
1 & -0.03537 & -0.000118 & 0 & 0.0004 & 0 \\
0 & 0 & 0 & 1 & 0 & 0 \\
0 & 0 & -605.16 & -4.92 & 0 & 0 \\
0 & 0 & 0 & 0 & 0 & 1 \\
0 & 0 & 0 & 0 & -3906.25 & -12.5
\end{bmatrix} x$$

is weakly coupled.

**2.18.** A singularly perturbed system is described by

$$\dot{x} = -x + z, \quad x(0) = -1$$
$$\varepsilon \dot{z} = x - 5z, \quad z(0) = 1$$

Find a boundary layer for this system.

**2.19.** For a linear discriptive variable system

$$\begin{bmatrix} -A_o & E_1 & 0 \\ 0 & -A_1 & E_2 \end{bmatrix} \begin{bmatrix} x(0) \\ x(1) \\ x(2) \end{bmatrix} = \begin{bmatrix} u(0) \\ u(1) \end{bmatrix}$$

where

$$A_0 = \begin{bmatrix} 1 & 0 \\ 1 & 1 \end{bmatrix}, \quad A_1 = \begin{bmatrix} k & 1 \\ 1 & 1 \end{bmatrix},$$

$$E_1 = \begin{bmatrix} 0 & k \\ k & 0 \end{bmatrix}, \quad E_2 = \begin{bmatrix} 0 & 1 \\ 1 & 0 \end{bmatrix}$$

find the values of $k$ such that the system is **(a)** solvable, **(b)** conditionable, and **(c)** both solvable and conditionable.

**2.20.** Repeat Example 2.4.4 with

$$E = \begin{bmatrix} 1 & 0 & 0 \\ 0 & 1 & 1 \\ 0 & 0 & 0 \end{bmatrix}, \quad A = \begin{bmatrix} 1 & 1 & 0 \\ 0 & 1 & 0 \\ 1 & 0 & 0 \end{bmatrix}$$

for a solvability check.

## References

Anderson, J. H. 1967. Geometrical approach to reduction of dynamical systems. *Proc. IEE* 114:1014–1018.

Aoki, M. 1968. Control of large-scale dynamic systems by aggregation. *IEEE Trans. Aut. Cont.* AC-13:246–253.

Aoki, M. 1971. Aggregation, in D. A. Wismer, ed., *Optimization Methods for Large-Scale Systems...with Applications*, chapter 5, pp. 191–232. New York: McGraw-Hill Book Co.

Aoki, M. 1978. Some approximation methods and control of large-scale systems. *IEEE Trans Aut. Cont.* AC-23:173–182.

Ardema, M. D. 1974. Singular perturbations in flight mechanics. NASA, TMX-62, p. 380.

Astani, K.; Iwazumi, T.; and Hattori, Y. 1971. Error estimation of prompt jump approximation by singular perturbation theory. *J. Nucl. Sci. Technol.* 8:653–656.

Avramović, B. 1979. Iterative algorithms for the time scale separation of linear dynamical systems, L. H. Fink and T. A. Trygar, eds., in *Systems Engineering for Power: Organizational Forms for Large-Scale Systems*, pp. 1.10–1.12, Vol. II, US DOE, Washington, D.C.

Bailey, F. N., and Ramapriyan, H. K. 1973. Bounds on suboptimality in the control of linear dynamic systems. *IEEE Trans. Aut. Cont.* AC-18:532–534.

Bertrand, P.; Gruca, A.; Michailesco, G.; and Siret, J. M. 1977. Sur l'utilisation de modeles reduits dans l'analyse et la commande de systemes complexes. *Proc. 4th IFAC Int. Symp.* (Fredriction, Canada). Pergamon, New York.

Brogan, W. L. 1974. *Modern Control Theory*, pp. 1–7. Quantum, New York.

Calović, M. 1971. Dynamical state space models of electric power systems. Dept. Elec. Engr., Univ. Illinois, Urbana, IL.

Chen, C. F., and Shieh, L. S. 1968. A novel approach to linear model simplification. *Int. J. Contr.* 8:561–570.

Chen, C. F., and Shieh, L. S. 1969. Continued fraction inversion by Routh's array. *IEEE Trans. Circuit Theory.* CT-16:197–202.

Chidambara, M. R. 1969. Two simple techniques for simplifying large dynamic systems. *Proc. JACC*, (Univ. Colorado, Boulder, CO).

Chipman, J. S. 1976. Estimation and aggregation in econometrics: An application of the theory of generalized inverse, in *Generalized Inverse and Applications*. Academic Press, New York.

Chow, J. H., and Kokotović, P. V. 1976. A decomposition of near-optimum regulators for systems with slow and fast modes. *IEEE Trans. Aut. Cont.* AC-21:701–705.

Cohen, D. S., ed. 1974. Mathematical aspects of chemical and biochemical problems and quantum chemistry. *SIAM-AMS Proceedings*, American Math. Soc., Providence, RI.

Cruz, J. B., Jr. 1976. Stackelberg strategies for multilevel systems, in Y. C. Ho and S. K. Mitter, eds., *Directions in Large Scale Systems*. Plenum, New York.

Davison, E. J. 1966. A method for simplifying linear dynamic systems. *IEEE Trans. Aut. Cont.* AC-12:119–121.

Davison, E. J. 1968. A new method for simplifying linear dynamic systems. *IEEE Trans. Aut. Cont.* AC-13:214–215.

DeCarlo, R., and R. Saeks. 1979. A root locus technique for interconnected systems. *IEEE Trans. Syst. Man. Cyber.* SMC-9:53–55.

Drenick, P. E. 1975. On the decomposition of state space. *IEEE Trans. Aut. Cont.* AC-20:269–271.

Edgar, T. F. 1975. Least squares model reduction using step response. *Int. J. Contr.* 22:261–270.

EISPAK. 1973. *Eigensystem Workshop.* Argone National Laboratory, Argone, IL.

Fortman, T. E., and Hitz, K. L. 1977. An Introduction to Linear Control Systems, pp. 654–661. Marcel Dekker, New York.

Francis, J. G. F. 1961. The QR transformation, Part I and II. *The Computer Journal* 4:265–271, 332–341.

Galiana, F. D. 1973. On the approximation of multiple-input multiple-output constant linear systems. *Int. J. Contr.* 17:1313–1324.

Gantmacher, F. R. 1966. Theorie des Matrices. Dunod, Paris, France.

Gelb, A., ed. 1974. *Applied Optimal Estimation.* MIT Press, Cambridge, MA.

Hadlock, C.; Jamshidi, M.; and Kokotović, P. V., 1970. Near optimum design of three time-scale systems. *Proc. 4th Princeton Conf.*, pp. 118–122. (Princeton, NJ).

Heineken, F. G.; Tsuchiya, H. M.; and Aris, R. 1967. On the mathematical status of the pseudo-steady-state hypothesis of biochemical kenetics. *Math. Biosciences* 1:95.

Hickin, J., and Sinha, N. K. 1980. Model reduction for linear multivariable systems. *IEEE Trans. Aut. Cont.* AC-25:1121–1127.

Hirzinger, G., and Kreisselmeier, G. 1975. On optimal approximation of high-order linear systems by low-order models. *Int. J. Contr.* 22:399–408.

Householder, A. S. 1964. *The Theory of Matrices in Numerical Analysis.* Blaisdell, New York.

Hutton, M. F., and Friedland, B. 1975. Routh approximations for reducing order of linear time-invariant systems. *IEEE Trans. Aut. Cont.* AC-20:329–337.

Jamshidi, M. 1972. A near-optimum controller for cold-rolling mills. *Int. J. Contr.* 16:1137–1154.

Jamshidi, M. 1974. Three-stage near-optimum design of nonlinear control processes. *Proc. IEE* 121:886–892.

Jamshidi, M. 1982. An overview on reduction of large-scale systems models. Submitted to *IFAC J. Automatica.*

Kelley, H. J., and Edelbaum, T. N. 1970. Energy climbs, energy turns and asymptotic expansions. *J. Aircraft* 7:93–95.

Khalil, H. K., and Kokotović, P. V. 1978. Control strategies for decision makers using different models of the same system. *IEEE Trans. Aut. Cont.* AC-23:289–297.

Khalil, H. K., and Kokotović, P. V. 1979a. D-stability and multi-parameter singular perturbation, *SIAM J. Contr. Optim.* 17:56–65.

Khalil, H. K., and Kokotović, P. V. 1979b. Control of linear systems with multi-parameter singular perturbations. *IFAC J. Automatica* 15:197–207.

Khalil, H. K., and Kokotović, P. V. 1979c. Decentralized stabilization of systems with slow and fast modes. *Proc. JACC* (Denver, CO).

Kokotović, P. V. 1972. Feedback design of large linear systems, in J. B. Cruz, Jr., ed., *Feedback Systems*, pp. 99–137. McGraw-Hill, New York.

Kokotović, P. V. 1979. Overview of multimodeling by singular perturbations, in L. H. Fink and T. A. Trygar, eds., *Systems Engineering for Power: Organizational Forms for Large-Scale Systems*, pp. 1.3–1.4. US DOE, Washington, D.C.

Kokotović, P. V.; O'Malley, R. E., Jr.; and Sannuti, P. 1976. Singular perturbations and order reduction in control theory—An overview. *IFAC J. Automatica* 12:123–132.

Kokotović, P. V.; Perkins, W. R.; Cruz, J. B.; and D'Ans, G. 1969. $\varepsilon$-coupling method for near-optimum design of large-scale linear systems. *Proc. IEE* 116:889–892.

Kokotović, P. V.; Allemong, J. J.; Winkelman, J. R.; and Chow, J. H. 1980. Singular perturbation and iterative separation of time scales. *IFAC J. Automatica* 16:23–34.

Kwatny, H. G., and Bhatt, A. D. 1979. The reduction of large-scale linear models, in L. H. Fink and T. A. Trygar, eds., *Systems Engineering for Power: Organizational Forms for Large-Scale Systems*, pp. 3.3–3.15. US DOE, Washington, D.C.

Lamba, S. S., and Rao, S. V. 1978. Aggregation matrix for the reduced order continued fraction expansion model of Chen&Shieh, *IEEE Trans. Aut. Cont.* AC-23:81–83.

Luenberger, D. G. 1977. Dynamic equations in descriptor form. *IEEE Trans. Aut. Cont.* AC-22:312–322.

Luenberger, D. G. 1978. Time-invariance descriptor systems. *IFAC J. Automatica* 14:473–480.

Mahmoud, M. S., and Singh, M. G. 1981. *Large-Scale Systems Modelling.* pp. 156–166. Oxford, England: Pergamon Press.

Malinvaud, E. 1956. L'Aggregation dans les models economiques. *Cahiers du Sémnaire d'Econometrive* 4:69–146.

Manke, J. W. 1979. Solvability of large-scale descriptor systems. in L. H. Fink and T. A. Trygar, eds., *Systems Engineering for Power: Organizational Forms for Large-Scale Systems*, pp. 4.1–4.53, Vol. I. US DOE, Washington, D.C.

Medanić, J. V.; Tse, E. C. Y.; and Perkins, W. R. 1978. A new approach to model reduction based on system output information structure. *Proc. 7th Triennial World Congress of IFAC*, Helsinki, Finland.

Medanić, J. V.; Tse, E. C. Y.; and Perkins, W. R. 1979. Model reduction based on system output information structure, in L. H. Fink and T. A. Trygar, eds., *Systems Engineering for Power: Organizational Forms for Large-Scale Systems*, pp. 1.3–1.4, Vol. II. US DOE, Washington, D.C.

Meier, L. and Luenberger, D. G. 1967. Approximation of linear constant systems. *IEEE Trans. Aut. Cont.* AC-12:585–588.

Mesarovic, M. D.; Macko, D.; and Takahara, Y. 1970. *Theory of Hierarchical Multilevel Systems.* Academic Press, New York.

Michailesco, G., and J. M. Siret. 1980. Comments on "Aggregation matrix for the reduced-order continued fraction expansion model of Chen and Shieh" and authors' reply, *IEEE Trans. Aut. Cont.* AC-25:133–134.

Milne, R. D. 1965. The analysis of weakly coupled dynamic systems. *Int. J. Contr.* 2:171–199.

Mishra, R. N., and Wilson, D. A. 1980. A new algorithm for optimal reduction of multivariable systems. *Int. J. Contr.* 31:443–466.

Nagaragan, R. 1971. Optimum reduction of large dynamic systems. *Int. J. Contr.* 14:1164–1174.

Penrose, R. 1955. A generalized inverse for matrices. *Proc. Cambridge Phil. Soc.* 51:406–413.

Pérez-Arriaga, I. J.; Schweppe, F. C.; and Verghese, G. C. 1980. Selective modal analysis: basic results. *Proc. IEEE Int. Conf. Circuits and Computers.* Port Chester, NY. pp. 649–656.

Pé ez-Arriaga, I. J.; Verghese, G. C.; and Schweppe, F. C. 1981. Determination of relevant state variables for selective modal analysis. *Proc. JACC.* Charlottesville, VA. paper TA-4F.

Phillips, R. G. 1979. A two-stage design of linear feedback controls, in L. H. Fink and T. A. Trygar, eds., *Systems Engineering for Power: Organizational Forms for Large-Scale Systems*, pp. 1.18–1.21, Vol. II. US DOE, Washington, D.C.

Rao, S. V., and Lamba, S. S. 1974. Suboptimal control of linear systems via simplified models of Chidambara, *Proc. Inst. Elec. Eng.* 121:879–882.

Riggs, J. B., and Edgar, T. F. 1974. Least squares reduction of linear systems impulse response. *Int. J. Contr.* 20:213–223.

Saeks, R., and DeCarlo, R. 1981. *Interconnected Dynamical Systems.* Marcel Dekker, New York.

Sage, A. P. 1977. *Methodologies for Large-Scale Systems.* McGraw-Hill, New York.

Sandell, N. R., Jr.; Varaiya, P.; Athans, M. J. and Safonov, M. G. 1978. *Survey of decentralized control methods for large scale systems, IEEE Trans. Aut. Cont.* AC-23:108–128 (special issue on large-scale systems).

Šiljak, D. D. 1978. *Large-Scale Dynamic Systems.* Elsevier North Holland, New York.

Sinha, N. K., and Berezani, G. T. 1971. Optimum approximation of high-order systems by low-order models. *Int. J. Contr.* 14:951–959.

Siret, J. M.; Michailesco, G.; and Bertrand, P. 1977a. Representation of linear systems by aggregated models. *Int. J. Contr.* 26:121–128.

Siret, J. M.; Michailesco, G.; and Bertrand, P. 1977b. Optimal approximation of high-order systems subject to polynomial inputs. *Int. J. Contr.* 26:963–971.

Stengel, D. N.; Luenberger, D. G.; Larson, R. E.; and Cline, T. S. 1979. A descriptor variable approach to modeling and optimization of large-scale systems, Report No. CONS-2858-T1. US DOE, Oak Ridge, TN.

Stewart, G. W. 1976. Simultaneous iteration method for computing invariant subspaces of non-Hamiltonian matrices. *Num. Math.* 25:123–136.

Tse, E. C. Y.; Medanić, J. V.; Perkins, W. R. 1977. Chained aggregation of linear time invariant systems. *Proc. JACC.* San Francisco, CA.

Tse, E. C. Y. 1978. Model reduction and decentralized control of large-scale systems using chained aggregation, Report DC-18, Decision and Control Lab., CSL, Univ. of Illinois, Urbana, IL.

Wasynczak, O., and DeCarlo, R. 1981. The component connection model and structure preserving model order reduction. *IFAC J. Automatica* 17:619–626.

Wilkinson, J. H. 1965. *The Algebraic Eigenvalue Problem*. Oxford University Press, Oxford, England.

Wilson, D. A. 1970. Optimum solution of model reduction problem. *Proc. IEE* 117:1161–1165.

Wilson, D. A. 1974. Model reduction for multivariable systems. *Int. J. Contr.* 20:57–64.

Wilson, D. A., and Mishra, R. N. 1979a. Optimal reduction of multivariable systems. *Int. J. Contr.* 20:57–64.

Wilson, D. A., and Mishra, R. N. 1979b. Optimal reduction of multivariable systems. *Int. J. Contr.* 29:267–278.

# Chapter 3

# Large-Scale Systems Modeling: Frequency Domain

## 3.1 Introduction

The realistic models of large-scale systems are so high in dimension that a direct simulation or design would be neither computationally desirable nor physically possible in many cases. A multiarea large-scale power system, for example, is a very high-dimensional system which is physically and geographically composed of several plants connected by tie lines. It therefore goes without saying that the reduction of system models is highly desirable. In Chapter 2, three general modeling philosophies for large-scale systems were introduced, all of which were concerned with time-domain models. Model reductions through aggregation, and singular and regular perturbation were discussed for large-scale linear time-invariant systems in state-space form

$$\dot{x}(t) = Ax(t) + Bu(t) \qquad (3.1.1)$$

$$y(t) = Cx(t) \qquad (3.1.2)$$

where $x$, $u$, and $y$ are $n$-, $m$-, and $r$-dimensional state, control, and output vectors, respectively. Alternatively, system (3.1.1)–(3.1.2) can be represented in frequency domain:

$$Y(s) = H(s)U(s) \qquad (3.1.3)$$

$$H(s) = C(sI - A)^{-1}B \qquad (3.1.4)$$

where $H(s)$ is the $(r \times m)$-dimensional transfer function matrix whose elements are rational functions of $s$, i.e.,

$$H_{ij}(s) = \frac{d_0 + d_1 s + \cdots + d_{n-1}s^{n-1}}{e_0 + e_1 s + \cdots + e_n s^n} = \frac{D(s)}{\Delta(s)} \qquad (3.1.5)$$

where $\Delta(s) = \det(sI - A)$ is the characteristic polynomial of the system and $D(s)$ is an $(n-1)$st order polynomial whose roots are the zeros of $H_{ij}(s)$. Alternatively, matrix $H(s)$ can be expressed as

$$H(s) = \frac{D_0 + D_1 s + \cdots + D_{n-1} s^{n-1}}{e_0 + e_1 s + \cdots + e_{n-1} s^{n-1}} \tag{3.1.6}$$

where $D_i$, $i = 0, 1, \ldots, n-1$ are constant $r \times m$ matrices.

Based on the domain in which a large-scale system model is represented, the model reduction methods are grouped into two initial categories: time domain and frequency domain (see Figure 2.1). The time-domain methods, commonly associated with state-space models (3.1.1)–(3.1.2), were discussed in Chapter 2. The frequency-domain methods associated with transfer function matrix representation (3.1.3)–(3.1.4) are discussed in this chapter. The frequency-domain methods are divided into two basic groups: single-input single-output systems (SISO) and multiinput, multioutput systems (MIMO). By far the greatest effort in model reduction techniques has been for SISO linear time-invariant systems in frequency domain, represented by the following rational function:

$$G(s) = \frac{d_0 + d_1 s + d_2 s^2 + \cdots + d_{n-1} s^{n-1}}{e_0 + e_1 s + e_2 s^2 + \cdots + e_n s^n} \tag{3.1.7}$$

The latter model reduction method is, in turn, divided into the following approaches: moment matching, Padé approximation, Routh approximation, continued fraction, error minimization, and mixed methods. Much of the material in this chapter is based on a survey by the author (Jamshidi, 1982).

## 3.2 Moment Matching

This method is based on determining a set of time functions for the full model and matching them to a simple model by choosing a number of appropriate parameters without having to obtain the full model's time or frequency responses (Paynter, 1956; Bosley and Lees, 1972). The technique is essentially a match of the time-moments of the full model's impulse response to those of the reduced model. Consider an $n$th-order transfer function of the large-scale system:

$$G(s) = \frac{a_{21} + a_{22} s + \cdots + a_{2, m+1} s^m}{1 + a_{12} s + a_{13} s^2 + \cdots + a_{1, n+1} s^n}, \quad m \leqslant n \tag{3.2.1}$$

It is desired to find a lower order transfer function for this system. A power series expansion of $e^{-st}$ about $s = 0$ results in the following expression for

$G(s)$:

$$G(s) = \int_0^\infty g(t) e^{-st}\, dt = \int_0^\infty g(t) \left\{ 1 - st + \frac{(st)^2}{2!} - \cdots \right\} dt$$

$$= \int_0^\infty g(t)\, dt - s \int_0^\infty t g(t)\, dt + s^2 \int_0^\infty \frac{t^2 g(t)}{2!}\, dt - \cdots \quad (3.2.2)$$

or

$$G(s) = c_0 + c_1 s + c_2 s^2 + \cdots \quad (3.2.3)$$

where

$$c_i = \frac{(-1)^i}{i!} \int_0^\infty t^i g(t)\, dt = \frac{(-1)^i}{i!} M_i \quad (3.2.4)$$

where $M_i$ is the $i$th time-moment of impulse response $g(t)$. Alternative derivation of moments and use of "cumulants" or Markov parameters instead of moments have been considered by Gibilaro and Lees (1969) and Bosley and Lees (1972).

Direct division of (3.2.1) yields

$$G(s) = a_{21} - a_{31} s + a_{41} s^2 - a_{51} s^3 + \cdots \quad (3.2.5)$$

In (3.2.5), $a_{21}$ is the zeroth-term coefficient of the numerator in (3.2.1), and the remaining coefficients are obtained from the following recursion:

$$a_{k,l} = a_{k-1,1} \cdot a_{1,l+1} - a_{k-1,l+1} \quad (3.2.6)$$

for $k = 3, 4, \ldots$, and $l = 1, 2, \ldots$ . Note that once a Routhian array is formed based on (3.2.6), the $j$th moment $M_j$ can be obtained by dividing $a_{j+1,1}$ by $j!$ for $j = 0, 1, 2 \ldots$ . The expansion coefficient $c_j$ is then obtained by $c_j = (-1)^j a_{j+2,1}$.

Let the full model be of the form (3.2.1); then by using (3.2.3), (3.2.5), and (3.2.6), Equation (3.2.7) is derived (Lal and Mitra, 1974). The $(n + m + 1)$-dimensional vector relation (3.2.7) can be rewritten in partitioned form:

$$\left[ \begin{array}{c} \hat{c}_1 \\ \hline \hat{c}_2 \end{array} \right] = \left[ \begin{array}{c|c} C_{11} & 0 \\ \hline C_{21} & C_{22} \end{array} \right] \left[ \begin{array}{c} \hat{a}_1 \\ \hline 0 \end{array} \right] + \left[ \begin{array}{c} \hat{a}_2 \\ \hline 0 \end{array} \right] \quad (3.2.8)$$

where $C_{11}$, $C_{21}$, and $C_{22}$ are $(m+1) \times n$, $n \times n$, and $n \times (m+1)$ matrices, respectively, and $\hat{c}_i$, $\hat{a}_i$, $i = 1, 2$, are vectors of $(m+1)$st and $n$th dimension defined by (3.2.7). Partitioning the set of two equations and solving for $\hat{a}_1$ and $\hat{a}_2$, one gets

$$\hat{a}_1 = C_{21}^{-1} \hat{c}_2, \ \hat{a}_2 = \hat{c}_1 - C_{11} C_{21}^{-1} \hat{c}_2 = \hat{c}_1 - C_{11} \hat{a}_1 \quad (3.2.9)$$

$n$th column

$(m+1)$th row

$$
\begin{bmatrix}
c_0 \\ c_1 \\ c_2 \\ \vdots \\ c_m \\ \hline c_{m+1} \\ c_{m+2} \\ \vdots \\ c_{m+n}
\end{bmatrix}
=
\begin{bmatrix}
0 & 0 & \cdots & -c_0 & 0 & 0 & \cdots & 0 \\
-c_0 & 0 & \cdots & -c_1 & -c_0 & 0 & \cdots & 0 \\
-c_1 & -c_0 & \cdots & & -c_1 & -c_0 & \cdots & \\
\vdots & \vdots & \cdots & & & \ddots & \ddots & \\
-c_{m-1} & -c_{m-2} & \cdots & & & \cdots & -c_0 & 0 \\
\hline
-c_m & -c_{m-1} & \cdots & & & \cdots & -c_1 & -c_0 \\
-c_{m+1} & -c_m & \cdots & & & & & \\
\vdots & \vdots & \cdots & & & & & \\
-c_{m+n-1} & -c_{m+n-2} & \cdots & & & & \cdots & -c_0
\end{bmatrix}
\times
\left(
\begin{bmatrix}
a_{12} \\ a_{13} \\ a_{14} \\ \vdots \\ a_{1,n+1} \\ \hline 0 \\ 0 \\ \vdots \\ 0
\end{bmatrix}
+
\begin{bmatrix}
a_{21} \\ a_{22} \\ a_{23} \\ \vdots \\ a_{2,m+1} \\ \hline 0 \\ 0 \\ \vdots \\ 0
\end{bmatrix}
\right)
$$

(3.2.7)

Once the moments $c_j, j = 0, 1, 2, \ldots$, are determined, coefficient matrix $C$ of (3.2.8) is defined and $\hat{a}_1$ and $\hat{a}_2$ are immediate from (3.2.9). Submatrix $C_{21}$ is normally nonsingular, and its singularity means that the given set of moments can be matched by a simpler model. The following example explains the moment matching method.

**Example 3.2.1.** Consider a third-order asymptotically stable system with a transfer function

$$G(s) = \frac{s^2 + 13s + 40}{s^3 + 13s^2 + 32s + 20} = \frac{2 + 0.65s + 0.05s^2}{1 + 1.6s + 0.65s^2 + 0.05s^3} \quad (3.2.10)$$

It is desired to find a reduced-order model for it.

SOLUTION: The closed-loop poles of the system are located at $-1$, $-2$, and $-10$. It is therefore reasonable to seek a second-order reduced model. Following the above discussions, the Routhian-type array for (3.2.10) becomes

$$
\begin{array}{llll}
1 & 1.6 & 0.65 & 0.05 \\
2 & 0.65 & 0.05 & \\
2.55 & 1.25 & 0.1 & \\
2.83 & 1.5575 & & \\
2.9705 & & &
\end{array}
\qquad (3.2.11)
$$

$$\vdots$$

which indicates that the first few expansion coefficients $c_j, j = 0, 1, \ldots$, are $c_0 = 2$, $c_1 = -2.55$, $c_2 = 2.83$, $c_3 = -2.9705$, etc. The denominator and numerator coefficients of the reduced-order model are obtained from (3.2.9), i.e.,

$$\hat{a}_1 = C_{21}^{-1}\hat{c}_2 = \begin{bmatrix} -c_1 & -c_0 \\ -c_2 & -c_1 \end{bmatrix}^{-1} \begin{bmatrix} c_2 \\ c_3 \end{bmatrix}$$

$$= \begin{bmatrix} 2.55 & -2 \\ -2.83 & 2.55 \end{bmatrix}^{-1} \begin{bmatrix} 2.83 \\ -2.9705 \end{bmatrix} = \begin{bmatrix} 1.5144 \\ 0.5171 \end{bmatrix} \quad (3.2.12a)$$

$$\hat{a}_2 = \hat{c}_1 - C_{11}\hat{a}_1 = \begin{bmatrix} c_0 \\ c_1 \end{bmatrix} - \begin{bmatrix} 0 & 0 \\ -c_0 & 0 \end{bmatrix} \begin{bmatrix} a_{12} \\ a_{13} \end{bmatrix}$$

$$= \begin{bmatrix} 2 \\ -2.55 \end{bmatrix} - \begin{bmatrix} 0 & 0 \\ -2 & 0 \end{bmatrix} \begin{bmatrix} 1.5144 \\ 0.5171 \end{bmatrix} = \begin{bmatrix} 2 \\ 0.48 \end{bmatrix} \quad (3.2.12b)$$

Therefore the second-order reduced model is

$$R_2(s) = \frac{a_{21} + a_{22}s}{1 + a_{12}s + a_{13}s^2} = \frac{2 + 0.48s}{1 + 1.5144s + 0.5171s^2} \quad (3.2.13)$$

which provides a pair of dominant poles at $s_{1,2} = -1.0$, $-1.925$, which indicates that a stable second-order reduced model results.

This result is not always obtainable. Moment matching is known for resulting in unstable reduced models for stable full models and vice versa. The following example illustrates this point.

**Example 3.2.2.** Consider a sixth-order asymptotically stable system with a transfer function

$$G(s) = \frac{0.6 + 1.55s + 2.016s^2 + 1.5s^3 + 0.6s^4 + 0.067s^5}{1 + 4.63s + 7.93s^2 + 6.67s^3 + 3s^4 + 0.7s^5 + 0.067s^6}$$

(3.2.14)

It is required to find a reduced-order model for it.

SOLUTION: The full model has closed-loop poles at $-0.5$, $-1$, $-2$, $-2 \pm j$, and $-3$. The coefficients of the expansion are $c_0 = 0.6$, $c_1 = -1.228$, $c_2 = 2.944$, $c_3 = -6.4$, etc. A second-order reduced model turns out to be

$$R_2(s) = \frac{0.6 - 0.0706s}{1 + 0.87s - 3.1s^2}$$

(3.2.15)

which provides a pair of poles at approximately $0.72$ and $-0.44$. It is seen that the method has resulted in an unstable model for the stable full model. The results were the same for reduced-order models $k = 3$, $4$, and $5$. In order to deal with this situation one can preassign one of the poles, say $s_1 = -1$, and find a new stable reduced-order model. As an example, consider the $k = 2$ case. The necessary equations for this reduced-order model following (3.2.7), (3.2.8) are

$$C_{21}\hat{a}_1 = \begin{bmatrix} -c_1 & -c_0 \\ -c_2 & -c_1 \end{bmatrix} \begin{bmatrix} a_{12} \\ a_{13} \end{bmatrix} = \begin{bmatrix} c_2 \\ c_3 \end{bmatrix}$$

(3.2.16)

$$\hat{a}_2 = \hat{c}_1 - C_{11}\hat{a}_1 = \begin{bmatrix} c_0 \\ c_1 \end{bmatrix} - \begin{bmatrix} 0 & 0 \\ -c_0 & 0 \end{bmatrix} \cdot \begin{bmatrix} a_{12} \\ a_{13} \end{bmatrix}$$

(3.2.17)

In order to guarantee a closed-loop pole at $s_1 = -1$, the last equation in (3.2.16) is changed to

$$-a_{12} + a_{13} = -1$$

(3.2.18)

and once the new equation and values of $c_i$, $i = 0, 1, 2, 3$, are used, the new set of equations are

$$\begin{bmatrix} 1.23 & -0.6 \\ -1 & 1 \end{bmatrix} \begin{bmatrix} a_{12} \\ a_{13} \end{bmatrix} = \begin{bmatrix} 2.95 \\ -1 \end{bmatrix},$$

$$\begin{bmatrix} a_{21} \\ a_{22} \end{bmatrix} = \begin{bmatrix} 0.6 \\ -1.23 \end{bmatrix} - \begin{bmatrix} 0 & 0 \\ -0.6 & 0 \end{bmatrix} \begin{bmatrix} a_{12} \\ a_{13} \end{bmatrix} \quad (3.2.19)$$

which results in the following second-order reduced model:

$$R_2(s) = \frac{0.6 + 0.408s}{1 + 3.73s + 2.73s^2}$$

(3.2.20)

with poles at $-0.36$ and $-1$.

Many other researchers have used or proposed modifications in or compared moment matching methods with other model reduction methods. Gibilaro (1967) and Johnson et al. (1971) have employed the moment matching technique by using the impulse response. Lees (1971) has extended the alternative moment matching of Gibilaro and Lees (1969) to invertible and oscillatory systems. Zakian (1973) has shown that the time-moment method for asymptotically stable systems is equivalent to a special case of Padé approximation.

## 3.3 Padé Approximation

The second model reduction method stems from the theory of Padé approximation, which was introduced by Padé (1892), extended by Wall (1948), and has been used for model reduction by many, including Baker et al. (1964) and Shamash (1974, 1975a, b, c). Before a formal presentation on this method is given, consider the following definition:

**Definition 3.1.** Consider a function

$$f(x) = c_0 + c_1 x + c_2 x^2 + \cdots \qquad (3.3.1)$$

and a rational function $[U_m(x)/V_n(x)]$, where $U_m(x)$ and $V_n(x)$ are $m$th- and $n$th-order polynomials in $x$, respectively, and $m \leqslant n$. The rational function $[U_m(\cdot)/V_n(\cdot)]$ is said to be a *Padé approximant* of $f(x)$ if and only if the first $(m+n)$ terms of power series expansions of $f(x)$ and $[U_m(x)/V_n(x)]$ are identical.

For the function $f(x)$ in (3.3.1) to be approximated, let the following Padé approximant be defined as

$$\frac{U_m(x)}{V_n(x)} = \frac{a_0 + a_1 x + a_2 x^2 + \cdots + a_m x^m}{b_0 + b_1 x + b_2 x^2 + \cdots + b_n x^n} \qquad (3.3.2)$$

For the first $(m+n)$ terms of (3.3.1) and (3.3.2) to be equivalent, it becomes apparent that the following set of relations must hold:

$$a_0 = b_0 c_0$$
$$a_1 = b_0 c_1 + b_1 c_0$$
$$a_2 = b_0 c_2 + b_1 c_1 + b_2 c_0 \qquad (3.3.3)$$
$$\cdots$$
$$a_m = b_0 c_m + b_1 c_{m-1} + \cdots + b_m c_0$$
$$0 = b_0 c_{m+1} + b_1 c_m + \cdots + b_{m+1} c_0 \qquad (3.3.4)$$
$$\cdots$$
$$0 = b_0 c_{m+n} + b_1 c_{m+n-1} + \cdots + b_{n-1} c_{m+1} + c_m$$

Once the coefficients $c_i$, $i = 0, 1, 2, \ldots$, are determined, (3.3.4) and (3.3.3) can be written in vector form:

$$
\begin{bmatrix}
c_{m+1} & c_m & & \cdots & & c_1 \\
c_{m+2} & c_{m+1} & c_m & \cdots & & c_2 \\
c_{m+3} & c_{m+2} & c_{m+1} & \cdots & & c_3 \\
\vdots & \vdots & & \ddots & & \vdots \\
& & & & c_m & \\
c_{m+n} & c_{m+n-1} & & \cdots & c_m & c_{m+1}
\end{bmatrix}
\begin{bmatrix}
b_0 \\ b_1 \\ b_2 \\ \vdots \\ b_{n-1}
\end{bmatrix}
=
\begin{bmatrix}
-c_0 \\ -c_1 \\ -c_2 \\ \vdots \\ -c_m
\end{bmatrix}
\quad (3.3.5)
$$

$$
\begin{bmatrix}
a_0 \\ a_1 \\ a_2 \\ \vdots \\ a_m
\end{bmatrix}
=
\begin{bmatrix}
c_0 & 0 & \cdots & & & & 0 \\
c_1 & c_0 & 0 & \cdots & & & 0 \\
c_2 & c_1 & c_0 & 0 & \cdots & & 0 \\
\vdots & \vdots & & & \ddots & 0 & \vdots \\
& & & & & & 0 \\
c_m & c_{m-1} & \cdots & & & c_1 & c_0
\end{bmatrix}
\begin{bmatrix}
b_0 \\ b_1 \\ b_2 \\ \vdots \\ b_{n-1}
\end{bmatrix}
$$

$$(3.3.6)$$

It must be noted that in the above reformulation of (3.3.4) and (3.3.3), $b_n = b_{m+1} = 1$. Moreover, in a more convenient compact form (3.3.5) and (3.3.6) are rewritten as,

$$C_1 \hat{b} = -\hat{c}, \quad \hat{a} = C_2 \hat{b} \qquad (3.3.7)$$

where $C_1$ and $C_2$ are $(n \times n)$ and $(m+1) \times (m+1)$ matrices, respectively, and $\hat{a}$, $\hat{b}$, and $\hat{c}$ are $(m+1)$-, $n$-, and $(m+1)$-dimensional column vectors.

**Example 3.3.1.** Consider the sixth-order system (3.2.14) of Example 3.2.2 rewritten as

$$G(s) = \frac{9 + 23.25s + 30.2s^2 + 22.25s^3 + 9s^4 + s^5}{15 + 69.5s + 119s^2 + 100s^3 + 45s^4 + 10.5s^5 + s^6} \qquad (3.3.8)$$

We would like to apply the Padé approximation method to find a reduced-order model.

SOLUTION: A power series expansion of $G(s)$ in (3.3.8) would result in

$$
\begin{aligned}
G(s) = {} & 0.60 - 1.230s + 2.95566s^2 - 6.45325s^3 \\
& + 13.45741s^4 - 25.540s^5 + 46.4s^6 \\
& - 85s^7 + 160s^8 - 307s^9 + \cdots
\end{aligned}
\qquad (3.3.9)
$$

Using the coefficients $c_i$, $i = 0, 1, 2, \ldots$, in (3.3.9) and forming the matrices $C_1$, $C_2$ and vector $\hat{c}$ in (3.3.7), the results obtained for $k$ as a second-, third-, and fourth-order reduced model are given in Table 3.1.

**Table 3.1** Results of Example 3.3.1 (Padé Approximation)

| $k$ th-Order Reduced Model, $R_k(s)$ | Closed-Loop Poles |
|---|---|
| $R_2(s) = \dfrac{-0.19543 + 0.2238s}{-0.3257 - 0.2947s + s^2}$ | $0.7368077, \ -0.442077$ |
| $R_3(s) = \dfrac{-0.16 - 0.389s + 0.095s^2}{-0.266 - 1.194s - 0.98s^2 + s^3}$ | $1.75, \ -0.385 \pm j0.064$ |
| $R_4(s) = \dfrac{-0.066 - 0.108s - 0.0986s^2 + 0.265s^3}{-0.11 - 0.4s - 0.45s^2 + 0.32s^3 + s^4}$ | $0.88, \ -0.355 \pm j0.358, \ -0.5$ |

As seen, the Padé approximation has also resulted in unstable reduced-order models for all cases. For the cases where unstable reduced-order models result, a scheme similar to that used for dealing with the unstable reduced models by time moments is applied. The retention of a full model's pole in this case calls for the approximation, in the sense of Padé, about more than one point (Shamash, 1975c). In fact, the Padé approximation discussed above was an approximation about $s = 0$. One can similarly preassign a given location for a reduced-order model closed-loop pole. Reconsider in Example 3.3.1 (see Table 3.1) the fourth-order reduced model where one of the four poles ends up on the right half-plane. In order to obtain a stable reduced-order model, preassign the first pole at $s = s_1 = -3$, corresponding to one of the full model's original poles. Under this condition the last equation in (3.3.4), or last row in (3.3.5), is replaced by

$$0 = b_0 + b_1 s_1 + b_2 s_1^2 + \cdots + b_n s_1^n \qquad (3.3.10)$$

which, for the particular example, becomes

$$0 = b_0 - 3b_1 + 9b_2 - 27b_3 + 81 \qquad (3.3.11)$$

The new application of Padé approximation with modified $C_1$ matrix in (3.3.7) results in the following fourth-order reduced model:

$$R_4(s) = \frac{1.3 \times 10^{-6} + 1.436s + 1.34s^2 + 1.358s^3}{2.1 \times 10^{-6} + 2.39s + 7.1404s^2 + 5.114s^3 + s^4} \qquad (3.3.12)$$

Note that there is a zero-pole cancellation in (3.3.12) at $s = 0$; hence, a third-order reduced model results:

$$R_3(s) = \frac{1.436 + 1.34s + 1.358s^2}{2.39 + 7.1404s + 5.114s^2 + s^3} \qquad (3.3.13)$$

with poles at $s = -0.492, \ -1.62$, and of course $-3$.

## 3.4 Routh Approximation

Thus far two model-reduction methods have been introduced. In this section a Routh approximation method is introduced.

Consider an $n$th-order transfer function:

$$G(s) = \frac{a_1 s^{n-1} + a_2 s^{n-2} + \cdots + a_n}{b_0 s^n + b_1 s^{n-1} + \cdots + b_n} \tag{3.4.1}$$

It is well known that an asymptotically stable system with a closed-loop transfer function (3.4.1) can be expanded in the following canonical fashion (Hutton and Friedland, 1975):

$$G(s) = \beta_1 f_1(s) + \beta_2 f_1(s) f_2(s) + \cdots + \beta_n f_1(s) f_2(s) \ldots f_n(s)$$

$$= \sum_{i=1}^{n} \beta_i \prod_{j=1}^{i} f_j(s) \tag{3.4.2}$$

where $\beta_i$, $i = 1, 2, \ldots, n$, and $f_k(s)$, $k = 2, 3, \ldots, n$, are determined by the following continued fraction:

$$f_k(s) = \cfrac{1}{\alpha_k s + \cfrac{1}{\alpha_{k+1} s + \cfrac{1}{\alpha_{k+2} s + \cfrac{1}{\ddots \atop \alpha_{n-1} s + \cfrac{1}{\alpha_n s}}}}} \tag{3.4.3}$$

and

$$f_1(s) = \frac{1}{1 + \alpha_1 s} \tag{3.4.4}$$

Equations (3.4.2) through (3.4.4) are called *alpha–beta expansions* of $G(s)$. The $n$ parameters $\alpha_k$, $k = 1, 2, \ldots, n$, of this expression can be found by forming the classical Routh table in the following fashion:

Alpha (Routh) Table

| | $b_0^0 = b_0$ | $b_2^0 = b_2$ | $b_4^0 = b_4$ | $b_6^0 = b_6$ $\cdots$ | |
|---|---|---|---|---|---|
| | $b_0^1 = b_1$ | $b_2^1 = b_3$ | $b_4^1 = b_5$ $\cdots$ | | |
| $\alpha_1 = b_0^0/b_0^1$ | $b_0^2 = b_2^0 - \alpha_1 b_2^1$ | $b_2^2 = b_4^0 - \alpha_1 b_4^1$ | $b_4^2 = b_6^0 - \alpha_1 b_6^1$ $\cdots$ | | |
| $\alpha_2 = b_0^1/b_0^2$ | $b_0^3 = b_2^1 - \alpha_2 b_2^2$ | $b_2^3 = b_4^1 - \alpha_2 b_4^2$ | | | |
| $\alpha_3 = b_0^2/b_0^3$ | $b_0^4 = b_2^2 - \alpha_3 b_2^3$ | $b_2^4 = b_4^2 - \alpha_3 b_4^3$ $\cdots$ | | | |
| $\alpha_4 = b_0^3/b_0^4$ | $b_0^5 = b_2^3 - \alpha_4 b_2^4$ $\cdots$ | | | | (3.4.5) |
| $\alpha_5 = b_0^4/b_0^5$ $\cdots$ | $\cdots$ | | | | |
| $\alpha_6 = b_0^5/b_0^6$ $\cdots$ | | | | | |
| $\vdots$ | | | | | |

The $\beta_i$ parameters can be similarly obtained using the coefficients of the numerator $a_j, j = 1, 2, \ldots, n$, as shown in (3.4.1):

Beta Table

| | $a_0^1 = a_1$ | $a_2^1 = a_3$ | $a_4^1 = a_5$ | $\cdots$ |
|---|---|---|---|---|
| | $a_0^2 = a_2$ | $a_2^2 = a_4$ | $a_4^2 = a_6$ | $\cdots$ |
| $\beta_1 = a_0^1/b_0^1$ | $a_0^3 = a_2^1 - \beta_1 b_2^1$ | $a_2^3 = a_4^1 - \beta_1 b_4^1$ | $\cdots$ | |
| $\beta_2 = a_0^2/b_0^2$ | $a_0^4 = a_2^2 - \beta_2 b_2^2$ | $a_2^4 = a_4^2 - \beta_2 b_4^2$ | $\cdots$ | |
| $\beta_3 = a_0^3/b_0^3$ | $a_0^5 = a_2^3 - \beta_3 b_2^3$ | $\cdots$ | | |
| $\beta_4 = a_0^4/b_0^4$ | $a_0^6 = a_2^4 - \beta_4 b_2^4$ | | | |
| $\beta_5 = a_0^5/b_0^5$ | $\cdots$ | | | |
| $\beta_6 = a_0^6/b_0^6$ | $\cdots$ | | | |
| $\vdots$ | | | | |

$$(3.4.6)$$

The recursive formula to compute the entries of alpha and beta tables can be obtained from

$$b_0^{i+1} = b_2^{i-1} - \alpha_i b_2^i$$

$$b_2^{i+1} = b_4^{i-1} - \alpha_i b_4^i \qquad (3.4.7)$$

$$\cdots$$

$$b_{n-i-2}^{i+1} = b_{n-i}^{i-1} - \alpha_i b_{n-i}^i, \quad i = 1, 2, \ldots, n-1$$

For the case when $n - i$ is odd, the last equation in (3.4.7) is replaced by

$$b_{n-i-1}^{i+1} = b_{n-i+1}^{i-1} \qquad (3.4.8)$$

and

$$\alpha_i = b_0^{i-1}/b_0^i, \quad i = 1, 2, \ldots, n \qquad (3.4.9)$$

$$a_{j-2}^{i+2} = a_j^i - \beta_i b_j^i, \quad j = \begin{cases} 2, 4, \ldots, n-i, \text{ for } n-i \text{ even} \\ 2, 4, \ldots, n-i-1, \text{ for } n-i \text{ odd} \end{cases} \qquad (3.4.10)$$

$$i = 1, 2, \ldots, n-2$$

and,

$$\beta_i = a_0^i/b_0^i \qquad (3.4.11)$$

The $k$th Routh reduced model using the alpha–beta expansion $R_k(s)$ for the full model $G(s)$ is found by truncating the expansion (3.4.2) and rearranging the retained terms as a rational transfer function. Truncating the continued fraction (3.4.3) after the $k$th term and denoting it by $g_{j,k}(s)$, the reduced model transfer function $R_k(s)$ is similar to (3.4.2):

$$R_k(s) = \sum_{i=1}^{k} \beta_i \prod_{j=1}^{i} g_{j,k}(s) \qquad (3.4.12)$$

where

$$g_{j,k}(s) = \cfrac{1}{\alpha_j s + \cfrac{1}{\alpha_{j+1}s + \cfrac{}{\phantom{x}\ddots\phantom{xxxxxxx}}}} \qquad (3.4.13)$$

$$\alpha_{k-1}s + \frac{1}{\alpha_k s}$$

Denote the numerator and denominator of $R_k(s)$ by $P_k(s)$ and $Q_k(s)$, respectively, defined below:

$$P_1(s) = \beta_1, \quad Q_1(s) = 1 + \alpha_1 s$$

$$P_2(s) = \beta_2 + \alpha_2\beta_1 s, \quad Q_2(s) = 1 + \alpha_2 s + \alpha_1\alpha_2 s^2 \qquad (3.4.14)$$

$$P_3(s) = (\beta_1 + \beta_3) + \alpha_3\beta_2 s + \alpha_2\alpha_3\beta_1 s^2, \quad Q_3(s) = 1 + (\alpha_1 + \alpha_3)s$$

$$+ \alpha_2\alpha_3 s^2 + \alpha_1\alpha_2\alpha_3 s^3$$

$$\vdots$$

and in general

$$P_k(s) = \alpha_k s P_{k-1}(s) + P_{k-2}(s) + \beta_k \qquad (3.4.15a)$$

$$Q_k(s) = \alpha_k s Q_{k-1}(s) + Q_{k-2}(s) \qquad (3.4.15b)$$

for $k = 1, 2, \ldots$, and

$$P_{-1}(s) = P_o(s) = 0, \quad Q_{-1}(s) = Q_o(s) = 1 \qquad (3.4.16)$$

The relations (3.4.15)–(3.4.16) along with the $\alpha$–$\beta$ tables are sufficient to find a $k$th-order reduced model. Hutton and Friedland (1975) mention that this reduced model preserves high-frequency characteristics, and for control application it is preferable to use reciprocal transfer function defined by

$$\hat{G}(s) = \frac{1}{s}G\left(\frac{1}{s}\right) = \frac{a_n s^{n-1} + \cdots + a_2 s + a_1}{b_n s^n + \cdots + b_1 s + b_o} \qquad (3.4.17)$$

which, if compared with (3.4.1), is simply $G(s)$ with $a_i, b_j$ coefficients reversing their orders. The Routh approximation can be summarized through the following algorithm:

*Algorithm 3.1.* Routh Approximation

   *Step 1:* Determine the reciprocal of the full model $\hat{G}(s)$.

   *Step 2:* Construct the $\hat{\alpha}$–$\hat{\beta}$ tables corresponding to $\hat{G}(s)$.

   *Step 3:* For a $k$th-order reduced model use recursive formulas (3.4.15) to find $\hat{R}_k(s) = \hat{P}_k(s)/\hat{Q}_k(s)$.

*Step 4:* Reverse the coefficients of $\hat{P}_k(s)$ and $\hat{Q}_k(s)$ back to find
$R_k(s) = P_k(s)/Q_k(s)$.

**Example 3.4.1.** Consider the sixth-order transfer function of Examples 3.2.2 and 3.3.1. It is desirable to find a $k$th-order reduced model for this system using the Routh algorithm.

SOLUTION: The $k$th approximant $R_k(s)$ can be found by Algorithm 3.1. The reciprocal transfer function $\hat{G}(s)$ is

$$G(s) = \frac{9s^5 + 23.25s^4 + 30.25s^3 + 22.5s^2 + 9s + 1}{15s^6 + 69.5s^5 + 119s^4 + 100s^3 + 45s^2 + 10.5s + 1} \quad (3.4.18)$$

The $\hat{\alpha}$ and $\hat{\beta}$ tables are

|  | 15 | 119 | 45 | 1 |  | 9 | 30.25 | 9 |
|---|---|---|---|---|---|---|---|---|
|  | 69.5 | 100 | 10.5 | 0 |  | 23.25 | 22.5 | 1 |
| $\hat{\alpha}_1 = 0.216$ | 97.4 | 42.7 | 1 | | $\hat{\beta}_1 = 0.13$ | 17.3 | 7.6 | 0 |
| $\hat{\alpha}_2 = 0.71$ | 69.5 | 9.8 | 0 | | $\hat{\beta}_2 = 0.24$ | 12.3 | 0.76 | |
| $\hat{\alpha}_3 = 1.4$ | 29.02 | 1 | | | $\hat{\beta}_3 = 0.25$ | 5.2 | 0 | |
| $\hat{\alpha}_4 = 2.4$ | 7.4 | 0 | | | $\hat{\beta}_4 = 0.424$ | 0.34 | | |
| $\hat{\alpha}_5 = 3.93$ | 1 | | | | $\hat{\beta}_5 = 0.704$ | | | |
| $\hat{\alpha}_6 = 7.4$ | | | | | | | | |

The resulting closed-loop poles of three reduced models are shown in Table 3.2. The results in this table indicate that all the reduced models are stable as expected from Routh's stability array. Furthermore, it is apparent that the less dominant poles of the full model are dropped and the dominant poles are retained—a desirable property.

For unstable transfer function $G(s)$, a shift of the imaginary axis would provide a modified asymptotically stable transfer function

$$\tilde{G}(s) = G(s + a) \quad (3.4.19)$$

where the real, positive parameter $a$ is chosen to be $a > R\{\lambda_m\}$, where $\lambda_m$ is the closed-loop pole with the highest positive real part. The next step would be to find $\tilde{R}_k(s)$ as usual and finally shift back the imaginary axis to its original position providing

$$R_k(s) = \tilde{R}_k(s - a) \quad (3.4.20)$$

the $k$th Routh approximant of an unstable system.

**Table 3.2.** Results of Reduced-Order Models Closed-Loop Poles Using Alpha–Beta Expansion Routh Technique for Example 3.4.1

| Routh Alpha–Beta Approximation | |
| --- | --- |
| $k$ th-Order Reduced Model | Closed-Loop Poles |
| $R_2(s) = \dfrac{0.24s + 0.0923}{s^2 + 0.71s + 0.1534}$ | $s_{1,2} = -0.355 \pm j0.165$ |
| $R_3(s) = \dfrac{0.38s^2 + 0.34s + 0.129}{s^3 + 1.616s^2 + 0.994s + 0.215}$ | $s_1 = -0.47, s_{2,3} = -0.57 \pm j0.356$ |
| $R_4(s) = \dfrac{0.664s^3 + 1.004s^2 + 0.806s + 0.31}{s^4 + 3.11s^3 + 4.0318s^2 + 2.385s + 0.515}$ | $s_1 = -0.525, s_2 = -0.765$ $s_{3,4} = -0.91 \pm j0.674$ |
| $G(s)$, full | $s_1 = -0.5, s_2 = -1, s_3 = -2,$ $s_{4,5} = -2 \pm j, s_6 = -3$ |

Another Routh-based model reduction scheme has been suggested by Krishnamurthy and Seshadri (1976, 1978). In this scheme, the Routh stability tables for the numerator and denominator are first constructed and then by considering any two rows, starting from the second rows on, a desired reduced-order model is obtained. Using the coefficients of the second and third rows a polynomial of $(n-1)$th or $(m-1)$th order can be constructed. Similarly an $(n-2)$th-order polynomial can be constructed by using the third and fourth rows of denominator's Routh table, etc. Although this scheme guarantees that a stable full model is reduced to a stable reduced one, it is a nonunique procedure in that several full models can have the same reduced model. This point has been experienced by the author and has also been brought up by Singh (1979).

## 3.5 Continued Fraction Method

Another model reduction method is the first (and second) Cauer continued fraction expansion proposed initially by Chen and Shieh (1968), which has been modified, applied to multiinput multioutput systems, and mixed with other methods by many others (Chen and Haas, 1968; Chuang, 1970; Chen and Shieh, 1970; Towill and Mehdi, 1970; Chen, 1972, 1974; Wright, 1973; Davidson and Lucas, 1974; Parthasarathy and Singh, 1975; Calfe and Healey, 1974; Lamba and Rao, 1978). Consider a SISO closed-loop transfer function:

$$G(s) = \frac{a_{21} + a_{22}s + a_{23}s^2 + \cdots + a_{2n}s^{n-1}}{a_{11} + a_{12}s + a_{13}s^3 + \cdots + a_{1,n+1}s^n} \tag{3.5.1}$$

The continued fraction proposed by Chen and Shieh (1968) which is equivalent to a Taylor series expansion about $s = 0$ (Chuang, 1970) is obtained by

$$G(s) = \cfrac{1}{\cfrac{a_{11}}{a_{21}} + s \cfrac{a_{31} + a_{32}s + \cdots}{a_{21} + a_{22}s + \cdots}}$$

$$= \cfrac{1}{\cfrac{a_{11}}{a_{21}} + \cfrac{s}{\cfrac{a_{21}}{a_{31}} + s \cfrac{a_{41} + a_{42}s + \cdots}{a_{31} + a_{32}s + \cdots}}} \qquad (3.5.2a)$$

$$= \cfrac{1}{h_1 + \cfrac{s}{h_2 + \cfrac{s}{h_3 + \cfrac{s}{h_4 + \cfrac{s}{\cdots}}}}} \qquad (3.5.2b)$$

where,

$$a_{31} = a_{12} - h_1 a_{22} \qquad\qquad a_{41} = a_{22} - h_2 a_{32}$$

$$a_{3,n-1} = a_{1n} - h_1 a_{2n} \qquad a_{4,n-1} = a_{2n} - h_2 a_{3n}$$

$$a_{3,n} = a_{1,n+1} \qquad\qquad\quad a_{4,n} = a_{2,n+1}$$

and

$$h_1 = a_{11}/a_{21}, h_2 = a_{21}/a_{31}, \ldots, h_i = a_{i,1}/a_{i+1,1} \cdots$$

In order to find a $k$th order reduced model it is necessary to keep the first $2k$ quotients in (3.5.2) and reconstruct $R_k(s)$ from it. The continued fraction, like the time moments and Padé approximation, often gives unstable reduced models for stable full models.

One of the better modifications of the original continued fraction expansion is due to Chuang (1970) which has carried out a Taylor series expansion for both $s = 0$ and $s = \infty$. This would, in effect, mean that the expansion begins from the constant term and then from the highest-order term. Thus the transfer function (3.5.2) would be reduced using the following expansion,

$$G(s) = \cfrac{1}{\cfrac{a_{11}}{a_{21}} + s \cfrac{a_{3n}s^{n-1} + a_{3,n-1}s^{n-2} + \cdots + a_{31}}{a_{2n}s^{n-1} + a_{2,n-1}s^{n-2} + \cdots + a_{21}}} \qquad (3.5.3)$$

$$= \cfrac{1}{\cfrac{a_{11}}{a_{21}} + \cfrac{s}{\cfrac{a_{2n}}{a_{3n}} + \cfrac{a_{41} + a_{42}s + \cdots + a_{4,n-1}s^{n-2}}{a_{31} + a_{32}s + \cdots + a_{3n}s^{n-1}}}}$$

where

$$a_{31} = a_{12} - h_1 a_{22} \qquad a_{41} = a_{21} - h_2 a_{31}$$

$$\cdots \qquad\qquad \cdots$$

$$a_{3,n-1} = a_{1n} - h_1 a_{2n} \quad a_{4,n-1} = a_{2,n-1} - h_2 a_{3,n-1}$$

$$a_{3n} = a_{1,n+1}$$

$$h_1 = a_{11}/a_{21}, h_2 = a_{2n}/a_{3n}, h_3 = a_{31}/a_{41}.$$

The continued fraction expansion would become,

$$G(s) = \cfrac{1}{h_1 + \cfrac{s}{h_2 + \cfrac{1}{h_3 + \cfrac{s}{h_4 + \cfrac{1}{\ddots}}}}} \tag{3.5.4}$$

Once again for a $k$th-order reduced model, the first $2k$ quotients of (3.5.4) are retained.

As mentioned earlier many authors have tried to modify and/or extend the continued fraction scheme. Chen (1972, 1974) Calfe and Healey (1974) have extended the method to the multivariable systems which will be discussed in Section 3.8. Wright (1973), Davidson and Lucas (1974) have proposed general expansion in place of the original second-order Cauer's expansion (3.5.2b). These later results, although sound, have less attractive computational features as mentioned by Parthasarathy and Singh (1975). A potentially attractive method from points of view of stability and computational efforts is the mixed Cauer expansion of Shieh and Goldman (1974). For the system whose transfer function is in the form of (3.5.1), the following combined first and second Cauer continued fraction expansion is proposed

$$G(s) = \cfrac{1}{h_1 + h_1^1 s + \cfrac{1}{\cfrac{h_2}{s} + h_2^1 + \cfrac{1}{h_3 + h_3^1 s + \cfrac{1}{\cfrac{h_4}{s} + h_4^1 + \cfrac{1}{\ddots}}}}} \tag{3.5.5a}$$

where

$$h_i = \frac{a_{i,1}}{a_{i+1,1}}, \quad h_i^1 = \frac{a_{i,n+2-i}}{a_{i+1,n+1-i}}, \quad i = 1, 2, 3, \ldots$$

with

$$a_{i+1,1} = 0 \quad \text{and} \quad a_{l,m} = a_{l-2,m+1} - h_{l-2} a_{l-1,m+1} - h_{l-2}^1 a_{l-1,m} \tag{3.5.5b}$$

for $l = 3, 4, \ldots, n+1$ and $m = 1, 2, \ldots$. The following example illustrates the continued fraction methods.

**Example 3.5.1.** Consider a third-order system example from Chuang (1970),

$$G(s) = \frac{8s^2 + 6s + 2}{s^3 + 4s^2 + 5s + 2} \qquad (3.5.6)$$

It is desired to find a reduced-order model using the three continued fraction methods discussed above.

SOLUTION: The system has three poles at $s = -1$, $-1$, and $-2$. A second-order reduced model for the original method (Chen and Shieh, 1968) $R_2(s)$, the modified scheme of Chuang (1970), $\tilde{R}_2(s)$ and mixed Cauer expansion of Shieh and Goldman (1974) $\hat{R}_2(s)$ turn out to be

$$R_2(s) = \frac{1.776s + 0.222}{-s^2 + 1.667s + 0.222} \qquad (3.5.7a)$$

$$\tilde{R}_2(s) = \frac{0.208s + 0.20}{0.026s^2 + 0.1085s + 0.20} = \frac{8s + 7.7}{s^2 + 4.15s + 7.7} \qquad (3.5.7b)$$

$$\hat{R}_2(s) = \frac{2.91s + 1.60}{0.364s^2 + 2.11s + 1.6} = \frac{8s + 4.4}{s^2 + 5.8s + 4.4} \qquad (3.5.7c)$$

As seen, the original method provides unstable reduced model while the other two do provide stable ones.

## 3.6 Error Minimization Methods

Another class of methods for model reduction has been based on the minimization of a measure of the error between the responses of the full and reduced models. One common measure is the square of the error between the frequency responses first proposed by Levy (1959) and later on by Nagarajan (1971), Hsia (1972), Rao and Lamba (1974) and Reddy (1976), among others. The other approach is the minimization of the square of the error between the step responses of full and reduced models proposed by Sinha and colleagues (1971a,b). The coefficients of the reduced model's numerator and denominator polynomials will act as the optimization parameters. In this section a brief overview on the frequency response error minimization methods will be made.

Consider a system with full model

$$G(s) = \frac{1 + a_1 s + a_2 s^2 + \cdots + a_m s^m}{1 + b_1 s + b_2 s^2 + \cdots + b_n s^n}, \qquad m < n \qquad (3.6.1)$$

where $a_1, \ldots, a_m, b_1, \ldots, b_n$ are constant coefficients. It is desired to find a reduced-order model

$$R(s) = \frac{1 + c_1 s + c_2 s^2 + \cdots + c_l s^l}{1 + d_1 s + d_2 s^2 + \cdots + d_k s^k} \qquad (3.6.2)$$

which approximates (3.6.1) over a range of frequency, say, $\omega_1 \leqslant \omega \leqslant \omega_2$. Levy (1959) proposed a minimization scheme based on the sum of $\varepsilon_r^2$, $\varepsilon_r = G(j\omega) - R(j\omega)$. Nagarajan (1971) treated the problem by minimizing a "feedback error correlation" performance index by considering the full model as a reference system. However, his method is restricted to systems with no numerator dynamics.

A more feasible scheme is due to Hsia (1972). The method begins by defining

$$E(\omega) = \left| \frac{G(j\omega)}{R(j\omega)} \right|^2 \qquad (3.6.3)$$

and expanding it in a Taylor's series about $\omega = 0$,

$$E(\omega) = E(0) + E^{(2)}(0) \frac{\omega^2}{2!} + E^{(4)}(0) \frac{\omega^4}{4!} + \cdots \qquad (3.6.4)$$

where $E(0) = 1$ by virtue of (3.6.1) and (3.6.2) and all the odd-order derivatives of $E(\omega)$ in (3.6.3) vanish. For a minimum error between the two models' frequency responses, it is required to have $E(\omega) = 1$, which implies that

$$E^{(2)}(0) = E^{(4)}(0) = \cdots = E^{(2i)}(0) = \cdots = 0 \qquad (3.6.5)$$

The function $E(\omega)$ in (3.6.3) can be rewritten by

$$E(\omega) = \left| \frac{G(j\omega)}{R(j\omega)} \right|^2 = \left| \frac{P(j\omega)}{Q(j\omega)} \right|^2 = \frac{P(j\omega)P(-j\omega)}{Q(j\omega)Q(-j\omega)}$$

$$= \frac{P_0 + P_2\omega^2 + P_4\omega^4 + \cdots}{Q_0 + Q_2\omega^2 + Q_4\omega^4 + \cdots} \qquad (3.6.6)$$

where $P_{2i}$ and $Q_{2i}$, $i = 0, 1, 2, \ldots$, are defined as

$$P_{2i} = \frac{1}{(2i)!} \left. \frac{d^{2i}[P(j\omega)P(-j\omega)]}{d\omega^{2i}} \right|_{\omega=0} = \sum_{j=0}^{2i} (-1)^{j+i} \frac{P^{(j)}(0)P^{(2i-j)}(0)}{j!(2i-j)!}$$

$$(3.6.7)$$

where

$$P^{(j)}(0) \triangleq \left. \frac{d^j P(s)}{ds^j} \right|_{s=0}$$

A similar expression can be found for the coefficients $Q_{2i}$ of (3.6.6):

$$Q_{2i} = \sum_{j=0}^{2i} (-1)^{j+i} \frac{Q^{(j)}(0)Q^{(2i-j)}(0)}{j!(2i-j)!}, \quad i = 1, 2, \ldots \qquad (3.6.8)$$

Since $P_0 = Q_0 = 1$, then (3.6.6) becomes

$$E(\omega) = 1 + \frac{(P_2 - Q_2)\omega^2 + (P_4 - Q_4)\omega^4 + \cdots}{1 + Q_2\omega^2 + Q_4\omega^4 + \cdots} \qquad (3.6.9)$$

Now comparing (3.6.9) with (3.6.4) and in view of (3.6.5), the following conditions would follow:

$$P_{2i} = Q_{2i}, \quad i = 1, 2, \ldots \qquad (3.6.10)$$

Depending on the number of unknown coefficients $c_1, c_2, \ldots, d_1, d_2, \ldots$, i.e., $l + k$, as many equations of the form (3.6.10) can be used. It is mentioned that the set of equations in (3.6.10) are nonlinear, and a real solution can usually be obtained (Hsia, 1972). By virtue of (3.6.6) and (3.6.1)–(3.6.2), it is clear that $P(s)$ and $Q(s)$ are polynomials of orders $(m + k)$ and $(n + l)$, respectively, which indicates that $P^{(i)}(s)$ and $Q^{(j)}(s)$ vanish for $i > m + k$ and $j > n + l$, i.e.,

$$P_{2r} = P_{2(m+k)}, \quad r > m + k, \quad Q_{2r} = Q_{2(n+l)}, \quad r > n + l \qquad (3.6.11)$$

implying that if $m = l$ and $n = k$, i.e., when $R(s)$ is to take on the form of $G(s)$, then (3.6.10) implies that $c_i = a_i$, $d_i = b_i$, $i = 1, 2, \ldots, m + n$, and $E(\omega)$ $= 1$ for all $\omega$. This is of course an expected result.

Another frequency response model reduction technique has been due to Reddy (1976), which is obtained by rewriting (3.6.1) and (3.6.2) in the domain of $\omega$ or

$$G(j\omega) = (F + j\omega I)/(M + j\omega L), \quad R(j\omega) = (A + j\omega B)/(C + j\omega D) \qquad (3.6.12)$$

where

$$F = 1 - a_2\omega^2 + a_4\omega^4 - \cdots, \quad I = a_1 - a_3\omega^2 + a_5\omega^4 - \cdots \qquad (3.6.13a)$$

$$M = 1 - b_2\omega^2 + b_4\omega^4 - \cdots, \quad L = b_1 - b_3\omega^2 + b_5\omega^4 - \cdots \qquad (3.6.13b)$$

and

$$A = 1 - c_2\omega^2 + c_4\omega^4 - \cdots, \quad B = c_1 - c_3\omega^2 + c_5\omega^4 - \cdots \qquad (3.6.14a)$$

$$c = 1 - d_2\omega^2 + d_4\omega^4 - \cdots, \quad D = d_1 - d_3\omega^2 + d_5\omega^4 - \cdots \qquad (3.6.14b)$$

Define the following four integral error functions:

$$E_1 = \int_{\omega_1}^{\omega_2} [F - A]^2 \, d\omega, \quad E_2 = \int_{\omega_1}^{\omega_2} [I - B]^2 \omega^2 \, d\omega \qquad (3.6.15)$$

$$E_3 = \int_{\omega_1}^{\omega_2} [M - C]^2 \, d\omega, \quad E_4 = \int_{\omega_1}^{\omega_2} [L - D]^2 \omega^2 \, d\omega \qquad (3.6.16)$$

which in effect means that the unknown reduced model coefficients are obtained by minimizing the integral of the deviations between the real and imaginary parts of the full and reduced models' numerator and denominator. The following example illustrates these two methods.

**Example 3.6.1.** Consider a fourth-order system:

$$G(s) = \frac{1 + s + 0.5s^2}{1 + 2.034s + 1.367s^2 + 0.367s^3 + 0.0334s^4} \qquad (3.6.17)$$

It is desired to use the methods of Hsia (1972) and Reddy (1976) to find a second-order system.

SOLUTION: The desired reduced-order model is $R(s) = (1 + c_1 s)/(1 + d_1 s + d_2 s^2)$. Utilizing the procedures of (3.6.6)–(3.6.10), equating $P_{2i} = Q_{2i}$, $i = 1, 2, 3$, leads to the following three equations in unknowns $c_1$, $d_1$, and $d_2$:

$$d_1^2 - 2d_2 + 8.136c_1 + c_1^2 - 6.871156 = 0 \quad (3.6.18)$$

$$-d_2^2 + 1.403156c_1^2 + 0.192533 = 0 \quad (3.6.19)$$

$$0.25d_1^2 - 0.5d_2 + 0.271475c_1 - 0.031187c_1^2 - 0.04337 = 0 \quad (3.6.20)$$

whose solutions are $d_1 = 1.233$, $d_2 = 1.085$, and $c_1 = 0.838$, leading to

$$R_2(s) = (1 + 0.838s)/(1 + 1.233s + 1.085s^2)$$

The reduction by Reddy's method over $0 \leqslant \omega \leqslant 2$ range is obtained by defining the parameters $A = 1$, $B = c_1$, $C = 1 - d_2\omega^2$, $D = d_1$, $F = 1 - 0.5\omega^2$, $I = 1$, $M = 1 - 1.367\omega^2$, and $L = 2.034 - 0.367\omega^2$. The necessary conditions $\partial E_i(c_1, d_1, d_2)/\partial c_1$, $i = 1, 2, 3, 4$, etc., lead to $d_1 = 1.1532$, $d_2 = 1.367$, and $c_1 = 1$. Thus, the reduced-order model is

$$\tilde{R}_2(s) = \frac{1 + s}{1 + 1.1532s + 1.367s^2} \qquad (3.6.21)$$

The two reduced models provided stable systems for the system. A frequency response comparison of these methods along with other schemes is presented in Section 3.9. It is noted that the computational requirements of these methods can be reduced substantially when there is a pole-zero cancellation in (3.6.6) or when some poles are preassigned.

## 3.7 Mixed Methods and Unstable Systems

One of the main issues in most model reduction methods discussed thus far is the unpredictable results of finding a stable reduced model from an unstable full model or an unstable reduced model for a stable full model.

The latter is due to the excitation of unretained modes through feedback, a characteristic similar to that of some aggregation methods discussed in Chapter 2. These problems have been dealt with in two different ways: a combination of Padé and Modal (pole assignment) approximations and a combination of Padé and Routh approximations. In this section these two mixed methods will be considered, while other mixed methods, such as continued fraction plus modal and continued fraction and Routh, which are reported for MIMO systems, will be considered in the next section.

### 3.7.1 Padé – Modal Method

The experience in model reduction using Padé approximation, as it was demonstrated in Section 3.3, shows that this technique may very well provide unstable reduced models. Using the Padé–Modal method one simply retains the dominant poles of the system, say $s_i$, $i = 1, 2, \ldots, l$, and finds the remaining $k - l$ poles by Padé approximation, where $k < n$ and $n$ is the order of the full model. Specifically it implies that the last $l$ rows of matrix $C_1$ in (3.3.5) or (3.3.7) will be replaced by the following set of $l$-equations satisfying the dominant poles $s_i$, $i = 1, 2, \ldots, l$:

$$\begin{vmatrix} 1 & s_1 & s_1^2 & \cdots & s_1^{n-1} \\ 1 & s_2 & s_2^2 & \cdots & s_2^{n-1} \\ \vdots & & & & \\ 1 & s_l & s_l^2 & \cdots & s_l^{n-1} \end{vmatrix} \tag{3.7.1}$$

and the right-hand side of (3.3.5) or (3.3.7) by

$$\left[ -s_1^n - s_2^n \cdots - s_l^n \right]^T \tag{3.7.2}$$

Depending on the choice of the dominant poles, a stable reduced-order model can be found by this mixed method (Shamash, 1975b). This point was already demonstrated in Example 3.3.1.

### 3.7.2 Padé – Routh Method

The combination of Padé and Routh approximations for order reduction has been proposed by Shamash (1974), among others. The approach is simply to construct an $\alpha$ table such as (3.4.5) for the denominator and find a stable reduced-order polynomial for it. However, a shortcoming of the original Routh approximation as suggested by Hutton and Friedland (1975) is having to go through two reciprocal processes in addition to constructing the $\alpha$ table. The latter difficulty is not so serious because this table is essentially the standard Routh–Hurwitz array, and the former problem can be avoided by a regrouping of the entries of $\alpha$ table as suggested by Krishnamurthy and Seshadri (1976) which gives the $\alpha$ coefficients of the full model without having to perform a reciprocal transformation. The construction of the $\beta$ table, which is more cumbersome than the $\alpha$ table, is avoided all together, since the numerator is now approximated by the Padé method. These points are illustrated in the following example.

**Example 3.7.1.** For the sixth-order theme example in (3.3.8) a second-order reduced model is sought using the mixed Padé–Routh method.

SOLUTION: We begin by constructing an $\alpha$ table similar to (3.4.5), except for the first two rows, which will become

$$b_0^0 = b_n \quad b_2^0 = b_{n-2} \cdots$$

$$b_0^1 = b_{n-1} \quad b_2^1 = b_{n-3} \cdots \qquad (3.7.3)$$

The resulting table for the system (3.3.8) becomes

| | | | |
|---|---|---|---|
| $b_0^0 = 15$ | $b_2^0 = 119$ | $b_4^0 = 45$ | $b_6^0 = 1$ |
| $b_0^1 = 69.5$ | $b_2^1 = 100$ | $b_4^1 = 10.5$ | |

$$\alpha_1 = \frac{15}{69.5} = 0.216 \quad b_0^2 = 97.4 \quad b_2^2 = 42.7 \qquad \cdots$$

$$\alpha_2 = \frac{69.5}{97.4} = 0.71 \quad b_0^3 = 69.5 \quad b_2^3 = 9.8 \qquad \cdots$$

$$\cdots \qquad \cdots \qquad \cdots$$

which is in fact the $\alpha$ table constructed for Example 3.4.1. Using the new regrouping of the $\alpha$ table, the reduced-order polynomials $Q_k(s)$ in (3.4.15) are now represented by

$$Q_k(s) = s^2 Q_{k-2}(s) + \alpha_k Q_{k-1}(s) \qquad (3.7.4a)$$

with $Q_{-1}(s) = 1/s$ and $Q_0(s) = 1$. For this example,

$$Q_2(s) = s^2 + \alpha_2 s + \alpha_1 \alpha_2 = s^2 + 0.71s + 0.154 \qquad (3.7.4b)$$

The second-order polynomial (3.7.4b) with roots at $s_{1,2} = -0.355 \pm j0.167$ approximates the sixth-order characteristic polynomial of the full model. Once the reduced model's denominator has been determined, the coefficients $\{b_0, b_1, \ldots\}$ are defined. For this example, $b_0 = 0.154$ and $b_1 = 0.71$ and the numerator coefficients $\{a_0 a_1 \ldots\}$ are obtained from (3.3.6), i.e.,

$$a_0 = b_0 c_0 = (0.154)(0.6) = 0.09$$

$$a_1 = b_0 c_1 + b_1 c_0 = (0.154)(-1.23) + (0.71)(0.6) = 0.24 \qquad (3.7.5)$$

which lead to the following reduced-order model:

$$R_2(s) = \frac{24s + 9}{100s^2 + 71s + 15} \qquad (3.7.6)$$

This mixed Padé–Routh method makes use of stable reduced polynomials for the denominator and takes advantage of computationally convenient schemes of the Padé method for the numerator. For unstable full models, the imaginary axis shifts sufficiently to the right so that the Routh approximation can be applied. The following example describes the use of the Padé–Routh method for an unstable system.

**Example 3.7.2.** Consider the following unstable third-order system:

$$G(s) = \frac{s^2 + 2s + 2}{s^3 + 6s^2 + 3s - 10} \tag{3.7.7}$$

It is required to find a second-order reduced model which preserves the instability of (3.7.7).

SOLUTION: The system has three poles at $s_1 = 1$, $s_2 = -2$, and $s_3 = -5$. In order to use Routh approximation the imaginary axis is shifted to the $(+1,0)$ point, resulting in a new characteristic polynomial:

$$\tilde{\Delta}(s) = s^3 + 9s^2 + 18s + 2 \tag{3.7.8}$$

Applying Routh's approximation to (3.7.8) provides $\alpha_1 = 1/9$ and $\alpha_2 = 81/40$ and a second-order reduced polynomial, $\tilde{\Delta}_2(s) = s^2 + 2.025s + 0.225$, which when shifted back to origin gives $\Delta_2(s) = s^2 + 0.025s - 0.8$. For this reduced denominator polynomial, using $b_0 = -0.8$ and $b_1 = 0.025$ and the first two expansion coefficients of (3.7.7), $c_0 = -0.2$ and $c_1 = -0.26$, the Padé approximation gives the following numerator coefficients: $a_0 = 0.16$ and $a_1 = 0.203$. The resulting second-order model is then

$$R_2(s) = \frac{40s + 32}{200s^2 + 5s - 160} \tag{3.7.9}$$

which has two poles at $s_1 = 0.88$ and $s_2 = -0.907$.

## 3.8  Multiinput–Multioutput Systems Reduction

Thus far all the techniques considered were limited to linear time-invariant SISO systems. In this section some of the model reduction methods via frequency domain which have been extended to take MIMO systems into account are discussed.

### 3.8.1  Matrix Continued Fraction Method

Chen (1972, 1974) and Shieh and Guadiano (1974) have extended the continued fraction method (Chen and Shieh, 1968) to the case of MIMO systems. The $(m \times r)$-dimensional transfer function matrix of a MIMO system with $m$ inputs and $r$ outputs introduced by (3.1.6) is rewritten in the following form:

$$H(s) = \left[ \sum_j A_{2j} s^{j-1} \right] \left[ \sum_i A_{1i} s^i \right]^{-1} \tag{3.8.1}$$

where the matrices $D_l$ and coefficients $e_l$, $l = 0, 1, \ldots$, in (3.1.6) have been replaced by the matrices $A_{2,l+1}$ and $A_{1,l+1} \triangleq e_l I_m$, and $I_m$ represents an $m \times m$ identity matrix. It is noted that the matrix continued fraction described here is restricted to systems with the same number of inputs as outputs, i.e., $m = r$; thus, all the matrices on the right side of (3.8.1) and $H(s)$ on the left are necessarily square and $m \times m$ dimensional. The matrix continued fraction of the Cauer second form applied to (3.8.1) results in:

$$H(s) = \left[ H_1 + \left[ H_2 \frac{1}{s} + \left[ H_3 + \left[ H_4 \frac{1}{s} + [\cdots]^{-1} \right]^{-1} \right]^{-1} \right]^{-1} \right]^{-1} \quad (3.8.2)$$

where $H_i$, $i = 1, 2, \ldots, 2k, k \leqslant n$ are matrix quotients and are evaluated through the following matrix Routh algorithm (Shieh and Gaudiano, 1974):

$$
\begin{array}{ll}
H_1 = A_{11} A_{21}^{-1} & 
\begin{array}{llll}
A_{11} & A_{12} & A_{13} & \cdots \\
A_{21} & A_{22} & A_{23} & \cdots \\
A_{31} & A_{32} & \cdots \\
A_{41} & \cdots
\end{array}
\end{array}
\quad (3.8.3)
$$

$$H_2 = A_{21} A_{31}^{-1}$$

$$H_3 = A_{31} A_{41}^{-1}$$

where

$$A_{ij} = A_{i-2, j+1} - H_{i-2} A_{i-1, j+1}, \quad i = 3, 4, \ldots, \quad j = 1, 2, \ldots$$

$$H_i = A_{i,1} (A_{i+1,1})^{-1}, \quad i = 1, 2, \ldots, 2J, J \leqslant n, \det(A_{i+1,1}) \neq 0 \quad (3.8.4)$$

The reduced model by the matrix continued fraction method is obtained by truncating after the $k$th quotient matrix $H_k$. For example, for a second-order reduction one has

$$M_2(s) = \left[ H_1 + \left[ \frac{1}{s} H_2 \right]^{-1} \right]^{-1} = H_2 [sI + H_1 H_2]^{-1} \quad (3.8.5)$$

The matrix continued fraction method has several limitations, namely, the number of outputs and inputs must be equal and, as demonstrated by Calfe and Healey (1974), it is possible for the reduced model characteristic polynomial to be of higher order than that of the full model's. Furthermore, the reduction of the MIMO systems by this and other methods yet to be discussed is a reduction in "output" and not the "state," which is an "aggregation" of system variables discussed in Chapter 2. In fact, as discussed by Marshall (1974), the state variables associated with the reduced model transfer function matrix $M_k(s)$ have no direct relation to the original full model's state variables.

### 3.8.2 Modal–Continued Fraction Method

An alternative method for the reduction of MIMO systems has been introduced by Shieh and Wei (1975) which retains the dominant poles of the full model and applies the matrix continued fraction method to find a reduced-order numerator matrix polynomial. The method eliminates the unpredictable results of the straight matrix continued fraction, such as providing higher order reduced models, but the restriction of having the number of inputs equal to the outputs remains. The method can be summarized by the following algorithm:

**Algorithm 3.2.** Modal–Continued Fraction Method

Step 1: Find the dominant poles of the system from $\Delta(s) = 0$ and construct the reduced model's common denominator

$$\Delta_k(s) = (s - \lambda_1)(s - \lambda_2)\ldots(s - \lambda_k) = \sum_{j=1}^{k+1} f_j s^{j-1}, \quad f_{k+1} = 1$$

(3.8.6)

and

$$A_{i,j} \triangleq f_j I_k, \quad j = 1, 2, \ldots, k; \quad A_{1,k+1} = I_k \qquad (3.8.7)$$

Step 2: Determine the matrix quotients $H_i$, $i = 1, 2, \ldots, k$, using (3.8.3) and (3.8.4).

Step 3: Calculate the reduced model's numerator matrix coefficients $A_{2,j}$, $j = 1, 2, \ldots, k$, from

$$A_{i+1,1} = H_i^{-1} A_{i,1}, \quad i = 1, 2, \ldots, k, \, k \leqslant n$$

$$A_{i+1,j+1} = H_i^{-1} \left[ A_{i,j+1} - A_{i+2,j} \right], \quad i = 1, 2, \ldots, k - j,$$

$$j = 1, 2, \ldots, k - 1 \qquad (3.8.8)$$

The reduced-order model transfer function matrix is given by

$$M_k(s) = \frac{1}{\Delta_k(s)} \left[ \sum_{j=1}^{k} A_{2,j} s^{j-1} \right] \qquad (3.8.9)$$

### 3.8.3 Padé – Modal Method

A third method of reducing large-scale MIMO systems is the combination of Padé approximation for the numerator's matrix coefficients and the retention of the full model's dominant poles for the denominator (Shamash 1975c). The method begins by expanding the full model's transfer function matrix

$$H(s) = \sum_{j=1}^{n} A_{2j} s^{j-1} \bigg/ \sum_{j=0}^{n+1} a_j s^{j-1} = \sum_{i=0}^{\infty} C_i s^i \qquad (3.8.10)$$

into a power series, where $C_i$, $i = 1, 2, \ldots$, are $m \times r$ constant matrices directly proportional to the $i$th moment of the system. Then the reduced order model is given by

$$M_k(s) = \sum_{j=1}^{k} E_j s^j / \Delta_k(s) \qquad (3.8.11)$$

where the reduced-order characteristic polynomial $\Delta_k(s)$ is defined in (3.8.6) and the coefficient matrices $E_j$, $j = 1, \ldots, k$, are obtained by

$$E_1 = f_1 C_0$$
$$E_2 = f_1 C_1 + f_2 C_0$$
$$E_3 = f_1 C_2 + f_2 C_1 + f_3 C_0 \qquad (3.8.12)$$
$$\vdots$$
$$E_k = f_1 C_{k-1} + f_2 C_{k-2} + \cdots + f_{k-1} C_1 + f_k C_0$$

which is the matrix version of the scalar numerator coefficients evaluation by Padé approximation defined by (3.3.3). This technique, as is demonstrated by the following example, is equivalent to the modal-continued fraction method discussed earlier. This result is of course expected, since for an asymptotically stable system the continued fraction method is a special case of Padé approximation.

**Example 3.8.1.** Consider a two-input two-output system which is a modification of a two-input single-output example of Hutton and Friedland (1975):

$$H(s) = \frac{A_{21} + A_{22}s + A_{23}s^2 + A_{24}s^3}{a_1 + a_2 s + a_3 s^2 + a_4 s^3 + a_5 s^4} \qquad (3.8.13)$$

where, $a_1 = 240$, $a_2 = 360$, $a_3 = 204$, $a_4 = 36$, $a_5 = 2$,

$$A_{21} = \begin{bmatrix} 2400 & 2000 \\ 4320 & 3200 \end{bmatrix}, \quad A_{22} = \begin{bmatrix} 1800 & 900 \\ 1440 & 1220 \end{bmatrix}$$

$$A_{23} = \begin{bmatrix} 496 & 488 \\ 528 & 396 \end{bmatrix}, \quad A_{24} = \begin{bmatrix} 28 & 30 \\ 12 & 24 \end{bmatrix} \qquad (3.8.14)$$

It is desired to find a second-order reduced model using matrix continued fraction, modal–continued fraction, and Padé–modal methods.

SOLUTION: The system's poles are $-1.197 \pm j0.69$ and $-7.8 \pm j1.358$. It is desired to keep two of these poles. Using the values of matrices $H_i$, $i = 1, 2$, in (3.8.3) and (3.8.5) leads to

$$M_2(s) = \frac{\begin{bmatrix} 9.8s + 2.3 & 7.6s + 1.9 \\ 16s + 4.2 & 12s + 3.1 \end{bmatrix}}{s^2 + 1.156s + 0.241} \qquad (3.8.15)$$

which provides a pair of poles at $-0.273$ and $-0.883$.

Next, the modal–continued fraction method is taken up by using $-1.97 \pm j0.69$ as dominant poles which, in view of (3.8.6), leads to $\Delta_2(s) = s^2 + 2.4s + 1.91$, $f_1 = 1.91$, $f_2 = 2.4$. Then using $H_i$, $i = 1,2$, from (3.8.3), $A_{21}$ and $A_{21}$ matrices become

$$A_{21} = H_1^{-1}A_{11} = \begin{bmatrix} 19.1 & 15.93 \\ 34.4 & 25.5 \end{bmatrix} \tag{3.8.16}$$

$$A_{22} = H_1^{-1}A_{12} - A_{31} = H_1^{-1}A_{12} - H_2^{-1}A_{31} = \begin{bmatrix} 9.74 & 3.28 \\ 3.07 & 3.44 \end{bmatrix} \tag{3.8.17}$$

leading to a reduced-order model

$$M_2(s) = \frac{\begin{bmatrix} 19.1 + 9.74s & 15.93 + 3.28s \\ 34.4 + 3.07s & 25.5 + 3.44s \end{bmatrix}}{s^2 + 2.4s + 1.91} \tag{3.8.18}$$

The Padé–modal reduction method is obtained by expanding (3.8.13) in a power series:

$$H(s) = C_0 + C_1 s + C_2 s^2 + \cdots \tag{3.8.19}$$

where

$$C_0 = \begin{bmatrix} 10 & 8.34 \\ 18 & 13.34 \end{bmatrix}, \quad C_1 = \begin{bmatrix} -7.5 & -8.75 \\ -21 & -14.91 \end{bmatrix}$$

Then the reduced-order model is given by $M_2(s) = (E_1 + sE_2)/(\Delta_2(s))$, where

$$E_1 = f_1 C_0 = 1.91 C_0 = \begin{bmatrix} 19.1 & 15.95 \\ 34.44 & 25.53 \end{bmatrix} \tag{3.8.20}$$

$$E_2 = f_1 C_1 + f_2 C_0 = 1.9 C_1 + 2.4 C_0 = \begin{bmatrix} 9.58 & 3.22 \\ 2.906 & 3.39 \end{bmatrix} \tag{3.8.21}$$

which except for round-off errors, leads to the same model as the modal–continued fraction (3.8.18).

## 3.9 Frequency Response Comparisons

In this section the frequency responses of various reduced models are compared with the full model's by way of two examples. A comparison on the advantages and disadvantages of the methods are discussed in the next section. The following example compares five model reduction methods used most commonly for SISO systems.

**Example 3.9.1.** Consider the sixth-order SISO system (3.2.14) discussed first in Example 3.2.2, using moment matching and henceforth used for demonstrating Padé approximation (Example 3.3.1), Routh approximation via alpha–beta expansions (Example 3.4.1), Routh's direct method (Krishnamurthy and Seshadri, 1976) and the continued fraction method (Section

3.5). It is desired to make a frequency response comparison of these reduction methods with the full model.

SOLUTION:  In order to facilitate the purpose of this example, the order of all reduced models was chosen to be identically three, i.e., $k = 3$. Table 3.3 shows a poles-zeros summary of the five methods and the full model. It is noted that for three cases (moment matching Padé, and continued fraction), unstable third-order models were obtained for the stable sixth-order full model. Figure 3.1 shows the Bode plots for the six models of Table 3.3. The closest response belongs to the method of Routh $\alpha-\beta$ expansion. Moment matching (shown by dashed line), Padé (shown by small dashes), and the continued fraction model (shown by dashes and small dots) provided negative phase margins, confirming the fact they provided unstable reduced models.

A frequency response comparison between the two methods of error minimization of Hsia (1972) and Reddy (1976), discussed in Section 3.6, revealed that both are rather close to the full model. The main advantage of Reddy's method is when the full model's poles are so close that no clear choice of dominant ones exists. However, this method has been known to provide unstable reduced models for such cases (El-Attar and Vidyasagar,

**Table 3.3.** A Comparison of Five Model Reduction Methods

| Trial | Method | Gain, $K$ | Numerator Polynomial (System zeros) | Denominator Polynomial (System poles) |
|---|---|---|---|---|
| 1 | Full Model | 1 | $s^5 + 9s^4 + 22.25s^3$ $+ 30.25s^2 + 23.25s + 9$ $(-0.51 \pm j0.98,$ $-0.96 \pm 0.53, -6)$ | $s^6 + 10.5s^5 + 45s^4 + 100s^3$ $+ 119s^2 + 69.5s + 15$ $(-0.5, -1, -2, -2 \pm j, -3)$ |
| 2 | Moment Matching[a] | 0.0094 | $s^2 - 44.1s - 35$ $(-0.782, 44.732)$ | $s^3 - s^2 - 1.75s - 0.55$ $(-0.5 \pm j0.085, 2)$ |
| 3 | Padé Approximation[a] | 0.095 | $s^2 - 4.1s - 1.7$ $(-0.376, 4.45)$ | $s^3 - 0.98s^2 - 1.194s - 0.27$ $(1.75, -0.385 \pm j0.064)$ |
| 4 | Routh $\alpha-\beta$ Expansion | 0.38 | $s^2 + 0.9s + 0.35$ $(-0.44 \pm j0.386)$ | $s^3 + 1.62s^2 + s + 0.216$ $(-0.47, -0.57 \pm j0.36)$ |
| 5 | Routh Direct | 0.295 | $s^2 + 0.7s + 0.46$ $(-0.35 \pm j0.58)$ | $s^3 + 1.17s^2 + 3.3s + 0.8$ $(-0.32, -0.42 \pm j0.725)$ |
| 6 | Continued Fraction[a] | 0.462 | $s^2 + 3.75s + 0.836$ $(-0.24, -3.51)$ | $s^3 - 6.2s^2 - 4.2s - 0.65$ $(-0.25, -0.382, 6.84)$ |

[a] Unstable reduced-order models.

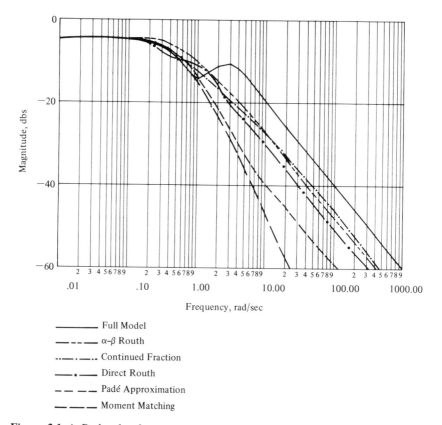

_____ Full Model

— — — — α–β Routh

..—.—.. Continued Fraction

—.—— Direct Routh

— — — — Padé Approximation

— —— Moment Matching

**Figure 3.1** A Bode plot frequency response comparison for five model reduction methods.

1978). Other schemes, such as the continued fraction (Shieh and Goldman, 1974) or modal schemes (Davison, 1966), are not even applicable, since the former technique allows only one zero at infinity and the latter requires the identification of dominant poles.

The following example provides a frequency response comparison of a MIMO system.

**Example 3.9.2.** Consider the two-input two-output fourth-order system (3.8.13)–3.8.14), which was reduced to a second-order system using the matrix continued fraction given by $M_2(s)$ in (3.8.15), the modal–continued fraction in (3.8.18), and the Padé–modal method in (3.8.18). It is desired to make a frequency response comparison of these models.

SOLUTION: All three models of this example are stable. The polar plot of the $h_{11}(s)$ elements of the full model (3.8.13) and reduced models (3.8.15) and

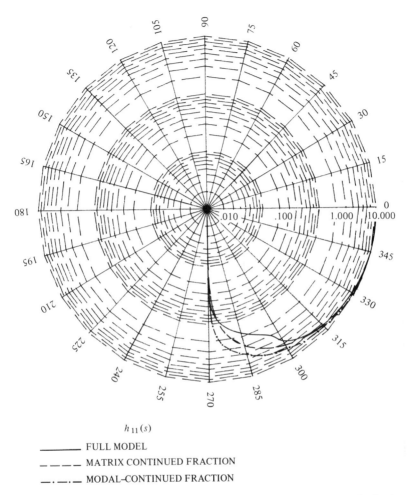

$h_{11}(s)$

——————  FULL MODEL

— — — —  MATRIX CONTINUED FRACTION

—.—.—  MODAL–CONTINUED FRACTION

**Figure 3.2** Polar plots for two multivariable systems model reduction methods.

(3.8.18) are shown in Figure 3.2. The polar plot indicates that the three plots are close, with the matrix continued fraction resulting in the better approximation, which indicates that this reduced model has a phase margin larger than the modal–continued fraction but less than that of the original model. This observation is further verified by comparing the phase margins of the four elements of the transfer function matrix $H(s)$ in (3.8.13), the matrix continued fraction reduced model $M_2(s)$ in (3.8.15), and the modal–continued fraction reduced model $M_2(s)$ in (3.8.18). It is clear that the stability is preserved by both methods with more deterioration of stability caused by the modal–continued fraction method, as indicated before.

**Table 3.4.** A General Comparison of 15 Aggregation Methods

*Frequency-Domain Aggregation Methods*

| Case | Method | Computational Efforts | Stability Preservation | Applicability to Multivariable Systems | Special Features | Other Comments |
|---|---|---|---|---|---|---|
| 1 | Moment Matching | Low | No | No | Most effective for inputs $\alpha_i t^i$. | It has been extended to "best" moment matching. |
| 2 | Padé Approximation | Low | No | No | Taylor series expansions of numerator and denominator. | Disadvantage is that poles of reduced model depend on both numerator and denominator of full model. |
| 3 | Routh $\alpha - \beta$ Expansions | Medium | Yes | Yes | Can handle unstable full models. Expansions belong to Padé expansions about one or more points. | |
| 4 | Routh Direct | Low | Yes | Yes | A matching Taylor series at $s = 0$. Can handle unstable full models. | |
| 5 | Continued Fraction | Low | No | Yes (but no. inputs must equal no. outputs) | A special case of 2 at $s = 0$. For stable cases is identical to moment matching method. | |
| 6 | Error Minimization | High | Yes | No | Commonly involves extended computations and often leads to iterative solution of nonlinear equations. | |
| 7 | Induced Norm Minimization | High | Yes | No | Effective for nondominant or all-dominant full models when other methods fail. | Good approximation for all $L_1$ or $L_\infty$ inputs involving Banach spaces. |

| # | Method | | | | | |
|---|--------|---|---|---|---|---|
| 8 | Mixed: Padé–Routh | Low | Yes | Yes | Routh expansion may fail for case of pole–zero cancellation. Straight Padé would not fail. | Denominator by Routh and numerator by Padé. Applicable to discrete time systems. |
| 9 | Mixed: Padé–Modal | Low | Yes | Yes | Accounts for unretained poles; has good transient and steady-state responses. | Applicable to discrete time systems. |
| *Time-Domain Aggregation Methods* | | | | | | |
| 10 | Exact | Low | No | Yes | May represent unrealistic reduced-order models. | |
| 11 | Modal | High | Yes | Yes | Computation of eigenvalues and eigenvectors is necessary. | |
| 12 | Minimum Realization | Low | Yes | Yes | Requires evaluation of system moments and Hankel matrix formulation. | Equivalent to continued fraction and moments matching methods. |
| 13 | Continued Fraction | Medium | No | Yes | Requires the usual Routhian-type array to set up the aggregation matrix. | |
| 14 | Chained | High | Yes | Yes | The Generalized Hessenberg form may not be conclusive and some QL algorithms are necessary. | Model reduction can be adjusted with the system structure. |
| 15 | Error Minimization | High | Yes | Yes | Requires the solution of a set of nonlinear algebraic equations. | $(F, G)$ structure is commonly fixed to cannonical form. |

## 3.10 Discussion and Conclusions

In this chapter nine model reduction methods for SISO and MIMO systems described in frequency domain were discussed. In the previous chapter, four general classes of time-domain aggregation methods were overviewed in Section 2.2. In this section, a general comparison is made among some fourteen aggregation methods. Table 3.4 gives a brief comparison of the model reduction of SISO systems with applicability to the MIMO case. The elements of this comparison are the computational efforts, stability (or instability) preservation, applicability to MIMO systems, special features and any other comments. From a computational point of view, methods 1, 2, 4, 5, 8, 9, 10, and 12 (moment matching, Padé approximation, Routh direct, continued fraction, Padé–Routh, Padé–modal, exact, and minimum realization) are all relatively easily implemented and their computer memory and time are minimal. On the other hand, the error minimization (cases 6 and 7), modal (case 11), and chained aggregation (case 14) schemes are very costly computationally. For these schemes, often a set of simultaneous nonlinear equations should be solved, the full set of eigenvalues and eigenvectors of large-scale system matrix must be calculated, or QR trans-formations need to be performed iteratively for minimum error, modal, or chained aggregations, respectively.

The issue of stability preservation is perhaps the most critical of all. The Routh-based methods (cases 3, 4, and 8) and the Padé–modal technique (case 9) seem to have little difficulty in guaranteeing stable (or unstable) reduced models for full models with similar property. A special case where the Routh–Hurwitz method (Appiah, 1979; Hutton and Friedland, 1975) will fail to give good approximations (still stable) is when there are some pole-zero cancellations in the full model.

The third important issue is the potential use of these various schemes for MIMO systems, under which virtually all large-scale systems fall. The two mixed methods (cases 8 and 9) of frequency-domain and all the time-domain techniques are the most suitable for MIMO systems. The continued fraction matrix form is also very attractive computationally, but it is restricted to systems with an equal number of inputs and outputs.

Based on the numerical experiments of these various methods, comments from other reports, and overviews (Bosely and Lees, 1972; Genesio and Milanese, 1975; Jamshidi, 1982) it is this author's understanding that the best methods are the mixed methods in which good features of two schemes are combined together. For example, in the Padé–Routh method (case 8), the desirable stability feature of Routh and the computational conveniences of Padé are put together to give a better method than any one of those individually. A potentially promising scheme is the "induced norm" mini-mization due to El-Attar and Vidyasagar (1978), which is theoretically sound, has been proven to give satisfactory time and frequency responses, and more importantly provides stable reduced models. Its most important shortcoming seems to be the lack of efficient and convenient computational algorithms or routines to handle large-scale cases. Its extension to MIMO cases does not pose any particular problems. The importance of this method would be more apparent when noting the fact that in virtually all reduction methods discussed in this chapter, it is assumed that the exact description of the full model is known and the reduction procedure plays the role of a tool. However, as also pointed by Genesio and Milanese (1975), the information required for obtaining the reduced model and a bound on its approximation error is much less than what is needed to fully describe an unreduced large-scale model which may not even be known in practice. A final note is that unfortunately no reduction method (time- or frequency-domain) exists to handle nonlinear or even time-varying systems. The linear time-invariant restriction is indeed too severe for most of the methods discussed here to make them a viable modeling alternative for large-scale systems.

## Problems

**3.1.** For a SISO system with a transfer function

$$G(s) = \frac{1 + 2s + 3s^2}{1 + s + 3s^2 + s^3}$$

find a reduced-order model using the moment matching method.

**3.2.** Use Padé approximation to reduce the following fourth-order system to a second- and third-order system:

$$G(s) = (4s^3 + 9s^2 + 18s + 24)/(s^4 + 3s^3 + 2s^2 + 12)$$

Is stability of the full model preserved?

**3.3.** A system with a transfer function

$$G(s) = (s^3 + 6s^2 + 11s + 6)/(s^4 + 17s^3 + 82s^2 + 130s + 100)$$

has a pair of dominant poles. Find a reduced-order system which preserves the dominant poles using Padé approximation.

**C3.4.** Use the Routh $\alpha-\beta$ expansion method to find a reduced-order model for

$$G(s) = (s^3 + s^2 + 80s + 220)/(s^4 + 4s^3 + 35s^2 + 80s + 210)$$

**3.5.** An unstable system has a transfer function

$$G(s) = (s^2 + 5s + 6)/(s^3 + s^2 - 2)$$

Find a second-order reduced model which preserves the instability using the following methods: (i) Routh, (ii) Padé, (iii) Padé–Routh, and (iv) modal–continued fraction.

**3.6.** Find a reduced model for the system

$$G(s) = (4s^2 + 3s + 1)/(s^3 + 2s^2 + 5s + 2)$$

using the continued fraction methods of Section 3.5.

**3.7.** Consider a sixth-order system

$$G(s) = \frac{(s^5 + 8s^4 + 20s^3 + 16s^2 + 3s + 2)}{(s^6 + 18.3s^5 + 102.42s^4 + 209.46s^3 + 155.94s^2 + 33.6s + 2)}$$

Find a second-order system with a root at $-2$ and a known parameter $d_1 = 18$ in Equation (3.6.2).

**3.8.** Repeat Example 3.7.1 for the system

$$G(s) = (s^3 + 10s^2 + 14s + 5)/(s^4 + 2s^3 + 5s^2 + 10s + 4)$$

Use the Padé–modal and Padé–Routh methods to find a second-order reduced model which would preserve the system's dominant poles.

**3.9.** For the system

$$G(s) = (s^2 + 2s + 2)/(s^3 + 12s^2 + 25s + 50)$$

Use the Padé–modal and Padé–Routh methods to find a second-order reduced model which would preserve the system's dominant poles.

**C3.10.** Consider a two-input two-output system with the following transfer function matrix:

$$H(s) = (A_{21} + A_{22}s + A_{23}s^2)/(a_1 + a_2s + a_3s^2 + a_4s^3)$$

where $a_1 = 120$, $a_2 = 320$, $a_3 = 180$, $a_4 = 2$.

$$A_{21} = \begin{bmatrix} 240 & 200 \\ 420 & 300 \end{bmatrix}, \quad A_{22} = \begin{bmatrix} 180 & 80 \\ 100 & 120 \end{bmatrix}, \quad A_{23} = \begin{bmatrix} 50 & 40 \\ 50 & 30 \end{bmatrix}$$

Find a second-order reduced model using matrix continued fraction.

**C3.11.** Repeat problem C3.10 using the modal–continued fraction method of Algorithm 3.2.

# References

Appiah, R. K. 1979. Padé methods of Hurwitz polynomial approximation with application to linear system reduction. *Int. J. Contr.* 29:39–48.

Baker, G. J., Jr.; Rushbrooke, G. S.; and Gilbert, H. E. 1964. *Phys. Review* 135:1272.

Bosley, M. J., and Lees, F. P. 1972. A survey of simple transfer function derivations from high-order state-variable models. *IFAC J. Automatica* 8:765–775.

Calfe, M. R., and Healey, M. 1974. Continued-fraction model-reduction technique for multi-variable systems. *Proc. IEE* 121:393–395.

Chen, C. F. 1972. Model reduction of multi-variable control systems by means of matrix continued fractions. *Proc. 5th IFAC Congress*, Paris, France, Paper 35.1.

Chen, C. F. 1974. Model reduction of multivariable control systems by means of continued fractions. *Int. J. Contr.* 20:225–238.

Chen, C. F., and Haas, I. J. 1968. Elements of Control Systems Analysis, p. 303. Prentice-Hall, Englewood Cliffs, NJ.

Chen, C. F., and Shieh, L. S. 1968. A novel approach to linear model simplification. *Int. J. Contr.* 8:561–570.

Chen, C. F., and Shieh, L. S. 1970. An algebraic method for control system design. *Int. J. Contr.* 11:717–739.

Chuang, S. C. 1970. Application of continued-fraction method for modelling transfer functions to give more accurate initial transient response. *Elect. Letters* 6:861–863.

Davidson, A. M., and Lucas, T. N. 1974. Linear system reduction by continued fraction expansion about a general point. *Elect. Letters* 10:271–273.

Davison, E. J. 1966. A method for simplifying linear dynamic systems. *IEEE Trans. Aut. Cont.* AC-12:119–121.

El-Attar, R. A. and Vidyasagar, M. 1978. Order reduction by $l_1$- and $l_\infty$-norm minimization. *IEEE Trans. Aut. Cont.* AC-23:731–734.

Genesio, R., and Milanese, M. 1976. A note on the derivation and use of reduced-order models. *IEEE Trans. Aut. Cont.* AC-21:118–122.

Gibilaro, L. G. 1967. Models for mixing vessels. Ph.D. thesis, Loughborough University of Technology, Loughborough, England.

Gibilaro, L. G., and Lees, F. P. 1969. The reduction of complex transfer function models to simple models using the method of moments. *Chem. Engr. Sci.* 24:85–93.

Hsia, T. C. 1972. On the simplification of linear systems. *IEEE Trans. Aut. Cont.* AC-17:372–374.

Hutton, M. F., and Friedland, B. 1975. Routh approximations for reducing order of linear, time-invariant systems. *IEEE Trans. Aut. Cont.* AC-20:329–337.

Jamshidi, M. 1982. An overview on the reduction of large-scale systems models. Submitted to *IFAC J. Automatica.*

Johnson, J. L.; Fan, L. T.; and Wu, Y. S. 1971. Comparison of moments, $s$-plane, and frequency response methods for analysing pulse testing data from flow systems. *Ind. Engr. Chem. Proc. Des. Dev.* 10:425–431.

Krishnamurthy, V., and Seshadri, V. 1976. A simple and direct method of reducing order of linear systems using Routh approximations in frequency domain. *IEEE Trans. Aut. Cont.* AC-21:797–799.

Krishnamurthy, V., and Seshadri, V. 1978. Model reduction using Routh stability criterion. *IEEE Trans. Aut. Cont.* AC-23:729–731.

Lal, M., and Mitra, R. 1974. Simplification of large system dynamics using a moment evaluation algorithm. *IEEE Trans. Aut. Cont.* AC-9:602–603.

Lamba, S. S., and Rao, S. V. 1978. Aggregation matrix for the reduced-order continued fraction expansion model of Chen and Shieh. *IEEE Trans. Aut. Cont.* AC-23:81–83.

Lees, F. P. 1971. The derivation of simple transfer function models of oscillating and inverting processes from the basic transformed equations using the method of moments. *Chem. Engr. Sci.* 26:1179–1186.

Levy, E. C. 1959. Complex-curve fitting. *IEEE Trans. Aut. Cont.* 4:37–43.

Marshall, S. A. 1974. Continued-fraction model-reduction technique for multivariable systems. *Proc. IEE* 121:1032.

Nagarajan, R. 1971. Optimum reduction of large dynamic system. *Int. J. Contr.* 14:1164–1174.

Padé, H. 1892. Sur la representation approachee d'une function par des fractions rationelles. *Annales Scientifiques de P'Ecole Normale Supieure*, Ser. 3 (Suppl.) 9:1–93.

Parthasarathy, R., and Singh, H. 1975. Comments on linear system reduction by continued fraction expansion about a general point. *Elect Letters.* 11:102.

Paynter, H. M. 1956. On an analogy between stochastic process and monotone dynamic systems, in G. Muller, ed., *Regelungstechnik Modern Theorien und ihre Verwendbarkeit.* R. Oldenbourg-Verlag, Munich.

Rao, S. V., and Lamba, S. S. 1974. A new frequency domain technique for the simplification of linear dynamic systems. *Int. J. Contr.* 20:71–79.

Rao, A. S., Lamba, S. S., and Rao, S. V. 1978. On simplification of unstable systems using Routh approximation technique. *IEEE Trans. Aut. Cont.* AC-23:943–944.

Reddy, A. S. S. R. 1976. A method for frequency domain simplification of transfer functions. *Int. J. Contr.* 23:403–408.

Shamash, Y. 1974. Stable reduced-order models using Padé-type approximations. *IEEE Trans. Aut. Cont.* AC-19:615–617.

Shamash, Y. 1975a. Model reduction using the Routh stability criterion and the Padé approximation technique. *Int. J. Contr.* 21:475–484.

Shamash, Y. 1975b. Linear system reduction using Padé approximation to allow retention of dominant modes *Int. J. Contr.* 21:257–272.

Shamash, Y. 1975c. Multivariable system reduction via modal methods and Padé approximation. *IEEE Trans. Aut. Cont.* AC-20:815–817.

Shieh, L. S., and Guadiano, F. F. 1974. Matrix continued fraction expansion and inversion by the generalized matrix algorithm. *Int. J. Contr.* 20:727–737.

Shieh, L. S., and Goldman, M. J. 1974. A mixed Cauer form for linear system reduction. *IEEE Trans. Sys. Man. Cyb.* SMC-4:584–588.

Shieh, L. S., and Wei, Y. J. 1975. A mixed method for multi-variable system reduction. *IEEE Trans. Aut. Cont.* AC-20:429–432.

Singh, V. 1979. Nonuniqueness of model reduction using the Routh approach. *IEEE Trans. Aut. Cont.* AC-24:650–651.

Sinha, N. K., and Pille, W. 1971a. A new method for reduction of dynamic systems. *Int. J. Cont.* 14:111–118.

Sinha, N. K., and Berezani, G. T. 1971b. Optimum approximation of high-order systems by low-order models. *Int. J. Contr.* 14:951–959.

Towill, D. R., and Mehdi, Z. 1970. Prediction of transient response sensitivity of high order linear systems using low order models. *Measurement Control* 3:T1–T9.

Wall, H. S. 1948. Analytic Theory of Continued Fractions. Van Nostrand, New York.

Wright, D. J. 1973. The continued fraction representation of transfer functions and model simplification. *Int. J. Contr.* 18:449–454.

Zakian, V. 1973. Simplification of linear time-invariant systems by moment approximations. *Int. J. Contr.* 18:455–460.

# Chapter 4
# Hierarchical Control
# of Large-Scale Systems

## 4.1 Introduction

The notion of a large-scale system, as it was briefly discussed in Chapter 1, may be described as a complex system composed of a number of constituents or smaller subsystems serving particular functions and shared resources and governed by interrelated goals and constraints (Mahmoud, 1977). Although interaction among subsystems can take on many forms, one of the most common one is hierarchical, which appears somewhat natural in economic, management, organizational, and complex industrial systems such as steel, oil, and paper. Within this hierarchical structure, the subsystems are positioned on levels with different degrees of hierarchy. A subsystem at a given level controls or "coordinates" the units on the level below it and is, in turn, controlled or coordinated by the unit on the level immediately above it. Figure 4.1 shows a typical hierarchical ("multilevel") system. The highest level coordinator, sometimes called the *supremal coordinator*, can be thought of as the board of directors of a corporation, while another level's coordinators may be the president, vice-presidents, directors, etc. The lower levels can be occupied by plant managers, shop managers, etc., while the large-scale system is the corporation itself. In spite of this seemingly natural representation of a hierarchical structure, its exact behavior has not been well understood mainly due to the fact that very little quantitative work has been done on these large-scale systems (March and Simon, 1958). Mesarovic et al. (1970) presented one of the earliest formal quantitative treatments of hierarchical (multilevel) systems. Since then, a great deal of work has been done in the field (Schoeffler and Lasdon, 1966; Beneveniste et al., 1976; Smith and Sage, 1973; Geoffrion, 1970; Schoeffler, 1971; Pearson, 1971; Cohen and Jolland, 1976; Sandell et al., 1978; Singh,

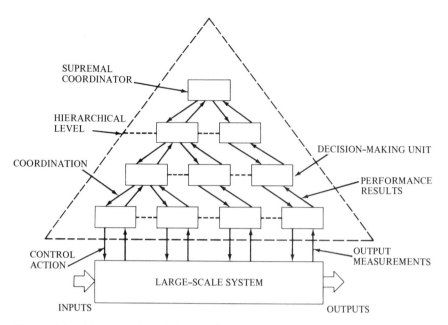

**Figure 4.1** A hierarchical (multilevel) control strategy for a large-scale system.

1980). For a relatively exhaustive survey on the multilevel systems control and applications, the interested reader may see the work of Mahmoud (1977).

In this section, a further interpretation and insight of the notion of hierarchy, the properties and types of hierarchical processes, and some reasons for their existence are given. An overall evaluation of hierarchical methods is presented in Section 4.6.

There is no uniquely or universally accepted set of properties associated with the hierarchical systems. However, the following are some of the key properties:

1. A hierarchical system consists of decision making components structured in a pyramid shape (Figure 4.1).
2. The system has an overall goal which may (or may not) be in harmony with all its individual components.
3. The various levels of hierarchy in the system exchange information (usually vertically) among themselves iteratively.
4. As the level of hierarchy goes up, the time horizon increases; i.e., the lower-level components are faster than the higher-level ones.

There are three basic structures in hierarchical (multilevel) systems depending on the model parameters, decision variables, behavioral and environmental aspects, uncertainties, and the existence of many conflicting goals or objectives.

1. Multistrata Hierarchical Structure: In this multilevel system in which levels are called *strata*, lower-level subsystems are assigned more specialized descriptions and details of the large-scale complex system than the higher levels.

2. Multilayer Hierarchical Structure: This structure is a direct outcome of the complexities involved in a decision making process. The control tasks are distributed in a vertical division (Singh and Titli, 1978), as shown in Figure 4.2. For the multilayer structure shown here, regulation (first layer) acts as a direct control action, followed by optimization (calculation of the regulators' set points), adaptation (direct adaptation of the control law and model) and self-organization (model selection and control as a function of environmental parameters).

3. Multiechelon Hierarchical Structure: This is the most general structure of the three and consists of a number of subsystems situated in levels such that each one, as discussed earlier, can coordinate lower-level units and be coordinated by a higher-level one. This structure, shown

**Figure 4.2** A multilayer control strategy for a large-scale system.

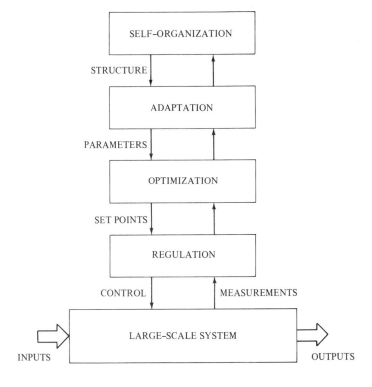

in Figure 4.1, considers conflicting goals and objectives between decision subproblems. The higher-level echelons, in other words, resolve the conflict goals while relaxing interactions among lower echelons. The distribution of control task in contrast to the multilayer structure described in Figure 4.2 is horizontal.

In addition to the vertical (multilayer) and horizontal (multiechelon) division of control task, a third division called a time or functional division is possible (Singh and Titli, 1978). In this division a given subsystem's functional optimization problem is decomposed into a finite number of single-parameter optimization problems at a lower level and results in a considerable reduction in computational effort. This scheme will be discussed in Section 4.5 in connection with the hierarchical control of discrete-time systems.

Before the scope of the present chapter is given, based on the above discussion, one can make a tentative conclusion that a successful operation of hierarchical systems is best described by two processes known as *decomposition* and *coordination*. The coordination process as applicable to most hierarchical systems is described in Section 4.2. Section 4.3 is concerned with the open-loop control of continuous-time hierarchical systems where coordination between two levels are considered. The closed-loop hierarchical control of large-scale systems is discussed in Section 4.4, including the notions of "interaction prediction" and "structural perturbation." In Section 4.5, the structural perturbation and interaction prediction approaches are extended to take on the discrete-time case with and without delay. Among the hierarchical control strategies discussed here are a three-level time-delay coordination algorithm by Tamura (1974, 1975) and a "costate coordination" or "costate prediction" scheme due to Mahmoud et al. (1977) and Hassan and Singh (1976a, 1977;). A number of numerical examples illustrate the various techniques presented. The near-optimum design of linear and nonlinear hierarchical systems are discussed in Chapter 6. Section 4.6 is devoted to further discussion and the evaluation of hierarchical control techniques.

## 4.2 Coordination of Hierarchical Structures

It was mentioned in the previous section that a large-scale system can be hierarchically controlled by decomposing it into a number of subsystems and then coordinating the resulting subproblems to transform a given intergrated system into a multilevel one. This transformation can be achieved by a host of different ways. However, most of these schemes are essentially a combination of two distinct approaches: the *model-coordination method* (or "feasible" method) and *goal-coordination method* (or "dual-feasible" method) (Mesarovic et al., 1969). In the next two sections, these methods are described for a two-subsystem static optimization (nonlinear programming) problem.

## 4.2.1 Model Coordination Method

Consider the following static optimization problem (Schoeffler, 1971):

$$\text{minimize } J(x, u, y) \tag{4.2.1}$$

$$\text{subject to } f(x, u, y) = 0 \tag{4.2.2}$$

where $x =$ vector of system (state) variables, $u =$ vector of manipulated (control) variables, and $y =$ vector of interaction variables between subsystems. Let the problem and its objective function be decomposed into two subsystems, i.e.,

$$J(x, u, y) = J_1(x^1, u^1, y^1) + J_2(x^2, u^2, y^2) \tag{4.2.3}$$

and

$$f^i(x^i, u^i, y^1, y^2) = 0, \quad i = 1, 2 \tag{4.2.4}$$

where $x^i$, $u^i$, and $y^i$ are vectors of system, manipulated, and interaction variables for $i$th subsystem, respectively. This decomposition has produced a performance function for each subsystem. However, through the vectors $y^i$, $i = 1, 2$, the subsystems are still interconnected. The objective of the model coordination method is to convert the integrated problem (4.2.1)–(4.2.2) into a two-level problem by fixing the interaction variables $y^1$ and $y^2$ at some value, say $w^i$, $i = 1, 2$, i.e.,

$$\text{Constrain } y^i = w^i, \quad i = 1, 2 \tag{4.2.5}$$

Under this situation the problem (4.2.1)–(4.2.2) may be divided into the following two sequential problems:

*First - Level Problem — Subsystem i*

$$\text{Find } K_i(w) = \min_{x^i, u^i} J_i(x^i, u^i, w^i) \tag{4.2.6}$$

$$\text{subject to } f^i(x^i, u^i, w^1, w^2) = 0 \tag{4.2.7}$$

*Second - Level Problem*

$$\min_{w} \text{mize } K(w) = K_1(w) + K_2(w) \tag{4.2.8}$$

The above minimizations are to be done, respectively, over the following feasible sets:

$$S_1^i = \{(x^i, u^i) : f^i(x^i, u^i, w) = 0\}, \quad i = 1, 2 \tag{4.2.9}$$

$$S_2^i = \{w^i : K_i(w^i) \text{ exists}\}, \quad i = 1, 2 \tag{4.2.10}$$

Figure 4.3 shows a two-level structure for the model coordination method.

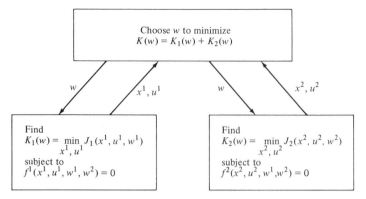

**Figure 4.3** A two-level solution of a static optimization problem using model coordination.

In this coordination procedure the variables $w^i$ which fix interaction variables $y^i$ are termed *coordinating variables*. Moreover, since certain internal interactions are fixed by adding a constraint to the mathematical model, this procedure is called model coordination. In other words, due to the fact that all intermediate variables $x$, $u$, and $y$ are present, it is alternatively termed "feasible decomposition method." Therefore, a system can operate with these intermediate values with a near-optimal performance. The first-level problems are constructed by fixing certain interacting variables in the original optimization problem, while assigning the task of determining these coordinating variables to the second level.

### 4.2.2 Goal Coordination Method

Consider the static optimization problem (4.2.1)–(4.2.2). In the goal coordination method the interactions are literally removed by cutting all the links among the subsystems. Let $y^i$ be the outgoing variable from the $i$th subsystem, while its incoming variable is denoted by $z^i$. Due to the removal of all links between subsystems, it is clear that $y^i \neq z^i$. Under this condition, $z^i$ acts as an arbitrary manipulated variable and should be chosen by the optimizing subsystems like $x$, $u$, and $y$. Moreover, the optimization problem considered in the previous section is completely decoupled into two subsystems due to the fact that their interactions are cut and their objective functions were already separated. In order to make sure the individual subproblems yield a solution to the original problem, it is necessary that the *interaction-balance principle* be satisfied, i.e., the independently selected $y^i$ and $z^i$ actually become equal (Mesarovic et al., 1969; Schoeffler, 1971).

Here again, the procedure is to decompose the problem into a number of decoupled subproblems which constitute the first-level problem. The second-level problem is to force the first-level subproblems to a solution for which the interaction-balance principle holds. Mathematically, this multi-level formulation can be set up by introducing a weighting parameter $\alpha$ which penalizes the performance of the system when the interactions do not balance. Hence, to the objective function (4.2.3) a penalty term is added:

$$J(x, u, y, z, \alpha) = J_1(x^1, u^1, y^1) + J_2(x^2, u^2, y^2) + \alpha^T(y - z)$$

$$(4.2.11)$$

where $\alpha$ is a vector of weighting parameters (positive or negative) which causes any interaction unbalance $(y - z)$ to affect the objective function. By introducing the $z$ variables, the system's equations are given by

$$f_1(x^1, u^1, y^1, z^2) = 0 \qquad (4.2.12)$$

$$f_2(x^2, u^2, y^2, z^1) = 0 \qquad (4.2.13)$$

The set of allowable system variables is defined by

$$S_0 = \{(x, u, y, z): f_1(\cdot) = f_2(\cdot) = 0\} \qquad (4.2.14)$$

Once the objective function (4.2.11) is minimized over the set $S_0$ it results a function,

$$K(\alpha) = \min_{x, u, y, z \in S_0} J(x, u, y, z, \alpha) \qquad (4.2.15)$$

After expanding the penalty term $\alpha^T(y - z) = \alpha_1^T(y^1 - z^1) + \alpha_2^T(y^2 - z^2)$ and considering the relations (4.2.11)–(4.2.13), the first-level problem is formulated as

Subsystem 1: $\quad \min_{x^1, u^1, y^1, z^2} J_1(x^1, u^1, y^1, z^2) + \alpha_1^T y^1 - \alpha_2^T z^2 \qquad (4.2.16)$

$\quad$ subject to $f_1(x^1, u^1, y^1,) = 0 \qquad (4.2.17)$

Subsystem 2: $\quad \min_{x^2, u^2, y^2, z^1} J_2(x^2, u^2, y^2, z^1) - \alpha_1^T z^1 + \alpha_2^T y^2 \qquad (4.2.18)$

$\quad$ subject to $f_2(x^2, u^2, y^2, z^1) = 0 \qquad (4.2.19)$

The second-level problem is to manipulate the coordinating variable $\alpha$ in order to derive the two-subsystems interaction error to zero, i.e.,

$$\min_\alpha e = \min_\alpha (y - z) \qquad (4.2.20)$$

It is clear from the second-level problem (Equation (4.2.20)) that the coordinating variable $\alpha$ is manipulated until the error $e$ approaches zero; i.e., the interaction balance is held by manipulating the objective functions of the first-level problems (4.2.16) and (4.2.18) through variable $\alpha$; hence, the name "goal coordination." Figure 4.4 shows the two-level solution via goal coordination. The reader should compare the two structures in Figures 4.3 and 4.4.

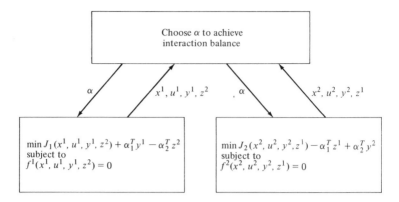

**Figure 4.4** A two-level solution of a static optimization problem using goal coordination.

It will be seen later that the coordinating variable $\alpha$ can be interpreted as a vector of Lagrange multipliers and the second-level problem can be solved through well-known iterative search methods, such as the gradient, Newton's, or conjugate gradient methods.

## 4.3 Open-Loop Hierarchical Control of Continuous-Time Systems

In this section the goal coordination formulation of multilevel systems is applied to large-scale linear continuous-time systems within the context of open-loop control. In addition to the interaction-balance approach another scheme known as the interaction prediction method is also discussed.

Let a large-scale dynamic interconnected system be represented by the following state equation:

$$\dot{x} = F(x, u, t), \quad x(t_o) = x_o \tag{4.3.1}$$

where $x$ and $u$ are $n \times 1$ and $m \times 1$ state and control vectors, respectively. It is assumed that the system consists of $N$ interconnected subsystems $s_i$, $i = 1, 2, \ldots, N$, and the $i$th subsystem's state equation is given by

$$\dot{x}_i = f_i(x_i, u_i, t) + g_i(x, t), \quad x_i(t_o) = x_{io} \tag{4.3.2}$$

where $x, u, x_i, u_i$ are respectively $n$-, $m$-, $n_i$-, and $m_i$-dimensional, $g_i(\cdot)$ represents the $i$th subsystem interaction and

$$x^T(t) = \left( x_1^T(t), x_2^T(t), \ldots, x_N^T(t) \right) \tag{4.3.3}$$

$$u^T(t) = \left( u_1^T(t), u_2^T(t), \ldots, u_N^T(t) \right) \tag{4.3.4}$$

The objective, in an optimal control sense, is to find control vectors $u_1, u_2, \ldots, u_N$ such that a cost function

$$J = G\big(x(t_f)\big) + \int_{t_o}^{t_f} h\big(x(t), u(t), t\big) \, dt \tag{4.3.5}$$

is minimized subject to (4.3.1) and a feasible domain

$$u(t) \in U(x(t), t) = \{u|v(x(t), u, t) \leqslant 0\} \qquad (4.3.6)$$

Through the assumed decomposition of system (4.3.1) into $N$ interconnected subsystems (4.3.2), a similar decomposition can be assumed to hold
for the cost function constraint (4.3.6) and the interaction $g_i(x, t)$ in (4.3.2),
i.e.,

$$J = \sum_i J_i = \sum_i \left\{ G_i\left(x_i(t_f)\right) + \int_{t_o}^{t_f} h_i\left(x_i(t), z_i(t), u_i(t), t\right) dt \right\}$$

$$(4.3.7)$$

$$v(x, u, t) = \sum_j v_j\left(x_j, u_j, t\right) \qquad (4.3.8)$$

$$g_i(x, t) = \sum_j g_{ij}\left(x_j, t\right) \qquad (4.3.9)$$

where $z_i(t)$ is a vector consisting of a linear (or nonlinear) combination of
the states of the $N$ subsystems. Under the above assumption of separation,
the large-scale system's optimal control problem (4.3.1), (4.3.5), and (4.3.6)
can be rewritten as

minimize

$$\sum_i J_i = \sum_i \left\{ G_i\left(x_i(t_f)\right) + \int_{t_o}^{t_f} h_i\left(x_i(t), z_i(t), u_i(t), t\right) dt \right\} \quad (4.3.10)$$

subject to

$$\dot{x}_i(t) = f_i\left(x_i(t), u_i(t), t\right) + \xi_i\left(z_i(t), t\right), \quad x_i(t_o) = x_{io}, \quad i = 1, 2, \ldots, N$$

$$(4.3.11)$$

$$\xi_i\left(z_i(t), t\right) = \sum_j g_{ij}\left(x_j(t), t\right), \quad i = 1, 2, \ldots, N \qquad (4.3.12)$$

$$\sum_j v_j\left(x_j, u_j(t), t\right) \leqslant 0 \qquad (4.3.13)$$

The above problem, known as a hierarchical (multilevel) control, was
demonstrated for a two-level optimization of a static problem in the
previous section. The application of two-level goal-coordination to large-
scale linear systems is given next.

### 4.3.1 Linear System Two-Level Coordination

Consider a large-scale linear time-invariant system:

$$\dot{x}(t) = Ax(t) + Bu(t), \quad x(0) = x_o \qquad (4.3.14)$$

It is assumed that (4.3.14) can be decomposed into

$$\dot{x}_i(t) = A_i x_i(t) + B_i u_i(t) + C_i z_i(t), \quad x_i(0) = x_{io} \qquad (4.3.15)$$

and the $k_i \times 1$ interaction vector

$$z_i(t) = \sum_{j=1}^{N} G_{ij} x_j \qquad (4.3.16)$$

is a linear combination of the states of the other $N-1$ subsystems, and $G_{ij}$ is an $n_i \times n_j$ matrix (Singh, 1980). The original system's optimal control problem is reduced to the optimization of $N$ subsystems which collectively satisfy (4.3.15)–(4.3.16) while minimizing

$$J = \sum_{i=1}^{N} \left\{ \frac{1}{2} x_i^T(t_f) Q_i x_i(t_f) + \frac{1}{2} \int_0^{t_f} \left[ x_i^T(t) Q_i x_i(t) + u_i^T(t) R_i u_i(t) \right. \right.$$

$$\left. \left. + z_i^T(t) S_i z_i(t) \right] dt \right\} \qquad (4.3.17)$$

where $Q_i$ are $n_i \times n_i$ positive semidefinite matrices, $R_i$ and $S_i$ are $m_i \times m_i$ and $k_i \times k_i$ positive definite matrices with

$$n = \sum_{i=1}^{N} n_i, \quad m = \sum_{i=1}^{N} m_i, \quad k = \sum_{i=1}^{N} k_i, \quad k_i \leqslant n_i \qquad (4.3.18)$$

The physical interpretation of the last term in the integrand of (4.3.17) is difficult at this point. In fact, the introduction of this term, as will be seen later, is to avoid singular controls. The "goal coordination" or "interaction balance" approach of Mesarvic et al. (1970) as applied to the "linear-quadratic" problem by Pearson (1971) and reported by Singh (1980) is now presented.

In this decomposition of a large interconnected linear system the common coupling factors among its $N$ subsystems are the "interaction" variables $z_i(t)$, which, along with (4.3.15)–(4.3.16), constitute the "coupling" constraints. This formulation has been called "global" by Benveniste et al. (1976) and is denoted by $s_G$. The following assumption is considered to hold. The global problem $s_G$ is replaced by a family of $N$ subproblems coupled together through a parameter vector $\alpha = (\alpha_1, \alpha_2, \dots, \alpha_N)^T$ and denoted by $s_i(\alpha)$, $i = 1, 2, \dots, N$. In other words, the global system problem $s_G$ is "imbedded" into a family of subsystem problems $s_i(\alpha)$ through an imbedding parameter $\alpha$ (Sandell et al., 1978) in such a way that for a particular value of $\alpha^*$, the subsystems $s_i(\alpha^*)$, $i = 1, 2, \dots, N$, yield the desired solution to $s_G$. In terms of hierarchical control notation, this imbedding concept is nothing but the notion of coordination, but in mathematical programming problem terminology, it is denoted as the "master" problem (Geoffrion, 1970). Figure 4.5 shows a two-level control structure of a large-scale system. Under this strategy, each local controller $i$ receives $\alpha_i^l$ from the coordinator (second-level hierarchy), solves $s_i(\alpha_i^l)$, and transmits

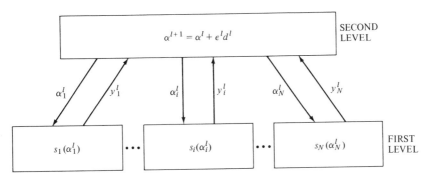

**Figure 4.5** The two-level goal-coordination structure for dynamic systems.

(reports) some function $y_i^l$ of its solution to the coordinator. The coordinator, in turn, evaluates the next updated value of $\alpha$, i.e.,

$$\alpha^{l+1} = \alpha^l + \varepsilon^l d^l \qquad (4.3.19)$$

where $\varepsilon^l$ is the $l$th iteration step size, and the update term $d^l$, as will be seen shortly, is commonly taken as a function of "interaction error":

$$e_i(\alpha(t), t) = z_i(\alpha(t), t) - \sum_{j=1}^{N} G_{ij} x_j(\alpha(t), t) \qquad (4.3.20)$$

The imbedded interaction variable $z_i(\cdot)$ in (4.3.20) can be considered as part of the control variable available to controller $i$, in which case the parameter vector $\alpha(t)$ serves as a set of "dual" variables or Langrange multipliers corresponding to interaction equality constraints (4.3.16). The fundamental concept behind this approach is to convert the original system's minimization problem into an easier maximization problem whose solution can be obtained in the two-level iterative scheme discussed above.

Let us introduce a dual function

$$q(\alpha) = \min_{x, u, z} \{ L(x, u, z, \alpha) \} \qquad (4.3.21)$$

subject to (4.3.15), where the Lagrangian $L(\cdot)$ is defined by

$$L(x, u, z, \alpha) = \sum_{i=1}^{N} \left\{ \frac{1}{2} x_i^T(t_f) Q_i x_i(t_f) + \frac{1}{2} \int_0^{t_f} \left[ x_i^T(t) Q_i x_i(t) \right. \right.$$

$$+ u_i^T(t) R_i u_i(t) + z_i^T(t) S_i z_i(t) \qquad (4.3.22)$$

$$\left. \left. + 2\alpha_i^T \left( z_i(t) - \sum_{j=1}^{N} G_{ij} x_j(t) \right) \right] dt \right\}$$

where the parameter vector $\alpha$ consists of $k$ Lagrange multipliers. In this way the original constrained (subsystems interactions) optimization problem is changed to an unconstrained one. In other words, the constraint (4.3.16) is satisfied by determining a set of Lagrange multipliers $\alpha_i$, $i = 1, 2, \ldots, k$. Under such cases, when the constraints are convex, Geoffrion (1971a, b) and Singh (1980) have shown that

$$\underset{\alpha}{\text{Maximize}}\, q(\alpha) \equiv \underset{u}{\text{Minimize}}\, J \qquad (4.3.23)$$

indicating that minimization of $J$ in (4.3.17) subject to (4.3.15)–(4.3.16) is equivalent to maximizing the dual function $q(\alpha)$ in (4.3.21) with respect to $\alpha$. To facilitate the solution of this problem, it is observed that for a given set of Lagrange multipliers $\alpha = \alpha^*$, the Lagrangian (4.3.22) can be rewritten as

$$
L(x, u, z, \alpha^*) = \sum_{i=1}^{N} \left\{ \frac{1}{2} x_i^T(t_f) Q_i x_i(t_f) + \frac{1}{2} \int_0^{t_f} \left[ x_i^T(t) Q_i x_i(t) \right. \right.
$$
$$
+ u_i^T(t) R_i u_i(t) + z_i^T S_i z_i(t) + 2 \alpha_i^{*T} z_i(t) \qquad (4.3.24)
$$
$$
\left. \left. - 2 \sum_{j=1}^{N} \alpha_j^{*T} G_{ji} x_i(t) \right] dt \right\} \triangleq \sum_{i=1}^{N} L_i(\cdot)
$$

which reveals that the decomposition is carried on to the Lagrangian in such a way that a sub-Lagrangian exists for each subsystem. Each subsystem would intend to minimize its own sub-Lagrangian $L_i$ as defined by (4.3.24) subject to (4.3.15) and using the Lagrange multipliers $\alpha^*$ which are treated as known functions at the first level of hierarchy. The result of each such minimization would allow one to determine the dual function $q(\alpha^*)$ in (4.3.21). At the second level, where the solutions of all first-level subsystems are known, the value of $q(\alpha^*)$ would be improved by a typical unconstrained optimization such as the Newton's method, the gradient method, or the conjugate gradient method. The reason for a gradient-type method is due to the fact that the gradient of $q(\alpha)$ is defined by

$$
\nabla_\alpha q(\alpha) \big|_{\alpha_i = \alpha_i^*} = z_i - \sum_{j=1}^{N} G_{ij} x_j \triangleq e_i, \quad i = 1, 2, \ldots \qquad (4.3.25)
$$

is nothing but the subsystems' interaction errors, which are known through first-level solutions, and $\nabla_x f$ defines the gradient of $f$ with respect to $x$. At the second level the vector $\alpha$ is updated as indicated by (4.3.19) and Figure 4.5. If a gradient (steepest descent) method is employed, the vector $d^l$ in (4.3.19) is simply the $l$th iteration interaction error $e^l(t)$. However, a superior technique from a computational point of view is the conjugate gradient defined by

$$d^{l+1}(t) = e^{l+1}(t) + \gamma^{l+1} d^{l}(t), \quad 0 \le t \le t_f \qquad (4.3.26)$$

where

$$\gamma^{l+1} = \frac{\int_0^{t_f} \left(e^{l+1}(t)\right)^T e^{l+1}(t) \, dt}{\int_0^{t_f} (e^l)^T e^l \, dt} \qquad (4.3.27)$$

and $d^o = e^o$. Once the error vector $e(t)$ approaches zero, the optimum hierarchical control is resulted. Below, a step-by-step computational procedure for the goal coordination method of hierarchical control is given.

*Algorithm 4.1.* Goal Coordination Method

Step 1:  For each first-level subsystem, minimize each sub-Lagrangian $L_i$ using a known Lagrange multiplier $\alpha = \alpha^*$. Since the subsystems are linear, a Riccati equation formulation[†] can be used here. Store solutions.

Step 2:  At the second level, a conjugate gradient iterative method similar to (4.3.26)–(4.3.27) is used to update $\alpha_*(t)$ trajectories like (4.3.19). Once the total system interaction error in normalized form

$$\text{Error} = \left( \sum_{i=1}^{N} \int_0^{t_f} \left\{ z_i - \sum_{j=1}^{N} G_{ij} x_j \right\}^T \left\{ z_i - \sum_{j=1}^{N} G_{ij} x_j \right\} dt \right) / \Delta t$$

$$(4.3.28)$$

is sufficiently small, an optimum solution has been obtained for the system. Here $\Delta t$ is the step size of integration.

Two examples follow that help to illustrate the goal coordination or interaction balance approach. The first example, which was first suggested by Pearson (1971) and further treated by Singh (1980), is used in a modified form. The second example represents the model of a multi-reach river pollution problem (Beck, 1974; Singh, 1975). The overall evaluation of the multilevel methods is deferred until Section 4.6, and the treatment of nonlinear multilevel systems is given in parts in Section 4.5 and Chapter 6.

---

[†]Readers unfamiliar with the Riccati formulation can consult Section 4.3.2 on Interaction Prediction Method.

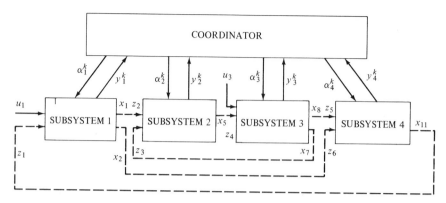

**Figure 4.6** A block diagram for system of Example 4.3.1.

**Example 4.3.1.** Consider a 12th-order system introduced by Pearson (1971) and shown in Figure 4.6 with a state equation

$$\dot{x} = \begin{bmatrix}
0 & 1 & 0 &   &   & 0 &   &   &   &   &   &   \\
0 & 0 & 1 &   & 0 &   &   & 0 &   & 0 & 0 & 0 \\
-3 & -2 & -1 &   &   &   &   &   &   & 0 & 1 & 0 \\
0 & 0 & 0 & 0 & 1 & 0 & 0 & 0 & 0 &   &   &   \\
0 & 0 & 0 & 0 & 0 & 1 & 0 & 0 & 0 &   & 0 &   \\
1 & 0 & 0 & -1 & -3 & -2 & 0 & 1 & 0 &   &   &   \\
  &   &   & 0 & 0 & 0 & 0 & 1 & 0 &   &   &   \\
  & 0 &   & 0 & 0 & 0 & 0 & 0 & 1 &   & 0 &   \\
  &   &   & 0 & 1 & 0 & -1 & -2 & -3 &   &   &   \\
0 & 0 & 0 &   &   &   & 0 & 0 & 0 & 0 & 1 & 0 \\
0 & 0 & 0 &   & 0 &   & 0 & 0 & 0 & 0 & 0 & 1 \\
0 & 1 & 0 &   &   &   & 1 & 0 & 0 & -3 & -2 & -1
\end{bmatrix} x$$

$$ + \begin{bmatrix}
0 & 0 \\
0 & 0 \\
1 & 0 \\
0 & 0 \\
0 & 0 \\
0 & 0 \\
0 & 0 \\
0 & 0 \\
0 & 1 \\
0 & 0 \\
0 & 0 \\
0 & 0
\end{bmatrix} u \qquad\qquad (4.3.29)$$

and a quadratic cost function

$$J = \int_0^{10} \{x^T(t)Qx(t) + u^T(t)Ru(t)\}\, dt \qquad (4.3.30)$$

with

$$Q = \text{diag}\{Q_1, Q_2, Q_3, Q_4\}, \quad R = \text{diag}\{R_1, R_2, R_3, R_4\}$$

where

$$Q_i = \text{diag}(1,1,0), \quad R_i = [1], \quad i = 1,2,3,4$$

The system output vector is given by

$$y = Cx = \begin{bmatrix} 1 & 0 & 0 & 0 & 0 & 0 \\ 0 & 1 & 0 & & & \\ & 0 & 1 & 0 & 0 & 0 & 0 \\ & & 0 & 1 & 0 & & \\ & 0 & & 0 & 1 & 0 & 0 & 0 \\ & & & 0 & 1 & 0 & \\ & 0 & & 0 & & 0 & 1 & 0 & 0 \\ & & & & & 0 & 1 & 0 \end{bmatrix} x$$

$$(4.3.31)$$

It is desired to find a hierarchical control strategy through the interaction balance (goal coordination) approach.

SOLUTION: From the schematic of the system shown in Figure 4.6 (dotted lines) and the state matrix in (4.3.29), it is clear that there are four third-order subsystems coupled together through six equality (number of dotted lines in Figure 4.6) constraints given by

$$\begin{aligned} e &= (e_1, e_2, e_3, e_4, e_5, e_6) \\ &= [(z_1 - x_{11}), (z_2 - x_1), (z_3 - x_7), (z_4 - x_5), (z_5 - x_8), (z_6 - x_2)] \end{aligned}$$

$$(4.3.32)$$

where $e_i$, $i = 1, 2, \ldots, 6$, represents the interaction errors between the four subsystems. The first-level subsystem problems were solved through a set of four third-order matrix Riccati equations

$$\dot{K}_i(t) = A_i^T K_i(t) + K_i(t) A_i - K_i(t) V_i K_i(t) + Q_i, \quad K_i(10) = 0$$

$$(4.3.33)$$

where $K_i(t)$ is an $n_i \times n_i$ positive-definite symmetric Riccati matrix and $V_i = B_i R_i^{-1} B_i^T$. The "integration-free," or "doubling," method of solving the differential matrix Riccati equation proposed by Davison and Maki (1973) and overviewed by Jamshidi (1980) was used on an HP-45 computer and a BASIC source program. The subsystems' state equations were solved by a standard fourth-order Runge–Kutta method, while the second-level iterations were performed by the conjugate gradient scheme (4.3.19),

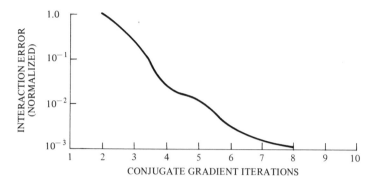

**Figure 4.7** Normalized interaction error vs congugate gradient iterations for Example 4.3.1.

(4.3.26)–(4.3.27) utilizing the cubic spline interpolation (Hewlett-Packard, 1979) to evaluate appropriate numerical integrals. The step size was chosen to be $\Delta t = 0.1$ as in earlier treatments of this example (Pearson, 1971; Singh, 1980). The conjugate gradient algorithm resulted in a decrease in error from 1 to about $10^{-3}$ in six iterations, as shown in Figure 4.7, which was in close agreement with previously reported results of a modified version of system (4.3.29) by Singh (1980). Now let us consider the second example.

**Example 4.3.2.** Consider a two-reach model of a river pollution control problem,

$$\dot{x} = \begin{bmatrix} -1.32 & 0 & \vline & 0 & 0 \\ -0.32 & -1.2 & \vline & 0 & 0 \\ \hline 0.90 & 0 & \vline & -1.32 & 0 \\ 0 & 0.9 & \vline & -0.32 & -1.2 \end{bmatrix} x + \begin{bmatrix} 0.1 & \vline & 0 \\ 0 & \vline & 0 \\ \hline 0 & \vline & 0.1 \\ 0 & \vline & 0 \end{bmatrix} u \quad (4.3.34)$$

where each reach (subsystem) of the river has two states—$x_1$ is the concentration of biochemical oxygen demand (BOD),* and $x_2$ is the concentration of dissolved oxygen (DO)—and its control $u_1$ is the BOD of the effluent discharge into the river. For a quadratic cost function

$$J = \frac{1}{2} \int_0^5 \left( x^T Q x + u^T R u \right) dt \quad (4.3.35)$$

with $Q = \text{diag}\{2, 4, 2, 4\}$ and $R = \text{diag }\{2, 2\}$, it is desired to find an optimal control which minimizes (4.3.35) subject to (4.3.34) and $x(0) = (1\ 1\ -1\ 1)^T$.

---

*The biochemical oxygen demand represents the rate of absorption of oxygen by decomposing organic matter.

SOLUTION: The two first-level problems are identical, and a second-order matrix Riccati equation is solved by integrating (4.3.33) using a fourth-order Runge–Kutta method for $\Delta t = 0.1$. The interaction error for this example reduced to about $10^{-5}$ in 15 iterations, as shown in Figure 4.8. The optimum BOD and DO concentrations of the two reaches of the river are shown in Figure 4.9.

### 4.3.2  Interaction Prediction Method

An alternative approach in optimal control of hierarchical systems which has both open- and closed-loop forms is the interaction prediction method based on the initial work of Takahara (1965), which avoids second-level gradient-type iterations. Consider a large-scale linear interconnected system which is decomposed into $N$ subsystems, each of which is described by

$$\dot{x}_i(t) = A_i x_i(t) + B_i u_i(t) + C_i z_i(t), \quad x_i(0) = x_{io}, \quad i = 1, 2, \ldots, N \quad (4.3.36)$$

where the interaction vector $z_i$ is

$$z_i(t) = \sum_{j=1}^{N} G_{ij} x_j(t) \quad (4.3.37)$$

The optimal control problem at the first level is to find a control $u_i(t)$ which

**Figure 4.8** Interaction error behavior for river pollution system of Example 4.3.2.

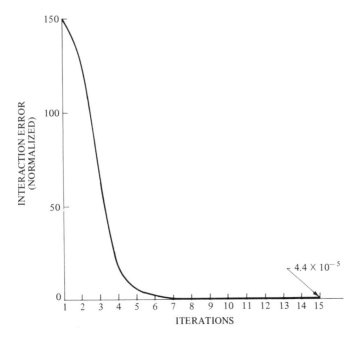

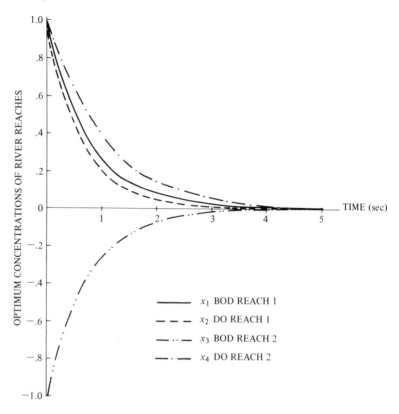

**Figure 4.9** Optimum BOD and DO concentrations for the two-reach model of a river pollution control problem in Example 4.3.2.

satisfies (4.3.36)–(4.3.37) while minimizing a usual quadratic cost function

$$J_i = \frac{1}{2} x_i^T(t_f) Q_i x_i(t_f) + \frac{1}{2} \int_0^{t_f} \{ x_i^T(t) Q_i x_i(t) + u_i^T(t) R_i(t) u_i(t) \} \, dt \quad (4.3.38)$$

This problem can be solved by first introducing a set of Lagrange multipliers $\alpha_i(t)$ and costate vectors $p_i(t)$ to augment the "interaction" equality constraint (4.3.37) and subsystem dynamic constraint (4.3.36) to the cost function's integrand; i.e., the $i$th subsystem Hamiltonian is defined by

$$H_i = \frac{1}{2} x_i^T(t) Q_i x_i(t) + \frac{1}{2} u_i^T(t) R_i u_i(t) + \alpha_i^T z_i$$

$$- \sum_{j=1}^{N} \alpha_j^T G_{ji} x_i + p_i^T (A_i x_i + B_i u_i + C_i z_i) \quad (4.3.39)$$

Then the following set of necessary conditions can be written:

$$\dot{p}_i = -\partial H_i / \partial x_i = -Q_i x_i - A_i^T p_i + \sum_{j=1}^{N} G_{ji}^T \alpha_i(t) \tag{4.3.40}$$

$$p_i(t_f) = \partial\left(\tfrac{1}{2} x_i^T(t_f) Q_i x_i(t_f)\right) / \partial x_i(t_f) = Q_i x_i(t_f) \tag{4.3.41}$$

$$\dot{x}_i(t) = \partial H_i / \partial p_i = A_i x_i(t) + B_i u_i(t) + C_i z_i(t), \quad x_i(0) = x_{io} \tag{4.3.42}$$

$$0 = \partial H_i / \partial u_i = R_i u_i(t) + B_i^T p_i(t) \tag{4.3.43}$$

where the vectors $\alpha_i(t)$ and $z_i(t)$ are no longer considered as unknowns at the second level, and in fact $z_i(t)$ is augmented with $\alpha_i(t)$ to constitute a higher-dimensional "coordination vector," which will be obtained shortly. For the purpose of solving the first-level problem, it suffices to assume $(\alpha_i^T(t) \mid z_i^T(t))$ as known. Note that $u_i(t)$ can be eliminated from (4.3.43),

$$u_i(t) = -R_i^{-1} B_i^T p_i(t) \tag{4.3.44}$$

and substituted into (4.3.40)–(4.3.42) to obtain

$$\dot{x}_i(t) = A_i x_i(t) - S_i p_i(t) + C_i z_i(t), \quad x_i(0) = x_{io} \tag{4.3.45}$$

$$\dot{p}_i(t) = -Q_i x_i(t) - A_i^T p_i(t) + \sum_{j=1}^{N} G_{ji} \alpha_i(t), \quad p_i(t_f) = Q_i x_i(t_f) \tag{4.3.46}$$

which constitute a linear two-point boundary-value (TPBV) problem and $S_i \triangleq B_i R_i^{-1} B_i^T$. It can be seen that this TPBV problem can be decoupled by introducing a matrix Riccati formulation. Here it is assumed that

$$p_i(t) = K_i(t) x_i(t) + g_i(t) \tag{4.3.47}$$

where $g_i(t)$ is an $n_i$-dimensional open-loop "adjoint," or "compensation," vector. If both sides of (4.3.47) are differentiated and $\dot{p}_i(t)$ and $\dot{x}_i(t)$ from (4.3.46) and (4.3.45) are substituted into it, making repeated use of (4.3.47) and equating coefficients of the first and zeroth powers of $x_i(t)$, the following matrix and vector differential equations result:

$$\dot{K}_i(t) = -K_i(t) A_i - A_i^T K_i(t) + K_i(t) S_i K_i(t) - Q_i \tag{4.3.48}$$

$$\dot{g}_i(t) = -\left(A_i - S_i K_i(t)\right)^T g_i(t) - K_i(t) C_i z_i(t) + \sum_{j=1}^{N} G_{ji}^T \alpha_j^T(t) \tag{4.3.49}$$

whose final conditions $K_i(t_f)$ and $g_i(t_f)$ follow from (4.3.41) and (4.3.47), i.e.,

$$K_i(t_f) = Q_i, \quad g_i(t_f) = 0 \tag{4.3.50}$$

Following this formulation, the first-level optimal control (4.3.44) becomes

$$u_i(t) = -R_i^{-1} B_i^T K_i(t) x_i(t) - R_i^{-1} B_i^T g_i(t) \tag{4.3.51}$$

which has a partial feedback (closed-loop) term and a feedforward (open-loop) term. Two points are made here. First, the solution of the differential matrix Riccati equation which involves $n_i(n_i + 1)/2$ nonlinear scalar equations is independent of the initial state $x_i(0)$. The second point is that unlike $K_i(t)$, $g_i(t)$ in (4.3.49), by virtue of $z_i(t)$, is dependent on $x_i(0)$. This property will be used in Section 4.4 to obtain a completely closed-loop control in a hierarchical structure.

The second-level problem is essentially updating the new coordination vector $(\alpha_i^T(t) \mid z_i(t))^T$. For this purpose, define the additively separable Lagrangian

$$L = \sum_{i=1}^{N} L_i = \sum_{i=1}^{N} \left( \frac{1}{2} x_i^T(t_f) Q_i x_i(t_f) + \int_0^{t_f} \left\{ \frac{1}{2} x_i^T(t) Q_i x_i(t) \right. \right.$$

$$+ \frac{1}{2} u_i^T(t) R_i u_i(t) + \alpha_i^T(t) z_i(t) - \sum_{j=1}^{N} \alpha_j^T(t) G_{ji} x_j(t) \quad (4.3.52)$$

$$\left. \left. + p_i^T(t) \left[ -\dot{x}_i(t) + A_i x_i(t) + B_i u_i(t) + C_i z_i(t) \right] \right\} dt \right)$$

The values of $\alpha_i(t)$ and $z_i(t)$ can be obtained by

$$0 = \partial L_i(\cdot)/\partial z_i(t) = \alpha_i(t) + C_i^T p_i(t) \quad (4.3.53)$$

$$0 = \partial L_i(\cdot)/\partial \alpha_i(t) = z_i(t) - \sum_{j=1}^{N} G_{ji} x_j(t) \quad (4.3.54)$$

which provide

$$\alpha_i(t) = -C_i^T p_i(t), \quad z_i(t) = \sum_{j=1}^{N} G_{ji} x_j(t) \quad (4.3.55)$$

The second-level coordination procedure at the $(l+1)$th iteration is simply

$$\begin{bmatrix} \alpha_i(t) \\ z_i(t) \end{bmatrix}^{l+1} = \begin{bmatrix} -C_i^T p_i(t) \\ \sum_{j=1}^{N} G_{ji} x_j(t) \end{bmatrix}^{l} \quad (4.3.56)$$

The interaction prediction method is formulated by the following algorithm.

**Algorithm 4.2.** Interaction Prediction Method for Continuous-Time Systems

Step 1: Solve $N$ independent differential matrix Riccati equations (4.3.48) with final condition (4.3.50) and store $K_i(t)$, $i = 1, 2, \ldots, N$.

Step 2: For initial $\alpha_i^l(t)$, $z_i^l(t)$ solve the "adjoint" equation (4.3.49) with final condition (4.3.50). Evaluate and store $g_i(t)$, $i = 1, 2, \ldots, N$.

*Step 3:* Solve the state equation

$$\dot{x}_i(t) = (A_i - S_i K_i(t)) x_i(t) - S_i g_i(t) + C_i z_i(t), \quad x_i(0) = x_{io}$$

(4.3.57)

and store $x_i(t)$, $i = 1, 2, \ldots, N$.

*Step 4:* At the second level, use the results of Steps 2 and 3 and (4.3.56) to update the coordination vector

$$\left[ \alpha_i^T(t) \,\vdots\, z_i^T(t) \right]^T$$

*Step 5:* Check for the convergence at the second level by evaluating the overall interaction error

$$e(t) = \sum_{i=1}^{N} \int_0^{t_f} \left\{ z_i(t) - \sum_{j=1}^{N} G_{ij} x_j(t) \right\}^T \left\{ z_i(t) - \sum_{j=1}^{N} G_{ij} x_j \right\} dt / \Delta t$$

(4.3.58)

It must be noted that depending on the type of digital computer and its operating system, subsystem calculations may be done in parallel and that the $N$ matrix Riccati equations at Step 1 are independent of $x_i(0)$, and hence they need to be computed once regardless of the number of second-level iterations in the interaction prediction algorithm (4.3.56). It is further noted that unlike the goal coordination methods, no $z_i(t)$ term is needed in the cost function, which was intended, as is discussed in next section, to avoid singularities.

The interaction prediction method, originated by Takahara (1965), has been considered by many researchers who have made significant contributions to it. Among them are Titli (1972), who called it the "mixed method" (Singh 1980), and Cohen et al. (1974), who have presented more refined proofs of convergence than those originally suggested. Smith and Sage (1973) have extended the scheme to nonlinear systems which will be considered in Chapter 6. A genuine comparison of the interaction prediction and goal coordination methods has been considered by Singh et al. (1975) which will be discussed in Section 4.6. The following two examples illustrate the interaction prediction method.

**Example 4.3.3.** Consider a fourth-order system

$$\dot{x} = \left[ \begin{array}{cccc} 2 & 0.1 & 0.01 & 0 \\ 0.2 & -1 & 0.10 & -0.5 \\ \hline 0.05 & 0.15 & 1 & 0.05 \\ 0 & -0.2 & -0.25 & -1.2 \end{array} \right] x + \left[ \begin{array}{cc} 1 & 0 \\ 0.1 & 0 \\ \hline 0 & 0.5 \\ 0 & 0.25 \end{array} \right] u \quad (4.3.59)$$

with $x(0) = (-1, 0.1, 1.0, -0.5)^T$ and a quadratic cost function with $Q = \text{diag}(2, 1, 1, 2)$, $R = \text{diag}(1, 2)$ and no terminal penalty. It is desired to use the interaction prediction method to find an optimal control for $t_f = 1$.

SOLUTION: The system was divided into two second-order subsystems, and steps outlined in Algorithm 4.2 were applied. At the first step, two independent differential matrix Riccati equations were solved by using both the doubling algorithm of Davison and Maki (1973) and the standard Runge–Kutta methods. The elements of the Riccati matrix were fitted in by quadratic polynomial in the Chebyschev sense (Newhouse, 1962) for computational convenience:

$$K_1(t) = \begin{bmatrix} 4.44 + 0.32t - 1.26t^2 & 0.09 + 0.007t - 0.027t^2 \\ 0.09 + 0.007t - 0.027t^2 & 0.5 + 0.034t - 0.141t^2 \end{bmatrix}$$

$$K_2(t) = \begin{bmatrix} 2.87 - 5.26t + 2.42t^2 & -0.1 + 0.16t - 0.054t^2 \\ -0.1 + 0.16t - 0.054t^2 & 0.73 + 0.118t - 0.83t^2 \end{bmatrix} \tag{4.3.60}$$

At the first level, a set of two second-order adjoint equations of the form (4.3.49) and two subsystem state equations as in Step 3 of Algorithm 4.2 using the fourth-order Runge–Kutta method and initial values

$$\alpha_1(t) = \begin{bmatrix} 0.5 \\ 0.5 \end{bmatrix}, \quad x_1(0) = \begin{bmatrix} -1 \\ 0.1 \end{bmatrix}, \quad z_1(t) = G_{12}x_2(0) = \begin{bmatrix} 0.01 \\ 0.35 \end{bmatrix}$$

$$\alpha_2(t) = \begin{bmatrix} 0.75 \\ 0.75 \end{bmatrix}, \quad x_2(0) = \begin{bmatrix} 1.0 \\ -0.5 \end{bmatrix}, \quad z_2(t) = G_{21}x_1(0) = \begin{bmatrix} -0.035 \\ -0.02 \end{bmatrix} \tag{4.3.61}$$

were solved. At the second level, the interaction vectors $[\alpha_{11}(t), \alpha_{12}(t), z_{11}(t), z_{12}(t)]^T$ and $[\alpha_{21}(t), \alpha_{22}(t), z_{21}(t), z_{22}(t)]^T$ were predicted using the recursive relations (4.3.56), and at each information exchange iteration the total interaction error (4.3.58) was evaluated for $\Delta t = 0.1$ and a cubic spline interpolator program. The interaction error was reduced to $3.5113456 \times 10^{-6}$ in six iterations, as shown in Figure 4.10. The optimum outputs for $C_i = (1\ 1)$ and control signals were obtained. Next, for the sake of comparison, the original system (4.3.59) was optimized by solving a fourth-order time-varying matrix Riccati equation by backward integration and solved for $x_i(t)$, $i = 1, 2, 3, 4$; $y_j(t)$ and $u_j(t)$, $j = 1, 2$. The outputs and control signals for both hierarchical and exact centralized cases are shown in Figure 4.11. Note the relatively close correspondence between the outputs for the original coupled and hierarchical decoupled systems. However, as one would expect, the two controls are different. When the decoupled the control signals are partially closed loop and partially open loop,

$$u_i(t) = -F_i x_i(t) + h_i(t) \tag{4.3.62}$$

For the overall system, a complete feedback structure results:

$$u(t) = -Fx(t) \tag{4.3.63}$$

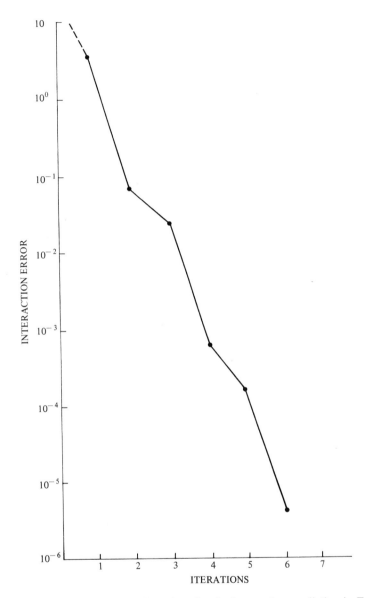

**Figure 4.10** Interaction error vs iterations for the interaction prediction in Example 4.3.3.

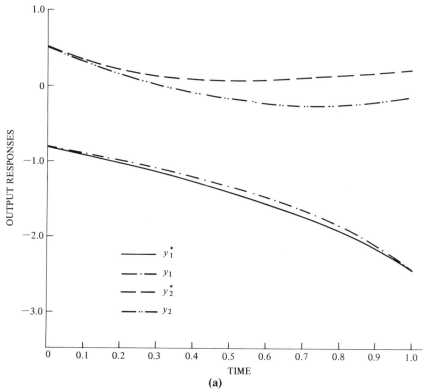

**Figure 4.11** The optimal (centralized) and suboptimal (interaction prediction) responses for Example 4.3.3: (a) outputs, (b) controls.

Now let us consider the second example.

**Example 4.3.4.** Consider an eighth-order system

$$\dot{x} = \begin{bmatrix}
-5 & 0 & 0 & 0 & 0.1 & -0.5 & -0.009 & 3 \\
0 & -2 & 0 & 0 & -0.29 & 0 & -0.3 & 0.48 \\
-0.08 & -0.11 & -3.99 & -0.93 & 0 & 0.1 & 0 & 0 \\
0 & 0 & 1.32 & -1.39 & -1 & -0.4 & 0 & 0 \\
0 & 0 & -0.1 & -0.4 & -0.2 & 0 & 0 & 0 \\
0 & 0 & 0 & 0 & 0 & -0.17 & 0 & 0 \\
0 & 0 & 0 & 0 & 0 & 0 & 0.5 & 0 \\
0 & 0 & 0 & 0 & 0 & 0.01 & 0 & -0.11
\end{bmatrix} x$$

$$+ \begin{bmatrix}
0 & 0 \\
0 & 0 \\
10 & 0 \\
0 & 0 \\
0 & 4 \\
0 & 0 \\
0 & 0 \\
0 & 0
\end{bmatrix} u \qquad\qquad (4.3.64)$$

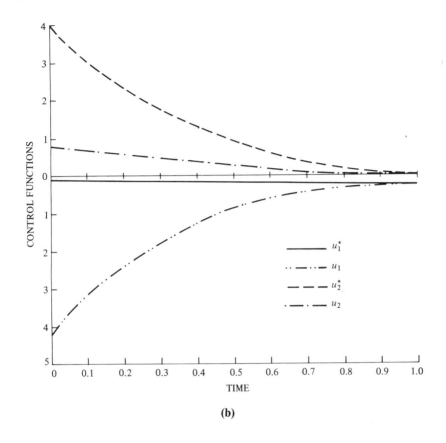

**(b)**

---

It is desired to use interaction prediction approach to find $u^*$.

SOLUTION: The system was decoupled into two fourth-order subsystems and $t_f = 2$, $\Delta t = 0.1$, $Q_1 = Q_2 = I_4$, $R_1 = R_2 = 1$ were chosen. The initial values of $\alpha_i^o(t)$, $i = 1,2$, and state $x(0)$ were assumed to be $\alpha_1^o(t) = (0.5 \quad 1 \quad -1 \quad 0)^T$, $\alpha_2^o(t) = (1 \quad 0 \quad -1 \quad 0)^T$, and $x(0) = (-1 \quad -0.5 \quad 1 \quad 0.5 \quad 1 \quad -1 \quad 0.5 \quad 0.5)^T$. The convergence was very rapid, as shown in Figure 4.12. In just four second-level iterations the interaction error reduced to $2 \times 10^{-4}$. In fact there was excellent convergence for a variety of $x(0)$ and $\alpha_i^o(t)$.

More applications of the interaction prediction method are given in the problems section.

### 4.3.3 Goal Coordination and Singularities

When the goal coordination method was discussed earlier in (4.3.15)–(4.3.17), it was mentioned that the positive definite matrices $S_i$ were

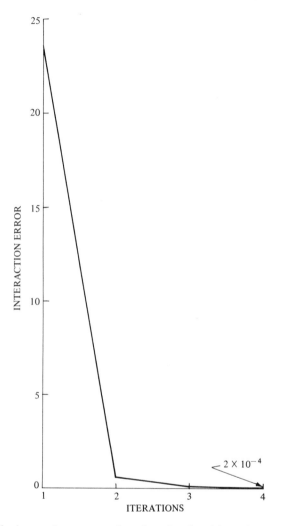

**Figure 4.12** The interaction error vs iterations for the eight-order system of Example 4.3.4.

introduced in the cost function (4.3.17) to avoid singularities. To see that this is in fact the case, let us reconsider the problem of minimizing $L_i$ in (4.3.24) subject to (4.3.15). Let the $i$th subsystem's Hamiltonian be

$$H_i(x_i, u_i, z_i, p_i, \alpha_i^*) = 1/2 x_i^T(t) Q_i x_i(t)$$
$$+ 1/2 u_i^T(t) R_i u_i(t) + 1/2 z_i^T(t) S_i z_i(t)$$
$$+ \alpha_i^{*T} z_i - \sum_{j=1}^{N} \alpha_j^{*T} G_{ji} x_i + p_i^T (A_i x_i + B_i u_i + C_i z_i)$$

$$(4.3.65)$$

As one of the necessary equations for the solution of the $i$th subsystem problem at the first level, we have

$$\partial H_i(\cdot)/\partial z_i = S_i z_i(t) + \alpha_i^*(t) + C_i^T p_i(t) = 0 \tag{4.3.66}$$

or

$$z_i(t) = - S_i^{-1}\left(C_i^T p_i(t) + \alpha_i^*(t)\right) \tag{4.3.67}$$

where a singular solution arises if the $z_i^T(t)S_i z_i(t)$ term does not appear in the cost function. Here two alternative approaches are given to avoid singularities at the first level. The following example illustrates the two approaches.

**Example 4.3.5.** Consider the following system:

$$\begin{aligned}
\dot{x}_1 &= - x_1 + x_2 + u_1, \quad x_1(0) = x_{10} \\
\dot{x}_2 &= - x_2 + u_2, \quad x_2(0) = x_{20}
\end{aligned} \tag{4.3.68}$$

It is desired to find $(u_1, u_2)$ such that (4.3.68) is satisfied while a quadratic cost function

$$J = 1/2 \int_0^1 \left(x_1^2 + x_2^2 + u_1^2 + u_2^2\right) dt \tag{4.3.69}$$

is minimized via the goal coordination method.

SOLUTION: From (4.3.68)–(4.3.69) it is seen that the system can be decomposed into two first-order subsystems,

$$\begin{aligned}
\dot{x}_1 &= - x_1 + u_1 + z_1, \quad x_1(0) = x_{10} \tag{4.3.70} \\
\dot{x}_2 &= - x_2 + u_2, \quad x_2(0) = x_{20} \tag{4.3.71}
\end{aligned}$$

with interaction constraint

$$z_1 = x_2 \tag{4.3.72}$$

The problem in its present form has the following Hamiltonian:

$$\begin{aligned}
H &= \left(\tfrac{1}{2}x_1^2 + \tfrac{1}{2}u_1^2 + \alpha z_1 - \alpha x_2 - p_1 x_1 + p_1 u_1 + p_1 z_1\right) \\
&\quad + \left(\tfrac{1}{2}x_2^2 + \tfrac{1}{2}u_2^2 - p_2 x_2 + p_2 u_2\right)
\end{aligned} \tag{4.3.73}$$

in which the interaction variable appears linearly. Thus, the application of goal coordination for the present formulation would lead to a singular problem, since $z_1$ appears linearly in (4.3.73). The following system reformulations of the problem would avoid singularities.

### 4.3.3.a Reformulation 1

Bauman (1968) suggests rewriting the interaction constraint (4.3.72) in quadratic form,

$$z_1^2 = x_2^2 \tag{4.3.74}$$

which would give the following necessary conditions for optimality at the first level:

$$0 = \partial H_1 / \partial u_1 = u_1 + p_1, \quad 0 = \partial H_1 / \partial z_1 = 2\alpha z_1 + p_1$$
$$-\dot{p}_1 = \partial H_1 / \partial x_1 = x_1 - p_1, \quad p_1(1) = 0 \tag{4.3.75}$$
$$\dot{x}_1 = \partial H_1 / \partial p_1 = -x_1 + u_1 + z_1, \quad x_1(0) = x_{10}$$

for first subsystem and

$$0 = \partial H_2 / \partial u_2 = u_2 + p_2$$
$$-\dot{p}_2 = \partial H_2 / \partial x_2 = x_2 - p_2, \quad p_2(1) = 0 \tag{4.3.76}$$
$$\dot{x}_2 = \partial H_2 / \partial p_2 = -x_2 + u_2, \quad x_2(0) = x_{20}$$

for the second subsystem. After the introduction of the Riccati formulation (4.3.75) and (4.3.76) will lead to

$$\dot{x}_1(t) = -\{1 + (1 + 1/\alpha)k_1(t)\}x_1(t), \quad x_1(0) = x_{10}$$
$$z_1(t) = -(\tfrac{1}{2}\alpha)k_1(t)x_1(t) \tag{4.3.77}$$
$$u_1(t) = -k_1(t)x_1(t)$$

and

$$\dot{x}_2(t) = -(1 + k_2(t))x_2(t), \quad x_2(0) = x_{20}$$
$$u_2(t) = -k_2(t)x_2(t) \tag{4.3.78}$$

where $k_i(t)$ is the $i$th subsystem scalar time-varying Riccati matrix. The coordination at the second level is achieved through the following iterations:

$$\alpha^{l+1}(t) = \alpha^l(t) + \varepsilon^l d^l(e(t))$$
$$e(t) = z_1^2(t) - x_2^2(t) \tag{4.3.79}$$

This reformulation would avoid singularities but makes the second-level iterations convergence very slow.

### 4.3.3.b Reformulation 2

Singh et al. (1976) suggest an alternative formulation which not only avoids singularities but also gives good convergence. The procedure is based on solving for $x$ in terms of the interaction vector $z$ and substituting it into the cost function; i.e., $z$ can be written in general as

$$z = Gx \text{ or } x = G^{-1}z \triangleq Vz \tag{4.3.80}$$

where $G$ is assumed to be nonsingular and the reformulated Hamiltonian is

$$H(\cdot) = \tfrac{1}{2}z^T(t)V^TQVz(t) + \tfrac{1}{2}u^T(t)Ru(t) + \alpha^Tz$$
$$- \alpha^TGx + p^T(Ax + Bu + Cz) \tag{4.3.81}$$

For the example under consideration, the matrix $G$ is singular, but a solution can still be found. Here the Hamiltonian is

$$H(\cdot) = \tfrac{1}{2}x_1^2 + \tfrac{1}{2}u_1^2 + \alpha z_1 - \alpha x_2 - p_1 x_1 + p_1 u_1 + p_1 z_1$$
$$+ \tfrac{1}{2}z_1^2 + \tfrac{1}{2}u_2^2 - p_2 x_2 + p_2 u_2$$

$$(4.3.82)$$

with first-level subsystem problems being

$$0 = \partial H / \partial u_1 = u_1 + p_1, \quad 0 = \partial H / \partial z_1 = z_1 + \alpha + p_1$$
$$- \dot p_1 = \partial H / \partial x_1 = x_1 - p_1, \quad p_1(1) = 0 \qquad (4.3.83)$$
$$\dot x_1 = \partial H / \partial p_1 = - x_1 + u_1, \quad x_1(0) = x_{10}$$

and

$$0 = \partial H / \partial u_2 = u_2 + p_2$$
$$- \dot p_2 = \partial H / \partial x_2 = - \alpha - p_2, \quad p_2(1) = 0 \qquad (4.3.84)$$
$$\dot x_2 = \partial H / \partial p_2 = - x_2 + u_2, \quad x_2(0) = x_{20}$$

The second subsystem can be solved immediately, since the $p_2$-costate equation is decoupled from $x_2$ and can be solved backward in time and substituted into the $x_2$ equation, which would, in effect, mean that the solution of a Riccati equation has been avoided for this particular example. For the first subsystem, however, following the formulation of first-level problems in interaction prediction (4.3.40)–(4.3.51), both a Riccati and an open-loop adjoint (compensation) vector equation such as (4.3.48) and (4.3.49) need to be evaluated. For this example, the first subsystem problem is

$$\dot x_1(t) = - \big(1 + 2k_1(t)\big)x_1(t) - 2g_1(t) - \alpha(t), \quad x_1(0) = x_{10}$$
$$\dot k_1(t) = - 2k_1(t) + 2k_1^2(t) - 1, \quad k_1(1) = 0$$
$$\dot g_1(t) = \big(1 + 2k_1(t)\big)g_1(t) + k_1(t)\alpha(t), \quad g_1(1) = 0 \qquad (4.3.85)$$
$$u_1(t) = - k_1(t)x_1(t) + g_1(t)$$

where two differential equations for $k_1(t)$ and $g_1(t)$ must be solved backward in time. Thus, while no auxiliary equation needs to be solved for the second subsystem, two such equations should be solved for the first subsystem. In general, this reformulation would require the solution of

$$\dot x = Ax - Sp - GQ^{-1}(p + \alpha), \quad x(0) = x_0$$
$$\dot p = - G^T\alpha + A^T p, \quad p(t_f) = 0 \qquad (4.3.86)$$
$$u = - R^{-1}B^T p, \quad z = - GQ^{-1}(p + \alpha)$$

which indicates that the costate vector $p$ equation is decoupled from $x$ and can be solved backward in time (eliminating a Riccati equation) and substituted in the top equation to find $x$. Since the $A$, $B$, $Q$, and $R$ matrices are block-diagonal, problem (4.3.86) can be decomposed into $N$ subsystem problems, provided that the term $(x^T(t)V^TQVz(t))$ is separable in $z$ where $V = G^{-1}$.

## 4.4 Closed-Loop Hierarchical Control of Continuous-Time Systems

The last section dealt with open-loop hierarchical control of continuous-time systems in which the control depended on the system's initial condition $x(t_0)$. The scheme nearest to a closed-loop structure was the interaction prediction method which resulted a partially closed-loop structure with an open-loop component which still depended on $x(t_0)$. Although one may always be able to measure $x(t_0)$, by the time an open-loop control is calculated and applied to the system, the initial state has most likely changed, thus resulting in unpredictable and undesirable responses. It is therefore worthwhile to construct closed-loop control laws which are independent of the initial state (Singh, 1980). The most likely case in which such a control structure is possible, as in nonhierarchical systems, is the linear quadratic regulator problem. Many authors have considered the problem of closed-loop control of hierarchical systems. Mesarovic et al. (1970) suggested a suboptimal structure which had an adaptive feature as the system evolves. Sage and his associates (Smith and Sage, 1973; Arafeh and Sage, 1974a, b) have used a similar suboptimal technique for the filter problem. Others (Cheneveaux, 1972; Cohen et al., 1972, 1974) have considered the problem and suggested either a "partial" feedback controller or "complete" feedback controls which involve off-line calculations of the overall coupled large-scale system. An attractive extension of the partial feedback algorithm of Cohen et al. (1974) which provides "complete" closed-loop structure based on off-line calculations of feedback gains and their on-line implementation is due to Singh (1980). Another attempt along this line, due to Šiljak and Sundareshan (Šiljak and Sundareshan, 1974, 1976a, b; Sundareshan, 1977; Šiljak, 1978), is based on obtaining local feedback controllers for each subsystem on the first level by ignoring the interactions; then a global controller at the second level is applied to minimize the interaction errors and improve the performance. This method emphasizes the structural perturbations categorized as "beneficial," "nonbeneficial," and "neutral" interconnections and their corresponding loss of performance.

In this section Singh's (1980) extension of the interaction prediction approach and the feedback control scheme of Šiljak and Sundareshan (1974, 1976a, b) and Sundareshan (1977) based on structural perturbation along with numerical examples are presented.

### 4.4.1 Closed-Loop Control via Interaction Prediction

In the previous section, the interaction prediction in its general sense was introduced with a partial closed-loop controller and an open-loop component given in (4.3.51). The main shortcoming of this structure is, as mentioned earlier, that the open-loop component depends on the initial state of the system and there is no apparent possibility for on-line implementation. To see this dependency of the open-loop component, let us consider the differential equation for the adjoint vector $g_i(t)$ in (4.3.49) and use (4.3.55) to eliminate $\alpha_i(t)$ and $z_i(t)$; i.e.,

$$\dot{g}_i(t) = -\left(A_i - S_i K_i(t)\right)^T g_i(t) - K_i(t) C_i \sum_{j=1}^{N} G_{ji} x_j(t)$$

$$- \sum_{j=1}^{N} G_{ji}^T C_j^T \left( K_j(t) x_j(t) - g_j(t) \right) \qquad (4.4.1)$$

which indicates that the vector $g_i(t)$ depends on the states of all the other subsystems and hence the initial state $x(t_0)$. The following theorem due to Singh (1980) relates the open-loop component

$$u^o(t) = -R^{-1} B^T g(t) \qquad (4.4.2)$$

to the state $x(t)$ for the overall system which can be used in a hierarchical structure of a regulator problem.

**Theorem 4.1.** *The open-loop adjoint vector $g(t)$ and state $x(t)$ are related through the following transformation:*

$$g(t) = M(t_f, t) x(t) \qquad (4.4.3)$$

PROOF: Rewriting the adjoint equations (4.4.1), the overall system's adjoint equation becomes

$$\dot{g}(t) = -\left(A - SK(t) + CG\right)^T g(t) - \left(K(t) CG + G^T C^T K(t)\right) x(t)$$

$$g(t_f) = 0 \qquad (4.4.4)$$

which can be represented in terms of its homogeneous and particular solutions,

$$g(t) = \Phi_1(t, t_0) g(t_0) - \int_{t_0}^{t} \Phi_1(t, \tau) \left( K(\tau) CG + G^T C^T K(\tau) x(\tau) \right) d\tau$$

$$(4.4.5)$$

where $\Phi_1(t, t_0)$ is the "state transition" matrix of $(A - SK(t) - CG)^T$. Note also that $K(t)$ is a block-diagonal matrix consisting of subsystems Riccati matrices, i.e., $K(t) = \text{diag}\{K_1(t), \ldots, K_i(t), \ldots, K_N(t)\}$. However, for the composite system,

$$\dot{x}(t) = Ax(t) + Bu(t) \qquad (4.4.6)$$

with standard quadratic cost

$$J = \frac{1}{2} \int_{t_0}^{t_f} \left[ x^T(t) Qx(t) + u^T(t) Ru(t) \right] dt \qquad (4.4.7)$$

the closed-loop optimal control system is well known:

$$\dot{x}(t) = (A - \tilde{S}P(t))x(t) \qquad (4.4.8)$$

or

$$x(t) = \Phi_2(t, t_0)x(t_0) \qquad (4.4.9)$$

where $P(t)$ is the $n \times n$-dimensional time-varying Riccati matrix for the composite system and $\Phi_2(t, t_0)$ is the state transition matrix corresponding to the feedback system matrix $(A - \tilde{S}K)$ and $\tilde{S} = BR^{-1}B^T$. Now if we substitute $x(t)$ from (4.4.9) in (4.4.5),

$$g(t) = \Phi_1(t, t_0)g(t_0) - \int_{t_0}^{t} \Phi_1(t, \tau)(K(\tau)CG$$

$$+ G^T C^T K(\tau))\Phi_2(\tau, t_0)x(t_0)\, d\tau \qquad (4.4.10)$$

Using the final condition $g(t_f)$ in (4.4.4) at $t = t_f$ and making use of the properties of the state transition matrix, (4.4.10) can be used to solve for $g(t_0)$:

$$g(t_0) = \Phi_1(t_0, t_f)\int_{t_0}^{t_f}\left[\Phi_1(t_f, \tau)(K(\tau)CG\right.$$

$$\left. + G^T C^T K(\tau))\Phi_2(\tau, t_0)\, d\tau\right]x(t_0) \qquad (4.4.11)$$

By moving the term $\Phi_1(t_0, t_f)$ inside the integral sign and taking advantage of product property of transition matrices, (4.4.11) is rewritten

$$g(t_0) = M(t_f, t_0)x(t_0) = \left\{\int_{t_0}^{t_f}\Phi_1(t_0, \tau)(K(\tau)CG\right.$$

$$\left. + G^T C^T K(\tau)\Phi_2(\tau, t_0)\, d\tau\right\}x(t_0) \qquad (4.4.12)$$

or

$$g(t) = M(t_f, t)x(t) \qquad (4.4.13)$$

which gives the desired relation. Q.E.D. ∎

A corollary of the above theorem can be stated as follows. For the time-invariant case as $t_f \to \infty$, constant $A$, $B$, $C$, $G$, $Q$, and $R$ matrices and time-invariant $g$ and $K$, $M$ becomes a constant transformation matrix (Sage, 1968). This corollary is used to find an approximate feedback law for the open-loop component.

The relation (4.4.13) is a sound theoretical property, but from an implementation point of view, it is not very desirable for a large-scale system because the overall system's Riccati differential equation must be solved and that defeats the original purpose of finding a control via hierarchical control. Singh (1980) has raised the point that for the time-invariant case, $M$ can be computed easily, since near $t = 0$, $M$ is constant while $x$ and $g$ are not. Therefore, it is suggested that if the first $n = \sum_{i=1}^{N} n_i$ values of $x(t_k)$ and $g(t_k)$ for $k = 0, 1, \ldots, n$ are evaluated and recorded, $M$ can be approximately given by

$$M = \tilde{G} X^{-1} \qquad (4.4.14)$$

where

$$\tilde{G} = \left[ g(t_0) \mid g(t_1) \mid \cdots \mid g(t_n) \right], \quad X = \left[ x(t_0) \mid x(t_1) \mid \cdots \mid x(t_n) \right]$$
$$(4.4.15)$$

and the inversion of $X$ is done off-line. Note that if a time-varying $M$ is desirable, it is possible to solve the problem with $n$ initial conditions, i.e., $x(t_0), x(t_{0+1}), \ldots$, and form $n \times n$ time-dependent matrices $\tilde{G}(t)$ and $X(t)$ to find $M(t)$ for each integration step. In summary, the resulting control for the composite system can be formulated by

$$u = -R^{-1}B^T K x - R^{-1} B^T g$$
$$= -R^{-1} B^T (K + M) x = -Fx \qquad (4.4.16)$$

It is noted that the above gains are all independent of $x(t_0)$, and the matrices $R$, $B$, $K$, and $M$ are obtained from decentralized calculations. The following example describes the above feedback law.

**Example 4.4.1.** Let us reconsider the system in Example 4.3.3 with $t_f = 4$, $G_{12}$, and $G_{21}$ matrices switched. It is desired to find a feedback gain matrix $F$.

SOLUTION: The decomposed system Riccati matrices at $t = 0$ are

$$K_1 = \begin{bmatrix} 4.440 & 0.093 \\ 0.093 & 0.498 \end{bmatrix}, \quad K_2 = \begin{bmatrix} 2.9067 & -0.1010 \\ -0.1010 & 0.7522 \end{bmatrix} \qquad (4.4.17)$$

The problem was simulated on an HP-9845 computer using BASIC. After six iterations of interaction prediction at the second level, $\tilde{G}$ and $X$ were determined to be

$$\tilde{G} = 10^{-1} \begin{bmatrix} -0.78 & -2.13 & -1.38 & 1.24 \\ -0.73 & -2.18 & -1.20 & 1.28 \\ -0.69 & -2.20 & -1.02 & 1.29 \\ -0.66 & -2.16 & -0.85 & 1.24 \end{bmatrix} \qquad (4.4.18)$$

$$X = \begin{bmatrix} 1.0 & -0.500 & -1.00 & 0.100 \\ 0.77 & -0.510 & -1.08 & -0.117 \\ 0.59 & -0.516 & -1.17 & 0.127 \\ 0.45 & -0.516 & -1.28 & 0.135 \end{bmatrix} \qquad (4.4.19)$$

the partial feedback matrix $M$ to be

$$M = \tilde{G} X^{-1} = \begin{bmatrix} 63.35 & -210.14 & 229.97 & -82.88 \\ 66.72 & -221.3 & 242.26 & -87.40 \\ 77.32 & -258.4 & 285.52 & -104.2 \\ 65.70 & -218.4 & 239.66 & -86.70 \end{bmatrix} \qquad (4.4.20)$$

and the overall approximate feedback gain matrix based on hierarchical control to be

$$F = R^{-1}B^T(K + M) = \begin{bmatrix} 74.5 & -232.1 & 254.2 & -91.6 \\ 27.5 & -91.89 & 102.0 & -36.82 \end{bmatrix}$$

$$(4.4.21)$$

## 4.4.2 Closed-Loop Control via Structural Perturbation

The second method of closed-loop control of a hierarchical system discussed here is based on the feedback control structure suggested by Šiljak and Sundareshan (1974, 1976a, b) and extensions by Sundareshan (1977) based on structural perturbations due to the interactions among subsystems in a large-scale system. Such perturbations may very well occur during the operation of the system, and the basic initial issue addressed by Šiljak and Sundareshan (1976a, b) is that assuming each subsystem has its own independent local controller, how reliable the overall system performance will be in the presence of structural perturbations. A classical example is a "power pool" in which each power company (subsystem) is responsible for the load, frequency regulation, and power generation within its own region while through tie lines it can exchange power with other companies (subsystems) resulting in variations in power among the companies which would affect the entire system's overall performance. Each subsystem has a feedback control structure consisting of a "local" component obtained through subsystem calculations and a "global" component which minimizes interaction errors and possibly improves the overall system performance.

Consider a large-scale linear time-invariant system described by $N$ subsystems:

$$\dot{x}_i(t) = A_i x_i(t) + B_i u_i(t) + \sum_{j=1}^{N} G_{ij} x_j(t), \quad x_i(t_0) = x_{i0} \quad (4.4.22)$$

for $i = 1, 2, \ldots, N$, where all matrices are defined earlier. Each subsystem has an immediate goal of finding a "local" controller $u_i^*(t)$ which minimizes an associated quadratic cost

$$J_i(t_0, x_i(t_0), u_i(t_0)) = \frac{1}{2} \int_{t_0}^{\infty} \left( x_i^T(t) Q_i x_i(t) + u_i^T(t) R_i u_i(t) \right) dt \quad (4.4.23)$$

while satisfying (4.4.22) with the interaction matrices $G_{ij}$ set to zero. It is assumed that although each subsystem is independent, they have a "goal harmony" in minimizing the overall system cost function

$$J(t_0, x(t_0), u(t_0)) = \sum_{i=1}^{N} J_i(t_0, x_i(t_0), u_i(t_0)) \quad (4.4.24)$$

Furthermore, it is assumed that the system possesses a complete decentralized information structure and each subsystem pair $(A_i, B_i)$ is completely controllable. For the decoupled subsystem,

$$\dot{x}_i(t) = A_i x_i(t) + B_i u_i(t), \quad i = 1, 2, \ldots, N \qquad (4.4.25)$$

and cost (4.4.23), the decentralized optimal control is given by

$$u_i^*(t) = - R_i^{-1} B_i^T K_i x_i(t) = - P_i x_i(t) \qquad (4.4.26)$$

where $K_i$ is the symmetric positive-definite solution of the algebraic matrix Riccati equation (AMRE)

$$A_i^T K_i + K_i A_i - K_i V_i K_i + Q_i = 0 \qquad (4.4.27)$$

where $V_i = B_i R_i^{-1} B_i^T$, the value of the corresponding optimal cost, is given by

$$J_i^*(t_0, x_i(t_0)) = \tfrac{1}{2} x_i^T(t_0) K_i x_i(t_0) \qquad (4.4.28)$$

for $i = 1, 2, \ldots, N$. Let the optimal performance function of the centralized system be denoted by $J^o(t_0, x(t_0))$. The decoupled system's cost

$$J^*(t_0, x(t_0)) = \sum_{i=1}^{N} J_i^*(t_0, x_i(t_0)) \qquad (4.4.29)$$

may, in general, be greater or less than $J^o(t_0, x(t_0))$, depending on the type of interconnection among subsystems. In fact, as Sundareshan (1977) points out and as we will see shortly through the following theorem, there is a useful class of interconnections for which $J^*(\cdot) \equiv J^o(\cdot)$. Before we introduce the theorem, the following definitions are given:

**Definition 4.1.** For a large-scale system consisting of $N$ subsystems with overall and decoupled performances $J^o(\cdot)$ and $J^*(\cdot)$, respectively, an interaction $G = \{g_{ij}\}$, $i, j = 1, 2, \ldots, N$, is said to be "nonbeneficial" if $J^*(\cdot) < J^o(\cdot)$.

**Definition 4.2.** An interaction $G$ is said to be "beneficial" if $J^*(\cdot) > J^o(\cdot)$.

**Definition 4.3.** The interaction $G$ is said to be "neutral" if $J^*(\cdot) = J^o(\cdot)$.

**Theorem 4.2.** *Let an $n \times n$ block-diagonal matrix $K = \text{block-diag}\{K_1, K_2, \ldots, K_N\}$, where $K_i$, $i = 1, 2, \ldots, N$, is the positive-definite symmetric solution of ith subsystem AMRE (4.4.27). Then the overall system's optimal performance index $J^o$ and the decoupled system optimal performance $J^*$ are equal if and only if the interaction matrix $G = \{g_{ij}\}$, $i, j = 1, 2, \ldots, N$, can be factorized by*

$$G = SK \qquad (4.4.30)$$

*where $S$ is a skew-symmetric matrix, i.e., $S = - S^T$.*

The proof of this theorem, due to Sundareshan (1977), is given below.

PROOF: Let $n \times n$ matrix $F$ be the solution of the following AMRE:

$$(A + G)^T F + F(A + G) - FVF + Q = 0 \qquad (4.4.31)$$

where $V = BR^{-1}B^T$, $A = \text{Block-diag}(A_1, A_2, \ldots, A_N)$, $B = \text{Block-diag}(B_1, B_2, \ldots, B_N)$, $R = \text{Block-diag}(R_1, R_2, \ldots, R_N)$, $Q = \text{Block-diag}(Q_1, Q_2, \ldots, Q_N)$ and $V = \text{Block-diag}(V_1, V_2, \ldots, V_N)$. It is clear that $J^o(t_0, x(t_0)) = 1/2 x^T(t_0) F x(t_0)$ if $F$ is positive-definite and symmetric. If $G$ satisfies (4.4.30), (4.4.31) reduces to

$$(A^T F + FA - FVF + Q) + (FSK + KS^T F) = 0 \qquad (4.4.32)$$

Since $K_i$, $i = 1, 2, \ldots, N$, are positive-definite and symmetric solutions of (4.4.27), then $K$ is the symmetric positive-definite solution of AMRE:

$$A^T K + KA - KVK + Q = 0 \qquad (4.4.33)$$

Now if Equations (4.4.32) and (4.4.33) are compared, it follows that $F = K$ satisfies (4.4.32) and is positive-definite and symmetric. Therefore, (4.4.30) implies that $J^o(\cdot) = 1/2 x^T(t_0) K x(t_0) = J^*(\cdot)$.

The reverse is also true. If $F$ is the symmetric positive-definite solution of (4.4.31), then by comparing (4.4.31) and (4.4.33), $F = K$ only if $KG + G^T K = 0$; hence, $KG = -G^T K = \hat{S}$, a skew-symmetric matrix. If we choose $\hat{S} = KSK$, the desirable condition (4.4.30) follows.   Q.E.D.   ∎

This theorem, as will be seen by the numerical examples, may be used to find a class of interaction matrix patterns for which the optimum overall system can be achieved by applying decentralized controls $u_i^*(t)$, i.e.,

$$\dot{x}_i(t) = (A_i - B_i P_i) x_i(t) + \sum_{j=1}^{N} G_{ij} x_j(t) \qquad (4.4.34)$$

for $i = 1, 2, \ldots, N$. It is noted that under condition (4.4.30) the local controllers not only optimize the overall system but also stabilize it. It must be emphasized that if the structural perturbation of the system is limited to (4.4.30), one can ignore the interactions and solve $N$ independent small-scale problems which provide both optimal and stabilizing control. However, in general, $G$ does not satisfy (4.4.30), and the application of $u_i^*(t)$ to the overall system will result in a performance

$$\hat{J}(t_0, x(t_0)) = \sum_{i=1}^{N} \hat{J}_i(t_0, x_i(t_0)) \qquad (4.4.35)$$

where $\hat{J}_i(t_0, x_i(t_0)) = J_i(t_0, x_i(t_0), u_i^*(t_0))$ for the composite system (4.4.34) is greater than or less than $J^*$, depending on whether the interaction matrix $G$ is nonbeneficial or beneficial in the sense of Definitions 4.1 and 4.2. Šiljak and Sundareshan (1976a,b) have determined bounds on the resulting performance suboptimality based on the interactions and have established multilevel schemes for minimizing interaction errors and improving on the performance. This is achieved by a so-called "corrective" control $u_i^c(t)$ in addition to the "local" decentralized control $u_i^*(t)$, i.e.,

$$u_i(t) = u_i^*(t) + u_i^c(t) \qquad (4.4.36)$$

where $u_i^*(t)$ is given by (4.4.26), while $u_i^c(t)$ is assumed to be

$$u_i^c(t) = - \sum_{j=1}^{N} H_{ij} x_j(t) \qquad (4.4.37)$$

where $H_{ij}$ is an $m_i \times n_j$ gain matrix for the feedback signals from the $j$th subsystem to the $i$th subsystem. The application of $u_i(t)$ in (4.4.36) to (4.4.22) using (4.4.26) and (4.4.37) yields

$$\dot{x}_i(t) = (A_i - B_i P_i) x_i(t) + \sum_{j=1}^{N} (G_{ij} - B_i H_{ij}) x_j(t) \qquad (4.4.38)$$

for $i = 1, 2, \ldots, N$. The corrective gain matrices $H_{ij}$ are obtained through

$$BH = B^p P \qquad (4.4.39)$$

where $P = \text{diag}\{P_1, P_2, \ldots, P_N\}$, $H = \{H_{ij}\}$, $i, j = 1, 2, \ldots, N$, and $B^p$ is an $n \times m$ perturbation in $B$. Note that matrix $B$ is block-diagonal, i.e., $B = \text{diag}\{B_1, B_2, \ldots, B_N\}$, while $B^p$ is not. By virtue of the above formulation of a structural perturbation, (4.4.38) can be reconstructed:

$$\dot{x}(t) = (A + G) x(t) - (B + B^p) P x(t) \qquad (4.4.40)$$

with $A = \text{diag}\{A_1, A_2, \ldots, A_N\}$. The closed-loop system (4.4.40) is influenced through the two components, i.e., "local" $BPx(t)$ and "corrector," or "global," $B^p P x(t)$. Figure 4.13 shows a schematic for the proposed multilevel control method. The local-global feedback control system (4.4.40) can be utilized to give an estimate on the performance index; i.e., once the perturbation matrix $B^p$ is determined, a bound on performance $\hat{J}$ results. The following theorem, due to Sundareshan (1977), provides the mechanism to achieve this.

**Theorem 4.3.** *For a nonsingular $(A + G)$ matrix, let a skew-symmetric matrix $S$ be the solution of the following matrix Lyapunov-type equation:*

$$S(A + G) + (A + G)^T S + G^T KA - A^T KG = 0 \qquad (4.4.41)$$

*with $K = \text{Block-diag}\{K_1, K_2, \ldots, K_N\}$, and let $n \times n$ matrix $\hat{K}$ given by*

$$\hat{K} = (S - KG)(A + G)^{-1} \qquad (4.4.42)$$

*be such that $(K + \hat{K})$ is a positive-definite matrix. Then an input matrix perturbation $B^p$ given by*

$$B^p = - (K + \hat{K})^{-1} \hat{K} B \qquad (4.4.43)$$

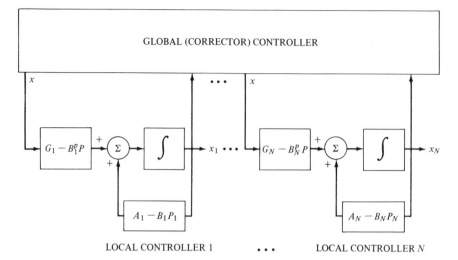

**Figure 4.13** A closed-loop multilevel state regulation structure.

*provides a performance index*

$$\hat{J}(t_0, x(t_0)) = \tfrac{1}{2} x^T(t_0)(K + \hat{K})x(t_0) \qquad (4.4.44)$$

*for the overall system* (4.4.40). *Moreover, the upper bound on the performance deviation*

$$\rho = (\hat{J} - J^*)/J^* \qquad (4.4.45)$$

*is given by* $\rho \leqslant \lambda_M(\hat{K})/\lambda_m(K)$, *where* $\lambda_m(\cdot)$ *and* $\lambda_M(\cdot)$ *represent the minimum and maximum of the eigenvalues of their associated matrix arguments, respectively.*

PROOF: Consider the following perturbed system:

$$\dot{x}(t) = (A + G)x(t) + (B + B^p)\hat{u}(t) \qquad (4.4.46)$$

and let $n \times n$ positive-definite and symmetric matrix $F$ be the solution of AMRE,

$$(A + G)^T F + F(A + G) - FV^p F + Q = 0 \qquad (4.4.47)$$

where $V^p = (B + B^p)R^{-1}(B + B^p)^T$. Clearly, the closed-loop control $\hat{u}(t)$ $= -R^{-1}(B + B^p)^T Fx(t)$ results in a minimum cost $\tfrac{1}{2}x^T(t_0)Fx(t_0)$ for the feedback control system

$$\dot{x}(t) = (A + G)x(t) - V^p Fx(t) \qquad (4.4.48)$$

However, since the desired closed-loop system is of the form (4.4.40), it is seen that for (4.4.48) to take on that form the following relation should hold:

$$R^{-1}(B + B^p)^T F = P = R^{-1}B^T K \qquad (4.4.49)$$

Since $K$ is a positive-definite and symmetric solution of (4.4.33), (4.4.49) can be used twice to rewrite (4.4.47):

$$G^T F + FG + A^T (F - K) + (F - K)A = 0 \qquad (4.4.50)$$

The relation (4.4.50) can be rewritten as

$$KG + (F - K)(A + G) = S \qquad (4.4.51)$$

where $S$ is a skew-symmetric matrix which satisfies (4.4.41), since $(F - K) = (S - KG)(A + G)^{-1}$ is a symmetric matrix. Now if we let $\hat{K} = (F - K)$, then, through direct substitution, it can be seen that $B^p$ defined in (4.4.43) in fact satisfies (4.4.49); therefore, the minimum cost is $\hat{J}(t_0, x(t_0)) = 1/2 x^T(t_0) F x(t_0) = 1/2 x^T(t_0)(K + \hat{K}) x(t_0)$, which is the desired cost (4.4.44) for the overall composite system (4.4.40). Moreover, it follows that the suboptimality index $\rho$ satisfies (4.4.45) and is given by

$$\rho \leqslant \lambda_M(\hat{K})/\lambda_m(K) \qquad (4.4.52)$$

for all $t_0$ and $x(t_0)$. Q.E.D. ∎

An immediate corollary of this theorem is that for a perturbation matrix $B^p$ given by (4.4.43), the control law

$$u(t) = -(P + H)x(t) \qquad (4.4.53)$$

is a stabilizing control for the original large-scale system. For the proof of this corollary, see Problem 4.5.

This combined global-local controller extends the earlier work of Šiljak and Sundareshan (1974) in the sense that (4.4.53) takes advantage of possible beneficial aspects of interconnection. The following examples illustrate the structural perturbation method. Further discussion on the method will be given in Section 4.6.

**Example 4.4.2.** Consider a simple second-order system,

$$\begin{aligned} \dot{x}_1 &= 2x_1 + u_1, \quad x_1(0) = 1 \\ \dot{x}_2 &= 4x_2 + u_2, \quad x_2(0) = 0.5 \end{aligned} \qquad (4.4.54)$$

with a $2 \times 2$ interaction matrix

$$G = \begin{bmatrix} g_{11} & g_{12} \\ g_{21} & g_{22} \end{bmatrix} \qquad (4.4.55)$$

whose elements are kept variable for illustrative purposes. For a quadratic cost function

$$J = \frac{1}{2} \int_0^\infty \left( x_1^2(t) + x_2^2(t) + u_1^2(t) + u_2^2(t) \right) dt \qquad (4.4.56)$$

we would like to investigate the effects of various interconnections.

SOLUTION: To begin with, assume that the system is completely decoupled, i.e., $G = 0$, and hence the solutions of two independent scalar AMRE's provide $K_1 = 4.24$ and $K_2 = 8.123$ and optimal local controllers

$$\begin{bmatrix} u_1^*(t) \\ u_2^*(t) \end{bmatrix} = \begin{bmatrix} -4.24 & 0 \\ 0 & -8.123 \end{bmatrix} \cdot \begin{bmatrix} x_1(t) \\ x_2(t) \end{bmatrix} \qquad (4.4.57)$$

with optimal decoupled performance index

$$J^* = \sum_{i=1}^{2} J_i^* = \frac{1}{2} \{ K_1 x_1^2(0) + K_2 x_2^2(0) \} = 3.1353 \qquad (4.4.58)$$

Next we consider the case of "neutral" interaction in which $\hat{J} = J^*$. Using $K = \text{diag}\{4.24, 8.123\}$ and an arbitrary skew-symmetric matrix

$$S = \begin{bmatrix} 0 & b \\ -b & 0 \end{bmatrix} \qquad (4.4.59)$$

(4.4.30) implies that

$$g_{11} = g_{22} = 0, \quad g_{12} = -1.915 g_{21} \qquad (4.4.60)$$

Thus, for any interaction matrix,

$$G = \begin{bmatrix} 0 & -1.915b \\ b & 0 \end{bmatrix} \qquad (4.4.61)$$

where $b$ is a nonzero constant, the performance index of the overall system does not improve any more. To see this we let $b = 1$ and solve a second-order AMRE for matrices,

$$(A + G) = \begin{bmatrix} 2 & -1.915 \\ 1 & 4 \end{bmatrix}, \quad B = \begin{bmatrix} 1 \\ 1 \end{bmatrix}, \quad Q = I_2, \quad R = I_2 \qquad (4.4.62)$$

with a solution

$$K^o = \begin{bmatrix} 4.23671007 & 0.00143700 \\ 0.00143700 & 8.12243780 \end{bmatrix} \qquad (4.4.63)$$

resulting in a performance $\hat{J} = \frac{1}{2} x^T(0) K^o x(0) = 3.13438$, which corresponds to the value of $J^*$ in (4.4.58) after rounding.

Next let us consider a case of "beneficial" interaction by assuming an interaction matrix

$$G = \begin{bmatrix} 5.5 & 6.2 \\ 5.5 & 12 \end{bmatrix} \qquad (4.4.64)$$

Using $G$, $A$, and $K = \text{diag}\{4.24, 8.123\}$, the linear-matrix equation (4.4.41) is solved for $S$,

$$S = \begin{bmatrix} 0 & 0.62044 \\ -0.62044 & 0 \end{bmatrix} \qquad (4.4.65)$$

and the corresponding $\hat{K}$, $K + \hat{K}$ matrices follow from (4.4.42):

$$\hat{K} = \begin{bmatrix} -2.7 & -0.558 \\ -2.2 & -5.240 \end{bmatrix}, \quad K + \hat{K} = \begin{bmatrix} 1.54 & -0.558 \\ -2.20 & 2.883 \end{bmatrix} \qquad (4.4.66)$$

which are negative- and positive-definite, respectively. The value of $\hat{J}$ is

$$\hat{J} = \tfrac{1}{2}x^T(0)(K + \hat{K})x(0) = 0.4409 \qquad (4.4.67)$$

which is much smaller than $J^*$ in (4.4.58). The suboptimality index for this case is $\rho = -0.85933$, with upper bound $\rho \leqslant -1.334$. The control for this case is

$$u(t) = u^*(t) + u^c(t) = u^*(t) - B^p P x$$

$$= \begin{bmatrix} -4.24 & 0 \\ 0 & -8.123 \end{bmatrix} \begin{bmatrix} x_1(t) \\ x_2(t) \end{bmatrix} + \begin{bmatrix} -12.34 & -11.88 \\ -12.64 & -23.82 \end{bmatrix} \begin{bmatrix} x_1(t) \\ x_2(t) \end{bmatrix}$$

$$(4.4.68)$$

whose first part is local (decentralized) control component and the second part is the corrective control component.

The remaining possible structural perturbation to be discussed is "nonbeneficial." Let us take an interaction matrix (or structural perturbation)

$$G = \begin{bmatrix} 0 & -1 \\ -2 & 0 \end{bmatrix} \qquad (4.4.69)$$

Using this perturbation, the skew-symmetric matrix $S$ from (4.4.41) becomes

$$S = \begin{bmatrix} 0 & -4.64 \\ 4.64 & 0 \end{bmatrix} \qquad (4.4.70)$$

and the resulting $K$ and $\hat{K}$ matrices become

$$\hat{K} = \begin{bmatrix} -0.1337 & -0.1337 \\ 13.92 & 3.48 \end{bmatrix}, \quad K + \hat{K} = \begin{bmatrix} 4.106 & -0.1337 \\ 13.92 & 11.604 \end{bmatrix}$$

$$(4.4.71)$$

with performance index $\hat{J} = \tfrac{1}{2}x^T(0)(K + \hat{K})x(0) = 6.95$. This value as compared with $J^* = 3.1353$ indicates that (4.4.69) is a nonbeneficial perturbation. The performance suboptimality index $\rho = 1.22$ and an upper bound $\rho \leqslant 0.674$.

The AMREs were solved by Newton's iterative formulation (Kleinman, 1968), while the Lyapunov-type equations were solved by an infinite series method given by Smith (1971). For a survey on the solutions of both equations, see Jamshidi (1980). Now consider a second example.

**Example 4.4.3.** This example deals with a two-reach segment of a river pollution problem considered in Example 4.3.2. Consider

$$\dot{x} = \begin{bmatrix} -1.32 & 0 & 0 & 0 \\ -0.32 & -1.2 & 0 & 0 \\ 0.9 & 0 & -1.32 & 0 \\ 0 & 0.9 & -0.32 & -1.2 \end{bmatrix} x + \begin{bmatrix} 0.1 & 0 \\ 0 & 0 \\ 0 & 0.1 \\ 0 & 0 \end{bmatrix} u \quad (4.4.72)$$

where each reach of the river is represented by two state variables, BOD (biochemical oxygen demand) and DO (dissolved oxygen). The remaining matrices were chosen as $Q = \text{diag}(1, 2, 1, 2)$ and $R = I_2$.

SOLUTION: Under decoupled conditions, the system can be considered as two one-reach subsystems:

$$\dot{x}_i = \begin{bmatrix} -1.32 & 0 \\ -0.32 & -1.2 \end{bmatrix} x_i + \begin{bmatrix} 0.1 \\ 0 \end{bmatrix} u_i, \quad i = 1, 2 \qquad (4.4.73)$$

with $Q_i = \text{diag}(1,2)$ and $R_i = 1$. For interaction matrix $G = 0$, the independent matrix Riccati equations lead to the following solutions:

$$K_1 = K_2 = \begin{bmatrix} 0.4038 & -0.1056 \\ -0.1056 & 0.8333 \end{bmatrix} \qquad (4.4.74)$$

and decentralized controllers

$$\begin{bmatrix} u_1^*(t) \\ u_2^*(t) \end{bmatrix} = - \begin{bmatrix} 0.0404 & -0.01056 & 0 & 0 \\ 0 & 0 & 0.0404 & -0.01056 \end{bmatrix} \begin{bmatrix} x_1(t) \\ x_2(t) \end{bmatrix} \qquad (4.4.75)$$

with $J^* = 0.5065$ for $x_i(0) = (1 \quad 0.5)^T$, $i = 1, 2$. The interaction matrix for

**Figure 4.14** Time responses for the structural perturbation in Example 4.4.3 showing exact optimum and approximate "$a$" "$e$" solutions: (a) states, (b) outputs, and (c) controls.

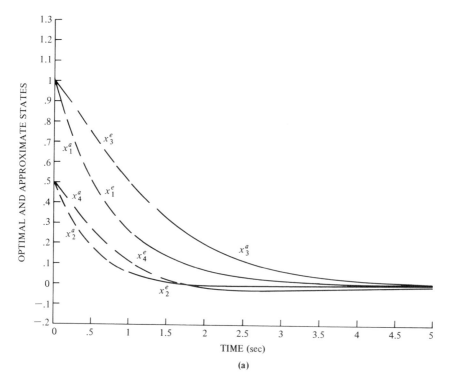

(a)

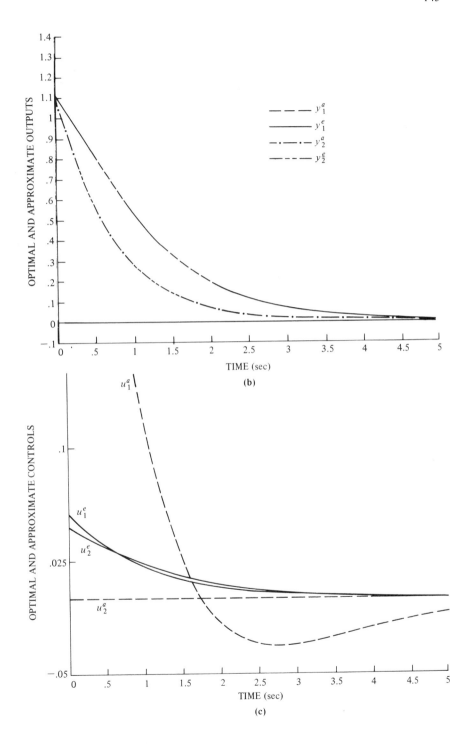

(b)

(c)

this example is

$$G = \begin{bmatrix} 0 & 0 & 0 & 0 \\ 0 & 0 & 0 & 0 \\ 0.9 & 0 & 0 & 0 \\ 0 & 0.9 & 0 & 0 \end{bmatrix} \qquad (4.4.76)$$

which may be neutral, beneficial, or nonbeneficial. In order to find out which case it is, we need to use Theorem 4.2 to factor $G$ as in (4.4.30). If we take $G$ defined by (4.4.76) and $K = $ Block-diag($K_1, K_2$), then the corresponding $S$ matrix becomes

$$S = \begin{bmatrix} 0 & 0 & 0 & 0 \\ 0 & 0 & 0 & 0 \\ 2.3 & 0.3 & 0 & 0 \\ 0.3 & 1.1 & 0 & 0 \end{bmatrix} \qquad (4.4.77)$$

which is not a skew-symmetric matrix, implying that the interaction matrix (4.4.76) is not neutral. In order to find out whether $G$ in (4.4.76) is beneficial or nonbeneficial, Theorem 4.3 and Equation (4.4.41) are used to find $S$:

$$S = \begin{bmatrix} 0 & 0 & -0.17 & 0.067 \\ 0 & 0 & -0.0238 & -0.38 \\ 0.17 & 0.0238 & 0 & 0.037 \\ -0.067 & 0.38 & -0.037 & 0 \end{bmatrix} \qquad (4.4.78)$$

and then by virtue of (4.4.42),

$$\hat{K} = \begin{bmatrix} 0.107 & -0.042 & 0.142 & -0.055 \\ -0.098 & 0.238 & -0.059 & 0.317 \\ 0.181 & -0.122 & 0.007 & -0.03 \\ -0.077 & 0.308 & 0.028 & 0 \end{bmatrix},$$

$$K + \hat{K} = \begin{bmatrix} 0.51 & -0.147 & 0.142 & -0.055 \\ -0.2 & 1.07 & -0.059 & 0.317 \\ 0.181 & -0.122 & 0.411 & -0.136 \\ -0.077 & -0.077 & 0.308 & 0.833 \end{bmatrix} \qquad (4.4.79)$$

and the value of $\hat{J} = 0.71937$ for $x(0) = (1 \quad 0.5 \quad 1 \quad 0.5)^T$, which indicates that the system's original interaction matrix is nonbeneficial. The global (corrector) controller is given by

$$u^c(t) = -B^p Px = -10^{-4} \begin{bmatrix} -3.55 & 0.93 & -12.4 & 3.25 \\ 1.77 & -4.63 & 0.8 & -0.2 \\ -15.2 & -4 & 4.2 & -1.1 \\ 1.32 & 3.45 & -24.2 & 0.63 \end{bmatrix} \begin{bmatrix} x_1 \\ x_2 \end{bmatrix}$$

$$(4.4.80)$$

with $\hat{J} = 0.71937$, the performance suboptimality index $\rho = 0.2960$, and upper bound of $\rho \leqslant 1.32$. The above performance index was also checked by the original system's cost function by solving a fourth-order AMRE, which provided the overall optimal system performance index as $J^o = 0.7132$, indicating that the proposed decentralized-global (corrector) control performance index is within less than 1% of the overall centralized optimum cost.

To check the original system's optimal control solution versus the combined decentralized global solution, the fourth-order system (4.4.72) was solved using

$$u_e = - R^{-1}B^TK^o x \qquad (4.4.81)$$

and

$$u_a = u^* + u_c \qquad (4.4.82)$$

with $x(0) = (1,0.5,1,0.5)^T$ and output matrix

$$C = \begin{bmatrix} 1 & 0.25 & 0 & 0 \\ 0 & 0 & 1 & 0.25 \end{bmatrix} \qquad (4.4.83)$$

The resulting $x_i(t)$, $i = 1,2,3,4$; $y_j(t)$, for $j = 1,2$ applying exact optimal control (4.4.81) and approximate optimal control (4.4.82) responses for $0 \leqslant t \leqslant 5.0$ and a step size $\Delta t = 0.1$ were found to be very close. The states and outputs of the fourth-order system utilizing two controls are undistinguishably close. Figure 4.14 indicates that the structural perturbation closed-loop control considered here is a good approximation. Further comments on this suboptimality are given in Section 6.5.

## 4.5 Hierarchical Control of Discrete-Time Systems

Thus far, the multilevel hierarchical control has been used for linear stationary continuous-time systems. In practice, however, many systems are neither linear nor continuous-time. In fact, many practical engineering systems, such as traffic control, water resources, and manufacturing processes, are both discrete and delayed in nature. Due to the importance of such applications, many researchers have made significant contributions in applying or extending hierarchical control to both nondelay discrete-time and time-delay discrete-time systems. In this section the extensions of hierarchical control to such systems in both linear and nonlinear forms are considered.

### 4.5.1 Three-Level Coordination for Discrete-Time Systems

This section deals with a three-level goal-coordination strategy suitable for discrete-time systems and their time-delay modifications. Such a strategy was first proposed by Tamura (1974, 1975) and treated further by Singh (1980).

Consider a large-scale linear discrete-time system

$$x(k+1) = Ax(k) + Bu(k), \quad x(0) = x_o \qquad (4.5.1)$$

where the usual definitions hold for $x$, $u$, $A$, and $B$. The optimal control problem is to find a sequence of discrete-time control vectors $u(k)$, $k = 0, 1, 2, \ldots, K - 1$ which minimizes a quadratic cost function

$$J = \frac{1}{2}x^T(K)Q(K)x(K) + \frac{1}{2}\sum_{k=0}^{K-1}\{x^T(k)Q(k)x(k) + u^T(k)R(k)u(k)\}$$

$$(4.5.2)$$

while (4.5.1) holds. Following the decomposition procedure discussed in Section 4.3, this problem can be reformulated by minimizing

$$J = \sum_{i=1}^{N}\left\{\frac{1}{2}x_i^T(K)Q_i(K)x_i(K) + \frac{1}{2}\sum_{k=0}^{K-1}\left[x_i^T(k)Q_i(k)x_i(k)\right.\right.$$

$$\left.\left. + z_i^T(k)S_i(k)z_i(k) + u_i^T(k)R_i(k)u_i(k)\right]\right\} \qquad (4.5.3)$$

while subsystem dynamic state equations

$$x_i(k+1) = A_i x_i(k) + B_i u_i(k) + C_i z_i(k), \quad x_i(0) = x_{io},$$

$$i = 1, 2, \ldots, N, \quad k = 0, 1, 2, \ldots, K - 1 \qquad (4.5.4)$$

and interaction relations

$$z_i(k) = \sum_{j=1}^{N} G_{ij}x_j(k), \quad k = 0, 1, \ldots, K - 1, \quad i = 1, 2, \ldots, N \quad (4.5.5)$$

are satisfied.

Following the decomposition of the Lagrangian and the duality of two-level strategy formulated by (4.3.21)–(4.3.22), let us define a dual function

$$q(\alpha) = \underset{x, u, z}{\text{Min}} \, L(x, u, z, \alpha) \qquad (4.5.6)$$

where

$$L(x, u, z, \alpha) = \sum_{i=1}^{N} L_i(x_i, u_i, z_i, \alpha_i)$$

$$\triangleq \sum_{i=1}^{N}\left\{\frac{1}{2}x_i^T(K)Q_i(K)x_i(K) + \frac{1}{2}\sum_{k=0}^{K-1}\left[x_i^T(k)Q_i(k)x_i(k)\right.\right.$$

$$+ z_i^T(k)S_i(k)z_i(k) + u_i^T(k)R_i(k)u_i(k)$$

$$\left.\left. + \alpha_i^T(k)z_i(k) - \sum_{j=1}^{N}\alpha_j^T G_{ji}x_i(k)\right]\right\} \qquad (4.5.7)$$

Through this decomposition, as in the continuous-time case, one can proceed to apply the two-level iterative procedure to improve on the values of the Lagrangian multipliers $\alpha_i$ using the gradient of the dual function $q(\alpha)$ as in (4.3.25):

$$\nabla_\alpha q(\alpha)|_{\alpha_i = \alpha_i^*} = z_i(k) - \sum_{j=1}^{N} G_{ij} x_j(k) = e_i(k) \qquad (4.5.8)$$

for $i = 1, 2, \ldots, N$; $k = 0, 1, 2, \ldots, K - 1$. Although one may proceed to use (4.5.8) and a few iterations of conjugate gradient or steepest descent to obtain a feasible and optimum solution, our objective here is to present a three-level modification of the problem due to Tamura (1974, 1975).

The essential point in this modification is to recognize the fact that the "first-level" solutions of a two-level structure can be obtained by utilizing the concepts of duality and decomposition instead of solving $N$ independent problems of minimizing $L_i$ defined by (4.5.7) and subject to (4.5.4)–(4.5.5). At this level, the sub-Lagrangian for every subsystem is further decomposed by the discrete-time index $k$, thereby reducing a "functional" optimization problem at the first level of a two-level structure to one of a "parametric" optimization at the first level of a three-level structure. This decomposition was mentioned in Section 4.1 under "time" or "functional" division of the control task. It can also be considered a "temporal" decomposition versus a "spatial" one in Section 4.3.

In order to determine the optimal strategy of this three-level structure, let us define a dual problem for minimizing $L_i(\cdot)$ in (4.5.7) subject to (4.5.4) as follows:

$$p(\beta_i) = \underset{x_i, u_i, z_i}{\text{Min}} \; L_i(x_i, u_i, z_i, \alpha_i^*, \beta_i) \} \qquad (4.5.9)$$

where

$$L_i(\cdot) = \frac{1}{2} x_i^T(K) Q_i(K) x_i(K) + \frac{1}{2} \sum_{k=0}^{K-1} \left[ x_i^T(k) Q_i(k) x_i(k) \right.$$
$$+ z_i^T(k) S_i(k) z_i(k) + u_i^T(k) R_i(k) u_i(k)$$
$$+ \beta_i^T(k)(A_i x_i(k) + B_i u_i(k) + C_i z_i(k) - x_i(k+1)) \right]$$
$$+ \alpha_i^{*T}(k) z_i(k) - \sum_{j=1}^{N} \alpha_j^{*T}(k) G_{ji} x_i(k) \qquad (4.5.10)$$

and $\beta_i$ is the $i$th subsystem Lagrange multiplier vector corresponding to dynamic equality constraint of (4.5.4), and all the other variables and parameters are defined earlier. The last constraint to be determined is the initial condition, also given by (4.5.4). In other words, the dual problem to minimizing $J$ in (4.5.3) subject to (4.5.4)–(4.5.5) is maximizing the dual function $p(\beta_i)$ defined by (4.5.9)–(4.5.10) and subject to (4.5.4) at a given $\beta_i = \beta_i^*, k = 1, 2, \ldots, N$. The gradient of $p(\beta_i)$ is similar to the continuous-time case, the error is satisfying equality constraint (4.5.4), i.e.,

$$\nabla_{\beta_i} p(\beta_i^*) = -x_i(k+1) + A_i x_i(k) + B_i u_i(k) + C_i z_i(k) \quad (4.5.11)$$

for $k = 0, 1, \ldots, K-1$, and $i = 1, 2, \ldots, N$, with $x_i(k)$ and $u_i(k)$ being the state and control vectors obtained from minimizing $L_i$ in (4.5.7) subject to (4.5.4) for a given $\beta_i = \beta_i^*$. Now let us define the Hamiltonian $H_i(\cdot)$ of the $i$th subsystem:

$$H_i(x_i(k), u_i(k), z_i(k), k) = \tfrac{1}{2} x_i^T(k) Q_i(k) x_i(k) + \tfrac{1}{2} u_i^T(k) R_i u_i(k)$$

$$+ \frac{1}{2} z_i^T(k) S_i z_i(k) + \alpha_i^{*T}(k) z_i(k) - \sum_{j=1}^{N} \alpha_j^{*T}(k) G_{ji} x_i(k)$$

$$+ \beta_i^{*T}(k) [A_i x_i(k) + B_i u_i(k) + C_i z_i(k)] \quad (4.5.12)$$

for $k = 0, 1, 2, \ldots, K-1$, and $i = 1, 2, \ldots, N$. Note that without loss of generality $R_i$ and $S_i$ matrices are assumed to be constant. By regrouping the last term $\beta_i^T(K-1) x_i(K)$ inside the bracket in (4.5.10) with $\tfrac{1}{2} x_i^T(K) Q_i(K) x_i(K)$ and adding the term $\beta_i(-1) x_i(0)$ to the sum inside the bracket with $\beta_i(-1)$ defined to be zero, the function $p(\beta_i)$ in (4.5.9) can be rewritten in terms of $H_i(\cdot)$, i.e.,

$$p(\beta_i) = \tfrac{1}{2} x_i^T(K) Q_i(K) x_i(K) - \beta_i^{*T}(K-1) x_i(K)$$

$$+ \sum_{k=0}^{K-1} \{ H_i(x_i(k), u_i(k), z_i(k), k) - \beta_i^{*T}(k-1) x_i(k) \} \quad (4.5.13)$$

The minimization problem at the first level is divided into three portions: for $k = 0$, $k = 1, 2, \ldots, K-1$, and $k = K$. For $k = 0$, the problem is defined as

$$\underset{u_i(0), z_i(0)}{\text{Minimize}} \; H_i(x_i(0), u_i(0), z_i(0), 0) \quad (4.5.14)$$

subject to

$$x_i(0) = x_{io} \quad (4.5.15)$$

In view of $H_i(x_i(k), u_i(k), z_i(k), k)$ in (4.5.12) for $k = 0$, the necessary conditions for the minimization problem (4.5.14)–(4.5.15) are

$$\nabla_{u_i}(0) H_i(\cdot) = R_i u_i(0) + B_i^T \beta_i^*(0) = 0 \quad (4.5.16)$$

$$\nabla_{z_i}(0) H_i(\cdot) = S_i z_i(0) + C_i^T \beta_i^*(0) + \alpha_i^*(0) = 0 \quad (4.5.17)$$

or

$$u_i(0) = -R_i^{-1} B_i^T \beta_i^*(0) \quad (4.5.18)$$

$$z_i(0) = -S_i^{-1} (C_i^T \beta_i^*(0) + \alpha_i^*(0)) \quad (4.5.19)$$

In a similar fashion, for the second portion $k = 1, 2, \ldots, K-1$, by virtue of (4.5.13), the minimization problem is

$$\underset{x_i(k), u_i(k), z_i(k)}{\text{Minimize}} \; \{ H_i(x_i(k), u_i(k), z_i(k), k) - \beta_i^{*T}(k-1) x_i(k) \} \quad (4.5.20)$$

which leads to the following relations (Singh, 1980; Tamura, 1974):

$$x_i(k) = - Q_i^{-1}(k)\left\{ A_i^T \beta_i^*(k) + \beta_i^*(k-1) + \sum_{j=1}^{N}\left[ \alpha_j^{*T}(k) G_{ji} \right]^T \right\} \quad (4.5.21)$$

$$u_i(k) = - R_i^{-1} B_i^T \beta_i^*(k) \quad\quad\quad\quad\quad\quad\quad\quad (4.5.22)$$

and

$$z_i(k) = - S_i^{-1}\left( C_i^T \beta_i^*(k) + \alpha_i^*(k) \right) \quad\quad\quad (4.5.23)$$

The final portion of the first-level minimization is defined by

$$\text{Minimize}\left\{ \tfrac{1}{2} x_i^T(K) Q_i(K) x_i(K) - \beta_i^{*T}(K-1) x_i(K) \right\} \quad (4.5.24)$$

which results in

$$x_i(K) = Q_i^{-1}(K) \beta_i^*(K-1) \quad\quad\quad\quad (4.5.25)$$

Therefore, by virtue of this three-level hierarchical structure, the large-scale optimal control problem defined by (4.5.3)–(4.5.5) can be solved by the following algorithm.

***Algorithm 4.3.*** Three-Level Coordination of Discrete-Time Systems

*Step 1:* At the first level, for given Lagrangian multiplier $\alpha_i^*(k)$, $\beta_i^*(k)$ sequences, (4.5.18)–(4.5.19), (4.5.21)–(4.5.22), and (4.5.25) can be used to find $x_i(k)$, $u_i(k)$, and $z_i(k)$ for $k = 0, 1, 2, \ldots, K$ and $i = 1, 2, \ldots, N$.

*Step 2:* At the second level, $x_i(k)$, $u_i(k)$, and $z_i(k)$ of the first level can be used along with the gradient of $p(\beta_i)$ in (4.5.11) to improve on the value of $\beta_i$, i.e.,

$$\beta_i^{*l+1}(k) = \beta_i^{*l}(k) + \delta_i^l f^l(k),$$

$$k = 0, 1, \ldots, K, \quad i = 1, 2, \ldots, N \quad (4.5.26)$$

where $f^l(k)$ is a function of gradient of $p(\beta_i^*)$, and again a simple gradient or conjugate gradient method can be used. Steps 1 and 2 are repeated alternatively until the optimal $\beta_i^*(k)$, $i = 1, 2, \ldots, N$, and $k = 0, 1, 2, \ldots, K$, are obtained.

*Step 3:* At level 3, the optimal $\beta_i^*(k)$ values can be used to improve on the values of $\alpha_i^*(k)$ using the gradient of $q(\alpha)$,

$$\alpha_i^{*l+1}(k) = \alpha_i^{*l}(k) + \varepsilon_i^l g_i^l(k),$$

$$k = 0, 1, \ldots, K, \quad i = 1, 2, \ldots, N \quad (4.5.27)$$

where $g_i^l(k)$ is a function of $\nabla_\alpha q(\alpha_i)$ given by (4.5.8).

152

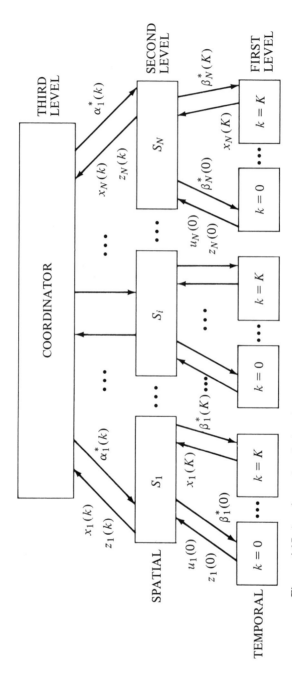

**Figure 4.15** A schematic of the three-level coordination structure proposed by Tamura (1974).

Once the above three steps are complete, the interaction errors defined by (4.5.8) and (4.5.11) would become zero and the optimal control of the original large-scale system is obtained (Singh, 1980). Figure 4.15 shows a schematic of the three-level modified coordination principle proposed by Tamura (1974). The above structure and algorithm is illustrated by the following example.

**Example 4.5.1.** Consider a third-order system,

$$\begin{bmatrix} x_1(k+1) \\ x_2(k+1) \\ \hline x_3(k+1) \end{bmatrix} = \begin{bmatrix} -0.1 & 0.05 & | & 0.05 \\ 0 & -0.2 & | & 0 \\ \hline 0.2 & -0.1 & | & -3 \end{bmatrix} \begin{bmatrix} x_1(k) \\ x_2(k) \\ \hline x_3(k) \end{bmatrix} + \begin{bmatrix} 0.25 & | & 0 \\ 0 & | & 0 \\ \hline 0 & | & 0 \end{bmatrix} \begin{bmatrix} u_1(k) \\ \hline u_2(k) \end{bmatrix}$$

$$(4.5.28)$$

with a cost function

$$J = \sum_{i=1}^{2} \left\{ \frac{1}{2} x_i^T(10) Q_i(10) x_i(10) + \sum_{k=0}^{9} \frac{1}{2} \left[ x_i^T(k) Q_i(k) x_i(k) \right. \right.$$

$$\left. \left. + z_i^T(k) S_i(k) z_i(k) + u_i^T(k) R_i(k) u_i(k) \right] \right\} \qquad (4.5.29)$$

where $Q_i(k) = 2I_{n_i}$, $R_i(k) = 0.5I_{m_i}$, $S_i(k) = I_{k_i}$, $n_1 = 2$, $n_2 = 1$, $m_1 = m_2 = 1$, $k_1 = 2$, $k_2 = 1$. It is desired to find an optimum control strategy through the three-level coordination Algorithm 4.3.

SOLUTION: The algorithm was simulated on an HP-9845 computer using BASIC and an initial condition $x(0) = (2 \ -3 \ 4)^T$. The results were generally very satisfactory, especially with respect to the interaction error between levels 2 and 3. Typical resulting error and states are shown in Figures 4.16 and 4.17. The interaction error between levels 1 and 2 reduced from 1,000 to 149 in some 50 iterations and the convergence was not as fast as the second-third levels interaction errors.

### 4.5.2 Discrete-Time Systems with Delays

In this section one of the more powerful algorithms for multilevel optimization of large linear discrete-time systems with delays in both state and control is presented. The problem was first introduced by Tamura (1974, 1975) and has been further applied by many others (Fallaside and Perry, 1975; Jamshidi and Heggen, 1980; Singh, 1980).

Consider the following large-scale discrete-time system with delays

$$x(k+1) = A_o x(k) + A_1 x(k-1) + A_2 x(k-2) + \cdots$$

$$+ A_s x(k-s) + B_o u(k) + B_1 u(k-1) + \cdots + B_s u(k-s)$$

$$(4.5.30)$$

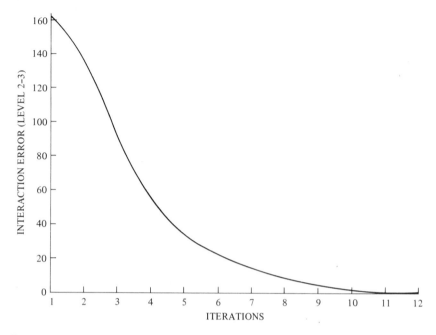

**Figure 4.16** Typical interaction errors of Example 4.5.1.

**Figure 4.17** Typical state trajectories for the third-order system of Example 4.5.1.

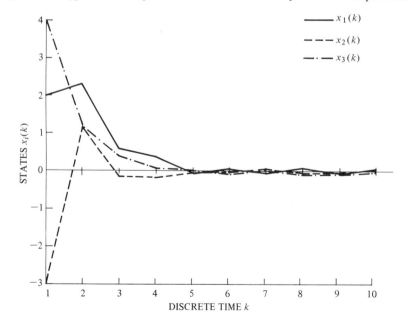

where $A_i$ and $B_i$, $k = 0, 1, 2, \ldots, s$, are $n \times n$ and $n \times m$ matrices, respectively, and $x$ and $u$ are $n$- and $m$-dimensional state and control vectors. The system (4.5.30) has $2s$ delayed terms; hence it requires $2s$ discrete-time initial functions, assumed to be zero without loss of generality:

$$x(k) = 0, \quad u(k) = 0, \quad -s \leqslant k < 0, \quad x(0) = x_0 \qquad (4.5.31)$$

Physical interpretation of initial functions in (4.5.31) for system (4.5.30) is that the system is operating at its steady-state and receives a disturbance at $k = 0$ and derives it to a known value $x_0$. The system cost function is assumed to be quadratic:

$$J = \frac{1}{2} x^T(K) Q(K) x(K) + \sum_{k=0}^{K-1} \frac{1}{2} \{ x^T(k) Q(k) x(k) + u^T(k) R(k) u(k) \}$$

$$(4.5.32)$$

where $Q(k)$ and $R(k)$ are both assumed to be positive-definite. The optimal control problem is to find a sequence of control vectors $u(0), u(1), \ldots, u(K-1)$ such that (4.5.32) is minimized while (4.5.30)–(4.5.31) and a set of inequality constraints

$$x_{\min} \leqslant x(k) \leqslant x_{\max} \qquad (4.5.33)$$

$$u_{\min} \leqslant u(k) \leqslant u_{\max} \qquad (4.5.34)$$

are satisfied. It goes without saying that a solution to the problem (4.5.30)–(4.5.34) in usual "centralized" methods by the application of the maximum principle, as it is demonstrated in Section 6.4, results in a TPBV (two-point boundary value) problem which involves both delay and advance terms, making the attainment of an optimum solution very difficult indeed, if not impossible. In the literature, there are several approximation techniques to deal with continuous-time systems with delay which will be discussed in Chapter 6. Here the objective is the application of hierarchical control via the interaction balance principle.

Following the formulation of discrete-time maximum principle (Dorato and Levis, 1971), let us define the Hamiltonian:

$$H(x(k), u(k), \lambda(k), k) = \tfrac{1}{2} \{ x^T(k) Q(k) x(k) + u^T(k) R(k) u(k) \}$$

$$+ \sum_{i=0}^{s} \lambda^T(k+i)(A_i x(k-i) + B_i u(k-i))$$

$$(4.5.35)$$

where $k = 0, 1, \ldots, K-1$, $\lambda(k)$ is a vector of Lagrange multipliers at $k$, and $\lambda(K), \lambda(K+1), \ldots$ are defined as zero vectors. In a manner similar to previous discussions regarding Equation (4.5.13) for a given vector $\lambda = \lambda^*$, the Lagrangian can be defined as

$$L(x, u, \lambda^*, k) = \tfrac{1}{2} x^T(K) Q(K) x(K) - \lambda^{*T}(K-1) x(K)$$
$$+ \sum_{k=0}^{K-1} \{ H(x(k), u(k), \lambda^*(k), k) - \lambda^*(k-1) x(k) \}$$

$$(4.5.36)$$

Thus the optimization problem is to minimize (4.5.36) subject to (4.5.33)–(4.5.34). As before, this problem can be altered to that of maximizing the minimum of $L(\cdot)$ with respect to $\lambda$. The power behind the "time-delay algorithm" of Tamura (1974) is the decomposition of this problem into $(K+1)$ independent minimization problems for a given $\lambda^*$, as in the three-level coordination formulation discussed in the last section, which reduces a "*functional*" optimization problem to a "*parametric*" one.

### 4.5.2.a  Problem $k = 0$

By virtue of (4.5.36), definition (4.5.35), and constraints (4.5.33)–(4.5.34), the optimization problem for $k = 0$ is

$$\operatorname*{Min}_{u(0)} H(x(0), u(0), \lambda(0)) = \operatorname{Min} \frac{1}{2} \{ x^T(0) Q(0) x(0) + u^T(0) R(0) u(0) \}$$
$$+ \sum_{i=1}^{s} \lambda^{*T}(i)(A_i x(0) + B_i u(0)) \qquad (4.5.37)$$

subject to

$$x(0) = x_o, \quad u_{\min} \leqslant u(0) \leqslant u_{\max} \qquad (4.5.38)$$

Now if $R(0)$ is assumed to be a diagonal matrix, the necessary conditions for (4.5.37)–(4.5.38) lead to a set of $m$ independent relations, each of which has an explicit solution given by setting $\partial H(\cdot)/\partial u(0) = 0$, i.e.,

$$u^*(0) = \operatorname{Sat}_u \left\{ - R^{-1}(0) \sum_{i=0}^{s} B_i^T \lambda^*(i) \right\} \qquad (4.5.39)$$

where the "saturation" function $\operatorname{Sat}_u(\cdot)$ is

$$\operatorname{Sat}_u(\sigma_j) = \begin{cases} u_{\max, j} & \text{if } \sigma_j > u_{\max, j} \\ \sigma_j & \text{if } u_{\min, j} \leqslant \sigma_j \leqslant u_{\max, j} \\ u_{\min, j} & \text{if } \sigma_j < u_{\min, j} \end{cases} \qquad (4.5.40)$$

and the index $j$ represents the $j$th element of control $u_j$, $j = 1, 2, \ldots, m$.

## 4.5.2.b  Problem $k = 1, 2, \ldots, K - 1$

The intermediate problem is defined by

$$\underset{x(k),\,u(k)}{\text{Min}}\ H(x(k), u(k), \lambda^*(k), k) - \lambda^{*T}(k-1)x(k) \qquad (4.5.41)$$

subject to

$$x_{\min} \leqslant x(k) \leqslant x_{\max} \qquad (4.5.42)$$

and

$$u_{\min} \leqslant u(k) \leqslant u_{\max} \qquad (4.5.43)$$

Once again, assuming that $R(k)$ and $Q(k)$ are diagonal, the partial derivatives $\partial H(\cdot)/\partial x_i(k)$ and $\partial H(\cdot)/\partial u_j(k)$ for $i = 1, 2, \ldots, n$ and $j = 1, 2, \ldots, m$ lead to a set of $n + m$ independent one-parameter equations whose general solution is

$$x^*(k) = \text{Sat}_x\left\{ -Q^{-1}(k)\left[ -\lambda^*(k-1) + \sum_{i=0}^{s} A_i^T \lambda^*(k+i) \right] \right\}$$

$$u^*(k) = \text{Sat}_u\left\{ -R^{-1}(k)\left[ \sum_{i=0}^{s} B_i^T \lambda^*(k+i) \right] \right\} \qquad (4.5.44)$$

where the $l$th element of the saturation function $\text{Sat}_x(\nu)$ is

$$\text{Sat}_x(\nu_l) = \begin{cases} x_{\max,\,l} & \text{if } \nu_l > x_{\max,\,l} \\ \nu_l & \text{if } x_{\min,\,l} \leqslant \nu_l \leqslant x_{\max,\,l} \\ x_{\min,\,l} & \text{if } \nu_l < x_{\min,\,l} \end{cases} \qquad (4.5.45)$$

## 4.5.2.c  Problem $k = K$

This problem is

$$\underset{x(K)}{\text{Min}}\left\{ \frac{1}{2} x^T(K)Q(K)x(K) - \lambda^{*T}(K-1)x(K) \right\} x(K) \qquad (4.5.46)$$

subject to

$$x_{\min} \leqslant x(K) \leqslant x_{\max} \qquad (4.5.47)$$

whose solution is similarly given by

$$x(K) = \text{Sat}_x\{ Q^{-1}(K)\lambda^*(K-1) \} \qquad (4.5.48)$$

The above so-called "time-delay algorithm" can be summarized as follows:

**Algorithm 4.4.**  Time-Delay Algorithm

*Step 1:* At level one, solve $K + 1$ analytic problems defined by (4.5.39)–(4.5.44) and (4.5.48) for a fixed set of Lagrange multipliers $\lambda(k) = \lambda^*(k)$, $k = 0, 1, \ldots, K - 1$.

Step 2: At level two, the value of $\lambda^*(k)$ is improved through a gradient-type iteration

$$\lambda^{*r+1}(k) = \lambda^{*r}(k) + \delta^r d^r(k) \qquad (4.5.49)$$

where $d^r(k)$ is a function of the error $e^r(k)$, i.e.,

$$d^r(k) = f(e^r(k))$$

$$= f\left\{\sum_{i=0}^{s} \left[ A_i x(k-i) + B_i x(k-i) \right] - x(k+1) \right\} \qquad (4.5.50)$$

which follows from our previous discussions, i.e., Equation (4.5.30).

The following example illustrates the time-delay algorithm.

**Example 4.5.2.** Consider a simple second-order system

$$\begin{bmatrix} x_1(k+1) \\ x_2(k+1) \end{bmatrix} = \begin{bmatrix} 2 & 0 \\ -1 & -1 \end{bmatrix} \begin{bmatrix} x_1(k) \\ x_2(k) \end{bmatrix} + \begin{bmatrix} 1 & 0 \\ 0 & 2 \end{bmatrix} \begin{bmatrix} x_1(k-1) \\ x_2(k-1) \end{bmatrix}$$

$$+ \begin{bmatrix} 0.5 & 0 \\ 1 & 0 \end{bmatrix} \begin{bmatrix} u_1(k) \\ u_2(k) \end{bmatrix} + \begin{bmatrix} 0 & 0.25 \\ 1 & 1 \end{bmatrix} \begin{bmatrix} u_1(k-1) \\ u_2(k-1) \end{bmatrix} \qquad (4.5.51)$$

with cost function

$$J = \frac{1}{2} x^T(5) Q(5) x(5) + \frac{1}{2} \sum_{k=0}^{4} \{ x^T(k) Q(k) x(k) + u^T(k) R(k) u(k) \}$$

$$(4.5.52)$$

constraints

$$\begin{bmatrix} 0 \\ 0 \end{bmatrix} \leqslant x(k) \leqslant \begin{bmatrix} 2 \\ 2 \end{bmatrix}, \quad \begin{bmatrix} -1 \\ -1 \end{bmatrix} \leqslant u(k) \leqslant \begin{bmatrix} 1 \\ 1 \end{bmatrix}, \quad x(0) = \begin{bmatrix} 0.5 \\ 0.5 \end{bmatrix} \qquad (4.5.53)$$

and $Q(5) = \text{diag}(1,2)$, $Q(k) = I_2$, and $R(k) = \text{diag}(1,0.5)$.

SOLUTION: The problem was solved for an error tolerance of 0.001, a step size of 0.1 for the conjugate gradient iteration, and $\lambda(0) = (0.1\ 0.1)^T$. The algorithm converged in 49 iterations, as shown in Figure 4.18. Several other initial $x(0)$ and $\lambda(0)$ were tried and the convergence was achieved in a similar fashion.

### 4.5.3 Interaction Prediction Approach

Consider the following linear discrete-time system in its state-space form,

$$x(k+1) = Ax(k) + Bu(k) + d(k), \quad x(0) = x_o \qquad (4.5.54)$$

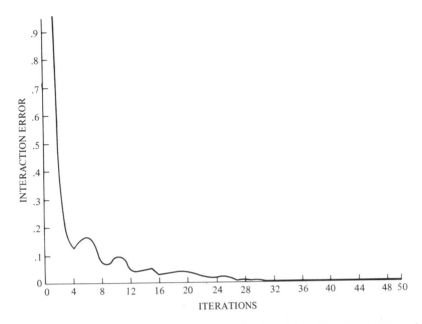

**Figure 4.18** Interaction error vs iterations for the time-delay algorithm in Example 4.5.2.

where $x(k)$, $u(k)$, and $d(k)$ are $n \times 1$, $m \times 1$, and $n \times 1$ state, control, and disturbance vectors, respectively. Let the system be decomposed into $N$ subsystems

$$x_i(k+1) = A_i x_i(k) + B_i u_i(k) + C_i z_i(k) + d_i(k), \quad x_i(0) = x_{io} \tag{4.5.55}$$

for $i = 1, \ldots, N$ and $x_i$, $u_i$, and $d_i$ are $n_i \times 1$, $m_i \times 1$, and $n_i \times 1$ state, control, and disturbance vectors of the $i$th subsystem, respectively. The vector $z_i(k)$, to be defined shortly, represents the interactions between the $i$th subsystem and the remaining $(N-1)$ subsystems. The matrices $A_i$, $B_i$, and $C_i$ are, respectively, $n_i \times n_i$, $n_i \times m_i$, and $n_i \times r_i$. The integer $r_i$ represents the number of incoming interactions to the $i$th subsystem. The optimal control problem can be stated as follows:

$$\max_{u_i, x_i} \left\{ J = \sum_{i=1}^{N} \sum_{k=1}^{N_f} q_i(u_i(k), x_i(k)) \triangleq \sum_{i=1}^{n} J_i(u_i, x_i) \right\} \tag{4.5.56}$$

subject to (4.5.55),

$$\underline{x}_i(k) \leqslant x_i(k) \leqslant \bar{x}_i(k), \quad \underline{u}_i(k) \leqslant u_i(k) \leqslant \bar{u}_i(k) \tag{4.5.57}$$

and

$$z_i(k) = \sum_{j=1}^{N} \left\{ D_{ij} u_j(k) + G_{ij} x_j(k) \right\} \qquad (4.5.58)$$

where $D_{ij}$ and $G_{ij}$ are the appropriate matrices between control $u_j(k)$, state $x_j(k)$, and the state $x_i(k+1)$, respectively.

Two solutions of the above optimization problem and its modified forms have already been presented. One is based on the time-delay algorithm due to Tamura (1975), which was discussed in the previous section. The other was discussed in Section 4.5.1 without the bounds (4.5.57) and utilizing the three-level discrete-time application of goal coordination. However, instead of utilizing those methods, the continuous-time interaction prediction method of Section 4.4.1 is extended to discrete-time, which has not received much attention in literature. Here again, we will ignore the bounds (4.5.57) for the time being. Moreover, the objective function (4.5.56) is assumed to be quadratic:

$$J_i = \frac{1}{2} \sum_{k=0}^{N_f - 1} \left\{ x_i^T(k) Q_i x_i(k) + u_i^T(k) R_i u_i(k) \right\} \qquad (4.5.59)$$

where weighting matrices $Q_i$ and $R_i$ follow the usual regulatory conditions. Consider the Lagrangian of the problem (4.5.55), (4.5.58)–(4.5.59):

$$\begin{aligned}
L = \sum_{i=1}^{N} L_i = \sum_{i=1}^{N} \Bigg\{ & \sum_{k=0}^{N_f - 1} \Bigg\{ \frac{1}{2} x_i^T(k) Q_i x_i(k) + \tfrac{1}{2} u_i^T(k) R_i u_i(k) + \lambda_i^T(k) z_i(k) \\
& - \sum_{j=1}^{N} \lambda_j^T(k) \left( D_{ji} u_j(k) + G_{ji} x_j(k) \right) \\
& + p_i^T(k+1) \left[ -x_i(k+1) + A_i x_i(k) + B_i u_i(k) + C_i z_i(k) + d_i(k) \right] \Bigg\} \Bigg\}
\end{aligned}$$

$$(4.5.60)$$

Here it is assumed that the Lagrangian $L$ is additively separable for $z_i$ and $\lambda_i$ trajectories. This would imply that for any given $z_i$ and $\lambda_i$, there are $N$ independent maximization problems, each with a sub-Lagrangian $L_i$. What is left is to find a mechanism for updating $z_i$ and $\lambda_i$. A necessary condition for this is

$$\partial L / \partial z_i = 0, \quad \partial L / \partial \lambda_i = 0 \qquad (4.5.61)$$

which result in

$$\lambda_i(k) + C_i^T p_i(k+1) = 0 \qquad (4.5.62)$$

$$z_i(k) - \sum_{j=1}^{N} \left( D_{ij} u_j(k) + G_{ij} x_j(k) \right) = 0 \qquad (4.5.63)$$

The coordination at the second level for this interaction prediction scheme would be

$$
\begin{bmatrix} \lambda_i(k) \\ z_i(k) \end{bmatrix}^{l+1} = \begin{bmatrix} -C_i^T p_i(k+1) \\ \sum_{j=1}^{N} \{ D_{ij} u_j(k) + G_{ij} x_j(k) \} \end{bmatrix}^{l} \tag{4.5.64}
$$

for $k = 1, 2, \ldots, N_f$, and $l$ is the iteration number. Here again it is noted that the computational effort at the second level is very small compared with that of the gradient, Newton, or conjugate gradient techniques.

For a known set of augmented interaction vectors $\left[ \lambda^{*T}(k) \mid z^{*T}(k) \right]$, the $i$th subsystem Hamiltonian is

$$
H_i(\cdot) = \tfrac{1}{2} x_i^T(k) Q_i x_i(k) + \tfrac{1}{2} u_i^T(k) R_i u_i(k)
$$

$$
+ \lambda_i^T(k) z_i(k) - \sum_{j=1}^{N} \lambda_j^T(k) \left( D_{ji} u_i(k) + G_{ji} x_j(k) \right)
$$

$$
+ p_i^T(k+1) \left[ A_i x_i(k) + B_i u_i(k) + C_i z_i(k) \right] \tag{4.5.65}
$$

Then the necessary conditions for optimality would lead to

$$
p_i(k) = \partial H_i(\cdot) / \partial x_i(k) = Q_i x_i(k) + A_i^T p_i(k+1)
$$

$$
- \sum_{j=1}^{N} \left( \lambda_j^T(k) G_{ji} \right)^T, \quad p_i(N_f) = 0 \tag{4.5.66}
$$

and

$$
0 = \partial H_i(\cdot) / \partial u_i(k) = R_i u_i(k) + B_i^T p_i(k+1) - \sum_{j=1}^{N} \left( \lambda_j^T(k) D_{ji} \right)^T \tag{4.5.67}
$$

or

$$
u_i(k) = - R_i^{-1} B_i^T p_i(k+1) + R_i^{-1} e_i(k) \tag{4.5.68}
$$

where

$$
e_i(k) = \sum_{j=1}^{N} \left( \lambda_j^T(k) D_{ji} \right)^T
$$

Let us assume that the costate $p_i(k)$ and state $x_i(k)$ are related by a linear vector equation

$$
p_i(k) = K_i(k) x_i(k) + g_i(k) \tag{4.5.69}
$$

Now eliminating $p_i(k)$ in (4.5.68), solving for $x_i(k+1)$, and substituting it in (4.5.66) while utilizing (4.5.69) and equating the coefficients of $x_i(k)$ and zeroeth-order terms would lead to the following Riccati and adjoint equations:

$$K_i(k) = Q_i + A_i^T K_i(k+1) E_i^{-1}(k) A_i, \quad K_i(N_f) = 0 \tag{4.5.70}$$

$$g_i(k) = A_i^T \left[ I - K_i(k+1) E_i^{-1}(k) F_i \right] g_i(k+1) - h_i(k), \quad g_i(N_f) = 0 \tag{4.5.71}$$

where

$$E_i(k) = I + F_i K_i(k+1)$$

$$F_i = B_i R_i^{-1} B_i^T$$

$$h_i(k) = A_i^T K_i(k+1) b_i(k) + f_i(k)$$

$$b_i(k) = E_i^{-1}(k) \left[ R_i^{-1} e_i(k) + C_i z_i(k) + d_i(k) \right] \tag{4.5.72}$$

$$f_i(k) = \sum_{j=1}^{N} \left( \lambda_j^T(k) G_{ji} \right)^T$$

Recalling the bounds (4.5.57), the expressions for $u_i(k)$ in (4.5.68) and $x_i(k+1)$ in (4.5.55) after eliminating $p_i(k+1)$ via (4.5.69), the following expressions are suggested for control and state vectors:

$$u_i(k) = \begin{cases} \underline{u}_i(k) & u_i(k) < \underline{u}_i(k) \\ -R_i^{-1} G_i(k) & \underline{u}_i(k) \leqslant u_i(k) \leqslant \bar{u}_i(k) \\ \bar{u}_i(k) & u_i(k) > \bar{u}_i(k) \end{cases} \tag{4.5.73}$$

where

$$G_i(k) = B_i^T \left[ K_i(k+1) x_i(k+1) + g_i(k+1) \right] - e_i(k) \tag{4.5.74}$$

and

$$x_i(k+1) = \begin{cases} \underline{x}_i(k+1) \cdots x_i(k+1) < \underline{x}_i(k+1) \\ L_i(k) x_i(k) + M_i(k) g_i(k+1) - b_i(k) \cdots x_i(k-1) \\ \quad\quad \leqslant x_i(k+1) \leqslant \bar{x}_i(k+1) \\ \bar{x}_i(k+1) \cdots x_i(k+1) > \bar{x}_i(k+1) \end{cases}$$

$$\tag{4.5.75}$$

where

$$L_i(k) = E_i^{-1}(k) A_i, \quad M_i(k) = E_i^{-1}(k) F_i \tag{4.5.76}$$

The discrete-time interaction prediction approach is summarized by the following algorithm.

**Algorithm 4.5.** Interaction Prediction Approach for Discrete-Time Systems

*Step 1:* At the second level set $l = 1$, assume initial values for $z_i(k) = z_i^*(k)$ and $\lambda_i(k) = \lambda_i^*(k)$, and pass them down to first level, $i = 1, \ldots, N$ and $k = 1, \ldots, N_f$.

*Step 2:* At the first level solve $N$ matrix Riccati equations (4.5.70) and store.

*Step 3:* Solve $N$ adjoint equations (4.5.71) and store for $k = 1, \ldots, N_f$.

*Step 4:* Using the stored values of $K_i(k)$, $g_i(k)$, (4.5.73)–(4.5.76), find and store $u_i(k)$ and $x_i(k)$, $i = 1, \ldots, N$ and $k = 1, \ldots, N_f$.

*Step 5:* Check for the convergence of (4.5.62)–(4.5.63) i.e., whether their left-hand sides are within $\varepsilon = 10^{-6}$ of zero. If not, use (4.5.64) to update $\lambda_i(k)$ and $z_i(k)$, increment $l = l + 1$, and go to Step 3.

*Step 6:* Stop.

An application of this algorithm is given in Example 4.5.3.


### 4.5.4 Structural Perturbation Approach

In this section the optimal hierarchical control scheme via structural perturbation of Section 4.4.2 for continuous-time systems is extended for discrete-time systems. For the sake of discussion, the discrete quantities are represented by index $i$ in a subscripted form and the subsystems by index $j$ in a superscripted form; e.g., $x_i^j$ represents the $j$th subsystem's state at $i$th interval. The present development, in part, follows the work of Sundareshan (1976).

Consider a large-scale discrete-time system which may consist of $M$ subsystems:

$$x_{i+1}^j = A_j x_i^j + B_j u_i^j + \sum_{k=1}^{M} G_{jk} x_i^k, \quad x_o^j = \xi_o^j \qquad (4.5.77)$$

for $j = 1, 2, \ldots, M$ and $i = 1, 2, \ldots, N$. In the above relation, $x_i^j$ and $u_i^j$ are $n_i$- and $m_i$-dimensional state and control vectors of the $j$th subsystem at $i$th interval. The $G_{jk}$ is the $n_j \times n_k$ interconnection matrix between the $j$th and $k$th subsystems. The relations of $A_j$, $B_j$, and $G_{jk}$ matrices are given below:

$$\begin{bmatrix} A_1 & G_{12} & & \\ G_{21} & A_2 & G_{23} & \\ & & \ddots & \\ & & & A_M \end{bmatrix}, \quad B = \begin{bmatrix} B_1 & & \\ & B_2 & \\ & & \ddots & \\ & & & B_M \end{bmatrix}$$

$$(4.5.78)$$

The optimal control problem would be to find control vectors $u_i^j$, $j = 1, 2, \ldots, M$, such that (4.5.77)–(4.5.78) are satisfied while minimizing a quadratic cost function

$$J^j\left(x_o^j, u_o^j\right) = \sum_{i=1}^{N} \left(x_i^{jT} Q_j x_i^j + u_{i-1}^{jT} R_j u_{i-1}^i\right) \tag{4.5.79}$$

where $Q_j$ and $R_j$ are $n_i \times n_i$ and $m_i \times m_i$ positive-semidefinite and positive-definite matrices, respectively. The optimal control problem, in its large-scale composite form, is to find an $m$-dimensional control $u^T = (u^{1T}, \ldots, u^{MT})$ which would satisfy the overall state equation

$$x_{i+1} = (A + G)x_i + Bu_i \tag{4.5.80}$$

where $A =$ Block-diag$(A_1, A_2, \ldots, A_M)$, $B =$ Block-diag$(B_1, B_2, \ldots, B_M)$, and $G = [G_{jk}]$, $j, k = 1, 2, \ldots, M$, while the cost

$$J(x_o, u_o) = \sum_{j=1}^{M} J^j\left(x_o^j, u_o^j\right) \tag{4.5.81}$$

is minimized. The solution of this problem requires the solution of a large-order Riccati equation (Dorato and Levis, 1971), and a single central controller would become necessary which may require too much, and often unnecessary or unavailable, information from all the states. In order to alleviate these problems, Sundareshan (1976) has proposed a hierarchical control which consists of a local and a global component, i.e.,

$$u_i = u_i^l + u_i^g \tag{4.5.82}$$

where the local control is given by

$$u_i^l = \left\{u_i^{1T}, u_i^{2T}, \ldots, u_i^{MT}\right\} \tag{4.5.83}$$

and each component $u_i^j$ is the optimal control of the $j$th decoupled subsystem problem defined by (4.5.77)–(4.5.78) and (4.5.79) which is obtained through a Riccati formulation as in (4.5.65)–(4.5.72). The $j$th subsystem local control is given by

$$u_i^j = - P_i^j x_i^j \tag{4.5.84}$$

where $P_i^j = - R_j^{-1} B_j^T K_{i+1}^j (I + S_j K_{i+1}^j)^{-1} A_j$ and $K_i^j$ is the positive-definite solution of the discrete matrix Riccati equation:

$$K_i^j = Q_j + A_j^T K_{i+1}^j \left(I + S_j K_{i+1}^j\right)^{-1} A_j, \quad K_N = 0 \tag{4.5.85}$$

where $S_j = B_j R_j^{-1} B_j^T$ and all other matrices are defined by (4.5.77)–(4.5.79). The global component $u_i^g$ is given by

$$u_i^g = - \Gamma x_i \tag{4.5.86}$$

where $\Gamma$ is an $m \times n$ gain matrix yet to be determined. Using the local and global controls defined by (4.5.84) and (4.5.86), the closed-loop composite system becomes

$$x_{i+1} = (A - BP_i)x_i + (G - B\Gamma)x_i \tag{4.5.87}$$

where $P_i = \text{Block-diag}(P_i^1, P_i^2, \ldots, P_i^M)$ and the term $(G - B\Gamma)$ is termed as the effective interconnection matrix $G_e$. The matrix $\Gamma$ should be chosen such that the norm $\|G - B\Gamma\|$ is minimized. The solution to this minimization problem is well known:

$$\Gamma = B^+ G \qquad (4.5.88)$$

where $B^+$ is the generalized inverse, i.e., $B^+ = (B^TB)^{-1}B^T$. The solution (4.5.88) is subject to the rank condition, $\text{rank}(B) = \text{rank}(BG)$. Thus, the global control component gain matrix is obtained from

$$\Gamma = (B^TB)^{-1}B^TG \qquad (4.5.89)$$

The above choice would in effect neutralize the interconnections, i.e., $\|G_e\| = 0$. The application of this hierarchical control to the large-scale interconnected discrete-time system would, in general, cause a deterioration of performance whose suboptimality degree is $\rho$ if the following inequality holds (Sundareshan, 1976):

$$\|G\| + \|L\| \leqslant \{\|L\|^2 + \rho\lambda_m(V)/\lambda_M(H_{i+1})\}^{1/2} \qquad (4.5.90)$$

where

$$L = [A_j - B_jP_j], \quad j = 1, 2, \ldots, M, \quad V = \text{Block-diag}(V_1, \ldots, V_M)$$
$$V_j = L_j^TQ_jL_j + P_i^{jT}R_jP_i^j, \quad H_i = (1+\rho)K_i + Q \qquad (4.5.91)$$

The terms $\lambda_m(D)$ and $\lambda_M(D)$ are, respectively, the minimum and maximum eigenvalues of matrix $D$. This control scheme is summarized by an algorithm.

*Algorithm 4.6.* Structural Perturbation Approach for Discrete-Time Systems

*Step 1:* Input all matrices $\{A_j, B_j, Q_j, R_j, G_{jk}\}$, initial states $x_o^j$, etc., $j = 1, \ldots, M$.

*Step 2:* For each subsystem $j$, solve (4.5.85) for Riccati matrix $K_i^j$, $i = 1, \ldots, N-1$, and store.

*Step 3:* Evaluate the local control components by solving (4.5.84).

*Step 4:* Solve (4.5.89) and use (4.5.86) for the global control component and form the overall control (4.5.82).

*Step 5:* Using the control $u$ and Equation (4.5.80), find state $x_i$, $i = 1, 2, \ldots, N$.

In sequel, Algorithms 4.5 (interaction prediction) and 4.6 (structural perturbation) are applied to a three-region energy resources system.

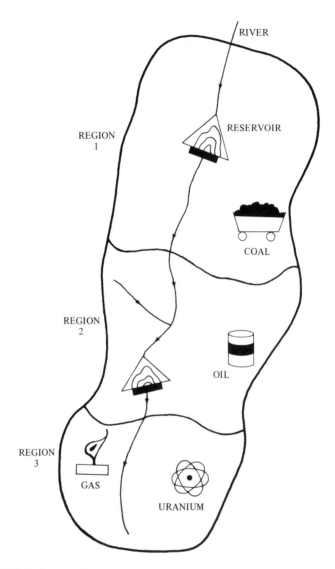

**Figure 4.19** A three-region energy resources system.

**Example 4.5.3.** Consider a three-region energy resources system shown in Figure 4.19. For this system, let the following discrete-time model hold:

$$x_{i+1} = \begin{bmatrix} A_1 & | & G_{12} & | & 0 \\ -- & | & -- & | & -- \\ G_{21} & | & A_2 & | & 0 \\ -- & + & -- & + & -- \\ 0 & | & 0 & | & A_3 \end{bmatrix} x_i + \begin{bmatrix} B_1 & | & 0 & | & 0 \\ -- & | & -- & | & -- \\ 0 & | & B_2 & | & 0 \\ -- & | & -- & + & -- \\ 0 & | & 0 & | & B_3 \end{bmatrix} u_i$$

where

$$\{A_1, B_1\} = \left\{ \begin{bmatrix} 1 & 1 & 1 \\ 0 & 0.5 & 0.75 \\ 0.75 & 0.5 & 1 \end{bmatrix}, \begin{bmatrix} 1 \\ 0 \\ 1 \end{bmatrix} \right\}$$

$$\{A_2, B_2\} = \left\{ \begin{bmatrix} 1 & 0.5 & 0.25 & 0 \\ 0 & 0.5 & 0 & 0.2 \\ 0.5 & 0 & 0.5 & 0.25 \\ 0 & 0.2 & 0.25 & 0.25 \end{bmatrix}, \begin{bmatrix} 0 \\ 1 \\ 1 \\ 0 \end{bmatrix} \right\} \qquad (4.5.92)$$

$$\{A_3, B_3\} = \left\{ \begin{bmatrix} 1 & 0.5 & 0.2 \\ 0.5 & 0.25 & 0.2 \\ 0.3 & 0.2 & 0.5 \end{bmatrix}, \begin{bmatrix} 0 \\ 1 \\ 1 \end{bmatrix} \right\}$$

$$G_{12} = \begin{bmatrix} 0 & 0 & 0 & 0 \\ 0 & 0.5 & 0 & 0 \\ 1.5 & 0 & 0 & 0 \end{bmatrix}, \quad G_{21} = \begin{bmatrix} 0 & 0 & 1 \\ 0 & 0.5 & 0 \\ 0 & 0 & 0 \\ 0 & 0 & 0 \end{bmatrix}$$

The quadratic cost function has weighting matrices $Q_1 = \text{diag}(1\ 10\ 1)$, $Q_2 = 5I_4$, $Q_3 = \text{diag}(10\ 1\ 10)$, and $R_j = 1$, $j = 1, 2, 3$. It is desired to apply Algorithms 4.5 and 4.6 to find a hierarchical allocation policy for the energy-resources system of (4.5.92).

SOLUTION: For the hierarchical control policies, three matrix Riccati equations of the form in (4.5.70) or (4.5.85) and three adjoint vector equations of the form in (4.5.71) were solved using an HP-9845 computer and BASIC. Based on the solutions of these and vector equations, three local control functions were obtained. Using the interation prediction method, an acceptable (within $10^{-4}$) convergence was reached with nine iterations. Using the structural perturbation method, Equation (4.5.89) was used to obtain the global control component and added to the vector of local controls to find the overall control (4.5.82). The resulting states and control function via the hierarchical control Algorithms 4.5 and 4.6 along with the optimum centralized trajectories which were obtained by solving a tenth-order discrete-time Riccati equation are shown in Figures 4.20 and 4.21, respectively.

The state and control responses for the interaction prediction (Algorithm 4.5) were closer to the optimum than those for the structural perturbation (Algorithm 4.6). However, the third subsystem's trajectories were closer than the other two. A reason for this may be the fact that the third subsystem is completely decoupled.

### 4.5.5 Costate Prediction Approach

In this section a computationally effective approach for hierarchical control of nonlinear discrete-time systems due to Mahmoud et al. (1977), Hassan and Singh (1976, 1977) is presented. The scheme is applied to nonlinear

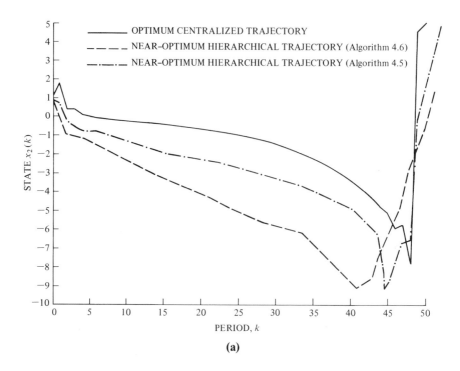

**(a)**

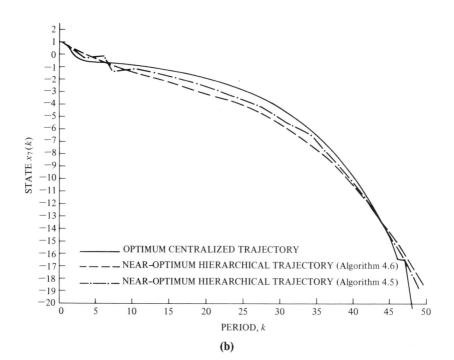

**(b)**

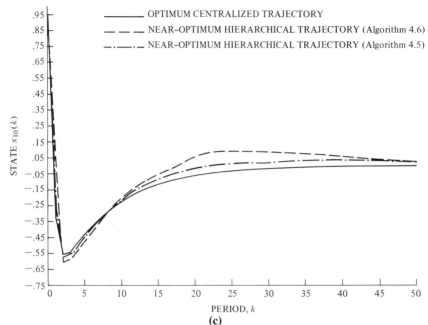

Figure 4.20 Optimum centralized and near-optimum hierarchical trajectories for Example 4.5.3: (a) state $x_2(t)$, (b) state $x_7(t)$, (c) state $x_{10}(t)$.

systems, and its linear extension is rather simple (see Problem 4.8). The hierarchical control of nonlinear continuous-time systems is considered in Chapter 6 (Section 6.3.1.) under the context of near-optimum design of large-scale systems.

Consider a nonlinear discrete-time system described by

$$x(k+1) = f(x, u, (k+1, k)), \quad x(0) = x_o \qquad (4.5.93)$$

with a quadratic cost function

$$J = \frac{1}{2} \sum_{k=0}^{K-1} \left( x^T(k)Qx(k) + u^T(k)Ru(k) \right) \qquad (4.5.94)$$

The procedure begins by rewriting the nonlinear state equation (4.5.93) as

$$x(k+1) = A(x, u, (k+1, k))x(k) + B(x, u, (k+1, k))u(k)$$
$$+ c(x, u, (k+1, k)) \qquad (4.5.95)$$

where $A(\cdot)$, $B(\cdot)$ are block diagonal matrices and

$$c(x, u, (k+1, k)) = C_1(x, u, (k+1, k))x(k) + C_2(x, u, (k+1, k))u(k)$$
$$(4.5.96)$$

It is noted that the reformulation (4.5.95)–(4.5.96) of the system (4.5.93) is

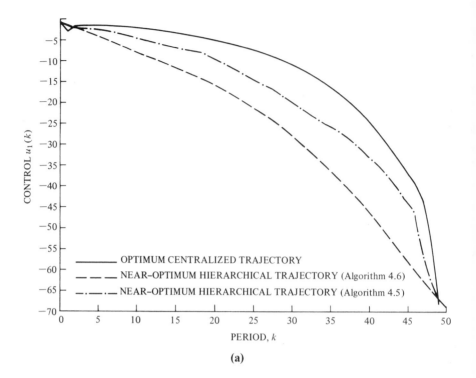

**(a)**

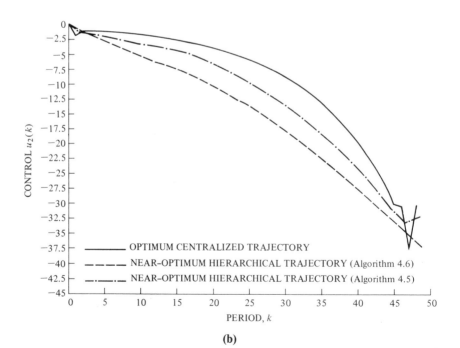

**(b)**

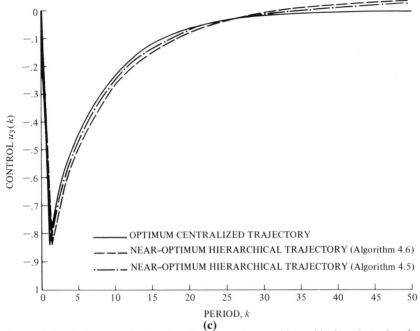

**Figure 4.21** Optimal centralized and near-optimum hierarchical trajectories for Example 4.5.3: (a) control $u_1(t)$, (b) control $u_2(t)$, (c) control $u_3(t)$.

always possible. Moreover, for $N$ blocks in $A$ and $B$, it is assumed that matrices $Q$ and $R$ also have $N$ blocks. The basic reason for the reformulation (4.5.95)–(4.5.96) is to provide "predicted" state and control vectors $x^*$ and $u^*$ to fix the arguments in the nonlinear coefficient matrices $A(\cdot)$, $B(\cdot)$, $C_1(\cdot)$, and $C_2(\cdot)$. Therefore, the problem (4.5.93)–(4.5.96) can be rewritten as

$$\min \tilde{J} = \frac{1}{2} \sum_{k=0}^{K-1} \left( x^T(k)Qx(k) + u^T(k)Ru(k) \right) \qquad (4.5.97)$$

subject to

$$x(k+1) = A(x^*, u^*, (k+1, k))x(k) + B(x^*, u^*, (k+1, k))u(k)$$
$$+ c(x^*, u^*, (k+1, k)) \qquad (4.5.98)$$
$$x^*(k) = x(k), \quad u^*(k) = u(k) \qquad (4.5.99)$$

The modified problem can be solved by defining a Hamiltonian:

$$H(\cdot) = \tfrac{1}{2}x^T(k)Qx(k) + \tfrac{1}{2}u^T(k)Ru(k)$$
$$+ p^T(k+1)\{A(x^*, u^*, (k+1, k))x(k)$$
$$+ B(x^*, u^*, (k+1, k))u(k) + c(x^*, u^*, (k+1, k))\}$$
$$+ \alpha^T(k)(x(k) - x^*(k)) + \beta^T(k)(u(k) - u^*(k)) \qquad (4.5.100)$$

In view of the assumptions made on matrices $A$, $B$, $C_1$, $C_2$, $Q$, and $R$, it is clear that the Hamiltonian $H(\cdot)$ in (4.5.100) is additively separable for given $x^*$ and $u^*$, i.e.,

$$H = \sum_{i=1}^{N} H_i = \sum_{i=1}^{N} \left\{ \frac{1}{2} x_i^T(k) Q x_i(k) + \frac{1}{2} u_i^T(k) R u_i(k) \right.$$
$$+ p_i^T(k+1)[A_i(\cdot)x_i(k) + B_i(\cdot)u_i(k)] + c_i(\cdot)\}$$
$$\left. + \alpha_i^T(k)[x_i(k) - x_i^*(k)] + \beta_i^T(k)[u_i(k) - u_i^*(k)] \right\} \quad (4.5.101)$$

The necessary conditions for optimality are given by

$$0 = \partial H_i / \partial u_i \tag{4.5.102}$$
$$x_i(k+1) = \partial H_i / \partial p_i(k+1) \tag{4.5.103}$$
$$p_i(k) = \partial H_i / \partial x_i(k) \tag{4.5.104}$$
$$0 = \partial H / \partial \alpha, \quad 0 = \partial H / \partial \beta \tag{4.5.105}$$
$$0 = \partial H / \partial x^*(k), \quad 0 = \partial H / \partial u^*(k) \tag{4.5.106}$$

Relation (4.5.102) yields an expression for $u_i(k)$,

$$u_i(k) = -R_i^{-1}\{B_i^T(x^*, u^*, (k+1, k)) p_i(k+1) + \beta_i(k)\} \tag{4.5.107}$$

and substituting $u_i(k)$ in Equation (4.5.103) yields a new expression for $x_i(k+1)$, i.e.,

$$x_i(k+1) = A_i(x^*, u^*, (k+1, k))x_i(k) - B_i(x^*, u^*, (k+1, k))$$
$$R_i^{-1}\{B_i^T(x^*, u^*, (k+1, k)) p_i^T(k+1) + \beta_i(k)\} + c_i(x^*, u^*, (k+1, k))$$
$$\tag{4.5.108}$$

with $x_i(0) = x_{io}$. The condition (4.5.104) gives the costate equation

$$p_i(k) = Q_i x_i(k) + A_i^T(x^*, u^*, (k+1, k)) p_i(k+1) + \alpha_i(k), \quad p_i(K) = 0 \tag{4.5.109}$$

and the necessary conditions (4.5.105) lead to the equality constraints (4.5.99), i.e.,

$$x^*(k) = x(k), \quad u^*(k) = u(k) \tag{4.5.110}$$

The first of the two conditions in (4.5.106) leads to an expression for $\alpha(k)$, i.e.,

$$\alpha(k) = \{F_x^T(x^*, u^*, x, (k+1, k)) + G_x^T(x^*, u^*, u, (k+1, k))$$
$$+ D_x^T(x^*, u^*, (k+1, k))\} p(k+1) \tag{4.5.111}$$

where

$$F_x(\cdot) = \partial z(\cdot)/\partial x^* \triangleq \partial\{A(x^*, u^*, (k+1,k))x(k)\}/\partial x^*$$
$$G_x(\cdot) = \partial y(\cdot)/\partial x^* \triangleq \partial\{B(x^*, u^*, (k+1,k))u(k)\}/\partial x^* \quad (4.5.112)$$
$$D_x(\cdot) = \partial c(x^*, u^*, (k+1,k))/\partial x^*$$

Finally, in order to obtain an expression for $\beta(k)$, the second condition in (4.5.106) yields

$$\beta(k) = \{F_u^T(x^*, u^*, x, (k+1,k)) + G_u^T(x^*, u^*, u, (k+1,k))$$
$$+ D_u^T(x^*, u^*, (k+1,k))\}p(k+1) \quad (4.5.113)$$

where $F_u(\cdot)$, $G_u(\cdot)$, and $D_u(\cdot)$ are derivatives of the expressions in the brackets of (4.5.112) with respect to $u^*$. The following algorithm summarizes the costate prediction method.

*Algorithm 4.7.* Costate Prediction Approach

*Step 1:* Set iteration index $l = 1$ and guess vectors $p^1$, $x^{*1}$, $u^{*1}$, and $\beta^1$.

*Step 2:* At the first-level, substitute $p^l(k)$, $x^{*l}(k)$, $u^{*l}(k)$, and $\beta^l(k)$, $k = 0,\dots,K-1$, in (4.5.107)–(4.5.108) to obtain $u_i^l(k)$ and $x_i^l(k)$ for $i = 1,2,\dots,N$. Similarly, use (4.5.111) to find $\alpha^l(k)$.

*Step 3:* At the second-level, use $x_i^l(k)$, $u_i^l(k)$, and (4.5.109)–(4.5.113) to update coordination vector, $q^l = (p_i^l, x^{*l}, u^{*l}, \beta^l)$, i.e.,

$$p_i^{l+1}(k) = Q_i x_i^l(k) + A_i^T(x^*, u^*, (k+1,k))p_i^{l+1}(k+1) + \alpha_i^l(k)$$

$$x^{*l+1}(k) = x^l(k)$$

$$u^{*l+1}(k) = u^l(k) \quad (4.5.114)$$

$$\beta^{l+1}(k) = \left\{ F_u^T(\cdot)\big|_{(x^{*l}, u^{*l}, x^l)} + G_u^T(\cdot)\big|_{(x^{*l}, u^{*l}, u^l)} + D_u^T(\cdot)\big|_{(x^{*l}, u^{*l})} \right\}$$
$$\times p(k+1)$$

*Step 4:* If $q^{l+1}(k) = q^l(k)$ for $k = 0,1,\dots,K-1$, stop and $u^{l+1}(k)$ is the optimal control. Otherwise go to Step 2.

Before this algorithm is illustrated by a numerical example, a few comments on the costate-prediction method are due. First, since the costate vector $p^l(k)$ is a component of the coordination vector $q^l(k)$, the first-level problem (Step 2) involves simple substitution and does not require the solution of a TPBV problem or even a Riccati equation. Moreover, the second-level problem (Step 3) is also rather trivial, requiring the substitution of $x$, $u$, and $\beta$ vectors which have been obtained from the previous iteration. Therefore, unlike the other multilevel formulations, such as the goal coordination and interaction prediction approaches, both the first- and second-level problems are mere substitution problems. The only question remaining is the nature of and/or conditions for the convergence of costate prediction. Hassan and Singh (1981) and Singh (1980) have proved theorems by which an open interval of time is obtained to guarantee convergence of the algorithm for the continuous-time case (see Problem 4.12). Similarly for the discrete-time case, Hassan and Singh (1976) in an unpublished report have given some conditions for the convergence. They have shown that Algorithm 4.7 converges uniformly over an interval $(0, K-1)$ if the following conditions hold: (i) $g$, $y$, $z$, and $C$ are bounded functions of $k$; and (ii) $z$, $y$, and $c$ in (4.5.112) are differentiable with respect to $x^*$ and $u^*$ for each $0 \leqslant k \leqslant K-1$ and their derivatives are also bounded functions of $k$ (Singh and Titli, 1978). Further discussion on costate coordination is given in Section 4.6.

The following example deals with an open-loop power system consisting of a synchronous machine connected to an infinite bus through a transformer and a transmission line. This system, in continuous-time form, is treated in detail in Section 6.3 and has been treated by many authors (Mukhopadhyay and Malik, 1973; Jamshidi, 1975; Hassan and Singh, 1977). For the sake of the present discussion, a discrete-time formulation of the original continuous-time model (Iyer and Cory, 1971) considered by Singh and Titli (1978) is used.

**Example 4.5.4.** Consider a sixth-order nonlinear discrete-time model of the open-loop synchronous machine system:

$$x_1(k+1) = x_1(k) + 0.05x_2(k)$$

$$x_2(k+1) = (1-0.05c_1)x_2(k) - 0.05c_2x_3(k)\sin x_1(k)$$
$$\qquad -0.025c_3\sin 2x_1(k) + (0.05/M)x_5(k)$$

$$x_3(k+1) = (1-0.05c_4)x_3(k) + 0.05x_6(k) + 0.05c_5\cos x_1(k) \qquad (4.5.115)$$

$$x_4(k+1) = (1-0.05K_3)x_4(k) + 0.05K_2x_2(k) + 0.05K_1u_1(k)$$

$$x_5(k+1) = (1-0.05K_5)x_5(k) + 0.05K_4x_4(k)$$

$$x_6(k+1) = (1-0.05K_7)x_6(k) + 0.05K_6u_2(k)$$

where $(c_1, c_2, c_3, c_4, c_5) = (2.1656, 13.997, -55.565, 1.03, 4.049)$, $(K_1, K_2,\ldots, K_7) = (9.4429, 1.0198, 5, 2.0408, 2.0408, 1.5, 0.5)$ and $M = 1$. Apply the costate prediction approach of Algorithm 4.7 to satisfy (4.5.115) starting with an initial state $x^T(0) = (0.7105\ 0.0\ 4.2\ 0.8\ 0.8\ 0.5)$ while minimizing a quadratic cost function

$$J = \frac{1}{2}\sum_{k=0}^{39}\left\{Q_{11}\left(x_1(k) - x_{f1}\right)^2 + Q_{33}\left(x_3(k) - x_{f3}\right)^2\right.$$
$$\left. + R_{11}\left(u_1(k) - u_{f1}\right)^2 + R_{22}\left(u_2(k) - u_{f2}\right)^2\right\} \qquad (4.5.116)$$

where $Q_{11} = Q_{33} = 0.2$ and $R_{11} = R_{22} = 1$.

SOLUTION: In order to apply Algorithm 4.7, system (4.5.115) must be reformulated in the form of Equation (4.5.98), i.e.,

$$x_1(k+1) = x_1(k) + 0.05x_2^*(k)$$
$$x_2(k+1) = (1-0.05c_1)x_2(k) - 0.05c_2x_3^*(k)\sin x_1^*(k)$$
$$\qquad - 0.025c_3\sin 2x_1^*(k) + (0.05/M)x_5^*(k)$$
$$x_3(x+1) = (1-0.05c_4)x_3(k) + 0.05x_6^*(k) + 0.05c_5\cos x_1^*(k) \qquad (4.5.117)$$
$$x_4(k+1) = (1-0.05K_3)x_4(k) + 0.05K_2x_2^*(k) + 0.05K_1u_1(k)$$
$$x_5(k+1) = (1-0.05K_5)x_5(k) + 0.05K_4x_4^*(k)$$
$$x_6(k+1) = (1-0.05K_7)x_6(k) + 0.05K_6u_2(k)$$

Additional equality constraints are

$$x_1^*(k) = x_i(k), \quad i=1,\ldots,6 \qquad (4.5.118)$$

This problem was simulated on an HP-9845 computer using BASIC. The necessary conditions of optimality through the Hamiltonian formulation leads to the following control, costate, and $\beta(k)$ vector equations:

$$u_1(k) = u_{f1} - 0.05K_1 p_4(k+1)$$
$$u_2(k) = u_{f2} - 0.05K_6 p_6(k+1) \qquad (4.5.119)$$

$$p_1(k) = 0.2(x_1(k) - x_{f1}) + p_1(k+1) + \alpha_1(k)$$
$$p_2(k) = (1-0.05c_1)p_2(k+1) + \alpha_2(k)$$
$$p_3(k) = 0.2(x_3(k) - x_{f3}) + p_3(k+1)(1-0.05c_4) + \alpha_3(k)$$
$$p_4(k) = (1-0.05K_3)p_4(k+1) + \alpha_4(k) \qquad (4.5.120)$$
$$p_5(k) = (1-0.05K_5)p_5(k+1) + \alpha_5(k)$$
$$p_6(k) = (1-0.05K_7)p_6(k+1) + \alpha_6(k)$$

with $p_i(K) = 0$, $i=1,\ldots,6$, and

$$\alpha_1(k) = -0.05c_2 p_2(k+1)x_3^*(k)\cos x_1^*(k) - 0.05c_3 p_2(k+1)$$
$$\qquad \cdot \cos 2x_1^*(k) - 0.05c_5 p_3(k+1)\sin x_1^*(k)$$
$$\alpha_2(k) = 0.05(p_1(k+1) - K_2 p_4(k+1))$$
$$\alpha_3(k) = -0.05c_2 p_2(k+1)\sin x_1^*(k) \qquad (4.5.121)$$
$$\alpha_4(k) = 0.05K_4 p_5(k+1) \qquad (4.5.121)$$
$$\alpha_5(k) = (0.05/M)p_2(k+1)$$
$$\alpha_6(k) = 0.05p_3(k+1)$$

In order to compare the results of this algorithm to those reported earlier (Hassan and Singh, 1977), the same values of parameters and initial values were chosen. Here $p(k) = x^*(k) = 0$ was chosen, and the algorithm converged in 86 second-level iterations. Figure 4.22 shows the optimum

176

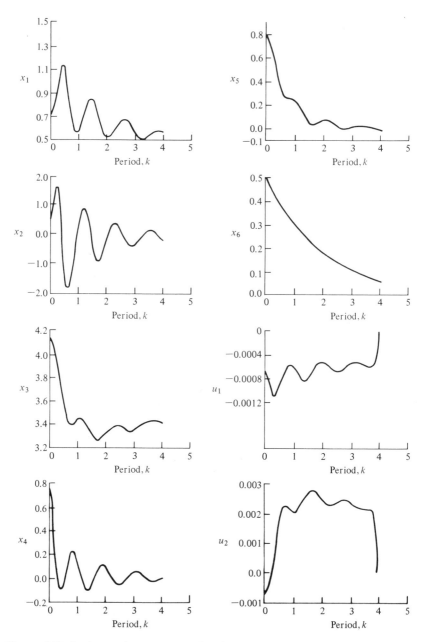

**Figure 4.22** Optimum time responses for the open-loop power system of Example 4.5.4.

responses for states and controls, which turned out to be identical to those reported earlier.

## 4.6 Discussion and Conclusions

In this section, the open- and closed-loop hierarchical control of continuous-time systems and hierarchical control of discrete-time systems will be discussed and compared. Some aspects, such as computer time, storage, information transfer requirements, and potential practical applicability, will be discussed and an attempt is made to point out advantages and disadvantages of each scheme.

The first method considered in this chapter was goal coordination, based on the interaction balance principle. The computational effort in the hierarchical control of a large-scale system reduces to that of a set of lower-order subsystems and a coordination procedure. The computational requirements of this method at the first level are normally much less than those of the original large-scale composite system. However, the overall computations depend heavily on the convergence characteristics of the second-level linear search iterations, e.g., gradient, Newton's, conjugate gradient, etc., methods. Since between each two successive second-level iterations, $N$ decoupled first-level problems must be solved, the slower the second-level problem's convergence is, the more times the $N$ first-level problems must be solved. In practice, one may use multiprocessors for the first level in an attempt to save computational time for the $N$ subsystems computations. Although this seems to be a good proposition and has been suggested by others (Singh, 1980), not many in the published literature support it (Sandell et al., 1978). An exception to this is due to Titli et al. (1978), who have used multiprocessors in the hierarchical control of a distributed parameter and a traffic control system. A major improvement in computations can be made when the first-level problems are both smaller and simpler. This latter observation is illustrated for coupled nonlinear systems with and without delays in Chapter 6. From the computer storage point of view, no significant limitations exist for the method. The scheme can handle constraints of inequality type on both the state and control, and, furthermore, the coordination at the second level has been shown (Varaiya, 1969) to converge to the optimum solution. The main disadvantage of goal coordination stems from the numerical convergence at the second level and its adverse effects on the first-level calculations mentioned before. Another shortcoming is the inadequacy of methods to find a near-optimum control in an attempt to avoid too many second-level iterations. A near-optimum control without convergence at the second level would be an unfeasible solution. Yet another difficulty is the need to add a quadratic term $z^TSz$ of the interaction vector $z$ in the cost function to avoid singular solutions. This problem, as demonstrated in Section 4.3.3, can, however, be avoided in two different ways.

Another hierarchical control technique discussed was the interaction prediction method. Based on its development in Section 4.3.2, it is clear that the second-level problem is much simpler here than in the goal coordination method. Furthermore, no possibility for a singular solution exists, and the computational experience of this author and others (Singh and Hassan, 1976) verify that the convergence at the second level is reasonably fast. Computationally, the interaction prediction method compares very favorably with the goal coordination approach. First from the storage point of view, the two methods are very similar. Both can be simulated in such a way so as to save on storage requirements by using a common block of memory for both levels. This was done for almost all illustrative examples of this chapter. From the computational viewpoint, for a number of reported applications (Singh and Titli 1978, Singh 1980), including the 12th-order system of Example 4.3.1, the interaction prediction method took on the order of one-quarter of the computer time of goal coordination. It should be mentioned, however, that the extent of computational benefits resulting from both the interaction prediction and goal coordination as compared to the original large-scale composite system depends on the format of the decomposition process. For example, if the 12th-order system of Example 4.3.1 had been decomposed into two sixth-order systems, the computational savings would not have been that appreciable. Another important point concerns the information structure between subsystems. An argument which can go against both the goal coordination and interaction prediction methods is the need for subsystems' full state information in a feedback configuration. Still another argument against the hierarchical control methods has been that they are insensitive with respect to modeling errors and component failure (Sandell et al., 1978). Part of the latter difficulty can be handled through the hierarchical control strategies for structural perturbations developed by Šiljak and Sundareshan (1976a, b).

The feedback control based on interaction prediction discussed in Section 4.4.1 has the advantages of being able to handle large interconnected systems regulator problem with a complete decentralized structure while the feedback gains remain independent of the initial conditions. The main disadvantage of this scheme is the extensive amount of off-line calculations for the finite-time case, as suggested in Section 4.4.1.

The feedback control based on structural perturbation presented in Section 4.4.2 is perhaps one of the first attempts to come up with a closed-loop control law for hierarchical systems. The method is relatively simpler than both the goal coordination and interaction prediction methods in that no second-level iterations or even simple updatings are involved. Moreover, no large-scale AMREs must be solved, but rather only a

Lyapunov-type equation, i.e., (4.4.41). Although the solution of a Lyapunov equation is much easier than a Riccati equation, when the system order is very large ($n > 200$), finding an efficient method with reasonable storage as well as computer time is questionable (Jamshidi, 1980). It has been argued by Sundareshan (1977) that all calculations are done off-line in contrast to the goal coordination which involves extensive on-line iterations on the first-level subsystems calculations. In this author's opinion, the best situation would be a balance between on-line and off-line calculations. The most interesting outcome of feedback control based on structural perturbation is that it takes possible beneficial effects of interactions into account. The establishment of a class of interconnection perturbations, which provide a foreseen effect on the overall system cost function, is a very useful flexibility for the coordinator. In spite of these advantages, it becomes clear that when the interconnection matrix $G$ is nonbeneficial, the near-optimality index $\rho$ in (4.4.45) may become very large. Under such conditions, it would be desirable to have an additional global controller, such as those of Šiljak and Sundareshan (1976a), which would neutralize the effects of the interactions. In all, the feedback control based on structural perturbation is an effective step in the right direction for closed-loop hierarchical control, although the total state information structure still remains the same.

In Section 4.5, the hierarchical control of discrete-time systems was considered. Five approaches were presented. In Section 4.5.1 the continuous-time version of goal coordination approach was extended to linear discrete-time systems. The computational behavior of this scheme is very similar to continuous-time goal coordination, which is heavily dependent upon the second-level problem's iterations. Moreover, both methods require the quadratic term in the cost function to avoid singularities. The only advantage of discrete-time over continuous-time goal coordination (Section 4.3.1) is that its first-level problem is very simple, as is evident from (4.5.21)–(4.5.23).

The time-delay algorithm discussed in Section 4.5.2 is perhaps the most appropriate goal coordination method for practical problems. The application of the algorithm to traffic control problems (Tamura, 1974, 1975) is excellent evidence of this. This algorithm as well as goal coordination have been used for the optimal management of water resources systems by many authors (Fallaside and Perry, 1975; Haimes, 1977; Jamshidi and Heggen, 1980). Perhaps the most striking benefit from the time-delay algorithm of Tamura (1974) is the fact that it avoids the solution of a TPBV problem, which involves both delay (in state vectors) and advance (in costate vectors) terms. This type of TPBV problem is a common difficulty with optimal control of time-delay systems by the maximum principle, which is discussed in Chapter 6, where a near-optimum solution is proposed. Further advantages of the method are the convenient handling of inequality constraints and avoiding the possibility of singular solutions, which is not always possible in goal coordination procedure.

In Section 4.5.3 the continuous-time version of the interaction prediction approach was extended to discrete-time systems for the first time in the author's best recollection. The first-level problem constitutes the solution of the discrete-time Riccati equation, which can prove to be rather time-consuming in a real-time situation. This scheme, tested numerically in Example 4.5.3, seems less effective than the costate prediction method of Section 4.5.5. The reasons for this are the convenient solutions of the costate prediction's first- and second-level problems. More specifically, for the system of Example 4.5.4, the first-level problem consists of straight substitutions on the right sides of 14 equations (six for states $x$, six for Lagrange multipliers $\beta$, and two for controls $u$), while the second-level problem involves six substitutions for the costate $p(k)$. The computational effort per iteration for this approach is a small fraction of that required for the other methods, such as discrete-time goal coordination (Section 4.5.1) and interaction prediction (Section 4.5.3). The costate prediction scheme can be easily extended to the linear case (see Problem 4.8) or continuous-time case (Problem 4.12). Jamshidi and Merryman (1982) have extended the costate-prediction method to take on continuous-time and discrete-time nonlinear systems with delays in state and control.

The other scheme considered in Section 4.5 was the structural perturbation approach of Section 4.5.4, which is computationally more attractive than goal coordination or interaction prediction due to its convenient scheme for obtaining a global (corrector) component for control vectors. Also, the solution of a discrete-time Riccati equation is sought only once for the $N$ subsystems. In other words, this scheme, as in its continuous-time version (Section 4.3.1), does not involve any iterations between first- or second-level hierarchies. The main difficulty with almost all of these hierarchical control schemes is that their convergence is not yet a settled issue. The only exception is perhaps continuous-time goal coordination (Varaiya, 1969). More discussions on hierarchical methods are in Section 6.7.

## Problems

**C4.1.** Consider a two-subsystem problem,

$$
\begin{bmatrix} \dot{x}_1 \\ \dot{x}_2 \\ \dot{x}_3 \\ \dot{x}_4 \end{bmatrix} = \begin{bmatrix} -1.5 & 0 & | & 0 & 0.1 \\ -0.5 & -1 & | & 0 & 0.2 \\ \hline 0.5 & 0 & | & -1.5 & 0 \\ 0 & 0.5 & | & -0.5 & -1 \end{bmatrix} \begin{bmatrix} x_1 \\ x_2 \\ x_3 \\ x_4 \end{bmatrix} + \begin{bmatrix} 0.1 & | & 0 \\ 0.1 & | & 0 \\ \hline 0 & | & 0.1 \\ 0 & | & 0.1 \end{bmatrix} \begin{bmatrix} u_1 \\ u_2 \end{bmatrix}
$$

Use the two-level goal coordination Algorithm 4.1 to find an optimum control which minimizes

$$J = \int_0^5 (x^T Q x + u^T R u)\, dt$$

$Q = \text{diag}(1,2,2,1)$, $R = I_2$, and $\Delta t = 0.1$. Use your favorite computer language and an integration routine such as Runge–Kutta to solve the associated differential matrix Riccati equation and the state equation.

**C4.2.** Algorithm 4.3 represents a goal coordination procedure for the hierarchical control of a large-scale discrete-time system. Consider the system

$$\begin{bmatrix} x_1(k+1) \\ x_2(k+1) \\ x_3(k+1) \\ x_4(k+1) \end{bmatrix} = \begin{bmatrix} -0.1 & 0.02 & 0 & 0.1 \\ 0.01 & -0.2 & 0 & 0 \\ 0.1 & 0 & -1 & 0 \\ 0 & 0 & 0 & -1 \end{bmatrix} \begin{bmatrix} x_1(k) \\ x_2(k) \\ x_3(k) \\ x_4(k) \end{bmatrix}$$

$$+ \begin{bmatrix} 0.2 & 0 \\ 0 & 0 \\ 0 & 0.1 \\ 0 & 0 \end{bmatrix} \begin{bmatrix} u_1(k) \\ u_2(k) \end{bmatrix}$$

with a cost function

$$J = \frac{1}{2} \sum_{i=1}^4 x_i(5) Q_i x_i(5) + \frac{1}{2} \sum_{k=0}^4 \left[ x^T(k) Q(k) x(k) + u^T(k) R(k) u(k) \right]$$

where $Q(k) = I_4$ and $R(k) = I_2$. Find the optimal hierarchical control of this system by decomposing it into two second-order subsystems.

**C4.3.** For a second-order discrete-time delay system

$$x_1(k+1) = 2x_1(k) + x_1(k-1) + u_1(k) + 0.5u_2(k-1)$$
$$x_2(k+1) = -2x_1(k) - x_2(k) + x_2(k-1) + u_1(k-1)$$
$$- u_2(k) - u_2(k-1)$$

where

$$\begin{bmatrix} 0 \\ 0 \end{bmatrix} \leqslant x(k) \leqslant \begin{bmatrix} 3 \\ 3 \end{bmatrix}, \quad \begin{bmatrix} -1 \\ -1 \end{bmatrix} \leqslant u(k) \leqslant \begin{bmatrix} 1 \\ 1 \end{bmatrix}$$

$$J = \frac{1}{2} x^T(7) \begin{bmatrix} 2 & 0 \\ 0 & 1 \end{bmatrix} x(7)$$

$$+ \frac{1}{2} \sum_{k=0}^6 \left[ x^T(k) \begin{bmatrix} 1 & 0 \\ 0 & 2 \end{bmatrix} x(k) + u^T(k) \begin{bmatrix} 0.5 & 0 \\ 0 & 1 \end{bmatrix} u(k) \right]$$

**Problems** (*continued*)

with initial conditions

$$x(k) = u(k) = 0, \quad -1 \leqslant k \leqslant 0, \quad x^T(0) = [1 \quad 1].$$

use the time-delay Algorithm 4.4 to find the optimal sequence $u^*(k)$, $k = 0, 1, \ldots, 6$. It is possible to solve this problem analytically; however, a computer implementation is more desirable for higher-order systems.

**C4.4.** Consider an interconnected system

$$\dot{x} = \begin{bmatrix} -1 & 0.5 & 0.1 & 0.5 & 0 \\ 0.1 & -2 & -0.5 & 0.2 & -0.1 \\ \hline 0.2 & 0 & -5 & 0.5 & -1 \\ 0.1 & -0.2 & 0 & -2 & 0 \\ 0.4 & 0.1 & -0.5 & 0 & -4 \end{bmatrix} x + \begin{bmatrix} 1 & 0 \\ 0 & 0 \\ \hline 0 & 0 \\ 0 & 1 \\ 0 & 1 \end{bmatrix} u$$

with cost function

$$J = \sum_{i=1}^{2} \frac{1}{2} \left[ x_i^T(2) Q_i x_i(2) + \int_0^2 \left( x_i^T(t) Q_i x_i(t) + u_i^T(t) R_i u(t) \right) dt \right]$$

with $Q_i = \text{diag}(2, 1, 1, 1, 1)$, $R_i = I_2$, and initial conditions $x^T(0) = [1 \quad 0 \quad 0.5 \quad -1 \quad 0]$, $\Delta t = 0.1$. Use the interaction prediction Algorithm 4.2 to find the optimal control $u^*(t)$ for the above problem.

**4.5.** Prove that the control law (4.4.53) is a stabilizing controller for the large-scale system (4.4.22). [*Hint:* $F = K + \hat{K}$ is a positive-definite solution of AMRE (4.4.47) for the perturbed system (4.4.46).]

**4.6.** Repeat Example 4.4.2 for the following system:

$$\dot{x}_1 = x_1 + u_1, \quad x_1(0) = 1$$
$$\dot{x}_2 = 2x_2 + u_2, \quad x_2(0) = 1$$

and a cost function

$$J = \frac{1}{2} \int_0^\infty \left( 2x_1^2 + x_2^2 + u_1^2 + u_2^2 \right) dt$$

**4.7.** For the system

$$\dot{x}_1 = x_1 + ax_2 + u_1, \quad x_1(0) = 1$$
$$\dot{x}_2 = x_2 + bx_1 + u_2, \quad x_2(0) = 0$$

and a quadratic cost function with weighting matrices $Q = R = I_2$, find regions in the $(b - a)$-plane where the interconnected system can be beneficial, neutral, and nonbeneficial.

**4.8.** Extend the costate prediction approach of Section 4.5.5 to a composite interconnected linear discrete-time system

$$x(k+1) = A(k)x(k) + B(k)u(k) + C(k)z(k)$$

where $A$ and $B$ are block-diagonal and $C$ is block-antidiagonal and $z(k)$ is the interconnection vector.

**4.9.** Use the costate prediction Algorithm 4.7 to find the optimum control for

$$x(k+1) = \begin{bmatrix} 0.9 & 0.2 \\ 0.1 & 0.1 - 0.1x_1(k) \end{bmatrix} x(k) + \begin{bmatrix} 0.1 & 0 \\ 0 & 0.2 \end{bmatrix} u(k)$$

with $x(0) = (10 \quad 5)^T$ and a cost function

$$J = \frac{1}{2} \sum_{k=0}^{20} \left( 0.1x_1^2(k) + 0.2x_2^2(k) + 0.1u_1^2(k) + 0.2u_2^2(k) \right)$$

**C4.10.** For a system with the matrices

$$A = \begin{bmatrix} -5 & 0.2 & 0.5 & 0.1 & 0 \\ 0 & -2 & 0.2 & 0 & 0 \\ 0.17 & 0 & -1 & 0 & 1 \\ 0 & -1 & 0 & -0.5 & 0 \\ -1 & 0 & -0.5 & 0 & -1 \end{bmatrix}, \quad B = \begin{bmatrix} 1 & 0 \\ 0 & 0 \\ 0 & 0 \\ 0 & 1 \\ 0 & 0 \end{bmatrix}$$

with $Q = \text{diag}(1,1,2,2,2)$ and $R = I_2$, find a hierarchical control law based on the structural perturbation method of Section 4.4.2. What is the value of the cost function deviation $\rho$? Use initial state $x(0) = [1 \quad 1 \quad 1 \quad 1 \quad 1]^T$.

**4.11.** Use Algorithm 4.6 on the structural perturbation approach for discrete-time systems to find the optimum control for

$$\begin{bmatrix} x_1(k+1) \\ x_2(k+1) \end{bmatrix} = \begin{bmatrix} -1 & 0.5 \\ 1 & -1 \end{bmatrix} \begin{bmatrix} x_1(k) \\ x_2(k) \end{bmatrix} + \begin{bmatrix} 1 & 0 \\ 0 & 1 \end{bmatrix} \begin{bmatrix} u_1(k) \\ u_2(k) \end{bmatrix}$$

with $x(0) = (1 \quad 1)^T$ and quadratic cost matrices $Q = I_2$, $R = 0.5I_2$.

**Problems** (*continued*)

**4.12.** Extend the discrete-time system's costate-prediction method of Section 4.5.5 to the continuous-time system

$$\dot{x}(t) = f(x(t), u(t), t)$$

$$J = \frac{1}{2} x^T(t_f) Q x(t_f) + \frac{1}{2} \int_0^{t_f} \left[ x^T(t) Q x(t) + u^T(t) R u(t) \right] dt$$

# References

Arafeh, S., and Sage, A. P. 1974a. Multi-level discrete time system identification in large scale systems. *Int. J. Syst. Sci.* 5:753–791.

Arafeh, S., and Sage, A. P. 1974b. Hierarchical system identification of states and parameters in interconnected power system. *Int. J. Syst. Sci.* 5:817–846.

Bauman, E. J. 1968. Multi-level optimization techniques with application to trajectory decomposition, in C. T. Leondes, ed., *Advances in Control Systems*, pp. 160–222.

Beck, M. B. 1974. The application of control and systems theory to problems of river pollution. Ph.D. thesis, University of Cambridge, Cambridge, England.

Benveniste, A.; Bernhard, P.; and Cohen, A. 1976. On the decomposition of stochastic control problems. IRIA Research Report No. 187, France.

Cheneveaux, B. 1972. Contribution a l'optimisation hierarchisée des systemes dynamiques. Doctor Engineer Thesis, No. 4. Nantes, France.

Cohen, G.; Benveniste, A.; and Bernhard, P. 1972. Commande hierarchisée avec coordination en ligne d'un systeme dynamique. *Renue Francaise d'Automatique, Informatique et Recherche Operationnelle.* J4:77–101.

Cohen, G.; Benveniste, A.; and Bernhard, P. 1974. Coordination algorithms for optimal control problems Part I. Report No. A/57, Centre d'Automatique, Ecole des Mines, Paris.

Cohen, G., and Jolland, G. 1976. Coordination methods by the prediction principle in large dynamic constrained optimization problems. *Proc. IFAC Symposium on Large-Scale Systems Theory and Applications*, Udine, Italy.

Davison, E. J., and Maki, M. C. 1973. The numerical solution of the matrix Riccati differential equation. *IEEE Trans. Aut. Cont.* AC-18:71–73.

Dorato, P., and Levis, A. H. 1971. Optimal linear regulators: The discrete-time case. *IEEE Trans. Aut. Cont.* AC-16:613–620.

Fallaside, F., and Perry, P. 1975. Hierarchical optimization of a water supply network. *Proc. IEE* 122:202–208.

Geoffrion, A. M. 1970. Elements of large-scale mathematical programming: Part I, Concepts, Part II, Synthesis of Algorithms and Bibliography. *Management Sci.* 16.

Geoffrion, A. M. 1971a. Duality in non-linear programming. *SIAM Review* 13:1–37.

Geoffrion, A. M. 1971b. Large-scale linear and nonlinear programming, in D. A. Wismer, ed., *Optimization Methods for Large Scale Systems*. McGraw-Hill, New York.

Haimes, Y. Y. 1977. *Hierarchical Analyses of Water Resources Systems*. McGraw-Hill, New York.

Hassan, M. F., and Singh, M. G. 1976. A two-level costate prediction algorithm for nonlinear systems. Cambridge University Engineering Dept. Report No. CUEDF-CAMS/TR(124).

Hassan, M. F., and Singh, M. G. 1977. A two-level costate prediction algorithm for nonlinear systems. *IFAC J. Automatica* 13:629–634.

Hassan, M. F., and Singh, M. G. 1981. Hierarchical successive approximation algorithms for non-linear systems. Part II. Algorithms based on costate coordination. *J. Large Scale Systems*. 2:81–95.

Hewlett-Packard Company, 1979. Interpolation: Chebyschev polynomial. System 9845 Numerical Analysis Library Part No. 9282-0563, pp. 247–256.

Iyer, S. N., and Cory, B. J. 1971. Optimization of turbogenerator transient performance by differential dynamic programming. *IEEE Trans. Power. Appar. Syst.* 90:2149–2157.

Jamshidi, M. 1975. Optimal control of nonlinear power systems by an imbedding method. *IFAC J. Automatica*. 11:633–636.

Jamshidi, M. 1980. An overview on the solutions of the algebraic matrix Riccati equation and related problems. *J. Large Scale Systems* 1:167–192.

Jamshidi, M., and Heggen, R. J. 1980. A multilevel stochastic management model for optimal conjunctive use of ground and surface water. *Proc. IFAC Symposium on Water and Related Land Resources Systems*. (Cleveland, OH).

Jamshidi, M., and Merryman, J. E. 1982. On the hierarchical optimization of retarded systems via costate prediction. *Proc. American Contr. Conf.*, pp. 899–904 (Arlington, VA).

Kleinman, D. L. 1968. On the iterative technique for Riccati equation computations. *IEEE Trans. Aut. Cont.* AC-13:114–115.

Mahmoud, M. S. 1977. Multilivel systems control and applications. *IEEE Trans. Syst. Man. and Cybern.* SMC-7:125–143.

Mahmoud, M. 1979. Dynamic feedback methodology for interconnected control systems. *Int. J. Contr.* 29:881–898.

Mahmoud, M.; Vogt, W.; and Mickle, M. 1977. Multi-level control and optimization using generalized gradients technique. *Int. J. Contr.* 25:525–543.

March, J. G., and Simon, H. A. 1958. *Organizations*. Wiley, New York.

Mesarovic, M. D.; Macko, D.; and Takahara, Y. 1969. Two coordination principles and their applications in large-scale systems control. *Proc. IFAC Congr.* Warsaw, Poland.

Mesarovic, M. D; Macko, D.; and Takahara, Y. 1970. *Theory of Hierarchical Multilevel Systems*. Academic Press, New York.

Mukhopadhyay, B. K., and Malik, O. P. 1973. Solution of nonlinear optimization problem in power systems. *Int. J. Contr.* 17:1041–1058.

Newhouse, A. 1962. Chebyschev curve fit. *Comm. ACM* 5:281.

Pearson, J. D. 1971. Dynamic decomposition techniques, in Wismer, D. A., ed., *Optimization Methods for Large-Scale Systems*. McGraw-Hill, New York.

Sage, A. P. 1968. *Optimum Systems Control*. Prentice Hall, Englewood Cliffs, NJ.

Sandell, N. R., Jr.; Varaiya, P.; Athans, M.; and Safonov, M. G. 1978. Survey of decentralized control methods for large scale systems. *IEEE Trans. Aut. Cont.* AC-23:108–128. (special issue on large scale systems).

Schoeffler, J. D., and Lasdon, L. S. 1966. Decentralized plant control. *ISA Trans.* 5:175–183.

Schoeffler, J. D. 1971. Static multilevel systems, in D. A. Wismer, ed., *Optimization Methods for Large-Scale Systems*. McGraw-Hill, New York.

Šiljak, D. D. 1978. *Large-Scale Dynamic Systems*. Elsevier North Holland, New York.

Šiljak, D. D., and Sundareshan, M. K. 1974. On hierarchical optimal control of large-scale systems. *Proc. 8th Asilomar Conf. Circuits Systems Computers*, pp. 495–502.

Šiljak, D. D., and Sundareshan, M. K. 1976a. A multi-level optimization of large scale dynamic systems. *IEEE Trans. Aut. Cont.* AC-21:79–84.

Šiljak, D. D., and Sundareshan, M. K. 1976b. Large-scale systems: Optimality vs. reliability. Internal Report, University of California, Berkeley, Department of Electrical Engineering.

Singh, M. G. 1975. River pollution control. *Int. J. Syst. Sci.* 6:9–21.

Singh, M. G. 1980. *Dynamical Hierarchical Control*, rev. ed. North Holland, Amsterdam, The Netherlands.

Singh, M. G., and Hassan, M. 1976. A comparison of two hierarchical optimisation methods. *Int. J. Syst. Sci.* 7:603–611.

Singh, M. G., and Titli, A. 1978. *Systems: Decomposition, Optimization and Control.* Pergamon Press, Oxford, England.

Singh, M. G.; Drew, A. W.; and Coales, J. F. 1975. Comparisons of practical hierarchical control methods for interconnected dynamical systems. *IFAC J. Automatica* 11:331–350.

Singh, M. G.; Titli, A.; and Galy, J. 1976. A method for improving the efficiency of the goal coordination method for large dynamical systems with state variable coupling. *Computers and Electrical Engineering* 2:339–346.

Smith, P. G. 1971. Numerical solution of the matrix equation $AX + XA^T + B = 0$. *IEEE Trans. Aut. Cont.* AC-16:278–279.

Smith, N. H., and Sage, A. P. 1973. An introduction to hierarchical systems theory. *Computers and Electrical Engineering* 1:55–71.

Sundareshan, M. K. 1976. Large-scale discrete systems: A two-level optimization scheme. *Int. J. Syst. Sci.* 7:901–909.

Sundareshan, M. K. 1977. Generation of multilevel control and estimation schemes for large-scale systems: A perturbation approach. *IEEE Trans. Syst. Man. Cyber.* SMC-7:144–152.

Takahara, Y. 1965. A multi-level structure for a class of dynamical optimization problems. M.S. thesis, Case Western Reserve University, Cleveland, OH.

Tamura, H. 1974. A discrete dynamic model with distributed transport delays and its hierarchical optimization to preserve stream quality. *IEEE Trans. Syst. Man. Cyber.* SMC-4:424–429.

Tamura, H. 1975. Decentralized optimization for distributed-lag models of discrete systems. *IFAC J. Automatica* 11:593–602.

Titli, A. 1972. Contribution à l'étude des structures de commande hierarchisées en vue de l'optimization des processes complexes, *These d'État*. No. 495, Toulouse, France.

Titli, A.; Singh, M. G.; and Hassan, M. F. 1978. Hierarchical optimization of dynamical systems using multiprocessors. *Computers and Electrical Engineering* 5:3–14.

Varaiya, P. 1969. A decomposition technique for non-linear programming. Internal Report, University of California, Berkeley, Department of Electrical Engineering.

# Chapter 5
# Decentralized Control of Large-Scale Systems

## 5.1 Introduction

In Chapter 1, the notion of decentralized control and its structure were briefly introduced. As it was mentioned then and is emphasized again here, the main motivation behind decentralized control is the failure of conventional methods of centralized control theory. Some fundamental techniques such as pole placement, state feedback, optimal control, state estimation and like of the latter theory requires complete information from all system sensors for the sake of feedback control. This scheme is clearly inadequate for feedback control of large-scale systems. Due to the physical configuration and high dimensionality of such systems, a centralized control is neither economically feasible nor even necessary. Therefore, in many applications of feedback control theory to linear large-scale systems some degree of restriction is assumed to prevail on the transfer of information. In some cases a total decentralization is assumed; i.e., every local control $u_i$ is obtained from the local output $y_i$ and possible external input $v_i$ (Sandell et al., 1978). In others, an intermediate restriction on the information is possible.

In this chapter, three major problems related to decentralized structure of large-scale systems are addressed. The first is decentralized stabilization. The problem of finding a state or an output feedback gain whereby the closed-loop system has all its poles on the left half-plane is commonly known as feedback "stabilization." Alternatively, the closed-loop poles of a controllable system may be preassigned through the state or output feedback. Clearly, the applications of these concepts in a decentralized fashion requires certain extensions which are discussed in Section 5.3.

The second problem addressed in this chapter is the decentralized "robust" control of large-scale linear systems with or without a known plant. This problem, first introduced by Davison (1976a,b,c,d) and known as "general servomechanism," takes advantage of the tuning regulators and dynamic compensators to design a feedback which both stabilizes and regulates the system in a decentralized mode. The notion of "robust" feedback control will be defined and discussed in detail later; however, for the time being a control is said to be robust if it continues to provide asymptotic stability and regulation under perturbation of plant parameters and matrices.

The third problem is stochastic decentralized control of continuous- and discrete-time systems. The scheme discussed here is based on the assumption of one sensor for each controller (channel or node) whose information, processed with a local Kalman estimator, is shared with all other controllers.

In Section 5.2, the three problems of decentralized stabilization, decentralized servomechanism, and decentralized stochastic control are mathematically formulated. Section 5.3 reviews some of the appropriate schemes for decentralized feedback stabilization, including the notions of "fixed modes," "fixed polynomials" (Wang and Davison, 1973), and their role in dynamic compensation. Also discussed are the stabilization of interconnected systems via local feedback (Sezer and Hüseyin, 1978) and the notion of "exponential stability" applied to decentralized systems. The stabilization of linear time-varying systems (Ikeda and Šiljak, 1980a,b) and the special case of time-invariant system stabilization will follow.

The decentralized servomechanism and robust control problems are discussed in Section 5.4. Several notions, such as "robust" control, steady-state "tracking" gain matrices, dynamic compensation through "tuning regulators" and their role in the existence of decentralized robust control (Davison, 1976b, 1978), are considered. Many algorithms are given, and numerical examples illustrate them. The notion of "sequentially stable" robust control (Davison and Gesing, 1979) concludes Section 5.4.

Stochastic decentralized control of continuous- and discrete-time systems are discussed in Section 5.5. Two computational schemes for this type of control are suggested.

Discussion on the three main problems considered in this chapter and their potential use in real large-scale systems is presented in Section 5.6. Further issues, such as decentralized optimal control and "sequential optimization" of servomechanism problems, are dealt with in Chapter 6.

## 5.2 Problems Formulation

Three important problems in the area of large-scale systems decentralized control are stated here.

### 5.2.1 Problem 1 — Decentralized Stabilization

Consider a large-scale linear TIV (time-invariant) system with $N$ local control stations (channels),

$$\dot{x}(t) = Ax(t) + \sum_{i=1}^{N} B_i u_i(t) \tag{5.2.1}$$

$$y_i(t) = C_i x, \quad i = 1, 2, \ldots, N \tag{5.2.2}$$

where $x$ is an $n \times 1$ state vector, and $u_i$ and $y_i$ are $m_i \times 1$ and $r_i \times 1$ control and output vectors associated with the $i$th control station, respectively. The original system control and output orders $m$ and $r$ are given by

$$m = \sum_{i=1}^{N} m_i, \quad r = \sum_{i=1}^{N} r_i \tag{5.2.3}$$

The decentralized stabilization problem is defined as follows: Obtain $N$ local output control laws, each with its independent dynamic compensator,

$$u_i(t) = H_i z_i(t) + K_i y_i(t) + L_i v_i(t) \tag{5.2.4}$$

$$\dot{z}_i(t) = F_i z_i(t) + S_i y_i(t) + G_i v_i(t) \tag{5.2.5}$$

so that the system (5.2.1)–(5.2.2) in its closed-loop form is stabilized. In (5.2.4)–(5.2.5) $z_i(t)$ is the $n_i \times 1$ output vector of the $i$th compensator, $v_i(t)$ is the $m_i \times 1$ external input vector for the $i$th controller, and matrices $H_i$, $K_i$, $L_i$, $F_i$, $S_i$, and $G_i$ are $m_i \times n_i$, $m_i \times r_i$, $m_i \times m_i$, $n_i \times n_i$, $n_i \times r_i$, and $n_i \times m_i$, respectively. Alternatively, the problem 1 can be restated as follows: Find matrices $H_i$, $K_i$, $L_i$, $F_i$, $S_i$, and $G_i$, $i = 1, 2, \ldots, N$ so that the resulting closed-loop system described by (5.2.1)–(5.2.2) has its poles in a set $\mathscr{L}$, where $\mathscr{L}$ is a nonempty symmetric open subset of complex $s$-plane (Davison, 1976a). It is clear that the membership of a closed-loop system pole $\lambda \in \mathscr{L}$ implies its complex conjugate $\lambda^* \in L$ in a prescribed manner.

### 5.2.2 Problem 2 — Decentralized Servomechanism

Consider a large-scale linear TIV system

$$\dot{x}(t) = Ax(t) + \sum_{i=1}^{N} B_i u_i(t) + E\omega(t) \tag{5.2.6}$$

$$y_i(t) = C_i x(t) + D_i u_i(t) + P_i \omega(t) \tag{5.2.7}$$

$$e_i(t) = y_i(t) - y_i^d(t), \quad i = 1, 2, \ldots, N \tag{5.2.8}$$

where $\omega(t)$ is a $q \times 1$ disturbance vector which may or may not be measurable, $y_i^d(t)$ is the $i$th controller's desired reference output, $e_i(t)$, $i = 1, 2, \ldots, N$, is the $i$th local control station error, and all the matrices are of appropriate dimensions. Let

$$
y^d = \begin{bmatrix} y_1^d \\ \vdots \\ y_N^d \end{bmatrix}, \quad P = \begin{bmatrix} P_1 \\ \vdots \\ P_N \end{bmatrix}, \quad e = \begin{bmatrix} e_1 \\ \vdots \\ e_N \end{bmatrix} \tag{5.2.9}
$$

and assume that $\mathrm{rank}(B_i) = m_i \geq 1$, $i = 1, 2, \ldots, N$. Furthermore, the disturbance vector $\omega$ is assumed to satisfy the following model:

$$
\dot{\sigma}_1 = \Omega_1 \sigma_1 \tag{5.2.10}
$$
$$
\omega = \Omega_2 \sigma_1
$$

where $\dim(\sigma_1) = \hat{n}_1$, pair $(\Omega_2, \Omega_1)$ is observable* and $\sigma(0)$ may or may not be available. The desired output $y^d$ is assumed to satisfy

$$
y^d = R\gamma, \quad \gamma = \Gamma_2 \sigma_2 \tag{5.2.11}
$$
$$
\dot{\sigma}_2 = \Gamma_1 \sigma_2
$$

where $\dim(\sigma_2) = \hat{n}_2$, pair $(\Gamma_2, \Gamma_1)$ is observable and $\sigma_2(0)$ is known.

The decentralized servomechanism problem, proposed by Davison (1976a, b, c, d, 1978), can be stated as follows: Find $N$ local output feedback control laws such that $\lim_{t \to \infty} e(t) = 0$ for all $x(0)$, $\sigma_1(0)$, and $\sigma_2(0)$ and the resulting closed-loop system is stable. It is further assumed that out of $r_i$ outputs of $i$th dynamic decentralized controller only $r_i^m (\leq r_i)$ outputs are measurable, i.e.,

$$
y_i^m(t) = C_i^m x(t) + D_i^m u_i(t) + P_i^m \omega \tag{5.2.12}
$$

The final assumption is that, for the sake of nontriviality,

$$
\mathrm{rank} \begin{bmatrix} E \\ P \end{bmatrix} = \mathrm{rank} \begin{bmatrix} \Omega_2 \end{bmatrix} = q
$$
$$
\mathrm{rank} \begin{bmatrix} R \end{bmatrix} = \mathrm{rank} \begin{bmatrix} \Gamma_2 \end{bmatrix} = \dim(\gamma) \tag{5.2.13}
$$
$$
\mathrm{rank} \begin{bmatrix} C_i^m \end{bmatrix} = \dim(y_i^m) = r_i^m, \quad i = 1, 2, \ldots, N
$$

The problem stated by (5.2.6)–(5.2.13) is known as robust decentralized control of general servomechanism (Davison 1976c), which will be precisely defined in Section 5.4.


### 5.2.3 Problem 3 — Decentralized Stochastic Control

In Section 5.5 two decentralized control schemes for continuous- and discrete-time large-scale systems are discussed. However, here the latter one is stated, while the former one is considered fully in Section 5.5.3. Consider

---

*For definition and discussion of observability, see Chapter 7.

a large-scale linear discrete-time system described by

$$x(k+1) = Ax(k) + \sum_{i=1}^{N} B_i u_i(k) + \xi(k) \qquad (5.2.14)$$

where $x(k)$ is the $n \times 1$ state vector at stage $k$, $u_i(k)$ is the $m_i \times 1$ control vector of the $i$th controller (channel or node) at stage $k$, $A$, $B_i$, $i = 1, 2, \ldots, N$, are known constant matrices, and $\xi(k)$ is a white noise with zero mean and known variance (Speyer, 1979):

$$E\{\xi(k)\xi^T(l)\} = V(k)\delta(k, l) \qquad (5.2.15)$$

where $\delta(\cdot, \cdot)$ is the Kronecker delta, $V(\cdot)$ is the variance and $E\{\cdot\}$ stands for the expected value. The measurement at each node or channel is assumed to follow

$$y_i(k) = C_i x(k) + \eta_i(k) \qquad (5.2.16)$$

where $y_i(k)$ is an $r_i \times 1$ measurement vector at node $i$ at stage $k$, $C_i$ is an $r_i \times n$ matrix, and $\eta_i(k)$ is a zero-mean white noise process assumed to be uncorrelated from each node to another and with a known variance

$$E\{\eta_i(k)\eta_l^T(k)\} = W_i(k)\delta(k, l) \qquad (5.2.17)$$

The problem can now be stated: Find $N$ decentralized controllers $u_i(k)$, $i = 1, 2, \ldots, N$, and $k = 1, \ldots, K$, such that (5.2.14)–(5.2.17) are satisfied, while the following cost functional is minimized:

$$J = E\left\{ \frac{1}{2} \sum_{k=1}^{K} \left[ x^T(k)Q(k)x(k) + \sum_{i=1}^{N} u_i^T(k)R_i u_i(k) \right] \right\} \qquad (5.2.18)$$

where the pair of matrices $Q(k)$, $R(k)$ are assumed to be positive-definite. The above problem along with its continuous-time as well as its centralized solution are discussed in Section 5.5.

## 5.3 Decentralized Stabilization

In this section the problem of stabilizing large-scale linear TIV and time-varying systems is presented. Conditions under which the overall system with decentralized control can be stabilized will be given. Decentralized stabilization has been an active field of research for large-scale systems. The discussions on this topic are restricted to linear time-invariant systems in the most part and are based on the works of Wang and Davison (1973), Davison (1976a, b, 1978, 1979), Šiljak (1978a, b), Corfmat and Morse (1976), Sezer and Hüseyin (1978, 1980), Saeks (1979), Huang and Sundareshan (1980), and Groumpos and Loparo (1980). Additional works on such subjects as large-scale linear systems with nonlinear interconnections (Sundareshan, 1977) and the results of Ikeda and Šiljak (1980a) for the time-varying systems and the case of time-invariant systems (Anderson and Moore, 1981) will also be considered.

## 5.3.1 Fixed Polynomials and Fixed Modes

The notions of fixed polynomials and fixed modes are generalizations of the "centralized" systems pole placement problem, in which any uncontrollable and unobservable mode of the system must be stable (Brasch and Pearson, 1970) to the decentralized case. The idea of fixed modes for decentralized control was introduced by Wang and Davison (1973) and further elaborated and used extensively with regard to the general servomechanism problem (Section 5.2.2) by Davison (1976a, b, c, d, 1978).

Consider the decentralized stabilization problem described by (5.2.1)–(5.2.5). The dynamic compensator (5.2.4)–(5.2.5) may be rewritten in compact form,

$$u(t) = Hz(t) + Ky(t) + Lv(t) \tag{5.3.1}$$
$$\dot{z}(t) = Fz(t) + Sy(t) + Gv(t) \tag{5.3.2}$$

where

$$H \triangleq \text{Block-diag}\{H_1, H_2, \ldots, H_N\}, \quad K \triangleq \text{Block-diag}\{K_1, K_2, \ldots, K_N\}$$
$$L \triangleq \text{Block-diag}\{L_1, L_2, \ldots, L_N\}, \quad F \triangleq \text{Block-diag}\{F_1, F_2, \ldots, F_N\}$$
$$S \triangleq \text{Block-diag}\{S_1, S_2, \ldots, S_N\}, \quad G \triangleq \text{Block-diag}\{G_1, G_2, \ldots, G_N\} \tag{5.3.3}$$

and

$$u^T(t) \triangleq \{u_1^T(t) : \cdots : u_N^T(t)\}, \quad z^T(t) \triangleq \{z_1^T(t) : \cdots : z_N^T(t)\}$$
$$y^T(t) = \{y_1^T(t) : \cdots : y_N^T(t)\}, \quad v^T(t) = \{v_1^T(t) : \cdots : v_N^T(t)\}$$

If the control (5.3.1)–(5.3.2) is applied to (5.2.1)–(5.2.2), the following augmented system results:

$$\begin{bmatrix} \dot{x}(t) \\ \dot{z}(t) \end{bmatrix} = \begin{bmatrix} A + BKC & BH \\ SC & F \end{bmatrix} \begin{bmatrix} x(t) \\ z(t) \end{bmatrix} + \begin{bmatrix} BL \\ G \end{bmatrix} v(t) \tag{5.3.4}$$

where

$$B = \begin{bmatrix} \underbrace{B_1}_{m_1} : \cdots : \underbrace{B_N}_{m_N} \end{bmatrix} \quad \text{and} \quad C = \begin{bmatrix} C_1 \\ \vdots \\ C_N \end{bmatrix} \begin{matrix} \} r_1 \\ \\ \} r_N \end{matrix} \tag{5.3.5}$$

As mentioned earlier, the problem is to find the control laws (5.3.1)–(5.3.2) so that the overall augmented system (5.3.4) is asymptotically stable. In other words, by way of local output feedback, the closed-loop poles of the decentralized system are required to lie on the left half of the complex $s$-plane. The following definitions and theorem provide the ground rules for this problem.

**Definition 5.1.** Consider the system $(C, A, B)$ describing (5.2.1)–(5.2.2) and integers $m_i$, $r_i$, $i = 1, 2, \ldots, N$, in (5.2.3). Let the $m \times r$ gain matrix $K$ be represented as a member of the following set of block-diagonal matrices:

$$\mathbf{K} = \left( K \mid K = \begin{array}{c} m_1 \left\{ \right. \end{array} \overbrace{\begin{bmatrix} \boxed{K_1} & & & \\ & \boxed{K_2} & & \\ & & \ddots & \\ & & & \boxed{K_N} \end{bmatrix}}^{r_1} \left. \begin{array}{c} \\ \\ \\ \} m_N \end{array} \right. \right) \qquad (5.3.6a)$$

where dim $(K_i) = m_i \times r_i$, $i = 1, 2, \ldots, N$. Then the "fixed polynomial" of $(C, A, B)$ with respect to $\mathbf{K}$ is the greatest common divisor (gcd) of the set of polynomial $|\lambda I - A - BKC|$ for all $K \in \mathbf{K}$ and is denoted by

$$\phi(\lambda; C, A, B, K) = \gcd\{|\lambda I - A - BKC|\} \qquad (5.3.6b)$$

**Definition 5.2.** For the system $(C, A, B)$ and the set of output feedback gains $K$ given by (5.3.6), the set of "fixed modes" of $(C, A, B)$ with respect to $K$ is defined as the intersection of all possible sets of the eigenvalues of matrix $(A + BKC)$, i.e.,

$$\Lambda(C, A, B, K) = \bigcap_{K \in \mathbf{K}} \lambda(A + BKC) \qquad (5.3.7)$$

where $\lambda(\cdot)$ denotes the set of eigenvalues of $(A + BKC)$. Note also that $K$ can take on the null matrix; hence the set of fix modes $\Lambda(\cdot)$ is contained in $\lambda(A)$. In view of Definition 5.1, the members of $\Lambda(\cdot)$, i.e., the "fixed modes," are the roots of the "fixed polynomials" $\phi(\cdot; \cdot)$ in (5.3.6b), i.e.,

$$\Lambda(C, A, B, K) = \{\lambda | \lambda \in s \text{ and } \phi(\lambda, C, A, B, K) = 0\} \qquad (5.3.8)$$

where $s$ denotes a set of values on the entire complex $s$-plane.

The following algorithm, due to Davison (1976a), provides a quick way of finding the fixed modes of a system $(C, A, B)$.

***Algorithm 5.1.*** Evaluation of Fixed Modes

  *Step 1:* Find all the eigenvalues of $A$, i.e., $\lambda(A)$.

  *Step 2:* Choose an arbitrary $m \times r$-dimensional $K \in \mathbf{K}$ (by either a pseudo-random number generator or other means) so that the norm $\|A\| \simeq \|BKC\|$.

  *Step 3:* Find $\sigma(A + BKC)$.

  *Step 4:* Then $\Lambda(C, A, B, K) \subset \lambda(A + BKC)$ with respect to $\mathbf{K}$, i.e., the fixed modes of $(C, A, B)$ are contained in those eigenvalues of $(A + BKC)$ which are common with the eigenvalues of $A$.

  *Step 5:* Steps 2 through 4 may be repeated until the fixed modes of $A$ are identified.

It turns out that the fixed modes of centralized system $(C, A, B, \tilde{K})$, where $\tilde{K}$ is $m \times r$, correspond to the uncontrollable and unobservable modes of the system (Wang and Davison, 1973). The following theorem provides the necessary and sufficient conditions for the stabilizability of a decentralized closed-loop system.

**Theorem 5.1.** *For the system* $(C, A, B)$ *in* (5.2.1)–(5.2.2) *and the class of block-diagonal matrices* $\mathbf{K}$ *in* (5.3.6a), *the local feedback laws* (5.2.4)–(5.2.5) *would asymptotically stabilize the system if and only if the set of fixed modes of* $(C, A, B, K)$ *is contained in the open left half s-plane, i.e.,* $\Lambda(C, A, B, K) \in s^-$, *where* $s^-$ *is the open LHP (left-half plane) s-plane.*

The proof of this theorem, which is based on Kalman's canonical structure theorem (Kalman, 1962) and three other lemmas, can be found elsewhere (Wang and Davison, 1973). An important corollary of Theorem 5.1 is that under the conditions of this theorem, a necessary and sufficient condition for a set of eigenvalues of $(A + BKC)$ to belong to a presubscribed set $\mathcal{L}$ is that $\Lambda(C, A, B, K) \subset \mathcal{L}$. The following examples illustrate the evaluation of the fixed modes of the system and check on the stability of decentralized control.

**Example 5.3.1.** Consider a system

$$\dot{x} = \begin{bmatrix} 0.5 & 0 & 1 & 0 \\ 0.1 & 1.2 & 0 & 0.1 \\ 0 & 0 & -1 & 0 \\ 0 & 0 & 0.4 & 0.75 \end{bmatrix} x + \begin{bmatrix} 0.85 & 0 \\ 0 & 1 \\ 0 & 1.25 \\ 1 & 0 \end{bmatrix} u \qquad (5.3.9)$$

$$y = \begin{bmatrix} 1 & 0 & 0 & 0 \\ 0 & 0 & 0.5 & 1 \end{bmatrix} x \qquad (5.3.10)$$

It is desired to find the fixed modes, if any, of this system.

SOLUTION: A program was written to simulate Algorithm 5.1. Here are the results of three iterations. The eigenvalues of $A$ are $\lambda(A) = (0.5, 1.2, -1, 0.75)$, which are the diagonal elements of $A$. For three arbitrary $(m \times r) = (2 \times 2)$-dimensional $K$ matrices,

$$K_i = \begin{bmatrix} k_1 & 0 \\ 0 & k_2 \end{bmatrix} = \begin{bmatrix} 2.248 & 0 \\ 0 & 32.458 \end{bmatrix}, \quad \begin{bmatrix} 1.2458 & 0 \\ 0 & 4.258 \end{bmatrix},$$

$$\begin{bmatrix} 2.3588 & 0 \\ 0 & -2.146 \end{bmatrix}, \quad i = 1, 2, 3 \qquad (5.3.11)$$

the respective eigenvalues of $(A + BKC)$ are

$$\lambda(A + BK_1C) = (1.0375 \pm j1.7866, 2.037, 1.20)$$

$$\lambda(A + BK_2C) = (1.966 \pm j1.196, 3.577, 1.20)$$

$$\lambda(A + BK_3C) = (1.66 \pm j0.759, -2.41, 1.20)$$

Clearly system (5.3.9)–(5.3.10) has a fixed mode $\lambda = 1.2$ and hence according to Theorem 5.1, this system *cannot* be stabilized by decentralized control with dynamic compensators.

**Example 5.3.2.** Consider a second-order system

$$\dot{x} = \begin{bmatrix} 0 & 0 \\ 1 & -2 \end{bmatrix} x + \begin{bmatrix} 0.2 & 0 \\ 0 & 0.5 \end{bmatrix} u, \quad y = \begin{bmatrix} 0 & 5 \\ 2 & 0 \end{bmatrix} x \qquad (5.3.12)$$

It is desired to check for stabilizability of this system under decentralized control.

SOLUTION: Utilizing Algorithm 5.1 it is found out that none of the eigenvalues of $(A + BKC)$ for several randomly chosen $K = \text{diag}\{k_1, k_2\}$ corresponded to $\lambda(A) = (0, -2)$. Thus it is concluded that this system can be stabilized through decentralized dynamic compensation which is discussed shortly and is illustrated by Example 5.3.4.

The following example makes an illustrative comparisons between decentralized and centralized control structures.

**Example 5.3.3.** Consider a seventh-order system

$$\dot{x} = \begin{bmatrix} 0 & 1 & 0 & 0 & 0 & 0 & 0 \\ 0 & 0 & 1 & 0 & 0 & 0 & 0 \\ -1 & -2 & -1 & 1 & 0 & 0 & 0 \\ 1 & 0 & 0 & -1 & -1 & 0 & 0 \\ 0 & 0 & 0 & 0 & 0 & 1 & 0 \\ 0 & 0 & 0 & 0 & 0 & 0 & 1 \\ 0 & 0 & 0 & -1 & -1 & -2 & -3 \end{bmatrix} x + \begin{bmatrix} 0 & 0 & 0 \\ 0 & 0 & 0 \\ 1 & 0 & 0 \\ 0 & 0 & 0 \\ 0 & 1 & 0 \\ 0 & 0 & 0 \\ 0 & 0 & 1 \end{bmatrix} u$$

$$(5.3.13)$$

$$y = \begin{bmatrix} 1 & 0 & 0 & 0 & 0 & 0 & 0 \\ 0 & 1 & 0 & 0 & 0 & 0 & 0 \\ 0 & 0 & 1 & 0 & 0 & 0 & 0 \\ 0 & 0 & 0 & 1 & 0 & 0 & 0 \\ 0 & 0 & 0 & 0 & 1 & 0 & 0 \end{bmatrix} x \qquad (5.3.14)$$

It is desired to investigate the advantages of a decentralized versus a centralized control structure.

SOLUTION: The $A$ matrix of this system has the following eigenvalues: $\lambda(A) = (-2.472, \ -0.322 \pm j1.43, \ -1.0, \ 0.24, \ -0.562 \pm j0.68)$. For the sake of output feedback gains, both decentralized and centralized structures are considered:

$$K_d = \begin{bmatrix} k_1 & 0 & 0 & 0 & 0 \\ 0 & k_2 & 0 & 0 & 0 \\ 0 & 0 & k_3 & k_4 & k_5 \end{bmatrix}, \quad K_c = \begin{bmatrix} k_{11} & k_{12} & k_{13} \\ k_{21} & k_{22} & k_{23} \\ k_{31} & k_{32} & k_{33} \end{bmatrix} \qquad (5.3.15)$$

For the above gain matrices with several randomly chosen entries, a fixed mode $\lambda = 1.0$ resulted. In fact, for several other possible decentralized structures like $K_d$, it was deduced that there is no particular advantage for using a more complex centralized controller. This result is most desirable for large-scale power systems, as reported for a 26th-order power system by Davison (1976a).

## 5.3.2 Stabilization via Dynamic Compensation

One of the earliest efforts in dynamically compensating centralized systems is due to Brasch and Pearson (1970) using output feedback. The problem can be briefly stated as follows: Consider a linear TIV system

$$\dot{x}(t) = Ax(t) + Bu(t) \tag{5.3.16}$$

$$y(t) = Cx(t) \tag{5.3.17}$$

It is desired to find a dynamic compensator

$$\dot{z}(t) = Fz(t) + Sy(t) \tag{5.3.18}$$

$$u(t) = Hz(t) + Ky(t) \tag{5.3.19}$$

so that the closed-loop system

$$\dot{x}(t) = (A + BKC)x(t) + BHz(t) \tag{5.3.20}$$

has a prescribed set of poles.

For the case of finding the dynamic compensator, let $n_c$ and $n_o$ be the smallest integers such that

$$\text{rank} \left[ B, AB, \ldots, A^{n_c}B \right] = n, \quad \text{rank} \left[ C^T, A^TC^T, \ldots, A^{Tn_o}C^T \right] = n \tag{5.3.21}$$

Now for convenience purposes let $\eta = \min(n_c, n_o)$, and $\Lambda_\eta = \{\lambda_1, \lambda_2, \ldots, \lambda_{n+\eta}\}$ be a set of arbitrary complex numbers with only restriction being that for each $\lambda_i$ with $\text{Im}(\lambda_i) \neq 0$, a complex conjugate pair $\lambda_i = \text{Re}(\lambda_i) \pm j\,\text{Im}(\lambda_i)$ is contained in $\Lambda_\eta$. Let us define the following augmented triplet $(C_\eta, A_\eta, B_\eta)$:

$$A_\eta = \begin{bmatrix} A & 0 \\ \hline 0 & 0 \end{bmatrix} \begin{matrix} \}n \\ \}\eta \end{matrix}, \quad B_\eta = \begin{bmatrix} B & 0 \\ \hline 0 & I \end{bmatrix} \begin{matrix} \}n \\ \}\eta \end{matrix}, \quad C_\eta = \begin{bmatrix} C & 0 \\ \hline 0 & I \end{bmatrix} \begin{matrix} \}r \\ \}\eta \end{matrix} \tag{5.3.22}$$

$$\underbrace{\quad}_{n}\underbrace{\quad}_{\eta} \qquad\qquad \underbrace{\quad}_{m}\underbrace{\quad}_{\eta} \qquad\qquad \underbrace{\quad}_{n}\underbrace{\quad}_{\eta}$$

The following theorem determines the existence of an output feedback gain for proper pole placement.

**Theorem 5.2.** *Let $(C, A, B)$ be a controllable and observable system, and let the triple $(C_\eta, A_\eta, B_\eta)$ be defined by (5.3.22) with $\eta = \min(n_c, n_o)$ and a set of prescribed poles $\Lambda_\eta = (\lambda_1, \lambda_2, \ldots, \lambda_{n+\eta})$. Then there exists a gain matrix $K$ such that the eigenvalues of $A_\eta + B_\eta K C_\eta$ are exact elements of $\Lambda_\eta$.*

The proof of this theorem with the aid of the properties of cyclic matrices can be found elsewhere (Brasch and Pearson, 1970). The above theorem, the canonical structure theorem of Kalman (1962), and the decentralized stabilization problem 1 of Section 5.2.1 have been used by Wang and Davison (1973) and Davison (1976a) to find a dynamic stabilizing compensator for a large-scale system under decentralized control. Consider that the set of $N$ dynamic compensators (5.2.4)–(5.2.5) and the triplet $(C_\eta, A_\eta, B_\eta)$ in (5.3.22) defines a real constant $(m + \eta) \times (r + \eta) K_\eta$ matrix,

$$
K_\eta =
\begin{bmatrix}
K_1 & & 0 & & H_1 & & 0 & \\
& K_2 & & & & H_2 & & \\
& & \ddots & & & & & \\
0 & & K_N & & 0 & & H_N & \\
S_1 & & & & F_1 & & & \\
& S_2 & 0 & & & F_2 & & \\
& 0 & \ddots & & & & \ddots & \\
& & & S_N & & & & F_N
\end{bmatrix}
\begin{matrix}
\} & m_1 \\
\} & m_2 \\
& \vdots \\
\} & m_N \\
\} & \eta_1 \\
\} & \eta_2 \\
& \vdots \\
\} & \eta_N
\end{matrix}
\quad (5.3.23)
$$

$$
\underbrace{r_1} \;\; \underbrace{r_2} \;\; \ldots r_N \qquad \underbrace{\eta_1} \;\; \underbrace{\eta_2} \ldots \qquad \underbrace{\eta_N}
$$

where $K_i$, $H_i$, $S_i$, $F_i$ are $m_i \times r_i$, $m_i \times \eta_i$, $\eta_i \times r_i$, and $\eta_i \times \eta_i$ submatrices, respectively, defined in (5.2.4)–(5.2.5); $m$ and $r$ are defined in (5.2.3); and $\eta = \Sigma_{i=1}^{N} \eta_i$. The following proposition summarizes the decentralized control pole placement problem.

**Proposition 5.1.** *Considering the triplets* $(C, A, B)$ *and* $(C_\eta, A_\eta, B_\eta)$ *defined above and the set of block-diagonal* **K** *in (5.3.6a), for any set of integers* $\eta_1, \eta_2, \ldots, \eta_N$ *with* $\eta_i \geq 0$, *the following two "fixed polynomials" are identical:*

$$
\phi(\lambda; C, A, B, K) = \phi(\lambda; C_\eta, A_\eta, B_\eta, K_\eta) \qquad (5.3.24)
$$

*where* $C_\eta$, $A_\eta$, $B_\eta$, *and* $K_\eta$ *are defined earlier. In other words, the greatest common divisor of* $\det(\lambda I - A - BKC)$ *and* $\det(\lambda I - A_\eta - B_\eta K_\eta C_\eta)$ *are the same.*

The proof of this proposition is given by Wang and Davison (1973). The result of this proposition and a matrix identity is used to place poles in decentralized output feedback controllers through dynamic compensation, which is illustrated by the following example.

**Example 5.3.4.** Let us consider the system in Example 5.3.2. It is desired to find a decentralized stabilizing output control such that a prescribed set of eigenvalues are achieved.

SOLUTION: For this example $\sigma(A) = (0, -2)$ and the matrix $A + BKC$ is

$$A + BKC = \begin{bmatrix} 0 & k_1 \\ 1 + k_2 & -2 \end{bmatrix} \qquad (5.3.25)$$

and $\eta = \min(n_c, n_o) = 1$; hence, $A_\eta$, $B_\eta$, $K_\eta$, and $C_\eta$ are

$$A_\eta = A_1 = \begin{bmatrix} 0 & 0 & | & 0 \\ 1 & -2 & | & 0 \\ \hline 0 & 0 & | & 0 \end{bmatrix}, \quad B_\eta = B_1 = \begin{bmatrix} 0.2 & 0 & | & 0 \\ 0 & 0.5 & | & 0 \\ \hline 0 & 0 & | & 1 \end{bmatrix}$$

$$\qquad (5.3.26)$$

$$C_\eta = C_1 = \begin{bmatrix} 0 & 5 & | & 0 \\ 2 & 0 & | & 0 \\ \hline 0 & 0 & | & 1 \end{bmatrix}, \quad K_\eta = K_1 = \begin{bmatrix} k_1 & 0 & | & h_1 \\ 0 & k_2 & | & 0 \\ \hline s_1 & 0 & | & f_1 \end{bmatrix}$$

where $k_1$, $k_2$, $s_1$, $h_1$, and $f_1$ are unknowns which can be found for a desired pole placement of the two decentralized controllers. The closed-loop matrix $A + BKC$ is given by (5.3.25) and $A_1 + B_1 K_1 C_1$ is

$$A_1 + B_1 K_1 C_1 = \begin{bmatrix} 0 & k_1 & | & 0.2h_1 \\ 1 + k_2 & -2 & | & 0 \\ \hline 0 & 5s_1 & | & f_1 \end{bmatrix} \qquad (5.3.27)$$

which, for the special case of $\eta = \eta_1 + \eta_2 = 1 + 0 = 1$, (5.3.26) is expressed by

$$A_1 + B_1 K_1 C_1 = \begin{bmatrix} A + BKC & | & B_1 h_1 \\ \hline s_1 C_1 & | & f_1 \end{bmatrix} \qquad (5.3.28)$$

which is in agreement with (5.3.4) for $v(t) = 0$ and a comparison between (5.3.25) and (5.3.27). The problem is to find $k_1$, $k_2$, $h_1$, $s_1$, and $f_1$ such that the augmented system has a preassigned set of poles for the decentralized system and compensator, say,

$$\Lambda_\eta = \Lambda_1 = \{-1 \pm j2, -1\} \qquad (5.3.29)$$

To achieve this, one notes the following matrix identity:

$$\det \begin{bmatrix} M_1 & | & M_{12} \\ \hline M_{21} & | & M_2 \end{bmatrix} = \det(M_1) \cdot \det(M_2 - M_{21} M_1^{-1} M_{12}) \qquad (5.3.30)$$

and applies it to

$$\det(\lambda I - A_1 - B_1 K_1 C_1) = \det(\lambda I - A - BKC)$$

$$\cdot \det \left[ (\lambda - f_1) - \begin{pmatrix} 0 & 5s_1 \end{pmatrix} (\lambda I - A - BKC)^{-1} \begin{pmatrix} 0.2h_1 \\ 0 \end{pmatrix} \right]$$

$$\qquad (5.3.31)$$

Choosing $k_1$ and $k_2$ such that the first two poles are appropriately placed, $k_1 = 1$ and $k_2 = -6$. The remaining unknowns may be obtained by setting the latter part of (5.3.31) equal to zero for $\lambda = \lambda_3 = -1$, i.e.,

$$\det\left[(\lambda - f_1) - \begin{pmatrix} 0 & 5s_1 \end{pmatrix}(\lambda I - A - BKC)^{-1}\begin{pmatrix} 0.2h_1 \\ 0 \end{pmatrix}\right]$$

$$= \det\left(\lambda - f_1 - \frac{-5h_1 s_1}{\lambda^2 + 2\lambda + 5}\right)\Bigg|_{\lambda = -1} = 0$$

(5.3.32)

or for arbitrary $s_1 = h_1 = 1$, $f_1 = 0.25$. Thus, the decentralized dynamic compensator controllers are

$$\dot{z}_1 = 0.25 z_1 + y_1, \quad z_1(0) = 0$$
$$u_1 = z_1 + y_1 \tag{5.3.33}$$
$$\dot{z}_2 = 0, \quad z_2(0) = 0$$
$$u_2 = -6 y_2 \tag{5.3.34}$$

Figure 5.1 shows a block diagram for the two-controller decentralized

**Figure 5.1** A block diagram for the two-controller decentralized system of Example 5.3.4.

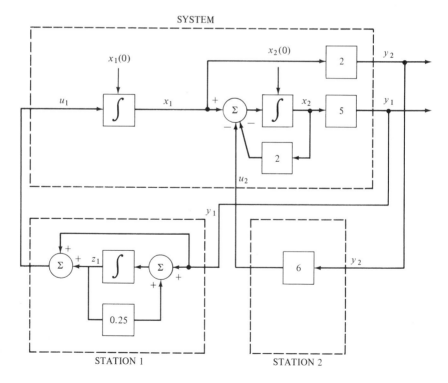

structure. Note that while Station 1 represents a dynamic compensator, Station 2 is a simple static feedback compensator. Note also that the eigenvalues of the combined system are not those specified by (5.3.29) for system with no compensation. In fact, for this decentralized system the closed-loop poles turned out to be $\lambda(\cdot) = -0.375 \pm j1.9$, $-1.0$ which are not too far from the desired locations.

Although the pole placement problem has been one of the most fruitful areas of research, there has not been an effective computational algorithm for the problem. In its frequency-domain framework, however, the problem has been very successful (Nyquist, 1932; Bode, 1940; Evans, 1950) within the context of Nyquist, Bode, and root locus plots. In the state-space case, by virtue of canonical transformation, SISO systems have been compensated (Chen, 1970). The multivariable case, considered by many authors (Simon and Mitter, 1968; Retallack and MacFarlane, 1970; Godbout, 1974; Seraji, 1980), reduces the problem to one of solving a set of nonlinear equations which may or may not be computationally effective.

The pole placement problem has also been taken up by Porter and Bradshaw (1978a, b, c, d), and Porter et al. (1979) have developed a software package for it. One of the more recent efforts in placing poles in dynamic compensation, due to Lee et al. (1979), takes advantage of unity rank gain matrices properties and proposes an algorithm for it. This algorithm, as pointed out by Porter (1980), can potentially lead to erroneous results where an infinite number of gain matrices may satisfy the algorithm. This was subsequently pointed out by Lee et al. (1980).

The pole placement schemes for centralized systems are not easily applicable to decentralized systems in general. Such methods can be used separately for each decentralized station in such a way that the $n$ eigenvalues of the system are divided into $N$ groups corresponding to the $N$ controllers. Then utilizing such stabilizing schemes, $K_i$, $i = 1, 2, \ldots, N$, gains are obtained which results in an overall closed-loop matrix $A - \sum_{i=1}^{N} BK_iC_i$.

### 5.3.3 Stabilization via Local State Feedback

In this section a large-scale system is stabilized by local state feedback without a formal pole placement through dynamic compensation as discussed in the previous section. Several authors have attempted to stabilize a large composite system using one form of feedback or another, i.e., state or output. Araki (1976) and Ramussen and Michel (1976) give necessary and/or sufficient conditions for the stability of the large-scale system in terms of low-order subsystems. These conditions will be formally introduced in Chapter 7. Davison (1974) has shown that a SISO system with unknown nonlinear time-varying interactions with a particular structure can be stabilized. Šiljak and Vukcevic (1976a, b, 1978), Šiljak (1978a, b), and Ikeda and Šiljak (1980b) have proposed elegant methods of stabilization which are based on either local/global controllers or the solutions of subsystem matrix Riccati equations and certain interaction conditions which lead to "exponential stability." These schemes are considered in Sections 5.3.4 and 5.3.5, respectively. Another result of Šiljak and his colleagues, in both time-varying and time-invariant cases, will be discussed in Section 5.3.7. In this section a state feedback stabilization scheme due to Sezer and Hüseyin (1978) which preassigns closed-loop poles and finds a set of local and global feedback gains based on diagonally dominant matrices (Rosenbrock, 1974) will be given.

Consider a set of $N$ linear time-invariant systems,

$$\dot{x}_i(t) = A_i x_i(t) + B_i u_i(t) \tag{5.3.35}$$

$$y_i(t) = C_i x_i(t), \quad i = 1, 2, \ldots, N \tag{5.3.36}$$

where matrices $A_i$, $B_i$, and $C_i$ are $n_i \times n_i$-, $n_i \times m_i$-, and $r_i \times n_i$-dimensional, respectively. The following local control laws are suggested:

$$u_i(t) = P_i x_i(t) + \sum_{\substack{j=1 \\ j \neq i}}^{N} F_{ij} y_j + v_i \tag{5.3.37}$$

for $i = 1, 2, \ldots, N$, and $P_i$ is the $i$th subsystem local state feedback gain matrix. The matrices $F_{ij}$, $i, j = 1, 2, \ldots, N$ are gains from other subsystems outputs which include subsystems interactions and $v_i$ is an external reference input for the $i$th subsystem. When the decentralized control laws (5.3.37) are applied to the system, its closed-loop composite form becomes

$$\dot{x}(t) = (A + BP + BFC)x(t) + Bv(t) \tag{5.3.38}$$

where $A$, $B$, $C$, and $P$ are block-diagonal matrices with $A_i$, $B_i$, $C_i$, and $P_i$, $i = 1, 2, \ldots, N$, respectively, as their diagonal blocks, $v$ is a column matrix consisting of $v_i$, $i = 1, 2, \ldots, N$, and the $m \times r$ matrix $F$ has a form

$$F = \begin{bmatrix} 0 & F_{12} & \cdots & F_{1N} \\ F_{21} & 0 & \cdots & F_{2N} \\ \vdots & \vdots & & \vdots \\ F_{N1} & F_{N2} & & 0 \end{bmatrix} \tag{5.3.39}$$

The following theorem provides the condition for the stabilization of the composite closed-loop system (5.3.55).

**Theorem 5.3.** *If each subsystem (5.3.35) is completely controllable for $i = 1, 2, \ldots, N$, then a set of local decentralized feedback gain matrices $P_i$ in (5.3.37) can be chosen such that the composite system (5.3.38) is stable.*

In order to prove this theorem, the following two lemmas are proved first (Sezer and Hüseyin, 1978).

**Lemma 5.1.** *Consider two monic polynomials $p(s)$ and $q(s)$ where all the roots (zeros) of $q(s)$ are in the open left half s-plane $s^-$. Let $r(s)$ be any polynomial so that*

$$\deg(p(s)) + \deg(q(s)) > \deg(r(s)) \qquad (5.3.40)$$

*Then the coefficients of $p(s)$ can be chosen such that all the zeros of $f(s) = p(s)q(s) + r(s)$ are in $s^-$.*

PROOF: Let $p(s)$ be represented by

$$p(s) = s^n + p_1 s^{n-1} + \cdots + p_n = s^n + p_1 \beta(s) \qquad (5.3.41)$$

where $\beta(s)$ is a monic polynomial with $\deg(\beta(s)) = n - 1$. Then

$$f(s) = s^n q(s) + p_1 \beta(s) q(s) + r(s) \qquad (5.3.42)$$

Now consider when $p_1 \to \infty$. Since $\deg(s^n q(s) + r(s)) = \deg(\beta(s)q(s)) + 1$, from the rules of plotting root locus (D'Azzo and Houpis, 1981), it follows that one zero of $f(s)$ approaches $-\infty$, while the remaining zeros approach those of $\beta(s)q(s)$. However, since the zeros of $q(s)$ are in $s^-$, by choosing a large value for $p_1$ and zeros of $\beta(s)$ in $s^-$, the result follows. Q.E.D. ■

Now consider the following lemma.

**Lemma 5.2.** *Theorem 5.3 is true for $N = 2$.*

PROOF: When $N = 2$, the composite system (5.3.38) becomes

$$\dot{x}(t) = \begin{bmatrix} A_1 + B_1 P_1 & B_1 F_{12} C_2 \\ B_2 F_{21} C_1 & A_2 + B_2 P_2 \end{bmatrix} x(t) + \begin{bmatrix} B_1 & 0 \\ 0 & B_2 \end{bmatrix} v(t) \qquad (5.3.43)$$

Let us choose $P_1$ such that all eigenvalues of $A_1 + B_1 P_1$ are in $s^-$, and furthermore, let the matrix $H_2$, $\tilde{A}_2 = H_2^{-1} A_2 H_2$, $\tilde{B}_2 = H_2^{-1} B_2$, $\tilde{C}_2 = C_2 H_2$, transform the pair $(\tilde{A}_2, \tilde{B}_2)$ into canonical form. The structure of such a transformation matrix will be defined shortly in this section (Luenberger, 1967; Chen, 1970). If $k_{21} \geqslant k_{22} \geqslant \cdots \geqslant k_{2m_2}$ are the controllability indices of the pair $(A_2, B_2)$, then

$$\tilde{A}_2 = \begin{bmatrix} \tilde{A}_{211} & \cdots & \tilde{A}_{21m2} \\ \vdots & & \vdots \\ \tilde{A}_{2m21} & \cdots & \tilde{A}_{2m2m2} \end{bmatrix}^*, \quad \tilde{B}_2 = \begin{bmatrix} \tilde{B}_{21} \\ \vdots \\ \tilde{B}_{2m2} \end{bmatrix} \cdot D_2,$$

$$\tilde{C}_2 = \begin{bmatrix} \tilde{C}_{21} & \cdots & \tilde{C}_{2m2} \end{bmatrix} \qquad (5.3.44)$$

---

$^*\tilde{A}_{2ij}$ stands for the $(i, j)$th block of the second subsystem.

where

$$\tilde{A}_{2jj} = \left[ \begin{array}{c|c} 0 & I \\ \hline \multicolumn{2}{c}{-a_{2jj}^T} \end{array} \right] \in R^{k2j \times k2j}$$

$$\tilde{A}_{2jk} = \left[ \begin{array}{c} 0 \\ -\tilde{a}_{2jl}^T \end{array} \right] \in R^{k2j \times k2l} \qquad (5.3.45)$$

$$\tilde{B}_{2j} = \left[ \begin{array}{c} 0 \\ e_j^T \end{array} \right] \in R^{k2j \times m2}$$

and $D_2 \in R^{m2 \times m2}$ is a nonsingular matrix, $\tilde{a}_{2jl}^T$ are row vectors, and $e_j^T$ is the $j$th row of the unit matrix $I_{m2}$. Now let

$$P_2 = D_2^{-1} \tilde{P}_2 H_2^{-1} \qquad (5.3.46)$$

where $\tilde{P}_2$ is partitioned as

$$\tilde{P}_2 = \left[ \tilde{P}_{21} \quad \cdots \quad \tilde{P}_{2m2} \right] \qquad (5.3.47)$$

Let $\tilde{P}_{2r}$ be chosen such that

$$\tilde{A}_{2jr} + \tilde{B}_{2j} \tilde{P}_{2r} = 0 \qquad (5.3.48)$$

i.e., $\tilde{a}_{2jr}^T + e_j^T \tilde{P}_{2r} = 0$, for all $j \neq r$, $r = 1, \ldots, m_2$. Therefore, all rows of $P_{2r}$ are fixed except the $r$th row. Let

$$-\tilde{a}_{2rr}^T + e_r^T \tilde{P}_{2r} = -\tilde{a}_{2rr}^T, \quad r = 1, \ldots, m_2 \qquad (5.3.49)$$

Then using (5.3.44)–(5.3.49) in (5.3.43) the following matrices are similar:

$$A + BFC + BP \sim \left[ \begin{array}{cccc} \hat{A}_1 & B_1 F_{12} \tilde{C}_{21} & \cdots & B_1 F_{12} \tilde{C}_{2m2} \\ \tilde{B}_{21} D_2 F_{21} C_1 & \hat{A}_{211} & & 0 \\ \vdots & \vdots & & \vdots \\ \tilde{B}_{2m2} D_2 F_{21} C_1 & 0 & & \hat{A}_{2m2m2} \end{array} \right]$$

$$(5.3.50)$$

where $\sim$ stands for matrix similarity and the $\hat{A}_{2jj}$ have the same structures as $\tilde{A}_{2jj}$ except that the $-\tilde{a}_{2jj}^T$ are replaced by $-\hat{a}_{2jj}^T$, $j = 1, \ldots, m_2$. Now let

$$G_j = \left| \begin{array}{cccc} \hat{A}_1 & B_1 F_{12} \tilde{C}_{21} & \cdots & B_1 F_{12} \tilde{C}_{2j} \\ \tilde{B}_{21} D_2 F_{21} C_1 & \hat{A}_{211} & & 0 \\ \vdots & \vdots & & \vdots \\ \tilde{B}_{2j} D_2 F_{21} C_1 & 0 & & \hat{A}_{2jj} \end{array} \right|, \quad j = 1, \ldots, m_2 \quad (5.3.51)$$

and

$$d_j(s) = |sI - G_j|, \quad j = 1, \ldots, m_2 \tag{5.3.52}$$

It is noted that $G_{m2} \sim A + BFC + BP$. Using column operations, it is easily seen that

$$d_j(s) = \begin{bmatrix} sI - \hat{A}_1 & -B_1 F_{12}\tilde{c}_{21}(s) & \cdots & -B_1 F_{12}\tilde{c}_{2j}(s) \\ -e_1^T D_2 F_{21} C_1 & \hat{a}_{211}(s) & & 0 \\ \vdots & \vdots & & \vdots \\ -e_j^T D_2 F_{21} C_1 & 0 & & \hat{a}_{2jj}(s) \end{bmatrix} \tag{5.3.53}$$

where

$$\hat{a}_{2rr}(s) = s^{p2r} + \hat{a}_{2rr}^T \begin{bmatrix} 1 \\ s \\ \vdots \\ s^{p2r-1} \end{bmatrix}, \quad r = 1, \ldots, j$$

and

$$\tilde{c}_{2r}(s) = \tilde{C}_{2r} \begin{bmatrix} 1 \\ s \\ \vdots \\ s^{p2r-1} \end{bmatrix}, \quad r = 1, \ldots, j$$

It follows from (5.3.49) that one can arbitrarily choose the coefficients of $\hat{a}_{2rr}(s)$ by selecting the $r$th row of $\tilde{P}_{2r}$ properly. Now through induction, it is shown that by properly choosing the coefficients $\hat{a}_{2rr}(s)$, $r = 1, \ldots, m2$, such that all zeros of each $d_j(s)$, $j = 1, \ldots, m2$ are in $s^-$.

1. For $j = 1$

$$d_1(s) = \begin{vmatrix} sI - A_1 & -B_1 F_{12}\tilde{c}_{21}(s) \\ -e_1^T D_2 F_{21} C_1 & \hat{a}_{211}(s) \end{vmatrix}$$

$$= \hat{a}_{211}(s)|sI - \hat{A}_1| + \begin{vmatrix} sI - \hat{A}_1 & -B_1 F_{12}\tilde{c}_{21}(s) \\ -e_1^T D_2 F_{21} C_1 & 0 \end{vmatrix} \tag{5.3.54}$$

Now if one identifies $p(s) = a_{211}(s)$, $q(s) = |sI - A_1|$, and the second term in (5.3.54) as $r(s)$, the result follows from Lemma 5.1.

2. Let the coefficients of $a_{2jj}(s)$, $j = 1, \ldots, r - 1$, be chosen such that the zeros of $d_{r-1}(s)$ are all in $s^-$. Now by writing $d_r(s)$ as the sum of $a_{2rr}(s) d_{r-1}(s)$ and a lower degree polynomial as in case 1, the proof follows from Lemma 5.1. This completes the proof of Lemma 5.2. Q.E.D. ∎

PROOF OF THEOREM 5.3. The proof is provided through induction again.

1. $N = 2$: Lemma 5.2.
2. Assume that any composite system composed of interconnecting $r - 1$ subsystems can be stabilized by local state feedback in the subsystems. Then a composite system composed of interconnecting $r$ subsystems can be thought of as an interconnection of any one of the subsystems with the subcomposite system formed by the remaining $r - 1$ subsystems and the proof follows from Lemma 5.2. Q.E.D. ∎

In sequel, an algorithm based on pole placement via output feedback (Paraskevopoulos, 1976, 1980) and modified by Sezer and Hüseyin (1978) is given to stabilize a composite large-scale system. The modified algorithm requires that the subsystems matrices $(A_i, B_i, C_i)$ be transformed into Luenberger (1967) canonical form $(\tilde{A}_i, \tilde{B}_i, \tilde{C}_i)$, which is briefly explained first. The stabilization algorithm would follow.

Let the characteristic polynomial of a single-input system $\dot{x} = Ax + bu$, $y = Cx$ be

$$p(s) = s^n + a_{n-1}s^{n-1} + \cdots + a_1 s^1 + a_o \qquad (5.3.55)$$

then an algorithm due to Chen (1970) transforms the system to $\dot{\tilde{x}} = \tilde{A}\tilde{x} + \tilde{b}u$, $y = \tilde{C}\tilde{x}$, where

$$\tilde{A} = H^{-1}AH, \quad \tilde{b} = H^{-1}b, \quad \tilde{C} = CH \qquad (5.3.56)$$

where column vectors of the transformation matrix are

$$h^n = b$$
$$h^{n-1} = Ab + a_{n-1}b$$
$$h^{n-2} = A^2b + a_{n-1}Ab + a_{n-2}b \qquad (5.3.57)$$
$$\vdots$$
$$h^1 = A^{n-1}b + a_{n-1}A^{n-2}b + \cdots + a_1 b$$

and

$$H = \left[ h^1 | h^2 | \cdots | h^n \right]$$

***Algorithm 5.2.*** Stabilization via Local State Feedback

*Step 1:*  Use (5.3.55)–(5.3.57) to transform each subsystem $(A_i, B_i, C_i)$ into controllable canonical from $(\tilde{A}_i, \tilde{B}_i, \tilde{C}_i)$ with controllability indices $k_{i1} \geqslant \cdots k_{im_i}$.

*Step 2:*  For each subsystem $i$, choose a set of prespecified eigenvalues, i.e., define a diagonal matrix

$$G_i = \mathrm{diag}(\lambda_1, \lambda_2, \ldots, \lambda_{n_i}) \qquad (5.3.58)$$

for $i = 1, 2, \ldots, N$.

*Step 3:* Define a set of $N$ $n_i \times n_i$ nonsingular matrices $W_i$:

$$W_i \triangleq \begin{bmatrix} w_{i1}^T \\ w_{i1}^T G_i^{ki1-1} \\ \vdots \\ w_{im_i}^T \\ \vdots \\ w_{im_i}^T G_i^{kimi-1} \end{bmatrix} \tag{5.3.59}$$

where $w_{ij}$ is a column vector whose $j$th block is all ones and the remaining blocks are zero, i.e.,

$$w_{ij} = \begin{bmatrix} 0 \cdots 0 \cdots |1 & 1 & \cdots & 1| \cdots |0 \cdots 0 \end{bmatrix}^T$$

*Step 4:* For a composite transformation matrix $H = \text{diag}\{H_1,\ldots,H_N\}$ and matrix $W = \text{diag}\{W_1,\ldots,W_N\}$, the composite system's closed-loop matrix is given by

$$A_c = W^{-1}H^{-1}(A + BFC + BP)HW$$
$$= \begin{bmatrix} G_1 & W_1^{-1}\tilde{B}_1 F_{12}\tilde{C}_2 W_2 & \cdots & W_1^{-1}\tilde{B}_1 F_{1N}\tilde{C}_N W_N \\ W_2^{-1}\tilde{B}_2 F_{21}\tilde{C}_1 F_1 & G_2 & \cdots & W_2^{-1}B_2 F_{2N}\tilde{C}_N W_N \\ \vdots & & & \vdots \\ W_N^{-1}B_N F_{N1}C_1 W_1 & \cdots & \cdots & G_N \end{bmatrix} \tag{5.3.60}$$

*Step 5:* Test whether $A_c$ is diagonally dominant, i.e., either row dominant:

$$|\hat{a}_{ii}| \gg \sum_{\substack{j=1 \\ j \neq i}}^{n} |\hat{a}_{ij}| \tag{5.3.61}$$

or column dominant:

$$|\hat{a}_{jj}| \gg \sum_{\substack{i=1 \\ i \neq j}}^{n} |\hat{a}_{ij}| \tag{5.3.62}$$

If either one of the two conditions (5.3.61) or (5.3.62) are met, the local feedback matrices $P_i$ are obtained from

$$P_i = \tilde{S}_i \tilde{B}_i^T (\tilde{W}_i - \tilde{A}_i) H_i^{-1} \tag{5.3.63}$$

where

$$\tilde{S}_i = \left( \tilde{B}_i^T \tilde{B}_i \right)^{-1}, \quad \tilde{W}_i = W_i G_i W_i^{-1} \tag{5.3.64}$$

If $A_c$ is not diagonally dominant, Steps 2 through 5 must be repeated.

The above algorithm is illustrated by the following example.

**Example 5.3.5.** Consider the following two subsystems:

$$(A_1, B_1, C_1) = \left\{ \begin{bmatrix} 2 & 1 \\ -4 & -3 \end{bmatrix}, \begin{bmatrix} 1 \\ 2 \end{bmatrix}, \begin{bmatrix} 1 & 2 \\ 0 & 1 \end{bmatrix} \right\} \tag{5.3.65}$$

$$(A_2, B_2, C_2) = \left\{ \begin{bmatrix} 0 & 1 & 0 \\ 0 & 0 & 1 \\ 6 & 5 & -2 \end{bmatrix}, \begin{bmatrix} 0 & 1 \\ 1 & 0 \\ 0 & 1 \end{bmatrix}, [1 \quad 1 \quad 1] \right\}$$

with $(m_1 + m_2) \times (r_1 + r_2)$-dimensional

$$F = \begin{bmatrix} 0 & | & F_{12} \\ \hline F_{21} & | & 0 \end{bmatrix} = \begin{bmatrix} 0 & 0 & | & f_{12} \\ \hline f_{211} & f_{212} & | & 0 \\ f_{213} & f_{214} & | & 0 \end{bmatrix} \tag{5.3.66}$$

It is desired to find two local state feedback control laws to stabilize the system.

SOLUTION: A careful view of the two subsystems indicates that both are controllable and moreover the second subsystem is already in controllable canonical form. The subsystems' open-loop poles are $\lambda(A_1) = \{1, -2\}$ and $\lambda(A_2) = (2, -1, -3)$. Following the steps of Algorithm 5.2, the transformation matrices are

$$H_1 = \begin{bmatrix} 5 & 1 \\ -8 & 2 \end{bmatrix}, \quad H_2 = \begin{bmatrix} 1 & 0 & 0 \\ 0 & 1 & 0 \\ 0 & 0 & 1 \end{bmatrix} \tag{5.3.67}$$

which give the following controllable canonical forms:

$$(\tilde{A}_1, \tilde{B}_1, \tilde{C}_1) = \left\{ \begin{bmatrix} 0 & 1 \\ 2 & -1 \end{bmatrix}, \begin{bmatrix} 0 \\ 1 \end{bmatrix}, \begin{bmatrix} -11 & 5 \\ -8 & 2 \end{bmatrix} \right\} \tag{5.3.68}$$

$$(\tilde{A}_1, \tilde{B}_2, \tilde{C}_2) = (A_2, B_2, C_2) \tag{5.3.69}$$

Let $G_1 = \text{diag}(-2, -5)$, $G_2 = \text{diag}(-8, -10, -15)$; hence,

$$W_1 = \begin{bmatrix} w_{11}^T \\ w_{11}^T G_1^1 \end{bmatrix} = \begin{bmatrix} 1 & 1 \\ -2 & -5 \end{bmatrix}, \quad W_2 = \begin{bmatrix} 1 & 0 & 0 \\ 0 & 1 & 0 \\ 0 & 0 & 1 \end{bmatrix}$$

Next using $H = \text{diag}(H_1, H_2)$ and $W = \text{diag}(W_1, W_2)$ and (5.3.56), the closed-loop matrix $A_c$ becomes

$$A_c = W^{-1}H^{-1}(A + BFC + BP)HW$$

$$= \begin{bmatrix} -2 & 0 & \vdots & \varepsilon_{121} & \varepsilon_{121} & \varepsilon_{121} \\ 0 & -5 & \vdots & -\varepsilon_{121} & -\varepsilon_{121} & -\varepsilon_{121} \\ \cdots & \cdots & + & \cdots & \cdots & \cdots \\ \varepsilon_{211} & \varepsilon_{212} & \vdots & -8 & 0 & 0 \\ \varepsilon_{213} & \varepsilon_{214} & \vdots & 0 & -10 & 0 \\ \varepsilon_{215} & \varepsilon_{216} & \vdots & 0 & 0 & -15 \end{bmatrix} \qquad (5.3.70)$$

where $\varepsilon_{121} = f_{12}/3$, and

$$\begin{bmatrix} \varepsilon_{211} & \varepsilon_{212} \\ \varepsilon_{213} & \varepsilon_{214} \\ \varepsilon_{215} & \varepsilon_{216} \end{bmatrix} = F_{21} \begin{bmatrix} -21 & -36 \\ -12 & -18 \end{bmatrix} \qquad (5.3.71)$$

Instead of iterating about Steps 2–5 in determining $\varepsilon_{ijk}$ values so that $A_c$ is diagonally dominant, an arbitrary set of values are chosen for these parameters. Let

$$\varepsilon_{121} = 2/30, \quad \varepsilon_{211} = \varepsilon_{212} = 0.2, \quad \varepsilon_{213} = \varepsilon_{214} = 0.25,$$

$$\varepsilon_{215} = \varepsilon_{216} = 0.375$$

and use (5.3.71) to find $F_{21}$:

$$F_{21} = \begin{bmatrix} 0.022 & -0.0562 \\ 0.0275 & -0.07025 \\ 0.04125 & -0.1054 \end{bmatrix} \qquad (5.3.72)$$

The state feedback gain matrices are

$$P_1 = \tilde{S}_1 \tilde{B}_1^T (\tilde{W}_1 - \tilde{A}_1) H_1^{-1} = [-4.23 \quad -1.39] \qquad (5.3.73)$$

$$P_2 = \tilde{S}_2 \tilde{B}_2^T (\tilde{W}_2 - \tilde{A}_2) H_2^{-1} = \begin{bmatrix} 0 & -10 & 0 \\ -4 & 0 & -7.5 \end{bmatrix}$$

A possible block diagram for the stabilized closed-loop system is shown in Figure 5.2. The thick connections represent vector values, and $v_i$, $i = 1, 2$, represent external reference inputs. It is noted that the local feedback gain matrices $P_i$, $i = 1, 2$, have relatively higher values as compared with the output feedback gain matrices $F_{12}$ and $F_{21}$. In other words, stabilization has been achieved by high local state feedback gains and low output feedback gains from other subsystems (i.e., weakening interactions).

Further comments on this method are given in Section 5.6.

### 5.3.4 Stabilization via Multilevel Control

In this section a decentralized stabilization scheme based on multilevel control (Chapter 4) using local and global controllers is described. This method is based on the works of Šiljak (1978b), Ikeda and Šiljak (1980b), and Sezer and Šiljak (1981b).

210

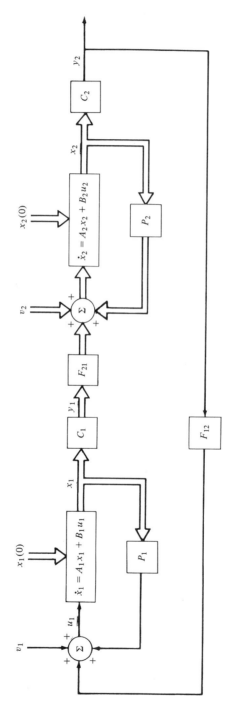

**Figure 5.2** A block diagram for the stabilized composite system of Example 5.3.5.

Consider a linear time-invariant system represented in "input-decentralized" form

$$\dot{x}_i(t) = A_i x_i(t) + b_i u_i(t) + \sum_{\substack{j=1 \\ j \neq i}}^{N} G_{ij} x_j(t), \quad i=1,\ldots,N \quad (5.3.74)$$

where all vectors and matrices are of appropriate dimensions and the pairs $(A_i, b_i)$ are controllable. It is desired to apply a decentralized multilevel control

$$u_i(t) = u_i^l(t) + u_i^g(t) \quad (5.3.75)$$

with the $i$th local control $u_i^l(t)$ and global control $u_i^g(t)$ to be chosen in the following feedback forms:

$$u_i^l(t) = -k_i^T x_i(t) \quad (5.3.76a)$$

$$u_i^g(t) = -\sum_{\substack{j=1 \\ j \neq i}}^{N} k_{ij}^T x_j(t) \quad (5.3.76b)$$

where $k_i$ and $k_{ij}$ are $n_i$- and $n_j$-dimensional constant vectors. Applying (5.3.76a) and (5.3.76b) to (5.3.74) results in the closed-loop system

$$\dot{x}_i(t) = \left(A_i - b_i k_i^T\right) x_i(t) + \sum_{\substack{j=1 \\ j \neq i}}^{N} \left(G_{ij} - b_i k_{ij}^T\right) x_j(t), \quad i=1,\ldots,N \quad (5.3.77)$$

It is noted that since each pair $(A_i, b_i)$ is controllable, a feedback gain vector $k_i$ can be always obtained to assign particular eigenvalues to $(A_i - b_i k_i^T)$ at desired locations $-\sigma_i^1 \pm j\omega_i^1, \ldots, -\sigma_i^r \pm j\omega_i^r, -\sigma_i^{r+1}, \ldots, -\sigma_i^{n_i - r}$, where $r = 0, 1, \ldots, n_i/2$ and $\sigma_i^p > 0$ for $p = 1, 2, \ldots, n_i - r$. Then each decoupled subsystem

$$\dot{x}_i(t) = \left(A_i - b_i k_i^T\right) x_i = \hat{A}_i x_i, \quad i=1,\ldots,N \quad (5.3.78)$$

is stabilized with a degree of exponential stability

$$\alpha_i = \min_p \sigma_i^p, \quad p = 1, 2, \ldots, n_i - r \quad (5.3.79)$$

The essential point of this stabilization scheme, as discussed by Šiljak (1978b), is that through relatively simple classical techniques each subsystem is stabilized and then through aggregating their stability properties into a single scalar Lyapunov function, the stability of the original large-scale system is deduced. This point will be elaborated further in this and the next section. The stability of interconnected systems will be considered in Chapter 7.

The construction of this aggregate model for the interconnected system (5.3.78) is achieved by the proper choice for a Lyapunov function. Let us apply a modal decomposition (transformation) to the uncoupled closed-loop subsystem (5.3.78) to obtain

$$\dot{\hat{x}}_i(t) = \Lambda_i \hat{x}_i(t) \tag{5.3.80}$$

where

$$x_i(t) = M_i \hat{x}_i(t) \tag{5.3.81}$$

$$\Lambda_i = M_i^{-1} \hat{A}_i M_i \tag{5.3.82}$$

and the transformation (modal) matrix $M_i$ is given by (See Problem 2.6)

$$M_i = \left[ \operatorname{Re}\{\xi_i^1\} \;\middle|\; \operatorname{Im}\{\xi_i^1\} \;\middle|\; \cdots \;\middle|\; \operatorname{Re}\{\xi_i^r\} \;\middle|\; \operatorname{Im}\{\xi_i^r\} \;\middle|\; \xi_i^{2r+1} \;\middle|\; \cdots \;\middle|\; \xi_i^{n_i} \right] \tag{5.3.83}$$

and $\xi_i^m = \operatorname{Re}\{\xi_i^m\} + j \operatorname{Im}\{\xi_i^m\}$ and $\xi_i^{r+1}, \ldots$ are complex, real distinct (or generalized) eigenvectors of the decoupled subsystem's closed-loop matrix $\hat{A}_i$. The quasidiagonal matrix $\Lambda_i$ for the $i$th subsystem can take on the form

$$\Lambda_i = \text{Block-diag} \left\{ \begin{bmatrix} -\sigma_i^1 & \omega_i^1 \\ -\omega_i^1 & -\sigma_i^1 \end{bmatrix}, \ldots, \begin{bmatrix} -\sigma_i^r & \omega_i^r \\ -\omega_i^r & -\sigma_i^r \end{bmatrix}, -\sigma_i^{r+1}, \ldots, -\sigma_i^{n_i-r} \right\} \tag{5.3.84}$$

A choice for the aggregated Lyapunov function for the $i$th subsystem is $v_i : R^{n_i} \to R^+$, i.e.,

$$v_i(\hat{x}_i) = \left( \hat{x}_i^T \hat{P}_i \hat{x}_i \right)^{1/2} \tag{5.3.85}$$

where

$$\hat{P}_i \Lambda_i + \Lambda_i^T \hat{P}_i + \hat{H}_i = 0 \tag{5.3.86}$$

and

$$\hat{P}_i = \beta_i I_i, \quad \hat{H}_i = 2\beta_i \operatorname{diag} \left\{ \sigma_i^1, \sigma_i^1, \ldots, \sigma_i^r, \sigma_i^r, \sigma_i^{r+1}, \ldots, \sigma_i^{n_i-r} \right\} \tag{5.3.87}$$

In (5.3.87), $\beta_i$ is an arbitrary positive constant and $I_i$ is an $n_i \times n_i$ identity matrix. Šiljak (1978b) has shown that the Lyapunov function (5.3.85) provides an exact estimate of $\alpha_i$ given in (5.3.79). The aggregate Lyapunov function $v : R^n \to R_+^N$ given by

$$v = (v_1, v_2, \ldots, v_N)^T \tag{5.3.88}$$

is obtained for the transformed system (5.3.77)

$$\dot{\hat{x}}_i(t) = \Lambda_i \hat{x}_i(t) + \sum_{\substack{j=1 \\ j \neq i}}^{N} \left( \hat{G}_{ij} - \hat{b}_i \hat{k}_{ij}^T \right) \hat{x}_j(t), \quad i = 1, \ldots, N \tag{5.3.89}$$

and using the Lyapunov functions $v_i(\hat{x}_i)$ defined in (5.3.85). In (5.3.89) we have $\hat{G}_{ij} = M_i^{-1} G_{ij} M_j$, $\hat{b}_i = M_i^{-1} b_i$, $\hat{k}_{ij}^T = k_{ij}^T M_j$. Using the vector version of the "Comparison Principle" (Šiljak, 1978b), the aggregate model is represented by

$$\dot{v} \leqslant \hat{S}v \tag{5.3.90}$$

where the $N \times N$ constant aggregation matrix $\hat{S}$ has the elements $\hat{s}_{ij}$

$$\hat{s}_{ij} = -\delta_{ij}\alpha_i + \hat{\gamma}_{ij} \tag{5.3.91}$$

and $\delta_{ij}$ is the Kronecker delta, $\alpha_i$ is given by (5.3.79), and

$$\hat{\gamma}_{ij} = \lambda_M^{1/2}\left\{\left(\hat{G}_{ij} - \hat{b}_i \hat{k}_{ij}^T\right)^T\left(\hat{G}_{ij} - \hat{b}_i \hat{k}_{ij}^T\right)\right\} \tag{5.3.92}$$

The term $\lambda_M\{\cdot\}$ represents the maximum eigenvalue of its matrix argument. Then by applying Sevastyanov–Kotelyanskii condition

$$(-1)^m \begin{vmatrix} -\alpha_1 + \hat{\gamma}_{11} & \hat{\gamma}_{12} & \cdots & \hat{\gamma}_{1m} \\ \hat{\gamma}_{21} & -\alpha_2 + \hat{\gamma}_{22} & & \hat{\gamma}_{2m} \\ \vdots & & \ddots & \\ \hat{\gamma}_{m1} & \hat{\gamma}_{m2} & & -\alpha_m + \hat{\gamma}_{mm} \end{vmatrix} > 0, \quad m = 1, 2, \ldots, N$$

$$\tag{5.3.93}$$

it can be proved (Šiljak, 1978b) that the origin is an "exponentially connectively stable"* equilibrium point in the large for the system (5.3.89). One way to satisfy conditions (5.3.93) is to choose $\hat{k}_{ij}$ in (5.3.89) such that the subsystems' interconnections strengths represented by the nonnegative numbers $\hat{\gamma}_{ij}$ are minimized. Using the Moore–Penrose generalized inverse of $\hat{b}_i$ (Langenhop, 1967), the interconnecting gains are given by

$$\hat{k}_{ij}^0 = \left[\left(\hat{b}_i^T \hat{b}_i\right)^{-1} \hat{b}_i^T \hat{G}_{ij}\right]^T \tag{5.3.94}$$

where $(\hat{b}_i^T \hat{b}_i)^{-1}\hat{b}_i^T$ is the generalized inverse of $\hat{b}_i$. Using these choices for gains $\hat{k}_{ij}$, the overall system (5.3.89) becomes

$$\dot{\hat{x}}_i(t) = \Lambda_i \hat{x}_i(t) + \left[I_i - \hat{b}_i\left(\hat{b}_i^T \hat{b}_i\right)^{-1} \hat{b}_i^T\right] \sum_{\substack{j=1 \\ j \neq i}}^{N} \hat{G}_{ij} \hat{x}_j, \quad i = 1, 2, \ldots, N \tag{5.3.95}$$

where $I_i$ is an $n_i \times n_i$ identity matrix. In order to check the stability of this system, it suffices to check the conditions (5.3.93) using the optimal aggregate matrix $S^o = (s_{ij}^o)$ defined by (5.3.91) and parameters $\gamma_{ij}$, which are now defined by

$$\hat{\gamma}_{ij} = \hat{\gamma}_{ij}^o = \lambda_M^{1/2}\left\{\hat{G}_{ij}^T\left[I_i - \hat{b}_i\left(\hat{b}_i^T \hat{b}_i\right)^{-1} \hat{b}_i^T\right]^T\left[I_i - \hat{b}_i\left(\hat{b}_i^T \hat{b}_i\right)^{-1} \hat{b}_i^T\right]\hat{G}_{ij}\right\} \tag{5.3.96}$$

---

*For a definition of connective stability see Section 7.2.3.

Šiljak (1978b) has provided two theorems which essentially, through (5.3.93), guarantee the stability of a large-scale system $\dot{x} = Ax + Bu$ using the feedback gains $k_i^T$ and $k_{ij}^T$ thus obtained. The following algorithm illustrates this stabilization scheme.

*Algorithm 5.3.* Stabilization via Multilevel Control

*Step 1:* Use a transformation similar to (5.3.55)–(5.3.57) to represent the system in its companion (canonical) input-decentralized form.

*Step 2:* Use any simple pole placement scheme to find local state feedback gains $k_i^T$ for each subsystem controllable pair $(A_i, b_i)$, $i = 1, \ldots, N$.

*Step 3:* Using new decoupled subsystems closed-loop matrices $\hat{A}_i = (A_i - b_i k_i^T)$, determine the transformation (modal) matrices $M_i$ in (5.3.83) and evaluate the transformed vectors and matrices $\hat{b}_i$ and $\hat{G}_{ij}$ for $i, j = 1, \ldots, N; \ i \neq j$.

*Step 4:* Evaluate the interconnection gains $\hat{k}_{ij}^o$ using (5.3.94) and obtain the overall system state equations (5.3.95).

*Step 5:* To check stability of the overall system, use aggregate matrix $\hat{S}$ defined by (5.3.91) and (5.3.96) to check for conditions (5.3.93).

*Step 6:* If conditions (5.3.93) are not satisfied, Steps 2 through 4 can be repeated using local subsystem feedback gains based on larger values of $\alpha_i$ in (5.3.79).

*Step 7:* Stop.

The following fifth-order system is used to illustrate this algorithm.

**Example 5.3.6.** Consider an interconnected system

$$\dot{x} = \begin{bmatrix} 0 & 1 & 0 & 1 & 1 \\ 0 & 0 & 1 & 0.1 & 1 \\ 4 & -1 & 2 & 0 & 0.5 \\ 0.4 & 0.2 & 0 & 0 & 1 \\ 0.5 & 0.2 & 1 & -1 & 2 \end{bmatrix} x + \begin{bmatrix} 0 & 0 \\ 0 & 0 \\ 1 & 0 \\ 0 & 0 \\ 0 & 1 \end{bmatrix} u \qquad (5.3.97)$$

The system matrix $A$ has its eigenvalues at $(3.5, 0.47 \pm j1.56, -0.21 \pm j0.6)$, which indicates that the system is unstable. Use Algorithm 5.3 to stabilize (5.3.97) using multilevel control.

SOLUTION: For a $3 \times 2$ decomposition of the system, it is clear that the system (5.3.97) would be already in input-decentralized and companion form. The eigenvalues of the two $3 \times 3$ and $2 \times 2$ companion submatrices $A_1$ and $A_2$ are $\lambda\{A_1\} = \{-0.157 \pm j1.3, 2.31\}$ and $\lambda\{A_2\} = \{1, 1\}$. Let the desired poles for the decoupled subsystems closed-loop submatrices $\hat{A}_i$, $i = 1, 2$, be at

$$\lambda\{\hat{A}_1\} = \{-5 \pm j2, -10\}, \quad \lambda\{\hat{A}_2\} = \{-2 \pm j\} \tag{5.3.98}$$

which would provide local feedback gains

$$k_1^T = (294 \quad 128 \quad 22), \quad k_2^T = (4 \quad 6) \tag{5.3.99}$$

The transformation matrices $M_1$ and $M_2$ of Step 3 of Algorithm 5.3 turn out to be

$$M_1 = \begin{bmatrix} 0.02497 & 0.02378 & -0.00995 \\ -0.01724 & -0.06896 & 0.09950 \\ 1 & 0 & -0.99500 \end{bmatrix}, \quad M_2 = \begin{bmatrix} 0.4 & 0.2 \\ 1 & 0 \end{bmatrix} \tag{5.3.100}$$

which lead to the following interconnected subsystems:

$$\dot{x}_i = \begin{bmatrix} -5 & 2 & 0 \\ -2 & -5 & 0 \\ 0 & 0 & -10 \end{bmatrix} \hat{x}_1 + \begin{bmatrix} -94.34 & -20.70 \\ 84.40 & 21.43 \\ -95.32 & -20.80 \end{bmatrix} \hat{x}_2 + \begin{bmatrix} -2.45 \\ 1.12 \\ -3.46 \end{bmatrix} u_1^g \tag{5.3.101}$$

$$\dot{x}_2 = \begin{bmatrix} -2 & -1 \\ 1 & -2 \end{bmatrix} \hat{x}_2 + \begin{bmatrix} 0.98 & -0.002 & -0.98 \\ 1.83 & -0.025 & -1.90 \end{bmatrix} \hat{x}_1 + \begin{bmatrix} 1 \\ 2 \end{bmatrix} u_2^g$$

Note that the system is still not identical to the system (5.3.89). Thus, what remains to be found are the global controls $u_i^g$, $i = 1,2$. However, before the gains $k_{ij}^{oT}$ are obtained, an investigation is made on the effects of the global controls by setting the gain vectors $\hat{k}_{12}$ and $\hat{k}_{21}$ to zero and checking the stability conditions (5.3.93). From (5.3.79) and (5.3.101), it is clear that $\alpha_1 = 5$ and $\alpha_2 = 2$, while by using (5.3.92) and (5.3.101) one computes $\hat{\gamma}_{12} = 2.97$ and $\hat{\gamma}_{21} = 162.5$. The aggregate matrix $\hat{S}$ in (5.3.90) becomes

$$\hat{S} = \begin{bmatrix} -5 & 2.97 \\ 162.5 & -2 \end{bmatrix} \tag{5.3.102}$$

which violates the stability conditions (5.3.93). Thus, the local feedback controls would not stabilize the overall system.

Now by utilizing (5.3.94) and Step 4 of Algorithm 5.3, the interconnection gains turn out to be

$$\hat{k}_{12}^{oT} = (34.05 \quad 7.6), \quad \hat{k}_{21}^{oT} = (0.93 \quad -0.01 \quad -0.95) \tag{5.3.103}$$

which, when used to replace the global controls $u_i^g$, $i = 1,2$, using (5.3.77), yields the subsystems (5.3.101) as

$$\begin{bmatrix} \dot{x}_1 \\ \hline \dot{x}_2 \end{bmatrix} = \begin{bmatrix} -5 & 2 & 0 & | & -10.96 & -2.04 \\ -2 & -5 & 0 & | & 46.24 & 12.9 \\ 0 & 0 & -10 & | & 22.70 & 5.61 \\ \hline 0.05 & 0.008 & -0.03 & | & -2 & -1 \\ -0.024 & -0.004 & 0.016 & | & 1 & -2 \end{bmatrix} \begin{bmatrix} \hat{x}_1 \\ \hline \hat{x}_2 \end{bmatrix} \tag{5.3.104}$$

The system provides parameters $\hat{\gamma}_{12} = 0.066$ and $\hat{\gamma}_{21} = 54.5$ and hence an aggregate matrix $\hat{S}$,

$$\hat{S}^o = \begin{bmatrix} -5 & 0.066 \\ 54.5 & -2 \end{bmatrix} \tag{5.3.105}$$

which satisfies the stability conditions (5.3.93). In fact, the eigenvalues of the closed-loop matrix in (5.3.104) turn out to be $(-5.06 \pm j2.2, -1.97 \pm j0.86, -9.93)$, indicating that system (5.3.97) has been stabilized by a two-level control scheme.

The above formulation for a decentralized stabilization scheme by multi-level control has been restricted to single inputs. The extension to multivariable systems follows the above development rather closely. This is considered in part in the next section under exponential stabilization.

### 5.3.5 Exponential Stabilization

In this section a decentralized stabilization procedure with a prescribed degree $\alpha$ for the closed-loop composite system is considered. Much of this section is based on the works of Sundareshan (1977) and Šiljak (1978b).

Consider an input-decentralized large-scale system consisting of $N$ subsystems:

$$\dot{x}_i(t) = A_i x_i(t) + B_i u_i(t) + g_i(t, x), \quad i = 1, \ldots, N \tag{5.3.106}$$

where each decoupled subsystem $(A_i, B_i)$ is assumed to be completely controllable, $g_i(\cdot, \cdot): R \times R^n \to R^{n_i}$ describes the interaction function between the $i$th subsystem and the other $N - 1$ and all matrices have appropriate dimensions. The problem is to find a state feedback decentralized control $u_i(t) = \psi_i(t, x)$ such that all the solutions of the compensated system

$$\dot{x}_i(t) = A_i x_i(t) + B_i \psi_i(t, x) + g_i(t, x), \quad i = 1, \ldots, N \tag{5.3.107}$$

satisfy $x_i(t)\exp(-\alpha t) \to 0$ as $t \to \infty$, where $\alpha > 0$ is the prescribed degree of exponential stability. An exponential stabilized system is formally defined as follows:

**Definition 5.3.** The system

$$\dot{x} = Ax + Bu \tag{5.3.108a}$$

$$y = Cx \tag{5.3.108b}$$

is called "exponentially stabilizable" by a control law $u = Px + Fy$ if for any prespecified positive number $\alpha$, a feedback gain matrix $P$ exists such that the closed-loop system state $x(t)$ satisfies

$$\|x(t_k)\| \leqslant \gamma \|x(t_{k-1})\|\exp\{-\alpha(t_k - t_{k-1})\} \tag{5.3.109}$$

for a positive number $\gamma$, all $t$, and $t_k \geqslant t_{k-1}$.

In sequel, a completely decentralized scheme for the solution of the above problem is given.

Let the interactions $g_i(t, x)$ be zero for (5.3.106) to provide a set of completely decoupled linear subsystems

$$\dot{x}_i(t) = A_i x_i(t) + B_i u_i(t), \quad i = 1, \dots, N \qquad (5.3.110)$$

It is well known (Kwakernaak and Sivan, 1972) that each of the subsystems in (5.3.110) can be exponentially stabilized with a prescribed degree $\alpha$ by control functions

$$u_i(t) = - B_i^T K_i x_i(t) \qquad (5.3.111)$$

where the $K_i$ is an $n_i \times n_i$ symmetric positive-definite solution of the algebraic matrix Riccati equation (AMRE),

$$(A_i + \sigma I_i)^T K_i + K_i(A_i + \alpha I_i) - K_i S_i K_i + Q_i = 0 \qquad (5.3.112)$$

where $S_i = B_i B_i^T$, $Q_i = C_i^T C_i$ is a nonnegative definite matrix such that the pair $(A_i, C_i)$ is completely observable and $I_i$ is an $n_i \times n_i$ identity matrix. Under these conditions each closed-loop subsystem

$$\dot{x}_i(t) = (A_i - S_i K_i) x_i(t), \quad i = 1, \dots, N \qquad (5.3.113)$$

has the property that $x_i(t) \exp(-\alpha t) \to 0$ as $t \to \infty$. What is left is to find conditions on the interactions $g_i(t, x)$ such that with the completely decentralized controls (5.3.111) the overall system (5.3.106) is exponentially stabilized within the above contex, i.e., the system

$$\dot{x}_i(t) = (A_i - S_i K_i) x_i(t) + g_i(t, x), \quad i = 1, \dots, N \qquad (5.3.114)$$

has the same property with respect to $\exp(-\alpha t)$. The above equations can be combined to obtain a description for the composite system

$$\dot{x}(t) = (A - SK) x(t) + g(t, x) \qquad (5.3.115)$$

where $A = \text{Block-diag}(A_1, \dots, A_N)$, $S = \text{Block-diag}(S_1, \dots, S_N)$, and $K = \text{Block-diag}(K_1, \dots, K_N)$. The following two theorems, due to Sundareshan (1977), set up conditions for decentralized exponential stabilization with respect to the structural arrangement of interconnections or the strength (the magnitude of information flow) of interconnections among various subsystems.

**Theorem 5.4.** *If the interconnection vector $g(t, x)$ can be represented by*

$$g(t, x) = [H(t, x) - W(t, x)] Kx(t) \qquad (5.3.116a)$$

*where $H(\cdot, \cdot)$ and $W(\cdot, \cdot)$ are two $n \times n$ arbitrary skew-symmetric and symmetric matrix functions, respectively, and if the $n \times n$ matrix*

$$U(t, x) = P + 2KW(t, x)K \qquad (5.3.116b)$$

*is negative definite, then the system (5.3.115) is exponentially stable with degree $\alpha$. In (5.3.115), $P = \text{Block-diag}(P_1, \dots, P_N)$, where $P_i = Q_i + K_i S_i K_i$.*

PROOF: The proof proceeds with the aid of the Lyapunov stability theory. Let $v(x) = x^T(t)Kx(t)$ be a potential Lyapunov function for (5.3.115). Since each $K_i$, $i = 1, \ldots, N$, is positive-definite, $v(x)$ is also positive-definite. Taking time derivative of $v(x)$ along the trajectories of (5.3.115), one obtains

$$\dot{v}(x) = x^T(t)\left[(A - SK)^T K + K(A - SK)\right]x(t) + x^T(t)Kg(t, x)$$
$$+ g^T(t, x)Kx(t) \tag{5.3.117}$$

Now by using the AMRE (5.3.112) in its augmented form, (5.3.117) can be simplified to

$$\dot{v}(x) = x^T(t)(-2\alpha K - P)x(t) + x^T(t)Kg(t, x) + g^T(t, x)Kx(t) \tag{5.3.118}$$

Using the expression for $g(t, x)$ from (5.3.116a) and the properties of matrix functions $H(\cdot, \cdot)$ and $W(\cdot, \cdot)$, (5.3.118) is simplified even further to

$$\dot{v}(x) = x^T(t)\left[-2\alpha K - P - 2KW(t, x)K\right]x(t) \tag{5.3.119}$$

Now in view of the negative-definiteness assumption of $U(t, x)$ in (5.3.116b), (5.3.119) can be changed to an inequality

$$\dot{v}(x) \leqslant -2\alpha v(x) \tag{5.3.120}$$

for all $n \times 1$ $x$ vectors. By integrating (5.3.120) and making use of definitions of $v(x)$ and $v(x(t_0))$, it will lead to

$$\|x(t)\| \leqslant \gamma \|x(t_0)\|\exp(-\alpha(t - t_0)) \tag{5.3.121}$$

for all $t \geqslant t_0$ and $\gamma = \lambda_M^{1/2}(K)\lambda_m^{-1/2}(K)$, where $\lambda_M(\cdot)$ and $\lambda_m(\cdot)$ represent, respectively, the maximum and minimum eigenvalues of their matrix arguments. Thus, the system (5.3.115) is exponentially stable with a prescribed degree $\alpha$. Q.E.D. ∎

The case when the interaction term $g_i(t, x)$ is linear would result in simpler conditions (see Problem 5.7). Theorem 5.5 provides conditions for exponential stability in terms of the strength of the interconnections.

**Theorem 5.5.** *If the interconnections $g_i(t, x)$ satisfy the inequality*

$$\|g_i(t, x)\| \leqslant \sum_{j=1}^{N} \gamma_{ij}\|x_j\|, \quad i = 1, \ldots, N \tag{5.3.122}$$

*for all $(t, x) \in R^{n+1}$, where $\gamma_{ij}$ are $N^2$ nonnegative numbers, and if $\gamma = \sum_{i=1}^{N}\sum_{j=1}^{N}\gamma_{ij}$ satisfy*

$$\min_i\left(\lambda_m(P_i)\right) \geqslant 2\gamma \max_i\left(\lambda_M(K_i)\right) \tag{5.3.123}$$

*the composite system (5.3.115) is exponentially stable with degree $\alpha$.*

PROOF: The proof of this theorem closely follows that of Theorem 5.4. Making a choice of Lyapunov function $v(x) = x^T(t)Kx(t)$ and evaluating $\dot{v}(x)$ as before, one obtains

$$\dot{v}(x) = x^T(t)(-2\alpha K - P)x(t) + 2g^T(t, x)Kx(t) \quad (5.3.124a)$$

The time derivative of $v(x)$ satisfies the exponential stability condition

$$\dot{v}(x) \leqslant -2\alpha v(x) \quad (5.3.124b)$$

for all $x \in R^n$ if

$$x^T(t)Px(t) \geqslant 2g^T(t, x)Kx(t) \quad (5.3.125)$$

for $x \in R^n$. Moreover, utilizing triangular-type inequality and (5.3.122), it is easy to observe that

$$\|g(t, x)\| \leqslant \sum_{i=1}^{N} \|g_i(t, x)\| \leqslant \sum_{i=1}^{N}\sum_{j=1}^{N} \gamma_{ij}\|x_j\| \leqslant \gamma\|x\| \quad (5.3.126)$$

which implies that condition (5.3.123) is sufficient to ensure (5.3.125). Therefore, (5.3.124b) holds and the theorem has been proved. Q.E.D. ∎

It is noted again that if the interconnection vector is linear, i.e., $g(t, x) = G(t)x(t)$, then the parameter $\gamma$ in (5.3.123) can be obtained simply as $\gamma = \text{Sup}_{t \in R}\lambda_M^{1/2}(G^T(t)G(t))$. Moreover, it is possible to generate simpler stabilizing controls through the solution of matrix Lyapunov equations instead of more difficult matrix Riccati equations (see Problem 5.9). The following example illustrates the complete decentralized exponential stabilization method.

**Example 5.3.7.** Consider a fourth-order system

$$\dot{x} = \begin{bmatrix} 0 & 0 & \vdots & 0 & -0.1 \\ 0.5 & -1 & \vdots & 0.15 & 0 \\ -- & -- & -- & -- & -- \\ -0.1 & 0 & \vdots & 1 & -0.1 \\ 0 & 0.15 & \vdots & 2 & -0.8 \end{bmatrix} x + \begin{bmatrix} 1 & \vdots & 0 \\ 0 & \vdots & 0 \\ -- & -- & -- \\ 0 & \vdots & 1 \\ 0 & \vdots & 0.2 \end{bmatrix} u \quad (5.3.127)$$

with eigenvalues $\lambda\{A\} = \{-0.26 \pm j0.18, 1.07, -1.36\}$. It is desired to exponentially stabilize this system through complete decentralized control.

SOLUTION: The two decoupled subsystems $(A_1, B_1)$ and $(A_2, B_2)$ are completely controllable. Using an $\alpha = 2$ and $Q_i = 2I_2$, $i = 1, 2$, the AMREs (5.3.112) are solved by the Newton's iterative method using the generalized inverse initialization scheme (Jamshidi, 1980):

$$K_1 = \begin{bmatrix} 1.48 & 0.198 \\ 0.198 & 0.98 \end{bmatrix}, \quad K_2 = \begin{bmatrix} 3 & 0.37 \\ 0.37 & 1 \end{bmatrix} \quad (5.3.128)$$

with eigenvalues $\lambda\{K_1\} = \{0.912, 1.55\}$ and $\lambda\{K_2\} = \{0.93, 3.07\}$. The two decentralized controls turn to be $u_1 = -1.48x_1 - 0.198x_2$ and $u_2 = -3.08x_3 -$

$0.6x_4$. Since the subsystems' interconnections are linear, the value of $\gamma = \lambda_M^{1/2}(G^TG) = 0.15$. The magnitudes of the eigenvalues of $P_i$, $i = 1, 2$, are

$$\lambda\{P_1\} = \lambda\{Q_1 + K_1S_1K_1\} = \lambda\left\{\begin{bmatrix} 4.2 & 0.29 \\ 0.29 & 2.04 \end{bmatrix}\right\}\{2, 4.24\} \quad (5.3.129)$$

and

$$\lambda\{P_2\} = \lambda\{Q_2 + K_2S_2K_2\} = \lambda\left\{\begin{bmatrix} 11.45 & 1.76 \\ 1.76 & 2.33 \end{bmatrix}\right\} = \{2, 11.78\} \quad (5.3.130)$$

Therefore, the terms of condition (5.3.123) would become

$$\min_i\left(\lambda_m(P_i)\right) = 2, \quad \max_i\left(\lambda_M(K_i)\right) = 3.07, \quad \gamma = \lambda_M^{1/2}(G^TG) = 0.15$$

$$(5.3.131)$$

which leads to

$$\min_i\lambda_m(P_i) = 2 > 2(0.15)\max_i\lambda_M(K_i) = (0.3)(3.07) = 0.921 \quad (5.3.132)$$

indicating that the system (5.3.127) is exponentially stable in accordance to Theorem 5.5. Next, a structural perturbation was made on the interconnections, i.e., the $G$ matrix is assumed to take on a form given by

$$G(\varepsilon) = \begin{bmatrix} 0 & 0 & | & 0.5\varepsilon & -0.1 \\ 0 & 0 & | & 0.15 & -\varepsilon \\ - & - & - & - & - \\ -0.1 & 0.5\varepsilon & | & 0 & 0 \\ -\varepsilon & 0.15 & | & 0 & 0 \end{bmatrix} \quad (5.3.133)$$

The values of the perturbation parameter $\varepsilon$ were varied between $-1 \leqslant \varepsilon \leqslant 1$. The value of the right-hand side of (5.3.132) less the left-hand side value, i.e., $f(\varepsilon) = 3.07\gamma(\varepsilon) - 1$, was calculated. Clearly, for all values of $\varepsilon$ for which $f(\varepsilon) \leqslant 0$, the system can be stabilized exponentially. The plot of $f(\varepsilon)$ versus $\varepsilon$ is shown in Figure 5.3. For the set of all values of $\varepsilon$ such that $-0.246 \leqslant \varepsilon \leqslant 0.246$, the system is exponentially stabilized.

In a similar fashion to last section, one can use an additional global control $u_i^g(t)$ similar to (5.3.75) for each subsystem. Using a suitable negative state feedback form for $u_i^g(t) = -\phi_i(t, x)$, the composite system can be represented by

$$\dot{x}(t) = (A - SK)x(t) + [g(t, x) - B\phi(t, x)] \quad (5.3.134)$$

where $\phi^T(\cdot) = [\phi_1^T(\cdot), \ldots, \phi_N^T(\cdot)]$. A comparison of (5.3.134) and (5.3.115) indicates that, as in Chapter 4 under structural perturbations and discussions of the previous section, the global control would offset any perturbation of the interconnections. If $B$ is nonsingular, an obvious choice for

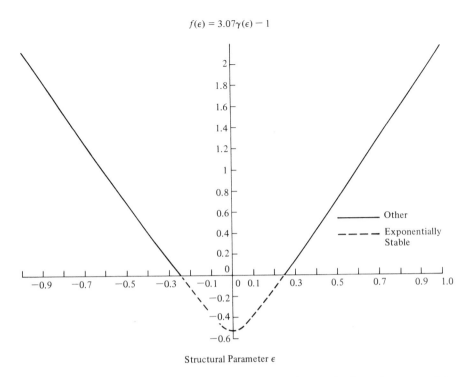

$f(\epsilon) = 3.07\gamma(\epsilon) - 1$

Structural Parameter $\epsilon$

**Figure 5.3** A graphical representation for structural perturbation of exponential stability in Example 5.3.7.

$\phi(\cdot, \cdot)$ would be

$$\phi(t, x) = B^{-1}g(t, x) \qquad (5.3.135)$$

For further discussions on the implications of the above relation and the case of linear interconnections, see Problem 5.5.

### 5.3.6 Stabilization via Dynamic Hierarchy

Thus far, four decentralized stabilization schemes based on dynamic compensation, local, and global controllers within a context of single-level or multilevel control formulations have been presented. The decentralized stabilization based on dynamic compensation, described by (5.3.1)–(5.3.2) and (5.3.4), would fail if there were an unstable fixed mode for the system relative to the class of block-diagonal matrices $K$ in (5.3.6a). On the other hand, the decentralized stabilization schemes of the previous three sections all require complete controllability of individual subsystems. A stabilization scheme which would effectively make a combination of dynamic compensation based on fixed modes (Wang and Davison, 1973) and multilevel control (Šiljak, 1978b) due to Groumpos and Loparo (1980) is discussed in this section. The scheme, called "dynamical hierarchical stabilization", interprets the external input $v(t)$ in (5.3.1) as a second-level global control component to stabilize the unstable fixed modes of the system relative to $K$ in (5.3.6a).

Consider two linear state feedback control laws

$$u_i(t) = P_i x_i(t) + P_{ic} x_c(t) \qquad (5.3.136)$$

$$u_c(t) = P_c x_c(t) + \sum_{i=1}^{N} P_{ci} x_i(t) \qquad (5.3.137)$$

where subscript $c$ stands for the coordinator. The matrices $P_i$, $P_{ic}$, $P_c$, and $P_{ci}$ are feedback gains of $n_i \times n_i$, $n_i \times n_c$, $n_c \times n_c$, and $n_c \times n_i$ dimensions, respectively. In the above relations, the first law is associated with the $i$th subsystem, while the second one is associated with a dynamic coordinator described by

$$\dot{x}_c(t) = A_c x_c(t) + \sum_{i=1}^{N} A_{ci} x_i(t) + B_c u_c(t) \qquad (5.3.138)$$

where $x_c$ and $u_c$ are $n_c$- and $m_c$-dimensional state and control vectors of the coordinator, respectively. Matrices $A_c$, $A_{ci}$, and $B_c$ are constant matrices of $n_c \times n_c$, $n_c \times n_i$, and $n_c \times m_c$ dimensions, respectively. If the control laws (5.3.136)–(5.3.137), which are called "structural hierarchical control," are applied to the structural state model of two-level dynamical hierarchical system (Groumpos 1980a, b),

$$
\begin{bmatrix} \dot{x}_1 \\ \dot{x}_2 \\ \vdots \\ \dot{x}_N \\ \dot{x}_c \end{bmatrix}
=
\begin{bmatrix}
A_1 & & & & A_{1c} \\
& A_2 & & 0 & A_{2c} \\
& 0 & \ddots & & \vdots \\
& & & A_N & A_{Nc} \\
A_{c1} & A_{c2} & \cdots & A_{cN} & A_c
\end{bmatrix}
\begin{bmatrix} x_1 \\ x_2 \\ \vdots \\ x_N \\ x_c \end{bmatrix}
$$

$$
+
\begin{bmatrix}
B_1 & & & \\
& B_2 & & \\
0 & & \ddots & \\
& & & B_N \\
& & & B_c
\end{bmatrix}
\begin{bmatrix} u_1 \\ u_2 \\ \vdots \\ u_N \\ u_c \end{bmatrix}
\qquad (5.3.139)
$$

the following closed-loop system configuration will result:

$$
\begin{bmatrix} \dot{x}_1(t) \\ \dot{x}_2(t) \\ \vdots \\ \dot{x}_N(t) \\ \dot{x}_c(t) \end{bmatrix}
$$

$$
= \begin{bmatrix} A_1 - B_1 P_1 & & & & A_{1c} - B_1 P_{1c} \\ & A_2 - B_2 P_2 & & & A_{2c} - B_2 P_{2c} \\ & & \ddots & & \vdots \\ & & & A_N - B_N P_N & A_{Nc} - B_N P_{Nc} \\ A_{c1} - B_c P_{c1} & A_{c2} - B_c P_{c2} & \cdots & A_{cN} - B_c P_{cN} & A_c - B_c P_c \end{bmatrix}
$$

$$
\times \begin{bmatrix} x_1(t) \\ x_2(t) \\ \vdots \\ x_N(t) \\ x_c(t) \end{bmatrix} \qquad (5.3.140)
$$

This closed-loop formulation, called "blocked arrow canonical form" (Groumpos and Loparo, 1980), shows a clear interdependence between the $N$ subsystems and the coordinator. The local control gain matrices $P_i$, $i = 1, \ldots, N$, can be found in a similar fashion to the previous two sections. The global control can be obtained as

$$
u^g(t) = \begin{bmatrix} u_1^g(t) \\ \vdots \\ u_N^g(t) \end{bmatrix} = \begin{bmatrix} P_{1c} \\ \vdots \\ P_{Nc} \end{bmatrix} x_c \qquad (5.3.141)
$$

where $x_c$ is the state of the coordinator whose dynamic is given by (5.3.138). Groumpos (1979) has shown that all fixed modes of the large-scale system can be stabilized through a proper choice of the dynamic coordinator. For example, if the system has unstable fixed modes, it is shown that a coordinator of at most $r$th dimension is necessary. This scheme, although sound, has not been well tested computationally, and its numerical applications are in unpublished reports (Groumpos, 1979).

### 5.3.7 General Stabilization Through Local State Feedback

Thus far, five methods for the stabilization of linear TIV large-scale systems have been proposed which are based on either decentralized pole placement, local feedback for composite systems, or multilevel control. The feedback gains in each method were fully or partially dependent on the pole assignment, unknown feedback gains of the $i$th subsystem from the other subsystems' measurable outputs, or the design of a global control to account for structural perturbation of interconnections. The exponential stabilization of linear time-invariant systems was introduced in Section 5.3.5. In this section the solutions of lower-order subsystem matrix differential Riccati equations are used, and the exponential stabilization is extended to time-varying systems. The results of Ikeda and Šiljak (1980a) for decentralized stabilization of time-varying systems are considered initially and then extended to the linear time-invariant case. The section is concluded by discussing the decentralized stabilization of time-invariant systems with unstable fixed modes using time-varying feedback control laws (Anderson and Moore, 1981).

#### 5.3.7.a Time-Varying Plant and Feedback Control

Consider a linear time-varying system consisted of $N$ subsystems,

$$\dot{x}_i(t) = A_i(t)x_i(t) + B_i(t)u_i(t) \tag{5.3.142}$$

$$y_i(t) = C_i x_i(t) \tag{5.3.143}$$

$i = 1, 2, \ldots, N$. The $A_i(t)$ and $B_i(t)$ matrices are assumed to be functions of time, $C_i$ is constant, and the dimensions of these matrices are $n_i \times n_i$, $n_i \times m_i$, and $r_i \times n_i$, respectively. The decentralized local state feedback law for each subsystem is assumed to be

$$u_i(t) = P_i(t)x_i(t) + \sum_{j=1}^{N} F_{ij}(t)y_j(t) \tag{5.3.144}$$

for $i = 1, 2, \ldots, N$. In (5.3.144), $P_i(t)$ is an $n_i \times n_i$ feedback gain matrix with the same properties as $A_i(t)$, to be discussed shortly, and $F_{ij}(t)$ is an $m_i \times r_j$ unknown feedback gain matrix from the $j$th subsystem output $y_j(t)$ to the $i$th local controller. Once controls (5.3.144) influence (5.3.142)–(5.3.143), one gets

$$\dot{x}_i(t) = \{A_i(t) + B_i(t)P_i(t)\}x_i(t) + \sum_{j=1}^{N} B_i(t)F_{ij}(t)y_j(t) \tag{5.3.145}$$

$$y_i(t) = C_i x_i(t), \quad i = 1, 2, \ldots, N \tag{5.3.146}$$

In the compact form, the closed-loop system becomes

$$\dot{x}(t) = \{A(t) + B(t)P(t) + B(t)F(t)C\}x(t)$$
$$= A_c(t)x(t) \tag{5.3.147}$$

with

$$u(t) = P(t)x(t) + F(t)y(t) \tag{5.3.148}$$

where $A(t)$, $B(t)$, $C$, and $P(t)$ are block-diagonal matrices of $n \times n$, $n \times m$, $r \times n$, and $n \times n$ dimensions, respectively, whose blocks are $A_i(t)$, $B_i(t)$, $C_i$, and $P_i(t)$. The $m \times r$ matrix $F(t)$ consists of $m_i \times r_i$-dimensional blocks. Ikeda and Šiljak (1980a) have given the necessary conditions for the existence of (5.3.148) based on subsystem controllability, which are similar to the conditions given for the stabilization of interconnected systems by Sezer and Hüseyin (1978), Sundareshan (1977), and Šiljak (1978b). However, before that, the following lemma due to Ikeda et al. (1976) will first be introduced.

**Lemma 5.3.** *For any uniformly completely controllable ith subsystem of the form (5.3.142), there exists a symmetric positive-definite solution to the following matrix Riccati equation:*

$$\dot{K}_i(t) = -(A_i + \delta I_i)^T K_i(t) - K_i(t)(A_i + \delta I_i) + K_i(t)S_i K_i(t) - \delta I_i \tag{5.3.149}$$

*with $S_i = B_i B_i^T$ and $K_i(t_f)$ known, which satisfies*

$$\alpha_i I_i \leqslant K_i(t) \leqslant \beta_i I_i \tag{5.3.150}$$

*for positive numbers $\alpha_i$, $\beta_i$; $\delta$ is a prespecified parameter.*

The following theorem gives the necessary conditions for exponential stabilizability of the system (see Definition 5.3).

**Theorem 5.6.** *The necessary condition for a composite system consisting of $N$ subsystems to be exponentially stable by the local decentralized laws (5.3.144) is that each subsystem be uniformly completely controllable, i.e., each pair $(A_i(t), B_i(t))$ is completely controllable, $i = 1, 2, \ldots, N$ and all $t$.*

PROOF: Since each subsystem is uniformly completely controllable by Lemma 5.3, there exists a matrix $K_i(t)$ which satisfies (5.3.149)–(5.3.150). Using this matrix, a local time-varying state feedback matrix $P_i(t)$ is defined by

$$P_i(t) = -\tfrac{1}{2}\eta_i(t)B_i^T(t)K_i(t) \tag{5.3.151}$$

where $\eta_i(t)$ is a scalar arbitrary function which is bounded and measurable on every finite time subinterval, satisfying

$$\eta_i(t) \geq 1 + \sum_{j=1}^{N} \|F_{ij}(t)C_j\|^2 \qquad (5.3.152)$$

for all $t$. Now consider a choice of a scalar Lyapunov function for the closed-loop system (5.3.147).

$$v(x) = x^T K x \qquad (5.3.153)$$

where $K = $ Block-diag($K_1, \ldots, K_N$). Following Lemma 5.3, it is clear that $v$ in (5.3.153) satisfies

$$\alpha\|x\|^2 \leq v(x) \leq \beta\|x\|^2 \qquad (5.3.154)$$

for all $t$ and $x$ in $R^{n+1}$, with $\|x\|$ denoting the Euclidean norm and $\alpha = \min_i \alpha_i$ and $\beta = \max_i \beta_i$. If $v(x)$ is differentiated with respect to time, and utilizing the system (5.3.147) and relations (5.3.149) and (5.3.152), one obtains

$$\dot{v}(x) = \sum_{i=1}^{N} \left( \dot{x}_i^T(t) K_i(t) x_i(t) + x_i^T(t) \dot{K}_i(t) x_i(t) + x_i^T(t) K_i(t) \dot{x}_i(t) \right)$$

$$\leq \sum_{i=1}^{N} \left[ x_i^T \left( -2\delta K_i - \sum_{j=1}^{N} \|F_{ij} C_j\|^2 K_i B_i B_i^T K_i - N I_i \right) x_i \right.$$

$$\left. + x_i^T K_i B_i \left( \sum_{j=1}^{N} F_{ij} C_j x_j \right) + \left( \sum_{j=1}^{N} F_{ij} C_j x_j \right)^T B_i^T K_i x_i \right]$$

$$\leq -2\delta \sum_{i=1}^{N} x_i^T K_i x_i - \sum_{i=1}^{N} \sum_{j=1}^{N} \left( \|F_{ij} C_j\|^2 \|B_i^T K_i x_i\|^2 \right.$$

$$\left. - 2\|F_{ij} C_j\| \|B_i^T K_i x_i\| \|x_j\| + \|x_j\|^2 \right)$$

$$\leq -2\delta v(x) - \sum_{i=1}^{N} \sum_{j=1}^{N} \left( \|F_{ij} C_j\| \|B_i^T K_i x_i\| - \|x_j\| \right)^2$$

$$\leq -2\delta v(x) \qquad (5.3.155)$$

The above relation implies that the local state feedback $P_i(t)$ defined by (5.3.151) and (5.3.152) guarantees that each $x(t)$ satisfies an exponential stability condition similar to (5.3.109) when parameter $\alpha$ is replaced by $\delta$. Thus, the system (5.3.147) is stabilized exponentially by the local control law (5.3.148). Q.E.D. ■

The following example illustrates this stabilization method.

**Example 5.3.8.** Consider a third-order system consisting of two subsystems

$$A_1(t) = \begin{bmatrix} -e^{-t} & 0 \\ 1 & 0.2t \end{bmatrix}, \quad B_1(t) = \begin{bmatrix} 1 \\ 0 \end{bmatrix}, \quad C_1 = [1 \quad 0]$$

$$A_2(t) = [0.5], \quad B_2(t) = [1], \quad C_2 = [1] \tag{5.3.156}$$

It is desired to exponentially stabilize this system for $0 \leqslant t \leqslant 1.0$.

SOLUTION: The first step in the solution is to solve the matrix Riccati equation (5.3.149) for, say, $\delta = 2$. A fourth-order Runge–Kutta integration method was used backward in time with $K_i(1) = 0$, $i = 1, 2$. A second-order fit through a Chebyschev algorithm (Newhouse, 1962) for $K_1(t)$ and $K_2(t)$ resulted

$$K_1(t) = \begin{bmatrix} 5.3 - 13t + 7.8t^2 & 4.4 - 6.5t + 2.05t^2 \\ 4.4 - 6.5t + 2.05t^2 & 19.8 - 47t + 28.2t^2 \end{bmatrix}$$

$$K_2(t) = 5.4 - 5.04t + 0.73t^2 \tag{5.3.157}$$

The application of the time-varying decentralized stabilization procedure for this example requires the determination of four gain matrices, $F_{11}(t)$, $F_{12}(t)$, $F_{21}(t)$, and $F_{22}(t)$ with dimensions $m_1 \times r_1$, $m_1 \times r_2$, $m_2 \times r_1$, and $m_2 \times r_2$. However, since for this example $m_1 = m_2 = r_1 = r_2 = 1$, $F_{ij}(t)$ gains are scalar functions. The composite $3 \times 3$ closed-loop matrix described by (5.3.147) for this example is

$$A_c(t) = \begin{bmatrix} -e^{-t} - \frac{1}{2}\eta_1(t)k_{11}(t) + f_{11}(t) & 0 & f_{12}(t) \\ 1 & 0.2t & 0 \\ f_{21}(t) & 0 & 0.5 - \frac{1}{2}\eta_2(t)K_2(t) + f_{22}(t) \end{bmatrix}$$

$$\tag{5.3.158}$$

where $k_{11}(t)$ is the 1-1 element of $K_1(t)$, with $K_2(t)$ defined in (5.3.157), and $f_{ij}(t)$ are arbitrarily chosen to be $f_{11}(t) = -5\exp(-t)$, $f_{12}(t) = -2.5$, $f_{21}(t) = 1$, and $f_{22}(t) = -4\exp(-t)$, and $\eta_i(t)$, $i = 1, 2$, were obtained by applying (5.3.152). In this way, the system's two unstable open-loop poles become stable for $0 \leqslant t \leqslant 1.0$. An exponential decay behavior of $\text{Re}\,\lambda_i\{A_c(t)\}$ versus time was experienced. The third pole remained essentially around zero.

Further comments regarding this stabilization scheme will continue in Section 5.6.

## 5.3.7.b Time-Invariant Plant and Feedback Control

As a special case of the decentralized exponential stabilization of a time-varying large-scale systems the time-invariant case is now discussed. Instead of repeating the development of last section, the following algorithm is presented for the TIV systems.

*Algorithm 5.4.* Decentralized Stabilization of Large-Scale Linear
TIV-Systems

*Step 1:* Choose a prespecified $\delta > 0$ and solve a set of AMREs for $K_i$,
$i = 1, 2, \ldots, N$:

$$(A_i + \delta I_i)^T K_i + K_i (A_i + \delta I_i) - K_i S_i K_i + \delta I_i = 0 \quad (5.3.159)$$

where $A_i$, $S_i = B_i B_i^T$, and $K_i$ are constant matrices of dimensions
$n_i \times n_i$.

*Step 2:* Evaluate $n_i \times n_i$ constant matrices $P_i$, $i = 1, 2, \ldots, N$:

$$P_i = -\eta_i B_i^T K_i \qquad\qquad (5.3.160)$$

where $\eta_i$ is an arbitrary positive parameter satisfying

$$\eta_i \geq 1 + \sum_{j=1}^{N} \|F_{ij} C_j\|^2 \qquad\qquad (5.3.161)$$

and $F_{ij}$ is an $m_i \times r_j$ constant gain matrix between the $j$th
subsystem output and the $i$th local controller. Choose potential
$F_{ij}$ matrices and evaluate $\eta_i$ using (5.3.161).

*Step 3:* Form closed-loop matrix

$$A + BP + BFC = \begin{bmatrix} A_1 & & \\ & \ddots & \\ & & A_n \end{bmatrix} + \begin{bmatrix} B_1 & & \\ & \ddots & \\ & & B_N \end{bmatrix} \begin{bmatrix} P_1 & & \\ & \ddots & \\ & & P_N \end{bmatrix}$$

$$+ \begin{bmatrix} B_1 & & \\ & \ddots & \\ & & B_N \end{bmatrix} \begin{bmatrix} F_{11} & \cdots & \\ \vdots & \ddots & \\ F_{N,N} & \end{bmatrix} \begin{bmatrix} C_1 & & \\ & \ddots & \\ & & C_N \end{bmatrix}$$

$$(5.3.162)$$

and check for its stability by evaluating its eigenvalues.

The following example illustrates this algorithm.

**Example 5.3.9.** Consider a two-subsystem problem,

$$\dot{x}_1(t) = \begin{bmatrix} 0 & 0 \\ 0.5 & -1 \end{bmatrix} x_1(t) = \begin{bmatrix} 1 \\ 0 \end{bmatrix} u_1(t), \quad y_1(t) = [1 \quad 0] x_1(t) \quad (5.3.163)$$

$$\dot{x}_2(t) = \begin{bmatrix} 1 & -0.1 \\ 2 & -0.8 \end{bmatrix} x_2(t) + \begin{bmatrix} 1 \\ 0.2 \end{bmatrix} u_2(t), \quad y_2(t) = [1 \quad 0.5] x_2(t)$$

$$(5.3.164)$$

It is desired to stabilize this system.

SOLUTION: To begin with, both subsystems are completely controllable, with an unstable mode existing in each subsystem, $\lambda_1 = 0$, $\lambda_3 = 0.88$. In general, even if the individual subsystems are stable, there is no guarantee that the composite system is stable; but even so, it is often desired to relocate closed-loop poles for overall system response improvements. Since the two subsystems matrices $(A_i, B_i)$ correspond to those considered in Example 5.3.7, the resulting Riccati matrices are already defined by (5.3.128). The results of a set of four different trials of stabilizing the system are shown in Table 5.1. The results indicate that for the first and fourth cases the system was stabilized through state feedback. Furthermore, note that for the fourth case shown in Table 5.1, two of the poles are much farther to the left of the $s$-plane, indicating that through the particular set of $F_{ij}$, $i, j = 1, 2$, matrices, the system has adapted two distinct modes, i.e., a "slow" and a "fast" one, a similar phenomenon to that in a singularly perturbed system of Section 2.3. Figure 5.4 shows a block diagram for the decentralized stabilization of the two-subsystem example.

There has been further research on the decentralized stabilization via connective stability by Šiljak and his associates (Ikeda and Šiljak, 1980b; Sezer and Šiljak, 1981a, b) which will be briefly discussed in Section 5.6.

### 5.3.7.c Time-Invariant Plant and Time-Varying Feedback Control

It was mentioned before that a shortcoming of decentralized time-invariant controllers is that they cannot stabilize a system with unstable fixed modes. In this section a result, due to Anderson and Moore (1981), where decentralized time-varying feedback controls are used to stabilize a time-invariant plant with unstable fixed modes, is briefly discussed. Here only a two-control station case is presented.

**Table 5.1** Results of Example 5.3.9

| No. | $F_{11}$ | $F_{12}$ | $F_{21}$ | $F_{22}$ | $\eta_1$ | $\eta_2$ | Closed-loop Poles |
|-----|----------|----------|----------|----------|----------|----------|-------------------|
| 1 | $-0.2$ | $-0.3$ | $0.1$ | $-0.25$ | $1.014$ | $1.0062$ | $-0.986 \pm j0.218$, $-0.83 \pm j937$ |
| 2 | $-0.4$ | $-0.15$ | $0.125$ | $-0.5$ | $1.026$ | $1.098$ | $0.054, 1.12$, $-1.02, -0.63$ |
| 3 | $-1.45$ | $0.28$ | $-0.45$ | $-1.0$ | $5.43$ | $2.6035$ | $0.896, 1.64$, $-1.08, -0.66$ |
| 4 | $-2.0$ | $-3.0$ | $1$ | $-2.5$ | $143.5$ | $63.03$ | $-148.4, -67.5$, $-1.1, -1.06$ |

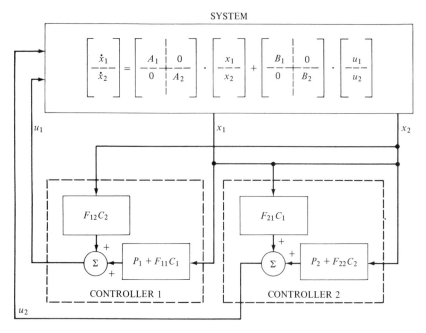

**Figure 5.4** A block diagram representation of state feedback stabilization in Example 5.3.9.

Consider a two-controller TIV system

$$\dot{x}(t) = Ax(t) + B_1 u_1(t) + B_2 u_2(t) \tag{5.3.165}$$

$$y_i = C_i x(t), \quad i = 1,2 \tag{5.3.166}$$

where the $i$th controller is assumed to have access to the past outputs $\{y_i(\cdot)\}$. Moreover, it is assumed that the system is completely controllable and observable at a fictitious centralized control and measurement station to avoid triviality, i.e., $\{A, (B_1 B_2)\}$ is controllable and $\{A, (C_1^T C_2^T)\}$ is observable. However, the system need not be both completely controllable and completely observable at either of the two stations. Anderson and Moore (1981) note that in order to devise a decentralized controller which would handle fixed modes, one has to sacrifice one of the properties of linearity or time-invariance. Following are conditions for the uniform controllability of the two-station decentralized control of system with fixed modes.

Let the second controller be given by

$$u_2(t) = K_2(t) y_2(t) \tag{5.3.167}$$

where $K_2(t)$ is assumed to be a periodic function with period $\Delta$. Then the system viewed from the first station can be represented by the triple

$\{A + B_2 K_2(t)C_2, B_1, C_1\}$. The uniform controllability and observability of this triplet is sought here. If the conditions for these properties are satisfied, it would imply that one can design an observer and linear state feedback which would stabilize the system.

Let $G(t, t + \Delta)$ denote the observability Grammian given by

$$G(t, t + \Delta) = \int_t^{t + \Delta} \phi_{K_2}^T(\tau, t) C_1^T C_1 \phi_{K_2}(\tau, t) \, d\tau \qquad (5.3.168)$$

where $\phi_{K_2}(\cdot, \cdot)$ is the transition matrix associated with $\{A + B_2 K_2(t)C_2\}$ and $\Delta$ is the period of $K_2(t)$. If the pair $(A, C_1)$ is observable, then a choice of $K_2(t) = 0$ suffices. Therefore, it is often assumed that $(A, C_1)$ is not observable. However, the following assumptions play a major role in the development to follow:

$$\{A, (C_1^T C_2^T)\} \text{ is observable} \qquad (5.3.169)$$

$$C_1(sI - A)^{-1} B_2 \neq 0 \qquad (5.3.170)$$

The above assumptions are called "centralized observability" and "connectivity", respectively, by Anderson and Moore (1981). If assumption (5.3.169) fails, then the pair $\{A + B_2 K_2(t)C_2, (C_1^T C_2^T)\}$ is not observable for all $K_2(t)$ and so would be $\{A + B_2 K_2(t)C_2, C_1\}$. The second assumption is significant only when $(A, C_1)$ is unobservable. Because, intuitively under this condition, station 1 needs to know something about what measurement the second station observes as well as its own direct observation to estimate the state. In other words, some of the second station's output, i.e., $C_2 x$, is fed back to control station 2 as $K_2(t)C_2 x$ and appears at observation station 1 through a nonzero transmission path with transfer matrix $C_1(sI - A)^{-1} B_2$. The following theorem, due to Anderson and Moore (1981), summarizes the above development.

**Theorem 5.7.** *Assume that the decentralized control system (5.3.165)–(5.3.166) is controllable and observable in the centralized sense. Let periodic function $K_2(t)$ with period $\Delta$ be the feedback gain matrix of the second station's output to its input. The pair $\{A + B_2 K_2(t)C_2, C_1\}$ is uniformly observable if the connectivity assumption (5.3.170) holds and $K_2(t)$ is piecewise constant, taking at least $m_2 + 1$ distinct values.*

The proof of this theorem in terms of two lemmas can be found in Anderson and Moore (1981).

Dual results can be obtained for controllability using the centralized controllability assumption on $\{A, (B_1, B_2)\}$ pairs. Also the above theorem can be similarly obtained for discrete-time systems (see Problem 5.13). Moreover, the case of $N$ controllers has been considered by Anderson and Moore (1981). The following example illustrates the use of this theorem.

**Example 5.3.10.** Consider a two-station system

$$\dot{x} = \begin{bmatrix} 1 & 0 & 0 \\ 0 & 1 & 0 \\ 0 & 0 & 3 \end{bmatrix} x + \begin{bmatrix} 0 & 0 \\ 1 & 0 \\ 0 & 0 \end{bmatrix} u_1 + \begin{bmatrix} 0 \\ 0 \\ 1 \end{bmatrix} u_2$$

$$y_1 = \begin{bmatrix} 0 & 0 & 1 \end{bmatrix} x, \quad y_2 = \begin{bmatrix} 0 & 1 & 0 \\ 1 & 0 & 0 \end{bmatrix} x \tag{5.3.171}$$

with a fixed mode and the required controllability and observability properties, which are not satisfied. It is desired to investigate the observability and
controllability of the closed-loop matrix $[A + B_2 K_2(t) C_2]$ for stabilization
purposes.

SOLUTION: Using an alternative criterion by Anderson and Clements (1981),
the fixed mode of this system can be easily checked. Here, since

$$\text{rank} \left. \begin{bmatrix} \lambda I - A & | & B_2 \\ ---- & + & -- \\ C_1 & | & 0 \end{bmatrix} \right|_{\lambda = 1} = 2 < n = 3$$

the value of $\lambda = 1$ is an unstable fixed mode. Now let the periodic function
$K_2(t)$ be defined by

$$K_2(t) = \begin{cases} \begin{bmatrix} 0 & 1 \end{bmatrix} \cdots 2k \leqslant t < 2k + 1 \\ \begin{bmatrix} 1 & 0 \end{bmatrix} \cdots 2k + 1 \leqslant t < 2k + 2 \end{cases}$$

for $k = 0, 1, \ldots$. Then the controllability and observability matrices for the
closed-loop matrix $[A + B_2 K_2(t) C_2]$ calculated analytically over the range
$2k \leqslant t < 2k + 2$ reveal that they are positive-definite. Hence, the pairs
$\{A + B_2 K_2(t) C_2, B_1\}$ and $\{A + B_2 K_2(t) C_2, C_1\}$ are controllable and observable, respectively.

This example illustrates how a simple periodic matrix function can be used
to help stabilize a decentralized system with an unstable fixed mode.
Further comments on this and other decentralized stabilization approaches
are given in Section 5.6.

## 5.4 Decentralized Robust Control

The second problem considered in this chapter is the decentralized robust
control of a large-scale linear system whose exact model may be unknown.
This problem, known as the "general servomechanism" was considered by
Davison (1976a, b, c, d, 1978, 1979) in various forms, e.g., within the context
of regulation (Davison, 1976a), as a general servomechanism problem
(Davison, 1976b), as the robust control of a linear TIV multivariable
problem (Davison, 1976c), as the decentralized robust control of unknown
systems (Davison, 1978) using tuning regulators (Davison, 1976d), and as a
sequentially stable robust controller (Davison and Gesing, 1979). Here we

are concerned with the decentralized robust control of the general servomechanism problem (Davison, 1978), sequentially stable robust controller (Davison and Gesing, 1979), and interconnected systems (Davison, 1979). These problems were stated in Section 5.2 by relations (5.2.6)–(5.2.13).

## 5.4.1 Constraints and Definitions

### 5.4.1.a Tuning Control Synthesis Constraints

The following set of constraints are suggested by Davison (1978) for the application of tuning regulators to the decentralized control problem.

1. A controller can be realized for only one control station at a given instant;
2. Once a controller has been determined and implemented for a specified station, it will not be changed; and
3. The closed-loop system remains stable throughout the control synthesis problem.

The application for the third constraint is clear, while the first two constraints are desirable for a vast class of large-scale systems, such as the chemical processes.

### 5.4.1.b Robust Decentralized Problem

Let us assume that a feasible (i.e., satisfying conditions 1 and 2 in Section 5.4.1.a) decentralized control is applied to the servomechanism problem (5.2.6)–(5.2.8) and the plant matrices $A$, $B$, $C$ are perturbed to $A + \Delta A$, $B + \Delta B$, and $C + \Delta C$, where

$$\Delta A \in \theta_\varepsilon, \Delta B \in \theta_\varepsilon, \Delta C \in \theta_\varepsilon, \text{ and } \theta_\varepsilon = \{a|,|a| < \varepsilon, \varepsilon > 0\} \qquad (5.4.1)$$

is a set of possible perturbations and $\varepsilon$ is not necessarily small. Furthermore, assume that $\varepsilon$ is chosen so that the resulting closed-loop system is stable, i.e., $\lim_{t \to \infty} \dot{x}(t) = 0$ for any $x(0)$ with $\sigma_1(0) = 0$ and $\sigma_2(0) = 0$. If a controller is then applied to the perturbed system such that the resulting closed-loop system is both asymptotically stable and regulated, i.e., $\lim_{t \to \infty} e(t) = 0$ for all appropriate $x(0)$, $\sigma_1(0)$, and $\sigma_2(0)$, then this controller is said to be "robust". With the above assumptions, a robust decentralized controller can thus be defined.

**Definition 5.4.** If a decentralized controller satisfies the tuning regulator constraints 1–3 discussed in Section 5.4.1.a, the asymptotic stability condition, the asymptotic regulation condition, and the perturbation condition, i.e., containment of $\Delta A$, $\Delta B$, and $\Delta C$ in (5.4.1), then it is said to be a "decentralized robust controller for the servomechanism problem with unknown plants."

### 5.4.2 Steady-State Tracking Gain Matrices and Their Evaluation

The steady-state tracking gain matrix is a measure of steady-state output of the system under the influence of different decentralized controls. Before these matrices are defined, let $\Lambda(s)$ and $\Delta(s)$ denote the minimal polynomials of disturbance and desired reference systems matrices $\Omega_1$ and $\Gamma_1$ in (5.2.10) and (5.2.11), respectively, i.e.,

$$\Lambda(s) = \det(sI - \Omega_1), \quad \Delta(s) = \det(sI - \Gamma_1) \qquad (5.4.2)$$

Let $\lambda_l, l = 1, 2, \ldots, \hat{\rho}$ denote the roots of the least common multiple of $\Lambda(s)$ and $\Delta(s)$, each of which is repeated $q_l$ times and is distinct from the others. It is further assumed that $\text{Re}(\lambda_l) = 0$, $l = 1, 2, \ldots, \hat{\rho}$ and that $\lambda_l, q_l, l = 1, 2, \ldots, \hat{\rho}$, are all known. It is emphasized that the $\lambda_l$ are the only values assumed to be known, i.e., the matrices $\Omega_1$, $\Omega_2$, $\Gamma_1$, $\Gamma_2$, and $R$ in (5.2.10)–(5.2.11) are not necessarily assumed to be known (Davison, 1978).

**Definition 5.5.** The steady-state tracking gain matrix $T_l(i, j)$ for $i, j = 1, 2, \ldots, N$, $l = 1, 2, \ldots, \hat{\rho}$, and the case of $m_i = r_i$, $i = 1, 2, \ldots, N$, is defined by

$$T_l(i, j) \triangleq \begin{cases} C_i(\lambda_l I_n - A)^{-1} B_i + D_i \text{ for } i = j \\ C_j(\lambda_l I_n - A)^{-1} B_i \text{ for } i \neq j \end{cases} \qquad (5.4.3)$$

Taking into account the discussion on the fixed modes and fixed polynomials in Section 5.3, where $m_i \times r_i$ input matrices $K_i$ are involved with rank $(K_i) = r_i$, the tracking gain matrices with respect to $K_i$, $T_l(i, j; K_i)$ for $m_i \geqslant r_i$, $i = 1, 2, \ldots, N$, are given by

$$T_l(i, j; K_i) = \begin{cases} C_i(\lambda_l I_n - A)^{-1} B_i K_i + D_i K_i & \text{for } i = j \\ C_j(\lambda_l I_n - A)^{-1} B_i K_i & \text{for } i \neq j \end{cases} \qquad (5.4.4)$$

It is noted that for the special case of $K_i = I_{r_i}$, $m_i = r_i$, $T_l(i, j; I_{r_i}) = T_l(i, j)$. Furthermore, $T_l(i, j)$ is the value of the transfer matrix between input $u_i$ and output $y_j$ evaluated at $s = \lambda_l$. Although one can evaluate the steady-state tracking gain matrices using (5.4.3) and (5.4.4), Davison (1976d, 1978) has suggested algorithms, called "experiments," which can be used to evaluate the steady-state tracking gain matrices.

### 5.4.2.a Evaluation of $T_1(i, j)$

In this situation it is assumed that $m_i = r_i$, $i = 1, 2, \ldots, N$, and two reference inputs are considered: (1) polynomial, $\lambda_1 = 0$, and (2) sinusoidal, $\lambda_{l, l+1} = \pm j\omega_l$. The algorithms corresponding to the first case are given here; the reader may refer to Davison (1978) for the algorithms corresponding to the second case.

**Algorithm 5.5.** Evaluation of Tracking Gain Matrix $T_1(i, j)$ with $\lambda_1 = 0$

*Step 1:* Let $u_i(t) = u_i^1$ where $u_i^1 \neq 0$ and $u_j(t) = 0, j = 1, 2, \ldots, N, \ j \neq i$, and apply them to the plant and find the constant steady-state output vectors $y_j^1$:

$$y_j^1 = \lim_{t \to \infty} y_j(t), \quad j = 1, 2, \ldots, N \qquad (5.4.5)$$

Note that $y_j^1$ is constant, since the plant is assumed to be stable.

*Step 2:* Let $u_i(t) = u_i^2$ where $u_i^2 \neq 0$ and $u_j(t) = 0, j = 1, 2, \ldots, N, \ j \neq i$, and apply them to the plant and find the constant steady-state output vectors $y_j^2$:

$$y_j^2 = \lim_{t \to \infty} y_j(t), \quad j = 1, 2, \ldots, N \qquad (5.4.6)$$

$\vdots$

*Step $m_i$:* Let $u_i(t) = u_i^{m_i}$ where $u_i^{m_i} \neq 0$ and $u_j(t) = 0, j = 1, 2, \ldots, N, \ j \neq i$, and apply them to the plant and find the constant steady-state output vectors $y_j^{m_i}$:

$$y_j^{m_i} = \lim_{t \to \infty} y_j(t), \quad j = 1, 2, \ldots, N \qquad (5.4.7)$$

Then $T_1(i, j)$ is obtained by

$$T_1(i, j) = \left( y_j^1, y_j^2, \ldots, y_j^{m_i} \right) \cdot \left( u_i^1, u_i^2, \ldots, u_i^{m_i} \right)^{-1} \qquad (5.4.8)$$

### 5.4.2.b Evaluation of $T_1(i, j, K_i)$

For this situation it is assumed that $m_i > r_i$, $i = 1, 2, \ldots, N$, and $K_i$ is an $(m_i \times r_i)$-dimensional input gain matrix given in advance.

**Algorithm 5.6.** Evaluation of Tracking Gain Matrix $T_1(i, j, K_i)$ with $\lambda_1 = 0$

*Step 1:* Let $u_i(t) = K_i u_i^1$, $u_i^1 \neq 0, j = 1, 2, \ldots, N, \ j \neq i$, and apply them to the plant and find the constant steady-state output vectors $y_i^1$ as in (5.4.5).

$\vdots$

*Step $m_i$:* Let $u_i(t) = K_i u_i^{m_i}$, $u_j(t) = 0, j = 1, 2, \ldots, N, \ j \neq i$, and apply them to the plant and find $y_j^{m_i}$ as defined by (5.4.7). Then $T_1(i, j, K_i)$ is obtained by an expression similar to (5.4.8).

The following example illustrates Algorithm 5.5.

**Example 5.4.1.** Consider a system

$$\dot{x} = Ax + \sum_{i=1}^{2} B_i u_i + E\omega \qquad (5.4.9)$$

$$y_i = C_i x + D_i u_i, \quad i = 1, 2 \qquad (5.4.10)$$

where

$$A = \begin{bmatrix} -0.4 & 0.2 & 0.6 & 0.1 & -0.2 \\ 0 & -0.5 & 0 & 0 & 0.4 \\ 0 & 0 & -2 & 0 & 0.2 \\ 0.2 & 0.1 & 0.5 & -1.25 & 0 \\ 0.25 & 0 & -0.2 & 0.5 & -1 \end{bmatrix},$$

$$E = [0], \quad D_i = [0], \quad i = 1, 2 \qquad (5.4.11)$$

$$B_1^T = C_1 = [1 \quad 0 \quad 0 \quad 0 \quad 0], \quad B_2^T = C_2 = [0 \quad 0 \quad 1 \quad 1 \quad 1]$$

It is desired to find $T_1(i, j)$, $i, j = 1, 2$, in two different ways.

SOLUTION: The $A$ matrix has its eigenvalues at $-0.26$, $-0.79 \pm j0.147$, $-1.45$, and $-1.85$, which indicates that the plant is stable. The steady-state tracking gain matrices $T_1(i, j)$, $i, j = 1, 2$ are evaluated using (5.4.3) directly and Algorithm 5.5 for $\lambda_1 = 0$.

Utilizing (5.4.3) would result in the following values:

$$\begin{aligned} T_1(1, 1) &= C_1(-A)^{-1}B_1 + D_1 = 2.67640 \\ T_1(1, 2) &= C_2(-A)^{-1}B_1 = 1.52676 \\ T_1(2, 1) &= C_1(-A)^{-1}B_2 = 1.18823 \\ T_1(2, 2) &= C_2(-A)^{-1}B_2 + D_2 = 3.91915 \end{aligned} \qquad (5.4.12)$$

Alternatively, Algorithm 5.5 can be used. Let

$$u_1(t) = u_1^1 = 1, \quad u_2(t) = 0$$

then

$$\begin{aligned} y_j^1 &= \lim_{t \to \infty} y_1(t) = \lim_{t \to \infty} C_1 x(t) = \lim_{t \to \infty} C_1 A^{-1}(-B_1 u_1^1) \\ &= [2.67640 \quad 1.52676], \quad j = 1, 2 \end{aligned} \qquad (5.4.13)$$

Next, let $u_1(t) = 0$, $u_2(t) = u_2^2 = 1$; then

$$y_j^2 = \lim_{t \to \infty} y_2(t) = \lim_{t \to \infty} C_2 A^{-1}(-B_2 u_2^2) = [1.18823 \quad 3.91915] \qquad (5.4.14)$$

Now using (5.4.8) four times gives

$$T_1(1, 1) = y_1^1(u_1^1)^{-1} = 2.67640, \quad T_1(1, 2) = y_2^1(u_1^1)^{-1} = 1.52676$$

$$T_1(2, 1) = y_1^2(u_2^2)^{-1} = 1.18823, \quad T_1(2, 2) = y_2^2(u_2^2)^{-1} = 3.91915 \qquad (5.4.15)$$

which check exactly with the values obtained by direct use of (5.4.3) given in (5.4.12).

## 5.4.3 Existence of Decentralized Robust Controllers

In this section the conditions under which a decentralized robust controller exists and its general structure for both known and unknown plants are provided. However, prior to this, the following preliminaries must be given. Let $\alpha_i$, $i = 1, 2, \ldots, q$, denote the coefficients of the input system's characteristic polynomial

$$\prod_{i=1}^{\hat{\rho}} (\lambda - \lambda_i)^{q_i} \triangleq \lambda^q + \alpha_q \lambda^{q-1} + \cdots + \alpha_2 \lambda + \alpha_1 \qquad (5.4.16)$$

where $q = \sum_{i=1}^{\hat{\rho}} q_i$. The input system can be represented by a controllable companion pair $(\tilde{a}, \tilde{b})$ defined by

$$\tilde{a} = \begin{bmatrix} 0 & 1 & 0 & \cdots & & 0 \\ 0 & 0 & 1 & 0 & \cdots & 0 \\ \vdots & & & & & \\ -\alpha_1 & -\alpha_2 & -\alpha_3 & & \cdots & -\alpha_q \end{bmatrix}, \quad \tilde{b} = \begin{bmatrix} 0 \\ 0 \\ \vdots \\ 1 \end{bmatrix} \qquad (5.4.17)$$

with $\dim(\tilde{a}) = q \times q$ and $\dim(\tilde{b}) = q \times 1$. Let $N$ controllable pairs $(\tilde{A}_i, \tilde{B}_i)$, $i = 1, 2, \ldots, N$, be defined by

$$\tilde{A}_i = \text{Block-diag}\{\tilde{a}, \tilde{a}, \ldots, \tilde{a}\}, \quad \tilde{B}_i = \text{Block-diag}\{\tilde{b}, \tilde{b}, \ldots, \tilde{b}\} \qquad (5.4.18)$$

each repeated $r_i$ times and whose dimensions are $q_{r_i} \times q_{r_i}$ and $q_{r_i} \times r_i$, respectively, and whose values depend on the particular class of inputs and/or disturbances and the number of outputs to be regulated. These matrices are used in the definition of the decentralized robust controller structure to be discussed shortly.

Let the following $2r \times (n + r)$-dimensional matrix $C^*$ be defined by

$$C^{*T} = \left( C_1^{*T}, C_2^{*T}, \ldots, C_N^{*T} \right) \qquad (5.4.19)$$

where

$$C_1^* = \begin{bmatrix} C_1 & 0 & 0 & \cdots & 0 \\ 0 & I_{r_1} & 0 & \cdots & 0 \end{bmatrix}$$

$$C_2^* = \begin{bmatrix} C_2 & 0 & 0 & 0 & \cdots & 0 \\ 0 & 0 & I_{r_2} & 0 & \cdots & 0 \end{bmatrix} \qquad (5.4.20)$$

$$\vdots$$

$$C_N^* = \begin{bmatrix} C_N & 0 & \cdots & 0 \\ 0 & 0 & \cdots & I_{r_N} \end{bmatrix}$$

with dimensions $2r_1 \times (n+r)$, $2r_2 \times (n+r), \ldots, 2r_N \times (n+r)$, respectively. Using (5.4.19)–(5.4.20) and the fixed modes of a system (Definition 5.1), the following theorem sets forth the conditions for the existence of a decentralized robust controller for a known plant of the form (5.2.6)–(5.2.8).

**Theorem 5.8.** *Let the plant (5.2.6)–(5.2.8) be known with a stable A matrix, and further assume that the outputs $y_i(t)$, $i = 1, 2, \ldots, N$, are measurable. Then there exists a decentralized robust controller with asymptotic regulation (i.e., $\lim_{t \to \infty} e(t) = 0$) for all disturbances $\omega$ defined by (5.2.10), all desired prespecified reference inputs defined by (5.2.11), and asymptotic stability of the closed-loop system if and only if the fixed modes of*

$$\{C^*, A^*, B^*\} = \left\{ C^*, \begin{pmatrix} A & 0 \\ C & \lambda_j I \end{pmatrix}, \begin{pmatrix} B \\ D \end{pmatrix} \right\}, \quad j = 1, 2, \ldots, \hat{\rho} \quad (5.4.21)$$

*with respect to K defined by (5.3.6a) of the input system do not contain any $\lambda_j$, $j = 1, 2, \ldots, \hat{\rho}$, respectively.*

A rather lengthy proof of this theorem can be found in Davison (1976c). The following example illustrates the use of Theorem 5.8.

**Example 5.4.2.** Consider the system

$$\dot{x} = \begin{bmatrix} -1 & 0 \\ 1 & -2 \end{bmatrix} x + \begin{bmatrix} 0.2 \\ 0 \end{bmatrix} u_1 + \begin{bmatrix} 0 \\ 0.5 \end{bmatrix} u_2 \quad (5.4.22a)$$

$$y = \begin{bmatrix} 0 & 5 \\ 2 & 0 \end{bmatrix} x \quad (5.4.22b)$$

It is desired to check whether a decentralized robust controller exists for the system.

SOLUTION: Utilization of conditions (5.4.21) requires the following matrices:

$$C^* = \begin{bmatrix} C_1^* \\ \overline{C_2^*} \end{bmatrix} = \begin{bmatrix} C_1 & 0 & 0 \\ 0 & 1 & 0 \\ \overline{C_2} & 0 & 0 \\ 0 & 0 & 1 \end{bmatrix} = \begin{bmatrix} 0 & 5 & 0 & 0 \\ 0 & 0 & 1 & 0 \\ 2 & 0 & 0 & 0 \\ 0 & 0 & 0 & 1 \end{bmatrix}$$

$$A^* = \begin{bmatrix} A & 0 \\ C & \lambda_j I \end{bmatrix} = \begin{bmatrix} -1 & 0 & 0 & 0 \\ 1 & -2 & 0 & 0 \\ 0 & 5 & \lambda_j & 0 \\ 2 & 0 & 0 & \lambda_j \end{bmatrix}, \quad B^* = \begin{bmatrix} B \\ D \end{bmatrix} = \begin{bmatrix} 0.2 & 0 \\ 0 & 0.5 \\ 0 & 0 \\ 0 & 0 \end{bmatrix}$$

It is thus required to check whether $\lambda_j = \lambda_1 = 0$ is a fixed mode of $(C^*, A^*, B^*)$ with respect to K defined by $K = \text{Block-diag}(K_1, K_2)$, $\text{dim}(K_1)$ $\text{dim}(K_2) = 1 \times 2$. This was done using Algorithm 5.1, and it was found that $\lambda_1 = 0$ was not contained in the appropriate set of fixed modes. Thus, it is concluded that a decentralized robust controller for the plant (5.4.22) does exist.

It is noted that if the plant matrix $A$ is unstable, condition (5.4.21) is extended to the following:

1. $(C_m, A, B)$ has no unstable fixed modes with respect to $K^m$:

$$K^m \triangleq \text{Block-diag}\{K_1, K_2 \ldots, K_N\} \qquad (5.4.23a)$$

where each $K_i$ has a dimension $m_i \times r_i^m$ and $r_i^m$ stands for the number of measurable outputs of the system.

2. The fixed modes of $\{C^*, A^*, B^*\}$ with respect to $K^*$,

$$K^* = \text{Block-diag}\{K_1, K_2, \ldots, K_N\} \qquad (5.4.23b)$$

with each $\dim(K_1) = m_i \times (r_i + r_i^m)$, $i = 1, 2, \ldots, N$, do not contain $\lambda_j$, $j = 1, 2, \ldots, \hat{\rho}$.

3. Each $y_i^m$ contains the actual outputs.

The following corollary, due to Davison (1978), gives a much simpler criterion for the existence of a decentralized robust controller for the case when $m_i = r_i$, $i = 1, 2, \ldots, N$.

**Corollary 5.1.** *For the existence of a decentralized robust controller for the system described in Theorem 5.8 with $m_i = r_i$, $i = 1, 2, \ldots, N$, a necessary and sufficient condition is*

$$\text{rank}\begin{bmatrix} A - \lambda_j I & B \\ C & D \end{bmatrix} = n + r, \quad j = 1, 2, \ldots, \hat{\rho} \qquad (5.4.24)$$

*This condition is equivalent to the situation where none of the eigenvalues $\lambda_j, j = 1, 2, \ldots, \hat{\rho}$, of the input system coincide with the "transmission zeros" of the system. The transmission zeros of the system with matrices $(C, A, B, D)$ are all the complex numbers, which satisfy (Davison and Wang, 1974)*

$$\text{rank}\begin{bmatrix} A - \lambda I & B \\ C & D \end{bmatrix} < n + \min(r, m) \qquad (5.4.25)$$

The following theorem gives the necessary and sufficient conditions for the existence of a decentralized robust controller for the case when the plant described by (5.2.6)–(5.2.8) is unknown.

**Theorem 5.9.** *Consider the system (5.2.6)–(5.2.8) with $m_i = r_i$ for $i = 1, 2, \ldots, N$, $i \neq i_1, i_2, \ldots, i_d$, and $m_i > r_i$ for $i = i_1, i_2, \ldots, i_d$, and a set of $m_i \times r_i$ input gain matrices $K_i$ for $i = i_1, i_2, \ldots, i_d$ with $\text{rank}(K_i) = r_i$. Then a necessary and sufficient condition for the existence of a decentralized robust controller for the case when the system is unknown is that there exists a number of* *distinct integers $c_1, c_2, \ldots, c_N$, each contained in the closed set $[1, 2, \ldots, N]$, such that the following $N$ successive rank conditions hold:*

1. $\operatorname{rank}\left[T_l\left(c_1, c_1; \tilde{K}_{c_1}\right)\right] = r_{c_1}, \quad l = 1, 2, \ldots, \hat{\rho}$          (5.4.26a)

2. $\operatorname{rank}\begin{bmatrix} T_l\left(c_2, c_2; \tilde{K}_{c_2}\right) & T_l\left(c_2, c_1; \tilde{K}_{c_2}\right) \\ T_l\left(c_1, c_2; \tilde{K}_{c_1}\right) & T_l\left(c_1, c_1; \tilde{K}_{c_1}\right) \end{bmatrix} = r_{c_1} + r_{c_2}, \quad l = 1, 2, \ldots, \hat{\rho}$

                                                                    (5.4.26b)

$$\vdots$$

$N$.   $\operatorname{rank}\begin{bmatrix} T_l\left(c_N, c_N; \tilde{K}_{c_N}\right) & \cdots & T_l\left(c_N, c_1; \tilde{K}_{c_N}\right) \\ T_l\left(c_{N-1}, c_N; \tilde{K}_{c_{N-1}}\right) & \cdots & T_l\left(c_{N-1}, c_1; K_{c_{N-1}}\right) \\ \vdots & & \vdots \\ T_l\left(c_1, c_N; \tilde{K}_{c_1}\right) & \cdots & T_l\left(c_1, c_1; \tilde{K}_{c_1}\right) \end{bmatrix}$

$$= \sum_{i=1}^{N} r_{c_i} = r, \quad l = 1, 2, \ldots, \hat{\rho} \quad (5.4.26c)$$

*where*

$$\tilde{K}_{c_i} = \begin{cases} I_{r_{ci}} & \text{for } c_i \neq i_1, i_2, \ldots, i_d \quad (\text{an identity matrix of } r_{c_i} \text{ dimension}) \\ K_{c_i} & \text{for } c_i = i_1, i_2, \ldots, i_d \end{cases}$$

                                                                       (5.4.26d)

In order to prove this theorem, the following lemmas must be considered first (Davison, 1978).

**Lemma 5.4.** *Consider the system (5.2.10)–(5.2.12) with controllers $c_1, c_2, \ldots, c_t$, and assume that gain matrices $K_i \in R^{m_i \times r_i}$, $i = c_1, c_2, \ldots, c_t$; then*

$$\operatorname{rank} \hat{A}(c_t, j) \triangleq \operatorname{rank}\begin{bmatrix} A - \lambda_j I & B_{c_1} K_{c_1} & \cdots & B_{c_t} K_{c_t} \\ C_{c_1} & D_{c_1} K_{c_1} & \cdots & 0 \\ \vdots & & & \\ C_{c_t} & 0 & \cdots & D_{c_t} K_{c_t} \end{bmatrix} = n + \sum_{i=1}^{t} r_{c_i},$$

$$j = 1, 2, \ldots, \hat{\rho} \qquad\qquad\qquad (5.4.27)$$

*if and only if*

$$\text{rank}\begin{bmatrix} T_j(c_t,c_t;K_{c_t}) & \cdots & T_j(c_t,c_1;K_{c_t}) \\ T_j(c_{t-1},c_t;K_{c_{t-1}}) & \cdots & T_j(c_{t-1},c_1;K_{c_{t-1}}) \\ \vdots & \ddots & \vdots \\ T_j(c_1,c_t;K_{c_1}) & \cdots & T_j(c_1,c_1;K_{c_1}) \end{bmatrix} = \sum_{i=1}^{t} r_{c_i},$$

$$j = 1,\ldots,\hat{\rho} \quad (5.4.28)$$

PROOF: Since $A$ is a stable matrix and $\text{Re}(\lambda_j) = 0$, $j = 1,\ldots,\hat{\rho}$, then $(A - \lambda_j I)$, $j = 1,\ldots,\hat{\rho}$, is nonsingular. The relation (5.4.28) is true if and only if

$$\text{rank}\begin{bmatrix} I_n & (A-\lambda_j I)^{-1}B_{c_1}K_{c_1} & \cdots & (A-\lambda_j I)^{-1}B_{c_t}K_{c_t} \\ C_{c_1} & D_{c_1}K_{c_1} & & 0 \\ \vdots & \vdots & & \vdots \\ C_{c_t} & 0 & & D_{c_t}K_{c_t} \end{bmatrix}$$

$$= n + \sum_{i=1}^{t} r_{c_i}, \quad j = 1,\ldots,\rho$$

$$(5.4.29)$$

or if and only if

$$\text{rank}\begin{bmatrix} I_n & (A-\lambda_j I)^{-1} \\ 0 & D_{c_1}K_{c_1} - C_{c_1}(A-\lambda_j I)^{-1}B_{c_1}K_{c_1} \\ \vdots & \\ 0 & -C_{c_t}(A-\lambda_j I)^{-1}B_{c_1}K_{c_1} \end{bmatrix}$$

$$\begin{aligned} \cdots & \quad (A-\lambda_j I)^{-1}B_{c_t}K_{c_t} \\ \cdots & \quad -C_{c_1}(A-\lambda_j I)^{-1}B_{c_t}K_{c_t} \\ \cdots & \quad D_{c_t}K_{c_t} - C_{c_t}(A-\lambda_j I)^{-1}B_{c_t}K_{c_t} \end{aligned} \Bigg] = n + \sum_{i=1}^{t} r_{c_i}$$

$$j = 1,\ldots,\hat{\rho}, \quad (5.4.30)$$

which is equivalent to (5.4.28). Q.E.D. ∎

**Lemma 5.5.** *Consider the system (5.2.10)–(5.2.12) and let gains $K_i \in R^{m_i \times r_i}$, $i = c_1,\ldots,c_{t+1}$, exist such that $\text{rank}(\hat{A}(c_{t+1}, j) = n + \sum_{i=1}^{t+1} r_{c_i}$, $j = 1,\ldots,\hat{\rho}$*

*(see Equation (5.4.27)), and $\tilde{A}$ given by*

$$
\tilde{A} \triangleq
\begin{bmatrix}
A & B_{c_1}K_{c_1}K^{c_1} & \cdots & B_{c_t}K_{c_t}K^{c_t} \\
\tilde{B}_{c_1}C_{c_1} & \tilde{A}_{c_1} + \tilde{B}_{c_1}D_{c_1}K_{c_1}K^{c_1} & & 0 \\
\vdots & \vdots & \ddots & \\
\tilde{B}_{c_t}C_{c_t} & 0 & \cdots & \tilde{A}_{c_t} + \tilde{B}_{c_t}D_{c_t}K_{c_t}K^{c_t}
\end{bmatrix}
\tag{5.4.31}
$$

*is stable. Then this implies that*

$$
\mathrm{rank}
\begin{pmatrix}
\tilde{A} - \lambda_k I & B_{c_{t+1}}K_{c_{t+1}} \\
C_{c_{t+1}} & D_{c_{t+1}}K_{c_{t+1}}
\end{pmatrix}
= n + q \sum_{i=1}^{t} r_{c_i} + r_{c_{t+1}}, \quad j = 1,\ldots,\hat{\rho} \tag{5.4.32}
$$

The proof of this lemma is given by Davison (1978). We can now prove Theorem 5.9.

PROOF OF NECESSITY OF THEOREM 5.9: From Lemma 5.4 there exists $t$ constant matrices $\hat{K}_{c_i}$, $i = 1,2,\ldots,t$, so that

$$
\mathrm{rank}
\begin{bmatrix}
T_j(c_t, c_t; \hat{K}_{c_t}) & \cdots & T_j(c_t, c_1; \hat{K}_{c_1}) \\
\vdots & & \\
T_j(c_1, c_t; \hat{K}_{c_t}) & \cdots & T_j(c_1, c_1; \hat{K}_{c_1})
\end{bmatrix}
= \sum_{i=1}^{t} r_{c_i}, \quad j = 1,\ldots,\hat{\rho}
$$

$$\tag{5.4.33}$$

it follows that for the existence of a robust decentralized controller for system (5.2.6)–(5.2.8) for the case when $t = 1,2,\ldots,N$, and satisfying the decentralized controller tuning constraint, it becomes necessary that conditions 1 through $N$ of (5.5.26) of Theorem 5.9 all hold. ∎

PROOF OF SUFFICIENCY OF THEOREM 5.9: The proof will be carried out by construction. Let matrix $A$ be stable and assume that condition 1 of Theorem 5.9 holds. Then by virtue of Lemma 5.5 it follows that there exists a centralized servocompensator to control $\{u_{c_1}^*, y_{c_1}, T_j^*(c_1, c_1; \hat{K}_{c_1})\}$ such that the resultant system remains stable at all times during the tuning procedure. Let us assume that this has, in fact, been done. Now assume that condition 2 of Theorem 5.9 holds. Then from Lemmas 5.4 and 5.5, $\mathrm{rank}(T_j^*(c_2, c_2; \hat{K}_{c_2})) = r_{c_2}$, $j = 1,\ldots,\hat{\rho}$, and moreover a centralized servocompensator exists to control $\{u_{c_2}^*, y_{c_2}, T_j^*(c_2, c_2; \hat{K}_{c_2})\}$ such that the resultant system remains stable for all the times during the tuning procedure. Again assume that this has been done. The above is now repeated a total of $N$ times until a centralized servocompensator is implemented to control $\{u_{c_N}^*, y_{c_N}, T_j^*(c_N, c_N; \hat{K}_{c_N})\}$. At this point, a decentralized controller for system (5.2.6)–(5.2.8) has been synthesized so that the closed-loop system remains stable all the times and asymptotic robust tracking takes place. Q.E.D. ∎

An interpretation of Theorem 5.9 is that if an ordered list of integers $c_1, c_2, \ldots, c_N$ can be obtained such that conditions (5.4.26) are satisfied, then the tuning procedure begins with decentralized controller $c_1$, followed by $c_2, \ldots$, until $c_N$. The following example illustrates this.

**Example 5.4.3.** Consider a sixth-order, three-controller system,

$$\dot{x} = \begin{bmatrix} -1 & 0.5 & -0.2 & 0.85 & 0.45 & 0.9 \\ 0 & -0.5 & -2 & 0.9 & 0.4 & 0.1 \\ 0.15 & 0 & -2 & -0.2 & 0.1 & 0.8 \\ 0 & 0.1 & -0.25 & -0.8 & 0 & 0.2 \\ -0.2 & 0.4 & 0 & -0.5 & -2 & 0.1 \\ 0.6 & -0.7 & 0 & 0.2 & 0 & -2.5 \end{bmatrix} x$$

$$+ \begin{bmatrix} 1 \\ 0 \\ 1 \\ 0 \\ 1 \\ 0 \end{bmatrix} u_1 + \begin{bmatrix} 1 & 0 \\ 1 & 0 \\ 1 & 0 \\ 1 & 1 \\ 0.5 & 1 \\ 0 & 1 \end{bmatrix} u_2 + \begin{bmatrix} 1 \\ 0.2 \\ 0.5 \\ 0 \\ 1 \\ 0.5 \end{bmatrix} u_3 \qquad (5.4.34)$$

$$y_i = c_i x + D_i u_i, \quad i = 1,2,3$$

$$c_1 = \begin{bmatrix} 1 & 1 & 0 & 0 & 0 & 0 \end{bmatrix}, \quad c_2 = \begin{bmatrix} 0 & 0 & 1 & 1 & 0 & 0 \end{bmatrix}$$

$$c_3 = \begin{bmatrix} 0 & 0 & 0 & 0 & 1 & 1 \end{bmatrix}, \quad K_1 = K_3 = 1$$

$$K_2 = \begin{bmatrix} 0.5 & 0.25 \end{bmatrix}^T, \quad D_1 = \begin{bmatrix} 1 \end{bmatrix}, \quad D_2 = \begin{bmatrix} 1 & 1 \end{bmatrix}, \quad D_3 = \begin{bmatrix} 0 \end{bmatrix}$$

It is desired to see whether the system (5.4.34) can be controlled by a decentralized robust controller.

SOLUTION: The system matrix has eigenvalues at $-0.397 \pm j0.1313$, $-0.888$, $-2.05$, $-2.536 \pm j0.5475$. The steady-state tracking gains can be obtained either by Algorithm 5.6 or Equation (5.4.4),

$$T_1(1,1;1) = -4.264, \quad T_1(1,2;1) = 0.274, \quad T_1(1,3;1) = 0.8441,$$

$$T_1(2,1; K_2) = 3.1773, \quad T_1(2,2; K_2) = 2.2451, \quad T_1(2,3; K_2) = 0.41746,$$

$$T_1(3,1;1) = -2.40715; \quad T_1(3,2;1) = 0.3806, \quad T_1(3,3;1) = 1.0354$$

for $\lambda_1 = 0$. Then the rank conditions (5.4.26) become

$$\text{rank}\begin{bmatrix} T_1(1,1;1) \end{bmatrix} = r_1 = 1$$

$$\text{rank}\begin{bmatrix} T_1(2,2; K_2) & T_1(2,1; K_2) \\ T_1(1,2;1) & T_1(1,1;1) \end{bmatrix} = r_1 + r_2 = 2$$

$$\text{rank}\begin{bmatrix} T_1(3,3;1) & T_1(3,2;1) & T_1(3,1;1) \\ T_1(2,3; K_2) & T_1(2,2; K_2) & T_1(2,1; K_2) \\ T_1(1,3;1) & T_1(1,2;1) & T_1(1,1;1) \end{bmatrix} = r_1 + r_2 + r_3 = 3$$

$$(5.4.35)$$

which indicates that the system can be controlled by a decentralized robust controller. Moreover, the first controller is tuned first, second next, and the third after that. It is noted that the list of ordered integers $(c_1, c_2, c_3) = (1, 2, 3)$ is not necessarily unique. This point is further elaborated in Example 5.4.4.

A direct observation of the conditions of Theorem 5.9 indicates that for the case of some $m_i < r_i$, no solution to the robust control problem exists.

The next section provides the structure of controllers and algorithms to find the solution for the servomechanism problem.

### 5.4.4 Control Structure and Algorithms

First of all, the decentralized robust controller structure for the case when the plant (5.2.6)–(5.2.8) is known and whose existence was set forth in Theorem 5.8 follows the control law of the tuning regulator of multivariable systems (Davison 1976b),

$$u_i = K_0^i \zeta_i + K^i \eta_i, \quad i = 1, 2, \ldots, N \tag{5.4.36}$$

where $\eta_i$ is a $q_{r_i} \times 1$ output vector of the "decentralized general servocompensator" which satisfies

$$\dot{\eta}_i = \tilde{F}_i \tilde{A}_i \tilde{F}_i^{-1} \eta_i + \tilde{F}_i \tilde{B}_i e_i \tag{5.4.37}$$

$$e_i = y_i - y_i^d \tag{5.4.38}$$

where $\tilde{A}_i$, $\tilde{B}_i$ are defined in (5.4.18) and $\tilde{F}_i$ is a $q_{r_i} \times q_{r_i}$ arbitrary nonsingular matrix. The vector $\zeta_i$ is the output of the "decentralized stabilizing compensator" whose inputs are $\tilde{y}_i = y_i - D_i u_i$ and $\eta_i$, $i = 1, 2, \ldots, N$, i.e.,

$$\zeta_i = \Delta_i^0 \zeta_i + \Delta_i^1 \zeta_i + \Delta_i^2 \tilde{y}_i \tag{5.4.39}$$

where $\Delta_i^j$, $j = 0, 1, 2$, are matrices of appropriate dimensions to be obtained. The gains $K_o^i$ and $K^i$ can be found through the decentralized stabilization scheme discussed in Section 5.3.2 to stabilize the following augmented system:

$$
\begin{bmatrix} \dot{x} \\ \dot{\eta}_1 \\ \vdots \\ \dot{\eta}_N \end{bmatrix} =
\begin{bmatrix}
A & 0 & \cdots & & 0 \\
\tilde{F}_1 \tilde{B}_1 C_1 & \tilde{F}_1 \tilde{A}_1 \tilde{F}_1^{-1} & 0 & & 0 \\
\vdots & & & \ddots & \\
\tilde{F}_N \tilde{B}_N C_N & 0 & \cdots & 0 & \tilde{F}_N \tilde{A}_N \tilde{F}_N^{-1}
\end{bmatrix}
\begin{bmatrix} x \\ \eta_1 \\ \vdots \\ \eta_N \end{bmatrix}
$$
$$
+ \begin{bmatrix}
B & 0 & 0 & \cdots & 0 \\
0 & \tilde{F}_1 \tilde{B}_1 D_1 & & & \\
& & \ddots & & \\
0 & & & & \tilde{F}_N \tilde{B}_N D_N
\end{bmatrix}
\begin{bmatrix} u_1 \\ u_2 \\ \vdots \\ u_N \end{bmatrix} \tag{5.4.40}
$$

with output vectors

$$\begin{bmatrix} \tilde{y}_i \\ \eta_i \end{bmatrix} = \begin{bmatrix} C_i x \\ \eta_i \end{bmatrix}, \quad i = 1, 2, \dots, N \tag{5.4.41}$$

The following algorithm, given by Davison (1976d), provides a robust feedback controller for desired inputs or disturbances of polynomial type; i.e., (5.4.16) has $k$ repeated roots $\lambda = 0$.

*Algorithm 5.7.* Robust Controller for Polynomial Inputs

Step 1: The first augmented states are formed from $x$ and

$$\dot{\eta}_1 = e$$

$$u = \alpha_1 K \eta_1 \tag{5.4.42}$$

with $K = [T_1(1, 1)]^+$, where " $+$ " represents the pseudo-inverse, and scalar $\alpha_1 > 0$ is obtained by a one-dimensional search such that the eigenvalues of the closed-loop matrix

$$A_{c_1} = \begin{bmatrix} A & \alpha_1 BK \\ C & \alpha_1 DK \end{bmatrix} \tag{5.4.43}$$

are at appropriate locations on the left-half $s$-plane for "maximum speed of response," i.e., desired settling time, overshoot, etc.

Step 2: Let $u = \alpha_2 K \eta_2$, $\dot{\eta}_2 = \eta_1$, and apply $u$ to the augmented closed-loop system of Step 1 and find $\alpha_2$ through the one-dimensional search to find desirable eigenvalues for the second augmented closed-loop matrix

$$A_{c_2} = \begin{bmatrix} A & \alpha_1^* BK & \alpha_2 BK \\ C & \alpha_1^* DK & \alpha_2 DK \\ 0 & I & 0 \end{bmatrix} \tag{5.4.44}$$

where $\alpha_1^*$ represents the desired value of $\alpha_1$ fixed at the end of Step 1.

$\vdots$

Step k: In a similar fashion let $u = \alpha_k K \eta_k$, $\dot{\eta}_k = \eta_{k-1}$ and apply $u$ to the $(k-1)$th closed-loop system such that $\alpha_k$ is obtained for a set of desired eigenvalues of $A_{c_{k-1}}$.

The overall control is thus given by

$$u = K \sum_{j=1}^{k} \alpha_j^* \eta_j \tag{5.4.45}$$

Algorithms for sinusoidal and combination of polynomial-sinusoidal disturbances can be found through the works of Davison (1976d).

The following algorithm provides procedures for checking the existence and synthesis of the decentralized robust controller for the case of unknown plants. The existence of a decentralized robust controller for the servomechanism problem in the general case where for some $i$, $i = 1, 2, \ldots, N$ $m_i > r_i$ and for the remaining values of $i$, $m_i = r_i$ was already demonstrated by Example 5.4.3. Assuming that the existence conditions (5.4.26) for a decentralized robust controller hold and a set of input gain matrices $K_i$ are determined and $\tilde{K}_{c_i}$ in (5.4.26d) are defined, the following algorithm suggested by Davison (1978) provides the necessary steps for the synthesis of the proposed controller.

**Algorithm 5.8.** Synthesis of Decentralized Robust Controller–Unknown Plant

*Step 1:* Beginning with controller $i = c_i$, $u_i = u_i^*$ for $i = 1, 2, \ldots, N$, $i \neq i_1, i_2, \ldots, i_d$, and $u_i = K_i u_i^*$ for $i = i_1, \ldots, i_d$, find a servocompensator using $y_{c_1}$, $T_l^*(c_1, c_1; \tilde{K}_{c_1})$ to obtain $u_{c_1}^*$ for the desired inputs (5.2.11) and disturbances (5.2.10). This is accomplished by a centralized servocompensator using an algorithm like Algorithm 5.7.

*Step 2:* Find the steady-state tracking gains $T_l^*(c_2, c_2; \tilde{K}_{c_2})$, $l = 1, 2, \ldots, \hat{\rho}$, for the augmented closed-loop system resulting from Step 1 using either Algorithm 5.6 or Equation (5.4.4). Obtain a centralized servocompensator using $y_{c_2}$ and $T_l^*(c_2, c_2; \tilde{K}_{c_2})$ to obtain $u_{c_2}^*$ through Algorithm 5.7.

$\vdots$

*Step N:* Find $T_l^*(c_N, c_N; \tilde{K}_{c_N})$, $l = 1, 2, \ldots, \hat{\rho}$, for the augmented closed-loop system resulting from Step N-1 using Algorithm 5.6 and obtain $u_{c_N}^*$ from Algorithm 5.7 using $y_{c_N}$ and $T_l^*(c_N, c_N; \tilde{K}_{c_N})$.

The following example illustrates the above algorithm and a number of comments regarding the nonuniqueness of the order list $(c_1, c_2, \ldots, c_N)$ and the criterion for a decentralized synthesis.

**Example 5.4.4.** Consider a servomechanism problem

$$\dot{x} = Ax + \sum_{i=1}^{2} B_i u_i + E\omega$$

$$y_i = c_i x + D_i u_i + P_i \omega, \quad i = 1, 2 \tag{5.4.46}$$

$$e_i = y_i - y_i^d$$

where nonzero vectors and matrices are

$$A = \begin{bmatrix} -1 & 0.1 \\ 0 & -2 \end{bmatrix}, \quad B_1 = \begin{bmatrix} 0 \\ 1 \end{bmatrix}, \quad B_2 = \begin{bmatrix} 1 \\ 0.5 \end{bmatrix}$$

$$c_1 = \begin{bmatrix} 1 & 0 \end{bmatrix}, \quad c_2 = \begin{bmatrix} 0 & 1 \end{bmatrix}, \quad D_1 = \begin{bmatrix} 1 \end{bmatrix}$$

with $D_2 = [0]$, $P_1 = P_2 = [0]$, $E^T = \begin{bmatrix} 0 & 0 \end{bmatrix}$, and $y_1^d = 0.5$, $y_2^d = -0.5$.

It is desired to find a decentralized robust controller which achieves asymptotic regulation with reasonably "fast" response speed and keeps the system stable at all times.

SOLUTION: For this system, $n = 2$, $N = 2$, $m_1 = m_2 = r_1 = r_2 = 1$; hence, we begin by applying Algorithm 5.5 for $l = 1$, $\lambda_l = 0$ to find the steady-state tracking gains $T_1(i, j)$, $i, j = 1, 2$. These values are obtained as follows. Let $u_1 = u_1^1 = 1$, $u_2 = 0$; then

$$y_1^1 = \lim_{t \to \infty} y_1(t) = 1.05, \quad y_2^1 = \lim_{t \to \infty} y_2(t) = 0.5$$

Then letting $u_2 = u_2^2 = 1$, $u_1 = 0$,

$$y_1^2 = \lim_{t \to \infty} y_1(t) = 1.025, \quad y_2^2 = \lim_{t \to \infty} y_2(t) = -0.25$$

Thus, $T_1(i, j)$, $i, j = 1, 2$, are $T_1(1, 1) = 1.05$, $T_1(1, 2) = 0.5$, $T_1(2, 1) = 1.025$, and $T_1(2, 2) = -0.25$. At this point, in an attempt to apply the rank conditions (5.4.26) for $N = 2$ and $l = 1$, one can note that for the present example

1.  $\text{rank} [T_1(1, 1)] = \text{rank} [T_1(2, 2)] = r_1 = r_2 = 1$

and

2.  $$\text{rank} \begin{bmatrix} T_1(2,2) & T_1(2,1) \\ T_1(1,2) & T_1(1,1) \end{bmatrix} = \text{rank} \begin{bmatrix} T_1(1,1) & T_1(1,2) \\ T_1(2,1) & T_1(2,2) \end{bmatrix}$$
$$= r_1 + r_2 = 2 \tag{5.4.47}$$

which indicates that the ordered list $(c_1, c_2, \ldots, c_N)$ can be either $(c_1, c_2)$ or $(c_2, c_1)$. In this application we first arbitrarily choose $(c_1, c_2)$ and then compare the results with the other choice $(c_2, c_1)$. By applying Step 1 of Algorithm 5.8, which, in turn, requires the implementation of an algorithm similar to Algorithm 5.7, the following robust controller is tuned for $u_{c_1} = u_1$, i.e.,

$$u_1 = -\alpha_1 [T_1^*(1,1)]^{-1} \eta_1 = -(1/1.05)\alpha_1 \eta_1 \tag{5.4.48}$$
$$\dot{\eta} = e_1 = y_1 - y_1^d = x_1 + u_1 - 0.5$$

which can be applied to the plant to provide a third-order augmented closed-loop system

$$\begin{bmatrix} \dot{x}_1 \\ \dot{x}_2 \\ \dot{\eta}_1 \end{bmatrix} = \begin{bmatrix} -1 & 0.1 & 0 \\ 0 & -2 & -\alpha_1/1.05 \\ 1 & 0 & -\alpha_1/1.05 \end{bmatrix} \begin{bmatrix} x_1 \\ x_2 \\ \eta_1 \end{bmatrix} + \begin{bmatrix} 0 \\ 0 \\ -0.5 \end{bmatrix} \tag{5.4.49}$$

**Table 5.2** Pattern of Closed-Loop Poles During the Tuning of the First Controller for Example 5.4.4

| $\alpha_1$ | Closed-Loop Poles | | |
|---|---|---|---|
| 0.025 | $-0.997$ | $-0.025$ | $-2.00$ |
| 0.10 | $-0.990$ | $-0.100$ | $-2.00$ |
| 0.15 | $-0.983$ | $-0.152$ | $-2.00$ |
| 0.25 | $-0.968$ | $-0.256$ | $-2.01$ |
| 0.50 | $-0.897$ | $-0.549$ | $-2.03$ |
| 0.60 | $-0.767 \pm j0.0274$ | | $-2.04$ |
| 0.625 | $-0.778 \pm j0.0887$ | | $-2.04$ |
| 0.65 | $-0.788 \pm j0.1214$ | | $-2.04$ |
| 0.70 | $-0.180 \pm j0.1665$ | | $-2.05$ |
| 0.75 | $-0.832 \pm j0.2000$ | | $-2.05$ |

A one-dimensional search for a set of eigenvalues which provides desirable "speed of response" can now be performed on (5.4.49). The resulting search is shown in Table 5.2 from which a value of $\alpha_1 = \alpha_1^* = 0.65$ is chosen arbitrarily for now.

Next, at the Step $N = 2$ of Algorithm 5.8, controller $u_{c_2} = u_2$ is now tuned as follows:

$$u_2 = -\alpha_2 \left[ T_1^*(2,2) \right]^{-1} \eta_2 = 8.4\alpha_2\eta_2$$
$$\dot{\eta}_2 = e_2 = y_2 - y_2^d = x_2 + 0.5$$
(5.4.50)

which once again can be applied to the augmented closed-loop system (5.4.49) in the presence of $u_2$ to obtain the following fourth-order system:

$$\begin{bmatrix} \dot{x}_1 \\ \dot{x}_2 \\ \dot{\eta}_1 \\ \dot{\eta}_2 \end{bmatrix} = \begin{bmatrix} -1 & 0.1 & 0 & 8.4\alpha_2 \\ 0 & -2 & -\alpha_1^*/1.05 & 4.2\alpha_2 \\ 1 & 0 & -\alpha_1^*/1.05 & 0 \\ 0 & 1 & 0 & 0 \end{bmatrix} \begin{bmatrix} x_1 \\ x_2 \\ \eta_1 \\ \eta_2 \end{bmatrix} + \begin{bmatrix} 0 \\ 0 \\ -0.5 \\ 0.5 \end{bmatrix}$$
(5.4.51)

Another one-dimensional search for parameter $\alpha_2$ with a fixed value $\alpha_1 = \alpha_1^* = 0.65$ gives a pattern for the closed-loop poles, i.e., eigenvalues of the matrix in (5.4.51), as shown in Table 5.3. It is noted that two of the poles, corresponding to $x_1$ and $x_2$, remained real, while the other, corresponding to $\eta_1$ and $\eta_2$, tended to become complex with negative real parts and eventually drive the system to instability. Figure 5.5 shows the time responses of $y_1(t)$ and $y_2(t)$ corresponding to $\alpha_1^* = 0.65$ and $\alpha_2^* = 0.046$. The decentralized robust controllers (5.5.48) and (5.5.50) provided asymptotic regulation with "settling times" of 20.8 and 21.0 seconds, respectively, for $y_1(t)$ and $y_2(t)$. Here the time at which the response reaches and remains within $\pm 5\%$ of its desired reference value is defined as the settling time.

**Table 5.3** Pattern of Closed-Loop Poles During the Tuning of the Second
Controller for Example 5.4.4

| $\alpha_2$ | Closed-Loop Poles | | | |
|---|---|---|---|---|
| 0.023 | $-0.409$ | $-0.064$ | $-1.10$ | $-2.05$ |
| 0.046 | $-0.1660 \pm j0.138$ | | $-1.23$ | $-2.05$ |
| 0.068 | $-0.1130 \pm j0.227$ | | $-1.32$ | $-2.07$ |
| 0.090 | $-0.0693 \pm j0.275$ | | $-1.40$ | $-2.08$ |
| 0.113 | $-0.0309 \pm j0.308$ | | $-1.46$ | $-2.09$ |
| 0.136 | $-0.0035 \pm j0.332$ | | $-1.52$ | $-2.10$ |
| 0.226 | $0.1175 \pm j0.383$ | | $-1.68$ | $-2.17$ |

Next, the other possible ordered list of controllers, i.e., $(c_1, c_2) = (2, 1)$
was used. The acceptable values of $\alpha_1$ and $\alpha_2$ were arbitrarily obtained to be
$\alpha_1 = \alpha_1^* = 0.5$ and $\alpha_2 = \alpha_2^* = 0.295$. The corresponding closed-loop poles of
the system turned out to be $-1.30 \pm j0.43$ and $-0.15 \pm j0.178$, which,
unlike the other ordered list, provided two complex conjugate pairs. The
system's output time responses are shown in Figure 5.6. The settling times
for this case turn out to be 33.3 and 22.6 seconds, respectively, for $y_1(t)$ and

**Figure 5.5** Output time responses $y_i(t)$ for the system of Example 5.4.4 with tuning
order $(1, 2)$.

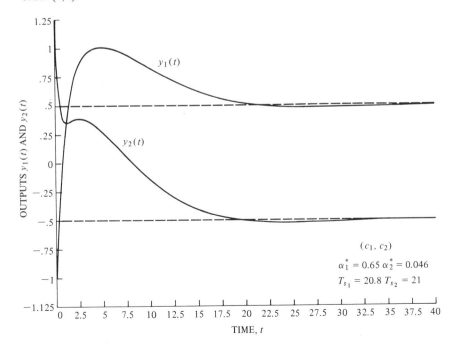

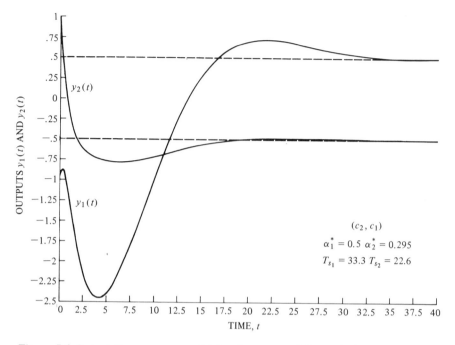

**Figure 5.6** Output time responses $y_i(t)$ for the system of Example 5.4.4 with tuning order (2, 1).

$y_2(t)$, which indicates that the second list, i.e., tuning the second controller first and the first one second, gave relatively slower speeds of response.

From a practical synthesis point of view, the most important issue with respect to the robust decentralized controller is perhaps the lack of a criterion under which the one-dimensional searches can be terminated. One possible way to terminate the case where a large-scale system is dominated by a pair of complex conjugate closed-loop poles is to use the graphical design and synthesis techniques of lead-lag compensators for SISO systems in frequency-domain. For a given set of desirable specifications, say a settling time $T_s$ of ten seconds and a maximum overshoot of 10%, a feasible domain for dominant closed-loop poles can be obtained on the complex plane. Then, the one-dimensional search in the domain of parameter $\alpha_{c_N}$ is terminated such that a pair of complex poles lie within the desirable region. A block diagram of the decentralized robust controller for Example 5.4.4 is shown in Figure 5.7.

### 5.4.5 Sequentially Stable Robust Controller

In this section, the notion of *sequential stability* introduced by Davison and Gesing (1979) is considered. This notion refers to a large-scale system's property in which a synthesis technique can be developed where one

251

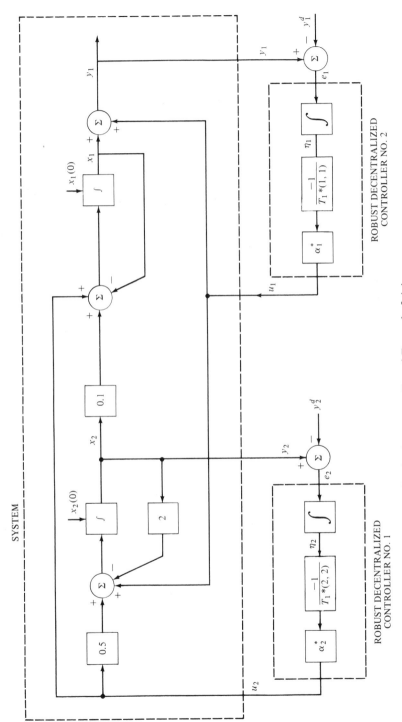

**Figure 5.7** A block diagram for the decentralized robust controller of Example 5.4.4.

controller after another is connected to the system until all $N$ stations are covered while the feedback system remains stable all times. The main motivation behind this notion is the impracticality of applying all decentralized controllers simultaneously due to time lags resulting from communication problems, etc. (Davison, 1979).

The problem considered here is basically the same as (5.2.6)–(5.2.8) with the additional constraint that out of $r$ system outputs only $r^m \leqslant r$ of them are measurable, i.e.,

$$y_i^m(t) = c_i^m x(t) + D_i^m u_i(t) + P_i^m \omega(t) \qquad (5.4.52)$$

where $y_i^m$ is an $r_i^m$-dimensional vector representing the outputs available for measurement at control station $i$. The existence conditions for a decentralized robust controller for system (5.2.6)–(5.2.8) and (5.4.52) was already discussed through relations (5.4.23) and has been applied to a general servomechanism problem by Davison (1976b). Furthermore, the structure of the controller is given by (5.4.36)–(5.4.39). In sequel, a sequentially stable robust decentralized controller is defined and conditions for its existence along with a synthesis algorithm are presented.

**Definition 5.6.** Consider the problem (5.2.6)–(5.2.8) and (5.4.52) and assume that $A$ is a stable matrix. Let $s^i$, $i = 1, 2, \ldots, N$, be a set of decentralized controllers whose inputs are $y_i^m$, $y_i^d$ and output $u_i$. If the closed-loop system resulting from applying the controllers $s^i$, $i = 1, 2, \ldots, N$, remains stable, then the controllers $s^i$ are called "sequentially stable" with respect to control stations applied in the order $1, 2, \ldots, N$.

It is noted that the difference between the robust controllers for a sequentially stable system and one with an unknown plant considered in Section 5.4.4 (see (5.4.26)) is that in the latter case a nonunique ordered list is obtained for tuning controllers one at a time, while in the former the order is fixed at $1, 2, \ldots, N$. The conditions for the existence of a sequentially stable robust decentralized controller are given by (5.4.24)–(5.4.25) and the asymptotic stability of $A$. For the special case when the reference inputs and disturbances are polynomial, i.e., when $\lambda_l = 0$, $l = 1, 2, \ldots, q$, an additional condition would be that the order of the decentralized stabilizing controller (5.4.36)–(5.4.39) be zero (Davison, 1979). The following algorithm provides a procedure for synthesising the sequentially stable controller for the case of polynomial inputs.

*Algorithm 5.9.* Synthesis of the Sequentially Stable Robust Controller with Polynomial Inputs

   *Step 1:* Apply $u_i(t) = K_i \hat{y}_i^m + L_i v_i(t)$, $i = 1, 2, \ldots, N$, to the plant, where $K_i$ is a small arbitrary feedback gain matrix chosen in such a way that

$$\text{Re}\left(\lambda\left\{A + \sum_{i=1}^{M} B_i K_i C_i^m\right\}\right) < 0 \qquad (5.4.53)$$

for all $M \in [1, 2, \ldots, N]$ and $L_i$ (rank $L_i = r_i$) are also arbitrarily chosen such that the following rank condition holds:

$$\text{rank}\begin{bmatrix} A + \displaystyle\sum_{i=1}^{N} B_i K_i C_i^m - \lambda_j I & B_1 L_1 & \cdots & B_k L_k \\ C_1 + D_1 K_1 C_1^m & D_1 L_1 & \cdots & 0 \\ \vdots & & \ddots & \\ C_k + D_k K_k C_k^m & 0 & \cdots & D_k L_k \end{bmatrix}$$

$$= n + \sum_{i=1}^{k} r_i, \quad j = 1, 2, \ldots, q \quad (5.4.54)$$

If $m_i = r_i$ for $i = 1, 2, \ldots, N$, $i \neq i_d$, then a good choice for $L_i = I_{r_i}$ for $i \neq i_d$ and $u_{i_d} = L_{i_d} u_{i_d}$ where $v_i$ is the input to the $i$th controller and $\hat{y}_i^m \triangleq y_i^m - D_i u_i$.

*Step 2:* Apply a decentralized controller

$$u_i = K_i \hat{y}_i^m + v_i, \quad v_i = -K^i \eta_i, \quad \dot{\eta}_i = e_i \qquad (5.4.55)$$

to the station $i = 1$ such that the closed-loop system is stable. It is noted that controller (5.4.55) is essentially the robust controller stemming from the tuning regulator for multivariable systems, as given by Algorithm 5.7.

*Step 3:* Repeat Step 2 for $i = 2, 3, \ldots, N$ sequentially until all stations are "tuned."

*Step 4:* The resulting controller asymptotically regulates the system.

Before this algorithm is illustrated by an example, it is noted that for the more general algorithm of Step 2 one can use the centralized servocompensator procedure of Davison and Goldenberg (1975). Furthermore, the sequential stabilizing controller discussed here is extended within a "sequential optimization" framework as a near-optimum design technique in Chapter 6.

**Example 5.4.5.** Consider a system

$$\dot{x} = \begin{bmatrix} -0.4 & 0.2 & 0.6 & 0.1 & -0.2 \\ 0 & -0.5 & 0 & 0 & 0.4 \\ 0 & 0 & -2 & 0 & 0.2 \\ 0.2 & 0.1 & 0.5 & -1.25 & 0 \\ 0.25 & 0 & -0.2 & 0.5 & -1 \end{bmatrix} x + \sum_{i=1}^{2} B_i u_i + E\omega$$

(5.4.56)

$$y_i = C_i x + D_i u_i + P_i \omega, \quad i = 1, 2,$$

where

$$B_1^T = C_1 = \begin{bmatrix} 1 & 1 & 0 & 0 & 0 \end{bmatrix}, \quad B_2^T = C_2 = \begin{bmatrix} 0 & 0 & 1 & 1 & 1 \end{bmatrix}$$
$$D_1 = D_2 = [1], \quad y_i^m = y_i, \quad i = 1, 2$$
$$(y_1^d, y_2^d) = (1, -1), \quad E^T = \begin{bmatrix} 1 & 0 & 1 & 0 & 1 \end{bmatrix}$$
$$P_i = [0], \quad i = 1, 2, \omega = 0.1$$

hence $\lambda_j = 0$, $j = 1$, $q = 1$. It is desired to find a sequentially stable robust decentralized controller for this system.

SOLUTION: The first thing one must do is to check the following conditions:

1. The triple $\langle C_m, A, B \rangle$ has no unstable fixed modes, with $A$ given in (5.4.56) and $B$ and $C_m$ as follows:

$$B^T = C_m = \begin{bmatrix} 1 & 1 & 0 & 0 & 0 \\ 0 & 0 & 1 & 1 & 1 \end{bmatrix} \qquad (5.4.57a)$$

This is accomplished by using the "fixed modes" in Algorithm 5.1 or by the rank condition of Anderson and Clements (1981). It is found that no unstable fixed mode exists.

2. The triplet $\langle C_m^*, A^*, B^* \rangle$ fixed modes do not contain $\lambda_1 = 0$, with

$$A^* = \begin{bmatrix} A & 0 \\ C & \lambda_j I \end{bmatrix}, \quad B^* = \begin{bmatrix} B \\ \hline -D \end{bmatrix} = \begin{bmatrix} 1 & 0 \\ 1 & 0 \\ 0 & 1 \\ 0 & 1 \\ 0 & 1 \\ \hline 1 & 0 \\ 0 & 1 \end{bmatrix} \qquad (5.4.57b)$$

$$C_m^* = \begin{bmatrix} C_1^m & 0 & \cdots & 0 \\ 0 & I_{r_1} & \cdots & 0 \\ \hline C_2^m & 0 & \cdots & 0 \\ 0 & 0 & \cdots & I_{r_2} \end{bmatrix} = \begin{bmatrix} 1 & 1 & 0 & 0 & 0 & 0 & 0 \\ 0 & 0 & 0 & 0 & 0 & 1 & 0 \\ \hline 0 & 0 & 1 & 1 & 1 & 0 & 0 \\ 0 & 0 & 0 & 0 & 0 & 0 & 1 \end{bmatrix}$$

(5.4.57c)

This condition was also checked to be the case using Algorithm 5.1.

The first step of Algorithm 5.9 begins by arbitrarily taking $u_2 = K_2 \hat{y}_2^m + L_2 v_2$, setting $L_2 = 1$, since $m_2 = r_2 = 1$, and $K_2$ is chosen as a small arbitrary gain such that conditions (5.4.53) hold. Step 2 indicates that $v_2$ can be obtained by (5.4.55):

$$v_2 = - K^2 \eta_2, \quad \dot{\eta}_2 = e_2 = y_2^m - y_2^d = C_2 x + D_2 u_2 + 1$$

$$= (I_{r_2} + D_2 K_2) C_2 x - D_2 K^2 \eta_2 + 1 \tag{5.4.58}$$

The results of these searches for $K_2$, $K^2$ for this system are $K_2 = 0.1$ and $K^2 = 0.15$.

Step 3 provides the following values for $u_1, v_1,$ and $\eta_1$:

$$u_1 = K_1 C_1 x - K^1 \eta_1, \quad v_1 = - K^1 \eta_1, \quad \dot{\eta}_1 = (I_{r_1} + D_1 K_1) C_1 x - D_1 K^1 \eta_1 - 1 \tag{5.4.59}$$

with resulting values $K_1 = -0.5$ and $K^1 = 1$, which provide a set of eigenvalues for the augmented closed-loop system

$$\begin{bmatrix} \dot{x} \\ \hline \dot{\eta}_2 \\ \hline \dot{\eta}_1 \end{bmatrix} = \begin{bmatrix} A + B_1 K_1 C_1 + B_2 K_2 C_2 & -B_2 K^2 & -B_1 K^1 \\ \hline (I_{r_2} + D_2 K_2) C_2 & -D_2 K^2 & 0 \\ \hline (I_{r_1} + D_1 K_1) C_1 & 0 & -D_1 K^1 \end{bmatrix} \begin{bmatrix} x \\ \hline \eta_2 \\ \hline \eta_1 \end{bmatrix} + \begin{bmatrix} E\omega \\ -y_2^d \\ -y_1^d \end{bmatrix} \tag{5.4.60}$$

equal to $\lambda_{1,2} = -1.117 \pm j0.994$, $\lambda_{3,4} = -0.383 \pm j0.673$, $\lambda_{5,6} = -1.623 \pm j0.136$, and $\lambda_7 = -0.752$.

The resulting outputs $y_i(t)$, $i = 1, 2$, are shown in Figure 5.8. It is seen that a generally robust regulation using $x^T(0) = (1 \quad -1 \quad 0 \quad -1 \quad 1)$ and $y_i$, $i = 1, 2$, given by

$$y_1 = C_1 x + D_1 u_1 = (0.5 \quad 0.5 \quad 0 \quad 0 \quad 0 \quad 0 \quad -1) \begin{bmatrix} x \\ \hline \eta_2 \\ \eta_1 \end{bmatrix}$$

$$y_2 = C_2 x + D_2 u_2 = (0 \quad 0 \quad 1.1 \quad 1.1 \quad 1.1 \quad -0.15 \quad 0) \begin{bmatrix} x \\ \hline \eta_2 \\ \eta_1 \end{bmatrix} \tag{5.4.61}$$

is achieved. The final structure of the robust sequentially stable decentralized controller is given by

$$u_1(t) = -0.5 y_1^m(t) - \int_0^t e_1(\tau) \, d\tau + u_1^0$$

$$u_2(t) = 0.1 y_2^m(t) - 0.15 \int_0^t e_2(\tau) \, d\tau + u_2^0 \tag{5.4.62}$$

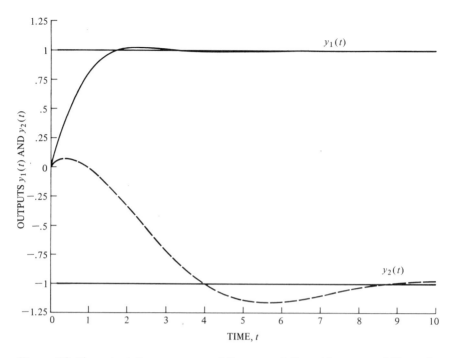

**Figure 5.8** The output time responses of the sequentially stable system of Example 5.4.5.

where $u_1^0, u_2^0$ can, in turn, be tuned to minimize a performance index in a "sequential optimization" technique, which is discussed in Chapter 6.

## 5.5 Decentralized Stochastic Control

In this section the third and final problem introduced in Section 5.2 is treated. Stochastic control of systems is of very immense practical importance. Here the control problem is addressed from a nondecentralized point of view, and then the decentralized version is discussed.

### 5.5.1 A Nondecentralized Solution

Consider the stochastic control problem described by (5.2.14)–(5.2.18) and let us review the general solution for the linear-quadratic Gaussian (LQG) problem. At each station (node) it is assumed that the following measurement vector is available, which is described by (5.2.16). Then it is well known (Bryson and Ho, 1969) that the $i$th control station has an input

$$u_i(k) = -\Lambda_i(k)\hat{x}(k) \qquad (5.5.1)$$

where the best estimate using all the information is given by

$$\hat{x}(k) \triangleq E\{x(k)/Y_1(k),\ldots,Y_N(k)\} \tag{5.5.2}$$

where $Y_i(k)$ defined by

$$Y_i(k) \triangleq \{y_i(l), l=1,\ldots,k\}, \quad i=1,\ldots,N \tag{5.5.3}$$

defines the measurement history. Following (5.5.1) and (5.5.2), it is clear that each station's optimal control is of the form

$$u_i(k) = \phi_i(Y_1(k),\ldots,Y_N(k),k) \tag{5.5.4}$$

The best estimate $\hat{x}_i(k)$ in (5.5.2) is assumed to propagate as

$$\hat{x}(k+1) = \bar{x}(k+1) + \sum_{i=1}^{N} K_i(k+1)(y_i(k+1) - C_i\bar{x}(k+1)) \tag{5.5.5}$$

where $\bar{x}(k+1) \triangleq E\{x(k+1)/Y_1(k),\ldots,Y_N(k)\}$ is given by

$$\bar{x}(k+1) = A\hat{x}(k) + \sum_{i=1}^{N} B_i u_i(k) \tag{5.5.6}$$

The Kalman gain $K_i(k)$ is given by

$$K_i(k) = P(k) C_i^T W_i^{-1}(k) \tag{5.5.7}$$

where $P(k)$ is the error variance given *all* information,

$$P(k) \triangleq E\{(\hat{x}(k) - x(k))(\hat{x}(k) - x(k))^T / Y_1(k),\ldots,Y_N(k)\} \tag{5.5.8}$$

which propagates as (Speyer, 1979)

$$P^{-1}(k+1) = M^{-1}(k+1) + \sum_{i=1}^{N} C_i^T W_i^{-1}(k+1)C_i, \quad P(K+1) \text{ given}$$

$$\tag{5.5.9}$$

where

$$M(k+1) \triangleq E\{(\bar{x}(k+1) - x(k+1))$$
$$\times (\bar{x}(k+1) - x(k+1))^T / Y_1(k),\ldots,Y_N(k)\} \tag{5.5.10}$$

propagates as

$$M(k+1) = AP(k)A^T + V(k), \quad M(1) \text{ given.} \tag{5.5.11}$$

The control gains are given by

$$\Lambda_i(k) = [R_i + B_i^T S(k+1) B_i]^{-1} B_i^T S(k+1) \tag{5.5.12}$$

where $S(k)$ is propagated backward in time and is given by

$$S(k) = A^T S(k+1) A - \sum_{i=1}^{N} \Lambda_i^T(k)(R_i + B_i^T S(k+1) B_i)\Lambda_i(k) + Q(k)$$

$$\tag{5.5.13}$$

The relations (5.5.1)–(5.5.13) constitute the complete solution to the LQG problem as applied to a stochastic control system. It is important to note that the estimator of (5.5.5) calculates data received at all the nodes. However, the objective of the decentralized system is to compute estimates of the state at each station by utilizing the data obtained only at that station.

### 5.5.2 A Decentralized Solution

The decentralized solution begins by dividing the best state estimate $\hat{x}(k)$ into two components: $\hat{x}^D(k)$, dependent on the incoming data, and $x^C(k)$, dependent on the control, i.e.,

$$\hat{x}(k) = \hat{x}^D(k) + x^C(k) \qquad (5.5.14)$$

where $x^C(k)$ is given by

$$x^C(k+1) = Ax^C(k) + \sum_{i=1}^{N} B_i u_i(k), \quad x^C(1) = \bar{x}(1) \qquad (5.5.15)$$

and $\bar{x}^D(1) = 0$, leading to

$$\hat{x}^D(k+1) = \bar{x}^D(k+1) + \sum_{i=1}^{N} K_i(k+1)\left(\tilde{y}_i(k+1) - C_i\bar{x}^D(k+1)\right)$$

$$(5.5.16a)$$

$$\bar{x}^D(k+1) = A\hat{x}^D(k) \qquad (5.5.16b)$$

where

$$\tilde{y}_i(k) \triangleq y_i(k) - C_i x^C(k) \qquad (5.5.17)$$

Through decomposition it can be shown (Speyer, 1979) that the decentralized system consists of a local Kalman filter processing the sensor data at each station. Let $\hat{x}_i^D(k) = E\{x^D(k)/Y_i(k)\}$ be the local estimate at station $i$ using measurement $Y_i(k)$ only, and let $P_i(k) = [(\hat{x}^D(k) - x_i^D(k))(\hat{x}^D(k) - x_i^D(k))^T/Y_i(k)]$ denote the error variance due to $Y_i(k)$. Using an additional local data-dependent vector $h_i(k)$, the estimate of the state given all data is given by

$$\hat{x}^D(k) = \sum_{i=1}^{N} \left[ P(k)P_i^{-1}(k)\hat{x}_i^D(k) + h_i(k) \right] \qquad (5.5.18)$$

where

$$\hat{x}_i^D(k) = \bar{x}_i^D(k) + P_i(k)C_i^T W_i^{-1}(k)\left[\tilde{y}_i(k) - C_i\bar{x}_i^D(k)\right] \qquad (5.5.19a)$$

$$\bar{x}_i^D(k) = A\hat{x}_i^D(k-1) \qquad (5.5.19b)$$

$$P_i^{-1}(k) = M_i^{-1}(k) + C_i^T W_i^{-1}(k)C_i \qquad (5.5.20)$$

$$h_i(k+1) = F(k+1)h_i(k) + G_i(k+1)\bar{x}_i^D(k+1), \quad h_i(1) = 0 \qquad (5.5.21)$$

$$F(k) = \left[I - \sum_{i=1}^{N} P(k)C_i^T W_i^{-1}(k)C_i\right]A = P(k)M^{-1}(k)A \qquad (5.5.22)$$

$$G_i(k+1) = P(k+1)M^{-1}(k+1)AP(k)P_i^{-1}(k)A^{-1}P(k+1)M_i^{-1}(k+1) \qquad (5.5.23)$$

assuming that $A$ is nonsingular. Now if one would define

$$\beta_i^l(k) = B_i^T S(k+1)\left[P(k)P_i^{-1}(k)\hat{x}_i^D(k) + h_i(k)\right] \qquad (5.5.24)$$

as the signal transmitted at mode $i$ to nodes $l = 1,\ldots,i-1,\ i+1,\ldots,N$ representing an $m_i \times 1$ vector, then the control vector $u_i(k)$ becomes

$$u_i(k) = -\left(R_i + B_i^T S(k+1)B_i\right)^{-1}\left\{\sum_{l=1}^{N}\beta_i^l(k) + B_i^T S(k+1)x^C(k)\right\} \qquad (5.5.25)$$

Here for $N$ scalar controls, each node transmits only $N-1$ numbers. However, in order to form $x^C(k+1)$, the controls $u_i(k)$ should be transmitted back from the $i$th station to stations $l = 1,\ldots,i-1, i+1,\ldots,N$ such that (5.5.15) is formed for the next step. Moreover, this transmission can be delayed up to one step, while $\beta_i^l$ is immediately required. On the other hand, for a centralized solution, the data are forwarded to the central processor, and, once processed, each station's control is transmitted back. In a decentralized system, a reduction in data transmission is achieved by transmitting the control vector instead of the data vector, especially when the data vector is larger than the control vector. Furthermore, note that for the special case when all $B_i$s are the same, no additional control transmission back to all nodes is needed because $\beta_i^l$ is the same for all $l = 1,\ldots,N$.

Chang (1980) has made use of a decomposition of the Kalman filter to reduce the computational effort in the above formulation of the stochastic decentralized control problem. From (5.5.24) it is clear that to construct $\beta_i(k)$, both $\hat{x}_i^D(k)$ and $h_i(k)$ must be generated locally. In sequel, it is shown that the required linear combination of $x_i^D(k)$ and $h_i(k)$ in (5.5.24) can be obtained directly by a linear difference equation. More precisely, let us rewrite (5.5.16) as follows:

$$\hat{x}^D(k+1) = \left(I - \sum_{j=1}^{N} K_i(k+1)C_i\right)\bar{x}^D(k+1) + \sum_{j=1}^{N} K_i(k+1)\tilde{y}_i(k+1)$$

$$= P(k+1)M^{-1}(k+1)A\bar{x}^D(k+1)$$

$$+ \sum_{j=1}^{N} K_i(k+1)\tilde{y}_i(k+1) \tag{5.5.26}$$

It is noted that (5.5.26) is a linear equation with various driving signals $\tilde{y}_i(k)$, $i = 1,\ldots,N$. Now define a new quantity $z_i(k)$ to be the component of $x(k)$ which is driven by $\tilde{y}_i(k)$ only, i.e.,

$$z_i(k+1) = P(k+1)M^{-1}(k+1)A\bar{z}_i(k+1) + K_i(k+1)\tilde{y}_i(k+1) \tag{5.5.27a}$$

$$\bar{z}_i(k+1) = Az_i(k), \quad z_i(1) = 0, \quad i = 1,\ldots,N \tag{5.5.27b}$$

What is needed to be shown is that

$$z_i(k) = P(k)P_i^{-1}(k)\hat{x}_i^D(k) + h_i(k) \tag{5.5.28}$$

is the desired linear combination in (5.5.24). If (5.5.28) holds, then (5.5.24) reads

$$\beta_i^I(k) = B_i^T S(k+1)z_i(k) \tag{5.5.29}$$

Now let us use (5.5.19) and (5.5.21) to express

$$P(k+1)P_i^{-1}(k+1)\hat{x}_i^D(k+1) + h_i(k+1)$$

$$= P(k+1)P_i^{-1}(k+1)\{\bar{x}_i^D(k+1)$$

$$+ P_i(k+1)C_i^T W_i^{-1}(k+1)[\tilde{y}_i(k+1) - C_i\bar{x}_i^D(k+1)]\}$$

$$+ P(k+1)M^{-1}(k+1)Ah_i(k)$$

$$+ G_i(k+1)\bar{x}_i^D(k+1) \tag{5.5.30}$$

If $G_i(k+1)$ is eliminated by (5.5.23) and (5.5.19b) is utilized, the right-hand side (RHS) of (5.5.30) becomes

$$\text{RHS}(5.5.30) = P(k+1)C_i^T W_i^{-1}(k+1)\tilde{y}_i(k+1)$$

$$+ P(k+1)M^{-1}(k+1)Ah_i(k)$$

$$+ P(k+1)M^{-1}(k+1)AP(k)P_i^{-1}(k)\hat{x}_i^D(k) + P(k+1)[P_i^{-1}(k+1)$$

$$- C_i^T W_i^{-1}(k+1)C_i - M^{-1}(k+1)]A\hat{x}_i^D(k) \tag{5.5.31}$$

which can be further reduced by utilizing (5.5.7) and (5.5.20) to read

$$P(k+1)P_i^{-1}(k+1)\hat{x}_i^D(k+1) + h_i(k+1)$$

$$= P(k+1)M^{-1}(k+1)A[P(k)P_i^{-1}(k)\hat{x}_i^D(k) + h_i(k)]$$

$$+ K_i(k+1)\tilde{y}_i(k+1) \tag{5.5.32a}$$

with

$$P(1)P_i^{-1}(1)\hat{x}_i^D(1) + h_i(1) = 0 \qquad (5.5.32b)$$

A comparison of (5.5.27) and (5.5.32) implies that the relation (5.5.28) is in fact correct. In this manner a considerable saving is made on the amount of computations involved. These points are discussed further in the Section 5.6. In the remainder of this section, the continuous-time case of the stochastic decentralized control is considered.

### 5.5.3 Solution of Continuous-Time System

Although the discrete-time version of the problem algorithm would most likely be used in practice due to band width limitations of data transmission and use of digital computers (see Problem 5.14), the continuous-time formulation of the state estimate from local state estimation is rather revealing. Here the problem is to find a set of $N$ local controls $u_i(t)$, $i = 1,\ldots,N$, such that a stochastic differential equation

$$dx = \left[ A(t)x + \sum_{i=1}^{N} B_i u_i(t) \right] dt + d\xi \qquad (5.5.33)$$

is satisfied, an objective functional

$$J = E\left\{ \tfrac{1}{2} \int_{t_0}^{t_f} \left[ x^T(t)Q(t)x(t) + \sum_{i=1}^{N} u_i^T(t)R_i(t)u_i(t) \right] dt \right\} \quad (5.5.34)$$

is minimized, and the local measurement sequence

$$dy_i = C_i(t)x(t)\,dt + d\eta_i \qquad (5.5.35)$$

where $\xi$ and $\eta_i$, $i = 1,\ldots,N$, are vector Brownian motion processes with zero variances and mean

$$E\{d\xi\,d\xi^T\} = V(t)\,dt\quad E\{d\eta_i\,d\eta_i^T\} = W_i(t)\,dt, \quad i = 1,\ldots,N \quad (5.5.36)$$

The matrices $Q(t)$ and $R_i(t)$ in (5.5.34) are assumed to be symmetric and positive-semidefinite and positive-definite, respectively. Let the measurement history be defined by

$$Y_i(t) \triangleq \{dy_i(\tau); 0 \leqslant \tau \leqslant t\}, \quad i = 1,\ldots,N \qquad (5.5.37)$$

Once again, the optimal control is assumed to have the general form

$$u_i(t) = \phi_i(Y_1(t),\ldots,Y_N(t),t) \qquad (5.5.38)$$

which indicates that each controller is a function of the information obtained over the entire network. In sequel, the nondecentralized and decentralized solutions of this problem are given.

### 5.5.3.a Nondecentralized Case

The solution of this case is well known (Bryson and Ho, 1969),

$$u_i(t) = -R_i^{-1}(t)B_i^T S(t)\hat{x}(t) \tag{5.5.39}$$

where $\hat{x}(t)$ is the conditional mean using the entire information set

$$\hat{x}(t) \triangleq E\{x(t)/Y_1(t),\ldots,Y_N(t)\} \tag{5.5.40}$$

Similar to the decentralized case of Section 5.5.2, let $\hat{x}$ be divided into a control and an estimation (data) state as

$$\hat{x}(t) = x^C(t) + \hat{x}^D(t) \tag{5.5.41}$$

where the data is processed by

$$d\hat{x}^D(t) = A\hat{x}^D(t)\,dt + P(t)\sum_{i=1}^{N}C_i^T(t)W_i^{-1}(t)\big(d\tilde{y}_i(t)$$

$$\qquad - C_i(t)\hat{x}^D(t)\,dt\big), \quad \hat{x}^D(0) = 0 \tag{5.5.42}$$

where

$$\tilde{y}_i(t) \triangleq y_i(t) - C_i(t)x^C(t) \tag{5.5.43}$$

and the control state propagates as

$$\dot{x}^C = Ax^C + \sum_{i=1}^{N}B_i(t)u_i(t), \quad x^C(0)\text{ given} \tag{5.5.44}$$

The error variance $P(t)$ under the access of all the information $Y(t)\triangleq [Y_1(t),\ldots,Y_N(t)]$ propagates as

$$\dot{P}(t) = A(t)P(t) + P(t)A^T(t) + V(t)$$

$$\qquad - P(t)\left[\sum_{i=1}^{N}C_i^T(t)W_i^{-1}(t)C_i(t)\right]P(t), \quad P(0)\text{ given}$$

$$\tag{5.5.45}$$

and the Riccati matrix associated with the controller, integrated backward in time, is given by

$$-\dot{S}(t) = A^T(t)S(t) + S(t)A(t) + Q(t)$$

$$\qquad - S(t)\left[\sum_{i=1}^{N}B_i(t)R_i^{-1}(t)B_i^T(t)\right]S(t), \quad S(t_f) = 0 \tag{5.5.46}$$

This completes the nondecentralization solution to the continuous-time problem.

## 5.3.3.b Decentralized Case

For this case, assume that the data at each station are processed by their own Kalman filter as

$$d\hat{x}_i^D(t) = A\hat{x}_i^D(t)\,dt + P_i(t)C_i^T(t)W_i^{-1}(t)$$
$$\cdot\left(d\tilde{y}_i(t) - C_i(t)\hat{x}_i^D(t)\,dt\right) \tag{5.5.47}$$

where $\tilde{y}_i(t)$ is still given by (5.5.43) and the local error variance $P_i(t)$ is based on the information $Y_i(t)$ only and propagates as

$$\dot{P}_i(t) = A(t)P_i(t) + P_i(t)A^T(t) + V(t) - P_i^T(t)C_i^T(t)W_i^{-1}(t)$$
$$\cdot C_i(t)P_i(t), \quad P_i(0) \text{ given} \tag{5.5.48}$$

Once all the data are available, the state estimate can be obtained as a linear function of the local estimate similar to (5.5.19), i.e.,

$$\hat{x}^D(t) = \sum_{i=1}^{N} \left\{ P(t)P_i^{-1}(t)\hat{x}_i^D(t) + h_i(t) \right\} \tag{5.5.49}$$

The dynamic equation for vector $h_i(t)$ can be obtained by taking the derivative of (5.5.49) with respect to time, eliminating $d\hat{x}^D(t)$, $d\hat{x}_i^D(t)$, and $\hat{x}^D(t)$ in terms of only $\hat{x}_i^D(t)$ by utilizing (5.5.42), (5.5.47), and (5.5.49), respectively, and then by using (5.5.45) and (5.5.48) for $\dot{P}(t)$ and $\dot{P}_i(t)$. Noting that the order of summation is interchangable, the dynamic equation for $h_i(t)$ is given by

$$\dot{h}_i(t) = \left[ A(t) - \sum_{i=1}^{N} P(t)C_i^T(t)W_i^{-1}(t)C_i(t) \right] h_i(t)$$
$$+ \left[ P(t)P_i^{-1}(t) - I \right] V(t)P_i^{-1}(t)\hat{x}_i^D(t) \tag{5.5.50}$$

Moreover, since $\hat{x}^D(0)$ and $\hat{x}_i^D(0)$ are null vectors, then

$$h_i(0) = 0 \tag{5.5.51}$$

The dependency of $h_i(t)$ on the process noise variance $V(t)$ can be seen to be explicit for the continuous-time formulation of $h_i(t)$. If $V(t) = 0$ for $0 \le t \le t_f$, then $h_i(t) = 0$. The additional term in (5.5.50) has a stabilizing effect, since it is negative semidefinite.

In a similar fashion to the discrete-time system case (5.5.25), the continuous-time controller is given by

$$u_i(t) = -R_i^{-1}(t)B_i^T(t)S(t)\left\{ \sum_{j=1}^{N} \left[ P(t)P_i^{-1}(t)\hat{x}_j^D(t) + h_j(t) \right] + x^C(t) \right\}$$
$$\tag{5.5.52}$$

Thus, at each station $(N - 1)$, continuous-time signals of the form

$$\beta_i^l(t) = B_l^T(t)S(t)\left[P(t)P_i^{-1}(t)\hat{x}_i^D(t) + h_i^l(t)\right] \qquad (5.5.53)$$

are transmitted to each station $l$ from the $j = 1,\ldots,l-1,\ l+1,\ldots,N$ other stations. Note also that at each node, $x^C(t)$ must be calculated for the purposes of control (5.5.52) and estimator (5.5.41). Once the control is obtained at each station, it will be transmitted to all the other $(N - 1)$ stations. Thus (5.5.44) is constructed at each station.

Other topics on decentralized stochastic control, such as "one-step sharing patterns," "fixed-structure controllers," "periodic coordination," and "decentralized state estimation" (Singh, 1981) are not considered here because of space limitations. However, these topics are briefly discussed in the next section, while decentralized state estimation will be discussed in detail in Section 6.6.

## 5.6 Discussion and Conclusions

Three important problems within the context of large-scale systems decentralization property were considered in this chapter. These problems were decentralized stabilization, decentralized robust servomechanism, and decentralized stochastic control. They are only three topics in large-scale systems design and synthesis. The primary motivations for these new developments are twofold. One is that straight application of centralized techniques, such as pole placement, identification, estimation, control, optimization, etc., are inappropriate due to the physical and natural characteristics of large-scale systems. The other is the vast number of areas in which the decentralized or hierarchical structures of large-scale systems fall into naturally. These areas of applications, which include economics, education, urban systems, transportation, power, energy, environment (including water resources systems) pose challenging problems for several years to come.

A usual condition for centralized stabilization of a system is the controllability and observability of the modes. The decentralized version of this, as discussed in Section 5.3.1, requires that the "fixed modes" of the systems be contained on the left-half $s$-plane. Following this important development, decentralized stabilization can be effectively and systematically achieved through a number of computational algorithms. In Section 5.3, eight decentralized stabilization schemes were discussed and four algorithms were presented. In Section 5.3.3 a typical stabilization scheme for composite systems via local state feedback was considered. The method is most effective for the case when the system's subsystems have small gains. Furthermore, the proposed Algorithm 5.2 is at best a trial-and-error approach, and a more systematic approach similar to QR or QL transformations is required to convert the close-loop matrix to a diagonally dominant form. The technique has been applied to serially connected systems, such as a hydraulic composite system by Sezer and Hüseyin (1978).

A typical decentralized stabilization approach based on multilevel control was given in Section 5.3.4. When a large-scale system is described in input-decentralized form, either by physical decomposition or input decentralization, the proposed control stabilizes the system through connective Lyapunov stability (see Chapter 7). In this scheme, each subsystem is stabilized through local controllers, while the effects of interconnections among subsystems are reduced through global controllers.

Another multilevel control scheme based on exponential stabilization of the linear state regulator was presented in Section 5.3.5. It was shown that a large-scale system in its input-decentralized form can be stabilized with a prescribed degree of stability if the system's interconnection pattern satisfies certain symmetry conditions (Theorem 5.4) or admits some norm bounds (Theorem 5.5). If the prescribed conditions are not satisfied by the existing interconnections, a higher-level controller can be used. Another decentralized stabilization scheme along the lines of reducing the influence of interconnections in an attempt to give more reliable decentralized controls is due to Huang and Sundareshan (1980). The schemes makes a modification of the objective function based on the maximum interconnection matrix leading to a modified linear state regulator for each subsystem similar to the exponential stabilization scheme.

A structural hierarchical control approach to decentralized control was discussed in Section 5.3.6. Although this scheme resembles the other multilevel control schemes, as in Sections 5.3.4 and 5.3.5, its main difference is in its construction of the global component of the overall control law. Through the use of a dynamic coordinator for the global controller, it may be possible to stabilize a system with unstable fixed modes without controllability of either subsystems or the overall system. Further comments on this scheme can be found in a report by Groumpos (1980b).

Perhaps the most effective stabilization procedure discussed in Section 5.3 is that of Ikeda and Šiljak (1980a) for linear time-varying systems in which a preassigned degree of stability can be achieved through local feedback. Other methods which require a high degree of subsystem stability, such as those reported by Šiljak and Vukcevic (1977) or Davison (1977), may fail to give proper stabilizing controllers unless for a particular control (Ikeda et al., 1972, 1976) or structure. This method was also applied to the time-invariant case in Section 5.3.7b, which is not reported elsewhere. There are many advantages about the proposed stabilization procedure. One is that the choice of feedback gains $K_i$ requires only information about the adjacent subsystems and does not depend on the interaction patterns as do some of the hierarchical methods of Sections 5.3.4 5.3.5, and Chapter 4. In fact, as far as the interconnections are concerned, only an upper bound on the interaction matrices is required (see Theorem 5.6). Ikeda and Šiljak

(1980a) point out that it is possible to use the same gain matrices $K_i$ to design a "connectively" stable system, i.e., a system which remains stable under interconnection perturbations. The notion of connective stability and the criterion for it are discussed in Chapter 7. The stabilization is not limited by all the state measurement; local state estimators can be used as well. However, like many others methods, this one fails if the $i$th subsystem output $y_i$ in (5.3.146) depends on both the state $x_i$ and control $u_i$.

The final decentralized stabilization scheme considered in this section was the use of time-varying feedback control laws for time-invariant systems as presented in Section 5.3.7c. The main outcome of this presentation, as proposed by Anderson and Moore (1981), is that in order to deal with decentralized control of systems with unstable fixed modes, one can widen the class of controllers by, for example, extending it to admit periodic time-varying gains. This method, which makes two assumptions—centralized controllability (or observability) and connectivity—has a good potential for decentralized stabilization of large-scale systems.

Before leaving the decentralized stabilization of large-scale systems, I would call the reader's attention to the more recent research results in this area by many authors, including Šiljak and his associates (Ikeda and Šiljak, 1980b; Sezer and Šiljak, 1981a, b). Ikeda and Šiljak (1980b) have proposed a decentralized stabilization scheme for large-scale systems represented in canonical (companion form) input-decentralized form for a wider class of interconnections than those already suggested (Davison, 1974; Šiljak and Vukcevic, 1976a, b; Sezer and Hüseyin, 1978). The decentralized stabilizability of the system can be easily checked by a simple inequality in terms of a set of integers which are, in turn, based on the structure of the interconnection matrix. Finally, Sezer and Šiljak (1981a, b) have proposed graph-theoretic-based structural decomposition and decentralized stabilization of large-scale systems. In Sezer and Šiljak (1981a) a large-scale system is decomposed into a causal (hierarchical) interconnection of input reachable subsystems whose stabilization problems are much simpler computationally. In Sezer and Šiljak (1981b) graph-theoretic conditions are obtained for decentrally connectively* stabilizable systems which are consequences of subsystems' autonomy preserved throughout the design procedure. This autonomy requirement constitutes an essential conceptual difference between this approach and the earlier one (Sezer and Šiljak, 1981a), where decentralization is used for computational efficiency of stabilization.

The second pertinent problem considered in this chapter was the decentralized servomechanism and its various properties. This problem addresses an important question: Can a system be compensated which posseses asymptotic tracking, stability, regulation, etc., without first identifying its model? Davison (1976d) refers to this problem as "compensator identifica-

---

*See Chapter 7 for discussions on connective stability.

tion," which, as seen in Section 5.4, provides asymptotically stable and regulated compensation independent of input disturbances, the plant's exact model parameters, and even order. The only assumption needed is that the system be open-loop stable. One of the attractive features of the decentralized servomechanism problem is the so-called "robustness" of the controllers. In other words, compensation is somewhat adaptive with respect to perturbations of plant matrices. The existence of robust controller was found to depend only on a set of tracking and steady-state parameters which can be easily calculated through simple numerical experiments (see Algorithms 5.5–5.6). The conditions further provide a nonunique prescribed order for tuning one controller at a time, thus providing a convenient one-dimensional search for compensator parameters to achieve "desirable" system transients. A significant extension of the decentralized servomechanism problem is sequential stability which is, in essence, a synthesis technique allowing the $N$ decentralized controllers to be connected in ascending order $1, 2, \ldots, N$, i.e., sequentially such that the system remains stable at all time. The basic motivation for this is based on the fact that simutaneous connection of all decentralized controllers is impossible (Davison, 1978).

The third problem considered in this chapter was decentralized stochastic control, which was discussed in Section 5.5. The main focus was on large-scale discrete-time systems. The decentralized LQG problem considered in this section showed that if the dimension of the control vector is smaller than that of the measurement vector and the state vector, then a minimum transmission between stations is that of a vector called $\beta_i^l(k)$, which is the dimension of the control at node $l$ sent from node $i$ at stage $k$. The main difficulty with this control is that this transmission must be made instantaneously. Moreover, since this transmission is not needed until stage $k+1$, the classical formulation can be extended to the one-step delayed information pattern (Singh, 1981) which allows delays in all transmissions. Therefore, with the restriction of having $\beta_i^l(k)$ delayed, the optimum system can still be derived where the necessary transmission is an $\beta_i^l(k)$ vector. The important point, as mentioned by Speyer (1979), is that $\beta_i^l(k)$ is used at stage $k+1$ but depends on the *measurement sequences up to* $k$. The control for the one-step delay sharing pattern would be

$$u_i(k+1) = \phi_i\big(y_i(k+1), Y_1(k), \ldots, Y_N(k), k\big) \qquad (5.6.1)$$

instead of (5.5.4). The effect of the one-step delay information pattern is an increase in cost over that of the classical information pattern. Moreover, the gains in the classical case follow the "certainty equivalence principle," while the one-step case depends on the noise variances only. For an extension to the $m$-step delay information sharing case and further discussions, the interested reader is referred to Singh (1981), where such topics as "fixed-structure controllers," "periodic coordination," and "feasibly decentralized control" are considered.

## Problems

**5.1.** Determine the fixed modes of the following system:

$$\dot{x} = \begin{bmatrix} -1 & 0 \\ 1 & -2 \end{bmatrix} x + \begin{bmatrix} 1 & 0 \\ 1 & 1 \end{bmatrix} u, \quad y = \begin{bmatrix} 1 & 0 \\ 0 & 2 \end{bmatrix} x$$

Is the system stabilizable under decentralized control?

**5.2.** Find a decentralized stabilizing output controller for the system

$$\dot{x} = \begin{bmatrix} 1 & 0 \\ 0.5 & -1 \end{bmatrix} x + \begin{bmatrix} 1 & 0 \\ 0 & 1 \end{bmatrix} u, \quad y = \begin{bmatrix} 1 & 0 \\ 0 & 1 \end{bmatrix} x$$

**5.3.** Consider the following two subsystems of an interconnected system:

$$(A_1, B_1, C_1) = \left( \begin{bmatrix} 1 & 0 & -1 \\ 0 & 2 & 1 \\ -1 & -2 & 0 \end{bmatrix}, \begin{bmatrix} 1 \\ 0 \\ 1 \end{bmatrix}, \begin{bmatrix} 1 & 0 & 1 \\ 0 & 1 & 0 \end{bmatrix} \right)$$

$$(A_2, B_2, C_2) = \left( \begin{bmatrix} 2 & 1 \\ -2 & 0 \end{bmatrix}, \begin{bmatrix} 1 & 0 \\ 0 & 1 \end{bmatrix}, \begin{bmatrix} 1 & 1 \end{bmatrix} \right)$$

Use Algorithm 5.2 to stabilize the system.

**C5.4.** Consider a three-subsystem problem

$$\dot{x}_1 = \begin{bmatrix} 0 & 0 \\ 1 & 0.5 \end{bmatrix} x_1 + \begin{bmatrix} 1 \\ 0 \end{bmatrix} u_1, \quad y_1 = \begin{bmatrix} 1 & 0 \end{bmatrix} x_1$$

$$\dot{x}_2 = -0.5 x_2 + u_2, \quad y_2 = x_2$$

$$\dot{x}_3 = \begin{bmatrix} 1 & -0.2 \\ 1 & -1 \end{bmatrix} x_3 + \begin{bmatrix} 1 \\ 1 \end{bmatrix} u_2, \quad y_3 = \begin{bmatrix} 1 & 1 \end{bmatrix} x_3$$

Use Algorithm 5.4 to find a decentralized stabilizing control for the system.

**5.5.** Consider the stabilization of a large-scale multivariable linear system $\dot{x} = Ax + Bu$ where the control vector consists of a local and a global control component, i.e., $u = u^l + u^g$. Use matrix Riccati formulation and discussions in Sections 5.3.4 and 5.3.5 to find an exponentially stabilizing control.

**C5.6.** Consider a two-subsystem interconnected time-varying system with the following matrices:

$$(A_1(t), B_1(t), C_1(t)) = \left( \begin{bmatrix} 0.25t & -t \\ 1 & te^{-t} \end{bmatrix}, \begin{bmatrix} t \\ -t \end{bmatrix}, \begin{bmatrix} 1 & 0 \end{bmatrix} \right)$$

$$(A_2(t), B_2(t), C_2(t)) = \left( \begin{bmatrix} 0 & -te^{-t} \\ t^2 & -t^2 \end{bmatrix}, \begin{bmatrix} 1 \\ 0 \end{bmatrix}, \begin{bmatrix} 0 & 1 \end{bmatrix} \right)$$

Use the method of Example 5.3.8 to stabilize this system exponentially for $0 \leqslant t \leqslant 2.5$ and $\Delta t = 0.1$. Plot the new eigenvalues $\lambda_i(t)$, $i = 1, 2, 3, 4$, and outputs $y_j(t)$, $j = 1, 2$, with an initial state

$$x_1^T(0) = \begin{bmatrix} 0 & 1 \end{bmatrix}, \quad x_2^T(0) = \begin{bmatrix} 0 & -1 \end{bmatrix}$$

**5.7.** State a corollary to Theorem 5.4 for the case of linear interconnections, i.e., $g_i(t, x) = \sum_{j=1}^{N} G_{ij} x_j$ and prove it.

**C5.8.** Repeat Example 5.3.7 for the system

$$\dot{x} = \begin{bmatrix} -1 & 0 & | & 0 & 0.5 \\ 0.2 & 0.5 & | & 0 & -0.2 \\ \hline 0.1 & 0 & | & -0.5 & 0.5 \\ 0 & 0.1 & | & 0.2 & 1 \end{bmatrix} x + \begin{bmatrix} 0 & | & 0 \\ 1 & | & 0 \\ \hline 0 & | & 0 \\ 0 & | & 1 \end{bmatrix} u$$

Choose an $\alpha = 2$ and $Q_i = 2I_2$, $i = 1, 2$. Check whether condition (5.3.123) is satisfied.

**5.9.** Extend Theorem 5.5 to the case of linear interconnection and use a matrix Lyapunov equation instead of a matrix Riccati equation.

**5.10.** Extend and prove Theorem 5.6 to the linear TIV case discussed in Section 5.3.7.b.

**C5.11.** For the system

$$\dot{x} = \begin{bmatrix} 0 & 1 & | & 0 & 1 & 0 \\ 2 & 1 & | & 1 & 0 & 0.5 \\ \hline 0 & 1 & | & 0 & 1 & 0 \\ 0 & 0 & | & 0 & 0 & 1 \\ 0 & 1 & | & -1 & 2 & -3 \end{bmatrix} x + \begin{bmatrix} 0 & | & 0 \\ 1 & | & 0 \\ \hline 0 & | & 0 \\ 0 & | & 0 \\ 0 & | & 1 \end{bmatrix} u$$

use Algorithm 5.3 to find a two-level stabilizing controller. Use $\lambda\{\hat{A}_1\} = \{-1, -2\}$ and $\lambda\{\hat{A}_2\} = \{-5 \pm j, -10\}$ as the desired poles for the two subsystems.

**5.12.** Repeat Example 5.4.1 for the following decentralized system:

$$\dot{x} = \begin{bmatrix} -1 & 0 \\ 1 & -2 \end{bmatrix} x + \begin{bmatrix} 1 \\ 0 \end{bmatrix} u_1 + \begin{bmatrix} 0 \\ 1 \end{bmatrix} u_2$$

$$y_1 = [1 \quad 0] x + u_1, \quad y_2 = [0 \quad 1] x_2 + u_2$$

**5.13.** Consider a third-order decentralized discrete-time system

$$x(k+1) = \begin{bmatrix} 2 & 0 & 0 \\ 0 & 2 & 0 \\ 0 & 0 & 3 \end{bmatrix} x(k) + \begin{bmatrix} 0 \\ 0 \\ 1 \end{bmatrix} u_1(k) + \begin{bmatrix} 0 \\ 0 \\ 1 \end{bmatrix} u_2(k)$$

$$y_1(k) = [1 \quad 0 \quad 0] X(k), \quad y_2(k) = [1 \quad 1 \quad 0] x(k)$$

Find a periodic feedback gain $K_2(k)$ for the second station with $0 \le k \le 2$ such that the system can be decentrally stabilized with its fixed mode.

**5.14.** Develop an algorithm for the decentralized stochastic control problem of Section 5.5.2 accounting for the computational savings due to $z_i(k)$ calculations instead of $\hat{x}_i^D(k)$ and $h_i(k)$.

**5.15.** Determine whether the system

$$\dot{x} = \begin{bmatrix} 1 & 2 \\ -1 & -1 \end{bmatrix} x + \begin{bmatrix} 1 \\ 1 \end{bmatrix} u_1 + \begin{bmatrix} 0 \\ 2 \end{bmatrix} u_2, \quad y_1 = [\, 1 \quad 0 \,] x, \quad y_2 = [\, 0 \quad 1 \,] x$$

with $K_1 = K_2 = 1$ can be controlled by a decentralized robust controller? [*Hint*: See Theorem 5.9 and Example 5.4.3.]

**C5.16.** Consider a servomechanism problem

$$\dot{x} = Ax + \sum_{i=1}^{2} B_i u_i + E\omega, \quad y_i = C_i x + D_i u_i + P_i \omega, \quad i = 1, 2$$

$$e_i = y_i - y_i^d$$

with

$$A = \begin{bmatrix} -1 & 0.1 \\ 0 & -1 \end{bmatrix}, \quad B_1 = \begin{bmatrix} 1 \\ 0 \end{bmatrix}, \quad B_2 = \begin{bmatrix} 0 \\ 1 \end{bmatrix}, \quad C_1 = C_2 = [\, 1 \quad 1 \,],$$

$$D_1 = [1],$$

$$D_2 = [0], \quad P_1 = P_2 = [0], \quad E^T = [\, 0 \quad 0 \,], \quad y_1^d = y_2^d = 1.$$

Find a decentralized robust controller which sustains asymptotic regulation with reasonable transient speeds. Use an appropriate initial state $x(0)$.

# References

Anderson, B. O. D., and Clements, D. J. 1981. Algebraic characterization of fixed modes in decentralized control. *IFAC J. Automatica* 17:703–712.

Anderson, B. O. D., and Moore, J. B. 1981. Time-varying feedback laws for decentralized control. *IEEE Trans. Aut. Cont.* AC-26:1133–1138. (See also *Proc. 19th IEEE CDC*, Albuquerque, NM.)

Araki, M. 1976. Input-output stability of composite feedback systems. *IEEE Trans Aut. Cont.* AC-21:254–259.

Bode, H. W. 1940. Feedback amplifier design. *Bell Syst. Tech. J.* 19.

Brasch, F. M., and Pearson, J. B. 1970. Pole placement using dynamic compensators. *IEEE Trans. Aut. Cont.* AC-15:34–43.

Bryson, A. E., Jr., and Ho, Y. C. 1969. *Applied Optimal Control*, pp. 428–429. Blaisdell Publ. Co., Waltham, MA.

Chang, T. S. 1980. Comments on "Computation and transmission requirements for a decentralized linear-quadratic-Gaussian control problem." *IEEE Trans. Aut. Cont.* AC-25:609–610.

Chen, C. T. 1970. *Introduction to Linear System Theory*. Holt, Rinehart and Winston, New York.

Corfmat, J. P., and Morse, A. S. 1976. Decentralized control of linear multi-variable systems. *IFAC J. Automatica* 12:479–495.

Davison, E. J. 1974. The decentralized stabilization and control of a class of unknown nonlinear time-varying systems. *IFAC J. Automatica* 10:309–316.

Davison, E. J. 1976a. Decentralized stabilization and regulation in large multivariable systems, in Y. C. Ho and S. K. Mitter, Eds., *Direction in Large-Scale Systems*, pp. 303–323. Plenum Press, New York.

Davison, E. J. 1976b. Multivariable tuning regulators: The feed-forward and robust control of a general servomechanism problem. *IEEE Trans. Aut. Cont.* AC-21:35–47.

Davison, E. J. 1976c. The robust decentralized control of a general servomechanism problem. *IEEE Trans. Aut. Cont.* AC-21:14–24.

Davison, E. J. 1976d. The robust control of a servomechanism problem for linear time-invariant multivariable systems. *IEEE Trans Aut. Cont.* AC-21:25–34.

Davison, E. J. 1977. The robust decentralized servomechanism problem with extra stabilizing control agents. *IEEE Trans. Aut. Cont.* AC-22:256–258.

Davison, E. J. 1978. Decentralized robust control of unknown systems using tuning regulators. *IEEE Trans. Aut. Cont.* AC-23:276–289.

Davison, E. J. 1979. The robust decentralized control of a servomechanism problem for composite systems with input-output interconnections. *IEEE Trans. Aut. Cont.* AC-24:325–327.

Davison, E. J., and Gesing, W. 1979. Sequential stability and optimization of large scale decentralized systems. *IFAC J. Automatica* 15:307–324.

Davison, E. J., and Goldenberg, A. 1975. Robust control of a general servomechanism problem: The servo compensator. *IFAC J. Automatica* 11:461–471.

Davison, E. J., and Wang, S. H. 1974. Properties and calculations of transmission zeros of linear multivariable systems. *IFAC J. Automatica* 10:643–658.

D'Azzo, J. J., and Houpis, C. H. 1981. *Linear Control System Analysis and Design — Conventional and Modern*. 2nd ed. McGraw-Hill, New York.

Evans, W. R. 1950. Control system synthesis by root locus methods. *AIEE Trans.* 69:66–69.

Godbout, L. F. 1974. Pole placement algorithms for multivariable systems. M.S. thesis., Dept. Elect. Engr., Univ. Conn., Tech. Report 74-3.

Groumpos, P. P. 1979. A state space approach to hierarchical systems. Ph.D. dissertation, State Univ. New York, Buffalo, NY.

Groumpos, P. P. 1980a. A structural state model for a two-level dynamical hierarchical system (DYHIS). *Proc. 23rd Midwest Symposium* (Toledo, OH), pp. 542–546.

Groumpos, P. P. 1980b. Dynamical hierarchical systems (DYHIS). Technical Report TR-ELE 80.1, Cleveland State University, Cleveland, OH.

Groumpos, P. P., and Loparo, K. A. 1980. Structural control of large scale systems. *Proc. 19th IEEE Conf. Dec. Contr.* (Albuquerque, NM), pp. 422–426.

Huang, P., and Sundareshan, M. K. 1980. A new approach to the design of reliable decentralized control schemes for large-scale systems. *Proc. IEEE Int. Conf. Circuits and Systems* (Houston, TX), pp. 678–680.

Ikeda, M., and Šiljak, D. D. 1980a. Decentralized stabilization of linear time-varying systems. *IEEE Trans. Aut. Cont.* AC-25:106–107.

Ikeda, M., and Šiljak, D. D. 1980b. On decentrally stabilizable large-scale systems. *IFAC J. Automatica* 16:331–334.

Ikeda, M.; Maeda, H.; and Kodama, S. 1972. Stabilization of linear systems. *SIAM J. Contr.* 10:716–729.

Ikeda, M.; Umefuji, O.; and Kodama, S. 1976. Stabilization of large-scale linear systems. *Trans. IECE Japan* (D) 59-D:355–362. Also in *Syst. Comput. and Contr.* 7 (1976):34–41.

Jamshidi, M. 1980. An overview on the solutions of the algebraic matrix Riccati equation and related problems. *J. Large Scale Systems* 1:167–192.

Kalman, R. E. 1962. Canonical structure of linear dynamical systems. *Proc. Nat. Acad. Sci.* 48:596–600.

Kwakernaak, H. W., and Sivan, R. 1972. Linear Optimal Control Systems. Wiley, New York.

Langenhop, C. E. 1967. On generalized inverses of matrices. *SIAM J. Appl. Math.* 15:1239–1246.

Lee, G; Jordan, D.; and Sohrwardy, M. 1979. A pole assignment algorithm for multivariable control systems. *IEEE Trans Aut. Cont.* AC-24:357–362.

Lee, G.; Jordan, D.; and Sohrwardy, M. 1980. Author's reply. *IEEE Trans. Aut. Cont.* AC-25:140.

Luenberger, D. G. 1967. Canonical forms for linear multivariable systems. *IEEE Trans. Aut. Cont.* AC-12:290–293.

Newhouse, A. 1962. Chebyschev curve fit. *Comm. ACM* 5:281.

Nyquist, H. 1932. Regeneration theory. *Bell Syst. Tech. J.* 2.

Paraskevopoulos, P. N. 1976. A general solution to the output feedback eigenvalue assignment problem. *Int. J. Contr.* 24:509–528.

Paraskevopoulos, P. N. 1980. On the design of PID output feedback controllers for linear multivariable systems. *IEEE Trans. Ind. Electr. Contr. Instr.* IECI-27:16–18.

Porter, B. 1980. Comments on "A pole assignment algorithm for multivariable control system." *IEEE Trans. Aut. Cont.* AC-25:139–140.

Porter, B., and Bradshaw, A. 1978a. Design of linear multivariable continuous-time output feedback regulators. *Int. J. Syst. Sci.* 9:445–450.

Porter, B., and Bradshaw, A. 1978b. Design of linear multivariable continuous-time tracking systems incorporating error-actuated dynamic controllers. *Int. J. Syst. Sci.* 9:627–637.

Porter, B., and Bradshaw, A. 1978c. Design of linear multivariable discrete-time output-feedback regulators. *Int. J. Syst. Sci.* 9:857–863.

Porter, B., and Bradshaw, A. 1978d. Design of linear multivariable discrete-time tracking systems incorporating error-actuated dynamic controllers. *Int. J. Syst. Sci.* 9:1079–1090.

Porter, B.; Bradshaw, A.; and Daintith, D. 1979. EIGENFRTRAC: A software package for the design of multivariable digital control systems. Report USAME/DC/102/79, Univ. Salford, Salford, England.

Ramussen, R. D., and Michel, A. N. 1976. Stability of interconnected dynamical systems described on Banach spaces. *IEEE Trans. Aut. Cont.* AC-21:464–471.

Retallack, D. G., and MacFarlane, A. G. J. 1970. Pole-shifting techniques for multivariable feedback systems. *Proc. IEE* 117:1037–1038.

Rosenbrock, H. H. 1974. *Computer Aided Control System Design.* Academic Press, London.

Saeks, R. 1979. On the decentralized control of interconnected dynamical systems. *IEEE Trans. Aut. Cont.* AC-24:269–271.

Sandell, N. R., Jr.; Varaiya, P.; Athans, M.; and Safonov, M. G. 1978. Survey of decentralized control methods for large-scale systems. *IEEE Trans. Aut. Cont.* AC-23:108–128.

Seraji, H. 1980. Design of pole-placement compensators for multivariable systems. *IFAC J. Automatica* 16:335–338.

Sezer M. E., and Hüseyin, Ö. 1978. Stabilization of linear time-invariant interconnected systems using local state feedback. *IEEE Trans. Syst. Man. Cyber.* SMC-8:751–756.

Sezer, M. E., and Hüseyin, Ö. 1980. On decentralized stabilization of interconnected systems. *IFAC J. Automatica*, 16:205–209.

Sezer, M. E., and Šiljak, D. D. 1981a. On structural decomposition and stabilization of large-scale control systems. *IEEE Trans. Aut. Cont.* AC-26:439–444.

Sezer, M. E., and Šiljak, D. D. 1981b. On decentralized stabilization and structure of linear large scale systems. *IFAC J. Automatica* 17:641–644.

Šiljak, D. D. 1978a. On decentralized control of large scale systems. *Proc. IFAC 7th World Congress* (Helsinki, Finland), pp. 1849–1856.

Šiljak, D. D. 1978b. Large Scale Dynamic Systems. Elsevier North Holland, New York.

Šiljak, D. D., and Sundareshan, M. K. 1976. A multilevel optimization of large-scale dynamic systems. *IEEE Trans. Aut. Cont.* AC-21:79–84.

Šiljak, D. D., and Vukcevic, M. B. 1976a. Multilevel control of large scale systems: Decentralization, stabilization, stimulation and reliability, in R. Aseks, ed., *Large Scale Dynamical Systems*, pp. 34–57. Point Lobos Press, Los Angeles.

Šiljak, D. D., and Vukcevic, M. B. 1976b. Large-scale systems: Stability, complexity, reliability. *J. Franklin Inst.* 301:49–69.

Šiljak, D. D., and Vukcevic, M. B. 1976c. Decentralization, stabilization and estimation in large scale systems. *IEEE Trans. Aut. Cont.* AC-21:363–366.

Šiljak, D. D., and Vukcevic, M. D. 1977. Decentrally stabilizable linear and bilinear large scale systems. *Int. J. Contr.* 26:289–305.

Simon, J. D. and Mitter, S. K. 1968. A theory of modal control. *Inform. Contr.* 13:316–353.

Singh, M. G. 1981. Decentralised Control, pp. 145–193. North Holland, Amsterdam.

Speyer, J. L. 1979. Computation and transmission requirements for a decentralized linear-quadratic-Gaussian control problem. *IEEE Trans. Aut. Cont.* AC-24:266–269.

Sundareshan, M. K. 1977. Exponential stabilization of large-scale systems: Decentralized and multilevel schemes. *IEEE Trans. Syst. Man. Cyber.* SMC 7:478–483.

Wang, S. H., and Davison, E. J. 1973. On the stabilization of decentralized control systems. *IEEE Trans. Aut. Cont.* AC-18:473–478. Also in Report No. 7213, Dept. Electrical Engineering, Univ. Toronto, Toronto, Canada.

# Chapter 6
# Near-Optimum Design
# of Large-Scale Systems

## 6.1 Introduction

One of the most significant motivations for the development of new design techniques suitable for large-scale systems has been the computational impracticality of direct application of optimal control or optimization theory. This impracticality is due to many system complexities, such as large dimensions, nonlinearities, coupling, time delays, and physical separation of components. One possibility, as seen in Section 2.2 and Chapter 3, is to simplify the model so that the application of optimal control theory is possible. Another possibility, as discussed in Section 2.3, is to develop near-optimum design techniques via perturbation of plant parameters while keeping the system model as realistic as possible. The perturbation of plant parameters leads to a decomposition in system structure which, as seen in Chapter 4, provides a number of subsystems interacting with each other in hierarchical fashion. Still another class of techniques is based on the decentralization of information structure which leads to some interesting stabilizing and robust control algorithms, as discussed in Chapter 5. Due to these characteristics of large-scale systems, the optimal control design of such systems are, in the most part, necessarily near-optimum in nature. The reduction of order, perturbation of parameters, decomposition of structure, omission of time delays, linearization of nonlinear terms, hierarchical interaction, and decentralization of control all would normally lead to near-optimality of system performance.

In this chapter the maximum principle of optimal control theory and optimization techniques are applied to various types of large-scale systems. Different applications of the maximum principle, such as the linear state regulator (matrix Riccati formulation), nonlinear optimal control systems (solution of two-point boundary value problems), and optimal control of systems with time-delay, will be utilized. Unconstrained optimization methods will be used to find optimal decentralized state and output feedback control laws. Since most design techniques require state feedback, decentralized estimation of large-scale systems is also considered.

The near-optimum design of large linear time-invariant systems based on aggregation, perturbation, hierarchical, and decentralized approaches is discussed in Section 6.2. Included in this section is the "sequential optimization" technique, which is a natural extension of "sequentially stable" robust decentralized control of linear systems discussed in Chapter 5.

In Section 6.3 the near-optimum control of nonlinear systems is discussed. The hierarchical control through interaction prediction is first introduced for nonlinear systems. Next a combination of perturbation and sensitivity methods is used to find a near-optimum control of an industrial process.

Three different approaches in the near-optimum control of systems with time delays are considered in Section 6.4. The first class of systems are those which are coupled time-delay and can be decomposed into unretarded (nondelay) subsystems. The large-scale systems, serially interconnected by delayed output terms, are optimally controlled next. This section is concluded by presenting an extension of goal-coordination formulation of hierarchical control to the large-scale systems with delay.

Section 6.5 deals with the important problem of near-optimality bounds or degrees of large-scale systems. It is important for the designer to have an estimate on the loss of system performance index by adapting a particular near-optimum technique. Near-optimality due to aggregation, perturbation, hierarchical control, nonlinearities, and time-delays are all considered. The decentralized state estimation of large-scale systems is considered next in Section 6.6. The concluding discussions are made in Section 6.7.

## 6.2 Near-Optimum Control of Linear Time-Invariant Systems

In this section a number of near-optimum control techniques based on model reduction methods (Chapters 2 and 3), hierarchical control (Chapter 4, and decentralized control (Chapter 5) for linear time-invariant systems are discussed, and numerous examples are given.

### 6.2.1 Aggregation Methods

A number of aggregated methods were discussed in Section 2.2 and Chapter 3. Here the aggregation procedure is addressed from an optimal control point of view. Consider a large-scale linear TIV system

$$\dot{x}(t) = Ax(t) + Bu(t), \quad x(0) = x_o \qquad (6.2.1)$$

with a quadratic cost functional

$$J = \frac{1}{2} \int_0^\infty \left( x^T(t)Qx(t) + u^T(t)Ru(t) \right) dt \qquad (6.2.2)$$

where $A$, $B$, $x$, and $u$ are $(n \times n)$-, $(n \times m)$-, $n$-, and $m$-dimensional system matrix, control matrix, state vector, and control vector, respectively, and $Q$ and $R$ are $n \times n$ nonnegative and $m \times m$ positive-definite matrices. The optimal control problem, treated extensively in literature, is to find a control vector $u^*(t)$ such that (6.2.1) is satisfied while the cost functional (6.2.2) is minimized. The solution to this so-called "state regulator" is well known (Kalman, 1960):

$$u^*(t) = -R^{-1}B^T Kx(t) \qquad (6.2.3)$$

where $K$ is an $n \times n$ symmetric positive-definite matrix solution of the following algebraic matrix Riccati equation (AMRE):

$$KA + A^T K - KSK + Q = 0 \qquad (6.2.4)$$

where $S = BR^{-1}B^T$. The solution of AMRE (6.2.4) is well documented, and a survey by Jamshidi (1980) reports at least eight different classes of solution techniques for it. In particular, some of the best methods are the Newton-based iterative scheme initialized by a parameter-imbedding method (Jamshidi, 1978) used to solve a 90th-order river-pollution system by Jamshidi (1980) and the Schur's vector transformation of the Hamiltonian matrix

$$H = \begin{bmatrix} A & -S \\ Q & -A^T \end{bmatrix} \qquad (6.2.5)$$

which has been successfully used for systems of order 64 to 104 (Laub, 1979). The latter method is constrained by the computer memory and is most effective for densed $A$ matrices. It is not my objective to give a detail treatment of various solution methods of AMRE (6.2.4); the reader can consult the overview (Jamshidi, 1980), which treats not only AMRE but also provides an exhaustive literature survey on differential, discrete-time, stochastic, and singularly-perturbed matrix Riccati as well as the Lyapunov-type equations.

For any value of $n$, the optimal control problem (6.2.1)–(6.2.2) and its solution (6.2.3)–(6.2.4) requires a set of at least $n(n+1)/2$ elemental values of the $n \times n$ symmetric Riccati matrix $K$. Clearly for a large $n$, the task of solving the AMRE (6.2.4) calls for considerable computational effort. Although there are some approximate solutions of the AMRE (6.2.4) through regular (Kokotović et al., 1969b) or singular perturbations (Yackel and Kokotović, 1973), here the approximation is assumed through the representation of the state model (6.2.1) by a "coarser" set of states called "aggregated" system,

$$\dot{z}(t) = Fx(t) + Gu(t), \quad z(0) = z_o \qquad (6.2.6)$$

where $z = Cx$ is the $l$-dimensional ($l < n$) aggregated state, $C$ is the $l \times n$ aggregation matrix, and $F$ and $G$ are $l \times l$ and $l \times m$ aggregated state and control matrices obtained from (see Section 2.2)

$$F = CAC^T(CC^T)^{-1}, \quad G = CB \tag{6.2.7}$$

One of the more popular aggregation procedures discussed in detail in Section 2.2.1 is the modal method originated by Davison (1966), which was considered as a special case of the aggregation technique due to Aoki (1968, 1978), which, in turn, is generalized by a chained aggregation scheme due to Tse et al. (1978). In sequel, the aggregation models described by (2.2.22)–(2.2.26) and (2.2.39)–(2.2.47) due to Davison (1966) and Chidambara (1969), respectively, are used within the context of near-optimum design of the original system.

For the full model, the optimal control is given by

$$u^*(t) = -R^{-1}B^TK_f x(t) = -F^* x(t) \tag{6.2.8}$$

where $K_f$ is the solution of the full model's AMRE

$$A^TK_f + K_f A - K_f SK_f + Q = 0 \tag{6.2.9}$$

where $S = BR^{-1}B^T$. The control for the aggregated model is

$$u^a(t) = -R^{-1}G^TK_a z(t) \tag{6.2.10}$$

where $K_a$ is the solution of the aggregated model's AMRE

$$F^TK_a + K_a F - K_a GR^{-1}G^TK_a + Q_a = 0 \tag{6.2.11}$$

Using the aggregation condition (2.2.5)–(2.2.6a), i.e., $CA = FC$, $G = CB$, pre- and postmultiplying (6.2.11) by $C^T$ and $C$, respectively, the aggregated model's AMRE becomes

$$A^T(C^TK_a C) + (C^TK_a C)A - (C^TK_a C)S(C^TK_a C) + C^TQ_a C = 0 \tag{6.2.12}$$

which is identical to the full model's AMRE (6.2.9) if the following relations hold:

$$K_f = C^TK_a C, \quad Q = C^TQ_a C \tag{6.2.13}$$

Using the pseudo-inverse of $C$, $Q_a$ can be written as

$$Q_a = (CC^T)^{-1}CQC^T(CC^T)^{-1} \tag{6.2.14}$$

Thus, the aggregated model's near-optimum control is given by

$$u^a(t) = -R^{-1}G^TK_a Cx(t) = -F_a x(t) \tag{6.2.15}$$

The following example illustrates this near-optimum control based on aggregation.

**Example 6.2.1.** Consider a fifth-order system

$$
\begin{bmatrix} \dot{x}_1 \\ \dot{x}_2 \\ \dot{x}_3 \\ \dot{x}_4 \\ \dot{x}_5 \end{bmatrix} = \begin{bmatrix} -0.2 & 0.5 & 0 & 0 & 0 \\ 0 & -0.5 & 1.6 & 0 & 0 \\ 0 & 0 & -14.28 & 85.71 & 0 \\ 0 & 0 & 0 & -25 & 75 \\ 0 & 0 & 0 & 0 & -10 \end{bmatrix} \begin{bmatrix} x_1 \\ x_2 \\ x_3 \\ x_4 \\ x_5 \end{bmatrix} + \begin{bmatrix} 0 \\ 0 \\ 0 \\ 0 \\ 30 \end{bmatrix} u
$$

$$(6.2.16)$$

which represents a voltage regulator system (Sannuti and Kokotović, 1969) and is also considered by Lamba and Rao (1974). It is desired to find an aggregated model for (6.2.16) and a near-optimum control with a quadratic cost

$$
J = \frac{1}{2} \int_0^\infty \left( 0.1x_1^2 + 0.01x_3^2 + 0.01x_5^2 + u^2 \right) dt \qquad (6.2.17)
$$

SOLUTION: A careful look at (6.2.16) indicates that since the system matrix is upper triangular, the eigenvalues are $-0.2$, $-0.5$, $-14.28$, $-25$, and $-10$. Thus a two-dimensional reduced-order model is sought. For a two-dimensional reduced model, the aggregation and aggregated matrices for (6.2.16) turn out to be

$$
C = \begin{bmatrix} 1 & 0 & -0.004 & -0.00224 & -0.336 \\ 0 & 1 & 0.115 & 0.40400 & 3.22 \end{bmatrix}
$$

$$
F = \begin{bmatrix} -0.2000 & 0.50 \\ 0.0087 & -0.58 \end{bmatrix}, \quad G = \begin{bmatrix} -10.08 \\ 96.60 \end{bmatrix}
$$

$$(6.2.18)$$

Using the full model's $\{A, B, Q, R\}$ matrices defined in (6.2.16)–(6.2.17), a fifth-order AMRE (6.2.9) is solved and an optimal feedback law is obtained:

$$
u^*(t) = -R^{-1}B^T K_f x(t) = -0.26x_1 - 0.11x_2 - 0.04x_3 - 0.15x_4 - 0.59x_5
$$

$$(6.2.19)$$

where $K_f$ corresponds to the full model's Riccati matrix. Next, by virtue of matrices $\{F, G, Q_a, R\}$ defined in (6.2.18), (6.2.17) and using (6.2.14) to find $Q_a = \text{diag}\langle 0.1, 0 \rangle$, a second-order AMRE is solved. A feedback law is obtained for the aggregated system

$$
u^a(t) = -R^{-1}G^T K_a z \qquad (6.2.20)
$$

which can result in an approximate feedback law

$$
u^a(t) = -R^{-1}G^T K_a C x = -0.60x_1 - 0.27x_2 - 0.0288x_3 - 0.096x_4 - 0.67x_5
$$

$$(6.2.21)$$

The two control laws (6.2.19) and (6.2.21) provide the optimum and near-optimum (aggregated) control whose control and output responses are shown in Figures 6.1 and 6.2, respectively. The initial state was chosen to be $x(0) = (0.5 \quad 0 \quad 0 \quad 0 \quad 0)^T$, and the output was $y = x_1$ in both cases.

In a similar fashion, a near-optimum control can be developed for the second aggregated model (2.2.39)–(2.2.47). Let us rewrite the quadratic cost (6.2.2) in the following form:

$$J = \frac{1}{2} \int_0^\infty \left\{ [z^T x_2^T] \begin{bmatrix} Q_1 & Q_{12} \\ Q_{12}^T & Q_2 \end{bmatrix} \begin{bmatrix} z \\ x_2 \end{bmatrix} + u^T Ru \right\} dt \qquad (6.2.22)$$

$$= \frac{1}{2} \int_0^\infty \left( z^T Q_1 z + 2 z^T Q_{12} x_2 + x_2^T Q_2 x_2 + u^T Ru \right) dt$$

which can be rewritten in terms of $z$ and $u$ by eliminating $x_2$ from it using (2.2.46):

$$J_l = \frac{1}{2} \int_0^\infty \left( z^T Q_l z + 2 z^T Su + u^T R_l u \right) dt \qquad (6.2.23)$$

**Figure 6.1** Optimal and aggregated control responses for Example 6.2.1.

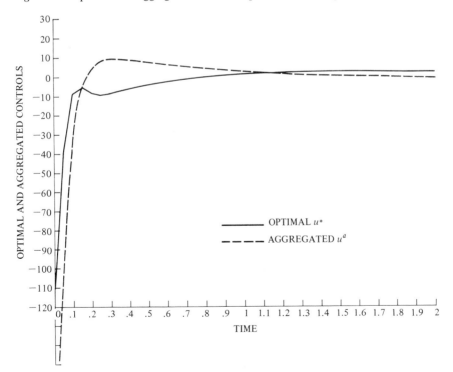

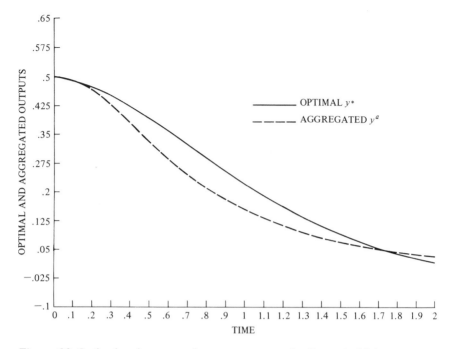

**Figure 6.2** Optimal and aggregated output responses for Example 6.2.1.

where $J_l$ represents the equivalent cost function (Rao and Lamba, 1974)

$$Q_l = Q_1 + 2Q_{12}N + N^T Q_2 N, \quad R_l = R + E^T Q_2 E, \quad S = Q_{12} E + N^T Q_2 E \tag{6.2.24}$$

In order to formulate a linear, quadratic problem from (2.2.47) and (6.2.23), let

$$u_l \triangleq R_l^{-1} S^T z + u \tag{6.2.25}$$

in (2.2.47),

$$\dot{z} = \left( F - GR_l^{-1} S^T \right) z + G u_l = F_l z + G u_l \tag{6.2.26}$$

and (6.2.23) becomes

$$J_l = \frac{1}{2} \int_0^\infty \left( z^T Q_l z + u_l^T R_l u_l \right) dt \tag{6.2.27}$$

The linear regulator problem for the aggregated system (6.2.26)–(6.2.27) for a $Q_l \geqslant 0$ and $R_l > 0$ results in

$$u_l^* = - R_l^{-1} G^T K_l z \tag{6.2.28}$$

where $K_l$ is the positive-definite solution of the AMRE,

$$F_l^T K_l + K_l F_l - K_l GR_l^{-1} G^T K_l + Q_l = 0 \tag{6.2.29}$$

The near-optimum control can thus be obtained as

$$u^a = u_I^* - R_I^{-1} S^T z = - R_I^{-1} (G^T K_I + S^T) z \qquad (6.2.30)$$

The following example illustrates this near-optimum control law.

**Example 6.2.2.** Consider the fourth-order system of Example 2.2.3:

$$\dot{x} = \begin{bmatrix} 0 & 1 & 0 & 0 \\ 0 & 0 & 1 & 0 \\ 0 & 0 & 0 & 1 \\ -0.6 & -9.22 & -33.32 & -11.3 \end{bmatrix} x + \begin{bmatrix} 0 \\ 1 \\ 0 \\ 1 \end{bmatrix} u \qquad (6.2.31)$$

with $x(0) = (1 \quad 1 \quad 1 \quad 1)^T$, cost function

$$J = \frac{1}{2} \int_0^\infty (x^T Q x + u^T R u) \, dt \qquad (6.2.32)$$

$Q = \text{diag}(5 \quad 4 \quad 2 \quad 1)$, and $R = 1$. It is desired to find a reduced-order model and a near-optimum control for it.

SOLUTION: A second-order reduced model $(F, G)$ was obtained in Example 2.2.3 as given by (2.2.50). The matrices $F_I$, $R_I$, and $Q_I$ are given by

$$F_I = \begin{bmatrix} 0 & 1 \\ -0.015 & -0.2324 \end{bmatrix}, \quad R_I = 1.14, \quad Q_I = \begin{bmatrix} 5.0 & 0.006 \\ 0.006 & 4.10 \end{bmatrix}$$
$$(6.2.33)$$

The near-optimum control law (6.2.30) resulting from the solution of a second-order AMRE becomes

$$u^a = - R_I^{-1} (G^T K_I + S^T) z = - 2.087 x_1 - 2.553 x_2 \qquad (6.2.34)$$

The optimal control was obtained by solving a fourth-order AMRE:

$$u^* = - 2.233 x_1 - 2.853 x_2 - 0.814 x_3 - 0.063 x_4 \qquad (6.2.35)$$

The performance indices for the particular initial condition turn out to be $J^* = 9.0062$ and $J^a = 9.1200$.

The results of this example motivate a number of comments. The reduced model has remained stable, and the corresponding near-optimum (aggregated) control law requires only two of the four states. This would mean that if the number of inaccessible states does not exceed the number of nondominant (fast) modes, this method would be appropriate. This is a contrasting point to the near-optimum law (6.2.15) for a fully modal aggregation. The degradation of the performance index is, of course, expected and its detail discussion is given in Section 6.5.

In a similar fashion a near-optimum control can be found for other aggregation methods considered in Section 2.2. Some of these applications are considered in the problem section of this chapter. Here one more example is considered to illustrate the aggregation via continued fraction discussed in Section 2.2.2.

**Example 6.2.3.** Consider the system of Example 2.2.4, whose full (fourth-order) and aggregated (second-order) models are defined by (2.2.72) and (2.2.74)–(2.2.75), respectively. It is required to find a near-optimum control law for this system.

SOLUTION: Using the full model's matrices, a fourth-order Riccati equation using $A$, $B$, $Q = I_4$, $R = 1$ is solved and an optimum feedback law results:

$$u^*(t) = -29.9x_1(t) - 45.8x_2(t) - 9.11x_3(t) - 0.543x_4(t) \quad (6.2.36)$$

A second-order AMRE can be solved using $F, G, Q_a = I_2$, $R = 1$ to obtain a feedback law for the aggregated system

$$u^a(t) = -0.332z_1(t) - 0.211z_2(t) \quad\quad\quad (6.2.37)$$

which can be used to find an approximate law for the full model using the aggregation matrix $C$ in (2.2.75):

$$u^a(t) = -29.9x_1(t) - 45.83x_2(t) - 9.11x_3(t) - 0.543x_4(t) \quad (6.2.38)$$

Figure 6.3 shows the optimum and near-optimum (aggregated) responses of the system as defined by (2.2.72b), $y^a(t) = C_l Cx(t)$ given in (2.2.75), and control vectors (6.2.36) and (6.2.38).

## 6.2.2 Perturbation Methods

The second principal class of model reduction methods is perturbation, which was discussed in Section 2.3. Here the concepts of regularly perturbed, singularly perturbed, and multi-time-scale systems are used to find near-optimum control of a large-scale system.

## 6.2.2.a Regular Perturbation

In this section a near-optimum control for a weakly coupled (regularly perturbed) large-scale system is developed, and a 17th-order example is used to illustrate the method. Consider the two subsystem "$\varepsilon$-coupled" system (2.3.2) with the $(A, B)$ pair

$$A(\varepsilon) = \left[\begin{array}{c|c} A_1 & \varepsilon A_{12} \\ \hline \varepsilon A_{21} & A_2 \end{array}\right], \quad B(\varepsilon) = \left[\begin{array}{c|c} B_1 & 0 \\ \hline 0 & B_2 \end{array}\right] \quad (6.2.39)$$

where $\varepsilon$ is a small positive parameter, $A_1$, $A_{12}$, $A_{21}$, $A_2$, $B_1$, and $B_2$ are $n_1 \times n_1$, $n_1 \times n_2$, $n_2 \times n_1$, $n_2 \times n_2$, $n_1 \times m_1$, and $n_2 \times m_2$ matrices, respectively, with $n = n_1 + n_2$ and $m = m_1 + m_2$. The corresponding AMRE (6.2.4) must be solved using (6.2.39) and matrices $Q$ and $R$ in (6.2.2). Here an additional approximation is obtained with regard to the accompanying

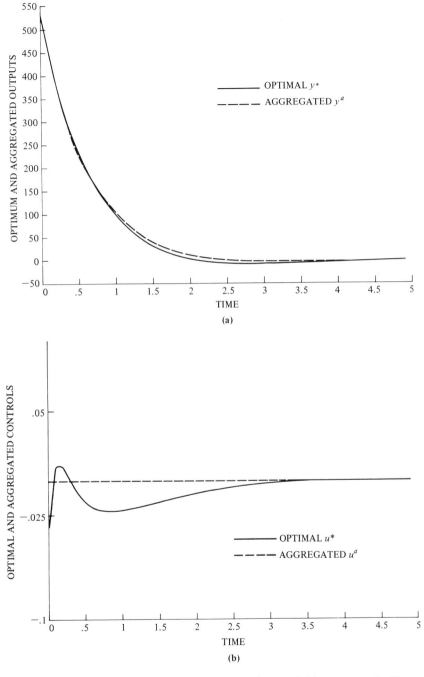

**Figure 6.3** Optimal and aggregated output (**a**) and control (**b**) responses for Example 6.2.3 using the continued fraction method.

Riccati matrix. An approximate solution to the AMRE (6.2.4) has been proposed by Kokotović et al. (1969b) and Kokotović (1972), which is based on a truncated MacLaurin series expansion in $\varepsilon$,

$$P \cong K(0) + \varepsilon K^1(0) + \cdots + \frac{\varepsilon^m}{m!} K^m(0) \qquad (6.2.40)$$

where $K^i(0) \triangleq \partial^i K(\varepsilon)/\partial \varepsilon^i |_{\varepsilon=0}$.

If $K(\varepsilon)$ is partitioned,

$$K = \begin{bmatrix} K_1 & \vdots & \varepsilon K_{12} \\ -- & -\vdots- & -- \\ \varepsilon K_{12}^T & \vdots & K_2 \end{bmatrix} \qquad (6.2.41)$$

and substituted into (6.2.40), three truncated series in $\varepsilon$ are obtained for $K_1$, $K_{12}$, $K_2$. It has been shown that the even-order partials of $K$ are diagonal, while the odd-order partials are antidiagonal, i.e.,

$$K^{2j} = \begin{bmatrix} K_1^{2j} & \vdots & 0 \\ -- & -\vdots- & -- \\ 0 & \vdots & K_2^{2j} \end{bmatrix}, \quad K^{2j+1} = \begin{bmatrix} 0 & \vdots & K_{12}^{2j+1} \\ ----- & -\vdots- & ----- \\ (K_{12}^{2j+1})^T & \vdots & 0 \end{bmatrix}, \quad j = 0,1,2\ldots$$

$$(6.2.42)$$

Now if $P$ in (6.2.40) is substituted in AMRE (6.2.4) for $K$, noting (6.2.41)–(6.2.42) and equating the coefficients of $\varepsilon^m$, $m = 0,1,2,\ldots$, it is deduced that $K_i^0$, $i = 1,2$, are solutions of

$$K_i^0 A_i + A_i^T K_i^0 - K_i^0 S_i K_i^0 + Q_i = 0 \qquad (6.2.43)$$

which are diagonal and correspond to $m = 0$. For $m = 1$, $K_{12}^1$ is the solution of

$$K_{12}^1 G_2 + G_1^T K_{12}^1 + F_{12}^0 = 0 \qquad (6.2.44)$$

where

$$\begin{aligned} G_i &= A_i - S_i K_i^0, \quad i = 1,2 \\ F_{12}^0 &= A_{21}^T K_2^0 + K_1^0 A_{12} \end{aligned} \qquad (6.2.45)$$

For $m = 2$, the block-diagonal matrices $K_i^2$ are the solution of

$$K_i^2 G_i + G_i^T K_i^2 + F_i^1 = 0, \quad i = 1,2 \qquad (6.2.46)$$

where

$$\begin{aligned} F_1^1 &= 2(A_{21} - S_2 K_{21}^1)^T K_{21}^1 + 2 K_{12}^1 A_{21}, \\ F_2^1 &= 2(A_{12} - S_1 K_{12}^1)^T K_{12}^1 + 2 K_{21}^1 A_{12} \end{aligned} \qquad (6.2.47)$$

and

$$K_{21}^1 = (K_{12}^1)^T$$

For $m = 3$ and 4, two sets of matrix equations similar to (6.2.44) and (6.2.46) are obtained for $K_{12}^3$ and $K_i^4$ except for the forcing terms, which are now $F_{12}^1$ and $F_i^2$, $i = 1, 2$, respectively. The following algorithm summarizes the near-optimum control of an "$\varepsilon$-coupled" system.

***Algorithm 6.1.*** Near-Optimum Control of "$\varepsilon$-Coupled" Systems

*Step 0:*      Solve two low-order AMREs (6.2.43) for $K_i^0$, $i = 1, 2$, and store.

*Step 1:*      Solve the Lyapunov-type* equations (6.2.44) for $K_{12}^1$ using $K_i^0$ and store.

*Step 2:*      Solve the Lyapunov equation (6.2.46) for $K_i^2$, $i = 1, 2$, and store.

$\vdots$

*Step m − 1:* Solve for antidiagonal block matrix $K_{12}^{m-1}$ and store.

*Step m:*     Solve for diagonal-block matrices $K_i^m$, $i = 1, 2$.

*Step m + 1:* The $m$th-order truncated Riccati matrix is obtained from (6.2.40) noting the diagonal properties (6.2.42).

*Step m + 2:* The near-optimum control is given by

$$u^a(t) = - R^{-1}B^T P x(t) \qquad (6.2.48)$$

where $R = \text{Block-diag}\{R_1, R_2\}$, $B = \text{Block-diag}\{B_1, B_2\}$.

The following example illustrates this technique.

**Example 6.2.4.** Consider the 17th-order system of Example 2.3.1, which represents a simplified model of a three-stand cold rolling mill (Figure 2.7) with the following partitions: $n_1 = 8$, $n_2 = 9$, $m_1 = 5$, and $m_2 = 7$. For computational purposes, let the payoff or winding reel radius have a value $r = 0.84$ ft., as defined in (2.3.5). Find a near-optimum feedback law for this system. The other matrices are $Q_1 = \text{diag}\langle 0.5, 0.5, 0.5, 1, 1, 5, 1, 5\rangle$, $Q_2 = \text{diag}\langle 1, 5, 1, 0.5, 0.5, 0.5, 1, 1, 5\rangle$, $R_1 = I_5$, and $R_2 = I_7$ (Jamshidi, 1972b).

SOLUTION: The results of Step 0 are

$$P = \left[\begin{array}{c|c} P_1 & P_{12} \\ \hline P_{12}^T & P_2 \end{array}\right] \cong \left[\begin{array}{c|c} K_1^0 + \varepsilon^2/2!K_1^2 & \varepsilon K_{12}^1 \\ \hline \varepsilon\left(K_{12}^1\right)^T & K_2^0 + \varepsilon^2/2!K_2^2 \end{array}\right] \qquad (6.2.49)$$

where symmetric matrices $P_i$, $K_i^0$, $i = 1, 2$, and matrix $P_{12}$ are given by (6.2.50). The matrices in (6.2.49) are used at Step 1 to find $K_{12}^1$, which in turn, is used to find $K_i^2$, $i = 1, 2$. Equation (6.2.51) is then used to obtain the

---

*For the numerical solution of a Lyapunov-type equation, see Algorithm 6.2.

$$P_1 = \begin{bmatrix}
-0.08 & -1.4 & -0.08 & -1.31 & -0.17 & -0.43 & -0.08 & -13.7 \\
 & 16.95 & -0.15 & 9.07 & -0.33 & -1.98 & -0.44 & -19.0 \\
 & & 0.7 & -0.14 & -0.02 & -0.04 & -0.08 & -1.46 \\
 & & & 26.0 & 3.52 & 1.44 & 3.3 & -21.0 \\
 & & & & 0.94 & 0.45 & 0.83 & -43.8 \\
 & & & & & 0.94 & -2.76 & -0.95 \\
 & & & & & & -7.8 & 0.03 \\
 & & & & & & & -233.0
\end{bmatrix}$$

$$K_1^0 = \begin{bmatrix}
1.11 & -0.03 & 0.05 & 0.03 & 0.12 & -0.376 & -0.09 & 0.526 \\
 & 18.87 & -0.003 & 11.04 & 0.07 & -1.91 & -0.51 & 1.066 \\
 & & 0.688 & 16.78 & 0.01 & -0.04 & -0.01 & 0.054 \\
 & & & 28.01 & 3.92 & 1.66 & 3.63 & 1.21 \\
 & & & & 10.22 & 0.50 & 0.93 & 0.24 \\
 & & & & & 0.85 & -3.06 & 0.07 \\
 & & & & & & -8.63 & -0.02 \\
 & & & & & & & 12.71
\end{bmatrix}$$

and

$$K_2^0 = \begin{bmatrix}
-8.78 & 0.0 & 0.0 & 0.0 & 0.0 & 0.0 & 0.0 & 0.0 & 0.0 \\
 & 23.32 & -2.39 & -0.16 & -0.01 & -0.02 & 0.90 & -0.35 & 0.75 \\
 & & -10.2 & 0.14 & -0.50 & 0.01 & 3.48 & -1.31 & 3.3 \\
 & & & 1.14 & -1.11 & 0.05 & -0.72 & 0.15 & -0.32 \\
 & & & & 20.70 & -0.11 & 12.9 & -1.0 & 0.92 \\
 & & & & & 0.73 & -0.07 & 0.02 & -0.032 \\
 & & & & & & 20.01 & -0.347 & -1.64 \\
 & & & & & & & 1.05 & 0.58 \\
 & & & & & & & & 0.12
\end{bmatrix}$$

(6.2.50)

$$
P_2 =
\begin{bmatrix}
-19.4 \\
0.03 & 32.93 \\
0.0 & -11.5 & -50.9 \\
0.0 & -0.2 & 0.65 & 1.13 \\
0.0 & -0.25 & -2.33 & -1.1 & 20.6 \\
0.0 & -0.02 & 0.06 & 0.04 & -0.11 & 0.73 \\
0.0 & 4.12 & 17.0 & -0.9 & 13.5 & -0.09 & 15.5 \\
0.0 & -1.55 & -6.44 & 0.22 & -1.23 & 0.02 & -1.76 & 0.4 \\
0.0 & 3.74 & 16.6 & -0.5 & 1.52 & -0.05 & -6.0 & 2.25 & -4.22
\end{bmatrix}
\tag{6.2.51}
$$

$$
P_{12} =
\begin{bmatrix}
0.02 & 0.57 & 0.0 & -0.25 & -0.03 & -0.03 & -0.05 & -0.07 & 0.0 \\
0.15 & 0.58 & -0.01 & -0.2 & -0.02 & -0.02 & -0.09 & -0.06 & 0.02 \\
0.0 & 0.75 & 0.0 & -0.02 & 0.0 & 0.0 & 0.0 & -0.01 & 0.0 \\
-0.36 & 0.76 & -0.01 & -0.19 & 0.05 & -0.02 & 0.02 & -0.07 & 0.0 \\
-0.1 & 0.16 & 0.0 & -0.04 & 0.02 & 0.0 & 0.03 & -0.01 & 0.0 \\
0.13 & 0.04 & 0.0 & -0.01 & 0.0 & 0.0 & 0.0 & 0.0 & 0.0 \\
0.0 & 0.0 & 0.0 & 0.0 & 0.0 & 0.0 & 0.0 & 0.0 & 0.0 \\
-10.44 & 8.4 & -0.03 & -2.1 & 1.05 & -0.25 & 1.32 & -0.73 & -0.08
\end{bmatrix}
\tag{6.2.51}
$$

near-optimum feedback control (6.2.52).

$$\begin{bmatrix} u_1 \\ \hline u_2 \end{bmatrix} = - \begin{bmatrix} R_1^{-1}B_1^T P_1 & | & R_1^{-1}B_1^T P_{12} \\ \hline R_2^{-1}B_2^T P_{21} & | & R_2^{-1}B_2^T P_2 \end{bmatrix} \begin{bmatrix} x_1 \\ \hline x_2 \end{bmatrix}$$

$$= - \begin{bmatrix} F_1 & | & F_{12} \\ \hline F_{21} & | & F_2 \end{bmatrix} \begin{bmatrix} x_1 \\ \hline x_2 \end{bmatrix} \tag{6.2.52}$$

The resulting $(12 \times 17)$-dimensional gain matrix is given by

$$F = \left[\begin{array}{ccccccc}
-0.02 & -0.45 & & -0.42 & & -0.14 & -4.38 \\
-0.45 & 5.4 & & 2.9 & -0.1 & -0.63 & -0.14 & -6.05 \\
& & 0.14 & & & & -0.29 \\
0.09 & 0.54 & & -4.0 & -1.01 & 3.38 & 9.48 & -0.04 \\
0.09 & 0.54 & & -4.0 & -1.01 & 3.38 & 9.48 & -0.04 \\
\hline
& -0.12 & & 0.29 & 0.1 & -0.1 & 8.62 \\
& -0.12 & & 0.29 & 0.1 & -0.1 & 8.62 \\
& & & & & & 0.0 \\
& & & & 0 & & 0.0 \\
-0.08 & -0.06 & & & & & -0.66 \\
0.0 & & & & & & 0.33 \\
0.0 & & & & & & 0.0
\end{array}\right.$$

$$\left.\begin{array}{ccccccccc}
0.0 & 0.22 & & -0.08 & & & & & \\
0.0 & 0.25 & & -0.06 & & & & & \\
0.0 & 0.0 & & & & 0 & & & \\
0.0 & 0.0 & & & & & & & \\
0.0 & 0.0 & & & & & & & \\
\hline
16.0 & & & & & & & & \\
16.0 & & & & & & & & \\
4.9 & 21.6 & -0.27 & 0.99 & 0.0 & -7.22 & 2.73 & -7.03 \\
4.9 & 21.6 & -0.27 & 0.99 & 0.0 & -7.22 & 2.73 & -7.03 \\
& 0.2 & 0.36 & -0.35 & 0.0 & -0.29 & 0.07 & -0.15 \\
-0.08 & -0.74 & -0.35 & 6.55 & 0.0 & 4.28 & -0.39 & 0.48 \\
0.0 & & & & & & & 0.0
\end{array}\right]$$

$$\tag{6.2.53}$$

## 6.2.2.b Singular Perturbation

In this section the near-optimum control of a large-scale linear TIV singularly perturbed system is considered. The problem can be defined as follows. Find control vector $u(t)$ such that a quadratic function

$$J = \int_0^{t_f} L(x, z, u)\, dt = \frac{1}{2} \int_0^{t_f} \{ x^T(t) Q_1 x(t) + z^T(t) Q_2 z(t) + u^T(t) R u(t) \}\, dt$$

$$\tag{6.2.54}$$

is minimized while the system model

$$\dot{x}(t) = h_s(x, z, u) = A_1 x(t) + A_{12} z(t) + B_1 u(t), \quad x(0) = x_o$$
$$\varepsilon \dot{z}(t) = h_f(x, z, u) = A_{21} x(t) + A_2 z(t) + B_2 u(t), \quad z(0) = z_o \qquad (6.2.55)$$

is satisfied, $A_2$ is a nonsingular matrix, and $\varepsilon$ is a small constant positive parameter.

The necessary conditions for optimality using Pontryagin's maximum principle lead to

$$\dot{x} = \partial H / \partial p = h_s(\cdot), \quad x(0) = x_o \qquad (6.2.56a)$$

$$\varepsilon \dot{z} = \partial H / \partial q = h_f(\cdot), \quad z(0) = z_o \qquad (6.2.56b)$$

$$\dot{p} = - \partial H / \partial x = Q_1 x - A_1^T p - A_{21}^T q, \quad p(t_f) = 0 \qquad (6.2.56c)$$

$$\varepsilon \dot{q} = - \partial H / \partial z = Q_2 z - A_{12}^T p - A_2^T q, \quad q(t_f) = 0 \qquad (6.2.56d)$$

$$0 = \partial H / \partial u = - Ru + B_1^T p + B_2^T q \qquad (6.2.56e)$$

where $H(\cdot)$ is the Hamiltonian function

$$H(x, z, p, q, u) = - L(x, z, u) + p^T h_s(x, z, u) + q^T h_f(x, z, u) \qquad (6.2.57)$$

Eliminating $u$ from (6.2.56e) and substituting it in (6.2.56a)–(6.2.56d) yields the following singularly perturbed TPBV problem:

$$\dot{x} = f(x, z, p, q, \varepsilon), \quad x(0) = x_o \qquad (6.2.58a)$$

$$\varepsilon \dot{z} = F(x, z, p, q, \varepsilon), \quad z(0) = z_o \qquad (6.2.58b)$$

$$\dot{p} = g(x, z, p, q, \varepsilon), \quad p(t_f) = 0 \qquad (6.2.58c)$$

$$\varepsilon \dot{q} = G(x, z, p, q, \varepsilon), \quad q(t_f) = 0 \qquad (6.2.58d)$$

where $f(\cdot)$, $F(\cdot)$, $g(\cdot)$, and $G(\cdot)$ are the sufficiently differentiable functions defined on the right-hand sides of (6.2.56a)–(6.2.56d) after eliminating $u(t)$ in (6.2.56e).

The original system's TPBV problem, given by (6.2.58), passes to the degenerate system by setting $\varepsilon = 0$, i.e.,

$$\dot{\hat{x}} = f(\hat{x}, \hat{z}, \hat{p}, \hat{q}, 0), \quad \hat{x}(0) = x_o \qquad (6.2.59a)$$

$$0 = F(\hat{x}, \hat{z}, \hat{p}, \hat{q}, 0) \qquad (6.2.59b)$$

$$\hat{p} = g(\hat{x}, \hat{z}, \hat{p}, \hat{q}, 0), \quad p(t_f) = 0 \qquad (6.2.59c)$$

$$0 = G(\hat{x}, \hat{z}, \hat{p}, \hat{q}, 0) \qquad (6.2.59d)$$

Note that in setting $\varepsilon = 0$ auxiliary conditions on $z$ and $q$ are lost so that it is not at all evident that the solution closely approximates that of the original system. In fact, a unique solution to the degenerate system may not even exist, in which case the analysis is somewhat more complicated. Without going through rigorous mathematical results (Wasow, 1965; Tupciev, 1962), some general characteristics are presented. The solutions to the full and degenerate systems are close on most of the interior of the interval $[0, t_f]$. Denoting solution of the degenerate system by $\hat{x}(t)$, $\hat{z}(t)$, $\hat{p}(t)$, $\hat{q}(t)$, the fact that $\hat{z}(0)$ and $z_o$ are in general different makes the above statement evident. Similar considerations can be given to $\hat{q}(t_f)$ and $q_{t_f} = 0$. Due to coupling effects, $\hat{z}(t_f)$ and $z(t_f)$, $\hat{q}(0)$ and $q(0)$ may differ significantly. This disparity at the endpoints is commonly referred to as "boundary layer behavior," as briefly discussed in Section 2.3.2.a. If no singular perturbation behavior were present, the standard Taylor series perturbation could be used. For some particularly convenient value $\varepsilon_o$ of the parameter $\varepsilon$, one computes the solution $y(t, \varepsilon)$, where $y^T = [x^T, z^T]$. The partial derivatives of the variables with respect to $\varepsilon$, i.e., "sensitivity functions," are then computed at $\varepsilon = \varepsilon_o$. A first-order Taylor series expansion of $y(t, \varepsilon)$ would be

$$y(t, \varepsilon) = y(t, \varepsilon_o) + \partial y(t, \varepsilon) / \partial \varepsilon|_{\varepsilon_o} (\varepsilon - \varepsilon_o) \qquad (6.2.60)$$

where $\partial y(t, \varepsilon) / \partial \varepsilon$ is the sensitivity function of $y$ with respect to $\varepsilon$. Here, due to the singularity in perturbation, the above Taylor series expansion cannot be used, since the derivatives may not even exist at $\varepsilon = \varepsilon_o = 0$. The proper expansion would be an asymptotic one and not a standard Taylor or MacLaurin expansion.

In sequel, formal construction of the asymptotic expansions is presented and the near-optimum control is obtained from them. A uniformly valid expansion on the closed interval $[0, t_f]$ is not, in general, a simple power series in $\varepsilon$. Consequently, a solution of this form cannot be assumed by substituting it into both sides of the equations, equating corresponding coefficients, and solving. However, such a procedure can in fact be used to obtain an expansion which is valid over most of the interval. Such expansion is commonly called "outer expansion" in fluid mechanics terminology. In this case the auxiliary conditions for the coefficient functions must be derived by a complicated procedure (Vasileva, 1952). This approach was applied to optimal control problems by Hadlock (1973), Hadlock et al. (1970), Sannuti and Kokotović (1969), Sannuti (1974), and Jamshidi (1976b). The uniformly valid expansion that is sought would be the sum of three power series in $\varepsilon$ shown as

$$y(t, \varepsilon) \simeq L(y) + \hat{y} + R(y) \qquad (6.2.61)$$

where $L(y)$ is a power series in $\varepsilon$ whose coefficients $L_i(y)$ are functions of the left-hand side expanded time argument (stretched time scale) $\tau = t / \varepsilon$, $\hat{y}$ is a power series in $\varepsilon$ whose coefficients $\hat{y}_i$ are functions of time argument $t$, and $R(y)$ is a power series in $\varepsilon$ whose coefficients $R_i(y)$ are functions of the right-hand side expanded time argument $\sigma = (t_f - t) / \varepsilon$. Denoting the state equations (6.2.56) after the elimination of control $u$ by $\dot{y} = \phi(y)$, one may proceed on substituting the sum $L(y) + \hat{y} + R(y)$ into both sides of the state equation and equate the coefficients to obtain appropriate equations for the series terms. To carry this last operation, an assumption is made that for each $i$, the coefficients $L_i(y)$ and $R_i(y)$ decay exponentially as their arguments increase. Let

$$x(t, \varepsilon) = \hat{x}(t, \varepsilon) + \varepsilon Lx(\tau, \varepsilon) + \varepsilon Rx(\sigma, \varepsilon) \qquad (6.2.62a)$$

$$p(t, \varepsilon) = \hat{p}(t, \varepsilon) + \varepsilon Lp(\tau, \varepsilon) + \varepsilon Rp(\sigma, \varepsilon) \qquad (6.2.62b)$$

$$z(t, \varepsilon) = \hat{z}(t, \varepsilon) + Lz(\tau, \varepsilon) + Rz(\sigma, \varepsilon) \qquad (6.2.62c)$$

$$q(t, \varepsilon) = \hat{q}(t, \varepsilon) + Lq(\tau, \varepsilon) + Rq(\sigma, \varepsilon) \qquad (6.2.62d)$$

Since the right boundary layer terms $Rx$, $Rp$, $Rz$, and $Rq$ are asymptotically negligible near $t = 0$, Equations (6.2.62) imply that the left boundary terms satisfy

$$dLx(\tau, \varepsilon)/d\tau = (dx/dt - d\hat{x}/dt)_{\tau = \varepsilon\tau}$$

$$= \hat{f}(Lx, Lp, Lz, Lq, \varepsilon, \tau) \qquad (6.2.63a)$$

$$dLp(\tau, \varepsilon)/d\tau = (dp/dt - d\hat{p}/dt)_{t = \varepsilon\tau}$$

$$= g(Lx, Lp, Lz, Lq, \varepsilon, \tau) \qquad (6.2.63b)$$

$$dLz(\tau, \varepsilon)/dt = (dz/dt - d\hat{z}/dt)_{t = \varepsilon\tau}$$

$$= \hat{F}(Lx, Lp, Lz, Lq, \varepsilon, \tau) \qquad (6.2.63c)$$

$$dLq(\tau, \varepsilon)/dt = (dq/dt - d\hat{q}/dt)_{t = \varepsilon\tau}$$

$$= \hat{G}(Lx, Lp, Lz, Lq, \varepsilon, \tau) \qquad (6.2.63d)$$

where $\hat{f}(\cdot) = f(\hat{x} + Lx, \hat{p} + Lp, \hat{z} + Lz, \hat{q} + Lq, \varepsilon, \varepsilon\tau) - f(\hat{x}, \hat{p}, \hat{z}, \hat{q}, \varepsilon, \varepsilon\tau)$, etc. In a similar manner, since the left-hand terms are negligible near $t = t_f$, it follows from (6.2.62a)–(6.2.62d) that

$$dRx(\sigma, \varepsilon)d\sigma = (d\hat{x}/dt - dx/dt)_{t = t_f - \varepsilon\sigma}$$

$$= \tilde{f}(Rx, Rp, Rz, Rq, \varepsilon, \sigma) \qquad (6.2.64a)$$

$$dRp(\sigma, \varepsilon)/d\sigma = (d\hat{p}/dt - dp/dt)_{t = t_f - \varepsilon\sigma}$$

$$= \tilde{g}(Rx, Rp, Rz, Rq, \varepsilon, \sigma) \qquad (6.2.64b)$$

$$dRz(\sigma, \varepsilon)/d\sigma = (d\hat{z}/dt - dz/dt)_{t = t_f - \varepsilon\sigma}$$

$$= \tilde{F}(Rx, Rp, Rz, Rq, \varepsilon, \sigma) \qquad (6.2.64c)$$

$$dRq(\sigma, u)/d\sigma = (d\hat{q}/dt - dq/dt)_{t = t_f - \varepsilon\sigma}$$

$$= \tilde{G}(Rx, Rp, Rz, Rq, \varepsilon, \sigma) \qquad (6.2.64d)$$

where $\tilde{f}(\cdot) = f(\hat{x}, \hat{p}, \hat{z}, \hat{q}, \varepsilon, \sigma) - f(\hat{x} + \varepsilon Rx, \hat{p} + \varepsilon Rp, \hat{z} + Rz, \hat{q} + Rq, \varepsilon, \sigma)$, etc. The actual differential equations for the boundary layer terms are obtained in greater detail for Example 6.2.5. Interested readers may refer to Sannuti (1974) or Hadlock (1973) for further insight. The outer expansion (degenerate) terms are of course obtained from Equations (6.2.59a)–(6.2.59d).

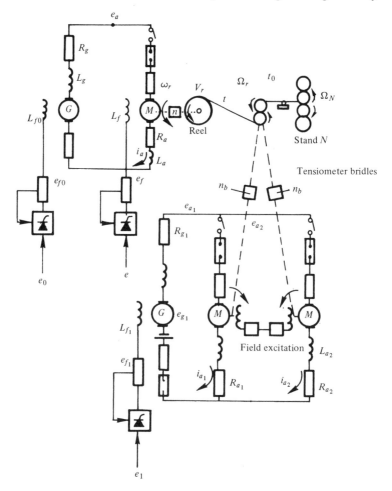

**Figure 6.4** A coiler system showing winding reel and delivery bridles for Example 6.2.5.

**Example 6.2.5.** The singular perturbation as a near-optimum control technique for large-scale systems is applied to a 12th-order coiler process in a continuous cold rolling mill discussed by Jamshidi (1976b) and shown in Figure 6.4.

SOLUTION: The method is explained in some detail and both left- and right-hand boundary layers are obtained. The coiler process dynamics depend on the winding-reel motor, generator, reel, bridle, bridle motor generator, and tensiometer. Table 6.1 presents a summary of state and control variables used in the system model. The state equation of the system

**Table 6.1** Example 6.2.5 State and Control Variables

| Vector | Winding Reel | Delivery Bridle |
|---|---|---|
| State Variables | | |
| Physical | $r, i_f, i_{fo}, \Omega_r, i_a$ | $i_{f_1}, \Omega_b, t_o, i_{a1}, i_{a2}, \Psi_1, \Psi_2{}^a$ |
| Mathematical | $y_1, y_2, y_3, y_4, y_8$ | $y_5, y_6, y_7, y_9, y_{10}, y_{11}, y_{12}$ |
| Control Variables | | |
| Physical | $e, e_o$ | $e_1$ |
| Mathematical | $u_1, u_2$ | $u_3$ |

$^a\Psi_1$ and $\Psi_2$ belong to the tensiometer.

is represented by

$$\dot{y} = Ay + Bu, \quad y(0) = y_o \tag{6.2.65}$$

where $y = (y_1, y_2, y_3, \ldots, y_{12})^T$, $u = (u_1, u_2, u_3)^T$. Based on the prior study of the plant parameters and experience with such processes (Jamshidi, 1972b), it is conjectured that the following set of slow and fast variables be chosen:

$$y = \left(x \mid z\right)^T = \left(r, i_f, i_{fo}, \Omega_r, i_{f1}, \Omega_b, t_o \; i_a, i_{a1}, i_{a2}, \Psi_1, \Psi_2\right)^T \tag{6.2.66}$$
$$u = \left(e, e_o, e_1\right)^T = \left(u_1, u_2, u_3\right)^T$$

The state equation (6.2.65) is now decoupled to

$$\dot{x} = A_1 x + B_1 u + C_1 z, \quad x(0) = x_o \tag{6.2.67}$$
$$\varepsilon \dot{z} = A_2 x + C_2 z, \quad z(0) = z_o \tag{6.2.68}$$

The optimization problem is to obtain an optimum control $u$ which would satisfy (6.2.66)–(6.2.68) while minimizing

$$J = \frac{1}{2} \int_0^1 \left(x^T Q_1 x + z^T Q_2 z + u^T R u\right) dt \tag{6.2.69}$$

The numerical values of the matrices $A_1$, $A_2$, $B_1$, $C_1$, $C_2$, $Q_1$, $Q_2$, and $R$ are given as follows:

$$A_1 = \begin{bmatrix} 0 & 0 & 0 & 0.004 & 0 & 0 & 0 \\ 0 & -0.3 & 0 & 0 & 0 & 0 & 0 \\ 0 & 0 & -0.3 & 0 & 0 & 0 & 0 \\ -2.3 & 0.5 & 0 & 0 & 0 & 0 & 0 \\ 0 & 0 & 0 & 0 & -0.3 & 0 & 0 \\ 0 & 0 & 0 & 0 & 0 & 0 & -0.2 \\ 0 & 0 & 0 & 0 & 0 & 23 & -1 \end{bmatrix}$$

$$A_2 = \begin{bmatrix} 0 & 0 & 12 & -8 & 0 & 0 & 0 \\ 0 & 26 & -3.4 & 0 & 0 & 0 & 0 \\ 0 & 0 & 1.4 & 0 & 0 & 0 & 0 \\ 0 & 0 & 0 & 0.8 & 0 & 0 & 0 \\ 0 & 0 & 0 & 0 & 0 & 0 & 0 \end{bmatrix}$$

$$B_1 = \begin{bmatrix} 0 & 0 & 0 \\ 0.3 & 0 & 0 \\ 0 & 0 & 0 \\ 0 & 0 & 0 \\ 0 & 0 & 0 \\ 0 & 0 & 0 \\ 0 & 0 & 0 \end{bmatrix} \quad C_2 = \begin{bmatrix} -1.2 & 0 & 0 & 0 & 0 \\ 0 & -0.9 & 0 & 0 & 0 \\ 0 & 0 & -1 & 0 & 0 \\ 0 & 0 & 0 & -1 & 0 \\ 0 & 0 & 0 & 1 & -4 \end{bmatrix}$$

$$\text{(6.2.70)}$$

$$Q_1 = \text{diag}(0 \quad 1 \quad 1 \quad 1 \quad 1 \quad 1 \quad 75)$$
$$Q_2 = \text{diag}(1 \quad 1 \quad 1 \quad 10 \quad 10)$$
$$R = I_3$$

$$C_1 = \begin{bmatrix} 0 & 0 & 0 & 0 & 0 \\ 0 & 0 & 0 & 0 & 0 \\ 0 & 0 & 0 & 0 & 0 \\ 0.5 & 0 & 0 & 0 & 0 \\ 0 & 0 & 0 & 0 & 0 \\ 0 & 0.07 & 0.12 & 0 & 0 \\ 0 & 0 & 0 & 0 & 0 \end{bmatrix}$$

The degenerate solution (outer expansion) is obtained through a Riccati formulation,

$$\dot{K} = A_3^T K + K A_3 - K S_1 K + Q_3, \quad K(1) = 0 \qquad \text{(6.2.71)}$$

where

$$A_3 = A_1 - C_1 C_2^{-1} A_2, \quad S_1 = B_1 R_1^{-1} B_1^T, \quad Q_3 = Q_1 + A_2^T (C_2^T)^{-1} Q_2 C_2^{-1} A_2$$

$$\text{(6.2.72)}$$

and $\hat{p} = K\hat{x}$. It is noted that $\hat{z}$ and $\hat{q}$ have been eliminated to lead to (6.2.72), which can be solved by backward integration (Jamshidi, 1980).

To obtain the differential equations for the boundary layer terms, one notes that the left- and right-hand terms in (6.2.61) are all series in $\varepsilon$, i.e.,

$$Lx(\tau, \varepsilon) = \sum_{i=0}^{\infty} L_i(x)\varepsilon^i, \quad Rx(\tau, u) = \sum_{i=0}^{\infty} R_i(x)\varepsilon^i$$

$$Lp(\sigma, \varepsilon) = \sum_{i=0}^{\infty} L_i(p)\varepsilon^i, \quad \text{etc.}$$

$$\text{(6.2.73)}$$

For simplicity of calculations, only the first two components of all $L_i$ and $R_i$ terms are assumed to exist. Making use of (6.2.63) and assumptions (6.2.73), the following differential equations for the left-hand side boundary layer terms result for the zeroth order:

$$dL_0x(\tau)/d\tau = C_1L_0z(\tau), \quad L_0x(0) = 0$$
$$dL_0p(\tau)/d\tau = -A_2^TL_0q(\tau), \quad L_0p(0) = 0$$
$$dL_0z(\tau)/d\tau = C_2L_0z(\tau), \quad L_0z(0) = z_0 - \hat{z}(0)$$
$$dL_0q(\tau)/d\tau = Q_2L_0z(\tau) - C_2^TL_0q(\tau), \quad L_0(0) = 0$$

$$(6.2.74)$$

The right-hand side term equations can be similarly obtained using (6.2.64) and (6.2.73), again for zeroth-order:

$$dR_0x(\sigma)/d\sigma = -C_1R_0z(\sigma), \quad R_0x(0) = 0$$
$$dR_0p(\sigma)/d\sigma = A_2^TR_0r(\sigma), \quad R_0p(0) = 0$$
$$dR_0z(\sigma)/d\sigma = -C_2R_0z(\sigma), \quad R_0z(0) = 0$$
$$dR_0q(\sigma)/d\sigma = -Q_2R_0z(\sigma) + C_2^TR_0q(\sigma), \quad R_0q(0) = q_1 - q(1)$$

$$(6.2.75)$$

Using the numerical values for the matrices in (6.2.74) and (6.2.75), the following exponentially decaying functions are obtained for the zeroth-order right- and left-hand side boundary layer terms

$$L_0z(\tau) = \begin{bmatrix} a_1e^{-1.2\tau} \\ a_2e^{-0.9\tau} \\ a_3e^{-\tau} \\ a_4e^{-\tau} \\ a_5(e^{-4\tau}+0.2e^{-\tau}) \end{bmatrix}, \quad L_0q(\tau) = -\begin{bmatrix} 0.83a_1e^{-1.2\tau} \\ 1.1a_2e^{-0.9\tau} \\ a_3e^{-\tau} \\ a_4e^{-\tau} \\ a_5(0.26e^{-4\tau}+0.2e^{-\tau}) \end{bmatrix},$$

$$L_0x(\tau) = \begin{bmatrix} 0 \\ 0 \\ 0 \\ -0.4a_1e^{-1.2\tau} \\ 0 \\ 0.084a_2e^{-0.9\tau}-12a_3e^{-\tau} \\ 0 \end{bmatrix}$$

$$(6.2.76)$$

$$L_0p(\tau) = -\begin{bmatrix} 0 \\ 32.3a_2e^{-0.9\tau}+1.53a_3e^{-\tau} \\ 8.4a_1e^{-1.2\tau}-4.2a_2e^{-0.9\tau} \\ -5.7a_1e^{-1.2}+0.78a_4e^{-\tau} \\ 0 \\ 0 \\ 0 \end{bmatrix}$$

where $a = (a_1 a_2 a_3 a_4 a_5)^T = L_0 z(0)$ and the right-hand side zeroth-order terms are

$$R_0 q(\sigma) = \begin{bmatrix} b_1 e^{-1.2\sigma} \\ b_2 e^{-0.9\sigma} \\ b_3 e^{-\sigma} \\ b_4(e^{-\sigma} - 0.2e^{-4\sigma}) \\ b_5 e^{-4\sigma} \end{bmatrix},$$

$$R_0 p(\sigma) = - \begin{bmatrix} 0 \\ 29b_1 e^{-0.9\sigma} - 1.5b_3 e^{-\sigma} \\ 10b_1 e^{-1.2\sigma} - 3.8b_2 e^{-0.9\sigma} \\ -6.9b_1 e^{-1.2\sigma} + b_4(0.78e^{-\sigma} + 0.16e^{-4\sigma}) \\ 0 \\ 0 \\ 0 \end{bmatrix}$$

where $b = (b_1 b_2 b_3 b_4 b_5)^T = R_0 q(0)$. Figures 6.5 through 6.7 show typical behavior of the slow and fast states and costate (adjoint) variables near the

**Figure 6.5** Reduced, first-order expansion and optimum responses for the strip tension ($y_7 = t_o$).

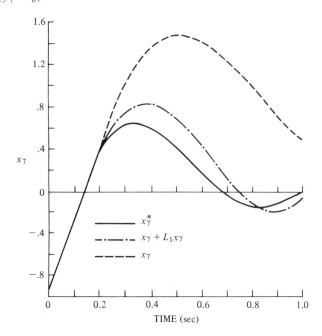

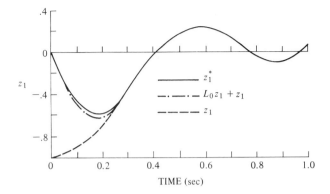

**Figure 6.6** Winding reel motor armature current $(z_1 = i_a)$ reduced, zeroth-order expansion and optimum responses.

endpoints and the rest of the interval. It is clear that the boundary level effect for the fast variables is quite pronounced. The optimum responses were obtained using the solution of a 12th-order matrix Riccati equation.

## 6.2.2.c The Multi-Time-Scale Approach

In Chapter 2 it was noted that a recent method of treating the optimal control of large-scale systems is multimodeling (Khalil and Kokotović, 1979a, b; Özgüner, 1979), where the system is decomposed into a slow and a number of fast subsystems. Both the decentralized and hierarchical controls

**Figure 6.7** Reduced, zeroth-order expansion and optimum responses for the adjoint variable (fast co-state).

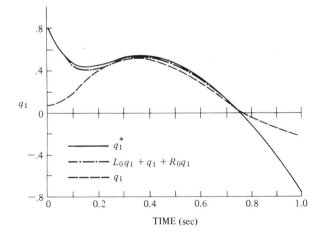

have been proposed. In this section the latter approach is briefly discussed, and a seventh-order example is used to illustrate it. Consider a large-scale system consisting of one slow and $N-1$ fast subsystems described by

$$\dot{x}_1 = A_{11}x_1 + \sum_{i=2}^{N} A_{1i}x_i + \sum_{i=1}^{N} B_{1i}u_i \tag{6.2.77}$$

$$\varepsilon \dot{x}_i = A_{i1}x_1 + A_{ii}x_i + B_{ii}u_i, \quad i = 2,\ldots,N \tag{6.2.78}$$

$$y_1 = C_{11}x_1, \quad y_i = C_{i1}x_1 + C_{ii}x_i \tag{6.2.79}$$

with a cost function

$$J = \frac{1}{2} \int_0^\infty \left( y^T y + \sum_{i=2}^{N} u_i^T R_i u_i \right) dt \tag{6.2.80}$$

In this formulation, the slow subsystem (6.2.77) acts as the coordinator at the second level and the other $N-1$ fast subsystems constitute the coordinator at the first level. This is similar to the dynamical hierarchical approach of decentralized stabilization of Section 5.3.6. The slow subsystem is influenced by $N-1$ local controls, $u_i$, $i = 2,\ldots,N$, given by

$$u_i = -F_{i1}x_1 - F_{ii}x_i, \quad i = 2,\ldots,N \tag{6.2.81}$$

where

$$F_{i1} \triangleq \left( I - R_i^{-1} B_{ii}^T K_{ii} A_{ii}^{-1} B_{ii} \right) R_i^{-1} \left( G_{oi}^T C_{oi} + B_{oi}^T K_1 \right) + \left( R_i^{-1} B_{ii}^T K_{ii} A_{ii}^{-1} A_{j1} \right) \tag{6.2.82}$$

$F_{ii} \triangleq R_i^{-1} B_{ii}^T K_{ii}$, $K_{ii}$ is $i$th fast subsystem's Riccati matrix,

$$0 = K_{ii}A_{ii} + A_{ii}^T K_{ii} - K_{ii}S_{ii}K_{ii} + C_{ii}^T C_{ii} \tag{6.2.83}$$

and $S_{ii} = B_{ii}R_i^{-1}B_{ii}^T$. The matrix $K_1$ is the slow subsystem Riccati matrix obtained from

$$0 = K_1 A + A^T K_1 - K_1 S K_1 + Q \tag{6.2.84}$$

The remaining matrices are

$$A = A_o - \sum_{i=2}^{N} B_{oi} R_i^{-1} G_{oi}^T C_{oi}, \quad S = \sum_{i=2}^{N} B_{oi} \left( R_i + G_{oi}^T G_{oi} \right) B_{oi}^T \tag{6.2.85a}$$

$$Q = C_o^T C_o - \sum_{i=2}^{N} C_{oi}^T G_{oi} \left( R_i + G_{oi}^T G_{oi} \right)^{-1} G_{oi}^T C_{oi}, \quad A_o = A_{11} - \sum_{i=2}^{N} A_{1i} A_{ii}^{-1} A_{i1} \tag{6.2.85b}$$

$$B_{oi} = B_{1i} - A_{1i} A_{ii}^{-1} B_{ii}, \quad C_{oi} = C_{i1} - C_{ii} A_{ii}^{-1} A_{i1} \tag{6.2.85c}$$

$$G_{oi} = -C_{ii} A_{ii}^{-1} B_{ii}, \quad i = 2,\ldots,N$$

Clearly, the original $n$th-order system optimal control problem has been reduced to $N$ linear regulators: one slow and $N-1$ fast problems. The existence conditions for these regulator problems are stabilizability and detectability of triplets $(C_{ii}, A_{ii}, B_{ii})$, $i = 2,\ldots,N$, and $(C_o, A_o, B_o)$. The following example illustrates the near-optimum control (6.2.81).

**Example 6.2.6.** Consider a seventh-order system

$$
\dot{x} = \left[\begin{array}{ccccccc}
0.2 & -1 & 0.1 & 0.1 & -0.1 & 0.3 & 0.1 \\
0.3 & -0.8 & 0.2 & 0.4 & -0.3 & -0.5 & -1 \\
-1 & 1 & -2.5 & 0 & 10 & 0 & 0 \\
4 & 5 & 2 & -10 & 2 & 0 & 0 \\
-10 & -20 & 8 & 5 & 10 & 0 & 0 \\
7.5 & 1 & 0 & 0 & 0 & 20 & 10 \\
-10 & 2.5 & 0 & 0 & 0 & -10 & 6
\end{array}\right] x
$$

$$
+ \left[\begin{array}{cc}
1 & -1 \\
0.25 & 0.1 \\
10 & 0 \\
5 & 0 \\
2.5 & 0 \\
0 & 10 \\
0 & 2
\end{array}\right] u
$$

$$
y = \left[\begin{array}{ccccccc}
1 & 1 & 0 & 0 & 0 & 0 & 0 \\
0.2 & 0.5 & 1 & 0.5 & 1 & 0 & 0 \\
0.1 & 0.1 & 0 & 0 & 0 & 2 & 1
\end{array}\right] x
\tag{6.2.86}
$$

Find a near-optimum control using the multi-time-scale method described above.

SOLUTION: Proceeding with the procedure discussed above, the system is assumed to be decomposed into a second-order slow and two fast subsystems of third and second order, as indicated by (6.2.86). Thus, it is assumed that the time-scale separation and/or weakly coupled conditions of Chapter 2 are somehow taken into account. The purpose of this example, in other words, is the construction of a near-optimum controller via the multi-time-scale approach of Özgüner (1979). The matrices $A$, $S$, $Q$, $K_1$, $K_{22}$, $K_{33}$ are

$$
A = \left[\begin{array}{cc} 1.78 & 1.41 \\ -0.38 & 1.12 \end{array}\right], \quad
S = \left[\begin{array}{cc} 2.02 & 0.46 \\ 0.46 & 0.95 \end{array}\right], \quad
Q = \left[\begin{array}{cc} 2.07 & 3.33 \\ 3.33 & 7.49 \end{array}\right]
$$

$$
K_1 = \left[\begin{array}{cc} 15.53 & -14.07 \\ -14.07 & 17.63 \end{array}\right], \quad
K_{22} = \left[\begin{array}{ccc} 1.224 & 0.521 & 2.242 \\ 0.521 & 0.228 & 0.984 \\ 2.242 & 0.984 & 4.801 \end{array}\right]
\tag{6.2.87}
$$

$$
K_{33} = \left[\begin{array}{cc} 7.843 & -5.307 \\ -5.307 & 13.596 \end{array}\right]
$$

The near-optimum controls when combined become

$$u^a = \begin{bmatrix} 9.35 & 4.64 & -2 & -0.88 & -3.93 & 0 & 0 \\ -16.41 & -4.93 & 0 & 0 & 0 & -6.78 & 2.58 \end{bmatrix} x$$

$$(6.2.88)$$

while the optimum control resulting from the solution of a seventh-order AMRE is

$$u^* = \begin{bmatrix} 6.5 & 8.92 & -2.7 & -1.07 & -6.2 & 0.61 & 0.045 \\ -6.65 & -0.90 & 0.4 & 0.155 & 1.06 & -7.4 & 2.22 \end{bmatrix} x$$

$$(6.2.89)$$

The respective time responses of the two control laws were reasonably close.

The method has been successfully applied to a seventh-order power system by Özgüner (1979). For further reading on the multi-time-scale approach, the reader is encouraged to refer to Khalil and Kokotović (1979b).

### 6.2.3 Hierarchical and Decentralized Methods

In Chapters 4 and 5 the hierarchical and decentralized controls were presented; several methods were discussed and supported by numerical examples. In this section, three of the methods for application to large-scale systems are presented. The first is the hierarchical control through structural perturbation discussed in detail in Section 4.4.2. Since the method has already been presented, only an illustrative example will be given here.

**Example 6.2.7.** Consider an eighth-order system which is a modified model for a power system:

$$\dot{x} = \begin{bmatrix} -5 & 0 & 0 & 0 & 4.75 & 0 & 0 & 0 \\ 0 & -2 & 0 & 0 & 0 & -2 & 0 & 0 \\ -0.08 & -0.11 & -3.99 & -0.93 & 0 & -0.07 & 0 & 9.1 \\ 0 & 0 & 1.32 & -1.39 & 0 & 0 & 0 & -0.28 \\ 0 & 0 & 0 & 0 & 0.2 & 0 & 0 & 0 \\ 0.17 & 0 & 0 & 0 & 0 & -0.1 & 0 & 0 \\ 0 & 0 & 0.2 & 0 & 0 & 0.01 & -0.5 & 0 \\ 0.01 & 0.01 & -0.6 & 0.12 & 0 & 0.01 & 0 & -0.11 \end{bmatrix} x$$

$$+ \begin{bmatrix} 0 & 0 \\ 0 & 0 \\ 10 & 0 \\ 0 & 0 \\ 0 & 4 \\ 0 & 0 \\ 0 & 0 \\ 0 & 0 \end{bmatrix} u \qquad (6.2.90)$$

It is required to find a near-optimum hierarchical control for this system by the structural perturbation of Section 4.4.2 using $Q = 4I_8$ and $R = 2I_2$.

SOLUTION: A careful inspection of the system (6.2.90) indicates that it can be decomposed into two fourth-order subsystems. Two independent fourth-order matrix Riccati equations were solved using $A_i$, $B_i$, $Q_i$, and $R_i$, $i = 1,2$. The feedback $P$ and the modified $B^p$ matrices turned out to be

$$P = \begin{bmatrix} -6.62 \times 10^{-3} & -9 \times 10^{-3} & 0.5338 & 0.205 & 0 & 0 & 0 & 0 & 0 \\ 0 & 0 & 0 & 0 & 0 & 0 & 0 & 0 & 1.365 \end{bmatrix}$$

$$B^p = \begin{bmatrix} -0.048 & -3.12 \\ -3.58 \times 10^{-3} & -2.13 \\ -1.025 & 0.06 \\ 0.184 & 3.3 \times 10^{-3} \\ -2.5 \times 10^{-3} & -3.7 \\ 4.5 \times 10^{-3} & -0.142 \\ -0.23 & 7.6 \times 10^{-4} \\ 0.43 & 0.011 \end{bmatrix} \qquad (6.2.91)$$

Based on the discussions made on structural perturbation in Section 4.4.2, the closed-loop system is

$$\dot{\hat{x}} = (A + G)\hat{x} - (B + B^p)P\hat{x} \qquad (6.2.92)$$

where the $-B^p\hat{x}$ represents the local control while $-B^pP\hat{x}$ is the "corrector," or "global," control to take systems interactions into account, and matrix $A + G$ is the system matrix in (6.2.90). The system (6.2.92) with an initial state $\hat{x}(0) = (1 \quad -1 \quad 1 \quad -1 \quad 1 \quad -1 \quad 1 \quad -1)^T$ was simulated and a cost function of $\hat{J} = 17.2687$ was obtained. For comparison purposes, an eighth-order AMRE was solved and an optimal centralized control was obtained to result in the following closed-loop system:

$$\dot{x}^* = (A + G - BF)x^* \qquad (6.2.93)$$

where

$$F = \begin{bmatrix} 5.7 \times 10^{-3} & 1.03 \times 10^{-2} & -1.12 & -0.322 \\ -0.335 & 2.24 \times 10^{-2} & 7.4 \times 10^{-4} & -2.2 \times 10^{-3} \end{bmatrix}$$

$$\begin{bmatrix} 1.85 \times 10^{-3} & 3.8 \times 10^{-3} & -0.136 & 0.386 \\ -1.62 & -0.83 & -3 \times 10^{-3} & -1.5 \times 10^{-2} \end{bmatrix}$$

with a cost function $J^* = 16.21$. A comparison between some of the states, i.e., $x_i^*$ and $\hat{x}_i$, $i = 1,3$, and 8, is shown in Figure 6.8. The responses of the two controllers are fairly close. Note that the optimal control requires the solution of $M = n(n+1)/2 = 36$ nonlinear simultaneous equations for the Riccati matrix, while the two subsystems combined need the solution of $n_1(n_1+1)/2 + n_2(n_2+1)/2 = 10 + 10 = 20$ equations with considerably less memory requirement.

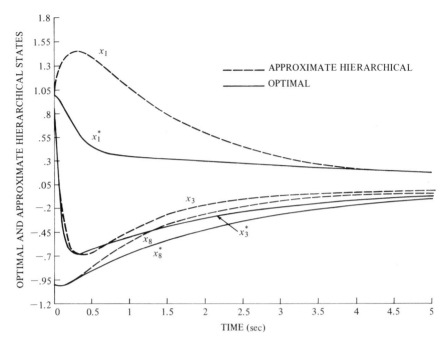

**Figure 6.8** A comparison of optimal and near-optimal states in a hierarchical control of Example 6.2.7.

The basic issues of decentralized control was presented in Chapter 5, where special emphasis was put on the "robust servomechanism" problem, which is not inherently an optimal control problem but rather a regulating (compensation) problem. The optimum and near-optimum decentralized control have been considered by many authors, among them are Chu (1974), Davison and Gesing (1979), Geromel and Bernussou (1979), Hassan et al. (1979), and Krtolica and Šiljak (1980). Chu (1974) has used local output feedback for the decentralized control of a string of coupled linear discrete-time systems utilizing bilateral $z$-transform (Melzer and Kuo, 1971; Ragazzini and Franklin, 1958). This method is most useful for transportation systems. Hassan et al. (1979) have applied the interaction prediction approach (Section 4.3.2) with a prespecified degree of stability and incorporating the structural perturbation (Section 4.4.2). This approach will be used in the next section for nonlinear large-scale systems. Krtolica and Šiljak (1980) have considered the problems of decentralized stochastic control and estimation with an estimate on the degradation of optimality, a discussion which is presented in Section 6.5. The remainder of this section is devoted to two algorithms for optimal decentralized control. One is a modification of the algorithm due to Geromel and Bernussou (1979) and the other is Sequential Optimization due to Davison and Gesing (1979), which is an extension of the sequentially stable robust control of the servomechanism problem (Section 5.4.5).

## 6.2.3.a Optimal Decentralized Control via Unconstrained Minimization

Consider a large-scale system described by a set of $N$ subsystems,

$$\dot{x}_i = A_{ii}x_i + B_iu_i + \sum_{j=1}^{N} A_{ij}x_j, \quad x_i(0) = x_{io}, \quad i = 1,\ldots,N \quad (6.2.94)$$

where $x_i$ and $u_i$ are $n_i$- and $m_i$-dimensional local state and control vectors, respectively. Geromel and Bernussou (1979) have proposed a set of $N$ totally decentralized control laws

$$u_i = -k_ix_i, \quad i = 1,2,\ldots,N \quad (6.2.95)$$

while minimizing a quadratic cost

$$J = \frac{1}{2}\sum_{i=1}^{N}\int_0^{\infty}\left(x_i^TQ_ix_i + u_i^TR_iu_i\right)dt \quad (6.2.96)$$

where each $Q_i$ and $R_i$ matrix pairs are positive-semidefinite and positive-definite, respectively. Defining the block and block-diagonal matrices

$$A = \{A_{ij}, i = 1,2,\ldots,N, j = 1,2,\ldots,N\}, \quad B = \text{Block-diag}(B_1, B_2,\ldots,B_N)$$

$$K = \text{Block-diag}(K_1, K_2,\ldots,K_N), \quad Q = \text{Block-diag}(Q_1, Q_2,\ldots,Q_N)$$

$$R = \text{Block-diag}(R_1, R_2,\ldots,R_N) \quad (6.2.97)$$

the above problem is reformulated as

$$\min_u : J = \frac{1}{2}\int_0^{\infty}\left(x^TQx + u^TRu\right)dt \quad (6.2.98)$$

$$\dot{x} = Ax + Bu, \quad x(0) = x_o \quad (6.2.99)$$

$$u = Kx \quad (6.2.100)$$

Unlike the Hamiltonian-based methods of optimizing with respect to the control function, the problem (6.2.98)–(6.2.100) can be solved through parameter optimization once the cost (6.2.98) as a function of $K$, i.e., $J(K)$, is obtained. This function can be obtained by

$$J(K) = \frac{1}{2}x_o^T\left(\int_0^{\infty}\Phi^T(t)(Q + K^TRK)\Phi(t)\,dt\right)x_o$$

$$= \text{tr}\left\{\frac{1}{2}\int_0^{\infty}\Phi^T(t)(Q + K^TRK)\Phi(t)\,dt(x_ox_o^T)\right\} \quad (6.2.101)$$

where $\Phi(t)$ is the transition matrix of closed-loop system, $\dot{x} = (A - BK)x$ and $\text{tr}\{\cdot\}$ represents trace of $\{\cdot\}$. With this expression for $J(K)$, the optimal decentralized control problem (6.2.98)–(6.2.100) is reduced to

$$\min_K J(K) = \text{tr}\{F(K)X_o\} \tag{6.2.102}$$

where $F(K)$ is the solution of the following matrix Lyapunov equation:

$$(A - BK)^T F + F(A - BK) + Q + K^T RK = 0 \tag{6.2.103}$$

and $X_o = x_o x_o^T$. Thus, the functional optimization problem with respect to $u(t)$ is reduced to a parametric one. This problem, however, depends on the initial state $x_o$ as formulated. In order to avoid this dependency, one can assume that $x_o$ is a random variable, and then an average value of $J(K)$ is chosen as the optimum cost. One possible way is to assume that $x_o$ is a uniformly distributed random variable, i.e., $X_o = E\{x_o x_o^T\} = (I/n)$, where $E\{\cdot\}$ is the expected value and $I$ is the identity matrix. Geromel and Bernussou (1979) have used the standard gradient method (Zoutendijk, 1970) and update $K$ by the so-called feasible direction matrix, which depends on the gradient of $J(K)$ with respect to $K$:

$$\nabla_K J(K) = G(K) = (RK - B^T F)P \tag{6.2.104}$$

where $P$ is obtained by a Lyapunov equation

$$(A - BK)P + P(A - BK)^T + X_o = 0 \tag{6.2.105}$$

and $F$ is the solution of (6.2.103). For a positive-definite solution of (6.2.103) and (6.2.105), the necessary and sufficient condition is that $(A - BK)$ be asymptotically stable (Barnett and Storey, 1970). Instead of using the feasible direction method, an algorithm is formed by using the well-known Davidon–Fletcher–Powell variable metric method (Fletcher and Powell, 1963). However, before the decentralized control algorithm is formally given, another algorithm for the iterative solution of the Lyapunov equation due to Davison and Man (1968) is considered. The following algorithm is presented without any further discussion.

***Algorithm 6.2.*** Solution of the Lyapunov Equation

*Step 1:* For the solution of a Lyapunov equation

$$A^T L + LA + S = 0 \tag{6.2.106}$$

where $A$ is a stable matrix, choose a step size $h = 10^{-4}/(2\|A\|)$ and set $L_o = hS$.

*Step 2:* Calculate the matrix

$$E = (I - hA/2 + h^2 A^2/12)^{-1}(I + hA/2 + h^2 A^2/12) \tag{6.2.107}$$

where $I$ is an identity matrix.

*Step 3:* Find the next value of $L$, i.e.,

$$L_{i+1} = (E^T)^{2^i} L_i E^{2^i} + L_i \qquad (6.2.108)$$

*Step 4:* Check if $\|\Delta L\| = \|L_{i+1} - L_i\| < \varepsilon$, a prespecified tolerance. If not, set $i = i + 1$ and go to Step 3.

*Step 5:* Stop.

It is emphasized that the above algorithm converges only if all the eigenvalues of $A$ have negative real parts. This algorithm was coded in BASIC, and it was found that in only ten iterations the algorithm converged to within six digits of accuracy. The following algorithm provides the solution for the desired optimal decentralized control problem.

**Algorithm 6.3.** Optimal Decentralized Control via Functional Minimization

*Step 1:* Select initial values $K = K_o$ and set $k = 0$.

*Step 2:* Solve Lyapunov equations (6.2.103) and (6.2.105) using $A$, $B$, $Q$, $R$, $X_o$, $K$ and Algorithm 6.2 for $P$ and $F$. Evaluate $J(K)$ and $G(K)$ using (6.2.102) and (6.2.104), respectively.

*Step 3:* Use the Fletcher–Powell method to update gain $K^k$

$$K^{k-\text{new}} = K^{k-\text{old}} + \varepsilon D^k \qquad (6.2.109)$$

where $D^k$ is the search direction during the $k$th iteration.

*Step 4:* Check whether convergence is achieved, e.g., $\|G(K_r^k)\| \leqslant \delta$, a prespecified tolerance value. If convergence is reached, stop; otherwise go to Step 2.

The above algorithm was also coded in BASIC and was used for optimal decentralized control system design. The following example illustrates this algorithm.

**Example 6.2.8.** Consider a fourth-order system

$$\dot{x} = \begin{bmatrix} 0 & 0.2 & 0.25 & 1 \\ -1 & -2 & 1 & 0 \\ -1 & 0.1 & 0.85 & 1 \\ 0.25 & -0.5 & 0 & -0.25 \end{bmatrix} x + \begin{bmatrix} 1 & 0 \\ 1 & 0 \\ 0 & 0.1 \\ 0 & 1 \end{bmatrix} u \qquad (6.2.110)$$

with a cost functional,

$$J = \frac{1}{2} \sum_{i=1}^{2} \int_0^{\infty} \left( x_i^T Q_i x_i + u_i^T R_i u_i \right) dt \qquad (6.2.111)$$

where $Q_i = 2I_{ni}$, $R_i = 2I_{mi}$ with $n_1 = n_2 = 2$ and $m_1 = m_2 = 1$. Find two decentralized gains $u_i = -K_i x_i$ such that $J$ is minimized.

SOLUTION: The two decentralized controllers are $u_1 = -K_1 x_1$ and $u_2 = -K_2 x_2$ with the following compact form

$$K = \begin{bmatrix} K_1 & 0 \\ 0 & K_2 \end{bmatrix} = \begin{bmatrix} k_{11} & k_{12} & 0 & 0 \\ 0 & 0 & k_{21} & k_{22} \end{bmatrix} \qquad (6.2.112)$$

Thus, there are four unknown gain parameters to be found. For a value of $X_o = I_4$ and two initial values of $K_o$,

$$K_o = \begin{bmatrix} 0.1 & 0.1 & 0 & 0 \\ 0 & 0 & 0.1 & 0.1 \end{bmatrix}, \quad K_o = \begin{bmatrix} 1 & 2 & 0 & 0 \\ 0 & 0 & 3 & 4 \end{bmatrix} \quad (6.2.113)$$

the Algorithm 6.3 converged in seven and 13 iterations, respectively. The resulting averaged optimum gain $K^*$ and the gradient matrix $\nabla_K J(K^*) = \partial J(K^*)/\partial K$ were found to be

$$K^* = \begin{bmatrix} 0.494 & 0.168 & 0 & 0 \\ 0 & 0 & 0.35 & 0.58 \end{bmatrix},$$

$$\nabla_K J(K^*) = \begin{bmatrix} -2.5 \times 10^{-3} & 1.4 \times 10^{-3} & 0 & 0 \\ 0 & 0 & 0.017 & 9.4 \times 10^{-3} \end{bmatrix}$$

$$(6.2.114)$$

which gives a $J^* = 1.0985$. The optimum decentralized control laws are then,

$$u_1^* = -0.494x_1 - 0.168x_2$$
$$u_2^* = -0.35x_3 - 0.58x_4 \qquad (6.2.115)$$

Further discussion on this algorithm and other examples are considered in Section 6.7 and Problem C6.4.


## 6.2.3.b  Decentralized Control via Sequential Optimization

In Section 5.4.5, the notion of sequentially stable robust control, proposed by Davison and Gesing (1979), was discussed, and Algorithm 5.9 was presented for it. In this section the sequentially stable robust controller is extended to an unconstrained optimization problem similar to the previous section's decentralized controller. Consider a large-scale system under the influence of $N$ decentralized controllers:

$$\dot{x} = Ax + \sum_{i=1}^{N} B_i u_i, \quad y_i = C_i x, \quad i = 1, 2, \ldots, N \qquad (6.2.116)$$

where $A$ is assumed to be stable and the control law is in a decentralized output feedback form

$$u_i = K_i y_i, \quad i = 1, 2, \ldots, N \qquad (6.2.117)$$

The sequentially stable control for this system was developed and is given by (5.4.45). The main problem of concern here is to add an optimizing controller to it, i.e., find a set of gains $\tilde{K}_i$ and $\tilde{K}^i$ such that an optimal control structure

$$u_i^* = u_i + \tilde{u}_i = K_i \hat{y}_i^m - K^i \eta_i + \tilde{K}_i \hat{y}_i^m - \tilde{K}^i \eta_i \qquad (6.2.118)$$

results while a quadratic cost

$$J\left(\tilde{K}_1, \tilde{K}^1, \ldots, \tilde{K}_N, \tilde{K}^N\right) = \mathrm{tr}\left\{ \frac{1}{2} \int_0^\infty \left( x^T Q x + \sum_{i=1}^N \tilde{u}_i^T R_i \tilde{u}_i \right) dt \right\} \qquad (6.2.119)$$

is minimized and the closed-loop system $\dot{x} = \{A + \sum_{i=1}^N B_i(K_i + \tilde{K}_i)\} x$ remains stable (Davison and Gesing, 1979). The term $\eta_i$ is the output of the $i$th compensator associated with control station $i$. Before the sequentially optimizing control algorithm is presented the following definition is given.

**Definition 6.1.** Sequentially Optimizing Controller. Consider a sequence of controls

$$u_i = K_i^j y_i, \quad i = 1, 2, \ldots, N, \quad j = 0, 1, \ldots \qquad (6.2.120)$$

which when applied to the system results in a sequentially stable closed-loop system $\dot{x} = (A + \sum_{i=1}^k B_i K_i^j C_i) x$ in the sense of Definition 5.6 for all $k \in [1, 2, \ldots, N]$ and $j = 0, 1, \ldots$ and such that

$$J\left( K_1^j, K_2^j, \ldots, K_i^j, K_{i+1}^{j-1}, \ldots, K_N^{j-1} \right)$$
$$\leqslant J\left( K_1^j, K_2^j, \ldots, K_{i-1}^j, K_i^{j-1}, K_{i+1}^{j-1}, \ldots, K_N^{j-1} \right) \qquad (6.2.121)$$

for $i = 1, 2, \ldots, N; j = 1, 2, 3, \ldots$. A sequence (6.2.120), if it exists, is called a "sequentially stabilizing" control.

The following algorithm provides the necessary steps for a sequentially stable optimizing decentralized control. The main deviation of this algorithm from that of Davison and Gesing (1979) is that here the direct search method of Rosenbrock (1960), which does not require the gradient vectors, is utilized rather than a conjugate gradient scheme suggested by Davison and Wang (1975). Moreover, the algorithm is described for the $\tilde{K}_i^j$ sequence for explanation purposes; the numerical examples, however, are solved for both $\tilde{K}^i$ and $\tilde{K}_i$ defined by (6.2.118).

*Algorithm 6.4.* Sequentially Optimizing Decentralized Controller

*Step 1:* Set $\tilde{K}_i^0 = 0$, $i = 1, 2, \ldots, N$; set $i = 0, j = 0$.

*Step 2:* Set $j = j + 1$, $i = i + 1$.

*Step 3:* Perform a prespecified number of direct search iterations of Rosenbrock's algorithm (Kuester and Mize, 1973) for $\tilde{K}_i^j$ and check the convergence condition $\| \tilde{K}_i^j - \tilde{K}_i^{j-1} \| \leqslant \varepsilon$. If $i > N$, stop. Otherwise go to Step 2.

Note that the optimizing function $J(\cdot)$, defined by (6.2.119), is obtained typically from the following Lyapunov equation:

$$\left( \tilde{A}_i^j + B_i \tilde{K}_i^j C_i \right)^T P_i^j + P_i^j \left( \tilde{A}_i^j + B_i \tilde{K}_i^j C_i \right) + \tilde{Q}_i^j + C_i^T \tilde{K}_i^{j^T} R_i \tilde{K}_i^j C_i = 0 \quad (6.2.122)$$

where

$$\tilde{A}_i^j \triangleq A + \sum_{k=i+1}^{N} B_k \tilde{K}_k^{j-1} C_k + \sum_{k=1}^{i-1} B_k \tilde{K}_k^j C_k$$

$$\tilde{Q}_i^j \triangleq Q + \sum_{k=i+1}^{N} C_k^T \tilde{K}_k^{j-1} R_k \tilde{K}_k^{j-1} C_k + \sum_{k=1}^{i-1} C_k^T \tilde{K}_k^{j^T} R_k \tilde{K}_k^j C_k \qquad (6.2.123)$$

and

$$\underset{\tilde{K}_i^j}{\mathrm{Min}\, J(\cdot)} = \underset{\tilde{K}_i^j}{\mathrm{Min\ tr}} \left\{ P_i^j \left( \tilde{K}_i^j \right) \right\} \qquad (6.2.124)$$

In the applications of this algorithm, the Lyapunov equation (6.2.122) was solved using the iterative method described by Algorithm 6.2. The following example illustrates the sequentially optimizing decentralized controller technique.

**Example 6.2.9.** Consider the system of Example 5.4.5, with a sequentially stable controller (5.4.62) already obtained. It is desired to find an additional sequentially optimizing component for each station, i.e.,

$$u_1^*(t) = -0.5 y_1^m(t) - \int_0^t e_1(\tau)\, d\tau + \tilde{u}_1 \qquad (6.2.125)$$

$$u_2^*(t) = 0.1 y_2^m(t) - 0.15 \int_0^t e_2(\tau)\, d\tau + \tilde{u}_2 \qquad (6.2.126)$$

while minimizing

$$J = \mathrm{tr} \left\{ \frac{1}{2} \int_0^\infty (x^T C^T C x + \tilde{u}^T \tilde{u})\, dt \right\} \qquad (6.2.127)$$

where

$$C = \begin{bmatrix} 1 & 1 & 0 & 0 & 0 \\ 0 & 0 & 1 & 1 & 1 \end{bmatrix}$$

Algorithm 6.4 along with Rosenbrock's (1960) minimization algorithm and Davison and Man's (1973) Lyapunov equation solution Algorithm 6.2 were

**Table 6.2**  Results of Example 6.2.9—Sequentially Optimizing
Decentralized Controller

| Iteration | $\tilde{K}_1^1$ | $\tilde{K}_1^2$ | $\tilde{K}_2^1$ | $\tilde{K}_2^2$ | $J$ |
|---|---|---|---|---|---|
| 0 | 0 | 0 | 0 | 0 | 0.044865 |
| 1 | $-0.2032$ | $-0.2032$ | 0 | 0 | 0.044755 |
| 2 | $-0.2032$ | $-0.2032$ | $-0.03077$ | $-0.03077$ | 0.044668 |
| 3 | $-0.2032$ | $-0.2370$ | $-0.03077$ | $-0.03077$ | 0.044668 |
| 4 | $-0.2032$ | $-0.2370$ | $-0.03077$ | $-0.03077$ | 0.044668 |

used on an HP-9845 computer with BASIC. The terms $\tilde{u}_i$, $i = 1, 2$, are first
rewritten by

$$\tilde{u}_1 = \tilde{K}_1^1 y_1^m + \tilde{K}_1^2 \int_0^\infty e_1(\tau)\, d\tau, \quad \tilde{u}_2 = \tilde{K}_2^1 y_2^m + \tilde{K}_2^2 \int_0^\infty e_2(\tau)\, d\tau$$

$$(6.2.128)$$

and thus the optimization is performed sequentially with respect to $\tilde{K}_1^1$, $\tilde{K}_1^2$,
$\tilde{K}_2^1$, and $\tilde{K}_2^2$. The results of the sequentially optimizing algorithm applied to
the fifth-order system are shown in Table 6.2. The algorithm converged in
just three iterations with a minimum cost of 0.044668. The optimal sequential stable decentralized controllers are then

$$u_1^*(t) = -0.7032\, y_1^m - 1.2370 \int_0^\infty e_1(\tau)\, d\tau$$

$$(6.2.129)$$

$$u_2^*(t) = 0.06923\, y_2^m - 0.18077 \int_0^\infty e_2(\tau)\, d\tau$$

which follows from (6.2.125)–(6.2.126), (6.2.128), and Table 6.2.

## 6.3 Near-Optimum Control of Large-Scale Nonlinear Systems

Throughout our discussions in Chapters 4 through 6, where the subject of
large-scale systems control has been discussed, the focus has been primarily
on large-scale linear TIV systems. In this section the case of nonlinear
systems is considered. A general approximate linearization scheme of optimally controlling nonlinear systems is first discussed. Then hierarchical and
perturbation control schemes will be discussed.

### 6.3.1 Near-Optimum Control via Sensitivity Methods

Consider a nonlinear system

$$\dot{x} = g(x, u), \quad x(0) = x_o \qquad (6.3.1)$$

where $x$, $u$, and $x_o$ are defined as before. The problem of finding an optimum control which satisfies (6.3.1) and minimizing a cost functional

$$J = L\left(x\left(t_f\right)\right) + \int_0^{t_f} V(x, u, t)\, dt \qquad (6.3.2)$$

has been of interest for several years. Although the optimization of this problem by the classical methods—gradient, Newton's second variation, etc.—is possible, near-optimum control laws have received special attention (Kelly, 1964; White and Cook, 1973; Garrard et al., 1967; Garrard, 1969, 1972; Garrard and Jordan, 1977; Werner and Cruz, 1968; Nishikawa et al., 1971; Kokotović et al., 1969a,b; Jamshidi, 1969, 1976a). Some of the methods suggested in literature have been "equivalent linearization" (White and Cook, 1973) and "approximate solution to the Hamilton–Jacobi–Bellman's equation" (Garrard et al., 1967; Garrard, 1969, 1972). Another approach is the so called "optimally adaptive" (Werner and Cruz, 1968), which minimizes the system cost functional regardless of plant parameters or initial condition variations. The control function is expanded in a MacLaurin's series of plant parameters and initial conditions. It has been asserted (Werner and Cruz, 1968) that for an $r$th-order truncation of the control function series, the optimum cost functional has been approximated up to $2r + 1$ terms. Another near-optimum control design developed by Nishikawa et al. (1971) takes on the general class of nonlinear systems given in Garrard et al. (1967) while making use of a similar parameter expansion as in the optimally adaptive control of Werner and Cruz (1968). The "optimally sensitive controller" (Kokotović et al., 1969a,b) is a first-order approximation of the optimally adaptive control which presents a convenient derivation of sensitivity equations from the maximum principle. Jamshidi (1969, 1976a) has extended the optimally sensitive control to a wider class of nonlinear systems than those considered by Garrard et al. (1967) and Nishikawa et al. (1971) while preserving the same order of approximation of the cost functional as in the optimally adaptive control. This method is briefly discussed here and a numerical example illustrates it.

Expanding (6.3.1) about a nominal (equilibrium) point, taken to be the origin for convenience, i.e., $x = 0$, $u = 0$, such that $g(0, 0) = 0$, then

$$\dot{x} = Ax + Bu + \varepsilon f(x, u) \qquad (6.3.3a)$$

where

$$A \triangleq \partial g / \partial x |x, u = 0 \qquad B \triangleq \partial g / \partial u |x, u = 0$$
$$f \triangleq g(x, u) - Ax - Bu \qquad (6.3.3b)$$

$\varepsilon \in [0, 1]$ is a scalar parameter and $A$ and $B$ are constant matrices of order $n \times n$ and $n \times m$, respectively. It is noted that for $\varepsilon = 0$, the nonlinear system (6.3.1) becomes linear, while for $\varepsilon = 1$, linearized system (6.3.3a) corresponds to the original system. This process of introducing a parameter in the original system in an attempt to "imbed" it in a family of similar problems such that the solution to one of its member (for $\varepsilon = 0$ in this case) is easily obtained. The scheme, known as "parameter imbedding," or "continuation" (Ortega and Rheinboldt, 1970), is to begin from the solution of the easy member in the family of problems by varying $\varepsilon$ from 0 to 1, until the solution of the desired problem is obtained. The uniqueness conditions for a solution to (6.3.3) are:

1. $x(\varepsilon)$, $u(\varepsilon)$ are continuously differentiable with respect to $\varepsilon$;
2. $f(\cdot)$ is continuously differentiable with respect to $x$ and $u$; and
3. $\partial f/\partial \varepsilon$ is continuous in $x$, $u$, and $\varepsilon$.

Now let us rewrite (6.3.3a) as

$$\dot{x}(t, \varepsilon) = h(x, u, t, \varepsilon) = Ax(t, \varepsilon) + Bu(t, \varepsilon) + \varepsilon f(x(t, \varepsilon), u(t, \varepsilon), \varepsilon) \quad (6.3.4)$$

$$x(t_o, \varepsilon) = x_o \quad (6.3.5)$$

Without loss of generality, the cost functional (6.3.2) is assumed to be quadratic:

$$J = \frac{1}{2}x^T(t_f, \varepsilon) Mx(t_f, \varepsilon) + \frac{1}{2}\int_0^{t_f}(x^TQx + u^TRu)\, dt \quad (6.3.6)$$

where $M$, $Q$, and $R$ satisfy the usual linear state regulator conditions. The necessary optimality conditions based on the maximum principle are

$$\dot{x} = H_p = h = Ax + Bu + \varepsilon f(x, u, \varepsilon), \quad x(t_0, \varepsilon) = x_0 \quad (6.3.7a)$$

$$\dot{p} = -H_x = -Qx - A^Tp - (\partial f/\partial x)^T p, \quad p(t_f, \varepsilon) = -Mx(t_f, \varepsilon) \quad (6.3.7b)$$

$$0 = H_u = -Ru + (B + \varepsilon(\partial f/\partial u))^T p \quad (6.3.8)$$

where

$$H = -\tfrac{1}{2}(x^TQx + u^TRu) + p^T(Ax + Bu + \varepsilon f(x, u, \varepsilon)) \quad (6.3.9)$$

is the Hamiltonian function and the subscripts denote vector gradients. Note that for nonzero values of $\varepsilon$, (6.3.7)–(6.3.9) represent a nonlinear TPBV problem whose solution is usually difficult to obtain. In order to overcome this difficulty let us differentiate (6.3.7)–(6.3.9) with respect to $\varepsilon$ and let $\varepsilon \to 0$, assuming that all conditions discussed above hold:

$$\dot{x}^1 = h_x x^1 + h_u u^1 + f, \quad x^1(t_0) = 0 \quad (6.3.10)$$

$$\dot{p}^1 = -H_{xx}x^1 - h_x^T p^1 - H_{xu}^T u^1 - f_x^T p, \quad p^1(t_f) = 0 \quad (6.3.11)$$

$$0 = H_{ux}^T x^1 + h_u^T p^1 + H_{uu}u^1 + f_u^T p \quad (6.3.12)$$

where $x^1 \triangleq \lim_{\varepsilon \to 0}\partial x(t, \varepsilon)/\partial \varepsilon$, similarly for $u^1$ and $p^1$, are sometimes referred to as first-order sensitivity functions (Kokotović et al., 1969a). Assuming that $H_{uu}$ is negative-definite, by eliminating $u^1$ in (6.3.10)–(6.3.11) by using (6.3.12), the following linear TPBV problem results:

$$\dot{x}^1 = Fx^1 + Ep^1 + \omega_0 \qquad (6.3.13)$$

$$\dot{p}^1 = Gx^1 - P^T p^1 + \delta_0 \qquad (6.3.14)$$

where

$$F = h_x - h_u H_{uu}^{-1} H_{ux}^T|_{\varepsilon \to 0} = A$$

$$G = H_{ux} H_{uu}^{-1} H_{ux}^T - H_{xx}|_{\varepsilon \to 0} = Q \quad \omega_0 = f - h_u H_{uu}^{-1} f_u p|_{\varepsilon \to 0} \qquad (6.3.15)$$

$$E = - h_u H_{uu}^{-1} h_u^T|_{\varepsilon \to 0} = BR^{-1} B^T \triangleq S, \quad \delta_0 = H_{xu}^T H_{uu}^{-1} f_u^T p - f_x p|_{\varepsilon \to 0}$$

It is well known (Kalman, 1960) that $x^1$ and $p^1$ are related by

$$p^1 = - Kx^1 + g_1 \qquad (6.3.16)$$

where $K$ is the symmetric positive-definite solution of the differential matrix Riccati equation (DMRE)

$$\dot{K} = - KA - A^T K + KSK - Q, \quad K(t_f) = M \qquad (6.3.17)$$

and $g_1$ is the solution of an adjoint vector equation

$$\dot{g}_1 = -(A - SK)^T g_1 + K\omega_0 + \delta_0 \qquad (6.3.18)$$

whose boundary condition in view of (6.3.11) and (6.3.16) is

$$g_1(t_f) = K(t_f) x^1(t_f) = Mx^1(t_f) \qquad (6.3.19)$$

Note that since only the final conditions of $K$ and $g_1$ are known, (6.3.17) and (6.3.18) must be solved backward in time.

Substituting $p^1$ of (6.3.16) in (6.3.13) results in

$$\dot{x}^1 = (A - SK)x^1 + Sg_1 + \omega_0 \qquad (6.3.20)$$

which can be solved for $x^1$. Considering (6.3.12) and (6.3.16), the first-order control sensitivity $u^1$ can be obtained:

$$u^1 = - R^{-1} B^T Kx^1 - R^{-1}(B^T g_1 + f_u^T p^0) = - R^{-1} B^T Kx^1 - \theta_1 \qquad (6.3.21)$$

where $p^0$ is the costate zeroth-order sensitivity or the costate vector itself which acts as the forcing function for the first-order terms evaluated along the "nominal trajectory." It is noted that (6.3.20)–(6.3.21) constitutes the first-order coefficients of the MacLaurin's series expansions of $x$ and $u$ in the parameter $\varepsilon$, i.e.,

$$x = x^0 + \varepsilon x^1 + \varepsilon^2 x^2/2! + \cdots, \quad u = u^0 + \varepsilon u^1 + \varepsilon^2 u^2/2! + \cdots \qquad (6.3.22)$$

The second-order terms $x^2$ and $u^2$ can be similarly obtained by differentiating (6.3.10)–(6.3.12) with respect to $\varepsilon$ and letting $\varepsilon \to 0$. This would require that the state, control, and costate vectors be continuously differentiable with respect to $\varepsilon$ as many times as the designer wishes, i.e.,

$$\dot{x}^i = (A - SK)x^i + Sg_i + \omega_{i-1} \qquad (6.3.23)$$

$$u^i = - R^{-1} B^T Kx^i - R^{-1}(B^T g_i + f_u^T p^{i-1}) = - R^{-1} B^T Kx^i - \theta_i \qquad (6.3.24)$$

for $i = 1, 2 \ldots$, where all coefficients are evaluated at $\varepsilon = 0$, i.e., along the "nominal trajectory." This is obtained by letting $\varepsilon \to 0$ in (6.3.7)–(6.3.8), which reduces the originally nonlinear TPBV problem to a linear regulator whose solution is

$$u^o = - R^{-1} B^T K x^o \qquad (6.3.25)$$

$$\dot{x}^o = (A - SK)x^o, \quad x^o(t_o) = x_o \qquad (6.3.26)$$

where $K$ is the solution of DMRE (6.3.17).

The proposed near-optimum control can now be shown to have an exact feedback and an approximate forward term. Substituting (6.3.25) and (6.3.24) in (6.3.23) results in the following:

$$u = - R^{-1} B^T K \sum_{i=0}^{\infty} \varepsilon^i x^i / i! - R^{-1} \sum_{i=1}^{\infty} \varepsilon^i \left( B^T g_i + f_u^T p^{i-1} \right) / i!$$

$$= - R^{-1} B^T K x - \sum_{i=1}^{\infty} \varepsilon^i \theta_i / i! \qquad (6.3.27)$$

Note that the second part of (6.3.27) was obtained in view of (6.3.22). The proposed $r$th-order near-optimum control can be obtained by truncating the second series in (6.3.27) after $r$ terms, i.e.,

$$u^r \simeq - R^{-1} B^1 K x - R^{-1} \sum_{i=1}^{r} \varepsilon^i \theta_i / i! \qquad (6.3.28)$$

which clearly shows that only the forward term contributes to the suboptimality of the control. Substituting (6.3.28) in (6.3.4) results

$$\dot{x}(t, \varepsilon) = (A - SK)x(t, \varepsilon) - BR^{-1} \sum_{i=1}^{r} \varepsilon^i \theta_i / i! + \varepsilon f(x(t, \varepsilon), u(t, \varepsilon,) \varepsilon)$$

$$(6.3.29)$$

It must be emphasized that by virtue of (6.3.25)–(6.3.26), (6.3.20)–(6.3.21), and (6.3.23)–(6.3.24) the homogeneous portions of all orders of the sensitivity functions remain the same. Furthermore, the solution of the $(i-1)$th terms should be used as the forcing function for evaluating the $i$th term. Figure 6.9 shows the structure of the proposed control, while the following algorithm provides the computational procedure.

*Algorithm 6.5.* Near-Optimum Control of Nonlinear Systems

*Step 1:* Input $A$, $B$, $Q$, $R$, $\varepsilon$, and $r$. Let $i = 1$.

*Step 2:* Solve DMRE (6.3.17) and store.

*Step 3:* Compute nominal state and control vectors using (6.3.25)–(6.3.26).

*Step 4:* Evaluate $(i-1)$th forcing terms $\delta_{i-1}$ and $\omega_{i-1}$ using (6.3.15) and the like.

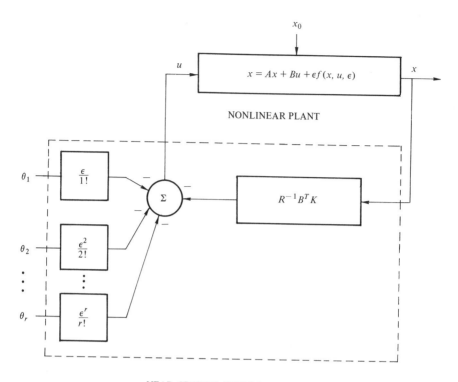

NEAR–OPTIMAL CONTROLLER

**Figure 6.9** Block diagram for the $r$th-order near-optimum controller.

*Step 5:* Compute the $i$th-order adjoint vector $g_i$ and sensitivity functions $x^i$, $p^i$, and $u^i$ using (6.3.20)–(6.3.21), (6.3.23), (6.3.24), and the like.

*Step 6:* Evaluate $i$th-order state and control vectors using (6.3.22).

*Step 7:* If $i = i + 1 \leqslant r$, go to Step 4.

*Step 8:* Stop.

The following example illustrates Algorithm 6.5.

**Example 6.3.1.** Consider a synthesis problem of a "control logic for a regulation system" (Garrard et al., 1967) whose torque source is a field control dc motor. The dynamic torque, field circuit equations are

$$J_L \frac{d^2(\delta\theta)}{dt^2} + B_L \frac{d(\delta\theta)}{dt} = (K_i E/R_a)i_f - (K_i K_b/R_a)\frac{d(\delta\theta)}{dt}i_f^2 \quad (6.3.30)$$

$$L_f \frac{di_f}{dt} + R_f i_f = e_f$$

In (6.3.30), $J_L$ = moment of inertia of the load, $\delta\theta$ = angular position error of the shaft, $B_L$ = friction loss coefficient, $\delta\dot{\theta} = \delta\omega$ is the angular velocity error of the shaft, $K_i$ = torque constant, $L_f$ = field resistance, $e_f$ = field voltage, $E$ = constant armature voltage, $R_a$ = armature resistance, and $K_b$ = back emf constant. Armature inductance has been neglected. The nonlinear term in (6.3.30) arises from the magnetization properties of the motor's ferromagnetic material. Equation (6.3.30) can be rewritten as

$$\dot{x}_1 = x_2$$
$$\dot{x}_2 = a_{22}x_2 + a_{23}x_3 - \varepsilon x_2 x_3^2 \qquad (6.3.31)$$
$$\dot{x}_3 = a_{33}x_3 + b_3 u$$

where $x_1 = \delta\theta$, $x_2 = \delta\omega$, $x_3 = i_f$, $u = e_f$, $a_{22} = -B_L/J$, $a_{23} = K_i E/J_L R_a$, $a_{33} = -R_f/L_f$, $b_3 = 1/L_f$, and $\varepsilon = K_i K_b/J_L R_a$. Since $R_a$ has a relatively large value, the magnitude of $\varepsilon$ is small compared to $a_{22}$ and $a_{23}$, and it is normally set equal to zero and the nonlinear term is neglected (Garrard et al., 1967). The performance index is $J = \frac{1}{2}\int_0^\infty (x'Qx + r_1 u^2)\, dt$. The control problem is to find a suitable near-optimum control which approximately minimizes $J$. For computational purposes, the same numerical values of previous work are used so that the result can be compared with those developed by Garrard et al. (1967) and the linearization scheme of White and Cook (1973):

$$\dot{x} = Ax + Bu + \varepsilon f(x) \qquad (6.3.32)$$

$$A = \begin{bmatrix} 0 & 1 & 0 \\ 0 & -0.2 & 2 \\ 0 & 0 & 5 \end{bmatrix}, \quad B = \begin{bmatrix} 0 \\ 0 \\ 1 \end{bmatrix}, \quad f = \begin{bmatrix} 0 \\ -x_2 x_3^2 \\ 0 \end{bmatrix}, \quad Q_1 = \begin{bmatrix} 2 & 0 & 0 \\ 0 & 2 & 0 \\ 0 & 0 & 2 \end{bmatrix}$$

$$r_1 = 1 \qquad (6.3.33)$$

and $\varepsilon = 0.20$. The nominal control and state trajectories are found from

$$u^o = -R^{-1}B^T K x^o = -1.41 x_1^o - 2.75 x_2^o - 11.16 x_3^o \qquad (6.3.34)$$

$$\dot{x}_1^o = x_2^o$$
$$\dot{x}_2^o = -0.2 x_2^o + 2 x_3^o \qquad (6.3.35)$$
$$\dot{x}_3^o = -1.41 x_1^o - 2.75 x_2^o - 6.16 x_3^o$$

Table 6.3 summarizes the cost functional $J$ for different initial conditions using the linearization scheme (White and Cook, 1973), suboptimal control using approximate solution of the Hamilton–Jacobi–Bellman's equation (Garrard et al., 1967), and the present method (Jamshidi 1976a). As seen from the table, the first-order near-optimum control proposed here results in the best overall performance. It is also noted that in view of Nishikawa et al. (1971) the optimum cost functional for the case $r = 0$ is approximated up to one term while for $r = 1$ it is approximated up to $2 + 1 = 3$ terms. Thus, it is not surprising that the $r = 1$ control law is closer to the exact

**Table 6.3**  Comparison of the Cost Functional of Example 6.3.1
Using Three Methods

| | Cost Functional $J$ Initial State $x_0$ | | |
|---|---|---|---|
| | $\begin{bmatrix} 0.10 \\ 0.10 \\ 0.10 \end{bmatrix}$ | $\begin{bmatrix} 0.25 \\ 0.25 \\ 0.25 \end{bmatrix}$ | $\begin{bmatrix} 0.50 \\ 0.50 \\ 0.50 \end{bmatrix}$ |
| Linearization (White and Cook, 1973) | 0.2293 | 1.1297 | 4.1941 |
| Approximate Hamilton–Jacobi– Bellman's equation (Garrard et al., 1967) | 0.2288 | 1.1259 | 4.0627 |
| Algorithm 6.3 | | | |
| $r = 0$ | 0.2165 | 1.0722 | 3.9520 |
| $r = 1$ | 0.2162 | 1.0712 | 3.9349 |

optimum solution. Further comments regarding this point are given in Section 6.5.

## 6.3.2  Hierarchical Control via Interaction Prediction

Recently the hierarchical control of nonlinear systems has received a great deal of attention. The straight application of goal coordination or interaction prediction to nonlinear systems does not, in general, provide a global sufficiency condition for optimum solution (Singh, 1980). The basic problem is that as a result of the lack of sufficiency condition in goal coordination, for example, there is a possibility for a "duality gap," i.e., a difference between the primal problem minimum and the dual problem maximum. In Chapter 4 where linear systems with linear interaction were considered it was deduced that the "duality gap" was zero. The fundamental reason behind this deduction was the theorem of Strong Lagrange Duality (Geoffrion, 1971), which requires that the interaction constraints be convex. However, the application of goal coordination to nonlinear systems, used by some authors (Bauman, 1968; Smith and Sage, 1973) does not have a guaranteed sufficiency condition, since the nonlinear interaction constraints are not convex in general.

There are at least two approaches where for certain special cases the goal coordination can be used where no duality gap would exist. First consider the following optimization problem:

$$\begin{aligned} \text{Maximize} \quad & J(x) \\ \text{Subject to} \quad & f(x) \in \phi \\ & x \in X \end{aligned} \qquad (6.3.36)$$

where $J(x)$ is a convex function, $X$ is a convex set, and $\phi$ has either of the two forms: $\phi = \{0\}$ or $\phi = \{v: v \leqslant 0\}$, $v \in R^m$. The dual problem is

$$\underset{\alpha \geqslant 0}{\text{Minimize}} \quad \underset{x \in X}{\text{Maximize}} \left\{ J(x) + \alpha^T f(x) \right\} \qquad (6.3.37)$$

For the case when $\phi\{v: v \leqslant 0\}$, problems (6.3.36) and (6.3.37) have the same solutions if $f(x)$ is a convex vector function (Javdan, 1976a). If $\phi = \{0\}$, the two problems can have the same solution only if $f(x)$ is linear (Whittle, 1971). Therefore, a more general convex constraints can be handled if the optimization problem has inequality constraints instead of equality constraints. One way to guarantee a solution for problems with equality constraints is to have all inequality constraints binding at optimum. More specifically, consider a modified version of the following problem:

$$\text{Maximize} \quad J(x) + u^T f(x)$$

$$\text{Subject to} \quad f(x) \leqslant 0, \quad x \in X, u \in R^m \qquad (6.3.38)$$

If a vector $u$ can be found such that inequality constraints in (6.3.38) are binding at optimum then the dual coordination would work for such a problem (Singh, 1980). Although it may not be an easy task to find a $u$ for a general convex problem which makes all inequalities binding at optimum, some attempts have been made to find a suitable $u$ for certain special cases. Javdan (1976a) has readily obtained a $u$ for certain quadratic constraints. The class of quadratic problems considered is one in which each second-order nonlinear term appears only once in the equality constraints. More insight in this approach can be obtained by referring to Javdan (1976a, b) or Singh (1980). An alternative approach for handling equality constraints is suggested by Simmons (1975) which assumes that there exist buffer stores between the interconnected subsystems. The basic idea here, due to Whittle (1971), is that one satisfy each interconnection constraint on the average instead of instantaneously. Under such average satisfaction of interconnection constraint, the strong Lagrangian principle works and the corresponding goal coordination solution is the best one. There are several examples where the goal coordination has been successfully applied. Bauman (1968) has applied it to a sliding mass system with linear interaction constraint and has used the modification on the constraints discussed in Section 4.2.6.a to avoid singular solutions. Singh (1980) has considered the same system and has used the modification of Titli et al. (1975) discussed in Section 4.3.3.b, to curb singularities. The remainder of this section is devoted to a new application of the interaction prediction method to nonlinear systems due to Hassan and Singh (1976) and Singh (1980). The method is applied to a sixth-order power system.

Following the linearization procedure of Section 6.3.1, for the sake of computational convenience, assume that the origin is an equilibrium point and linearize a large-scale nonlinear system $\dot{x} = h(x, u)$, $x(0) = x_o$ about it to obtain

$$\dot{x} = A_d x + B_d u + f(x, u), \quad x(0) = x_o \tag{6.3.39}$$

where

$$f(x, u) \triangleq A_o x + B_o u + h(x, u) - Ax - Bu$$

$$A = \partial h(\cdot)/\partial x^o, \quad B = \partial h(\cdot)/\partial u^o$$

similar to what is defined in (6.3.3b), $A_d$, $A_o$, $B_d$, and $B_o$ are, respectively, block-diagonal and block-off-diagonal parts of $A$ and $B$, i.e.

$$A_d \triangleq \text{Block-diag}(A_1, A_2, \ldots, A_N), \quad B_d = \text{Block-diag}(B_1, B_2, \ldots, B_N)$$

$$A_o = \begin{bmatrix} 0 & A_{12} & \cdots & A_{1N} \\ A_{21} & 0 & & \\ \vdots & & \ddots & \vdots \\ A_{N1} & \cdots & & 0 \end{bmatrix}, \quad B_o = \begin{bmatrix} 0 & B_{12} & \cdots & B_{1N} \\ B_{21} & 0 & & \\ \vdots & & \ddots & \vdots \\ B_{N1} & \cdots & & 0 \end{bmatrix}$$

$$\tag{6.3.40}$$

The optimal control problem is to find a control $u$ which satisfies (6.3.39) while minimizing a quadratic cost function

$$J = \frac{1}{2} \int_0^{t_f} (x^T Q x + u^T R u) \, dt \tag{6.3.41}$$

As in Chapter 4, it is assumed that the large-scale nonlinear system (6.3.39) can be decomposed into $N$ small-scale subsystems:

$$\dot{x}_i = A_i x_i + B_i u_i + f_i(x, u), \quad x_i(0) = x_{io} \tag{6.3.42}$$

Furthermore, for the sake of the present discussion, it is assumed that the cost (6.3.41) is separable, i.e.,

$$J = \sum_{i=1}^N J_i = \sum_{i=1}^N \frac{1}{2} \int_0^{t_f} (x_i^T Q_i x_i + u_i^T R_i u_i) \, dt \tag{6.3.43}$$

where $Q = \text{Block-diag}(Q_1, Q_2, \ldots, Q_N)$ and $R = \text{Block-diag}(R_1, R_2, \ldots, R_N)$ are, respectively, assumed to be positive-semidefinite and positive-definite.

Hassan and Singh (1976) and Singh (1980) suggest a two-level hierarchical structure in which the second level (coordinator) is assumed to provide composite state and control vectors $x = x^o$ and $u = u^o$ to the first level, which in view of (6.3.42), reduces the problem to $N$ independent problems:

$$\text{Minimize} \quad J_i = \frac{1}{2} \int_0^{t_f} (x_i^T Q_i x_i + u_i^T R_i u_i) \, dt \tag{6.3.44}$$

$$\text{Subject to} \quad \dot{x}_i = A_i x_i + B_i u_i + f_i(x^o, u^o), \quad x_i(0) = x_{io} \tag{6.3.45}$$

where $x^o$ and $u^o$ are initial values for the equivalent state and control vectors, respectively. These vectors, as will be seen shortly, would be periodically updated through an interaction prediction-type algorithm at the second level. Singh (1980) and Hassan and Singh (1976) further suggest adding two additional penalty terms in the cost function (6.3.44),

$$
\begin{aligned}
J_i^o = \frac{1}{2} \int_0^{t_f} & \left\{ x_i^T Q_i x_i + \left( x_i - x_i^o \right)^T V_i \left( x_i - x_i^o \right) + u_i^T R_i u_i \right. \\
& \left. + \left( u_i - u_i^o \right)^T W_i \left( u_i - u_i^o \right) \right\} dt \\
\triangleq \int_0^{t_f} & L_i \left( x_i, x_i^o, u_i, u_i^o \right) dt
\end{aligned}
\tag{6.3.46}
$$

for regulation purposes. The solutions to the first-level problems (6.3.45)–(6.3.46) follow the same Riccati formulation discussed in Section 6.3.1, except for two additional linear equality constraints:

$$
x_i - x_i^o = 0, \quad u_i - u_i^o = 0
\tag{6.3.47}
$$

Taking these two constraints into account, the $i$th subsystem Hamiltonian becomes

$$
\begin{aligned}
H_i^o = & - L_i \left( x_i, x_i^o, u_i, u_i^o \right) + p_i^T \left( A_i x_i + B_i u_i + f_i \left( x^o, u^o \right) \right) \\
& + \alpha_i^T \left( x_i - x_i^o \right) + \beta_i^T \left( u_i - u_i^o \right)
\end{aligned}
\tag{6.3.48}
$$

where $p_i$, $\alpha_i$, and $\beta_i$ are $n_i$-, $n_i$-, and $m_i$-dimensional costate vectors, Lagrange multiplier vectors corresponding to the additional equality constraints (6.3.47). Writing the necessary conditions of the maximum principle, assuming $p_i = -K_i x_i + g_i$, eliminating $u_i$ in the necessary conditions, and following a procedure similar to the derivations of sensitivity functions of (6.3.10)–(6.3.21), the optimum $i$th subsystem equation becomes

$$
\dot{x}_i = \left( A_i - \tilde{S}_i K_i \right) x_i + B_i d_i \left( g_i, u_i^o, \beta_i \right) + f_i \left( x^o, u^o \right)
\tag{6.3.49}
$$

where $K_i$ is the solution of the $i$th subsystem Riccati equation

$$
\dot{K}_i = -K_i A_i - A_i^T K_i + K_i \tilde{S}_i K_i - \tilde{Q}_i, \quad K_i \left( t_f \right) = 0
\tag{6.3.50a}
$$

$$
\tilde{S}_i = B_i \tilde{R}_i^{-1} B_i^T, \quad \tilde{R}_i = R_i + W_i
\tag{6.3.50b}
$$

$$
\tilde{Q}_i = Q_i + V_i
$$

function

$$
d_i ( \cdot ) = \tilde{R}_i^{-1} \left( B_i^T g_i + W_i u_i^o + \beta_i \right)
\tag{6.3.51}
$$

$g_i$ is the solution of the $i$th subsystem adjoint vector equation

$$
\dot{g}_i = - \left( A_i - \tilde{S}_i K_i \right)^T g_i + K_i B_i \left( W_i u_i^o - \beta_i \right) - K_i f_i \left( x^o, u^o \right) - \alpha_i,
$$

$$
g_i \left( t_f \right) = 0
\tag{6.3.52}
$$

and the optimum local control is

$$
u_i = - \tilde{R}_i^{-1} B_i^T K_i x_i + d_i \left( g_i, u_i^o, \beta_i \right)
\tag{6.3.53}
$$

The relations (6.3.49), (6.3.50), (6.3.52), and (6.3.53) constitute the essential computations at the first level, with the DMRE (6.3.50a) to be solved only once during all subsequent first-second level iterations. DMREs (6.3.50a) can be solved either by the "doubling" scheme (Davison and Maki, 1973) or by straight backward integration (Jamshidi, 1980).

The second-level problem is basically to try to find a set of Lagrange multipliers $\alpha_i(t)$, $\beta_i(t)$ for all $i = 1, 2, \ldots, N$ and $0 \leqslant t \leqslant t_f$ such that the constraints (6.3.47) are satisfied. In other words, $x_i^o$, $u_i^o$, $\alpha_i$, and $\beta_i$ must be updated based on a prediction mechanism. In order to reach this mechanism, it is noted that the $i$th subsystem Hamiltonian (6.3.48) must also be extremized with respect to $x_i^o$, $u_i^o$, $\alpha_i$, and $\beta_i$, i.e.,

$$\partial H_i^o / \partial \alpha_i = 0, \quad \partial H_i^o / \partial \beta_i = 0, \quad \partial H_i^o / \partial x_i^o = 0, \quad \partial H_i^o / \partial u_i^o = 0 \quad (6.3.54)$$

The above relations along with (6.3.47) give the desired interaction prediction iterations for the second level:

$$\alpha = \alpha(x, p) = V(x - x^o) + \left\{ A_o^T + \left[ \partial h(x^o, u^o) / \partial x^o \right]^T - A^T \right\} p \quad (6.3.55a)$$

$$\beta = \beta(u, p) = W(u - u^o) + \left\{ B_o^T + \left[ \partial h(x^o, u^o) / \partial u^o \right]^T - B^T \right\} p \quad (6.3.55b)$$

The above relations along with (6.3.47) give the desired interaction prediction iterations for the second level:

$$\begin{bmatrix} x^o \\ \alpha \\ u^o \\ \beta \end{bmatrix}^{l+1} = \begin{bmatrix} x^l \\ \alpha(x^l, p^l) \\ u^l \\ \beta(u^l, p^l) \end{bmatrix} \quad (6.3.56)$$

where the right-hand side of (6.3.56) is obtained by substituting the values of $x^l = (x_1^{Tl} x_2^{Tl} \cdots x_N^{Tl})^T$, $u^l = (u_1^{Tl} u_2^{Tl} \cdots u_N^{Tl})^T$ as well as $x^{ol}$ and $u^{ol}$ in (6.3.55).

The interaction errors can be expressed by the following;

$$\text{Error}_x^l = \left\{ \int_0^{t_f} \sum_{i=1}^{N} \| \Delta x_i^{ol} \|^2 \, dt \right\}^{1/2} \quad (6.3.57)$$

$$\text{Error}_\alpha^l = \left\{ \int_0^{t_f} \sum_{i=1}^{N} \| \Delta \alpha_i^l \|^2 \, dt \right\}^{1/2} \quad (6.3.58)$$

where

$$\Delta x_i^l = x_i^{ol+1} - x_i^{ol}, \quad \Delta \alpha_i^l = \alpha_i^{l+1} - \alpha_i^l \quad (6.3.59)$$

The application of the interaction prediction approach to nonlinear system (6.3.1) is summarized by the following algorithm.

**Algorithm 6.6.** Hierarchical Control of Large-Scale Nonlinear Systems via Interaction Prediction

*Step 1:* Start with initial values $x^o$, $u^o$, $\alpha$, and $\beta$ at level 2.

*Step 2:* Solve $N$ matrix Riccati equations of type (6.3.50a) for $K_i$, $i = 1, 2, \ldots, N$, and store at level 1.

*Step 3:* Solve $N$ adjoint vector equations of type (6.3.52) for $g_i$, $i = 1, 2, \ldots, N$, and store at level 1.

*Step 4:* Solve for $x_i, u_i$, $i = 1, 2, \ldots, N$, using (6.3.49) and (6.3.53), collate and store $x^T = (x_1^T x_2^T \cdots x_N^T)$, $u^T = (u_1^T u_2^T \cdots u_N^T)$, and transmit values to second level.

*Step 5:* Use the latest values of $x$, $u$, $x^o$, $u^o$ to predict new values of $x^o$, $u^o$, $\alpha$, and $\beta$ using (6.3.56).

*Step 6:* Check whether the interaction errors (6.3.57)–(6.3.58) are within some tolerance $\varepsilon$. If not, go to Step 3.

*Step 7:* Stop.

The following example illustrates this algorithm.

**Example 6.3.2.** Consider the open-loop model of a sixth-order power system which was originally developed by Iyer and Cory (1971) and further considered by Mukhopadhyay and Malik (1973) and Jamshidi (1975a):

$$\dot{x}_1 = x_2$$
$$\dot{x}_2 = -c_1 x_2 - c_2 x_3 \sin x_1 - 0.5 c_3 \sin 2x_1 + x_5/M$$
$$\dot{x}_3 = x_6 - c_4 x_3 + c_5 \cos x_1$$
$$\dot{x}_4 = k_1 u_1 - k_2 x_2 - k_3 x_4 \qquad\qquad (6.3.60)$$
$$\dot{x}_5 = k_4 x_4 - k_5 x_5$$
$$\dot{x}_6 = k_6 u_2 - k_7 x_6$$

where $x_1$ = rotor angle, $x_2$ = Park's transformation variable, $x_3$ = field flux linkage, $x_4$ = turbine's input steam power, $x_5$ = mechanical input torque, $x_6$ = normalized field voltage, $u_1$ = speeder gear setting, and $u_2$ = normalized exciter voltage. The cost function is

$$J = \int_0^2 \{(x_1 - 0.7105)^2 + x_2^2 + 0.1(x_3 - 5.604)^2$$
$$+ 0.5(x_4 - 0.8)^2 + 0.5(x_5 - 0.8)^2 + (x_6 - 2.645)^2$$
$$+ 100(u_1 - 0.4236)^2 + 10(u_2 - 0.8817)^2\} \, dt \qquad (6.3.61)$$

which indicates that the equilibrium point of the system is

$$x^o = ( 0.7105 \quad 0 \quad 5.604 \quad 0.8 \quad 0.8 \quad 2.645 )^T$$
$$u^o = ( 0.4236 \quad 0.8817 )^T \tag{6.3.62}$$

and the initial state was chosen as $x(0) = x^o$. It is desired to find the optimal control for this system by the hierarchical approach outlined in Algorithm 6.6.

SOLUTION: Numerical values for system (6.3.60) were calculated using the data by Mukhapadhyay and Malik (1973), $c_1 = 2.165$, $c_2 = 14$, $c_3 = -55.56$, $c_4 = 1.02$, $c_5 = 4.05$, $k_1 = 9.443$, $k_2 = 1.02$, $k_3 = 5$, $k_4 = 2.04$, $k_5 = 2.04$, $k_6 = 1.5$, $k_7 = 0.5$ and $M = 1.0$. The linearized matrices $A$ and $B$ are

$$A = \begin{bmatrix} 0 & 1 & 0 & 0 & 0 & 0 \\ -51.2 & -2.16 & -9.02 & 0 & 29.6 & 0 \\ -2.61 & 0 & -1.02 & 0 & 0 & 1 \\ 0 & -1.02 & 0 & -5 & 0 & 0 \\ 0 & 0 & 0 & 2.04 & -2.04 & 0 \\ 0 & 0 & 0 & 0 & 0 & -0.5 \end{bmatrix}$$

$$B = \begin{bmatrix} 0 & 0 \\ 0 & 0 \\ 0 & 0 \\ 9.443 & 0 \\ 0 & 0 \\ 0 & 1.5 \end{bmatrix} \tag{6.3.63}$$

The system was decomposed into two subsystems of orders $n_1 = 4$ and $n_2 = 2$ with $m_1 = m_2 = 1$. The solution, in accordance with Algorithm 6.6, was followed by solving two matrix Riccati equations using a fourth-order Runge–Kutta method and the elements of the corresponding Riccati matrices were fitted to third-order polynomials. The two subsystems Riccati formulations are summarized here:

*Subsystem 1:*

$$A_1 = \begin{bmatrix} 0 & 1 & 0 & 0 \\ -51.2 & -2.16 & -9.02 & 0 \\ -2.64 & 0 & -1.02 & 0 \\ 0 & -1.02 & 0 & -5 \end{bmatrix}, \quad B_1 = \begin{bmatrix} 0 \\ 0 \\ 0 \\ 9.443 \end{bmatrix},$$

$$\tilde{R}_1 = 100, \quad \tilde{Q}_1 = \text{diag}( 1 \quad 1 \quad 0.1 \quad 0.5 )$$

$$K_1(t) = \begin{bmatrix} \dfrac{\begin{array}{l} 9.94 - 2.4t + 4.5t^2 - 2.9t^2 \\[2pt] \end{array}}{} & \dfrac{\begin{array}{l} -0.15 + 0.8t - 1.25t^2 + 0.43t^2 \\[2pt] 0.2 - 0.071t + 0.133t^2 - 0.074t^2 \end{array}}{} \\[20pt] \rule{1cm}{0.4pt} & \rule{1cm}{0.4pt} \end{bmatrix}$$

$$\begin{bmatrix} \begin{array}{l} 1.62 - 0.18t + 0.44t^2 - 0.38t^3 \\ 10^{-2}(-5.8 + 2t - 3t^2 + 1.7t^2) \\ 0.71 - 0.07t + 0.02t^2 - 0.08t^3 \\[4pt] \rule{1cm}{0.4pt} \end{array} & \begin{array}{l} 0.03 - 0.024t + 0.043t^2 - 0.02t^3 \\ 10^{-3}(-3.3 + 3.4t - 5.8t^2 + 2.4t^3) \\ 10^{-3}(5 - 4.25t + 7.5t^2 - 3.3t^3) \\ 10^{-2}(5.3 - 4t + 7.3t^2 - 3.3t^3) \end{array} \end{bmatrix}$$

$$(6.3.64)$$

*Subsystem 2:*

$$A_2 = \begin{bmatrix} -2.04 & 0 \\ 0 & -0.5 \end{bmatrix}, \quad B_2 = \begin{bmatrix} 0 \\ 1.5 \end{bmatrix}, \quad \tilde{R}_2 = 10, \quad \tilde{Q}_2 = \text{diag}(0.5 \quad 1)$$

$$K_2(t) = \begin{bmatrix} 0.127 - 0.064t + 0.123t^2 - 0.06t^3 & 0 \\ 0 & 0.78 - 0.11t + 0.015t^2 - 0.77t^3 \end{bmatrix}$$

$$(6.3.65)$$

The algorithm was simulated on an HP-9845 computer using BASIC. The first-level problem is essentially to solve for the two subsystems adjoint vectors $g_i(t)$, $i = 1, 2$, by integrating (6.3.50) and (6.3.52) backward in time, integrating (6.3.49) for $x_i(t)$, $i = 1, 2$, forward in time, and evaluating $u_i(t)$ using (6.3.53). The second-level problem follows (6.3.56) and is obtained for this example from

$$x^{ol+1} = x^{ol} \tag{6.3.66a}$$

$$\alpha^{l+1} = V(x - x^o) + \left\{ A_o^T - A^T + \left[ \partial h(x^{ol}, u^{ol}) / \partial x^{ol} \right]^T \right\} p^l \tag{6.3.66b}$$

$$u^{ol+1} = u^{ol} \tag{6.3.66c}$$

$$\beta^{l+1} = W(u - u^o) + \left\{ B_o^T - B^T + \left[ \partial h(x^{ol}, u^{ol}) \partial u^{ol} \right]^T \right\} p^l \tag{6.3.66d}$$

where

$$\partial h(\cdot) / \partial x^o$$

$$= \begin{bmatrix} 0 & 1 & 0 & 0 & 0 & 0 \\ -c_2 x_2^o \cos x_1^o - c_3 \cos 2x_1^o & -c_1 & -c_2 \sin x_1^o & 0 & 1/M & 0 \\ -c_5 \sin x_1^o & 0 & -c_4 & 0 & 0 & 1 \\ 0 & -k_2 & 0 & -k_3 & 0 & 0 \\ 0 & 0 & 0 & k_4 & k_5 & 0 \\ 0 & 0 & 0 & 0 & 0 & -k_7 \end{bmatrix}$$

$$(6.3.67a)$$

$$\partial h(\cdot)/\partial u^o = B = \begin{bmatrix} 0 & 0 \\ 0 & 0 \\ 0 & 0 \\ k_1 & 0 \\ 0 & 0 \\ 0 & k_6 \end{bmatrix} \qquad (6.3.67b)$$

The interaction prediction method converged in 14 iterations. Typical responses, such as rotor angle $x_1(t)$, speeder gear setting $u_1(t)$, and exciter voltage versus time are shown in Figure 6.10. The results are in close agreement with the previous one-level optimization methods, such as quasi-linearization (Mukhopadhyay and Malik, 1973) and parameter imbedding (Jamshidi, 1975a). The latter approach is discussed in Section 6.3.3a.

The interaction prediction methods seem to be very promising due to their simple computational requirements. Below a brief outline of the convergence property of the method is given.

Singh (1980) and Hassan and Singh (1976) have established the following conditions:

1. $\|G\| < 1$
2. $(x, u, \alpha, \beta)$ and $h(x, u)$ are bounded functions of time

---

**Figure 6.10** Typical responses for the power system of Example 6.3.2: (a) rotor angle $x_1(t)$, (b) speeder gear setting $u_1(t)$, and (c) exciter voltage $u_2(t)$.

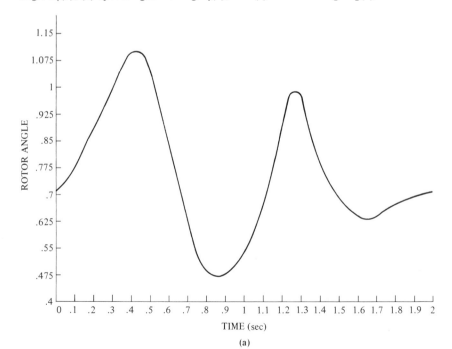

(a)

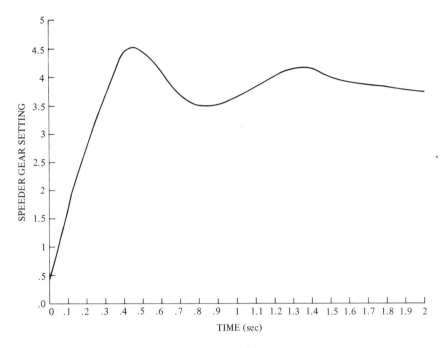

**Figure 6.10(b)**

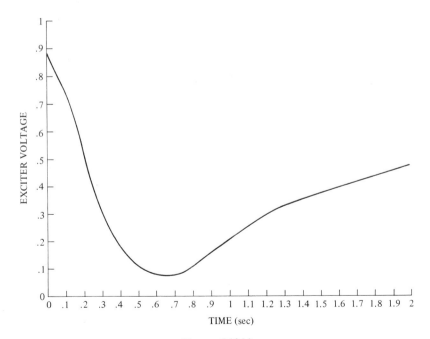

**Figure 6.10(c)**

3. $h(x, u)$ is a continuously differentiable function of $x$ and $u$ on $(0, t_f)$ and its derivatives are bounded, which provides a final time $t_f$ such that the second-level iterations (6.3.56) converge.                    (6.3.68)

In (6.3.68), the matrix $G$ is defined by

$$G \triangleq \begin{bmatrix} 0 & 0 & 0 & 0 \\ V & 0 & 0 & 0 \\ 0 & 0 & \tilde{R}^{-1}W & -\tilde{R}^{-1} \\ 0 & 0 & W - W\tilde{R}^{-1}W & W\tilde{R}^{-1} \end{bmatrix} \qquad (6.3.69)$$

It is noted by Singh and Hassan (1979) in their response to the comments of Mora-Camino (1979) that it is possible to choose $W$ in $\tilde{R} = R + W$ large enough as compared to $V$ in $\tilde{Q} = Q + V$ such that desirable convergence is achieved. This trend was verified in Example 6.3.2 for different $(W, V)$ combinations.

There are two definite advantages to using the interaction prediction method for the hierarchical control of nonlinear systems. One is the fact that, unlike goal coordination, this approach converges to the optimum solution provided that a long enough final period $t_f$ is chosen, as pointed out by Singh (1980). The second advantage is that the first-level problems are simple low-order linear ones which are centered around the solutions of accompanying matrix Riccati equations for all subsequent iterations. Moreover, the second-level problem consists of a series of simple substitutions.

On the other hand, this approach gives a local optimal solution unlike the goal coordination, which would give a global solution if there is no duality gap. The computational experiences of Singh (1980), Hassan and Singh (1976) and Hassan et al. (1979) indicate that the solution for a third-order synchronous machine example is no worse than the gradient and quasilinearization methods. This opinion is also shared by this author for the sixth-order example, where the results were quite comparable to the quasi-linearization method of Mukhopadhyay and Malik (1973) and the imbedding method of Jamshidi (1975a). The other basic shortcoming is the limitation of the quadratic form of the cost function. This difficulty can, however, be overcome by expanding a general cost function's integrand into a quadratic form and a nonlinear function. This scheme, suggested by Singh and Hassan (1978), is briefly considered.

To accompany the nonlinear system (6.3.36), let the following be the cost function which is to be minimized:

$$J = \int_0^{t_f} \gamma(x, u) \, dt \qquad (6.3.70)$$

which can be modified by

$$J^o = \frac{1}{2} \int_0^{t_f} \{ x^T Q x + u^T R u + 2\Gamma(x, u) + (u - u^o)^T W (u - u^o) \} \, dt \quad (6.3.71)$$

where $\Gamma(x, u) \triangleq \gamma(x, u) - \frac{1}{2}(x^T Q x - u^T R u)$ and the last term in (6.3.71) is added to help the convergence to the "desired" control $u^o$. Singh and Hassan (1978) have suggested using the desired point $(x^o, u^o)$ to fix $\Gamma(x^o, u^o)$, very much like fixing $f(x^o, u^o)$ in the system dynamics as seen in (6.3.45). Without going through the derivations of the optimal hierarchical control, we simply give the resulting equations which need to be solved for first- and second-level problems in composite but diagonal form. The matrix Riccati and vector adjoint equations for the first-level problem become

$$\dot{K} = -KA_d - A_d^T K + K\tilde{S}K - Q, \quad K(t_f) = 0 \tag{6.3.72}$$

$$\dot{g} = -\left(A_d - \tilde{S}K\right)^T g + KB_d(Wu^o - \beta) - Kf(x^o, u^o) - \alpha, \quad g(t_f) = 0 \tag{6.3.73}$$

where $\tilde{S} = B_d \tilde{R}^{-1} B_d^T$, $\tilde{R} = R + W$, $A_d$ and $B_d$ are defined in (6.3.40), $K =$ Block-diag$(K_1, K_2, \ldots, K_N)$, and $g = (g_1^T g_2^T \cdots g_N^T)^T$. The control vector and the closed-loop system equation for the first level would be identical to (6.3.53) and (6.3.49), respectively. The update equations for the second level differ from (6.3.55) as indicated here:

$$\alpha = \alpha(p) = Qx^o - \partial\gamma(x^o, u^o)/\partial x^o + \left(\partial h^T/\partial x^o - A_d^T\right)p(t) \tag{6.3.74}$$

$$\beta = \beta(u, p) = W(u - u^o) + \partial\gamma(x^o, u^o)/\partial u^o - Ru^o + \left(\partial h^T/\partial u^o - B_d^T\right)p(t) \tag{6.3.75}$$

An example for treating this approach can be found in Problem C6.6.

Singh (1980) has presented the heirarchical control of other problems of interest such as "tracking" or feedback forms for the local controllers. Some of these approaches are again considered as problems and are not formally treated here, since their derivations are similar.

### 6.3.3 Near-Optimum Control via Perturbation and Sensitivity Methods

In this section, the regular and singular perturbations discussed in Sections 6.2.2a and 2.3.2 along with the general sensitivity approach of Section 6.3.1 are used to find near-optimum control of a large nonlinear system.

Consider the state model of a nonlinear control system

$$\dot{y} = F(y, u), \quad y(0) = y_o \tag{6.3.76}$$

where $y$ and $u$ are, respectively, $n$-dimensional state and $m$-dimensional control vectors. In most realistic systems, the dimension $n$ is large and the model (6.3.76) is highly nonlinear and coupled. In general, a prohibitive amount of computation is required to find the optimal control. To initiate the near-optimum technique, it is assumed that (6.3.76) can be decoupled into $r$ subsystems:

$$dy_i/dt = F_i(y_i, u_i, \varepsilon a_i(y, u)), \quad i = 1, 2, \ldots, N \qquad (6.3.77)$$

where $\varepsilon$ is a positive-scalar coupling parameter, and $a_i(\cdot)$ are the coupling functions (interactions), relating the $i$th subsystem to the remaining subsystems. The term $\varepsilon a_i(\cdot)$ is the influence of other $n-1$ subsystems on the $i$th subsystem. When $\varepsilon \to 0$, the $N$ subsystems become completely decoupled, i.e.,

$$dy_i/dt = F_i(y_i, u_i), \quad i = 1, \ldots, N \qquad (6.3.78)$$

each having a much smaller dimension called the $i$th "nominal" subsystem. The $i$th nominal subsystem (6.3.78) can be further decomposed by conjecturing that its state components fall into a slow or fast category. Then by introducing a small scalar parasitic parameter $\mu$, the above conjecture can be mathematically formulated as

$$\dot{x}_i = f_i(y_i, u_i, \mu), \quad x_i(0) = x_{io} \qquad (6.3.79)$$

$$\mu \dot{z}_i = h_i(y_i, u_i, \mu), \quad z_i(0) = z_{io} \qquad (6.3.80)$$

where $y^T = (x^T z^T)$ and functions $f_i(\cdot)$ and $h_i(\cdot)$ stand for slow and fast proportions of the $i$th subsystem. Now by letting $\mu \to 0$, the dimension of the singularly perturbed system (6.3.79)–(6.3.80) further reduces, since the fast subprocess (6.3.80) of the $i$th subsystem becomes algebraic. Assuming that $z_i$ can be eliminated from (6.3.80) after $\mu \to 0$ and substituted in (6.3.79), the following $i$th "reduced"-order subprocess results:

$$\dot{\hat{x}}_i = f_i(\hat{x}_i, \hat{u}_i, 0) \qquad (6.3.81)$$

The basic control problem is to determine control functions for the $i$th reduced subprocess, $i = 1, \ldots, N$, coupled subsystems and the original large-scale system (Jamshidi, 1974). Without loss of generality, it is assumed that the cost function is quadratic and separative, i.e.,

$$J = \int_0^{t_f} \sum_{i=1}^{N} \left( y_i^T \hat{Q}_i u_i + u_i^T \hat{R}_i u_i \right) dt \qquad (6.3.82)$$

where $\hat{Q}_i$ and $\hat{R}_i$ are nonnegative-definite and positive-definite matrices, respectively. The optimal control problem is to find a sequence $u_i$ satisfying (6.3.77) and minimizing (6.3.82). The necessary optimality conditions on applying the maximum principle are given by the following set of canonical equations for the $i$th subsystem:

$$\dot{y}_i = H_{p_i}^T = F_i(y_i, u_i, \varepsilon a_i(y, u)) \qquad (6.3.83a)$$

$$\dot{p}_i = H_{y_i}^T = \hat{Q}_i y_i - \left( F_{iy_i} + \varepsilon \sum_{i=1}^{N} F_{i\alpha_i} a_{iy_i} \right)^T p_i, \quad p_i(t_f) = 0 \qquad (6.3.83b)$$

$$0 = H_{u_i}^T = -\hat{R}_i u_i + \left( F_{iu_i} + \varepsilon \sum_{i=1}^{N} F_{i\alpha_i} a_{iu_i} \right)^T p_i \qquad (6.3.83c)$$

where

$$H = \sum_{i=1}^{N} \left\{ p_i^T F_i - \frac{1}{2} \left( y_i^T \hat{Q}_i y_i + u_i^T \hat{R}_i u_i \right) \right\} \tag{6.3.84}$$

is the Hamiltonian function, $p_i$ is the $i$th subsystem costate vector, and the subscript $y_i$ in $F_{y_i}$ denotes vector gradient and $F_{i\alpha_i} \triangleq \partial F_i(\cdot)/(\varepsilon a_i)$. Equations (6.3.83) constitute a TPBV problem. Following the formulations of sensitivity functions of Section 6.3.1, $u_i$ can be approximated by a MacLaurin series

$$u_i \simeq \sum_{j=0}^{k} \varepsilon^j u_i^{(j)}/j! \tag{6.3.85}$$

where $u_i^{(j)} \triangleq \lim_{\varepsilon \to 0} \partial^j u_i / \partial \varepsilon^j$ is the $i$th control sensitivity function of $j$th order and $k$ is the order of approximation. The first-order terms of the $i$th subsystem are obtained by differentiating (6.3.83) with respect to $\varepsilon$ and letting $\varepsilon \to 0$, i.e.,

$$\dot{y}_i^{(1)} = F_{iy_i} y_i^{(1)} + F_{iu_i} u_i^{(1)} + F_{i\varepsilon} \tag{6.3.86a}$$

$$\dot{p}_i^{(1)} = \left( \hat{Q}_i - F_{iy_i}^1 \right) y_i^{(1)} - F_{iy_i}^T p_i^{(1)} - F_{iu_i}^1 u_i^{(1)} + \delta_i \tag{6.3.86b}$$

$$0 = F_{iy_i}^2 y_i^{(1)} + F_{iu_i}^T p_i^{(1)} + \left( F_{iu_i}^2 - \hat{R}_i \right) u_i^{(1)} + \gamma_i \tag{6.3.86c}$$

where $F^1 = F^1(y, p, u) = F_y^T p$, $F^2 = F^2(y, p, u) = F_u^T p$

$$\delta_i = \left( \sum_{i=1}^{N} F_{i\alpha_i} a_{iy_i} \right)^T p_i, \quad \gamma_i = \left( \sum_{i=1}^{N} F_{i\alpha_i} a_{iu_i} \right)^T p_i \tag{6.3.87}$$

Eliminating $u_i^{(1)}$ from (6.3.86c), the following TPBV problem is obtained:

$$\dot{y}_i^{(1)} = A_i y_i^{(1)} + S_i p_i^{(1)} + c_i, \quad y_i^{(1)}(0) = 0 \tag{6.3.88a}$$

$$\dot{p}_i^{(1)} = Q_i y_i^{(1)} - A_i^T p_i^{(1)} + d_i, \quad p_i^{(1)}(t_f) = 0 \tag{6.3.88b}$$

where $A_i$, $S_i$, $Q_i$, $c_i$, and $d_i$ are appropriate coefficient matrices and vectors expressed in terms of those in (6.3.86). Equations (6.3.88) constitute a linear TPBV problem whose solution by Riccati formulation is well known. If we let

$$p_i^{(1)} = -K_i y_i^{(1)} + g_i^1 \tag{6.3.89}$$

and pursue the derivation of Section 6.3.1, the following Riccati and adjoint equations result:

$$\dot{K}_i = -K_i A_i - A_i^T K_i + K_i S_i K_i - Q_i, \quad K_i(t_f) = 0 \tag{6.3.90}$$

$$\dot{g}_i^1 = -(A_i - S_i K_i)^T g_i^1 + K_i c_i + d_i, \quad g_i^1(t_f) = 0. \tag{6.3.91}$$

Thus, from (6.3.86c) and (6.3.89), the first-order coefficients are

$$u_i^{(1)} = -R_i^{-1} \left( F_{iy_i}^2 - F_{iu_i}^T K_i \right) y_i^{(1)} - R_i^{-1} \left( F_{iu_i}^T g_i^1 + \gamma_i \right) \tag{6.3.92}$$

where $y_i^{(1)}$ is obtained from

$$\dot{y}_i^{(1)} = (A_i - S_i K_i) y_i^{(1)} + K_i g_i^1 + c_i \qquad (6.3.93)$$

and

$$R_i = F_{iu_i}^2 - \hat{R}_i.$$

It must be noted that all coefficient matrices $A_i$, $S_i$, $R_i$, $Q_i$ and vectors $\gamma_i$, $\delta_i$, $c_i$ and $d_i$ are functions of the zeroth-order terms $y_i^{(0)}$ and $u_i^{(0)}$. Following the formulation of time scale decomposition, the zeroth-order term can be approximated by another MacLaurin series expansion in $\mu$:

$$u_i^{(0)} \cong \sum_{j=0}^{l} \mu^j \hat{u}_i^{(j)}/j! \qquad (6.3.94)$$

where $\hat{u}_i^{(j)} \triangleq \lim_{\mu \to 0} \partial^j u_i/\partial \mu^j$ and $l$ is the order of approximation. The necessary optimality conditions for the $i$th subsystem singular perturbation follows (6.2.58) and is given by

$$\dot{x}_i = f_i(x_i, z_i, u_i, \mu), \quad x_i(0) = x_{io} \qquad (6.3.95a)$$

$$\mu \dot{z}_i = h_i(x_i, z_i, u_i, \mu), \quad z_i(0) = z_{io} \qquad (6.3.95b)$$

$$\dot{q}_i = -H_{x_i} = v_i(x_i, z_i, q_i, r_i, \mu), \quad q_i(t_f) = q_{if} \qquad (6.3.95c)$$

$$\mu \dot{r}_i = -H_{z_i} = w_i(x_i, z_i, q_i, r_i, \mu), \quad r_i(t_f) = r_{if} \qquad (6.3.95d)$$

and the control $u_i$ can be obtained from (6.3.83c) after setting $\varepsilon = 0$. Now by letting $\mu \to 0$ in (6.3.95), the following "reduced" subsystem equations result:

$$\dot{\hat{x}}_i = f_i(\hat{x}_i, \hat{z}_i, \hat{u}_i, 0) \qquad (6.3.96a)$$

$$0 = h_i(\hat{x}_i, \hat{z}_i, \hat{u}_i, 0) \qquad (6.3.96b)$$

$$\dot{\hat{q}}_i = v_i(\hat{x}_i, \hat{z}_i, \hat{q}_i, \hat{r}_i, 0) \qquad (6.3.96c)$$

$$0 = w_i(\hat{x}_i, \hat{z}_i, \hat{q}_i, \hat{r}_i, 0) \qquad (6.3.96d)$$

The above equations have lost the auxiliary conditions on $z_i$ and $r_i$ by passing from the "nominal" ($\varepsilon = 0$, $\mu > 0$) subsystem to the "reduced" ($\varepsilon = 0$, $\mu = 0$) subprocess. The consequence of this loss, known as boundary layer behavior, was already given in some detail in Sections 6.2.2.b as well as 2.3.2.a. Under this condition, as discussed in Section 6.2.2.b, a standard MacLaurin series in $\mu$ is not adequate any more and an asymptotic expansion must be used. However, if the initial and final behavior of the fast variables are not significant compared with the remaining part of the interval $0 < t < t_f$, the degenerate reduced solution is a good approximation. This, as will be seen in a design Example 6.3.4, is the case. The computation of $\hat{u}_i^{(j)}$ of (6.3.94) is similar to $u^{(j)}$. By differentiating (6.3.95) with respect to $\mu$, letting $\mu \to 0$, and eliminating $\hat{z}_i^{(1)}$, $\hat{r}_i^{(1)}$, and $\hat{u}_i^{(1)}$, the following TPBV problem is obtained:

$$\dot{\hat{x}}_i^{(1)} = A_o \hat{x}_i^{(1)} + S_o \hat{q}_i^{(1)} + c_o \tag{6.3.97a}$$

$$\dot{\hat{q}}_i^{(1)} = Q_o \hat{x}_i^{(1)} - A_o^T \hat{q}_i^{(1)} + d_o \tag{6.3.97b}$$

where $A_o$, $S_o$, $Q_o$, and $d_o$ are similarly appropriate matrices and vectors. The procedure for obtaining $\hat{u}_i^{(1)}$ is similar to the previous case using a Riccati formulation.

The reduced subsystem equations (6.3.96) would reduce to the following TPBV problem after the elimination of $\hat{z}_i$, $\hat{r}_i$, and $\hat{u}_i$ by means of (6.3.96) and (6.3.83c) after setting $\varepsilon = 0$:

$$\dot{\hat{x}}_i = f_i(\hat{x}_i, \hat{q}_i), \quad \hat{x}_i(0) = x_{io} \tag{6.3.98a}$$

$$\dot{\hat{q}}_i = h_i(\hat{x}_i, \hat{q}_i), \quad \hat{q}_i(t_f) = q_{if} \tag{6.3.98b}$$

The solution of (6.3.98) is not by any means simple, because of the existence of split boundary conditions. The iterative schemes, such as Newton's gradient, or quasilinearization schemes are among the best known methods of solving (6.3.98), whose main difficulty is the need for a good initial guess. Another promising scheme is the use of the imbedding or "continuation" methods (D'Ans et al., 1970; Hontoir and Cruz, 1972; Jamshidi, 1972a). The application of the imbedding concept to AMRE is well documented in the literature (Kokotović and D'Ans, 1969; Jamshidi et al., 1970; Jamshidi and Böttiger, 1977; Jamshidi, 1972c, 1978, 1980). The application of the imbedding procedure for the case of the free end point problem is considered next.

### 6.3.3.a Imbedding Solution of a TPBV Problem

In this section a brief outline of the imbedding method of solving a set of TPBV problems is presented. Let the $2n$-dimensional TPBV problem for a free-end point case be

$$\dot{x} = f(x, p), \quad x(0) = x_o \tag{6.3.99a}$$

$$\dot{p} = g(x, p), \quad p(t_f) = 0 \tag{6.3.99b}$$

where $x$ and $p$ are, respectively, state and costate vectors, and the control $u = u(x, p)$ has presumably been eliminated by maximizing the corresponding Hamiltonian (Jamshidi, 1972 a, 1975 a). The imbedding scheme begins by introducing a parameter $k$ in the final time

$$t(k) = kt_f, \quad 0 \leqslant k \leqslant 1 \tag{6.3.100}$$

The introduction of this so-called imbedding parameter $k$ will place the original problem (6.3.99) into a family of TPBV problems:

$$\dot{x}(t, k) = f(x(t, k), p(t, k)) \tag{6.3.101a}$$

$$\dot{p}(t, k) = g(x(t, k), p(t, k)) \tag{6.3.101b}$$

$$x(0, k) = x_o, \quad p(t(k), k) = 0 \tag{6.3.102}$$

Assuming that $x$ and $p$ are continuously differentiable functions of $k$ (Ortega and Rheinboldt, 1970), (6.3.101) and (6.3.102) are differentiated with respect to $k$ to obtain the following "imbedded" TPBV problem:

$$\begin{bmatrix} \dot{\alpha}(t,k) \\ \dot{\beta}(t,k) \end{bmatrix} = \begin{bmatrix} f_x(x(t,k),p(t,k)) & f_p(x(t,k),p(t,k)) \\ g_x(x(t,k),p(t,k)) & g_p(x(t,k),p(t,k)) \end{bmatrix}$$
$$\cdot \begin{bmatrix} \alpha(t,k) \\ \beta(t,k) \end{bmatrix} \tag{6.3.103}$$

$$\alpha(0,k) = 0, \quad dp(t(k),k)/dk = 0 \tag{6.3.104}$$

where $\alpha(t,k) = \partial x(t,k)/\partial k$ and $\beta(t,k) = \partial p(t,k)/\partial k$. In order to find a suitable initial costate $p(0,k)$, it is necessary to find $\beta(0,k)$, given as

$$\beta(0,k) = -t_f \phi_{22}^{-1}(k) g(x_e(k), p_e(k)) \tag{6.3.105}$$

where

$$\Phi(0,k) = \begin{bmatrix} \phi_{11}(k) & \phi_{12}(k) \\ \phi_{21}(k) & \phi_{22}(k) \end{bmatrix}$$

is the transition matrix of (6.3.103) evaluated at $t = 0$ and $x_e(k) \triangleq x(t(k),k)$ and $p_e(k) \triangleq p(t(k),k)$. Once $\beta(0,k)$ is available, the initial costate can be obtained through a simple first-order integration in $k$, e.g., Euler's method,

$$p(0,k^{i+1}) = p(0,k^i) + \Delta k \beta(0,k^i) \tag{6.3.106}$$

where $\beta(0,k)$ is defined by (6.3.105). The imbedding method is summarized by Algorithm 6.7.

***Algorithm 6.7.*** Parameter Imbedding Solution of a TPBV Problem

*Step 1:* For $k^i = 0$, $t(0) = 0$, $p(0,0) = 0$, $\phi_{12}(0) = 0, \phi_{22}(0) = I_n$, and choose $\Delta k$.

*Step 2:* Use (6.3.105) and (6.3.106) to obtain $p(0,k^i)$.

*Step 3:* If $k^i = 1$, go to Step 6.

*Step 4:* $k^i = k^i + \Delta k$.

*Step 5:* Integrate (6.3.103) to find $\phi_{22}(k^i)$. Go to Step 2.

*Step 6:* Stop. The desired initial costate is $p(0,1)$.

The following example, taken from Jamshidi (1972a), illustrates the algorithm.

**Example 6.3.3.** Consider a second-order model of a continuous stirred tank reactor (CSTR) suggested by Luus and Lapidus (1967) and Birta and

Trushel (1969):

$$\dot{x}_1 = -(1+2x_1)+(x_2+0.5)\exp(25x_1/(x_2+2))$$
$$-(x_1+0.25)u, \quad x_1(0)=0.05$$
$$\dot{x}_2 = -x_2-(x_2+0.5)\exp(25x_1/x_2+2))+0.5, \quad x_2(0)=0.0 \quad (6.3.107)$$

where state variables $x_1$ and $x_2$ are the steady-state deviations of temperature and concentration and control variable $u$ is the coolant inflow. Associated with the state equations is a quadratic cost functional

$$J = \int_0^{0.78}\left(x_1^2+x_2^2+0.1u^2\right)dt \qquad (6.3.108)$$

This problem has been solved by Luus and Lapidus (1967), where a combination of gradients, using the first and second variations, is used to find the optimum trajectories. Birta and Trushel (1969) have also considered the CSTR problem and applied conjugate gradients and Davidon–Fletcher–Powell (Fletcher and Powell, 1963) methods to minimize the sum-square-error in the costate's final conditions. Here the same problem is solved using the imbedding Algorithm 6.7, and the results of the three methods are tabulated and compared.

Following the above formulation after eliminating $u$, the TPBV problem corresponding to (6.3.101) and (6.3.102) becomes

$$\dot{x} = f(x,p) = \begin{bmatrix} -2x_1+(x_2+0.5)\cdot e(x)+5(x_1+0.25)^2 p_1-0.5 \\ -x_2-(x_2+0.5)\cdot e(x)+0.5 \end{bmatrix}$$

$$(6.3.109a)$$

$$\dot{p} = g(x,p) = \begin{bmatrix} 2x_1+2p_1-5(x_1+0.25)p_1^2-50\left((x_2+0.5)/(x_2+2)^2\right) \\ \cdot(p_1-p_2)\cdot e(x) \\ 2x_1+p_2-(p_1-p_2)\cdot e(x) \end{bmatrix}$$

$$(6.3.109b)$$

$$x(0,k) = \begin{pmatrix} 0.05 \\ 0.0 \end{pmatrix}, \quad p(0.78k,k) = \begin{pmatrix} 0.0 \\ 0.0 \end{pmatrix} \qquad (6.3.110)$$

where $e(x) \triangleq e(x(t,k)) \triangleq \exp(25x_1(t,k)/(x_2(t,k)+2))$ and the optimal control is $u^* = u(x,p) = -5(x_1+0.25)p_1$. Note that for simplicity the $(t,k)$ arguments are omitted in (6.3.109).

The imbedded TPBV problem (6.3.103) can be easily derived from (6.3.109). In generating $\phi_{12}$ and $\phi_{22}$ from (6.3.103), it is clear that the coefficients depend on $x$ and $p$; thus, Equations (6.3.103) and (6.3.109) must be solved simultaneously. This amounts to a set of $2n(n+1)=4(3)=12$ differential equations for the CSTR example. The optimal control was obtained as a function of time, and the initial and final values of the costate and the performance index were computed. For comparison purposes, the

**Table 6.4** Results of the CSTR Model in Example 6.3.3

| Method | Initial Value Costate $p(0)$ | Final Value Costate $p(0.78)$ | Computed Performance Index $J$ | Unit Computer Time |
|---|---|---|---|---|
| Second Variation (Luus and Lapidus, 1967) | $-1.079215$ $-0.192443$ | $0.345621 \times 10^{-5}$ $-0.112393 \times 10^{-5}$ | $0.02661471$ | 3.32 min |
| Davidon–Fletcher–Powell (Birta and Trushel, 1969) | $-1.078170$ $-0.191786$ | Not available | $0.02660336$ | Not available |
| Parameter Imbedding $\Delta k = 0.10, N = 21$ (Algorithm 6.7) | $-1.071700$ $-0.289208$ | $6.15906 \times 10^{-9}$ $-0.63290 \times 10^{-9}$ | $0.02651277$ | 1.10 min |

second variation method of Luus and Lapidus (1967) was also implemented on the computer. A summary of available boundary conditions, performance index, and unit computer time for the three methods is presented in Table 6.4. Although some of the results for the other methods are not available, the data in Table 6.4 does indicate that the proposed imbedding method is competitive and certainly comparable.

## 6.3.3.b An Application of the Perturbation Method

The near-optimum control of the large interconnected system discussed in Section 6.3.3 is first summarized in terms of an algorithm and then applied to a physical system.

***Algorithm 6.8.*** Near-Optimum Control via Decomposition

Step 1: Apply the imbedding method (Algorithm 6.7) or Riccati formulation to Equations (6.3.98), respectively, depending on whether they are nonlinear or linear.

Step 2: Use Equations (6.3.83) with $\varepsilon = 0$ and (6.3.96) to obtain reduced subprocess state and control $\hat{x}_i^{(0)}$, $\hat{z}_i^{(0)}$, and $\hat{u}_i^{(0)}$.

Step 3: Solve (6.3.97) to find first-order terms $\hat{x}_i^{(1)}$, $\hat{q}_i^{(1)}$, and $\hat{u}_i^{(1)}$.

Step 4: Set $i = i + 1$; if $i < N$, go to Step 1.

Step 5: Use Equations (6.3.94)–(6.3.95) to find approximate nominal control and state $u_i = u_i^{(0)}$ and $x_i = x_i^{(0)}$; set $i = 1$.

Step 6: Using the nominal variables to compute all coefficient matrices, solve Equations (6.3.90) and (6.3.91) for Riccati matrix $K_i$ and adjoint vector $g_i^1$ and store.

Step 7: Obtain first-order terms $u_i^{(1)}$ and $y_i^{(1)}$ using (6.3.92) and (6.3.93).

Step 8: Determine control and state $u_i$ and $y_i$ using (6.3.85) and (6.3.83).

*Step 9:* Set $i = i + 1$; if $i < N$, go to Step 6.

*Step 10:* First-order near-optimum control is complete.

The following example illustrates this algorithm.

**Example 6.3.4.** In this example, the coiler process system of Figure 6.4 discussed in Example 6.2.5 with a new nonlinear model is reconsidered. The system dynamics depend on a winding-reel motor generator, reel, bridle, bridle motor generator, and tensiometer. Table 6.1 shows a summary of the state and control variables involved in each of these components.* The state model of the system is represented by (Jamshidi, 1971; Jamshidi, 1974)

$$\dot{y} = Ay + Bu + h(y) + d \qquad (6.3.111)$$

where $y = (y_1 y_2 \cdots y_{12})^T$ and $u = (u_1 u_2 u_2)^T$. The nonzero elements of $B$ and $d$ are $b_{21} = 0.33$, $b_{32} = b_{63} = 0.318$, and $d_1 = 0.0034$. The $A$ matrix is

$$A = \begin{bmatrix}
0 & 0 & 0 & -0.003 & 0 & & 0 & 0 & 0 & 0 & 0 & 0 \\
0 & -0.33 & 0 & 0 & 0 & & 0 & -0.205 & 0.076 & 0.118 & 0 & 0 \\
0 & 0 & 0 & 0 & 0 & & 23.4 & -0.973 & 0 & 0 & 0 & 0 \\
-1.95 & 0.241 & 0 & 0 & 0.241 & & -33.9 & 0 & -8.96 & 0 & 0 & 0 \\
0 & 0 & 121 & -83 & -12 & & 14.4 & 0 & 0 & -9.65 & 0 & 0 \\
& & & & & -0.32 & 0 & 7.78 & 0 & 0 & -10 & 0 \\
& & & & & 0 & 0 & 0 & 0 & 0 & 10 & -3.89 \\
& & & & & 0 & & & & & & \\
& & & & & 262 & & & & & & \\
& & & & & 0 & & & & & & \\
& & & & & 0 & & & & & & \\
& & & & & 0 & & & & & &
\end{bmatrix}$$

$$B = \begin{bmatrix}
0 & 0 & 0 \\
0.33 & 0 & 0 \\
0 & 0.32 & 0 \\
0 & 0 & 0 \\
0 & 0 & 0 \\
0 & 0 & 0.32 \\
& 0 &
\end{bmatrix} \qquad (6.3.112)$$

---

*The choices of states in this model are $y^T = [y_1 y_2 \cdots y_{12}] = [r, i_f, i_{fo}, \Omega_r, i_a, i_{f1}, \Omega_b, t_o, i_{a1}, i_{a2}, \Psi_1, \Psi_2]$.

while the nonzero elements of $h(\cdot)$ are

$$h_4 = \{-0.89y_1y_8 + 5(y_2 + y_5) - 8.1y_1 + y_2y_5$$
$$-0.1(y_1 + 1)^3(y_4 + 1)^3 - 31(y_7 + 1)\}/(20.7 + y_1^4)$$
$$h_8 = -0.42(1 + 0.04y_4) \qquad\qquad (6.3.113)$$

The physical configuration of the coiler system of Figure 6.4 involves two basic subsystems: the winding reel and the bridles. Let $y_r$ and $y_b$ denote the state vectors for the reel and the bridles subsystems, respectively, as defined earlier. With this reformulation of the state variables, the regular perturbation (weak coupling) of (6.3.111) leads to

$$\dot{y} = \begin{bmatrix} \dot{y}_r \\ \dot{y}_b \end{bmatrix} = \begin{bmatrix} A_r & 0 \\ 0 & A_b \end{bmatrix} \begin{bmatrix} y_r \\ y_b \end{bmatrix} + \begin{bmatrix} B_r & 0 \\ 0 & B_b \end{bmatrix} \begin{bmatrix} u_r \\ u_b \end{bmatrix} + \begin{bmatrix} h_r(y_r, \varepsilon a_r(y)) \\ h_b(y) \end{bmatrix} + \begin{bmatrix} d_r \\ d_b \end{bmatrix}$$
$$(6.3.114)$$

where $A_r$, $A_b$, $B_r$, and $B_b$ matrices follow immediately from (6.3.111). The nonzero elements of $h_r$ and $h_b$ are

$$h_{r4} = \{-0.89\varepsilon y_1y_8 + 5(y_2 + y_5) - 8.1y_1 + y_2y_5$$
$$-0.1(y_1 + 1)^3(y_4 + 1)^2 - 31\varepsilon(1 + y_7)^2\}/(20.7 + y_1^4)$$
$$h_{b3} = -0.42\varepsilon(1 + 0.04y_4)$$

If $\varepsilon \to 0$, (6.3.114) reduces to

$$\dot{y}_r = A_ry_r + B_ru_r + h_r(y_r)$$
$$\dot{y}_b = A_by_b + B_bu_b \qquad\qquad (6.3.115)$$

Note that the disturbance vectors are eliminated by introducing an open-loop control as follows: Let $u_r|_{\varepsilon=0} = u_r + u_{ro}$; then $B_ru_{ro} + d_r = 0$ assures an expression for $u_{ro}$. This completes the regular perturbation. To initiate the singular perturbation (strong coupling) a detailed knowledge of the plant parameters and experimental results are needed to gain an insight into the variables. Alternatively if experimental data are not available, mechanical, electromechanical, and electrical components of the processes are candidates for slow and fast subvectors. Here, by using the numerical data (Jamshidi, 1971), it can be seen that

$$\tau_{fo} = \tau_f = 3.14, \quad \tau_a = 0.086, \quad \tau_{a1} = 0.103, \quad \tau_{a2} = 0.112,$$
$$\tau_1 = 0.1 \text{ and } (1/h_s) = 9.26 \qquad\qquad (6.3.116a)$$

where $\tau_i$ are time constants associated with the field, armature circuits, or tensiometer. The large time constants are due to slow variations of flux linkage, reel radius, or moment of inertia and $h_s$ is the thickness of the strip. The small time constants are due to the presence of some "parasitic" parameters, such as armature inductance, resistance, or transducer dynamics. The presence of such parameters motivates the time-scale separation or singular perturbation of each subsystem. Introducing the slow and fast substates and a parameter $\mu$,

$$\mu = \max(h_s/2\pi, \tau_a, \tau_{a1}, \tau_{a2}, \tau_1) \qquad (6.3.116b)$$

The system equation (6.3.114) can be rewritten as

$$\dot{x}_r = \begin{bmatrix} 0 & 0 & 0 & -0.003 \\ 0 & -0.33 & 0 & 0 \\ 0 & 0 & 0 & 0 \\ -1.95 & 0.241 & 0 & 0 \end{bmatrix} x_r - \begin{bmatrix} 0 \\ 0 \\ 0 \\ 0.241 \end{bmatrix} z_r$$

$$+ \begin{bmatrix} 0 & 0 \\ 0.33 & 0 \\ 0 & 0.318 \\ 0 & 0 \end{bmatrix} u_r + \begin{bmatrix} 0 \\ 0 \\ 0 \\ h_4 \end{bmatrix} \qquad (6.3.117a)$$

$$\mu\dot{z}_r = [\,0 \quad 0 \quad 12.1 \quad -8.3\,]x_r - 1.2z_r \qquad (6.3.117b)$$

with

$$h_4 = \left\{5(x_2 + z_1) - 8.1x_1 + x_2z_1 - \mu r_o^3(1 + x_1)3 \cdot (1 + x_4)^2\right\}/(20.7 + r_0^4 y_1^4)$$

and

$$\dot{x}_b = \begin{bmatrix} -0.32 & 0 & 0 \\ 0 & 0 & -0.205 \\ 0 & 23.4 & -0.973 \end{bmatrix} x_b + \begin{bmatrix} 0 & 0 & 0 & 0 \\ 0.0757 & 0.118 & 0 & 0 \\ 0 & 0 & 0 & 0 \end{bmatrix} z_b$$

$$+ \begin{bmatrix} 0.318 \\ 0 \\ 0 \end{bmatrix} u_b \qquad (6.3.118a)$$

$$\mu\dot{z}_b = \begin{bmatrix} 26.2 & -3.39 & 0 \\ 0 & 1.44 & 0 \\ 0 & 0 & 0.778 \\ 0 & 0 & 0 \end{bmatrix} x_b + \begin{bmatrix} -0.896 & 0 & 0 & 0 \\ 0 & -0.965 & 0 & 0 \\ 0 & 0 & -1 & 0 \\ 0 & 0 & 1 & -3.89 \end{bmatrix} z_b$$

$$\qquad (6.3.118b)$$

where $\mu = 0.1$ and

$$y_r = \left(x_r^T \mid z_r^T\right)^T = \left(\hat{r}\hat{i}_f \hat{i}_{fo}\Omega_r \mid i_a\right)^T$$

$$y_b = \left(x_b^T \mid z_b^T\right)^T = \left(\hat{i}_1\hat{\Omega}_b\hat{i}_o \mid \hat{i}_{a1}\hat{i}_{a2}\Psi_1\Psi_2\right)^T \qquad (6.3.119)$$

when $\mu = 0$, (6.3.117b), and (6.3.118b) become algebraic, from which the fast variables $z_r$ and $z_b$ can be eliminated to give

$$\dot{\hat{x}}_r = A_1 \hat{x}_r + B_1 \hat{u}_r + f(x_r)$$

$$= \begin{bmatrix} 0 & 0 & 0 & -0.003 \\ 0 & -0.33 & 0 & 0 \\ 0 & 0 & 0 & 0 \\ -1.95 & 0.241 & -2043 & 1.667 \end{bmatrix} \hat{x}_r = \begin{bmatrix} 0 & 0 \\ 0.33 & 0 \\ 0 & 0.318 \\ 0 & 0 \end{bmatrix} u_r$$

$$+ \begin{bmatrix} 0 \\ 0 \\ 0 \\ 2.4x_2(x_3 - 0.686x_4) \end{bmatrix} \qquad (6.3.120)$$

and

$$\dot{\hat{x}}_b = A_2 \hat{x}_b + B_2 \hat{u}_b$$

$$= \begin{bmatrix} -0.318 & 0 & 0 \\ 2.21 & -0.11 & -0.205 \\ 0 & 23.4 & -0.973 \end{bmatrix} \hat{x}_b + \begin{bmatrix} 0.318 \\ 0 \\ 0 \end{bmatrix} \hat{u}_b \quad (6.3.121)$$

Equations (6.3.120) and (6.3.121) are the reduced models of the reel and delivery bridles subsystems, respectively.

This problem was simulated on a CDC-1600 digital computer using FORTRAN and the following initial conditions:

$$y_r^T(0) = \begin{pmatrix} 0 & -0.025 & 0.025 & -0.1 & | & 0.95 \end{pmatrix}$$

$$y_b^T(0) = \begin{pmatrix} 0.025 & 0.025 & -0.1 & | & 0.64 & 0.037 & -0.08 & -0.2 \end{pmatrix}$$

$$(6.3.122)$$

The weighting matrices in the integrand of the cost functions were chosen as

$$\text{Reel:} \quad Q_r = \text{diag}( 1 \quad 1 \quad 1 \quad 0 \quad 0), \quad R_r = I_2$$
$$\text{Bridle:} \quad Q_b = \text{diag}( 1 \quad 1 \quad 75 \quad 0 \quad 0 \quad 0 \quad 0), \quad R_b = 1$$

$$(6.3.123)$$

Since the reel subsystem reduced model of (6.3.120) is nonlinear, the imbedding technique of Algorithm 6.7 was applied to the following TPBV problem:

$$\begin{bmatrix} \dot{\hat{x}}_r \\ \dot{\hat{p}}_r \end{bmatrix} = \begin{bmatrix} A_1 & | & B_1 R_r^{-1} B_1^{-1} \\ \hline Q_r & | & -(A_1 + f_{\hat{x}}) \end{bmatrix} \begin{bmatrix} \hat{x}_r \\ \hat{p}_r \end{bmatrix} + \begin{bmatrix} f(\hat{x}_r) \\ \hline 0 \end{bmatrix} \qquad (6.3.124)$$

with

$$\hat{x}_r^T(0) = ( -0.025 \quad 0.025 \quad -0.10), \quad \hat{p}_r^T(1) = ( 0 \quad 0 \quad 0)$$

$$(6.3.125)$$

The reel subsystem reduced-model control is given by

$$\hat{u}_r = R_r^{-1}B_1^T\hat{p}_r \qquad (6.3.126)$$

The resulting initial and corresponding final conditions of the adjoining vector $\hat{p}_r$ obtained from applying the imbedding method were $\hat{p}_r^T(0) = (0.0171 \quad -0.062 \quad 0.0113)$ and $\hat{p}_r^T(1) = (-0.062 \quad 0.537 \quad 1.973)^T \times 10^{-6}$. With the above value of $p_r(0)$, the TPBV problem of (6.3.124) is reduced to an initial-value problem; hence, (6.3.126) will give the resulting control $u_r$ as a function of time. The bridle reduced model of (6.3.121) is linear; hence, a Riccati matrix solution will give a feedback solution for the control $\hat{u}_b$ as

$$\hat{u}_b = -R_b^{-1}B_2^T K_2\hat{x}_b = -(2.68 \quad 55.6 \quad 3.76)\hat{x}_b \qquad (6.3.127)$$

Thus, the result of the first part of the technique is an open-loop control (6.3.126) for the reel and a closed-loop control (6.3.127) for the bridle subsystems. The second part of the design involves evaluation of control–sensitivity functions with respect to parameter $\mu$. For the reel subsystem of (6.3.117), the TPBV problem of (6.3.88) has to be solved. The coefficient matrices $A_{ri}$ and $S_{ri}$, and vectors $c_i$ and $d_i$, depend on the reduced model states, and hence time, because the nonlinear function $h_4$ in (6.3.117) depends on $x_r$ and $\mu$. Therefore, a time-varying Riccati solution $K_r(t)$, as well as a linear adjoint $g_r^1(t)$ equation, needs to be solved to give the first-order control sensitivity

$$\hat{u}_r^{(1)} = -R_r^{-1}B_1^T\left(K_r\hat{x}_r^{(1)} + g_r^1\right) \qquad (6.3.128)$$

where the state sensitivity function $x_r^{(1)}$ is

$$\dot{\hat{x}}_r^{(1)} = \left(A_r(t) - S_r K_r(t)\right)\hat{y}^{(1)} + S_r g_r^1(t) + c_r(t) \qquad (6.3.129)$$

The sensitivity function $\hat{u}_r^{(1)}(t)$ in (6.3.128) along with the reduced-model control $\hat{u}_r$ in (6.3.126) will result in an open-loop near-optimum control (see Equation (6.3.94)) for the reel subsystem. The bridle subsystem in (6.3.121) constitutes a linear singularly perturbed system whose feedback near-optimum control is, in fact, possible. This is a special case of systems involving a singular-perturbation characteristic. Instead of approximating the control as in (6.3.94), the high-order Riccati matrix $K_b(\mu)$, now a function of $\mu$, is approximated by a truncated MacLaurin series following Algorithm 6.1:

$$K_b(\mu) \simeq K_b(0) + \left.\frac{\partial K_b}{\partial \mu}\right|_{\mu=0} \qquad (6.3.130)$$

where

$$K_b(0) = \left.\begin{bmatrix} K_2 & | & \mu H_2 \\ --- & -|- & --- \\ \mu H_2^T & | & \mu K_2 \end{bmatrix}\right|_{\mu=0} = \begin{bmatrix} K_2 & | & 0 \\ -- & -L & - \\ 0 & | & 0 \end{bmatrix}$$

and $K_2$ was already calculated, as is evident from (6.3.127). We rewrite (6.3.118) as

$$d\hat{x}_b/dt = A_3\hat{x}_b + C_1\hat{z}_b + B_2\hat{u}_b$$

$$\mu \, d\hat{z}_b/dt = A_4\hat{x}_b + C_2\hat{z}_b \tag{6.3.131}$$

where matrices $A_3$, $A_4$, $B_2$, $C_1$, and $C_2$ are defined by (6.3.118). The computation of $\partial K/\partial \mu|_{\mu=0}$ can be summarized by the following equations (Sannuti and Kokotović, 1969):

$$0 = W_3 C_2 + C_2^T W_3 - C_1^T K_2 D_1 - D_1^T K_2^T C_1 \tag{6.3.132}$$

$$0 = -W_2 C_2 - W_b C_1 - A_4^T W_3 + A_3^T K_2 D_1 - K_2 S_2 K_2 D_1 + (dK_2/dt) D_1 \tag{6.3.133}$$

$$d\dot{W}_b/dt = -W_b(A_3 - S_2 K_2) - (A_3 - S_2 K_2)^T W_b$$
$$\quad - (W_2 A_4 + A_4^T W_2) \tag{6.3.134}$$

$$W_b(T) = 0$$

where $W_b = \lim_{\mu \to 0}(\partial K_2/\partial \mu)$; $W_i = \lim_{\mu \to 0}(\partial H_i/\partial \mu)$; $i = 2,3$; $D_2 = C_1 C_2^{-1}$; and $K_2$ is the time-varying matrix Riccati solution for the reduced model (6.3.121). Note that the algebraic Lyapunov-type equation (6.3.132) is solved first for $W_3$. Substituting $W_3$ in (6.3.133) yields a linear algebraic equation in $W_b$ and $W_2$ with time-varying coefficients. Finally, by the use of the resulting Equation (6.3.133) to eliminate $W_2$ in (6.3.134), a time-varying Lyapunov-type differential equation is obtained, which is then solved for $W_b$. The nominal control for the bridle subsystem is

$$u_b^0 \simeq -R_b^{-1}B_2^T(K_2 + \mu W_b), \quad \hat{x}_b = -\mu^2 R_b^{-1}B_2^T W_2 z_b \tag{6.3.135}$$

This completes the computations up to Step 5 of Algorithm 6.8. Procedure for Steps 6–8 are similar to the nominal control of the reel subsystem where matrix Riccati equation (6.3.90) and time-varying linear adjoint equation (6.3.91) have to be solved successively once all the nominal states are available. Figure 6.11 represents typical responses of the bridle subsystem control (reduced, nominal, and optimum). The optimum responses were obtained by solving a seventh-order Riccati equation corresponding to (6.3.118). The zeroth- and first-order responses resulted from applying reduced and nominal controls, namely, (6.3.118) with $\mu = 0.10$, to the original plant. Figure 6.12 presents the reel subsystem responses, where the optimum responses were obtained by applying the imbedding Algorithm 6.7 to the fifth-order nonlinear plant to (6.3.117).

A systematic use of regular perturbation (subsystem decomposition), singular perturbation (time-scale decomposition), and sensitivity functions is made to develop a near-optimum design method. Both decoupling schemes contribute significantly to the reduction of computation and memory stor-

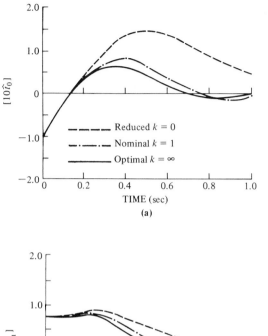

**Figure 6.11** Bridle subsystem time responses: **(a)** tension error and **(b)** armature current error.

age in all-digital-computer simulation of large-scale systems. The computation time for simulating the original 12th-order system on a CDC1600 computer was about 90 minutes for the process time considered in the simulation. Comparable computer time for the bridle and reel subprocesses were, respectively, seven and five minutes. Similar computational time differences were observed on an IBM/1130 computer. The near-optimum control is obtained in terms of subsystem computations only, which are often of a much lower order.

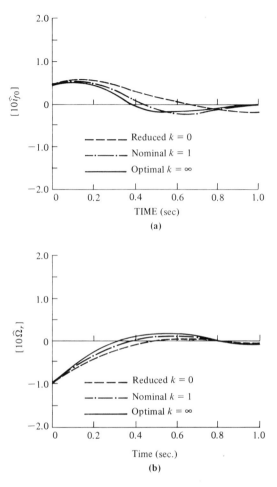

**Figure 6.12** Reel subsystem time responses: (a) field current error and (b) angular velocity error.

## 6.4 Near-Optimum Control of Large-Scale Time-Delay Systems

The control of systems with time-delay have been of considerable concern because many industrial plants have inherent delays. Rolling mills, production processes, water resources and quality systems, traffic control systems and chemical reactors are only a few systems whose mathematical models are described most exactly by time-delay differential equations. The extension of the maximum principle to time-delay systems has been developed by Kharatishivili (1961). The corresponding TPBV problem for such systems involves both delay (in state) and advance (in costate) terms whose exact solution is practically impossible. The primary concern of most proposed methods of solving time-delay systems has been to avoid solving the associated TPBV problem.

For linear time-delay processes with a quadratic cost function, Krasovskii (1963) has developed expressions for the optimal cost function and the controller. The method of Krasovskii (1963) has been formulated more conveniently by reducing the control of the time-delay system to the solution of a set of successively coupled partial differential equations (Eller et al., 1969). The above method is not only limited to linear systems but, as also mentioned in Aggarwal (1970), it is computationally cumbersome. Another method is the sensitivity approach (Inoue et al., 1971), in which the state, costate and control are expanded in terms of the delay itself and the series coefficients are obtained by nondelay system solutions. Another deviation from this method (Sannuti, 1970; Inoue et al., 1971) is to subdivide the delay into a number of equally spaced subintervals and approximate the time-delay problem by a singularly perturbed one.

The parameter imbedding approach to the solution of linear time-delay systems proposed by Jamshidi and Malek-Zavarei (1972), Chan and Perkins (1973), and Jamshidi and Razzaghi (1975) forms a family of problems, one of which is not delayed while the last member of the family corresponds to the original problem. The concept of regular perturbation or coupling has been applied to linear and nonlinear time-delay systems by Jamshidi (1973). The latter method is on the same line as the sensitivity approach of Inoue et al. (1971). It extends the optimal control method for coupled systems (Kokotović and Singh, 1971) to coupled time-delay systems. Malek-Zavarei (1980a) applied a sensitivity approach to obtain the suboptimal control for nonstationary linear systems with delay in both the state and the control and with quadratic cost. The suboptimal control is in the form of an exact closed-loop and some truncated-series open-loop terms, where all the series coefficients were calculated in a recursive manner from nondelay system computations.

Another approach is based on a transformation, first introduced by Bate (1969) and independently proposed by Slater and Wells (1972). The basic idea behind this approach is the transformation of the original linear time-delay system into a nondelay and nonhomogeneous system with the same optimal control and cost functional. This method was extended and incorporated in a systematic three-stage design method of nonlinear time-delay systems by Jamshidi (1975b).

Still another approach for suboptimal control of time-delay systems is to treat the delay terms as extra inputs to linear nondelay systems which must be optimized in each step of an iterative procedure. Gracovetsky and Vidyasagar (1973) used this method for suboptimal control of systems with a single state delay. Malek-Zavarei (1980b) applied this procedure to suboptimal control of systems with multiple state and control delays. The procedure can be extended to the case with time-varying delays. It can also be extended to the case where the delay terms are nonlinear, provided that some of the nonlinearities satisfy the Lipschitz condition.

The subject of time delays was first introduced in Chapter 4, where the time-delay algorithm of Tamura (1974) was introduced. As a result of the ever increasing importance of time delays in the models of some important industrial and environmental large-scale systems, the subject is discussed further in this section.

Large-scale systems involving time delays have been the subject of recent investigation by some authors (Anderson, 1979; Singh, 1980; Ikeda and Šiljak, 1980; Jamshidi and Malek-Zavarei, 1981). Jamshidi and Malek-Zavarei (1981) have considered the suboptimal control of a large-scale time-delay system. Here the system is decomposed into several subsystems and a procedure similar to that of Malek-Zavarei (1980b) is applied to determine the suboptimal control. It is noted that in most large-scale systems a natural decomposition exists which can be applied. This method also produces a suboptimal control which is partly closed-loop and partly open-loop.

In this section, three approaches for near-optimum control of large-scale time-delay systems are introduced. The first is based on the decomposition of linear and nonlinear systems with delay based on the approach due to Jamshidi (1973). The next approach deals with the hierarchical control of a serial time-delay system in which the delayed state of one subsystem acts as an input to the next one down the line and so on (Singh, 1980). The last approach is the application of a hierarchical control's goal coordination to large-scale time-delay systems due to Jamshidi and Malek-Zavarei (1981).

### 6.4.1 Near-Optimum Control of Coupled Time-Delay Systems

Consider a large-scale time-delay system consisting of a set of $N$ coupled subsystems:

$$\dot{z}_1 = h_1\big(z_1, w_1, \varepsilon c_1(z, z(t-\lambda), w, w(t-\lambda), t), t\big)$$
$$\dot{z}_2 = h_2\big(z_2, w_2, \varepsilon c_2(z, z(t-\lambda), w, w(t-\lambda), t), t\big)$$
$$\vdots \qquad\qquad (6.4.1)$$
$$\dot{z}_N = h_N\big(z_N, w_N, \varepsilon c_N(z, z(t-\lambda), w, w(t-\lambda), t), t\big)$$

where $z = [z_1^T z_2^T \cdots z_N^T]^T$ and $w = [w_1^T w_2^T \cdots w_N^T]^T$ are state and control vectors, respectively, $\varepsilon$ is a scalar coupling parameter, and $\lambda$ is the delay, not necessarily small. The problem is to find a control $w$ composed of $w_i$, $i = 1, 2, \ldots, N$ which satisfies (6.4.1) with appropriate boundary conditions and minimize a separable cost functional

$$J = \int_{t_0}^{t_f} \sum_{i=1}^{N} L_i(z_i, w_i, t)\, dt \qquad (6.4.2)$$

Assuming sufficient continuity and differentiability of $w$ with respect to $\varepsilon$, the MacLaurin series expansion for $w_i$ has the form

$$w_i \simeq \sum_{j=1}^{K} \frac{\varepsilon^j}{j!} w_i^{(j)}, \quad i = 1, 2, \ldots, N \tag{6.4.3}$$

where $w_i^{(j)} \triangleq \lim_{\varepsilon \to 0} \partial^j w_i / \partial \varepsilon^j$. The computation of coefficients of series (6.4.3), as in the nondelayed case (Kokotović and Singh, 1971), involves uncoupled and, for this case, unretarded subsystems solutions.

To illustrate the near-optimum control for this class of large-scale systems it is assumed, without any loss of generality, that there are two subsystems involved in (6.4.1), i.e., $N = 2$. Letting $z_1 = x$, $z_2 = y$, $w_1 = u$, $w_2 = v$, $c_1(\cdot) = a(\cdot)$, $c_2(\cdot) = b$, $h_1 = f$, and $h_2 = g$, the state models for the subsystem $x$ and subsystem $y$ become

$$\dot{x} = f(x, u, \alpha) = f(x, u, \varepsilon a(x, x', y, y', u, u', v, v')) \tag{6.4.4a}$$

$$\dot{y} = g(y, v, \beta) = g(y, v, \varepsilon b(x, x', y, y', u, u', v, v')) \tag{6.4.4b}$$

where dimensions of $x$ and $y$ are, respectively, $n_1$ and $n_2$ and the prime on the variables defines delayed quantities. The initial functions for (6.4.4) are

$$x(\tau) = \phi(\tau), \quad t_0 - \lambda \leqslant \tau \leqslant t_0 \tag{6.4.5a}$$

$$y(\tau) = \psi(\tau), \quad t_0 - \lambda \leqslant \tau \leqslant t_0 \tag{6.4.5b}$$

Assuming at $L_1(\cdot) = F(\cdot)$ and $L_2(\cdot) = G(\cdot)$ in (6.4.2), the necessary conditions for the optimality of the coupled time-delay systems (6.4.4)–(6.4.5) reduces to the following two time-delay and advance sets of TPBV problems (Kharatishivili, 1961):

$$\dot{x} = H_p^T = f \tag{6.4.6a}$$

$$\dot{p} = -H_x^T - H_{x'}^T(s) = F_x^T - (f_x + \varepsilon f_x a_x)^T p - \varepsilon(g_\beta b_x)^T q$$
$$\qquad - \varepsilon \{ (f_\alpha a_{x'})^T p + (g_\beta b_{x'})^T q \}|_s \cdots \quad t \in I_1 \tag{6.4.6b}$$

$$\qquad = -H_x^T = F_x^T - (f_x + \varepsilon f_\alpha a_x)^T p - \varepsilon(g_\beta b_x)^T q \cdots \quad t \in I_2 \tag{6.4.6c}$$

$$0 = H_u^T + H_{u'}^T(s) = -F_u^T + (f_u + \varepsilon f_\alpha a_u)^T p + \varepsilon(g_\beta b_u)^T q$$
$$\qquad + \varepsilon \{ (f_\alpha a_{u'})^T p + (g_\beta b_{u'})^T q \}|_s \cdots \quad t \in I_1 \tag{6.4.6d}$$

$$\qquad = H_u^T = -F_u^T + (f_u + \varepsilon f_\alpha a_u)^T p + \varepsilon(g_\beta b_u)^T q \cdots \quad t \in I_2 \tag{6.4.6e}$$

$$\dot{y} = H_q^T = g \tag{6.4.7a}$$

$$\dot{q} = -H_y^T - H_{y'}^T(s) = G_y^T - (g_y + \varepsilon g_\beta b_y)^T q - \varepsilon(f_\alpha a_y)^T p$$
$$\qquad - \varepsilon \{ (g_\beta b_{y'})^T q + (f_\alpha a_{y'})^T p |_s \cdots \quad t \in I_1 \tag{6.4.7b}$$

$$= - H_y^T = G_y^T - \left( g_y + \varepsilon g_\beta b_y \right)^T q - \varepsilon \left( f_\alpha a_y \right)^T p \cdots \quad t \in I_2 \quad (6.4.7c)$$

$$0 = H_v^T + H_{v'}^T(s) = - G_v^T + \left( g_v + \varepsilon g_\beta b_v \right)^T q + \varepsilon \left( f_\alpha a_v \right)^T p$$

$$+ \varepsilon \left\{ \left( g_\beta b_{v'} \right)^T q + \left( f_\alpha a_{v'} \right)^T p \right\}|_s \cdots \quad t \in I_1 \quad (6.4.7d)$$

$$= H_v^T = - G_v^T + \left( g_v + \varepsilon g_\beta b_r \right)^T q + \varepsilon \left( f_\alpha a_v \right)^T p \cdots \quad t \in I_2 \quad (6.4.7e)$$

where $I_1: t_0 \leqslant t \leqslant t_f - \lambda$, $I_2: t_f - \lambda \leqslant t \leqslant t_f$, $s = t + \lambda$, $H = - F - G + p^T f + q^T g$ is the Hamiltonian function, and    and $q$ are, respectively, costates of $x$ and $y$. The final values of costates $p(t_f)$ and $q(t_f)$ are zero vectors.

Jamshidi (1973) has proved four assertions regarding the reduction of the linear and nonlinear time-delay, time-advanced TPBV problems as well as their respective sensitivity functions TPBV problems to two independent uncoupled unretarded TPBV problems as $\varepsilon \rightarrow 0$.

**Assertion 6.1.** At $\varepsilon = 0$ the necessary conditions (6.4.6) and (6.4.7) reduce to two independent TPBV problem for the two uncoupled unretarded systems.

PROOF: At $\varepsilon = 0$, none of the functions $f$, $f_x$, and $f_v$ depend on $x'$, $y$, $y'$, $u'$, $v$, and $v'$. Similarly, none of the functions $g$, $g_y$, and $g_v$ depend on $y'$, $x$, $x'$, $v'$, $v$, and $u'$. Thus,

$$\dot{x} = f, \quad x(t_0) = \phi(t_0) \qquad (6.4.8a)$$

$$\dot{p} = F_x^T - f_x^T p, \quad p(t_f) = 0 \qquad (6.4.8b)$$

$$0 = - F_u^T + f_u^T p \qquad (6.4.8c)$$

$$\dot{y} = g, \quad y(t_0) = \psi(t_0) \qquad (6.4.9a)$$

$$\dot{q} = G_y^T - g_y^T q, \quad q(t_f) = 0 \qquad (6.4.9b)$$

$$0 = - G_v^T + g_v^T q \qquad (6.4.9c)$$

The solutions of TPBV problems (6.4.8) and (6.4.9) provide $u^{(0)}$ and $v^{(0)}$, which are the zeroth-order terms of series in (6.4.3). Q.E.D. ■

**Assertion 6.2.** If the solution from the necessary conditions for terms $j = 0, 1, 2, \ldots, i - 1$ is known, the necessary conditions for the $i$th term reduces to two independent unretarded TPBV problems. Furthermore, the homogeneous parts of these problems remains unchanges for $i \geqslant 1$.

PROOF: Differentiate (6.4.6) $i$ times with respect to $\varepsilon$ and let $\varepsilon \to 0$; then the following TPBV problem is obtained for subsystem $x$:

$$\dot{x}^{(i)} = f_x x^{(i)} + f_u u^{(i)} + X^i \tag{6.4.10a}$$

$$\dot{p}^{(i)} = \left( F_{xx} - f_x^1 \right) x^{(i)} - f_x^T p^{(i)} + \left( F_{xu} - f_u^1 \right) u^{(i)} + P_1^i \cdots \quad t \in I_1 \tag{6.4.10b}$$

$$= \left( F_{xx} - f_x^1 \right) x^{(i)} - f_x^T p^{(i)} + \left( F_{xu} - f_u^1 \right) u^{(i)} + P_2^i \cdots \quad t \in I_2 \tag{6.4.10c}$$

$$0 = \left( f_x^2 - F_{ux} \right) x^{(i)} + f_u^T p^{(i)} + \left( f_u^2 - F_{uu} \right) u^{(i)} + U_1^i \cdots \quad t \in I_1 \tag{6.4.10d}$$

$$= \left( f_x^2 - F_{ux} \right) x^{(i)} + f_u^T p^{(i)} + \left( f_u^2 - F_{uu} \right) u^{(i)} + U_2^i \cdots \quad t \in I_2 \tag{6.4.10e}$$

where $x^{(i)}(0) = 0$ and $p^{(i)}(t_f) = 0$, $f^1 = f^1(x, p, v)$, and $f^2 = f^2(x, p, v)$, respectively, denote vectors $f_x^T p$ and $f_u^T p$. It must also be noted that nonhomogeneous parts $X^i$, $P^i$, and $U^i$ do not depend on $x^{(i)}$, $p^{(i)}$, $u^{(i)}$, $y^{(i)}$, $q^{(i)}$, or $v^{(i)}$. A similar procedure will lead to a TPBV problem for subsystem $y$:

$$\dot{y}^{(i)} = g_y y^{(i)} + g_v v^{(i)} + Y^i \tag{6.4.11a}$$

$$\dot{q}^{(i)} = \left( G_{yy} - g_y^1 \right) y^{(i)} - g_y^T q^{(i)} + \left( G_{yv} - g_v^1 \right) v^{(i)} + Q_1^i \cdots \quad t \in I_1 \tag{6.4.11b}$$

$$= \left( G_{yy} - g_y^1 \right) y^{(i)} - g_y^T q^{(i)} + \left( G_{yv} - g_v^1 \right) v^{(i)} + Q_2^i \cdots \quad t \in I_2 \tag{6.4.11c}$$

$$0 = \left( g_y^2 - G_{vy} \right) y^{(i)} + g_v^T q^{(i)} + \left( g_v^2 - G_{vv} \right) v^{(i)} + V_1^i \cdots \quad t \in I_1 \tag{6.4.11d}$$

$$= \left( g_y^2 - G_{vy} \right) y^{(i)} + g_v^T q^{(i)} + \left( g_v^2 - G_{vv} \right) v^{(i)} + V_2^i \cdots \quad t \in I_2 \tag{6.4.11e}$$

Similar comments apply to $Y^i$, $Q^i$, and $V^i$.

It is noted that the only unknown in TPBV problems (6.4.10) and (6.4.11) are $x^{(i)}$, $p^{(i)}$, $u^{(i)}$ and $y^{(i)}$, $q^{(i)}$, $v^{(i)}$, respectively. Thus, the solution of the necessary conditions for the $i$th terms of the control truncated series (6.4.3) reduces to two independent TPBV problems. Furthermore, due to the characteristic of sensitivity equations, the homogeneous parts of (6.4.10) and (6.4.11) remain the same for all $i = 1, 2, \ldots, k$. Q.E.D.  ∎

For the case when (6.4.4) is linear,

$$\dot{x} = Ax + Bu + \varepsilon a(\cdot)$$
$$= Ax + Bu + \varepsilon \left( A_1 y + A_2 y' + A_3 x' + B_1 v + B_2 u' + B_3 v' \right) \tag{6.4.12a}$$

$$\dot{y} = Dy + Ev + \varepsilon b(\cdot)$$
$$= Dy + Ev + \varepsilon \left( D_1 x + D_2 x' + D_3 y' + E_1 u + E_2 u' + E_3 v' \right) \tag{6.4.12b}$$

with the initial functions given by (6.4.5). The cost function is the usual quadratic form

$$J = \frac{1}{2} \int_{t_0}^{t_f} \left( x^T Q_1 x + y^T Q_2 y + u^T R_1 u + v^T R_2 v \right) dt \qquad (6.4.13)$$

where $Q_i$, $R_i$, $i = 1, 2$, have the usual regulating conditions. The necessary conditions for optimality are similar to those discussed for nonlinear system:

$$\dot{x} = H_p^T = Ax + Bu + \varepsilon a(\cdot), \quad x(\tau) = \phi(\tau) \qquad (6.4.14a)$$

$$\dot{p} = Q_1 x - A^T p - \varepsilon A_1^T q - \varepsilon A_3^T p(t + \lambda) - \varepsilon D_3^T q(t + \lambda) \cdots \quad t \in I_1 \quad (6.4.14b)$$

$$= Q_1 x - A^T p - \varepsilon D_1^T q, \quad p(t_f) = 0 \cdots \quad t \in I_2 \qquad (6.4.14c)$$

$$0 = -R_1 u + B^T p + \varepsilon E_1^T q + \varepsilon B_3^T p(t + \lambda) + \varepsilon E_2^T q(t + \lambda) \cdots$$

$$t \in I_1 \quad (6.4.14d)$$

$$= -R_1 u + B^T p + \varepsilon E_1^T q \cdots \quad t \in I_2 \qquad (6.4.14e)$$

Similarly for "subsystem $y$":

$$\dot{y} = H_q^T = Dy + Ev + \varepsilon b(\cdot), \quad y(\tau) = \psi(\tau) \qquad (6.4.15a)$$

$$\dot{q} = Q_2 y - D^T q - \varepsilon A_1^T p - \varepsilon D_3^T q(t + \lambda) - \varepsilon A_3^T p(t + \lambda) \cdots \quad t \in I_1 \quad (6.4.15b)$$

$$= Q_2 y - D^T q - \varepsilon A_1^T p, \quad q(t_f) = 0 \cdots \quad t \in I_2 \qquad (6.4.15c)$$

$$0 = -R_2 v + E^T q + \varepsilon B_1^T p + \varepsilon E_3^T q(t + \lambda) + \varepsilon B_2^T p(t + \lambda) \cdots$$

$$t \in I_1 \quad (6.4.15d)$$

$$= -R_2 v + E^T q + \varepsilon B_1^T p \cdots \quad t \in I_2 \qquad (6.4.15e)$$

In a similar fashion, the following two assertions are given for the linear system case.

**Assertion 6.3.** At $\varepsilon = 0$, the necessary conditions (6.4.14) and (6.4.15) reduce to two independent linear TPBV problems for the two subsystems.

PROOF: At $\varepsilon = 0$, it follows from (6.4.14) and (6.4.15) that subsystem $x$

$$\dot{x} = Ax + Bu \qquad (6.4.16a)$$

$$\dot{p} = Q_1 x - A^T p \qquad (6.4.16b)$$

$$0 = -R_1 u + B^T p \qquad (6.4.16c)$$

and subsystem $y$

$$\dot{y} = Dv + Ev \qquad (6.4.17a)$$

$$\dot{q} = Q_2 y - D^T q \qquad (6.4.17b)$$

$$0 = -R_2 v + E^T q \qquad (6.4.17c)$$

It is clear that the above problems are independent of each other, and furthermore their solutions constitute the zeroth-order terms $u^{(0)}$ and $v^{(0)}$, given as

$$u^{(0)} = -R_1^{-1}B^T K x^{(0)} \qquad (6.4.18a)$$

$$v^{(0)} = -R_2^{-1}E^T P y^{(0)} \qquad (6.4.18b)$$

where $K$ and $P$ are the solutions of the following two matrix Riccati equations:

$$\dot{K} = -A^T K - KA + KSK - Q_1, \quad K(t_f) = 0 \qquad (6.4.19)$$

$$\dot{P} = -D^T P - PD + PTP - Q_2, \quad P(t_f) = 0 \qquad (6.4.20)$$

where $S = BR_1^{-1}B^T$ and $T = ER_2^{-1}E^T$. Q.E.D. ∎

**Assertion 6.4.** If the solutions from the necessary conditions for the $j$th terms, $j = 0, 1, 2, \ldots, i-1$, are known, the necessary conditions for the $i$th term reduces to two independent linear unretarded TPBV problems. Furthermore the homogeneous parts of all solutions remain the same throughout.

PROOF: Differentiate (6.4.14) $i$ times with respect to $\varepsilon$ and let $\varepsilon \to 0$; then the following TPBV problem is obtained for subsystem $x$:

$$\dot{x}^{(i)} = Ax^{(i)} + Bu^{(i)} + X^i \qquad (6.4.21a)$$

$$\dot{p}^{(i)} = Q_1 x^{(i)} + A^T u^{(i)} + P_1^i \cdots \quad t \in I_1 \qquad (6.4.21b)$$

$$= Q_1 x^{(i)} - A^T u^{(i)} + P_2^i \cdots \quad t \in I_2 \qquad (6.4.21c)$$

$$0 = -R_1 u^{(i)} + B^T p^{(i)} + U_1^i \cdots \quad t \in I_1 \qquad (6.4.21d)$$

$$= -R_1 u^{(i)} + B^T p^{(i)} + U_2^i \cdots \quad t \in I_2 \qquad (6.4.21e)$$

where $x^{(i)}(t_0) = p^{(i)}(t_f) = 0$ and nonhomogeneous parts $X^i$, $P^i$, and $U^i$ do not depend on the $i$th terms. A similar procedure will result in a TPBV problem for subsystem $y$:

$$\dot{y}^{(i)} = Dy^{(i)} + Ev^{(i)} + Y^i \qquad (6.4.22a)$$

$$\dot{q}^{(i)} = Q_2 Y^{(i)} - D^T q^{(i)} + Q_1^i \cdots \quad t \in I_1 \qquad (6.4.22b)$$

$$= Q_2 y^{(i)} - D^T q^{(i)} + Q_2^i \cdots \quad t \in I_2 \qquad (6.4.22c)$$

$$0 = -R_2 v^{(i)} + E^T q^{(i)} + V_1^i \cdots \quad t \in I_1 \qquad (6.4.22d)$$

$$= -R_2 v^{(i)} + E^T q^{(i)} + V_2^i \cdots \quad t \in I_2 \qquad (6.4.22e)$$

This completes the proof. Q.E.D. ∎

In sequel, two algorithms are given for near-optimum control of linear and nonlinear coupled time-delay systems.

***Algorithm 6.9.*** Near-optimum Control of Nonlinear Coupled Time-Delay Systems

*Step 1:* Calculate the zeroth-order (unretarded) terms from (6.4.8) and (6.4.9).

*Step 2:* a. Solve two matrix Riccati equations:

$$\dot{K}_x = - K_x A_x - A_x^T K_x + K_x S_x K_x - Q_x, \quad K_x(t_f) = 0 \quad (6.4.23)$$

$$\dot{K}_q = - K_y A_y - A_y^T K_y + K_y S_y K_y - Q_y, K_y(t_f) = 0 \quad (6.4.24)$$

b. Solve the linear adjoint equations

$$\dot{g}_x^1 = - (A_x - S_x K_x)^T g_x^1 - K_x L_x^1 + l_x^i \cdots \quad t \in I_1 \quad (6.4.25a)$$

$$= - (A_x - S_x K_x)^T g_x^1 - K_x L_x^2 + l_x^2 \cdots \quad t \in I_2 \quad (6.4.25b)$$

$$\dot{g}_y^1 = - (A_y - S_y K_y)^T g_y^1 - K_y L_y^1 + l_y^1 \cdots \quad t \in I_1$$

$$= - (A_y - S_y K_y)^T g_y^1 - K_y L_y^2 + l_y^2 \cdots \quad t \in I_2 \quad (6.4.26b)$$

$$g_x^1(t_f) = 0, \quad g_y^1(t_f) = 0$$

c. Obtain $x^{(1)}$ and $y^{(1)}$ from

$$\dot{x}^{(1)} = (A_x - S_x K_x) x^{(1)} - S_x g_x^1 + L_x^1 \quad (6.4.27)$$

$$\dot{y}^{(1)} = (A_y - S_y K_y) y^{(1)} - S_y g_y^1 + L_y^1 \quad (6.4.28)$$

with $x^{(1)}(t_0) = 0$, $y^{(1)}(t_0) = 0$ and $u^{(1)}$ and $v^{(1)}$ obtained from

$$u^{(1)} = - (\Gamma_x + \Pi_x K_x) x^{(1)} - \eta_x^1 - \Pi_x g_x^1 \cdots \quad t \in I_1 \quad (6.4.29a)$$

$$= - (\Gamma_x + \Pi_x K_x) x^{(1)} - \eta_x^2 \cdots \quad t \in I_2 \quad (6.4.29b)$$

$$v^{(1)} = - (\Gamma_y + \Pi_y K_y) y^{(1)} - \eta_y^2 - \Pi_y g_y^1 \cdots \quad t \in I_1 \quad (6.4.30a)$$

$$= - (\Gamma_y + \Pi_y K_y) y^{(1)} - \eta_y^2 \cdots \quad t \in I_2 \quad (6.4.30b)$$

Expressions for $A_x$, $S_x$, $Q_x$, $\Gamma_x$, $\Pi_x$, $L_x^1$, $L_x^2$, $l_x^1$, $l_x^2$, $\eta_x^1$, $\eta_x^2$, etc. are (Jamshidi, 1973)

$$A_x = f_x - f_u \left( f_u^2 - F_{uu} \right)^{-1} \left( f_x^2 - F_{ux} \right)$$

$$S_x = f_u \left( f_u^2 - F_{uu} \right)^{-1} f_u^T$$

$$Q_x = \left( F_{xx} - f_x^1 \right) - \left( F_{xu} - f_u^1 \right) \left( f_u^2 - F_{uu} \right)^{-1} \left( f_x^2 - F_{ux} \right)$$

$$\Gamma_x = \left( f_u^2 - F_{uu} \right)^{-1} \left( f_x^2 - F_{ux} \right)$$

$$\Pi_x = \left( f_u^2 - F_{uu} \right)^{-1} f_u^T$$

$$L_x^1 = f_\alpha a - f_u \left( f_u^2 - F_{uu} \right)^{-1} U_1^1$$

$$L_x^2 = f_\alpha a - f_u \left( f_u^2 - F_{uu} \right)^{-1} U_2^1 \qquad (6.4.31)$$

$$l_x^1 = Q_c - \left( F_{xu} - f_u^1 \right) \left( f_u^2 - F_{uu} \right)^{-1} U_1^1$$

$$l_x^2 = Q_c - \left( F_{xu} - f_u^1 \right) \left( f_u^2 - F_{uu} \right)^{-1} U_2^1$$

$$\eta_x^1 = \left( f_u^2 - F_{uu} \right)^{-1} U_1^1$$

$$\eta_x^2 = \left( f_u^2 - F_{uu} \right)^{-1} U_2^1$$

where $Q_c \equiv - \left( f_\alpha^1 a + a_x^T f_\alpha^T p + b_x^T g_\beta^T q \right)$.

*Step j(j > 2):* Solve the linear adjoint equations similar to (6.4.25) and (6.4.26) for $g_x^j$ and $g_y^j$ using the same Riccati solution as in (6.4.23) and (6.4.24):

$$\dot{x}^{(j)} = \left( A_x - S_x K_x \right) x^{(j)} - S_x g_x^j + L_x^j \qquad (6.4.32)$$

$$\dot{y}^{(j)} = \left( A_y - S_y K_y \right) y^{(j)} - S_y g_y^j + L_y^j \qquad (6.4.33)$$

with a similar expression for $v^{(j)}$ and $u^{(j)}$ as in (6.4.29) and (6.4.30).

*Step j + 1:* The control vectors are given by expressions (6.4.40)–(6.4.44). Stop.

**Algorithm 6.10.** Near-Optimum Control of Linear Coupled Time-Delay Systems

*Step 1:* Using (6.4.16) and (6.4.17) and Riccati equations (6.4.19) and (6.4.20), obtain the zeroth-order terms.

*Step 2:* a. Obtain the adjoint equations

$$\dot{g}_x^1 = -(A - SK)^T g_x^1 - KL_x^1 + l_x^1 \cdots \quad t \in I_1 \quad (6.4.34a)$$

$$= -(A - SK)^T g_x^1 - KL_x^2 + l_x^2 \cdots \quad t \in I_2 \quad (6.4.34b)$$

$$\dot{g}_y^1 = -(D - TP)^T g_y^1 - PL_y^1 + l_y^1 \cdots \quad t \in I_1 \quad (6.4.35a)$$

$$= -(D - TP)^T g_y^1 - PL_y^2 + l_y^2 \cdots \quad t \in I_2 \quad (6.4.35b)$$

where $L_x^i = X^i - BR_1^{-1}U_i^1$, $l_x^i = Q^i$, $L_y^i = Y^i - ER_2^{-1}V_i^1$, $i = 1,2$.
b. Then $x^{(1)}$, $y^{(1)}$, $u^{(1)}$, and $v^{(1)}$ are obtained from

$$\dot{x}^{(1)} = (A - SK)^T x^{(1)} + Sg_x^1 + L_x^1 \qquad (6.4.36)$$

$$\dot{y}^{(1)} = (D - TP)^T y^{(1)} - Tg_y^1 + L_y^1 \qquad (6.4.37)$$

$$u^{(1)} = -R_1^{-1}B^T Kx^{(1)} + R_1^{-1}U_1^1 + R_1^{-1}B^T g_x^1 \cdots \quad t \in I_1 \quad (6.4.38a)$$

$$= -R_1^{-1}B^T Kx^{(1)} - R_1^{-1}U_1^2 \cdots \quad t \in I_2 \qquad (6.4.38b)$$

$$v^{(1)} = -R_2^{-1}E^T Py^{(1)} + R_2^{-1}V_1^1 + R_2^{-1}E^T g_y^1 \cdots \quad t \in I_1 \quad (6.4.39a)$$

$$= -R_2^{-1}E^T Py^{(1)} - R_2^{-1}V_1^2 \cdots \quad t \in I_2 \qquad (6.4.39b)$$

*Step j(j > 2):* This step is similar to the corresponding step of the nonlinear case.

Note that based on the expressions for $u^{(i)}$ and $v^{(i)}$ in both linear and nonlinear system (6.4.29), (6.4.30), (6.4.38), (6.4.39), the control structure has the following general forms:

$$u = -\alpha_x x + \sum_{i=1}^{N} \frac{\varepsilon^i}{i!} \beta_{xi} \cdots \quad t \in I_1 \qquad (6.4.40a)$$

$$= -\alpha_x x + \sum_{i=1}^{N} \frac{\varepsilon^i}{i!} \gamma_{xi} \cdots \quad t \in I_2 \qquad (6.4.40b)$$

$$v = -\alpha_y y + \sum_{i=1}^{N} \frac{\varepsilon^i}{i!} \beta_{yi} \cdots \quad t \in I_1 \qquad (6.4.41a)$$

$$= -\alpha_y y + \sum_{i=1}^{N} \frac{\varepsilon^i}{i!} \gamma_{yi} \cdots \quad t \in I_2 \qquad (6.4.41b)$$

where

$$\alpha_x = (\Gamma_x + \Pi_x K_x)\cdots \quad \text{nonlinear} \qquad (6.4.42a)$$

$$= R_1^{-1}B^T K \cdots \quad \text{linear} \qquad (6.4.42b)$$

$$\beta_{xi} = -\eta_{xi}^1 + \Pi_x g_x^i \cdots \quad \text{nonlinear} \qquad (6.4.43a)$$

$$= -R_1^{-1}U_1^i + B_1^{-1}B'g_x^i \cdots \quad \text{linear} \qquad (6.4.43b)$$

$$\gamma_{xi} = -\eta_{xi}^2 \cdots \quad \text{nonlinear} \qquad (6.4.44a)$$

$$= -R_1^{-1}U_2^i \cdots \quad \text{linear} \qquad (6.4.44b)$$

Similar terms can be obtained for subsystem $y$.

The following two examples illustrate the two algorithms.

**Example 6.4.1.** Consider a simple nonlinear coupled time-delay system

$$\dot{x}_1 = x_2 + w_1, \quad \dot{x}_2 = -x_1 - 0.8x_2 - x_2(t-0.1) - x_1^3 + w \quad (6.4.45)$$

with

$$x_1(\tau) = 1 + \tau, \quad x_2(\tau) = -1 - \tau \cdots \quad -0.1 \leqslant \tau \leqslant 0.0 \quad (6.4.46)$$

In order to be able to decouple the state model (6.4.45), let control $w = u + \varepsilon v = \varepsilon u + v$ and $x = x_1$ and $y = y_1$; then

$$\dot{x} = f(x, u, \varepsilon a(\cdot)) = u + \varepsilon(y + v) \qquad (6.4.47a)$$

$$\dot{y} = g(y, v, \varepsilon b(\cdot)) = -0.8y + v + \varepsilon(u - x - x^3 - y(t-0.1)) \quad (6.4.47b)$$

Note that (6.4.47) is now in the general couple time-delay systems of (6.4.4). The cost function is chosen to be quadratic, with $L_1 = F = \frac{1}{2}(x^2 + u^2)$, $L_2 = G = \frac{1}{2}(y^2 + v^2)$, and $t_f = 2.0$ sec.

The result of the zeroth-order terms can be obtained from a pair of linear TPBV problems

$$\dot{x}^{(0)} = -p^{(0)}, \quad \dot{y}^{(0)} = -0.8y^{(0)} + q^{(0)} \qquad (6.4.48a)$$

$$\dot{p}^{(0)} = x^{(0)}, \quad \dot{q}^{(0)} = y^{(0)} - 0.8q^{(0)} \qquad (6.4.48b)$$

based on the solutions of the associated pair of Riccati equations similar to (6.4.23) and (6.4.24):

$$x^{(0)}(t) = -\exp(-t), \quad p^{(0)}(t) = \exp(-t), \quad u^{(0)}(t) = \exp(-t) \qquad (6.4.49a)$$

$$y^{(0)}(t) = \exp(-1.28t), \quad q^{(0)}(t) = -0.48\exp(-1.28t)$$

$$v^{(0)}(t) = -0.48\exp(-1.28) \qquad (6.4.49b)$$

The first-order adjoint vectors are

$$g_x^1(t) = -0.2533\exp(-t) + 0.44\exp(-1.28t) + 0.336\exp(-3.28t)$$

$$(6.4.50)$$

$$g_y^1(t) = -0.532\exp(-1.28t) + 0.88\exp(-t) - 0.234\exp(-3t)$$

$$\cdots 0 \leqslant t \leqslant 1.9 \quad (6.4.51\text{a})$$

$$= -1.532\exp(-1.28t) + 0.88\exp(-t) - 0.234\exp(-3t) \quad \cdots 1.9 \leqslant t \leqslant 2.0$$

$$(6.4.51\text{b})$$

The suboptimal controls $u$ and $v$ after truncating the forcing functions after the first term are

$$u \simeq x + \varepsilon g_x^1(t) \tag{6.4.52a}$$

$$v \simeq -y + \varepsilon g_y^1(t) \tag{6.4.52b}$$

The state equations are then

$$\dot{x} \simeq -x - \varepsilon g_x^1 - \varepsilon^2 g_y^1 \tag{6.4.53a}$$

$$\dot{y} \simeq -1.8y - \varepsilon\left(2x + x^3 + y(t-0.1) - \varepsilon g_x^1\right) + \varepsilon g_y^1 \tag{6.4.53b}$$

with initial functions (6.4.46). Figure 6.13 shows the suboptimal state and control of the nonlinear plant. The near-optimum performance index turned out to be $J'' = 1.0$.

**Example 6.4.2.** Consider the following linear coupled time-delay system:

$$\dot{x}_1 = -x_1 + x_2 + 0.2x_1(t-0.1) + w \tag{6.4.54a}$$

$$\dot{x}_2 = -x_1 - x_2 - 0.1x_2(t-0.1) + w \tag{6.4.54b}$$

with initial functions $x_1(\tau) = x_2(\tau) = 1.0$, $-0.1 \leqslant \tau \leqslant 0$.

In a similar fashion as in the nonlinear plant example, one may let $x = x_1$, $y = x_2$, and $w = u + \varepsilon v = \varepsilon u + v$ in the two equations of (6.4.54). The following coupled linear systems result:

$$\dot{x} = -x + u + \varepsilon a(\cdot) = -x + u + \varepsilon\left(2x(t-0.1) + y + v\right) \tag{6.4.55a}$$

$$\dot{y} = -y + v + \varepsilon b(\cdot) = -y + v + \varepsilon\left(-x - 0.1y(t-0.1) + u\right) \tag{6.4.55b}$$

The cost function is

$$J = \frac{1}{2}\int_0^1 \left(x^2 + y^2 + u^2/3 + v^2/3\right) dt \tag{6.4.56}$$

The Riccati equations (6.4.19) and (6.4.20) become

$$\dot{k} = -2k + 3k^2 - 1, \quad k(1) = 0 \tag{6.4.57a}$$

$$\dot{p} = -2p + 3p^2 - 1, \quad p(1) = 0 \tag{6.4.57b}$$

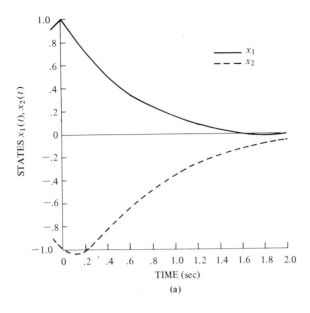

(a)

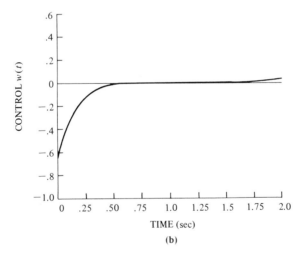

(b)

**Figure 6.13** Time responses for the nonlinear time-delay system of Example 6.4.1: (a) states and (b) control.

Using the solutions of these equations, the responses of the decoupled systems, i.e., zeroth-order terms, are easily obtained:

$$x^{(0)}(t) = y^{(0)}(t) = \exp(-4t), \quad p^{(0)}(t) = q^{(0)}(t) = -\exp(-4t)$$
$$u^{(0)}(t) = v^{(0)}(t) = -3\exp(-4t) \tag{6.4.58}$$

The first-order adjoint vectors follow form (6.4.34) and (6.4.35) as

$$g_x^1(t) = -0.47 \times 10^{-4}\exp(4t) + 0.17\exp(-4t), \quad 0 \leqslant t \leqslant 0.9 \tag{6.4.59a}$$
$$= -0.61 \times 10^{-4}\exp(4t) + 0.19\exp(-4t), \quad 0.9 \leqslant t \leqslant 1.0 \tag{6.4.59b}$$
$$g_y^1(t) = -0.18 \times 10^{-3}\exp(4t) + 0.565\exp(-4t), \quad 0 \leqslant t \leqslant 0.9 \tag{6.4.60a}$$
$$= -0.18 \times 10^{-3}\exp(4t) + 0.562\exp(-4t), \quad 0.9 \leqslant t \leqslant 1.0 \tag{6.4.60b}$$

The suboptimal controls, when truncating after one term, are

$$u \simeq -3x - 3\varepsilon g_x^1(t) \tag{6.4.61a}$$
$$v \simeq -3y - 3\varepsilon g_y^1(t) \tag{6.4.61b}$$

The state model using the controls in (6.4.61) will become

$$\dot{x} \simeq -4x - 2\varepsilon y + 0.2\varepsilon x(t - 0.1) - 3\varepsilon\left(g_x^1 + \varepsilon g_y^1\right) \tag{6.4.62a}$$
$$\dot{y} \simeq -4y - 4\varepsilon x - 0.1\varepsilon y(t - 0.1) - 3\varepsilon\left(\varepsilon g_x^1 + g_y^1\right) \tag{6.4.62b}$$

with $x(0) = y(0) = 1$. Figure 6.14 shows the state and control responses for a one-term truncation series. The near-optimum performance index turned out to be $J^n = 0.79$. All the computations were done on an IBM/1130 computer using FORTRAN.

The coupling procedure described here is computationally attractive, since all the calculations are based on lower-order unretarded and decoupled subsystems. For the two coupled subsystem formulation, it was shown that a near-optimum controller can be obtained which has an exact feedback portion and an approximate forward term. This result is of course expected, since all sensitivity methods give such near-optimum controls. Also, as in the unretarded nonlinear case discussed in Section 6.3.1, only one low-order Riccati equation must be solved, regardless of the order of approximation. The only extra computation required for each new approximation is the solution of the linear adjoint vector equation.

### 6.4.2 Near-Optimum Control of Serial Time-Delay Systems

In this section the hierarchical control of a linear large-scale system with a serial structure and time-delay linear interaction shown in Figure 6.15 is considered. The state and output equations of this system are represented

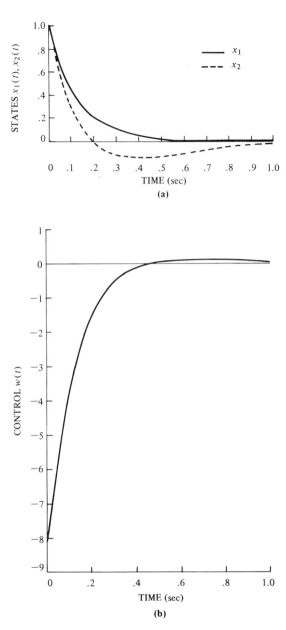

**Figure 6.14** Time responses for the linear time-delay system of Example 6.4.2: **(a)** states and **(b)** control.

358

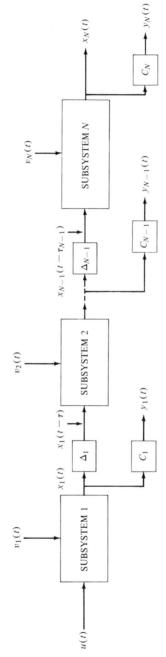

**Figure 6.15** A block diagram respresentation of a serial time-delay system.

by

$$\dot{x}_1(t) = A_1 x_1(t) + B_1 u_1(t) + v_1(t)$$
$$y_1(t) = C_1 x_1(t)$$
$$\dot{x}_2(t) = A_2 x_2(t) + B_2 u_2(t) + D_2 x_1(t - \tau_1) + v_2(t)$$
$$y_2(t) = C_2 x_2(t) \qquad\qquad\qquad\qquad\qquad (6.4.63)$$
$$\vdots$$
$$\dot{x}_N(t) = A_N x_N(t) + B_N u_N(t) + D_N x_{N-1}(t - \tau_{N-1}) + v_N(t)$$
$$y_N(t) = C_N x_N(t)$$

where $x_i(t)$, $y_i(t)$, and $u_i(t)$ are $n_i$-, $r_i$-, and $m_i$-dimensional state, output, and control vectors, respectively, $v_i(t)$ is the $i$th subsystem external input, and $\tau_i$, $i = 1, 2, \ldots, N-1$, are the delays between the $N$ subsystems. The cost function to be minimized is

$$J = \frac{1}{2} \sum_{i=1}^{N} \{ y_i(t_f) - y_i^*(t_f) \}^T F_i \{ y_i(t_f) - y_i^*(t_f) \}$$
$$+ \frac{1}{2} \int_0^{t_f} \sum_{i=1}^{N} \{ (y_i - y_i^*)^T Q_i (y_i - y_i^*) + u_i^T R_i u_i \} \, dt \qquad (6.4.64)$$

where $y_i^* = y_i^*(t)$, $i = 1, 2, \ldots, N$, are the desired outputs of the $N$ subsystems and the bracketed term outside the integral sign corresponds to the terminal output penalty function. For the sake of nontriviality, it is assumed that $t_f > \tau_1 + \cdots + \tau_{N-1}$. The application of the maximum principle of time-delay systems, as demonstrated earlier, results in a set of $2n$ TPBV problems with delay and advance terms which is clearly impractical. Any other approach, such as dynamic programming, as demonstrated by Singh (1980), is still formidable and computationally unfeasible.

The approach which seems most suitable is an approximate optimum solution based on hierarchical control. Under a hierarchical structure, the first-level problem would be to minimize

$$J_i = \frac{1}{2} \left( y_i(t_f) - y_i^*(t_f) \right)^T F_i \left( y_i(t_f) - y_i^*(t_f) \right)$$
$$+ \frac{1}{2} \int_0^{t_f} \{ (y_i - y_i^*)^T Q_i (y_i - y_i^*) + u_i^T R_i u_i \} \, dt \qquad (6.4.65)$$

subject to

$$\dot{x}_i(t) = A_i x_i(t) + B_i u_i(t) + D_i x_{i-1}(t - \tau_{i-1}) + v_i(t) \qquad (6.4.66)$$
$$y_i(t) = C_i x_i(t) \qquad\qquad\qquad\qquad\qquad\qquad (6.4.67)$$

Then assuming that the disturbance $v_i(t)$ and an estimate $\hat{x}_{i-1}(t - \tau_{i-1})$ of $x_{i-1}(t - \tau_{i-1})$ is transferred down from the second level, the first-level problem (6.4.65)–(6.4.67) can be readily solved through a Riccati formulation. Under such conditions, the second-level problem would be an iterative search to reduce the interaction error between $x_j(t - \tau_j)$ and $\hat{x}_j(t - \tau_j)$ for $j = 1, 2, \ldots, N - 1$ to a small value. Such approaches as "goal coordination" or "interaction prediction" discussed in Sections 4.2.1 and 4.2.5 may well be used. The near-optimum scheme suggested by Singh (1980) is to stop the second-level iteration once the state of any given subsystem $x_i(t)$ becomes known and simply transfer down an estimate $\hat{x}_i(t - \tau_i)$ as an extra known external input to be incorporated in the optimization of the $(i+1)$th problem. Thus, the $i$th subsystem optimization at the first level given by (6.4.65)–(6.4.67) after replacing $x_{i-1}(t - \tau_{i-1})$ by $\hat{x}_{i-1}(t - \tau_{i-1})$ would be summarized as

$$u_i(t) = - R_i^{-1} B_i^T \{ K_i(t) x_i(t) + g_i(t) \} \tag{6.4.68}$$

where Riccati matrix $K_i(t)$ and adjoint vector $g_i(t)$ are obtained from

$$\dot{K}_i(t) = - K_i(t) A_i - A_i^T K_i(t) + K_i(t) S_i K_i(t) - C_i^T Q_i C_i \tag{6.4.69a}$$

$$K_i(t_f) = C_i^T F_i C_i \tag{6.4.69b}$$

$$\dot{g}_i(t) = - (A_i - S_i K_i(t))^T g_i(t) + K_i(t) w_i(t) - C_i Q_i y_i^*(t) \tag{6.4.70a}$$

$$g_i(t_f) = C_i^T F_i y_i^*(t_f) \tag{6.4.70b}$$

where $S_i = B_i R_i^{-1} B_i^T$ and

$$\begin{aligned} w_i(t) &= v_i(t) + D_i \hat{x}_{i-1}(t - \tau_{i-1}), \quad \text{for } i = 2, 3, \ldots, N \\ &= v_i(t), \quad \text{for } i = 1 \end{aligned} \tag{6.4.71}$$

The closed-loop system becomes

$$\dot{x}_i(t) = (A_i - S_i K_i(t)) x_i(t) + D_i \hat{x}_{i-1}(t - \tau_{i-1}) + v_i(t) \tag{6.4.72}$$

The near-optimum control of the serial time-delay system is summarized by the following algorithm.

**Algorithm 6.11.** Near-Optimum Control of a Serial Time-Delay System

Step 1: Set $i = 1$ and input $t_f, A_i, B_i, v_i, \ldots$.

Step 2: Solve $K_i(t)$ and $g_i(t)$ using (6.4.69) and (6.4.70) and store.

Step 3: Integrate (6.4.72) to compute $x_i(t)$ and store
$\hat{x}_i(t - \tau_i) = x_i(t - \tau_i)$.

Step 4: If $N < i = i + 1$, go to Step 2.

Step 5: Stop.

The following example illustrates Algorithm 6.11.

**Example 6.4.3.** Consider a three-subsystem serial time-delay system defined by the following state and output equations:

*Subsystem 1:*

$$\dot{x}_1 = A_1 x_1 + B_1 u_1 + v_1, \quad y_1 = C_1 x_1 \qquad (6.4.73)$$

$$A_1 = \begin{bmatrix} 0 & 0.1 \\ -1 & -1 \end{bmatrix},$$

$$B_1 = \begin{bmatrix} 1 \\ 1 \end{bmatrix}, \quad v_1 = \begin{bmatrix} 1.5 \\ 0.2 \end{bmatrix}, \quad C_1 = [1 \quad 0.1]$$

$$Q_1 = R_1 = F_1 = [1], \quad t_o = 0, \quad t_f = 4, \quad x_1(0) = [1 \quad -1]^T$$

*Subsystem 2:*

$$\dot{x}_2 = A_2 x_2 + B_2 u_2 + D_2 x_1(t - \tau_1) + v_2, \quad y_2 = C_2 x_2 \qquad (6.4.74)$$

$$A_2 = \begin{bmatrix} 0 & 0 & 0.1 \\ 0.1 & -1 & 0.2 \\ 1 & 0.85 & -0.9 \end{bmatrix}, \quad B_2 = \begin{bmatrix} 1 & 0 \\ 0 & 1 \\ 0 & 1 \end{bmatrix}$$

$$v_2 = \begin{bmatrix} 0 \\ 0 \\ -1 \end{bmatrix}, \quad D_2 = \begin{bmatrix} 0.15 & -0.2 \\ 0.25 & 0.8 \\ 0.1 & -0.1 \end{bmatrix}$$

$$Q_2 = F_2 = [2] \quad R_2 = 2I_2, \quad C_2 = [10.5 \quad 0.1], \quad \tau_1 = 0.05$$

$$x_2(0) = [1 \quad 0.5 \quad -1]^T$$

*Subsystem 3:*

$$\dot{x}_3 = A_3 x_3 + B_3 u_3 + D_3 x_2(t - \tau_2) + v_2, \quad y_3 = C_3 x_3 \qquad (6.4.75)$$

$$A_3 = \begin{bmatrix} 0.1 & 0.5 & -0.25 \\ 0.5 & 0 & 0.8 \\ -1 & 1 & -2 \end{bmatrix}, \quad B_3 = \begin{bmatrix} 1 \\ 0 \\ 1 \end{bmatrix}, \quad v_3 = \begin{bmatrix} 1.2 \\ 1 \\ -1 \end{bmatrix},$$

$$D_3 = \begin{bmatrix} 1 & 0.2 & 0.5 \\ -0.5 & 0.1 & 0.8 \\ 0.75 & 1 & -1 \end{bmatrix}$$

$$Q_3 = R_3 = [2], \quad F_3 = [0.5], \quad C_3 = [2 \quad 1 \quad 1]$$

$$\tau_2 = 0.1, \quad x_3(0) = [1 \quad -0.5 \quad 1]^T$$

It is desired to find the optimal controls for the three subsystems using Algorithm 6.11.

SOLUTION: As the first step, one should solve three differential matrix Riccati equations (6.4.69). This was done on an HP-9845 computer using a fourth-order Runge–Kutta method, and the solutions were fit in second-order polynomials. The step size of 0.05 was chosen to conveniently recover the delayed quantities defined in (6.4.74) and (6.4.75). Next the adjoint equation (6.4.70) was solved for $i = 1$, 2, and 3. The resulting optimal controls and outputs for the three subsystems are shown in Figure 6.16.

### 6.4.3 Hierarchical Control of a Nonserial Time-Delay System

Consider a large-scale time-delay system

$$\dot{x}(t) = A(t)x(t) + B(t)u(t) + C(t)x(t - h_x) + D(t)u(t - h_u), \quad t \geqslant t_o$$

(6.4.76a)

$$x(t) = \eta(t), \quad t_o - h_x \leqslant t \leqslant t_o, \quad u(t) = \alpha(t), \quad t_o - h_u \leqslant t \leqslant t_o \quad (6.4.76b)$$

where $x(t) \in R^n$ and $u(t) \in R^m$ are, respectively, state and control vectors; $A(t)$, $B(t)$, $C(t)$, and $D(t)$ are real, piecewise-continuous matrices of appropriate dimensions defined on the appropriate intervals; $t_o$ is the initial process time; $\eta(t)$ and $\alpha(t)$ are specified initial functions; and $h_x$ and $h_u$ are

---

**Figure 6.16** Output and control time responses of the serially time-delayed Example 6.4.4: **(a)** Subsystem 1, **(b)** Subsystem 2 and **(c)** Subsystem 3.

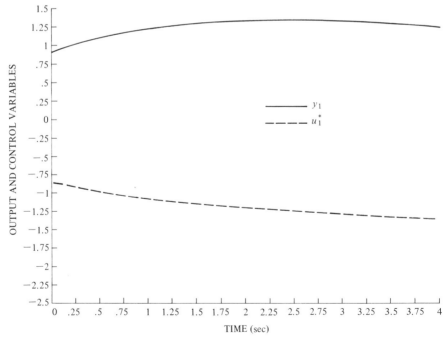

(a)

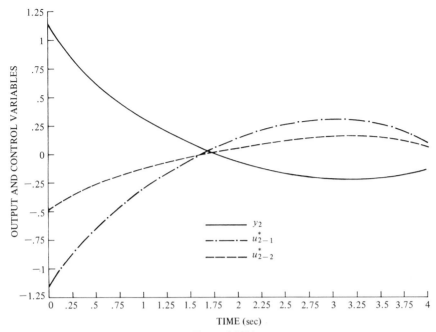

**Figure 6.16(b)**

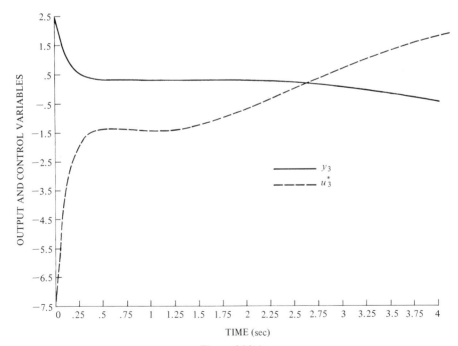

**Figure 6.16(c)**

constant positive scalars. The cost functional to be minimized is

$$J = \frac{1}{2}x^T(t_f)Fx(t_f) + \frac{1}{2}\int_{t_o}^{t_f}\left[x^T(t)Q(t)x(t) + u^T(t)R(t)u(t)\right]dt \quad (6.4.77)$$

where matrix $F$ is symmetric positive-semidefinite; the matrix $Q(t)$ is symmetric positive-semidefinite and piecewise-continuous; and the matrix $R(t)$ is symmetric, positive-definite, and piecewise-continuous. The problem is to find a control $u(t)$, $t_0 \leq t \leq t_f$, which for fixed final time $t_f$ and free final state $x(t_f)$ minimizes the cost functional $J$ in (6.4.77).

Assume that the state vector $x$ and the control vector $u$ are decomposed as follows (Jamshidi and Malek-Zavarei, 1982):

$$x = \left[x_1^T, x_2^T, \ldots, x_N^T\right]^T \quad (6.4.78)$$

$$u = \left[u_1^T, u_2^T, \ldots, u_N^T\right]^T \quad (6.4.79)$$

where $x_i \in R^{n_i}$, $u_i \in R^{m_i}$, $i = 1, 2, \ldots, N$, and

$$\sum_{i=1}^{N} n_i = n, \quad \sum_{i=1}^{N} m_i = m \quad (6.4.80)$$

The initial vector functions $\eta(t)$ and $\alpha(t)$ will be partitioned accordingly. The matrices $A$, $B$, $C$, $D$, $F$, $q$, and $R$ will also be partitioned accordingly. We denote the $i$th block row of matrix $A$ by $A_i$ and the $ij$ block of matrix $A$ by $A_{ij}$, $i, j = 1, 2, \ldots, N$. Also let $\hat{A}_i = A_i$ with $A_{ii}$ be set to zero, i.e.,

$$\hat{A}_i = [A_{i1}, A_{i2}, \ldots, A_{i,i-1}, 0, A_{i,i+1}, \ldots, A_{iN}] \quad (6.4.81)$$

Similar notation applies to matrix $\hat{B}_i$.

With the above notation, the $i$th subsystem, $i = 1, 2, \ldots, N$, becomes

$$\dot{x}_i(t) = A_{ii}(t)x_i(t) + B_{ii}(t)u_i(t) + z_i(t), \quad t \geq t_0 \quad (6.4.82)$$

$$x_i(t_0) = \eta_i(t_o) \quad (6.4.83)$$

where

$$z_i(t) = \hat{A}_i(t)x(t) + \hat{B}_i(t)u(t) + C_i(t)x(t - h_x) + D_i(t)u(t - h_u) \quad (6.4.84)$$

Also the cost functional (6.4.77) is assumed to be represented by

$$J = \sum_{i=1}^{N} J_i \quad (6.4.85)$$

where

$$J_i = \frac{1}{2}x_i^T(t_f)\left[F_{ii}x_i(t_f) + 2f_i(t_f)\right]$$
$$+ \frac{1}{2}\int_{t_o}^{t_f}\{x_i^T(t)\left[Q_{ii}(t)x_i(t) + 2q_i(x(t))\right]$$
$$+ u_i^T(t)\left[R_{ii}(t)u_i(t) + 2r_i(u(t))\right]\}\,dt \quad (6.4.86)$$

and

$$f_i(\hat{x}_i(T)) = \tfrac{1}{2}F_i\hat{x}_i(T), \quad q_i(\hat{x}_i(t)) = \tfrac{1}{2}Q_i\hat{x}_i(t), \quad r_i(\hat{u}_i(t)) = \tfrac{1}{2}R_i\hat{u}_i(t)$$

(6.4.87)

No constraints need to be put on the method of system decomposition. However, often a natural decomposition exists for any given large-scale system. If this is not the case, it is partitioned in such a way so that, on the average, a maximum number of zeros occur in the off-diagonal blocks of the matrices $A$, $B$, $C$, $D$, $F$, $Q$, and $R$ or the system would be weakly coupled within the context of nondelay systems (Milne, 1965).

In sequel, an iterative procedure is proposed to determine a near-optimum control for the problem defined by (6.4.76)–(6.4.77). In each iteration the delay terms and the terms due to interdependence between subsystems will appear as known, forcing functions obtained in the previous iteration. More precisely, in iteration $k$ the following nondelay optimal control problem is solved:

$$\dot{x}_i^k = A_{ii}x_i^k + B_{ii}u_i^k + z_i^{k-1}, \quad t \geqslant t_o$$

(6.4.88a)

$$x_i^k(t_o) = \eta_i(t_o)$$

(6.4.88b)

$$J_i^k = \frac{1}{2}x_i^{kT}(t_f)\left[F_{ii}x_i^k(t_f) + 2f_i^{k-1}\left(x_i^k(t_f)\right)\right]$$

$$+ \frac{1}{2}\int_{t_o}^{t_f}\left\{x_i^{kT}\left[Q_{ii}x_i^k + 2q_i^{k-1}(x^k)\right]\right.$$

$$\left. + u_i^{kT}\left[R_{ii}u_i^k + 2r_i^{k-1}(u^k)\right]\right\}dt$$

(6.4.89)

where

$$z_i^{k-1} = \hat{A}_i x^{k-1} + \hat{B}_i u^{k-1} + C_i x^{k-1}(t - h_x) + D_i u^{k-1}(t - h_u)$$

(6.4.90a)

and

$$x_i^k(t) = \eta_i(t), \quad t_o - h_x \leqslant t \leqslant t_o, \quad k = 1, 2, \ldots$$

(6.4.90b)

$$u_i^k(t) = \alpha_i(t), \quad t_o - h_u \leqslant t \leqslant t_o, \quad k = 1, 2, \ldots$$

(6.4.90c)

Note that dependence on $t$ has been omitted whenever it does not cause ambiguity. In order to initiate the iterations, we let

$$x_i^o(t) = \psi_{ii}(t, t_o)\eta_i(t_o), \quad u_i^o(t) = h_i(t), \quad t \geqslant t_o$$

(6.4.91)

where $\psi_{ii}(t, t_o)$ is the state transition matrix corresponding to system matrix $A_{ii}(t) - B_{ii}R_{ii}^{-1}B_{ii}^T K_{ii}(t)$, $h_i(t)$ is an arbitrary continuous function, and $K_{ii}(t)$ is the symmetric positive-definite solution to the DMRE

$$\dot{K}_{ii} + K_{ii}A_{ii} + A_{ii}^T K_{ii} - K_{ii}S_{ii}K_{ii} + Q_{ii} = 0, \quad K_{ii}(t_f) = F_{ii}$$

(6.4.92)

where $S_{ii} = B_{ii}R_{ii}^{-1}B_{ii}^T$.

The following theorem justifies the above procedure.

**Theorem 6.1.** *Consider the sequence of linear state equations (6.4.88) with (6.4.90) and 6.4.91) and the associated cost function (6.4.89). Suppose that for the kth iteration the optimal state trajectory $x_i^{*k}$ and the optimal control $u_i^{*k}$ are obtained. Then the sequence of n-dimensional state vectors $[x_1^{*k}, x_2^{*k}, \ldots, x_N^{*k}]^T$ and m-dimensional control vectors $[u_1^{*k}, u_2^{*k}, \ldots, u_n^{*k}]^T$ uniformly converge, respectively to $x^*(t)$ and $u^*(t)$, the optimal state trajectory and the optimal control for the optimization problem defined by (6.4.76) and (6.4.77).*

The proof of this theorem, due to Jamshidi and Malek-Zavarei (1982), is given after the following lemma is established.

**Lemma 6.1.** *Consider the system of delay-differential equations*

$$\dot{x}_i(t) = A_{ii}(t) x_i(t) + \hat{A}_i(t) x(t) + C_i(t) x(t - h_x), \quad t \geq t_0 \qquad (6.4.93a)$$

$$x_i(t) = \eta_i(t), \quad t_0 - h_x \leq t \leq t_0, \quad i = 1, 2, \ldots, N \qquad (6.4.93b)$$

*where $A_{ii}(t)$, $\hat{A}_i(t)$, and $C_i(t)$, $i = 1, 2, \ldots, N$, are real piecewise-continuous matrices defined previously; vectors $x$ and $x_i$ are defined in (6.4.78), and $h_x$ is a constant real positive scalar. Then the sequence of vector functions $\{x_i^k(t)\}$, $i = 1, 2, \ldots, N$, defined by*

$$x_i^o(t) = \phi_{ii}(t, t_0) \eta_i(t_0), \quad t_0 \leq t \leq t_f \qquad (6.4.94a)$$

$$x_i^k(t) = \phi_{ii}(t, t_0) \eta_i(t_0)$$
$$+ \int_{t_0}^{t_f} \phi_{ii}(t, \tau) \left[ \hat{A}_i(\tau) x^{k-1}(\tau) + C_i(\tau) x^{k-1}(\tau - h_x) \right] d\tau$$

$$t_0 \leq t \leq t_f, \quad k = 1, 2, \ldots \qquad (6.4.94b)$$

$$x_i^k(t) = \eta_i(t), \quad t_0 - h_x \leq t \leq t_0, \quad k = 0, 1, 2, \ldots \qquad (6.4.94c)$$

*where $\phi_{ii}(t, \tau)$ denotes the state transition matrix corresponding to the system matrix $A_{ii}(t)$, and $\hat{A}_i(t)$, defined in (6.4.81), converges uniformly to the solution of (6.4.93).*

PROOF: Equations (6.4.93) for $i - 1, 2, \ldots, N$ imply

$$\dot{x}(t) = A_d(t) x(t) + \hat{A}(t) x(t) + C(t) x(t - h_x), \quad t_0 \leq t \leq t_f \qquad (6.4.95a)$$

where $A_d(t) = \text{diag}(A_{ii}(t))$ and $\hat{A}(t) = A(t)$ where the block diagonals and $A_{ii}(t)$ are zero matrices. Also, equations (6.4.93b) for $i = 1, 2, \ldots, N$ imply

$$x(t) = \eta(t), \quad t_0 = h_x \leq t \leq t_0 \qquad (6.4.95b)$$

In the same manner, using equations (6.4.94), the sequence

$$x^k(t) = \left[ x_1^{kT}(t), x_2^{kT}(t), \ldots, x_N^{kT}(t) \right]^T \qquad (6.4.96)$$

will be defined by

$$x^o(t) = \phi_d(t, t_o)\eta(t_o), \quad t \geq t_o \tag{6.4.97a}$$

$$x^k(t) = \phi_d(t, t_o)\eta(t_o) + \int_{t_o}^t \phi_d(t, \tau)\left[\hat{A}(\tau)x^{k-1}(\tau) + C(\tau)x^{k-1}(\tau - h_x)\right] d\tau$$

$$k = 1, 2, \ldots, \quad t \geq t_o \tag{6.4.97b}$$

$$x^k(t) = \eta(t), \quad t_o - h_x \leq t \leq t_o, \quad k = 0, 1, 2, \ldots \tag{6.4.97c}$$

where

$$\phi_d(t, \tau) = \text{diag}(\phi_{ii}(t, \tau)) \tag{6.4.97d}$$

It will be shown that the sequence of vector functions $\{x^k(t)\}$ defined above uniformly converges to the solution of (6.4.95). Equation (6.4.97b) yields

$$x^2(t) - x^1(t) = \int_{t_o}^t \phi_d(t, \tau)\{\hat{A}(\tau)[x^1(\tau) - x^o(\tau)]$$

$$+ C(\tau)[x^1(\tau - h_x) - x^o(\tau - h_x)]\} d\tau \tag{6.4.98a}$$

which implies

$$\|x^2(t) - x^1(t)\| \leq M\int_{t_o}^t \{N_a\|x^1(\tau) - x^o(\tau)\|$$

$$+ N_c\|x^1(\tau - h_x) - x^o(\tau - h_x)\|\} d\tau \tag{6.4.98b}$$

where

$$M = \underset{t, \tau \in [t_o, t_f]}{\text{Sup}} \|\phi_d(t, \tau)\|, \quad N_a = \underset{\tau \in [t_o, t_f]}{\text{Sup}} \|\hat{A}(\tau)\|, \quad N_c = \underset{\tau \in [t_o, t_f]}{\text{Sup}} \|C(\tau)\|$$

$$\tag{6.4.99a}$$

It is convenient to choose a norm $\|\cdot\|$ such that $\|\phi_d(t_o, t_o)\| = \|I\| = 1$. This then guarantees that $M \geq 1$. Let

$$L = \underset{t \in [t_o - h_x, t_o]}{\text{Sup}} \|\eta(t)\| \tag{6.4.99b}$$

Then from (6.4.97) we have

$$\|x^1(t) - x^o(t)\| \leq M\left[N_a\int_{t_o}^t \|x^o(\tau)\| d\tau + N_c\int_{t_o}^t \|x^o(\tau - h_x)\| d\tau\right]$$

$$= M\bigg\{N_a\int_{t_o}^t \|\phi_d(\tau, t_o)\eta(t_o)\| d\tau$$

$$+ N_c\bigg[\int_{t_o}^{t_o + h_x} \|\eta(\tau - h_x)\| d\tau$$

$$+ \int_{t_o + h_x}^t \|\phi(\tau - h_x, t_o)\eta(t_o)\| d\tau\bigg]\bigg\}$$

$$\leq M\{N_a[ML(t - t_o)] + N_c[Lh_x + ML(t - t_o - h_x)]\}$$

$$\leq M^2L(N_a + N_c)(t - t_o), \quad t_o \leq t \leq t_f \tag{6.4.100}$$

Using (6.4.100), (6.4.98b) implies that

$$\|x^2(t) - x^1(t)\| \leqslant M^3 L (N_a + N_c)^2 (t - t_o)^2 / 2, \quad t_o \leqslant t \leqslant t_f \qquad (6.4.101)$$

and, by induction,

$$\|x^k(t) - x^{k-1}(t)\| \leqslant M^{k+1} L (N_a + N_c)^k (t - t_o)^k / k!, \quad t_o \leqslant t \leqslant t_f \qquad (6.4.102)$$

Applying the triangle inequality one has, for any $r$,

$$\|x^{k+r}(t) - x^k(t)\| \leqslant \sum_{i=k+1}^{k+r} \left[ M^{i+1} L (N_a + N_c)^i \frac{(t - t_o)^i}{i!} \right]$$

$$\leqslant ML \left[ M (N_a + N_c)(t - t_o) \right]^{k+1} \exp \left[ M (N_a + N_c)(t - t_o) \right], \quad t_o \leqslant t \leqslant t_f \qquad (6.4.103)$$

Therefore, the sequence $\{x^k(t)\}$ is uniformly convergent. The limit of this sequence is clearly the solution to (6.4.95), and the lemma is proved. Q.E.D. ∎

PROOF OF THEOREM 6.1: Consider the $i$th subproblem defined by Equations (6.4.88)–(6.4.89). Note that $z_i^{k-1}(t)$ is known in the $k$th iteration and acts as an extra perturbing input in the $k$th state equation. The Hamiltonian function for this problem is

$$H_i^k = \tfrac{1}{2} x_i^{kT} \left( Q_{ii} x_i^k + 2q_i^{k-1} \right) + \tfrac{1}{2} u_i^{kT} \left( R_{ii} u_i^k + 2r_i^{k-1} \right)$$
$$+ p_i^{kT} \left( A_{ii} x_i^k + B_{ii} u_i^k + z_i^{k-1} \right)$$

where $p_i^k(t)$ is the corresponding costate vector and $q_i^k$ and $r_i^k$ are defined in (6.4.89). The necessary and sufficient conditions for optimality are

$$\dot{p}_i^k = -\frac{\partial H_i^k}{\partial x_i^k} = -Q_{ii} x_i^k - q_i^{k-1} - A_{ii}^T p_i^k, \quad t \geqslant t_o \qquad (6.4.104a)$$

$$p_i^k(t_f) = \frac{\partial}{\partial x_i^k(t_f)} \left\{ \tfrac{1}{2} x_i^{kT}(t_f) \left[ F_{ii} x_i^k(t_f) + 2f_i(t_f) \right] \right\} = F_{ii} x_i^k(t_f) + f_i(t_f)$$

$$\qquad (6.4.104b)$$

$$0 = \frac{\partial H_i^k}{\partial u_i^k} = R_{ii} u_i^k + r_i^{k-1} + B_{ii}^T p_i^k, \quad t \geqslant t_o \qquad (6.4.104c)$$

Equations (6.4.88a) and (6.4.104a) can be decoupled by defining the adjoint vectors $g_i^k(t)$, $k = 1, 2, \ldots$, as follows:

$$p_i^k = K_{ii} x_i^k + g_i^k, \quad t_o \leqslant t \leqslant t_f \qquad (6.4.105)$$

where $K_{ii}$ is the symmetric positive-definite solution to the DMRE (6.4.92).

Equations (6.4.104) and (6.4.105) imply that

$$\dot{g}_i^k = -(A_{ii} - S_{ii}K_{ii})^T g_i^k - K_{ii}\gamma_i^{k-1} - q_i^{k-1} \qquad (6.4.106a)$$

where

$$\gamma_i^{k-1} = -D_{ii}R_{ii}^{-1}r_i^{k-1} + z_i^{k-1} \qquad (6.4.107)$$

The boundary condition for Equation (6.4.106a) can be determined by comparison of (6.4.105) for $t = t_f$ with (6.4.104b) which yields

$$g_i^k(t_f) = f_i(t_f), \quad K_{ii}(t_f) = F_{ii} \qquad (6.4.106b)$$

Note that the second condition of (6.4.106b) conforms with that of (6.4.92). From (6.4.104c) and (6.4.105), the optimal control for the $k$th optimization problem can be written as

$$u_i^{*k} = -R_{ii}^{-1}(B_{ii}^T p_i^k + r_i^{k-1}) = -R_{ii}^{-1}B_{ii}^T K_{ii}x_i^{*k} - R_{ii}^{-1}B_{ii}^T g_i^k - R_{ii}^{-1}r_i^{k-1}$$

$$(6.4.108)$$

Hence, from (6.4.88a) and (6.4.108), the optimal state trajectory $x_i^{*k}(t)$ is the solution to

$$\dot{x}_i^{*k} = [A_{ii} - S_{ii}K_{ii}]x_i^{*k} - S_{ii}g_i^k + \gamma_i^{k-1} \qquad t_o \leqslant t \leqslant t_f \quad (6.4.109)$$

From (6.4.106a), note that $g_i^k(t)$ depends on known functions and $z_i^{k-1}$. The solution to (6.4.109) with boundary condition (6.4.88b) is

$$x_i^{*k}(t) = \psi_{ii}(t, t_o)\eta_i(t_o) + \int_{t_o}^t \psi_{ii}(t, \tau)\big[-S_{ii}(\tau)g_i^k(\tau) + \gamma_i^{k-1}(\tau)\big]d\tau,$$

$$t_o \leqslant t \leqslant t_f, \quad k = 1, 2, \dots \quad (6.4.110)$$

Comparison of (6.4.91) with (6.4.94a) and (6.4.110) with (6.4.94b) shows that the sequence $\{x_i^{*k}(t)\}$ converges uniformly. Also, the sequences $\{g_i^k(t)\}$ and $\{u_i^{*k}(t)\}$ converge because, from (6.4.106a) and (6.4.108), these sequences are related to $\{x_i^{*k}(t)\}$ by continuous transformations. From Lemma 6.1, the limit of the sequence $x_i^{*k}(t)$ is the solution to

$$\dot{x}_i^* = [A_{ii} - S_{ii}K_{ii}]x_i^* - S_{ii}g_i - B_{ii}R_{ii}^{-1}r_i$$
$$+ A_i x^*(t) + B_i u^* + C_i x^*(t - h_x) + D_i u^*(t - h_u), \quad t_o \leqslant t \leqslant t_f$$

$$(6.4.111a)$$

$$x_i^*(t) = \eta_i(t), \quad t_o - h_x \leqslant t \leqslant t_o \qquad (6.4.111b)$$

$$u_i^*(t) = \alpha_i(t), \quad t_o - h_u \leqslant t \leqslant t_o \qquad (6.4.111c)$$

where $x_i^*(t)$, $u_i^*(t)$, and $g_i(t)$ are, respectively, the limits of the sequences $\{x_i^{*k}(t)\}$, $\{u_i^{*k}(t)\}$, and $\{g_i^k(t)\}$. From (6.4.108),

$$u_i^* = -R_{ii}^{-1}B_{ii}^T K_{ii}x_i^* - R_{ii}^{-1}B_{ii}^T g_i - R_{ii}^{-1}r_i \qquad (6.4.112)$$

substituting $u_i^*(t)$ from (6.4.112) for $u_i(t)$ in (6.4.82) and comparing the result with (6.4.111a) shows that $x_i^*(t)$ and $u_i^*(t)$ are, respectively, the optimal state trajectory and the optimal control for the $i$th optimization subproblem defined by (6.4.82)–(6.4.83) and (6.4.86) for $i = 1, 2, \ldots, N$. Or, equivalently,

$$x^*(t) = \left\{ x_1^{T*}(t), \ldots, x_N^{T*}(t) \right\} \qquad (6.4.113a)$$

and

$$u^*(t) = \left\{ u_1^{T*}(t), \ldots, u_N^{T*}(t) \right\} \qquad (6.4.113b)$$

are, respectively, the optimal state trajectory and the optimal control for the optimization problem defined by (6.4.76) and (6.4.77). Thus the theorem is proved. Q.E.D. ∎

The following algorithm summarizes the hierarchical control of a large-scale time-delay system.

*Algorithm 6.12.* Near-Optimum Control of a Large-Scale Linear Time-Varying Time-Delay System

*Step 1:* Solve (6.4.92) to obtain $K_{ii}(t)$ and store.

*Step 2:* Determine $x_i^o(t)$ and $u_i^o(t)$ from (6.4.91). Set $i = 1$, $k = 1$.

*Step 3:* Use $x_i^{k-1}$, $u_i^{k-1}$ and (6.4.90b), (6.4.90c) in (6.4.90a) to obtain $z_i^k(t)$, $t \geqslant t_o$.

*Step 4:* Solve the $i$th optimal control subproblem to find $x_i^{*k}(t)$ and $u_i^{*k}(t)$, $t \geqslant t_o$, as described by (6.4.111) and (6.4.112).

*Step 5:* If $i = i + 1 < N$, go to Step 3.

*Step 6:* Form $x^k(t)$ and $u^k(t)$ as in (6.4.78)–(6.4.79). If $\max_{t_o \leqslant t \leqslant t_f} \{ \| x^k(t) - x^{k-1}(t) \| \} \leqslant \varepsilon$ and $\max_{t_o \leqslant t \leqslant t_f} \{ \| u^k(t) - u^{k-1}(t) \| \} \leqslant \varepsilon$, for all $t_o \leqslant t \leqslant t_f$, where $\varepsilon$ is a prespecified small constant, stop. Otherwise, set $k = k + 1$ and go to Step 3.

A discussion on the performance indices of this and all other near-optimum controllers is given next.

## 6.5 Bounds on Near-Optimum Cost Functional

Thus far, several optimum and near-optimum control techniques have been presented. As a result of the various complexities of large-scale systems, such as high dimension, nonlinearities, specific structures (e.g., hierarchical and decentralized), time delays, etc., an exact optimal control is neither computationally desirable nor even possible in many cases. Thus, whether it is through model reduction, structural decomposition, approximation of nonlinearities, time delays, or parameter sensitive series expansion, a degree of degradation of the optimal cost function is the price that one has to pay. The general problem of the performance index sensitivity with respect to the variations in plant parameters, initial conditions, uncertainties in measurements, and the model has been considered by several authors (Popov, 1960; Dorato, 1963; Rissanen, 1966; Werner and Cruz, 1968; McClamroch et al., 1969; Kokotović and Cruz, 1969; Kokotović, 1972; Bailey and Ramapriyan, 1973; Weissenberger, 1974; Malek-Zavarei and Jamshidi, 1975; Šiljak and Sundareshan, 1976; Laub and Bailey, 1976; Šiljak, 1978a, b; Singh, 1980). Dorato (1963) has presented a procedure for analysis of performance index sensitivity to small plant parameter variations by introducing the so-called "performance index sensitivity vector." Werner and Cruz (1968) have established a relation between approximations in optimal control and the optimal performance index of the system under the influence of uncertain parameters. They have asserted that a truncation up to the $r$th term of the series expansion of control in plant parameters corresponds to a truncation up to the $(2r + 1)$th terms of the series expansion of the optimal performance index. McClamroch et al. (1969) have studied the sensitivity of the optimal performance index to large plant parameter variations in linear systems by introducing the concept of $\rho$-sensitivity. A system is said to be $\rho$-sensitive with respect to a certain "class" of variations if the value of the performance index does not increase by more than a factor of $\rho$ for variations in that class. Bailey and Ramapriyan (1973) have studied the bounds of performance with respect to model uncertainties due to weak coupling. Aoki (1968, 1971, 1978) has given bounds on the performance index degradation due to model aggregation. Kokotović et al. (1969b), Kokotović and Cruz (1969), and Kokotović (1972) have extended the assertion of Werner and Cruz (1968) for linear weakly coupled systems. Malek-Zavarei and Jamshidi (1975) have extended the $\rho$-sensitivity approach of McClamroch et al. (1969) to take into account the sensitivity of the performance index with respect to time delays.

In this section some of the earlier and more recent results on the bounds and degradation of the near-optimum cost functional due to aggregation, perturbation, expansion of sensitivity functions, nonlinearities, and delays will be discussed.

### 6.5.1 Near-Optimality Due to Aggregation

The aggregation methods were first introduced in Section 2.2 within the context of large-scale system modeling via time-domain. The optimal control of large-scale systems through aggregation was considered in Section 6.2.1. In this section, bounds on the cost function of near-optimum control due to aggregation (Aoki, 1968, 1978) are presented.

The application of the near-optimum control $u^a(t)$ in (6.2.15) to the full model $\dot{x} = Ax + Bu$, a cost function (6.2.2), and a weighing matrix $Q = Q_a$ in (6.2.14) results in a value

$$J^a = \tfrac{1}{2} x_o^T P_a x_o \qquad (6.5.1)$$

where $x_o$ is the initial state and $P_a$ is the positive-definite solution of the following Lyapunov equation:

$$S_a^T P_a + P_a S_a + G_a = 0 \qquad (6.5.2)$$

where $S_a = A - BF_a$, $G_a = C^T F_a^T R F_a C + Q$, $F_a$ is defined by (6.2.15), and $C$ is the aggregation matrix. The optimal cost function is

$$J^* = \tfrac{1}{2} x_o^T K_f x_o \qquad (6.5.3)$$

where $K_f$ is the Riccati matrix of the full model (6.2.9). If we let $P_a = K_f + D$, it can be shown that $D$ satisfies (Aoki, 1971)

$$S_a^T D + DS_a + \Delta S \Delta = 0 \qquad (6.5.4a)$$

where $S = BR^{-1}B^T$ and $\Delta = K_f - K_l = K_f - C^T K_a C$, satisfying

$$0 = S_l^T \Delta + \Delta S_l - \Delta S \Delta + Q - C^T Q_a \qquad (6.5.4b)$$

with $Q_a$ defined in (6.2.14) and $S_l = A - SK_l$. If all the eigenvalues of $S_a$ have negative real parts, i.e., if the aggregated control $u^a$ in (6.2.15) stabilizes the full model, then a positive-definite (or positive-semidefinite) $D$ can be uniquely determined from (6.5.4a). The right-hand side of (6.5.4b) is nonnegative-definite, and from the relation of $\Delta$ in (6.5.4b) with respect to $D$ in (6.5.4a), it follows that

$$D = P_a - K_f \geqslant 0 \quad \text{or} \quad K_f \leqslant P_a \qquad (6.5.5a)$$

and

$$\Delta = K_f - K_l \geqslant 0 \quad \text{or} \quad K_f \geqslant K_l. \qquad (6.5.5b)$$

The relations (6.5.5) indicate that

$$J^l \leqslant J^* \leqslant J^a \qquad (6.5.5c)$$

which is the desired bound on the cost function. The following example illustrates this bound condition on $J^*$ while $J^l$ in (6.5.5c) is $J^l = \tfrac{1}{2} x_o^T K_l x_o$.

**Example 6.5.1.** Consider a fifth-order system:

$$\dot{x} = \begin{bmatrix} -1 & 0 & 0.01 & 0.05 & 0.25 \\ 0 & -4 & 0 & 0.45 & 0.1 \\ -0.088 & 0.2 & -10 & 0 & 0.22 \\ 1 & 0 & 0.075 & -4 & 0.05 \\ 0.11 & 0.2 & 0.999 & 0.44 & -3 \end{bmatrix} x + \begin{bmatrix} 1 & 0.5 \\ 0 & 1 \\ 0.5 & 0.9 \\ 2 & 0.75 \\ 1 & 1 \end{bmatrix} u$$

$$(6.5.6)$$

The eigenvalues of matrix $A$ are $-10.03$, $-0.952$, $-0.2996$, $-4.073$, and $-3.95$. A third-order aggregated model for this system consisting of mode two, an average of first and fourth modes, and an average of third and fifth modes, can be obtained by choosing an aggregation matrix

$$C = \begin{bmatrix} \frac{1}{2} & 0 & 0 & \frac{1}{2} & 0 \\ 0 & 1 & 0 & 0 & 0 \\ 0 & 0 & \frac{1}{2} & 0 & \frac{1}{2} \end{bmatrix} \qquad (6.5.7a)$$

The aggregated matrices $F, G$ are obtained from (2.2.7) and (2.2.6a):

$$(F, G) = \left( \begin{bmatrix} -1.975 & 0 & 0.1925 \\ 0.45 & -4 & 0.1 \\ 0.231 & 0.2 & -5.8905 \end{bmatrix}, \begin{bmatrix} 1.5 & 0.625 \\ 0 & 1 \\ 0.75 & 0.95 \end{bmatrix} \right)$$

$$(6.5.7b)$$

The weighting matrices are chosen as $Q = I_5$ and $R = I_2$. It is desired to find the bounds on the optimal cost function.

SOLUTION: The optimal cost equation (6.5.3), was obtained by solving a fifth-order AMRE using $(A, B, Q, R)$ and an initial state $x_o = (1 \quad -1 \quad 0 \quad -1 \quad 1)^T$, i.e., $J^* = 0.4034917$. Next a third-order AMRE using $(F, G, Q_a, R)$ was solved for the aggregated system Riccati matrix $K_a$, and with the help of $F_a$ defined by (6.2.15) and $Q_a$ defined by (6.2.14), the Lyapunov equation (6.5.2) can be solved for $P_a$. The resulting upper bound, given by (6.5.1), turns out to be $J^a = 0.4145285$. In a similar fashion, $J^l$ turns out to be $J^l = 0.0810435$. Thus, aggregation done on system (6.5.6) results in a bound $0.0810435 < J^* < 0.4145286$ or a 3% degradation of the cost function.

## 6.5.2 Near-Optimality Due to Perturbation

Perturbation, in both regular and singular forms, was introduced in Section 2.3 as a modeling approach. The near-optimum controls were obtained through perturbation in Section 6.2.2. Algorithm 6.1 gave a near-optimum solution to a set of two weakly coupled ($\varepsilon$-coupled) subsystems. It was shown that the solution to the full model Riccati equation is expressed as a MacLaurin series expansion in $\varepsilon$. For the suboptimality caused by $\varepsilon$-coupling, it has been shown (Kokotović, 1972; Kokotović and Cruz, 1969; Kokotović et al., 1969b) that for an $r$th-order expansion of the Riccati matrix, the resulting performance index $J^a$ approximates the optimal cost $J^*$ up to $(2r + 1)$ terms of its expansion. For instance, in Example 6.2.4, for a three-term expansion of the Riccati matrix $P$ in (6.2.49), the approximate cost $J^a$ matches the first seven terms of the optimal cost. The remainder of this section is devoted to the performance bounds obtained by Ramapriyan

(1970) and Bailey and Ramapriyan (1973). Consider a system

$$\dot{x} = Ax + Bu, \quad y = Cx \tag{6.5.8}$$

with a cost functional

$$J = \frac{1}{2} \int_0^\infty \left( y^T Q y + u^T R u \right) dt \tag{6.5.9}$$

The optimal control is $u^* = -R^{-1}B^T Kx = F^* x$ and the optimal cost is $J^* = \frac{1}{2} x_o^T K x_o$, where $K$ is the solution of the following AMRE

$$A^T K + KA - KSK + C^T QC = 0 \tag{6.5.10}$$

with $S = BR^{-1}B^T$. Now assume that the system matrix $A$ is decoupled into $A = A_n + A_o$, where $A_n$ and $A_o$ are the nominal (or block-diagonal) and uncertain (or off-diagonal) portions of $A$, respectively. The feedback control for the nominal case, i.e., $A = A_n$ is assumed to be $u^a = -R^{-1}B^T K_n x = -F_a x$, where $K_n$ is the solution of nominal AMRE

$$A_n^T K_n + K_n A_n - K_n S K_n + C^T QC = 0 \tag{6.5.11}$$

It is known that the approximate cost function $J^a = \frac{1}{2} x_o^T P_a x_o$ where $P_a$ is the solution of the following Lyapunov equation

$$P_a S_a + S_a^T P_a + G_a = 0 \tag{6.5.12}$$

where $S_a = A - BF_a$ and $G_a = F_a^T RF_a + C^T QC$. Bailey and Ramapriyan (1973) have proved that the optimal cost $J^*$ is bounded by

$$p_2 J^n \leqslant J^* \leqslant J^a \leqslant p_1 J^n \tag{6.5.13}$$

where $J^n = \frac{1}{2} x_o^T K_n x_o$, $p_1 = (1 + \lambda_M)^{-1}$ and $p_2 = (1 + \lambda_m)^{-1}$ and $\lambda_M = \max_i\{\lambda_i(H_n)\}$, $\lambda_m = \min_i\{\lambda_i(H_n)\}$ with

$$H_n = \left( F_a^T RF_a + C^T QC \right)^{-1} \left( K_n A_o + A_o^T K_n \right) \tag{6.5.14}$$

The following example illustrates the bound on the optimal cost $J^*$.

**Example 6.5.2.** Reconsider the fifth-order system of Example 6.5.1 and find the range on the cost function due to a $2 \times 2$ and $3 \times 3$ decomposition.

SOLUTION: Consider the system $A$ matrix given by (6.5.6) rewritten as

$$A = A_n + A_o = \begin{bmatrix} -1 & 0 & 0 & 0 & 0 \\ 0 & -4 & 0 & 0 & 0 \\ 0 & 0 & -10 & 0 & 0.22 \\ 0 & 0 & 0.075 & -4 & 0.05 \\ 0 & 0 & 0.999 & 0.44 & -3 \end{bmatrix}$$

$$+ \begin{bmatrix} 0 & 0 & 0.01 & 0.05 & 0.25 \\ 0 & 0 & 0 & 0.45 & 0.1 \\ -0.088 & 0.2 & 0 & 0 & 0 \\ 1 & 0 & 0 & 0 & 0 \\ 0.11 & 0.2 & 0 & 0 & 0 \end{bmatrix} \tag{6.5.15}$$

The nominal or decoupled solution of the AMRE (6.5.11) using the same values for $B$, $Q$, and $R$ as in Example 6.5.1 results in $J^n = 0.4030237$. The optimum cost function is already known to be $J^* = 0.4034917$. The approximate cost, i.e., when $u^a = - R^{-1}B^T K_n x$ is applied to the coupled unperturbed system (6.5.8), was found by solving a fifth-order Lyapunov equation (6.5.12) using $A$ and $K_n$, i.e., $J^a = 0.4116365$. The values of $p_1$ and $p_2$ turned out to be 1.2975 and 1.00, respectively. It is clear that the bound on $J^*$ as defined by (6.5.13) does check, i.e., $p_2 J^n = 0.403237 < 0.4034917 = J^* \leqslant J^a = 0.4116365 \leqslant p_1 J^n = 0.5229232$. It must be noted that the cost function bound (6.5.13) developed by Bailey and Ramapriyan (1973) differs from the assertion of Werner and Cruz (1968) that $J^a$ approximates $J^*$ up to $2r + 1$ terms. The latter is not a bound condition in the sense discussed in this section.

### 6.5.3 Near-Optimality in Hierarchical Control

The degree of near-optimality in the hierarchical control systems can be estimated in two ways. The first is based on the system's structural perturbation due to the interactions between subsystems (Šiljak and Sundareshan, 1976; Šiljak, 1978b). The second approach stems from the relation between the suboptimal indices of the primal and dual problems (Singh, 1980).

### 6.5.3.a Structural Perturbation

The first approach was discussed in some detail in Section 4.4.2, and the near-optimality index $\rho$ was introduced by Equations (4.4.45). As it was discussed then and as is still the case here, the near-optimality index depends on the strength of the interconnection term. This method, which stems from the works of Popov (1960) and Rissanen (1966), is in fact similar to the approach of Bailey and Ramapriyan (1973) discussed in the previous section and to that of Weissenberger (1974). In sequel, a fundamental relation between the near-optimality index $\rho$ and the interaction term due to Šiljak and Sundareshan (1976) is given.

Consider a large-scale system decomposed into $N$ subsystems:

$$\dot{x}_i = f_i(x_i, u_i^d, t) + g_i(x, t), \quad i = 1, \ldots, N \qquad (6.5.16)$$

where $g_i(\cdot)$ represents the interaction term and $u_i^d$ and $x_i$ are the $i$th local decoupled subsystem control vector and its corresponding state vector. The term $f_i(\cdot)$ represents the decoupled subsystems dynamics

$$\dot{x}_i = f_i(x_i, u_i^d, t) \qquad (6.5.17)$$

Let the local optimal control law which satisfies (6.5.17) while minimizing

$$J_i = k_i(x_i(t_f), t_f) + \int_{t_o}^{t_f} G_i(x_i(t), u_i^d(t), t)\, dt \qquad (6.5.18)$$

be given by

$$u_i^d(t) = F_i^d(x_i, t) \tag{6.5.19}$$

In (6.5.18) $k_i(\cdot)$ is the penalty term which, along with $G_i(\cdot)$, is assumed to be functions of class $C^2$ in the arguments of Šiljak and Sundareshan (1976). Each optimal local decoupled control $u_i^{d*} = F_i^\alpha(x_i, t)$ results in an optimal cost

$$J_i^{d*}(x_{io}, t_o) = J_i\left(x_{io}, F_i^d(x_{io}, t_o), t_o\right) \tag{6.5.20}$$

In Section 4.4.2 it was deduced that, depending on the structural properties, the performance index

$$J(x_o, u^d, t_o) = \sum_{i=1}^{N} J_i\left(x_{io}, u_i^d, t_o\right) \tag{6.5.21}$$

may be neutral, beneficial, or nonbeneficial depending on the interconnections (Sundareshan, 1977b). The application of decoupled local control laws (6.5.19) would not, of course, result in the optimal performance

$$J^*(x_o, t_o) = \sum_{i=1}^{N} J_i^*(x_{io}, t_o) \tag{6.5.22}$$

unless in the case when all $g_i(\cdot) = 0$ for $i = 1, 2, \ldots, N$. The value of the performance index when (6.5.19) is applied in the presence of $g_i(\cdot)$ can be denoted by

$$\hat{J}(x_o, t_o) = \sum_{i=1}^{N} \left\{ k_i\left(\hat{x}_i(t_f), t_f\right) + \int_{t_o}^{t_f} G_i\left(x_i(t), F_i^d(\hat{x}_i, t), t\right) dt \right\} \tag{6.5.23}$$

which would clearly satisfy the inequality

$$\hat{J}(x_o, t_o) \geqslant J^*(x_o, t_o) \tag{6.5.24}$$

for all $x_o$ and $t_o$ belonging to a bounded region in $R^{n+1}$. Following the discussions of Section 4.4.2, if there exists a number $\rho > 0$ such that

$$\hat{J}(x_o, t_o) \leqslant (1 + \rho)J^*(x_o, t_o) \tag{6.5.25}$$

holds, then the system (6.5.16) with control laws (6.5.19) is defined to be near-optimum with index $\rho$ (Šiljak and Sundareshan, 1976). Šiljak (1978a), using the Hamilton–Jacobi equation, has proved that if the condition

$$\{\operatorname{grad} V(x, t)\}^T g(x, t) \leqslant (\rho/(1 + \rho))G\left(x, F^d(x, t), t\right) \tag{6.5.26}$$

holds, then the large-scale composite system

$$\dot{x}_i = f_i\left(x_i, F_i^d(x_i, t), t\right) + g_i(x, t) \tag{6.5.27}$$

is near-optimal with index $\rho$. In (6.5.26), $V(\cdot)$ is the sum of $N$ optimal indices $V_i(\cdot)$ and assumed to belong to class $C^2$. Equation (6.5.25) has two important interpretations: (i) for given interactions $g_i(x, t)$, one can determine the corresponding near-optimality index $\rho$, and (ii) to guarantee a given index of near-optimality $\rho$, the relation puts a constraint on the interactions. A special case of (6.5.16) consists of linear subsystems and nonlinear interactions:

$$\dot{x}_i = A_i x_i + B_i u_i + g_i(x, t), \quad i = 1, \ldots, N \qquad (6.5.28)$$

with a quadratic cost

$$J_i(x_{io}, u_i^d, t_o) = \frac{1}{2} \int_0^\infty e^{2\alpha t}\left(x_i^T(t)Q_i x_i(t) + u_i^T(t)R_i u_i(t)\right) dt \quad (6.5.29)$$

where $\alpha$ is the degree of exponential stability following the development of Section 4.4.2. The interaction-near-optimality index relation is

$$\|g_i(x, t)\| \leqslant \sum_{j=1}^N \xi_{ij}\|x_j\| \qquad (6.5.30a)$$

where $\zeta = \Sigma_{i,j}\xi_{ij}$ is given by

$$\zeta \leqslant (\rho/(1 + \rho))\lambda_m(P)/\lambda_M(K) \qquad (6.5.30b)$$

and $P = \text{Block-diag}(P_1, P_2, \ldots, P_N)$, $K = \text{Block-diag}(K_1, K_2, \ldots, K_N)$, $P_i = K_i S_i K_i + Q_i$, $S_i = B_i R_i^{-1} B_i^T$, and $K_i$ is the Riccati matrix for the $i$th subsystem satisfying

$$K_i \tilde{A}_i + \tilde{A}_i^T K_i - K_i S_i K_i + Q_i = 0 \qquad (6.5.31)$$

with $\tilde{A}_i = A_i + \alpha I_i$. Several examples in Section 4.4.2 and problems at the end of Chapter 4 were devoted to the above discussions. For the case when $g_i(x, t)$ is also linear, as in (4.4.22), the interaction matrix $G$ was seen to play a major role in the degree of near-optimality. Šiljak (1978b), and Šiljak and Sundareshan (1976) have introduced the notion of "connective" near-optimality as follows. The system (6.5.27) with $u_i^d = L_i^d x_i$ is said to be connectively near-optimal with index $\rho$ if it is near-optimal with index $\rho$ for all interconnection matrices $G(t)$. The following example illustrates connective near-optimality.

**Example 6.5.3.** Consider a second-order system

$$\dot{x}_i = 3x_1 - 5x_2 + u_1, \quad x_1(0) = 1 \qquad (6.5.32)$$
$$\dot{x}_2 = -3x_1 + 8x_2 + u_2, \quad x_2(0) = 1$$

with a quadratic cost

$$J = \frac{1}{2} \int_0^\infty \left(x_1^2 + x_2^2 + u_1^2 + u_1^2\right) dt \qquad (6.5.33)$$

It is desired to find the index of near-optimality and study the connective near-optimality of the system.

SOLUTION: The system's optimal controls are

$$u_1^* = -5.20x_1 + 6.77x_2$$
$$u_2^* = 6.77x_1 - 17.32x_2$$

(6.5.34a)

which provide the closed-loop system

$$\dot{x}_1 = -2.20x_1 + 2.77x_2$$
$$\dot{x}_2 = 3.77x_1 - 9.32x_2$$

(6.5.34b)

Let (6.5.32) be decomposed into two subsystems,

$$\dot{x}_1 = 3x_1 + u_1$$
$$\dot{x}_2 = 8x_2 + u_2$$

(6.5.35)

with interactions $-5x_2$ and $-3x_1$, respectively. Should the composite system (6.5.32) be expected to undergo a structural perturbation, then the optimal control would result in a closed-loop system

$$\dot{x}_1 = -2.20x_1 + 6.77x_2$$
$$\dot{x}_2 = 6.77x_1 - 9.32x_2$$

(6.5.36)

which causes instability. However, using the hierarchical control scheme discussed here and in Section 4.4.2, would give a stabilizing controller under structural perturbation (see Sections 5.3.4 and 5.3.5). Moreover, the cost to pay is the near-optimality of the performance index, to be obtained next. For the present system, the composite performance index $J^o = 4.4866$, while the decoupled $J^* = J_1^* + J_2^* = 11.11$ through solving two scalar Riccati equations for $k_1 = 6.162$ and $k_2 = 16.062$. Following the conditions of Theorem 4.3, $S$ and $\hat{K}$ turned out to be

$$S = \begin{bmatrix} 0 & 26.64 \\ -26.64 & 0 \end{bmatrix}, \quad \hat{K} = \begin{bmatrix} 19.15 & 19.15 \\ 19.16 & 11.97 \end{bmatrix}$$

(6.5.37)

which provide a $\hat{J} = \frac{1}{2}x_o^T(K + \hat{K})x_o = 45.83$, and the near-optimality index of (4.4.45) is $\rho = 0.76$ and $\hat{J} \leqslant (1 + \rho_{max})J^* = 5.7J^*$.

## 6.5.3.b Lagrange Duality

Let us assume that the optimum performance of a primal problem, defined in Section 4.3.1, be $J^*$ and the corresponding near-optimal value be $J^s$; then it is known that

$$I^s \leqslant I^* = J^* \leqslant J^s$$

(6.5.38)

where $I^*$ and $I^s$ are the optimal and near-optimal performance indices of the dual problem, respectively. The bounds in (6.5.38) can be obtained by the following development due to Singh (1980). Consider the primal problem

$$\text{Minimize}_{u(t)} \quad J = \frac{1}{2}\int_0^{t_f}(x^T(t)Qx(t)+u^T(t)Ru(t))\,dt \qquad (6.5.39)$$

$$\text{Subject to} \quad \dot{x}=Ax+Bu, \quad x(0)=x_o \qquad (6.5.40)$$

where $x$ and $u$ are the collated state and control vectors of subsystems states and controls $x_i, u_i, i=1,2,\dots,N$. The dual function of the primal problem (6.5.39)–(6.5.40) is

$$I = \text{Max}_{p(t)}\left\{\text{Min}_{x(t),u(t)}\int_0^{t_f}\left[x^TQx+u^TRu+p^T(Ax+Bu-\dot{x})\right]dt\right\} \qquad (6.5.41)$$

where $p(t)$ is the adjoint vector. In order to find an explicit value for $I$, the minimum value in (6.5.41) is evaluated next. Let the Hamiltonian of the primal problem be

$$H = \tfrac{1}{2}(x^TQx+u^TRu)+p^T(Ax+Bu) \qquad (6.5.42)$$

and consider the necessary conditions for optimality:

$$\dot{p}=-\partial H/\partial x=-Qx-A^Tp, \quad p(t_f)=0 \qquad (6.5.43)$$

$$0=\partial H/\partial u=Ru+B^Tp \qquad (6.5.44)$$

Using the integration by parts, the last term of the integrand in (6.5.41) is expressed by

$$\int_0^{t_f}p^T\dot{x}\,dt = -p^T(0)x_o-\int_0^{t_f}x^T(Qx+A^Tp)\,dt \qquad (6.5.45)$$

Now using the expression for $u$ in (6.5.44), substituting it in (6.5.41), and considering (6.5.45), the dual problem cost function becomes

$$I = \max_p\left\{p^T(0)x_o+\int_0^{t_f}(x^TQx-\tfrac{1}{2}p^TSp)\,dt\right\} \qquad (6.5.46)$$

where $S=BR^{-1}B^T$ and $p$ is defined in (6.5.43).

In order to find lower bound $I^s$, the value of $p$ is replaced by $Kx$, where $K$ is the solution of the accompanying Riccati equation, and the maximization procedure is ignored (Singh 1980):

$$I^s = \frac{1}{2}x_o^TKx_o=\frac{1}{2}\int_0^{t_f}x^T(t)(Q-2K(t)SK(t))x(t)\,dt \qquad (6.5.47)$$

where $K(t)$ is the solution of the desired DMRE. The following example illustrates the duality approach for hierarchical control of a serially coupled system.

**Example 6.5.4.** Consider two first-order serially coupled systems

$$\dot{x}_1=x_1+u_1, \quad x_1(0)=1$$
$$\dot{x}_2=2x_2+u_2+x_1, \quad x_2(0)=1 \qquad (6.5.48a)$$

with

$$J = \frac{1}{2} \int_0^5 \left( x_1^2 + x_2^2 + u_1^2 + u_2^2 \right) dt \qquad (6.5.48b)$$

It is desired to find a bound on the optimum performance $J^*$.

SOLUTION: For this problem three DMREs were solved for the two subsystems and the composite system and were fitted to second-order polynomials, i.e.,

$$k_1(t) = 2.162 + 0.643t - 0.205t^2,$$

$$k_2(t) = 3.717 + 1.254t - 0.379t^2 \qquad (6.5.49a)$$

$$K(t) = \begin{bmatrix} 2.42 + 0.78t - 0.24t^2 & 0.914 + 0.362t - 0.103t^2 \\ 0.914 + 0.362t - 0.103t^2 & 3.5 + 1.14t - 0.35t^2 \end{bmatrix} \qquad (6.5.49b)$$

The system was simulated on an HP-9845 computer using BASIC and the optimum and near-optimum costs $J^*, I^s, J^s$ and states $x^*$ and $x^s$ were computed. The resulting values of performance indices turned out to be $I^s = 4.01416$, $J^s = 5.15419$, and $J^* = 4.45102$, which clearly indicates that

$$I^s = 4.01416 < I^* = 4.45102 = J^* < J^s = 5.15419 \qquad (6.5.50)$$

The results of this simple example indicates that the hierarchical near-optimum control of serial systems is a fairly reasonable one.

### 6.5.4 Near-Optimality in Time-Delay Systems

In Section 6.4 the near-optimal control of time-delay systems was considered. Two cases were distinguished. The first was based on the decomposition of a large-scale time-delay systems into nondelayed and decoupled subsystems. The second was the hierarchical control of serially and nonserially time-delayed coupled systems. In this section, the variation of the performance index with respect to the perturbations of the delayed terms in the state equation and the time-delay itself is considered. The development here is based on the work of Malek-Zavarei and Jamshidi (1975).

Consider a linear time-delay system

$$\dot{x}(t) = Ax(t) + Bu(t) + Cx(t - \tau) \qquad (6.5.51a)$$

$$x(t) = \eta(t), \quad -\tau \leqslant t \leqslant 0 \qquad (6.5.51b)$$

where $A$, $B$, $C$, $x$, and $u$ are matrices and vectors of appropriate dimensions and $\tau$ is the time delay, assumed to be known. Let us assume that, due to plant parameter variations, the system (6.5.51) is alternatively modeled by

$$\dot{x}(t) = Ax(t) + Bu(t), \quad x(0) = x_o \qquad (6.5.52)$$

or

$$\dot{x}(t) = (A + C)x(t) + Bu(t), \quad x(0) = \eta(0) \qquad (6.5.53)$$

In the first case, a perturbation in delayed state form has taken place, while, in the second one the delay $\tau$ itself is a perturbation. The main issue is then to investigate the corresponding variations of the system performance index

$$J = \frac{1}{2} \int_0^\infty \{ x^T(t) Q x(t) + u^T(t) R u(t) \} \, dt \qquad (6.5.54)$$

due to the above perturbations.

The relationships between $J$ and perturbations of the delayed term $Cx(t - \tau)$ and the delay $\tau$ are developed through the concept of $\rho$-sensitivity (McClamroch et al., 1969) and the linear control law proposed by Krasovskii (1963) and Ross and Flügge-Lotz (1969). The latter approach to optimization of time-delay systems provides a sufficient condition which leads to a set of Riccati-type partial differential equations which do not involve delay or advance terms, unlike the maximum principle approach.

Under plant perturbations, let the system (6.5.52) be changed to (6.5.51a) through an unknown perturbation matrix $C$, which is assumed, however, to belong to a class $\xi$ where $0 \in \xi$ so that it is possible to have an errorless system. The optimal control of (6.5.52) and (6.5.54) is well known, i.e., $u = -R^{-1}B^T K_o x$, where $K_o$ is the solution of the AMRE.

$$A^T K_o + K_o A - K_o S K_o + Q = 0 \qquad (6.5.55)$$

where $S = BR^{-1}B^T$. Malek-Zavarei and Jamshidi (1975) have asserted that since the $C$ matrix is unknown, the initial function $\eta(t)$ can be approximated by

$$\eta(t) = \exp\{(A - SK_o)t\} x_o \qquad (6.5.56)$$

The following definition and theorem, proposed by Malek-Zavarei and Jamshidi (1975), set forth the conditions for performance index sensitivity with respect to perturbation matrix $C$.

**Definition 6.2.** For a real number $\rho$ and some perturbation class $\xi$, the system (6.5.51) and cost functional (6.5.54) are said to be $\rho$-sensitive if for each $x_o$, $J^p \leqslant \rho J^o$ for all matrices $C \in \xi$, where $J^p$ and $J^o$ denote the optimal values of $J$ in (6.5.54) evaluated, respectively, along the trajectories of (6.5.52) and (6.5.51) with initial function (6.5.56).

**Theorem 6.2.** *The system (6.5.51) and (6.5.56) and cost function (6.5.54) are $\rho$-sensitive in the sense of Definition 6.2 if and only if for each perturbation matrix $C \in \xi$, the matrix $\rho K_o - K_1(C)$ is positive-definite, where $K_o$ satisfies (6.5.55) and*

$$K_1(C) = k_1 + 2 \int_{-\tau}^0 k_2(s) \exp\{(A - SK_o)s\} \, ds$$

$$+ \int_{-\tau}^0 \int_{-\tau}^0 \exp(A - SK_o)^T S k_3(r, s) \exp\{(A - SK_o)r\} \, dr \, ds$$

$$(6.5.57)$$

*where*

$$A^T k_1 + k_1 A - k_1 S k_1 + k_2(0) + k_2^T(0) + Q = 0 \qquad (6.5.58)$$

$$- dk_2(s)/ds + A^T k_2(s) - k_1 S k_2(s) + k_3^T(0, s) = 0, \quad -\tau \leqslant s \leqslant 0 \qquad (6.5.59)$$

$$\partial k_3(r, s)/\partial r + \partial k_3(r, s)/\partial s + k_2^T(r) S k_2(s) = 0, \quad -\tau \leqslant r, s \leqslant 0 \qquad (6.5.60)$$

*with boundary conditions*

$$k_1 C = k_2(-\tau), \quad C^T k_2(s) = k_3(-\tau, s), \quad -\tau \leqslant s \leqslant 0 \qquad (6.5.61)$$

PROOF: For the errorless system, i.e., $C = 0$, the optimal cost function (6.5.54) is $J^o = \frac{1}{2} x_o^T K_o x_o$, where $K_o$ satisfies (6.5.55). When $C \neq 0$, the optimal cost is given by (Krasovskii, 1963; Ross and Flügge-Lotz, 1969)

$$J^p = \frac{1}{2} x_o^T k_1 x_o + x_o^T \int_{-\tau}^0 k_2(s) x(s) \, ds + \int_{-\tau}^0 \int_{-\tau}^0 x^T(s) k_3(r, s) x(r) \, dr \, ds \qquad (6.5.62)$$

where matrices $k_1$, and $k_2$, and $k_3$ satisfy (6.5.58)–(6.5.60). Using (6.5.56), one can write

$$J^p = \frac{1}{2} x_o^T K_1(C) x_o \qquad (6.5.63)$$

where $K_1(C)$ is given by (6.5.57). Therefore, $J^p \leqslant \rho J^o$ if and only if the matrix $\rho K_o - K_1(C)$ is positive-semidefinite. Q.E.D. ∎

A corollary of this theorem that follows for the necessity and sufficiency of $\rho$-sensitivity of system (6.5.53) and cost functional (6.5.54) with respect to matrix $C$ is that $\rho K_o - k_1$ is positive-semidefinite, where $K_o$ satisfies (6.5.55) and $k_1$ satisfies

$$(A + C)^T k_1 + k_1(A + C) - k_1 S k_1 + Q = 0 \qquad (6.5.64)$$

For the second perturbation, the system (6.5.51) is assumed to change to (6.5.53) for a small time delay $\tau$. The matrix $C$ is considered to be known for this case and the delay $\tau \in [0, T_1]$, some error interval. The following definition and theorem provide the conditions for the second perturbation.

**Definition 6.3.** For a real number $\rho$ and some perturbation interval $[0, T_1]$, the system (6.5.53) and cost functional (6.5.54) are said to be $\rho$-sensitive if for each $x_o$, $J^p \leqslant \rho J^o$ for all $\tau \in [0, T_1]$ where $J^p$ and $J^o$ are the optimal cost $J$ evaluated, respectively, along the trajectories of (6.5.53) and (6.5.51) with initial function $x(t) = \eta(0), -\tau \leqslant t \leqslant 0$.

**Theorem 6.3.** *A necessary and sufficient condition for the system (6.5.53) with cost functional (6.5.54) to be $\rho$-sensitive in the sense of Definition 6.3 for* *each delay $\tau \in [0, T_1]$ with $T_1$ sufficiently small is the positive-semidefinite-ness of the matrix $L_o - \rho L_1(\tau)$, where*

$$(A+C)^T L_o + L_o(A+C) - L_o SL_o + Q = 0 \qquad (6.5.65)$$

$$L_1(\tau) = k_1 + 2\int_{-\tau}^{0} k_2(s)\,ds + \int_{-\tau}^{0}\int_{-\tau}^{0} k_3(r,s)\,dr\,ds \qquad (6.5.66)$$

*and the matrices $k_1$, $k_2$, and $k_3$ satisfy (6.5.58)–(6.5.61).*

PROOF: If the delay $\tau$ is neglected, and the optimal value of the cost function (6.5.54) is given by $J^p = \frac{1}{2}x_o^T L_o x_o$, where $L_o$ satisfies (6.5.65). Moreover, in a similar fashion to the proof of Theorem 6.2, the optimal cost (6.5.54) evaluated along the trajectory of system (6.5.51) with initial function $x(t) = \eta(0)$, $-\tau \leqslant t \leqslant 0$, is $J^o = \frac{1}{2}x_o^T L_1(\tau)x_o$, where $L_1(\tau)$ satisfies (6.5.66). Hence, $J^p \leqslant \rho J^o$ if and only if the matrix $L_o - \rho L_1(\tau)$ is positive-semidefinite. Q.E.D. ∎

The following examples considered by Malek-Zavarei and Jamshidi (1975) illustrate the performance index $\rho$-sensitivity of time-delay systems described above.

**Example 6.5.5.** Consider a linear time-delay system

$$\dot{x}(t) = -2x(t) + cx(t-1) + u(t) \qquad (6.5.67)$$

and cost

$$J = \frac{1}{2}\int_{0}^{\infty}(10x^2 + 2u^2)\,dt \qquad (6.5.68)$$

where $c$ is the perturbation parameter. It is desired to evaluate the $\rho$-sensitivity of (6.5.68) if (6.5.67) represents a variation of $\dot{x}(t) = -2x(t) + u(t)$, $x(0) = 1$.

SOLUTION: The initial function for (6.5.67) is $\eta(t) = \exp\{-(2 + K_o)t\}$, where $K_o = 1$ is the solution of AMRE (6.5.55); thus, $\eta(t) = \exp(-3t)$. According to Theorem 6.2, the necessary and sufficient condition for the $\rho$-sensitivity is the positive-semidefiniteness of $\rho K_o - K_1(c)$ or $\rho K_o \geqslant K_1(c)$ where $K_1(c)$ is evaluated from (6.5.57). This boundary value problem was solved by the finite difference method (Salvadori and Baron, 1964) using FORTRAN on an IBM 1130 computer. Figure 6.17 shows the resulting $K_1(c)$ as a function of $c$. Note that for any perturbation $c$, the system is $\rho$-sensitive in the sense of Definition 6.2 for $\rho \geqslant K_1(c)$. For example, for the unperturbed case, $c = 0$, $\rho = 1$, which is expected. For $c = 0.3$, the system is $\rho$-sensitive for $\rho \geqslant 0.4$. Alternatively, for a fixed value of $\rho = 0.5$, the class of perturbations which gives that bound on the performance is $\xi = (c : c \leqslant 0.3)$.

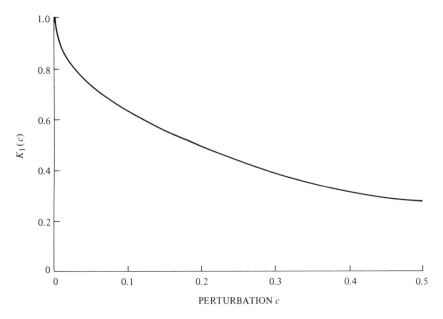

**Figure 6.17** The function $K_1(c)$ as a function of perturbation parameter $c$ for Example 6.5.5.

**Example 6.5.6.** Consider a linear time-delay system

$$\dot{x}(t) = -x(t) - x(t-\tau) + u(t), \quad x(t) = \exp(t), \quad -\tau \leqslant t \leqslant 0 \quad (6.5.69)$$

with cost function (6.5.68). Assume that (6.5.69) is approximated by $\dot{x}(t) = -2x(t) + u(t)$, $x(0) = 1$. It is desired to study the sensitivity of $J$ for the perturbations of delay $\tau$ in (6.5.69).

SOLUTION: Theorem 6.3 was used with $L_o$ in (6.5.65) becoming 1 and $L_1(\tau)$ was calculated by (6.5.66). The value of $J^p \leqslant J^o$ if and only if $L_o - \rho L_1(\tau) \geqslant 0$ or $\rho \leqslant 1/L_1(\tau)$. The response of $1/L_1(\tau)$ versus $\tau$ is shown in Figure 6.18. It is noted again that for a given perturbation in delay $\tau$, the system (6.5.69) is $\rho$-sensitive in the sense of Definition 6.3 for all $\rho < 1/L_1(\tau)$. As an example, if $\tau$ is perturbed to 0.8, then the system is $\rho$-sensitive for $\rho \leqslant 1.35$. Alternatively, for $\rho \leqslant 1.1$, then $\tau$ must belong to interval $\tau \in [0, 0.5]$. Finally, note that for nondelay case, $\tau = 0$, $\rho = 1$, as expected.

## 6.5.5 Near-Optimality in Nonlinear Systems

The last case whose degree of near-optimality is considered is a nonlinear system. The development in this section follows the work of Laub and Bailey (1976) which extends the linear case (Bailey and Ramapriyan, 1973)

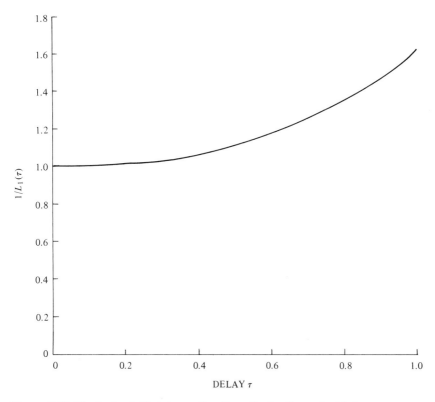

**Figure 6.18** The factor $1/L_1(\tau)$ as a function of $\tau$ for Example 6.5.6.

discussed in Section 6.5.2. The general class of nonlinear systems examined in Section 6.3 is considered again.

Consider first a linear dynamic system

$$\dot{x} = Ax + Bu, \quad x(0) = x_o \qquad (6.5.70)$$

and cost function

$$J(x_o, u) = \int_0^\infty g(x, u, t)\, dt \qquad (6.5.71)$$

where $g(\cdot)$ is a nonnegative function, continuously differentiable in its arguments. It is assumed that a unique feedback control law

$$u = k_n(x(t), t), \quad t \geqslant 0 \qquad (6.5.72)$$

exists for the problem (6.5.70)–(6.5.71). Now let the system (6.5.70) be perturbed by a nonlinear term

$$\dot{x} = Ax + Bu + f(x, u, t), \quad x(0) = x_o \qquad (6.5.73)$$

with cost function (6.5.71). Further assume that another unique feedback control law

$$u = k(x(t), t), \quad t \geqslant 0 \tag{6.5.74}$$

exists for (6.5.73) and (6.5.71). If the control (6.5.72) is applied to (6.5.73), a near-optimal cost functional results which is to be studied here. Let this cost function be $J^a$,

$$J^a = J^a(x, t) = \int_t^\infty g(\phi(\tau; x, k_n, t), k_n, \tau) \, d\tau \tag{6.5.75}$$

while $J^*$ and $J^n$ are defined by

$$J^* = J^*(x, t) = \int_t^\infty g(\phi(\tau; k, t), k, \tau) \, d\tau \tag{6.5.76}$$

$$J^n = J^n(x, t) = \int_t^\infty g(\psi(\tau; k_n, t), k_n, t) \, dt \tag{6.5.77}$$

where $\psi(\cdot)$ and $\phi(\cdot)$ are the state trajectories of (6.5.70) and (6.5.73), respectively. Laub and Bailey (1976) have presented the following definition and subsequent lemma to estimate bounds on $J^*$ similar to linear case (6.5.13).

**Definition 6.4.** The system (6.5.70) is said to be weakly coupled by a perturbation $f$ if there exists a scalar parameter $\mu > 0$ such that

$$g_n - J_x^{nT} f_n \geqslant \mu > 0 \tag{6.5.78}$$

holds for all $x$ in its feasible domain. The terms $f_n$ and $g_n$ denote, respectively, $f(x, k_n, t)$ and $g(x, k_n, t)$ and $J_x$ correspond to the gradient of $J$ with respect to $x$.

**Lemma 6.2.** *If the system (6.5.70) is weakly perturbed by $f$, then there exists a parameter $p_1$ such that $J^a \leqslant p_1 J^n$.*
*An estimate for $p_1$ is given by*

$$p_1 = \max_{(t, x) \in L} g_n / (g_n - J_x^{nT} f_n) = 1/(1 - r) \tag{6.5.79}$$

*where $L$ is the feasible domain of $(t, x)$ and $r = max_{(t, x) \in L, x \neq 0}(J_x^{nT} f_n / g_n)$. It is noted, however, that unlike the linear case, a lower bound is not available for here. A crude lower bound $p_2$ has been suggested by Laub and Bailey (1976):*

$$p_2 = \min_{\substack{(t, x) \in L \\ x \neq 0}} g_n / (g_n - J_x^{nT} f_n) \tag{6.5.80}$$

*If the cost function (6.5.71) is assumed to be quadratic, i.e., $g(x, u, t) = \frac{1}{2}(x^T Q x + u^T R u)$, then $u$ in (6.5.72) becomes $u = k_n(\cdot) = -R^{-1} B^T K$, where $K$ is the positive-definite solution of the system $(A, B, Q, R)$ Riccati equation. The value of $J^n = \frac{1}{2} x_o^T K x_o$ and the weakly perturbed condition*

(6.5.78) *becomes*

$$\tfrac{1}{2}x^T(Q + KSK)x - x^TKf(x, k_n(\cdot)) \geqslant \mu > 0 \qquad (6.5.81)$$

*and the parameter r in (6.5.79) would be*

$$r = \max_{\substack{x \in R^n \\ x \neq 0}} \{x^TKf(\cdot)/[\tfrac{1}{2}x^T(Q + KSK)x]\} \qquad (6.5.82)$$

The following example illustrates the above development on the near-optimality of nonlinear systems.

**Example 6.5.7.** Consider the third-order nonlinear system of Example 6.3.1,

$$\dot{x}_1 = x_2, \quad x_1(0) = 0.1$$
$$\dot{x}_2 = -0.2x_2 + 2x_3 - 0.2x_2x_3^2, \quad x_2(0) = 0.1 \qquad (6.5.83)$$
$$\dot{x}_3 = 5x_3 + u, \quad x_3(0) = 0.1$$

which represents the "logic control of a regulation system" and has been used by some authors (Garrard et al., 1967; Jamshidi, 1976a). A near-optimum control for this system via the sensitivity method of Section 6.3.1 was designed (see Table 6.3) and an approximate value of $J^a = 0.2162$ was obtained for the cost function. It is desired to find a bound on the index $J^a$ using Lemma 6.2.

SOLUTION: The near-optimum feedback control law $u_n = k_n(x(t))$ is given by (6.3.34), i.e.,

$$u_n = -R^{-1}B^TKx_n = [-1.41 \quad -2.75 \quad -11.16]x_n \qquad (6.5.84)$$

stemming from a third-order AMRE whose solution is

$$K = \begin{bmatrix} 4.7135 & 4.3260 & 1.4050 \\ 4.3260 & 7.9540 & 2.7.200 \\ 1.4050 & 2.7200 & 11.1154 \end{bmatrix} \qquad (6.5.85)$$

using the matrices $A, B$ in (6.5.83), $Q = 2I_3$, and $R = 1$. The unperturbed system cost turned out to be $J^n = 0.2036175$. Next an unconstrained minimization method due to Rosenbrock (1960) was used twice to find $p_1$ and $p_2$ defined by (6.5.79), (6.5.80), and 30 function evaluations. The results turned out to be $p_1 = 1.7441$ and $p_2 = 0.25$, thus bounding $J^a$ by

$$p_2J^n = 0.051 < J^a = 0.2162 < 0.3552 = p_1J^n \qquad (6.5.86)$$

The above formulation can be used for hierarchical control of nonlinear systems as well. This plus other points are considered as problems at the end of this chapter.

## 6.6  State Estimation in Large-Scale Systems

The primary topic discussed in this chapter has been the near-optimum design of large-scale systems. Unlike the nonoptimum designs of Section 5.3, this design has been based exclusively on state feedback. However, it is a well-known fact that the states are not always available for measurement and, as in the non-large-scale systems, states must be estimated. This brief section, therefore, is devoted to some extensions of state estimation and observer design to large-scale systems. The topic of observability of large-scale systems will be discussed in Chapter 7.

Luenberger (1966) first proposed an "observer" or "estimator" to estimate the system state variable $x$ by $\hat{x}$ for such applications as state feedback. Much effort has gone into the design of estimators, in particular for the linear TIV systems. Yuskel and Bongiorno (1971) and Kwakernaak and Sivan (1972) are among many who have proposed suitable procedures for this task. However, the straight application of "centralized" system estimator design schemes for large-scale systems is infeasible, as brought up by Sundareshan (1977), among others. For one reason, the number of computations for a large-scale system would be prohibitive, and, perhaps even more important, for a large-scale system whose structure is most naturally represented in decentralized form, a single observer is not feasible. Furthermore, unlike centralized systems, the decentralized estimation procedure, as will be seen, requires testing for the observability of only a set of isolated subsystems.

Many authors have considered the state estimation of large-scale systems in input decentralized fashion. Among them are Aoki and Li (1972), Šiljak and Vukcević (1976, 1978), Šiljak (1978a, 1978b), and Sundareshan (1977). In this section we concentrate on the recent works of Sundareshan (1977) and Šiljak (1978b) because of their convenient implementation and computation.

Consider an $n$th-order large-scale system represented by $N$ interconnected subsystems:

$$\dot{x}_i(t) = A_i x_i(t) + B_i u_i(t) + g_i(t, x) \qquad (6.6.1)$$

$$y_i(t) = C_i x_i(t), \quad i = 1, 2, \ldots, N \qquad (6.6.2)$$

where all vectors and matrices are appropriately defined and $g_i(\cdot)$ is the interaction function between the $i$th subsystem and the rest of the system. It is assumed that each pair $(C_i, A_i)$ is completely observable for $i = 1, 2, \ldots, N$. If there were no interaction among the subsystems, i.e., $g_i(t, x) = 0$ for each subsystem, a local estimator would result:

$$\dot{\hat{x}}_i(t) = (A_i - P_i C_i)\hat{x}_i(t) + P_i y_i(t) + B_i u_i \qquad (6.6.3)$$

where $x_i(t)$ and $u_i(t)$ satisfy

$$\dot{x}_i(t) = A_i x_i(t) + B_i u_i(t) \qquad (6.6.4)$$

$$y_i(t) = C_i x_i(t) \qquad (6.6.5)$$

In (6.6.3) $P_i$ is an $n_i(\dim A_i)$-by-$r_i(\dim C_i)$-dimensional gain matrix which must be chosen so that the desired degree of convergence in the estimation error $e_i(t) = x_i(t) - \hat{x}_i(t)$ is achieved. Kwakernaak and Sivan (1972) have shown that for a convergence of at least $e_i(t)\exp(-\alpha t)$, $\alpha > 0$ and $t \to \infty$, $P_i$ must be chosen by

$$P_i = H_i C_i^T \tag{6.6.6}$$

where $H_i$ is the symmetric positive-definite solution of the AMRE

$$H_i(A_i^T + \alpha I_i) + (A_i + \alpha I_i)H_i - H_i D_i H_i + Q_i = 0 \tag{6.6.7}$$

where $D_i = C_i^T C_i$ and $Q_i \geq 0$.

In this case the estimation error for (6.6.3) is obtained by subtracting (6.6.3) from (6.6.4) to get

$$\dot{e}_i(t) = (A_i - H_i C_i^T C_i)e_i(t) \tag{6.6.8}$$

which decay at least as fast as $\exp(-\alpha t)$. The following example illustrates this point.

**Example 6.6.1.** Consider the $i$th decoupled subsystem of a large-scale system:

$$\dot{x}_i(t) = \begin{bmatrix} -1 & -0.25 & 1 \\ 0 & -2 & 0.5 \\ 0.4 & 0 & 0.1 \end{bmatrix} x_i(t) + \begin{bmatrix} 0 \\ 0.1 \\ 1 \end{bmatrix} u_i(t)$$

$$y_i(t) = \begin{bmatrix} 1 & 0 & 1 \end{bmatrix} x_i(t) \tag{6.6.9}$$

Study the exponential decay of this subsystem's estimation error for two values of $\alpha = 0.1$, 1.0.

SOLUTION: The AMRE (6.6.7) must be solved for two values of $\alpha$ using the $A_i$ and $C_i$ matrices in (6.6.9). The resulting solutions are

$$H_i(0.1) = \begin{bmatrix} 0.094 & -0.00817 & 0.1800 \\ -0.00817 & 0.027 & -0.013 \\ 0.1800 & -0.013 & 0.666 \end{bmatrix}$$

$$H_i(1.0) = \begin{bmatrix} 0.262 & -0.039 & 0.362 \\ -0.039 & 0.059 & -0.0065 \\ 0.362 & -0.0065 & 1.8468 \end{bmatrix} \tag{6.6.10}$$

Using the values of $H_i(\alpha)$ in (6.6.10) and (6.6.8) with $e_i(0) = (-1.0, -1.0, -0.75)^T$, the resulting values of the $e_i(t)$ versus time for $0 \leq t \leq 5.0$ are shown in Figure 6.19. The estimation errors for the $i$th subsystem for the two cases are quite distinguishable, especially for the first and third components and fairly close for the second one. In general the exponential decay of the estimation errors are clearly shown.

As effective as the decentralized estimation (6.6.3) may seem, since interactions do not play any role in it, an alternate estimation scheme must

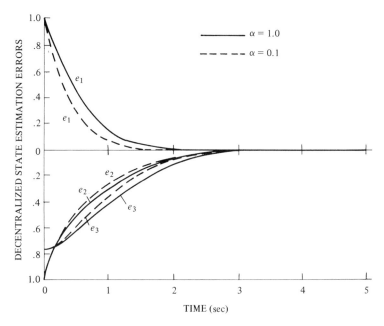

**Figure 6.19** The exponential convergence of the estimation errors $e_i(t)$ versus time for the decoupled subsystem of Example 6.6.1.

be proposed. The basic objective would then be to modify the completely decentralized estimation (6.6.3) in such a way that the same degree of convergence for estimation error $e_i$ would result for system (6.6.1)–(6.6.2). The following theorem provides the first step toward this direction.

**Theorem 6.4.** *Consider the large-scale system* (6.6.1)–(6.6.2) *with a set of linear interconnections*

$$g_i(t, x) = \sum_{j=1}^{N} G_{ij} x_j(t) \qquad (6.6.11)$$

*and a composite interaction matrix* $G = \{G_{ij}\}$, $i, j = 1, 2, \ldots, N$ *which satisfy*

$$\text{rank}\left[\frac{C}{G}\right] = \text{rank}[C] = r = \sum_{i=1}^{N} r_i \qquad (6.6.12)$$

*Then a set of decentralized estimators*

$$\dot{\hat{x}}_i(t) = (A_i - P_i C_i)\hat{x}_i(t) + P_i y_i(t) + B_i u_i(t) + \sum_{j=1}^{N} \tilde{P}_{ij} y_j(t) \qquad (6.6.13)$$

*for* $i = 1, 2, \ldots, N$, *with* $\tilde{P}_{ij}$ *being an* $n_i \times r_j$ *submatrix whose composite form*

$\tilde{P}$ *satisfies*

$$\tilde{P} = GC^T(CC^T)^{-1} \qquad (6.6.14)$$

*have a converging rate proportional to* $exp\{-\alpha t\}$.

The following proof due to Sundareshan (1977b) is now given.

PROOF: Let the gains $P_i$ in (6.6.6) be chosen such that the decentralized observation approach (6.6.3) or, equivalently,

$$\dot{\hat{x}}(t) = (A - PC)\hat{x}(t) + Py(t) + Bu(t) \qquad (6.6.15)$$

has a convergence degree of $\alpha$. In the above equation, $\hat{x}^T = (\hat{x}_1^T \hat{x}_2^T \dots \hat{x}_N^T)$ and $P = \text{Block-diag}(P_1 P_2 \dots P_N)$ and the spectrum $(A - PC)C$ has the property $\{s: \text{Re}(s) \leqslant -\alpha\}$. Following the rank condition (6.6.12), $G$ can be expressed as $G = \tilde{P}C$, where $\tilde{P}$ is given by (6.6.14), and therefore (Chen, 1970)

$$\text{rank}\begin{bmatrix} C \\ CA \\ \vdots \\ CA^{n-1} \end{bmatrix} = \text{rank}\begin{bmatrix} C \\ C(A+G) \\ \vdots \\ C(A+G)^{n-1} \end{bmatrix} \qquad (6.6.16)$$

However, since the pairs $(A_i, C_i)$ are assumed to be completely observable and $A$ and $C$ are block-diagonal matrices, the composite system observability matrix on the left-hand side of (6.6.16) is of full rank. Therefore, the pair $((A+G), C)$ is also completely observable, which implies that a gain matrix $K \in R^{n \times r}$ can be chosen such that a prescribed degree of convergence for the estimation scheme

$$\dot{\hat{x}}(t) = (A + G - KC)\hat{x}(t) + Ky(t) + Bu(t) \qquad (6.6.17)$$

for the composite system (6.6.1)–(6.6.2) is achieved. Now if $K$ is chosen as $K = P + \tilde{P}$, it will result in a spectrum $(A + G - KC)$ identical to the spectrum $(A - PC)$, hence ensuring a convergence degree $\alpha$ for the estimation scheme (6.6.17). Finally, it is easy to see that under this condition the estimation scheme (6.6.17) reduces to that of (6.6.13). Q.E.D. ∎

Although the decentralized estimator (6.6.3) requires the solutions of low-order AMREs (6.6.7) only the modified estimator (6.6.13) needs the outputs of other subsystems. In sequel, we discuss an alternative decentralized estimator which was proposed independently by Sundareshan (1977) and Šiljak (1978a) which depends on the estimated states of all the other subsystems instead of their normal outputs. The work of Sundareshan (1977), which provides necessary conditions for the existence of such an estimation procedure, is first presented, and then the actual estimation is applied to an example using Šiljak's (1978a,b) method based on the "separation property" of decentralized estimators formulation which is computationally more convenient in this author's opinion.

**Theorem 6.5.** *For the decentralized estimation of a large-scale system, let the following Lipschitz-type conditions hold for the interactions:*

$$\|g_i(t, x) - g_i(t, \tilde{x})\| \leq \sum_{j=1}^{N} \delta_{ij} \|x_j - \tilde{x}_j\| \qquad (6.6.18)$$

*for all* $t$, $x$, *and* $\tilde{x}$, $i = 1, 2, \ldots, N$, *and* $\delta_{ij}$ *are real nonnegative numbers. Furthermore, let* $\tilde{E}_i$ *be an arbitrary* $(n_i \times n_i)$*-dimensional symmetric, positive-definite matrix and* $\tilde{F}_i$ *an* $n_i \times n_i$ *matrix satisfying the following Lyapunov equation:*

$$\tilde{A}_i^T \tilde{F}_i + \tilde{F}_i \tilde{A}_i + \tilde{E}_i = 0 \qquad (6.6.19)$$

*Matrix* $\tilde{A}_i = A_i - H_i C_i^T C_i + \alpha I_i$ *and*

$$\min_i \{\lambda_m(\tilde{E}_i)\} \geq 2\delta \max_i \{\lambda_M(\tilde{F}_i)\} \qquad (6.6.20)$$

*where* $\lambda_m(\cdot)$ *and* $\lambda_M(\cdot)$ *correspond to the minimum and maximum eigenvalue of their arguments, respectively, and*

$$\delta = \sum_{i=1}^{N} \sum_{j=1}^{N} \delta_{ij} \qquad (6.6.21)$$

*Then the state estimation through*

$$\dot{\hat{x}}_i(t) = \left(A_i - H_i C_i^T C_i\right)\hat{x}_i(t) + H_i C_i^T y_i(t) + B_i u_i(t) + g_i(t, \hat{x}) \qquad (6.6.22)$$

*has a convergence degree* $\alpha$, *i.e.,* $e(t)$ *decays by at least* $\exp(-\alpha t)$.

PROOF: First let us assume that through the choice of $P_i$ from (6.6.6), an estimation scheme (6.6.3) results in a convergence degree of $\alpha$. Now by using (6.6.1)–(6.6.2) and (6.6.22), it is possible to find an expression for the error systems:

$$\dot{e}_i(t) = \left(A_i - H_i C_i^T C_i\right)e_i(t) + g_i(t, x) - g_i(t, \hat{x}) \qquad (6.6.23)$$

for $i = 1, 2, \ldots, N$. These expressions can be equivalently expressed as

$$e(t) = (A - HC^T C)e(t) + h(t, x, \hat{x}) \qquad (6.6.24)$$

where $h(t, x, \hat{x}) = [h_1^T(\cdot) \cdots h_N^T(\cdot)]^T$ with $h_i(t, x, \hat{x}) = g_i(t, x) - g_i(t, \hat{x})$. Now since Equation (6.6.19) holds for every index $i$, the latter set of equations can be written as

$$\tilde{A}^T \tilde{F} + \tilde{F} \tilde{A} + \tilde{E} = 0 \qquad (6.6.25)$$

where $\tilde{A} = (A - HC^TC + \alpha I) = \text{Block-diag}(\tilde{A}_1 \ldots \tilde{A}_N)$, $\tilde{F} = \text{Block-diag}(\tilde{F}_1 \ldots$
$\tilde{F}_N)$ and $\tilde{E} = \text{Block-diag}(\tilde{E}_1 \ldots \tilde{E}_N)$. Now let $v(e) = e^T(t)\tilde{F}e(t)$ be a
Lyapunov function for the error system (6.6.24). Then using (6.6.25) one has

$$\dot{v}(e) = e^T(t)\{(A - HC^TC)^T\tilde{F} + \tilde{F}(A - HC^TC)\}e(t) + 2h^T(t, x, \hat{x})\tilde{F}e(t)$$
$$= e^T(t)(-2\alpha\tilde{F} - \tilde{E})e(t) + 2h^T(t, x, \hat{x})\tilde{F}e(t) \qquad (6.6.26)$$

Therefore,

$$\dot{v}(e) \leqslant -2\alpha v(e) \qquad (6.6.27)$$

if

$$e^T(t)\tilde{E}e(t) \geqslant 2h^T(t, x, \hat{x})\tilde{F}e(t) \qquad (6.6.28)$$

for all $n$-dimensional $e(t)$. However, using (6.6.18) it is easy to note that

$$\|h(t, x, \hat{x})\| \leqslant \sum_{i=1}^{N} \|h_i(t, x, \hat{x})\| \leqslant \sum_{i=1}^{N} \sum_{j=1}^{N} \delta_{ij}\|e_j\| \leqslant \delta\|e\| \qquad (6.6.29)$$

Thus, condition (6.6.20) is sufficient to ensure (6.6.28). Hence (6.6.27) holds,
which proves the theorem. Q.E.D. ∎

Note Theorem 6.5 is general for any time-varying interaction $g_i(t, x)$. For
the special case of linear interactions with time-invariant $G_{ij}$ matrices
(6.6.11), an estimate for $\delta$ is suggested:

$$\delta = \lambda_M^{1/2}(G^TG) \qquad (6.6.30)$$

where $G = [G_{ij}]$, $i, j = 1, 2, \ldots, N$. The following example illustrates this.

**Example 6.6.2.** Consider a fourth-order system

$$\dot{x}(t) = \begin{bmatrix} -1 & 0 & 5 \times 10^{-3} & 10^{-4} \\ -0.5 & -1.1 & 10^{-3} & 10^{-2} \\ 5 \times 10^{-4} & -8 \times 10^{-4} & -3 & -1 \\ 2.5 \times 10^{-3} & -8 \times 10^{-3} & 0.8 & -2 \end{bmatrix} x(t)$$

$$+ \begin{bmatrix} 1 & 0 \\ 0 & 0 \\ 0 & 1 \\ 0 & 1 \end{bmatrix} u(t) \qquad (6.6.31)$$

$$y(t) = \begin{bmatrix} 1 & 0 & 0 & 0 \\ 0 & 0 & 0 & 1 \end{bmatrix} x(t) \qquad (6.6.32)$$

Check the decentralized estimation conditions set forth by Theorem 6.5.

SOLUTION: From the structure of the system matrix in (6.6.31), one can
choose to decouple the system into two second-order subsystems. Let us

choose an estimation convergence degree of $\alpha = 1$, and if the AMRE (6.6.7) is solved for the two subsystems using a $Q_i = \text{diag}\{0.1, 0.1\}$, the following results:

$$H_1(1) = \begin{bmatrix} 0.552 & -0.209 \\ -0.209 & 0.274 \end{bmatrix} \quad H_2(1) = \begin{bmatrix} 0.0263 & 3.3 \times 10^{-3} \\ 3.3 \times 10^{-3} & 0.0456 \end{bmatrix}$$

$$(6.6.33)$$

Now choosing two arbitrary matrices $\tilde{E}_1 = \text{diag}\{2, 2\}$, $\tilde{E}_2 = \text{diag}\{1, 1\}$ and solving the Lyapunov equation (6.6.19) for $\tilde{F}_i(\alpha)$, $i = 1, 2$, the following results:

$$\tilde{F}_1(1) = \begin{bmatrix} 1.8122 & -0.810 \\ -0.810 & 12.36 \end{bmatrix}, \quad \tilde{F}_2(1) = \begin{bmatrix} 0.432 & 0.362 \\ 0.362 & 0.755 \end{bmatrix} \quad (6.6.34)$$

In order to check for exponential convergence of the decentralized estimation error at a rate $\exp(-t)$, condition (6.6.20) for $i = 1, 2$ must be checked. Utilizing (6.6.30), the value of $\delta = \lambda_M^{1/2}(G^T G) = 1.007 \times 10^{-2}$. The eigenvalues of $\tilde{E}_i$ and $\tilde{F}_i$, $i = 1, 2$, are

$$\lambda\{\tilde{E}_1\} = \{1, 1\}, \quad \lambda\{\tilde{F}_1\} = \{1.75, 12.42\}$$

$$\lambda\{\tilde{E}_2\} = \{2, 2\}, \quad \lambda\{\tilde{F}_2\} = \{0.197, 0.99\}$$

then the condition (6.6.20) is

$$\min_i \{\lambda_m(\tilde{E}_i)\} = 1 \geqslant 2\delta \max_i \{\lambda_M(\tilde{F}_i)\} = 2(1.007 \times 10^{-2})(12.42) = 0.25$$

$$(6.6.35)$$

and it is satisfied; hence, the states of system (6.6.31), when decomposed into two second-order subsystems, can be estimated with a convergence rate $\exp(-t)$. Note that if the system (6.6.31) were decomposed into $1 \times 1$ and $3 \times 3$ subsystems, the condition (6.6.20) would most likely be violated. In fact, if some elements of the interaction submatrices of (6.6.31) are changed or increased, i.e., for a new $G$ matrix,

$$G = \begin{bmatrix} 0 & 0 & 0 & 0 \\ 0 & 0 & 5 \times 10^{-2} & 2 \times 10^{-2} \\ 0 & 0 & 0 & 0 \\ 0 & 8 \times 10^{-2} & 0 & 0 \end{bmatrix} \quad (6.6.36)$$

then $\delta = \lambda_M^{1/2}\{G^T G\} = \lambda_M^{1/2}\{0, 0, 6.5 \times 10^{-3}, 2.9 \times 10^{-3}\} = 0.0806$, and this value is large enough to violate (6.6.20). Thus, for any given value of $\alpha$, it is in fact possible to find a class of interaction matrices such that an specified rate of convergence in decentralized form is guaranteed, provided of course that each pair $\{C_i, A_i\}$ is completely observable for $i = 1, 2, \ldots, N$.

We will now formulate the optimal decentralized feedback control based on the estimated state error and decoupled subsystem Riccati matrix solutions as formulated by Šiljak (1978a). Consider the estimated state equation (6.6.22) and assume linear time-invariant interactions

$$\dot{\hat{x}}_i = \left( A_i - H_i C_i^T C_i \right)\hat{x}_i + H_i C_i^T y_i(t) + \sum_{j=1}^{N} G_{ij}\hat{x}_j + B_i u_i \quad (6.6.37)$$

for $i = 1, 2, \ldots, N$. Now in controlling the systems

$$\dot{x}_i = A_i x_i + B_i u_i + \sum_{j=1}^{N} G_{ij} x_j \quad (6.6.38)$$

it is suggested to use

$$u_i = v_i - L_i \hat{x}_i \quad (6.6.39)$$

instead of the usual

$$u_i = v_i - L_i x_i \quad (6.6.40)$$

where $v_i$ is the reference input, $L_i = R_i^{-1} B_i^T K_i$, and $K_i$ is the solution of

$$K_i \left( A_i^T + \alpha I_i \right) + \left( A_i + \alpha I_i \right) K_i - K_i S_i K_i + Q_i = 0 \quad (6.6.41)$$

with $S_i = B_i R_i^{-1} B_i^T$. The performance index is in the quadratic form

$$J_i\left(0, x_i(0), u_i\right) = \int_0^\infty e^{2\alpha t}\left( x_i^T Q_i x_i + u_i^T R_i u_i \right) dt \quad (6.6.42)$$

Substituting (6.6.39) in (6.6.37) and (6.6.38), the following closed-loop equations for the state $x_i$ and its estimation $\hat{x}_i$ result:

$$\dot{\hat{x}}_i = \left( A_i - H_i D_i - S_i K_i \right)\hat{x}_i + \sum_{j=1}^{N} G_{ij}\hat{x}_j + H_i D_i x_i + B_i v_i \quad (6.6.43)$$

$$\dot{x}_i = A_i x_i + \sum_{j=1}^{N} G_{ij} x_j - S_i K_i \hat{x}_i + B_i v_i \quad (6.6.44)$$

which can be rewritten in composite form (6.6.45) (see p. 396) where $D_i = C_i^T C_i$, $i = 1, 2, \ldots, N$. Now by applying the transformation

$$
\begin{bmatrix} x_1 \\ \vdots \\ x_N \\ \hline e_1 \\ \vdots \\ e_N \end{bmatrix}
=
\begin{bmatrix} I_n & 0 \\ \hline I_n & -I_n \end{bmatrix}
\begin{bmatrix} x_1 \\ \vdots \\ x_N \\ \hline \hat{x}_1 \\ \vdots \\ \hat{x}_N \end{bmatrix}
\quad (6.6.46)
$$

$$
\begin{bmatrix}
\dot{x}_1 \\
\dot{x}_2 \\
\cdots \\
\dot{x}_N \\
\hline
\dot{\hat{x}}_1 \\
\dot{\hat{x}}_2 \\
\cdots \\
\dot{\hat{x}}_N
\end{bmatrix}
=
\left[
\begin{array}{cccc|cccc}
A_1 & G_{12} & \cdots & G_{1N} & -S_1 K_1 & 0 & \cdots & 0 \\
G_{21} & A_2 & & \cdots & 0 & -S_2 K_2 & \cdots & 0 \\
\cdots & & \ddots & & \cdots & & \ddots & \cdots \\
G_{N1} & \cdots & & A_n & 0 & 0 & \cdots & -S_N K_N \\
\hline
H_1 D_1 & 0 & \cdots & 0 & A_1 - H_1 D_1 - S_1 K_1 & G_{12} & \cdots & G_{1N} \\
0 & H_2 D_2 & \cdots & 0 & G_{21} & A_2 - H_2 D_2 - S_2 K_2 & \cdots & \cdots \\
\cdots & & \ddots & & \cdots & & \ddots & \cdots \\
0 & 0 & \cdots & H_N D_N & G_{N1} & \cdots & & A_N - H_N D_N - S_N K_N
\end{array}
\right]
\times
\begin{bmatrix}
x_1 \\
\cdots \\
x_N \\
\hline
\hat{x}_1 \\
\cdots \\
\hat{x}_N
\end{bmatrix}
+
\begin{bmatrix}
B_1 v_1 \\
B_2 v_2 \\
\cdots \\
B_N v_N \\
\hline
B_1 v_1 \\
B_2 v_2 \\
\cdots \\
B_N v_N
\end{bmatrix}
\tag{6.6.45}
$$

to (6.6.45), a desirable separation between $x$ and $e$ results:

$$
\begin{bmatrix}
\dot{x}_1 \\
\vdots \\
\dot{x}_N \\
-\,-\,- \\
\dot{e}_1 \\
\vdots \\
\dot{e}_N
\end{bmatrix}
$$

$$
=
\left[
\begin{array}{ccc|ccc}
A_1 - S_1 K_1 & \cdots & G_{1N} & S_1 K_1 & \cdots & 0 \\
 & \ddots & & & \ddots & \\
G_{N1} & & A_N - S_N I_N & 0 & & S_N K_N \\
\hline
 & & & A_1 - H_1 D_1 & \cdots & G_{1N} \\
 & 0 & & & \ddots & \\
 & & & G_{N1} & & A_N - H_N D_N
\end{array}
\right]
$$

$$
\times
\begin{bmatrix}
x_1 \\
\vdots \\
x_N \\
-\,-\,- \\
e_1 \\
\vdots \\
e_N
\end{bmatrix}
+
\begin{bmatrix}
B_1 v_1 \\
\vdots \\
B_N v_N \\
-\,-\,- \\
B_1 v_1 \\
\vdots \\
B_N v_N
\end{bmatrix}
\tag{6.6.47}
$$

The following algorithm finds the optimal states of a large-scale system based on decentralized estimation and control.

***Algorithm 6.13.*** Decentralized Estimation of Large-Scale Systems

*Step 1:* Solve $2N$ low-order AMREs (6.6.7) and (6.6.41) for $H_i$, $K_i$ and evaluate $S_i K_i$, $i = 1, 2, \ldots, N$.

*Step 2:* Integrate a set of $n$ simultaneous equations for $e_i(t)$, $i = 1, 2, \ldots, N$, using the lower partition of (6.6.47) and $e_i(0) = x_i(0)$. Store $e_i(t)$.

*Step 3:* Integrate a set of $n$ simultaneous equations for $x_i(t)$, $i = 1, 2, \ldots, N$, using the upper partition of (6.6.47) and $e_i(t)$ and $x_i(0)$.

The following example illustrates the decentralized estimation algorithm.

**Example 6.6.3.** Consider the fifth-order system

$$\dot{x}(t) = \begin{bmatrix} -1.5 & 0.1 & 0 & 0.6 & 0.4 \\ -0.3 & 0 & 0.2 & -0.1 & 0.2 \\ -0.25 & 0 & -1 & -0.25 & 1 \\ 0.1 & -0.2 & 0 & -2 & 0.5 \\ 0.5 & 0 & 0.4 & 0 & 0.1 \end{bmatrix} x(t) + \begin{bmatrix} 0 & 0 \\ 1 & 0 \\ 0 & 0 \\ 0 & 0.1 \\ 0 & 1 \end{bmatrix} u(t)$$

(6.6.48)

$$y(t) = \begin{bmatrix} 1 & 1 & 0 & 0 & 0 \\ 0 & 0 & 1 & 0 & 1 \end{bmatrix} x(t)$$

(6.6.49)

It is desired to find $x(t)$ and $y(t)$ for zero reference inputs and step inputs $v_i(t) = 0.5$, $i = 1, 2$.

SOLUTION: In an attempt to solve the estimation problem, the system (6.6.48) is divided into a second- and a third-order subsystem as shown, i.e., $(n_i, m_i, r_i) = (2, 1, 1)$, $(3, 1, 1)$ for $i = 1, 2$. The first step of Algorithm 6.13 calls for $K_i$ and $H_i$ using a value of $\alpha = 1$. It is noted that the second subsystem was already considered in Example 6.6.1, and in fact the value of Riccati matrix $H_2(\alpha) = H_2(1)$ is given in (6.6.10). The remaining Riccati matrices are

$$K_1(1) = \begin{bmatrix} 0.1824 & -0.3872 \\ -0.3872 & 2.0112 \end{bmatrix}, \quad H_1(1) = \begin{bmatrix} 0.3163 & -0.8621 \\ -0.8621 & 3.50 \end{bmatrix}$$

$$K_2(1) = \begin{bmatrix} 0.4877 & -0.0733 & 0.9225 \\ -0.0733 & 0.0634 & -0.1054 \\ 0.9225 & -0.1054 & 2.8634 \end{bmatrix}$$

(6.6.50)

The second and third steps of Algorithm 6.13 were achieved by integrating the separated error subsystems (lower partition of (6.6.47))

$$\begin{bmatrix} \dot{e}_1 \\ \dot{e}_2 \end{bmatrix} = \begin{bmatrix} A_1 - H_1 D_1 & G_{12} \\ G_{21} & A_2 - H_2 D_2 \end{bmatrix} \begin{bmatrix} e_1 \\ e_2 \end{bmatrix} + \begin{bmatrix} B_1 v_1 \\ B_2 v_2 \end{bmatrix}$$

(6.6.51)

with $e(0) = (1, \quad 0, \quad 1-1, \quad 0)$ and state subsystems

$$\begin{bmatrix} \dot{x}_1 \\ \dot{x}_2 \end{bmatrix} = \begin{bmatrix} A_1 - S_1 K_1 & G_{12} \\ G_{21} & A_2 - S_2 K_2 \end{bmatrix} \begin{bmatrix} x_1 \\ x_2 \end{bmatrix} + \begin{bmatrix} S_1 K_1 & 0 \\ 0 & S_2 K_2 \end{bmatrix} \begin{bmatrix} e_1 \\ e_2 \end{bmatrix} + \begin{bmatrix} B_1 v_1 \\ B_2 v_2 \end{bmatrix}$$

(6.6.52)

with $x(0) = (1, 0, 1 \quad -1, 0)^T$. The resulting typical estimation errors, states,

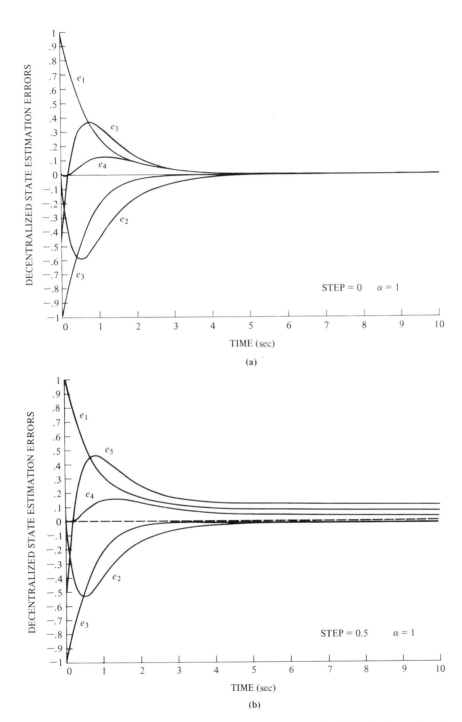

**Figure 6.20** The estimation errors, $e_i(t)$ vs time for Example 6.6.3: **(a)** Step = 0 and **(b)** Step = 0.5.

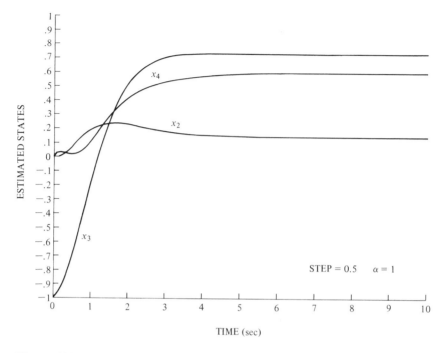

**Figure 6.21** Typical estimated states for Example 6.6.3.

and system outputs are shown in Figures 6.20–6.22. The estimation errors for step inputs of zero and 0.5 are shown in Figure 6.21. The convergence of the estimation depends on several factors. One is the value of $\alpha$; another is the strength of interaction matrices $G_{12}$ and $G_{21}$; and the third is the value of input disturbance or size of the step. Therefore, the behavior of the estimation error $e_i(t)$, $i = 1, 2$, shown in Figures 6.20a, b is rather expected. Typical estimated states for the zero and input of 0.5 step are shown in Figure 6.21. The two subsystems outputs for the zero and 0.5 inputs are shown in Figure 6.22. The regulation behavior of the outputs for the first case is expected. The outputs of the $\alpha = 1$, 0.5 step and $G_{ij}$ interaction matrices are compared with a weaker interaction $0.1G_{ij}$ in Figure 6.22b. Note that as the interaction strength gets weaker, the outputs get closer to the desired output of 0.5. This behavior is also predictable because of the fact that the present system does not actually satisfy the decentralized estimation conditions set forth by Theorem 6.4. Even for the reduction of every element of interaction matrices $G_{12}$ and $G_{21}$ by a factor of 10, the conditions still were not satisfied; but it was a step closer to the convergence at a rate of $\exp(-t)$.

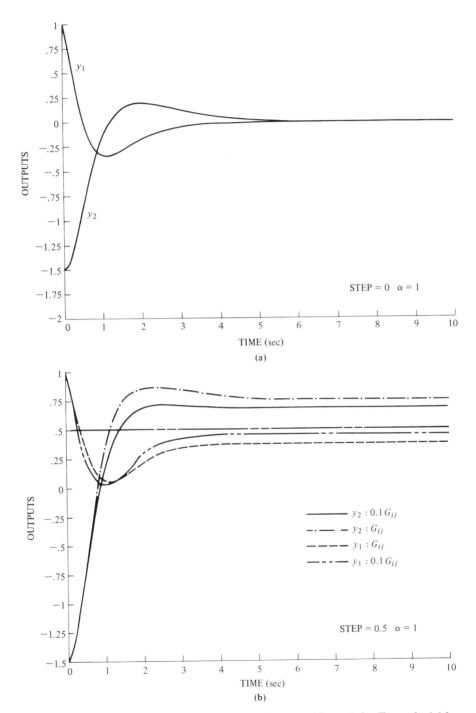

**Figure 6.22** Two subsystem outputs $y_1(t)$ and $y_2(t)$ with $\alpha = 1$ for Example 6.6.3:
(a) for Step = 0 and (b) for two interaction matrices and Step = 0.5.

## 6.7  Discussion and Conclusions

Chapter 6 can be considered a review of the first five chapters of the text from an optimal control point of view. The notions and topics developed in those chapters were used to control and/or optimize various types of large-scale systems in this chapter. The only other related topic to control was the state estimation of large-scale systems discussed in Section 6.6.

The two main classes of model reduction techniques, i.e., aggregation and perturbation, were considered first. It was seen that no matter how a given large-scale system is aggregated, the aggregation procedure—exact, modal, continued fraction, minimum realization, time- or frequency-domain based—a near-optimum feedback controller can always be obtained provided that an aggregation matrix is available. In the cases where the aggregation matrix $C$ is not apparent, one can follow the procedure outlined in Section 2.2, where a controllable pair $(F, G)$ for the aggregated system is found and then by using the controllability and modified controllability matrices $W_A$ and $W_F$ of $\{B, A\}$ and $\{G, F\}$, respectively, an aggregation matrix $C$, given by Equation (2.2.12), is obtained.

The main difficulty in both aggregation and perturbation approaches of large-scale systems, as has been mentioned previously, is determining the exact procedure by which a system should be aggregated or perturbed. Partial answers to these questions can be found in the works of Mahapatra (1977, 1979), Rao et al., (1979), Tse et al. (1978), and Elrazaz (1982) for aggregation and Kokotović et al. (1980) and Elrazaz and Sinha (1979) for perturbation. The common denominator in the application of all reduction schemes is, of course, the loss of optimality and a degradation of the objective function. Rao and Lamba (1974) have also applied linear state regulator theory to aggregated linear TIV systems.

The balance of Section 6.2 was devoted to the determination of a near-optimum control for a large-scale system via hierarchical and decentralized control methods. Three simple and conveniently applicable methods of structural perturbation (Šiljak 1978b), optimal decentralized control via unconstrained minimization due to Geromel and Bernussou (1979), and the sequential optimization of Davison and Gesing (1979) were discussed. The various numerical examinations of these methods presented both in Section 6.2 and experienced by this and other authors bear the fact that they are readily applicable for at least demonstration of the concepts.

The near-optimum control of large-scale nonlinear systems was considered in Section 6.3. One of the few computationally efficient optimal control approaches for nonlinear systems is based on the parameter sensitivity methods discussed in Section 6.3.1. An essentially feedback control structure resulted for nonlinear systems. It is noted that to obtain the $i$th-order near-optimum control, only $(i - 1)$th terms are needed which will act as forcing functions for $i$th-order sensitivity functions. The basic difficulty with its implementation stems from the fact that for each new order of approximation, a number of partial differentiations of the TPBV problem representing the previous order is needed. This difficulty may be eliminated by comparing the cost function and corresponding responses resulting from each new order of approximation with the previous one. If the new approximation does not improve the performance a great deal, the search for a design closer to the optimum can be terminated.

The next topic in the design of large nonlinear systems was the hierarchical control via interaction prediction, which was discussed in Section 6.3.2. The main advantages of this method, as briefly outlined before, are twofold. One is that for a long enough $t_f$ the approach converges to an optimum solution (Singh, 1980), while the other is that computational efforts are rather minimal and applicable with existing methods. Specifically, the first-level problems are centered around time-varying matrix Riccati formulations for which efficient integration-free methods have been introduced (Davison and Maki, 1973). The second-level problem is free of convergence difficulties of linear iterations and is based on a simple substitution. However, the method converged to a local optimal solution, unlike the goal coordination which gave a global solution in the absence of a duality gap.

The regular and singular perturbations and sensitivity methods were combined in a systematic fashion in Section 6.3.3 to design nonlinear systems. Both structural and time-scale decompositions were used.

The concept of coupling and perturbation for time-delay systems was introduced in Section 6.4.1. A large-scale time-delay system is decomposed into a number of lower-order nondelay subsystems which can be easily solved by available methods.

The application of hierarchical control to large-scale time-delay systems was considered in Sections 6.4.2 and 6.4.3. An important special class of large-scale composite systems interconnected by delayed subsystem outputs, termed serial time-delay, was considered in Section 6.4.2. The extension of hierarchical control to nonserial time-delay system within the context of goal coordination was considered next. It was proved that the proposed two-level iterative algorithm converges uniformly to the optimum solution of the large-scale time-delay system. Jamshidi and Wang (1982) have extended the interaction prediction algorithm to linear and nonlinear time-delay systems with convergence proof and application. The next topic, considered in Section 6.5, was the degree of near-optimality of different design techniques. A detailed survey of the topic was undertaken in this section. In each case, a bound on the performance index was obtained. A basic discussion of each case were then presented.

The final section of this chapter, Section 6.6, dealt with the important problem of state estimation of large-scale systems. Theorems 6.4 and 6.5 provided Lipschitz-type conditions on the system interactions whereby a prescribed degree of convergence on the estimation can be achieved. These conditions are adequate for both linear time-invariant and linear time-varying as well as nonlinear interactions. However, except for the time-invariant case, a quick check on these conditions is computationally difficult. The decentralized estimation as proposed by Šiljak (1978a) turned out to be very computationally attractive by utilizing the separation transformation (6.6.46), which conveniently separated state estimation and state feedback problems.

## Problems

**C6.1.** Consider a fourth-order system

$$\dot{x} = \begin{bmatrix} 0 & 1 & 0 & 0 \\ 0 & 0 & 1 & 0 \\ 0 & 0 & 0 & 1 \\ -10.1 & -9.07 & -12.41 & -7.2 \end{bmatrix} x + \begin{bmatrix} 0 \\ 0 \\ 0 \\ 1 \end{bmatrix} u$$

with $x^T(0) = (1 \quad -1 \quad 1 \quad -1)$ and cost function

$$J = \frac{1}{2} \int_0^\infty \left( x^T Q x + u^T R u \right) dt$$

with $Q = \operatorname{diag}(1,2,3,4)$ and $R = 1$. Find a second-order aggregated model using the modal aggregation method and then find the near-optimum feedback control law and the corresponding cost function.

**6.2.** Consider a singularly perturbed system

$$\dot{x} = -x + z + u, \quad x(0) = 1$$
$$\varepsilon \dot{z} = -z + u, \quad x(0) = 1, \quad \varepsilon = 0.1$$

and a cost function

$$J = \frac{1}{2} \int_0^\infty \left( x^2 + z^2 + u^2 \right) dt$$

Find (a) the left-hand boundary layer for this system and (b) the near-optimum control by methods of Section 6.2.2.b.

**C6.3.** Consider an $\varepsilon$-coupled system

$$\dot{x} = \left[ \begin{array}{cc|cc} -5 & 0.1 & 0 & -0.01 \\ 0 & -1 & 0 & 0 \\ \hline 0 & 0 & -0.5 & 0.1 \\ 0 & 0.05 & 0 & -0.1 \end{array} \right] x + \left[ \begin{array}{cc|cc} 1 & 0 \\ 0 & 0 \\ \hline 0 & 0 \\ 0 & 1 \end{array} \right] u$$

with a cost function

$$J = \frac{1}{2} \int_0^\infty \left( x^T \left[ \begin{array}{c|c} Q_1 & 0 \\ \hline 0 & Q_2 \end{array} \right] x + u^T \left[ \begin{array}{c|c} R_1 & 0 \\ \hline 0 & R_2 \end{array} \right] u \right) dt$$

with $Q_1 = 2I_2$, $Q_2 = I_2$, $R_1 = R_2 = 1$. Apply Algorithm 6.1 to find a near-optimum controller for this system.

**C6.4.** Find an optimal control for the system

$$\dot{x} = \begin{bmatrix} 0 & 0.1 & 1 \\ -1 & -1 & 0 \\ 0.5 & -0.5 & -0.5 \end{bmatrix} x + \begin{bmatrix} 1 & 0 & 0 \\ 0 & 1 & 0 \\ 0 & 0 & 1 \end{bmatrix} u$$

with a cost function

$$J = \frac{1}{2} \sum_{i=1}^{2} \int_0^\infty \left( x_i^T Q_i x_i + u_i^T R_i u_i \right) dt$$

where $Q_i = I_{n_i}$, $R_i = 2I_{m_i}$ with $n_i = m_i = 1$, $i = 1, 2, 3$, using Algorithm 6.3.

**C6.5.** Repeat Example 6.2.9 for the system of Example 5.4.4 to find an optimal sequentially stable control.

**C6.6.** Use Algorithm 6.6 to find a hierarchical control for the problem

$$\dot{x} = \begin{bmatrix} -1 & 0.2 \\ 0 & -1 \end{bmatrix} x + \begin{bmatrix} 1 \\ 1 \end{bmatrix} u + \begin{bmatrix} x_1^2 x_2 \\ x_2^2 x_1 \end{bmatrix}, \quad x(0) = \begin{bmatrix} 1 \\ 1 \end{bmatrix}$$

$$J = \int_0^2 \left( x_1^2 x_2^2 + x_1^3 + x_2^3 + u^2 x_1^2 + u^2 x_2^2 + x_1^2 + x_2^2 + u^2 \right) dt$$

[*Hint:* Use the developments following Equations (6.3.70)–(6.3.75).]

**C6.7.** Consider the coupled time-delay system

$$\dot{x} = -x + 0.1y - 0.1x(t - 0.1) + u$$
$$\dot{y} = -x - 0.5y - y(t - 0.1) + v$$

with initial functions $x(a) = y(a) = -1$, $-0.1 \leq a \leq 0$. Use Algorithm 6.10 to find a near-optimum controller for the system with the cost

$$J = \frac{1}{2} \int_0^\infty \left( x^2 + y^2 + u^2 + v^2 \right) dt$$

**6.8.** Find a bound on the performance index in the system of Example 6.2.1.

**C6.9.** For the system

$$\dot{x} = \left[ \begin{array}{cc|cc} -1 & 0 & 0 & 0.5 \\ 0.2 & -0.5 & 0 & -0.2 \\ \hline 0.1 & 0 & -0.5 & 0.5 \\ 0 & 0.1 & 0 & -2 \end{array} \right] x + \left[ \begin{array}{c|c} 0 & 0 \\ 1 & 0 \\ \hline 0 & 0 \\ 0 & 1 \end{array} \right] u$$

$$y = \left[ \begin{array}{cc|cc} 1 & 1 & 0 & 0 \\ 0 & 0 & 1 & 1 \end{array} \right] x$$

use decentralized estimation Algorithm 6.13 to find $x(t)$ and $y(t)$ with step inputs $v_i(t) = 1$, $i = 1, 2$, and $x^T(0) = (1 \quad 0 \quad -1 \quad 0)$.

# References

Aggarwal, J. K. 1970. Computational of optimal control for time-delay. Systems. *IEEE Trans. Aut. Cont.* AC-15:683–685.

Anderson, B. D. O. 1979. Time delays in large-scale systems. *Proc. CDC.* (Ft. Lauderdale, FL).

Aoki, M. 1968. Control of large-scale dynamic systems by aggregation. *IEEE Trans. Aut. Cont.* AC-13:246–253.

Aoki, M. 1971. Aggregation, in D. A. Wismer, Ed., *Optimization Methods for Large-Scale Systems... with Applications*, chapter 5, pp. 191–232. McGraw-Hill, New York.

Aoki, M. 1978. Some approximation methods and control of large scale systems. *IEEE Trans. Aut. Cont.* AC-23:173–182.

Aoki, M., and Li, M. T. 1972. Partial reconstruction of state vectors in decentralized dynamic systems. *IEEE Trans. Aut. Cont.* AC-18:289–292.

Bailey, F. N., and Ramapriyan, H. K. 1973. Bounds on suboptimality in the control of linear dynamic systems. *IEEE Trans. Aut. Cont.* AC-18:532–534.

Barnett, S., and Storey, C. 1970. *Matrix Methods in Stability Analysis.* T. Nelson, London.

Bate, R. 1969. The optimal control of systems with transport lag. in C. T. Leondes, ed., *Advances in Control Systems*, vol. 7. Academic Press, New York.

Bauman, E. J. 1968. Multi-level optimization techniques with application to trajectory decomposition, in C. T. Leondes, ed., *Advances in Control Systems*, vol. 6. Academic Press, New York.

Birta, L. G., and Trushel, P. J. 1969. A comparative study of four implementations of a dynamic optimization scheme. *Simulation J.* 13:89–97.

Chan, H. C., and Perkins, W. R. 1973. Optimization of time delay systems using parameter imbedding. *IFAC J. Automatica* 9:257–261.

Chen, C. T. 1970. Introduction to linear system theory. New York: Holt, Rinehart and Winston, New York.

Chidambara, M. R. 1969. Two simple techniques for simplifying large dynamic systems. *Proc. JACC* (Boulder, CO).

Chu, K. C. 1974. Optimal decentralized regulation for a string of coupled systems. *IEEE Trans. Aut. Cont.* AC-19:243–246.

D'Ans, G.; Hontoir, Y.; and Jamshidi, M. 1970. A manifold-imbedding solution of optimal control problems. *Proc. 8th Allerton Conf.* (Monticello, IL), pp. 564–575.

Davison, E. J. 1966. A method for simplifying linear dynamic systems. *IEEE Trans. Aut. Cont.* AC-11:93–101.

Davison, E. J., and Gesing, W. 1979. Sequential stability and optimization of large scale decentralized systems. *IFAC J. Automatica* 15:307–324.

Davison, E. J., and Maki, M. C. 1973. The numerical solution of the matrix Riccati differential equations. *IEEE Trans. Aut. Cont.* AC-18:71–73.

Davison, E. J., and Man, F. T. 1968. The numerical solution of $A^T Q + QA = -C$. *IEEE Trans. Aut. Cont.* AC-13:448–449.

Davison, E. J., and Wang, P. 1975. A robust conjugate-gradient algorithm which minimizes $\mathcal{L}$-functions. *IFAC J. Automatica* 11:297–308.

Dorato, P. 1963. On sensitivity in optimal control systems. *IEEE Trans. Aut. Cont.* AC-8:256–257.

Eller, D. H.; Aggarwal, J. K.; and Bank, H. T. 1969. Optimal control of linear time-delay systems. *IEEE Trans. Aut. Cont.* AC-14:678–687.

Elrazaz, Z. S. 1982. The choice of the reduced-model order. *Proc. Amer. Contr. Conf.* (Arlington, VA), pp. 1063–1067.

Elrazaz, Z. S., and Sinha, N. K. 1979. On the selection of the dominant poles of a system to be retained in a low-order model. *IEEE Trans. Aut. Cont.* AC-24:792–793.

Fletcher, R., and Powell, M. J. D. 1963. A rapidly convergent descend method for minimization. *Computer J.* 6:163–168.

Garrard, W. L. 1969. Additional results on suboptimal feedback control on nonlinear system. *Int. J. Cont.* 10:657–663.

Garrard, W. L. 1972. Suboptimal feedback control for nonlinear system. *IFAC J. Automatica* 8:219–221.

Garrard, W. L.; McClamroch, N. H.; and Clark, L. G. 1967. An approach to suboptimal feedback control of nonlinear systems. *Int. J. Cont.* 5:425–435.

Garrard, W. L., and Jordan, J. M. 1977. Design of nonlinear automatic flight control systems. *IFAC J. Automatica* 13:497–505.

Geoffrion, A. M. 1971. Duality in nonlinear programming. *SIAM Review* 13:1–37.

Geromel, J. C., and Bernussou, J. 1979. An algorithm for optimal decentralized regulation of linear quadratic interconnected systems. *IFAC J. Automatica* 15:489–491.

Gracovetsky, S. A., and Vidyasagar, M. 1973. Suboptimal control of neutral systems. *Int. J. Cont.* 18:121–128.

Hadlock, C. R. 1973. Existence and dependence on a parameter of solution of nonlinear two-point boundary-value problems. *J. Differential Equations* 14:498–517.

Hadlock, C. R., Jamshidi, M. and Kokotović, P. V. 1970. Near-optimum design of three time-scale systems. *Proc. 4th Princeton Conf.* (Princeton, NJ), pp. 118–122.

Hassan, M. F., and Singh, M. G. 1976. The optimization of nonlinear systems using a new two level method. *IFAC J. Automatica* 12:359–363.

Hassan, M. F.; Singh, M. G.; and Titli, A. 1979. Near optimal decentralized control with a pre-specified degree of stability. *IFAC J. Automatica*. 15:483–488.

Hontoir, Y. and Cruz, J. B., Jr. 1972. Manifold imbedding algorithm for optimization problems. *IFAC J. Automatica* 8:581–588.

Ikeda, M., and Šiljak, D. D. 1980. Decentralized stabilization of large-scale systems with time delay. *J. Large Scale Systems* 1:273–279.

Inoue, K.; Akashi, H.; Ogino, K.; and Sawaragi, Y. 1971. Sensitivity approaches to optimization of linear systems with time delay. *IFAC J. Automatica* 7:671–679.

Iyer, S. N., and Cory, B. J. 1971. Optimization of turbo-generator transient performance by differential dynamic programming. *IEEE Trans. Power. Appar. Syst.* PAS-90:2149–2157.

Jamshidi, M. 1969. A near-optimal controller for nonlinear systems. *Proc. 7th Allerton Conf. on Circuits and Systems* (Monticello, IL), pp. 169–180.

Jamshidi, M. 1971. An integrated near-optimum control for cold rolling mills. CSL Report R-499, Univ. Illinois, Urbana, IL.

Jamshidi, M. 1972a. On the imbedding solution of a class of optimal control problems. *IFAC J. Automatica* 8:637–640.

Jamshidi, M. 1972b. A near-optimum controller for cold rolling mills. *Int. J. Contr.* 16:1137–1154.

Jamshidi, M. 1972c. A parameter adjustable regulator for a winding process. *Int. J. Contr.* 15:725–736.

Jamshidi, M. 1973. Suboptimal control of coupled time-delay systems. *Int. J. Contr.* 17:995–1008.

Jamshidi, M. 1974. Three-stage near-optimum design of nonlinear-control processes. *Proc. IEE* 121:886–892.

Jamshidi, M. 1975a. Optimal control of nonlinear power systems by an imbedding method. *IFAC J. Automatica* 11:633–636.

Jamshidi, M. 1975b. A three-stage design of nonlinear control systems with time-delay. *Int. J. Contr.* 21:753–762.

Jamshidi, M. 1976a. A feedback near-optimum control for nonlinear systems. *Inform. Contr.* 32:75–84.

Jamshidi, M. 1976b. Application of three time-scale near-optimum design to control systems. *Aut. Cont. Theory and Appl.* 4:7–13.

Jamshidi, M. 1978. An imbedded initialization of Newton's algorithm for matrix Riccati equation. *IFAC J. Automatica* 14:167–170.

Jamshidi, M. 1980. An overview on the algebraic matrix Riccati equation and related problems. *J. Large Scale Systems* 1:167–192.

Jamshidi, M., and Böttiger, F. 1977. A parameter imbedding solution of algebraic matrix Riccati equation. *Int. J. Contr.* 25:271–281. See also *Proc. JACC* (W. Lafayette, IN) 1976.

Jamshidi, M.; D'Ans, G.; and Kokotović, P. V. 1970. Application of a parameter-imbedded Riccati equation. *IEEE Trans. Aut. Cont.* AC-15:682–683.

Jamshidi, M., and Malek-Zavarei, M. 1972. Suboptimal design of linear control systems with time delay. *Proc. IEE* 119:1743–1746.

Jamshidi, M., and Malek-Zavarei, M. 1981. A hierarchical optimization method of large-scale time-delay systems. *Proc. 20th IEEE Conf. Dec. Contr.* (San Diego, CA), pp. 1303–1304.

Jamshidi, M., and Malek-Zavarei, M. 1982. Hierarchical control of large-scale time-delay systems. Submitted for publication to *J. Large Scale Systems*.

Jamshidi, M., and Razzaghi, M. 1975. Optimization of linear systems with input time-delay. *Kybernetika* 11.

Jamshidi, M., and Wang, C.-M. 1982. Optimal hierarchical control of nonlinear large-scale time-delay systems. *Proc. IEEE Int. Large-Scale Systs. Symp.* (Virginia Beach, VA), pp. 258–262.

Javdan, M. R. 1976a. On the use of Lagrange duality in multi-level optimal control. *Proc. IFAC Symposium on Large Scale Systems Theory and Appl.* (Udine, Italy).

Javdan, M. R. 1976b. Extension of dual coordination to a class of nonlinear systems. *Int. J. Contr.* 24:551–571.

Kalman, R. E. 1960. Contribution to the theory of optimal control. *Bol. Soc. Math.*, 2nd Ser. 5:102–118.

Kelly, J. J. 1964. An optimal guidance approximation theory. *IEEE Trans. Aut. Cont.* 9:375.

Khalil, H. K., and Kokotović, P. V. 1979a. D-stability and multiparameter singular perturbation. *SIAM J. Contr.* 17:56–65.

Khalil, H. K., and Kokotović, P. V. 1979b. Control of linear systems with multi-parameter singular perturbations. *IFAC J. Automatica* 15:197–207.

Kharatishivili, G. L. 1961. The maximum principle in the theory of optimal processes with time lags. *Dokl. Akad. Nauk SSSR* 136:39–42.

Kokotović, P. V. 1972. Feedback design of large linear systems, in J. B. Cruz, Jr., Ed., *Feedback Systems*, pp. 99–137. McGraw-Hill, New York.

Kokotović, P. V., and Cruz, J. B., Jr. 1969. An approximate theorem for linear optimal regulator. *J. Math. Anal. Appl.* 27:249–252.

Kokotović, P. V., and D'Ans, G. 1969. Parameter imbedding design of linear optimal regulators. *Proc. 3rd Princeton Conf.* (Princeton, NJ), pp. 378–379.

Kokotović, P. V., and Singh, G. 1971. Optimization of coupled nonlinear systems. *Int. J. Contr.* 14:51–

Kokotović, P. V.; Allemong, J. J.; Winkelman, J. R.; and Chow, J. H. 1980. Singular perturbation and iterative separation of time scales. *IFAC J. Automatica* 16:23–33.

Kokotović, P. V.; Cruz, J. B., Jr.; Heller, J. E.; and Sannuti, P. 1969a. Synthesis of optimally sensitive systems. *Proc. IEEE* 56:1318.

Kokotović, P. V.; Perkins, W. R.; Cruz, J. B., Jr.; and D'Ans, G. 1969b. ε-coupling method for near optimum desing of large scale linear systems. *Proc. IEE* 116:889–892.

Krasovskii, N. N. 1963. Optimal processes in systems with time lag. *Proc. 2nd IFAC Congress* (Basel, Switzerland), pp. 327–332.

Krtolica, R., and Šiljak, D. D. 1980. Suboptimality of decentralized stochastic control and estimation. *IEEE Trans. Aut. Cont.* AC-25:76–83.

Kuester, J. L., and Mize, J. H. 1973. *Optimization Techniques with FORTRAN*, pp. 320–330. McGraw-Hill, New York.

Kwakernaak, H. W., and Sivan, R. 1972. *Linear Optimal Control Systems*. Wiley, New York.

Lamba, S. S., and Rao, S. V. 1974. On suboptimal control via the simplified model of Davison. *IEEE Trans. Aut. Cont.* AC-19:448–450.

Laub, A. J. 1979. A Schur method for solving algebraic Riccati equations. *IEEE Trans. Aut. Cont.* AC-24:913–921.

Laub, A. J., and Bailey, F. N. 1976. Suboptimality bounds and stability in the control of nonlinear dynamic systems. *IEEE Trans. Aut. Cont.* AC-21:396–399.

Luenberger, D. G. 1966. Observers for multivariable systems. *IEEE Trans. Aut. Cont.* AC-11:190–197.

Luus, R., and Lapidus, L. 1967. The control of nonlinear systems, Part II: Convergence by combined first and second variation. *Am. Inst. Chem. Engr. J.* 15:108–113.

Mahapatra, G. B. 1977. A note on selecting a low-order system by Davison's model simplification technique. *IEEE Trans. Aut. Cont.* AC-22:677–678.

Mahapatra, G. B. 1979. A futher note on selecting a low-order system using the dominant eigenvalue concept. *IEEE Trans. Aut. Cont.* AC-24:135–136.

Malek-Zavarei, M. 1980a. Near-Optimum design of nonstationary linear systems with state and control delays. *J. Optimization Theory and Applications*, 30:73–88.

Malek-Zavarei, M. 1980b. Suboptimal control of systems with multiple delays. *J. Optimization Theory and Applications* 30:621–633.

Malek-Zavarei, M., and Jamshidi, M. 1975. Sensitivity of linear time-delay systems to parameter variations. *IFAC J. Automatica* 11:315–319.

Marshall, S. A., and Owens, D. H. 1975. Comment on "Suboptimal control of linear systems via models of Chidambara." *Proc. IEE* 122:759–760.

McClamroch, N. H.; Clark, L. G.; and Aggarwal, J. K. 1969. Sensitivity of linear control systems to large parameter variations. *IFAC J. Automatica* 5:257–263.

Melzer, S. M., and Kuo, B. C. 1971. Optimal regulation of systems described by a countably infinite number of objects. *IFAC J. Automatica* 7:359–366.

Milne, R. D. 1965. The analysis of weakly coupled dynamic systems. *Int. J. Contr.* 2:171–199.

Mora-Camino, F. 1979. Comments on Optimization of non-linear systems using a new two level method. *IFAC J. Automatica* 15:125–126.

Mukhopadhyay, B. K., and Malik, O. P. 1973. Solution of nonlinear optimization problems in power systems. *Int. J. Contr.* 17:1041–1058.

Nishikawa, Y.; Sannomiya, N.; and Tokura, H. L. 1971. Suboptimal design of a nonlinear feedback system. *IFAC J. Automatica* 7:703–712.

Ortega, J. M., and Rheinboldt, W. C. 1970. *Iterative Solution of Nonlinear Equations in Several Variables*, pp. 230–235. Academic Press, New York.

Özgüner, Ü. 1979. Near-optimal control of composite systems: The multi time-scale approach. *IEEE Trans. Aut. Contr.* AC-24:652–656.

Popov, V. M. 1960. Criterion of quality for nonlinear controlled systems. *Proc. 1st IFAC Congress* (Moscow, USSR), pp. 173–176.

Ragazzini, J. R., and Franklin, G. F. 1958. *Sampled-Data Control Systems*. McGraw-Hill, New York.

Ramapriyan, H. K. 1970. A study of coupling in interconnected systems. Ph.D. dissertation, Univ. Minnesota, Minneapolis, MN.

Rao, S. V., and Lamba, S. S. 1974. Suboptimal control of linear systems via simplified models of Chidambara. *Proc. IEE* 121:879–882.

Rao, A. S.; Lamba, S. S.; and Rao, S. V. 1979. Comments on a note on selecting a low-order system by Davison's model simplification technique. *IEEE Trans. Aut. Cont.* AC-24:141–142.

Rissanen, J. J. 1966. Performance deterioration of optimum systems. *IEEE Trans. Aut. Cont.* AC-11:530–532.

Rosenbrock, H. H. 1960. An automatic method for finding the greatest or least value of a function. *Computer J.* 3:175–184.

Ross, D. W., and Flügge-Lotz, I. 1969. An optimal control problem for systems with differential difference equation dynamics. *SIAM J. Contr.* 7:609–623.

Salvadori, M. G., and Baron, M. L. 1964. *Numerical Methods in Engineering*. Prentice-Hall, Englewood Cliffs, NJ.

Sannuti, P. 1970. Near-optimum design of time-lag systems by singular perturbation method. *Proc. JACC* (Atlanta, GA), Paper No. 20-A.

Sannuti, P. 1974. Asymptotic series solution of singularly perturbed optimal control problems. *IFAC J. Automatica* 10:183–194.

Sannuti, P., and Kokotović, P. V. 1969. Near-optimum design of linear systems by a singular perturbation method. *IEEE Trans. Aut. Cont.* AC-14:15–21.

Šiljak, D. D. 1978a. On decentralized control of large scale systems. *Proc. IFAC 7th World Congress* (Helsinki, Finland), pp. 1849–1856.

Šiljak, D. D. 1978b. *Large-Scale Dynamic Systems Stability and Structure.* Elsevier North Holland, New York.

Šiljak, D. D., and Sundareshan, M. K. 1976. A multilevel optimization of large scale dynamic systems. *IEEE Trans. Aut. Cont.* AC-21:79–84.

Šiljak, D. D., and Vukcević, M. B. 1976. Decentralization, stabilization and estimation in large scale systems. *IEEE Trans. Aut. Cont.* AC-21:363–366.

Šiljak, D. D., and Vukcević, M. B. 1978. On decentralized estimation. *Int. J. Contr.* 27:113–131.

Simmons, M. 1975. The decentralized profit maximisation of inter-connected production systems. Report CUED/F Control/TR101, Cambridge University Engineering Dept., Cambridge, England.

Singh, M. 1980. *Dynamical Hierarchical Control.* Rev. Ed. North-Holland, Amsterdam.

Singh, M. G., and Hassan, M. F. 1978. Hierarchical optimization for non-linear dynamical systems with non-separable cost functions. *IFAC J. Automatica* 14:99–101.

Singh, M. G., and Hassan, M. F. 1979. Author's reply. *IFAC J. Automatica* 15:126–128.

Slater, G. L., and Wells, W. R. 1972. On the reduction of optimal time-delay systems to ordinary ones. *IEEE Trans. Aut. Cont.* AC-17:154–155.

Smith, N. J., and Sage, A. P. 1973. An introduction to hierarchical systems theory. *Computers and Electrical Engineering* 1:55–71.

Sundareshan, M. K. 1977. Generation of multilevel control and estimation schemes for large-scale systems: A perturbation approach. *IEEE Trans. Syst. Man. Cyber.* SMC-7:144–152.

Tamura, H. 1974. A discrete dynamic model with distributed transport delays and its hierarchical optimization to preserve stream quality. *IEEE Trans. Syst. Man. Cyber.* SMC-4:424–429.

Titli, A.; Galy, J.; and Singh, M. G. 1975. Methodes de decompositon-coordination en calcul des variations et couplage par variables des etats. *Revue Francaise d' Automatique. Informatique et Recherche Operationnelle.* J4

Tse, E. C. Y.; Medanic, J. V.; and Perkins, W. R. 1978. Generalized Hessenberg transformations for reduced-order modeling of large-scale systems. *Int. J. Contr.* 27:493–512.

Tupciev, V. A. 1962. Asymptotic behavior of the solutions of a boundary-value problem for systems of a small parameter in the derivatives. *Soviet Mathematics* 3:612–616.

Vasileva, A. B. 1952. On differential equations depending on a small parameter. *Mat. Sb.* 31:590–603.

Wasow, W. R. 1965. *Asymptotic Expansions for Ordinary Differential Equations.* Wiley-Interscience, New York.

Weissenberger, S. 1974. Tolerance of decentrally optimal controllers to nonlinearity and coupling. *Proc. 12th Allerton Conf. Circuits and Systems* (Monticello, IL), pp. 87–95.

# Chapter 7
# Structural Properties
# of Large-Scale Systems

## 7.1 Introduction

The high dimensionalities, nonlinearities, and complexities of interconnection in large-scale systems provide computational and analytical difficulties not only in modeling, control, or optimization but also in the fundamental issues of stability, controllability, and observability. As the dimension of the system increases, the problem of assessing these structural properties become much more difficult. In this chapter these three important properties of system theory from the large-scale systems viewpoint are briefly considered.

When the stability of large-scale system is of concern, one basic approach, consisting of three steps, has prevailed: decompose a given large-scale system into a number of small-scale subsystems, analyze each subsystem using the classical stability theories and methods, and combine the results leading to certain restrictive conditions with the interconnections and reduce them to the stability of the whole. This approach has been termed the "composite system method" by Araki (1978) and many others.

One of the earliest efforts regarding the stability of composite systems is due to Bailey (1966), which assumed a Lyapunov function for each subsystem; then using the theory of the vector Lyapunov function (Šiljak, 1972a; Matrosov, 1972), the stability of the composite system was checked (Moylan and Hill, 1978). Others (Araki and Kondo, 1972; Michel and Porter, 1972) have constructed a scalar Lyapunov function as a weighted sum of the Lyapunov functions of the individual subsystems. This line of work has given rise to the so-called "Lyapunov methods." These methods have been extended by many authors, including Michel (1975a, b), Rasmussen and Michel (1976a, b), and Šiljak (1976).

An alternative approach, known as "input-output method," describes each subsystem by a mathematical relation or an operator on functional space, and then functional analysis methods are employed. Porter and Michel (1974) and Cook (1974) considered the situation where subsystems have finite gain and are conic, which is a generalization of Zames's (1966) single-loop results (Moylan and Hill, 1978). The input-output stability has been extended by several authors, including Sundareshan and Vidyasagar (1975), Araki (1976), and Lasley and Michel (1976a, b).

A basic issue involved in interconnected systems stability is the question of how large the interactions magnitudes and strength can be before the stability of the composite system is affected? Furthermore, as mentioned by Sandell et al. (1978), in some systems a strong coupling exists between various subsystems which makes a major contribution to stability. Such issues lead us to connective stability, which is essentially the extension of stability, in the sense of Lyapunov, to take into account the structural perturbations (Šiljak, 1972a, b, 1978). We already saw in Chapters 4 and 6 that when a system is expected to undergo structural perturbations, the interactions have major effects on control and estimation (observability) and, just as important, stability.

A system is said to be "completely state controllable" if it is possible to find an unconstrained control vector $u(t)$ that would transfer any initial state $x(t_o)$, for any $t_o$, to any final state $x(t_f)$, say origin, in a finite time interval $t_o \leqslant t \leqslant t_f$. Observability, on the other hand, is a concept related to the determination of the state from the measurement of output. A system is said to be "completely observable" at any time $t_o$ if it is possible to determine $x(t_o)$ by measuring $y(t)$ over the interval $t_o \leqslant t \leqslant t_1$. Consider a linear TIV system

$$\dot{x}(t) = Ax(t) + Bu(t) \tag{7.1.1}$$

$$y(t) = Cx(t) + Du(t) \tag{7.1.2}$$

where $x$, $u$, and $y$ are $n$-, $m$-, and $r$-dimensional state, control, and output vectors, respectively, and $A$, $B$, $C$, and $D$ are constant matrices of appropriate dimensions. The standard criteria for checking controllability and observability of this system are the following two rank conditions (Kalman, 1961):

$$\text{rank } P = \text{rank}\{ B \quad AB \quad \cdots \quad A^{n-1}B \} = n \tag{7.1.3}$$

$$\text{rank } Q = \text{rank}\{ C^T \quad A^TC^T \quad \ldots \quad (A^T)^{n-1}C^T \} = n \tag{7.1.4}$$

where $P$ and $Q$ are the $n \times nm$ controllability and $n \times nr$ observability matrices, respectively. These conditions are useful and computationally simple only if $n$ is small, i.e., less than 10. However, if the system is large in scale or has particular inherent properties which make these two conditions difficult to check, alternative criteria are required.

The bulk of research in the controllability and observability of large-scale systems falls into four main problems: controllability and observability of composite systems, controllability (and observability) of decentralized systems, structural controllability, and controllability of singularly perturbed systems.

The controllability and observability of composite (series, parallel, and feedback) systems was first considered by Gilbert (1963), where the controllability and observability of the system was studied in terms of those of the subsystems. Since that initial work, many researchers have considered this problem; among them are Chen and Desoer (1967), Rosenbrock (1970), Brasch et al. (1971), Klamka (1972, 1974), Yonemura and Ito (1972), Bhandarkar and Fahmy (1972), Graselli (1972), Wang and Davison (1973a, b), Wolovich and Huang (1974), Hautus (1975), Davison (1976, 1977), Porter (1976), Sezer and Hüseyin (1977, 1979).

The "structural controllability" has been introduced by Lin (1974) which determines the controllability of the pair $(A, b)$ through the properties of system structure through the graph of $(A, b)$. Structural controllability has been further considered by many other authors, including Shields and Pearson (1976), Corfmat and Morse (1975), Glover and Silverman (1975), and Davison (1977). The graph theoretic concepts have also been used by Davison (1976) for composite systems.

It therefore bears repeating that the stability, controllability, and observability of large-scale systems have been of concern to many researchers in the field, with stability being perhaps the most dominant one. The literature on these topics is indeed so vast that a dedicated text can be written on any of these subjects. Consequently, it is well beyond the scope of this book to go into great detail. However, we attempt to present here the most relevant methods of testing large-scale systems stability, controllability, and observability. In specific, two fundamental techniques, one of Lyapunov and the other the input-output method, are introduced in Sections 7.2 and 7.3, respectively. An important extension of Lyapunov stability, i.e., connective stability, is also considered in Section 7.2. The topics considered in Section 7.4 are controllability and observability of composite systems, including the new notion of connectability approach. Structural controllability and observability of large-scale systems are discussed in Section 7.5. Section 7.6 deals with controllability of singularly perturbed systems. This and other pertinent materials, such as dissipative systems stability along with a comparative discussion on the topics, are presented in Section 7.7.

## 7.2 Lyapunov Stability Methods

One of the most celebrated methods of investigating system stability is the direct method of Lyapunov. In simple terms, the method is described as follows: For a given system, a scalar function $v(x, t)$ known as Lyapunov function (sometimes representing a system's total energy) is found in terms of the state variables; then based on the properties of $v(x,t)$ and its time derivative $\dot{v}(x,t)$, various conclusions may be made regarding the system stability. It is assumed here that the reader is already familiar with the basic notions of Lyapunov stability, and our main purpose here is to point out how the Lyapunov method may be applied to large-scale interconnected systems. The next section provides the necessary definitions and a statement of the problem, while Section 7.2.2 gives a few criteria for checking the stability of large-scale systems.

## 7.2.1 Definitions and Problem Statement

The following definitions are necessary elements in the understanding of stability criteria set forth in Section 7.2.2.

**Definition 7.1.** A scalar real-valued function $v(x,t)$ of state $x$ and time $t$ is said to be "positive-definite" if there is a nondecreasing real-valued function $\hat{v}(x,t)$ such that $\hat{v}(0,0)=0$ and $0<\hat{v}(x,t)\leqslant v(x,t)$ for all $x\neq 0$. The function $v(x,t)$ is further called radially unbounded if $\hat{v}(\infty,t)=\infty$. The single bars $|\ |$ denote the Euclidean norm defined by $|x|=(x_1^2+\cdots+x_n^2)^{1/2}$.

**Definition 7.2.** A positive-definite function $v(x,t)$ is called "decrescent" if a nondecreasing function $\tilde{v}(|x|)$ exists such that $\tilde{v}(0)=0$ and $v(x,t)\leqslant\tilde{v}(|x|)$. A function which is positive-definite, decrescent, and radially unbounded is denoted by pdu.

**Definition 7.3.** An $n\times n$ matrix $A$ is said to be an "$M$-" or "Metzler matrix" if the following equivalent conditions hold:

1. All principle minors of $A$ are positive.
2. All leading principle minors of $A$ are positive.
3. For a vector $x$ (or $y$) whose elements are all positive, the elements of $Ax$ (or $A^Ty$) are all positive.
4. $A^{-1}$ exists and all its elements are nonnegative.
5. Re $\{\lambda_i(A)\}>0$ for $i=1,2,\ldots,n$.
6. A diagonal matrix $B=\text{diag}(b_1,\ldots,b_n)$, $b_i>0$, exists such that $BA+A^TB$ is a positive-definite matrix. This condition is sometimes termed Lyapunov-type.

**Definition 7.4.** A real square matrix $\Omega$ is called an "$M$-matrix" if there is a diagonal matrix $\tilde{D}=\text{diag}(\tilde{d}_1,\ldots,\tilde{d}_N)$ with $\tilde{d}_i>0$ such that $\tilde{D}-\Omega^T\tilde{D}\Omega$ is a positive-definite matrix (Araki, 1975).

With the above preliminary definitions presented, the system whose stability is of concern is now defined. Consider a large-scale unforced system described by

$$\text{Lss:} \quad \dot{x} = f(x, t) \tag{7.2.1}$$

which is assumed to consist of $N$ subsystems,

$$\text{Css:} \quad \dot{x}_i = f_i(x_i, t) + g_i(x, t), \quad i = 1, \ldots, N \tag{7.2.2}$$

where $x_i, f_i(\cdot)$, and $g_i(\cdot)$ satisfy $x = (x_1^T \cdots x_N^T), f = \{f_1^T(\cdot) + g_1^T(\cdot) \cdots f_N^T(\cdot) + g_N^T(\cdot)\}$. The notations Lss and Css refer, respectively, to the original large-scale system (7.2.1) and composite subsystem representation (7.2.2). A further assumption is that the origin $x_e = 0$ is an equilibrium state, i.e.,

$$f(0, t) = 0, \quad f_i(0, t) = 0, \quad g_i(0, t) = 0 \tag{7.2.3}$$

for $i = 1, 2, \ldots, N$. The set of $N$ composite subsystems (7.2.2) can be rewritten as

$$\dot{x}_i = f_i(x_i, t) + u_i \tag{7.2.4}$$

by the substitution of $u_i = g_i(x, t)$, which in effect represents an interaction or interconnection input into the $i$th subsystem. When the $i$th subsystem is completely decoupled,

$$\text{Iss:} \quad \dot{x}_i = f_i(x_i, t) \tag{7.2.5}$$

then it is referred to as an isolated subsystem for the sake of our discussions. Furthermore, the present discussion is restricted to stability with respect to the equilibrium point $x_e = 0$ or $x_{ie} = 0$, $i = 1, \ldots, N$. The following definitions define uniform stability, uniform asymptotic stability, and uniform asymptotic stability in the sense of Lyapunov.

**Definition 7.5.** For a positive-definite, decrescent function $v(x, t)$ of system state $x$ and time $t$, the equilibrium point $x_e = 0$ of (7.2.1) is said to be "uniformly stable" if $-\dot{v}(x, t)|_{(\text{Lss})} \geqslant 0$ for all $x$ and $t$. Note that the notation $k(\cdot)|_{(\text{Lss})}$ means that the arguments of $k(\cdot)$ are evaluated along the trajectories of the large-scale system in (7.2.1).

**Definition 7.6.** In view of Definition 7.5, the equilibrium point $x_e = 0$ is "uniformly asymptotically stable" if $-\dot{v}(x, t)|_{(\text{Lss})} > 0$ and uniformly a.s.i.L. (asymptotically connectively stable in the Large) if, in addition, $v(x, t)$ is radially unbounded (Definition 7.1). The function $v(x, t)$ of Definitions 7.5 and 7.6 is called a Lyapunov function.

After the above developments and definitions, the problem can be stated as follows: For a large-scale system Lss defined by (7.2.1), which can be decomposed into $N$ subsystems Css (7.2.2) with isolated subsystems Iss

(7.2.5) and interconnections $u_i$ defined in (7.2.4), under what conditions is the original composite system (Lss) a.s.i.L.? This problem is usually approached in two different ways. One is to assume a Lyapunov function $v_i(x_i, t)$ for the isolated subsystems Iss (7.2.5), which are presumably obtained more easily than the original system and use a weighted sum

$$v(x, t) = \sum_{i=1}^{N} c_i v_i(x_i, t) \qquad (7.2.6)$$

as a potential Lyapunov function for the Lss (7.2.1). In (7.2.6) the coefficients $c_i$, $i = 1, \ldots, N$ are positive constants. This approach has been considered by many authors in the field, Araki and Kondo (1972), Grujić and Šiljak (1973a, b), and Thompson (1970) to name a few. The other approach is to define a vector Lyapunov function $v = (v_1(x_1, t) \ldots v_N(x_N, t))$ and by virtue of the Metzler matrices properties and positive-definite decrescent and radially unbounded functions (Definitions 7.1–7.3) appropriate conditions are attached to $\dot{v}$ for stability of the Lss (7.2.1). The latter approach, not considered here, had been considered originally by Bailey (1966) and later by Cuk and Šiljak (1973), Matrosov (1972), Piontkovskii and Rutkovskaya (1967), and Šiljak (1972a, b, 1974a, b, 1975).

Referring back to the weighted sum of (7.2.6), as long as each $v_i(x_i, t)$ is positive-definite, decrescent, and radially unbounded (pdu), the Lss composite system Lyapunov function $v(x, t)$ is also pdu. Therefore, in view of Definitions 7.5 and 7.6, the only condition to be checked is the negative-definiteness of $\dot{v}|_{(Lss)}$. Differentiating (7.2.6) yields

$$\dot{v}(x, t)|_{(Lss)} = \sum_{i=1}^{N} c_i \dot{v}_i(x_i, t)|_{(Lss)} \qquad (7.2.7)$$

where

$$\dot{v}_i(\cdot)|_{(Lss)} = \partial v_i / \partial t + (\partial v_i / \partial x_i)^T (f_i(x_i, t) + g_i(x, t))$$

$$= \dot{v}_i(\cdot)|_{(Iss)} + (\partial v_i / \partial x_i)^T g_i(x, t) \qquad (7.2.8)$$

and the gradient

$$\partial v_i / \partial x_i = (\partial v_i / \partial x_{i1}, \ldots, \partial v_i / \partial x_{in_i}) \qquad (7.2.9)$$

with $n_i$ being the order of the $i$th subsystem and $x_{ij}$, $j = 1, 2, \ldots, n_i$, representing the $j$th element of the $i$th subsystem state vector. The above development suggests the following algorithm for analyzing a composite large-scale system which has been suggested by several authors (Sandell et al., 1978, Araki, 1978).

*Algorithm 7.1.* Lyapunov Stability of Large-Scale Composite Systems

*Step 1:* Decompose the Lss (7.2.1) into $N$ subsystems Css (7.2.2), assume a Lyapunov function $v_i(x_i, t)$ for each isolated subsystem Iss (7.2.5), and obtain a bound for $\dot{v}_i(\cdot)|_{(Iss)}$.

*Step 2:* Find a bound for each interconnection or interaction term $g_i(x,t)$, $i = 1,\ldots,N$.

*Step 3:* Obtain a condition for the existence of positive constants $c_i$, $i = 1,\ldots,N$, such that the negative-definiteness of (7.2.7) is guaranteed from the above bounds.

The next section provides two theorems which provide stability criteria for Css (7.2.2).

## 7.2.2 Stability Criteria

The uniform stability in the sense of Lyapunov for Css (7.2.2) has been extensively treated by many authors, including Araki (1978), who has presented one of the more conveniently applicable approaches. Here two of Araki's results will be given.

**Theorem 7.1.** *The large-scale system Lss (7.2.1) represented by composite subsystems Css (7.2.2) is uniformly a.s.i.L. if the following conditions hold:*

1. *For each Iss there is a pdu function $v_i(x_i,t)$ such that*

$$\dot{v}_i(x_i,t)|_{(\text{Iss})} \leqslant -a_i\{w_i(x_i)\}^2 \qquad (7.2.10)$$

$$|\partial v_i(\cdot)/\partial x_i| \leqslant w_i(x_i) \qquad (7.2.11)$$

   *where $a_i$, $i = 1,\ldots,N$ are positive constants and $w_i(x_i)$ is a positive-definite function.*
2. *The interconnection terms are bounded by*

$$|g_i(x,t)| \leqslant \sum_{j=1}^{N} b_{ij} w_j(x_j) \qquad (7.2.12)$$

   *where $b_{ij}$ are nonnegative constants.*
3. *The $N \times N$ matrix $E = (e_{ij})$ given by*

$$e_{ii} = a_i - b_{ii}, \quad e_{ij} = -b_{ij}, \quad i \neq j \qquad (7.2.13)$$

   *is an M-matrix; i.e. the leading principle minors of $E$ are all positive:*

$$D_i \triangleq \det \begin{bmatrix} e_{11} & \cdots & e_{1i} \\ \vdots & \ddots & \vdots \\ e_{i1} & \cdots & e_{ii} \end{bmatrix} > 0, \quad i = 1,\ldots,N \qquad (7.2.14)$$

PROOF: Through condition 3 and recalling Definition 7.3, one can choose $d_i > 0$ such that $DE + E^T D$ is a positive-definite matrix where $D = \text{diag}(d_1,\ldots,d_N)$. Define $v(x,t)$ by (7.2.6). Then $v(x,t)$ is a pdu function.

Using (7.2.7)–(7.2.13), one can obtain

$$\dot{v}(x,t)|_{(Lss)} \leq \sum_{i=1}^{N} d_i \left[ -a_i w_i(x_i)^2 + w_i \left( x_i \sum_{j=1}^{N} b_{ij} w_j(x_j) \right) \right]$$

$$= -\frac{1}{2} \sum_{i=1}^{N} \sum_{j=1}^{N} (d_i e_{ij} + d_j a_{ji}) w_i(x_i) u_j(x_j) \quad (7.2.15)$$

Now since $DE + E^T D$ is positive-definite, the right-hand side of (7.2.15) is a negative-definite function of $x$. Thus, Lss is uniformly a.s.i.L by Definition 7.6. Q.E.D. ■

Before the use of the above theorem is illustrated by examples, it is worthwhile to interpret the three conditions of Theorem 7.1. Condition 1 implies that each isolated subsystem is a.s.i.L. with $v_i(x_i, t)$ as its Lyapunov function. A common candidate for $v_i(x_i, t)$ is a quadratic function. The constant $a_i$ is considered as the degree of stability in view of the fact that it gives a lower bound for the decrease in $\dot{v}$ with respect to $w_i^2(x_i)$. Moreover, the constants $b_{ij}$ in (7.2.12) indicate the interconnections strength in the sense that they provide an upper bound with respect to $w_i^2(x_i)$. Condition 3 indicates that the diagonal elements of $E$ are, in general, larger than the off-diagonal ones. As a whole, Theorem 7.1 indicates that if the subsystems are stable to a degree larger than the strength of the interconnections, then the composite system is stable.

**Example 7.2.1.** Consider a fifth-order system decomposed into third- and second-order subsystems:

$$\dot{x} = \begin{bmatrix} \dot{x}_1 \\ -- \\ \dot{x}_2 \end{bmatrix} = \begin{bmatrix} -1 & 0.1 & 0.2 & | & 0.1 & 0.2 \\ 0.2 & -2 & 0.5 & | & 0.1 & 0.1 \\ 0.1 & -1 & -3 & | & 0.5 & 0.4 \\ -- & -- & -- & -- & -- & -- \\ 1 & 0 & 1 & | & -4 & 0.2 \\ 0.2 & 0.5 & 0 & | & 1 & -5 \end{bmatrix} \begin{bmatrix} x_1 \\ -- \\ x_2 \end{bmatrix} \quad (7.2.16)$$

It is desired to check its stability by means of Theorem 7.1.

SOLUTION: Since the two subsystems are linear and the $A_i$, $i = 1, 2$, are stable matrices, the following Lyapunov functions $v_i(x_i, t)$ and positive-definite functions $w_i(x_i)$ are chosen:

$$v_i(x_i, t) = x_i^T P_i x_i, \quad w_i(x_i) = \alpha_i \left( x_i^T Q_i x_i \right)^{1/2} \quad (7.2.17)$$

for $i = 1, 2$ and $P_i, Q_i$ satisfy

$$P_i A_i + A_i^T P_i + Q_i = 0 \quad (7.2.18)$$

Choosing $Q_1 = I_3$ and $Q_2 = 2I_2$ in an arbitrary fashion, two solutions of

(7.2.18) provide

$$P_1 = \begin{bmatrix} 0.508 & 0.023 & 0.032 \\ 0.023 & 0.254 & -0.006 \\ 0.032 & -0.006 & 0.168 \end{bmatrix}, \quad P_2 = \begin{bmatrix} 0.26 & 0.03 \\ 0.03 & 0.20 \end{bmatrix} \quad (7.2.19)$$

A value of $\alpha_i = 1/a_i^2$ where $a_i = \max_{x_i \neq 0}(|2P_i x_i|/(x_i^T Q_i x_i)^{1/2}$ would guarantee condition (7.2.10) of Theorem 7.1. Furthermore, if we choose $b_{11} = b_{22} = 0$,

$$b_{12} = \max_{x_2 \neq 0} \left\{ |G_{12} x_2| / \alpha_2 \left( x_2^T Q_2 x_2 \right)^{1/2} \right\}$$

and

$$b_{21} = \max_{x_1 \neq 0} \left\{ |G_{21} x_1| / \alpha_1 \left( x_1^T Q_1 x_1 \right)^{1/2} \right\}$$

the condition (7.2.12) would be satisfied. In above formulation, $G_{12}$ and $G_{21}$ are the off-diagonal interaction submatrices defined in (7.2.16). These four maximation procedures were performed through a coordinate rotation method due to Rosenbrock (1960), and the results after a few iterations were, $\alpha_1 = -1.0255$, $a_1 = 0.9509$, $\alpha_2 = 0.38$, $a_2 = 6.93$, $b_{21} = 1.387$, and $b_{12} = 1.28$. Using these parameters, the matrix $E$ in (7.2.13) becomes

$$E = \begin{bmatrix} 0.9509 & -1.280 \\ -1.3870 & 6.930 \end{bmatrix} \quad (7.2.20)$$

which is clearly a Metzler matrix. Thus we conclude that composite systems (7.2.16) is uniformly a.s.i.L. according to Theorem 7.1. This checks with the application of Lyapunov stability to the overall system whose eigenvalues are $-0.9$, $-2.32 \pm j0.54$, $-4.52$, $-4.94$.

**Example 7.2.2.** Consider a second-order nonlinear system

$$\dot{x}_1 = -2/3 x_1^3 + g_1(x, t)$$

$$\dot{x}_2 = -1/3 x_2^3 + g_2(x, t) \quad (7.2.21)$$

where the interaction terms $g_i(x)$, $i = 1, 2$, will be defined shortly. Check for a.s.i.L.

SOLUTION: This example has been inspired by a similar example by Araki (1978). It turns out that this system's isolated subsystems fall within the class of $\dot{x}_i = \psi_i(x_i)$ such that $0 < \psi_i(x_i)x_i$, $x_i \neq 0$, and $\bar{\psi}_i(x_i) = \int_0^{x_i} \psi_i(\tau)\,d\tau \to \infty$ as $|x_i| \to \infty$. A set of possible choices for $v_i(x_i, t)$ and $w_i(x_i)$ are $v_i(x_i, t) = \bar{\psi}_i(x_i)$ and $w_i(x_i) = |\psi_i(x_i)|$. Using these values, the condition (7.2.10) would be satisfied for all $a_i \leq 12$, $i = 1, 2$. If the interaction values are assumed to be $g_i(x, t) = C_i \psi_i(x_i) + \hat{g}_i(x, t)$, where $\hat{g}_i(\cdot)$ is not dependent on $x_i$, then by appropriate choices of positive constants $c_i$ and parameter $b_{ij}$, condition (7.2.12) can also be satisfied.

Theorem 7.1 assumes that all isolated subsystems Iss (7.2.5) are a.s.i.L., which is a rather strong assumption. The following theorem provides the stability criteria using a weaker set of assumptions.

**Theorem 7.2.** *The large-scale system Lss* (7.2.1) *represented by composite subsystem Css* (7.2.2) *is uniformly a.s.i.L. if the following conditions hold:*

1. *For each Iss there is a pdu function* $v_i(x_i, t)$ *such that*

$$\dot{v}_i(x_i, t)|_{(Iss)} \leqslant - a_i\{w_i(x_i)\}^2 - z_i(x_i) \qquad (7.2.22)$$

   *where* $a_i$, $i = 1, \ldots, N$, *are positive constants and* $w_i(x_i)$ *and* $z_i(x_i)$ *are positive-semidefinite and positive-definite functions, respectively.*
2. *The interconnection terms satisfy*

$$\left(\partial v_i(x_i, t)/\partial x_i\right)^T g_i(x, t) \leqslant w_i(x_i) \sum_{j=1}^{N} b_{ij} w_j(x_j) \qquad (7.2.23)$$

3. *The $N \times N$ matrix E defined by* (7.2.13) *is an M-matrix.*

The proof of this theorem is similar to Theorem 7.1 and is left to the reader as an exercise (see Problem 7.7). It is noted that $w_i(x_i)$ in (7.2.22) can be positive-semidefinite due to $z_i(x_i)$ and $b_{ij}$, and, hence, $a_i$ can be negative, since $(\partial v_i/\partial x_i)^T g_i$ is estimated directly. This development would allow the isolated subsystems Iss (7.2.5) to be unstable. The following example illustrates the application of Theorem 7.2.

**Example 7.2.3.** Consider a second-order nonlinear interconnected system

$$\dot{x}_1 = 0.25x_1 - x_1 \cos x_2 + 0.2x_2 \sin x_1 x_2$$
$$\dot{x}_2 = x_2 - x_2 \sin x_1 + 0.125x_1 \cos x_1 x_2 \qquad (7.2.24)$$

Check if it is a.s.i.L.

SOLUTION: In this example $n_1 = n_2 = 1$ and $N = 2$. The two isolated subsystems $\dot{x}_1 = 0.25x_1$ and $\dot{x}_2 = x_2$ are unstable, which implies that Theorem 7.1 is not applicable. Let $v_i(x_i, t) = x_i^2/2$ and $w_i(x_i) = |x_i|$, $i = 1, 2$, and follow the conditions (7.2.22) and (7.2.23) for $z_i(x_i)$, any arbitrary positive-definite function. The resulting parameters are $a_1 = 0.25$, $a_2 = 1$, $b_{11} = b_{22} = -1$, $b_{12} = 0.2$, and $b_{21} = 0.125$. With these values, the $E$ matrix in (7.2.13) is

$$E = \begin{bmatrix} 1.25 & -0.2 \\ -0.125 & 2 \end{bmatrix} \qquad (7.2.25)$$

which is clearly an M-matrix.

There are several possibilities of extending the above results by changing the assumptions on $\dot{v}_i$, $g_i$ and redefining elements $e_{ij}$ of $E$. For further details, the reader can consult the work of Araki (1978).

### 7.2.3 Connective Stability

An important issue in large-scale systems is the perturbation in its structure, either intentionally (by design) or unintentionally (by fault). The hierarchical optimum and near-optimum control of large-scale systems under structural perturbation were already discussed in Chapters 4 and 6. Another basic issue is how such structural perturbations affect the overall system stability. This notion, termed connective stability by Šiljak (1972a), has been developed extensively in a book subsequently (Šiljak, 1978). The object of this section is to introduce this notion and present a criterion for connective stability.

#### 7.2.3.a System Structure and Perturbation

Consider a linear large-scale unforced system

$$\dot{x} = Ax \qquad (7.2.26)$$

where $A$ is an $n \times n$ matrix whose elements $a_{ij}$ represent the extent of influence that state or "agent" $x_i$ puts on state $x_j$ for $i, j = 1, \ldots, n$. In order to examine the structure of such a system, let $n = 3$ and rewrite (7.2.26) as

$$\begin{aligned}
\dot{x}_1 &= a_{11}x_1 + a_{12}x_2 + a_{13}x_3 \\
\dot{x}_2 &= a_{21}x_1 + a_{22}x_2 + a_{23}x_3 \\
\dot{x}_3 &= a_{31}x_1 + a_{32}x_2 + a_{33}x_3
\end{aligned} \qquad (7.2.27)$$

whose relations can be shown by a "directed graph" or simply a "diagraph" shown in Figure 7.1. The points or nodes on the graph represent subsystem (or system) states, while the directed lines correspond to the elements of matrix $A$, the extent of the influence of one state on itself or another state. Now suppose that $a_{31} = 0$ in (7.2.27), which implies that matrix $A$ is

$$A = \begin{bmatrix} a_{11} & a_{12} & a_{13} \\ a_{21} & a_{22} & a_{23} \\ 0 & a_{23} & a_{33} \end{bmatrix} \qquad (7.2.28)$$

This perturbation indicates that the interaction from $x_1$ to $x_3$ is nonexistent. This can be shown by introducing a $3 \times 3$ so-called "interconnection matrix" $G$ defined by

$$\tilde{G} = \begin{bmatrix} 1 & 1 & 1 \\ 1 & 1 & 1 \\ 0 & 1 & 1 \end{bmatrix} \qquad (7.2.29)$$

which is a binary matrix whose entry $\tilde{g}_{ij}$ is one if $x_j$ "influences" $x_i$ and zero otherwise. The diagraph corresponding to this structural perturbation is shown in Figure 7.2a. Similarly, other perturbations are possible by changing the unity elements of $\tilde{G}$ in (7.2.29) to zero. For example, if $a_{21} = a_{22} =$

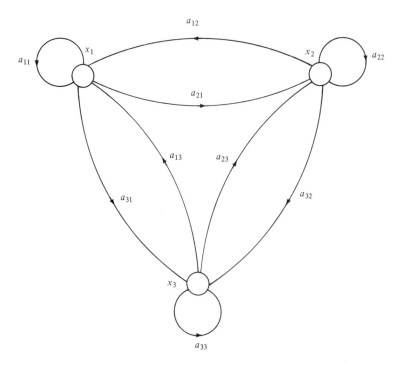

**Figure 7.1** A diagraph representing a three-dimensional interconnected system.

$a_{23} = a_{33} = 0$, $\tilde{G}$ is changed to

$$G_1 = \begin{bmatrix} 1 & 1 & 1 \\ 0 & 0 & 1 \\ 0 & 0 & 0 \end{bmatrix} \qquad (7.2.30)$$

whose diagraph is shown in Figure 7.2b. If the three states are disconnected from each other, i.e.,

$$G_2 = \begin{bmatrix} 1 & 0 & 0 \\ 0 & 1 & 0 \\ 0 & 0 & 1 \end{bmatrix} \qquad (7.2.31)$$

it would correspond to the diagraph in Figure 7.2c. The case in which there is a "Total disconnection" occurs when the interconnection matrix is null, i.e.,

$$G_3 = \begin{bmatrix} 0 & 0 & 0 \\ 0 & 0 & 0 \\ 0 & 0 & 0 \end{bmatrix} \qquad (7.2.32)$$

as shown in Figure 7.2d. The interconnection matrix $\tilde{G}$ given by (7.2.29) is termed the "fundamental interconnection matrix" by Šiljak (1972a, 1978), since all other interaction matrices, such as $G_i$, $i = 1, 2, 3$, in (7.2.30)–(7.2.32)

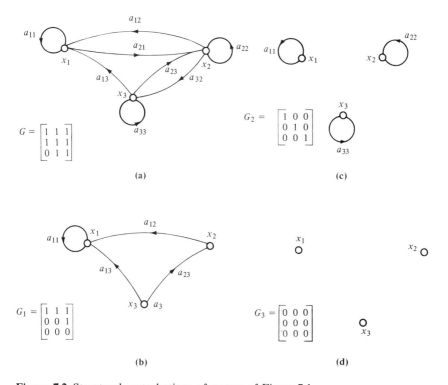

**Figure 7.2** Structural perturbations of system of Figure 7.1.

can be obtained from it by replacing unit elements with zeros. With this introduction to structural perturbation, the notion of connective stability is now considered.

Let the $a_{ij}$, $i, j = 1, 2, 3$, elements of (7.2.27) be represented by

$$a_{ij} = \begin{cases} -\alpha_i + \tilde{g}_{ij}\Delta a_{ii}, & i = j \\ \tilde{g}_{ij}\Delta a_{ij}, & i \ne j \end{cases} \qquad (7.2.33)$$

where $\tilde{g}_{ij}$ are the elements of the fundamental interconnection matrix $G$ in (7.2.29), $\alpha_i$ represent system's basic structure, and $\Delta a_{ij}$ correspond to the perturbations. The following definition can now be given.

**Definition 7.7.** The equilibrium point $x_e = 0$ is said to be "connectively stable" for a system if it is stable for all interconnection matrices $G$.

In order to achieve the connective stability, it suffices to prove the stability for the "fundamental interconnection matrix" $\tilde{G}$ (Šiljak, 1978). This is achieved by the so-called "comparison principle" (Birkhoff and Rota, 1962). This principle is described briefly as follows: Let a continuous function $y(t)$ satisfy the differential inequality

$$\dot{y}(t) \leqslant h(y,t) \qquad (7.2.34)$$

where $h(y,t)$ satisfies a Lipschitz condition

$$|h(y,t) - h(z,t)| \leqslant L|y-z| \qquad (7.2.35)$$

for any two pairs $(y,t)$ and $(z,t)$, and $L$ is called the Lipschitz constant. Furthermore, let $w(t)$ be the solution of the differential equation

$$\dot{w}(t) = h(w,t) \qquad (7.2.36)$$

with initial value $w(t_0) = y(t_0)$; then

$$y(t) \leqslant w(t), \quad t \geqslant 0 \qquad (7.2.37)$$

## 7.2.3.b  A Connective Stability Criterion

In this section a connective stability criterion due to Šiljak (1978) along with a numerical example is given. Let the model of a large-scale unforced system be

$$\dot{x} = F(x,t) \qquad (7.2.38)$$

where $x$ is the $n$-dimensional state vector, $F$ is a function from $R^n \times \mathfrak{I}$ to $R^n$ and $x_e = 0$ is a unique equilibrium point, i.e., $F(0,t) = 0$ for all $t \in \mathfrak{I}$, $\mathfrak{I}$ is the time interval $(t_o, +\infty)$. Let the system (7.2.38) be represented by a set of $N$ interconnected subsystems

$$\dot{x}_i = F_i(x_i, \tilde{g}_{i1}x_1, \ldots, \tilde{g}_{iN}x_N, t) \qquad (7.2.39)$$

where $x_i$ is $n_i$-dimensional state and $\tilde{g}_{ij}$ are elements of the $(N \times N)$-dimensional interaction matrix $G \in \tilde{G}$. There are various stability definitions within the framework of connectiveness. Below, various connective stability points are defined mathematically.

**Definition 7.8.** The equilibrium point $x_e = 0$ of system (7.2.38) is "connectively stable" if for every $\sigma > 0$, there is a number $\varepsilon > 0$ such that if

$$\|x_o\| < \varepsilon \qquad (7.2.40)$$

then

$$\|x(t; x_o, t_o)\| < \sigma \qquad (7.2.41)$$

for all interconnections $G \in \tilde{G}$.

In the above definition, $\varepsilon$ is considered a function of $\sigma$ and $t_o$, i.e., $\varepsilon(t_o, \sigma)$. However, if for each $\sigma > 0$ there is an $\varepsilon(\sigma)$ independent of $t_o$, condition (7.2.40) implies (7.2.41) for all $G \in \tilde{G}$; then $x_e = 0$ is said to be "uniformly connectively stable." It is noted that connective stability thus defined is a local concept because it is appropriate only near $x_e = 0$. In many applications it is not only necessary to have $x(t;, x_o, t_o)$ bounded but also to

converge to the equilibrium point after some disturbance occurs. The
following definition considers this situation.

**Definition 7.9.** The equilibrium point $x_e = 0$ of system (7.2.38) is "asymptotically connectively stable" if it is connectively stable and in addition
there is a number $\delta > 0$ such that if $\|x_o\| < \delta$, then

$$\lim_{t \to +\infty} x(t; x_o, t_o) = 0 \qquad (7.2.42)$$

for all interactions $G \in \tilde{G}$.

This stability is also a local concept because one does not know a priori
how small $\delta$ can be chosen. However, in many cases the focus is on $\delta$ being
arbitrarily large and fixed at that value. Then the system is said to be
"asymptotically connectively stable in the Large." This is the stability for
which a criterion will be given.

Assume that system (7.2.38) is decomposed into $N$ interconnected subsystems

$$\text{Css:} \quad \dot{x}_i = f_i(x_i, t) + h_i(x, t), \quad i = 1, \ldots, N \qquad (7.2.43)$$

where $f_i(x_i, t)$ represents the $i$th decoupled or isolated subsystem

$$\text{Iss:} \quad \dot{x}_i = f_i(x_i, t) \qquad (7.2.44)$$

and $h_i(x_i, t)$ is the interaction of the $i$th subsystem with the remaining ones:

$$h_i(x, t) = h_i(g_{i1}x_1, \ldots, g_{iN}x_n, t) \qquad (7.2.45)$$

where $g_{ij}$ are elements of the $N \times N$ interaction matrix $G$. The functions
$f_i(x_i, t)$ and $g_i(x, t)$ are further assumed to satisfy $f_i(0, t) = 0$ and $g_i(0, t) = 0$
for all $t \in \mathfrak{T}$. Before the stability criterion is given, the following definitions
are considered.

**Definition 7.10.** A function $\psi(\varepsilon)$ belongs to a "comparison class" $K_\varepsilon$ if
$\psi \in C(\mathfrak{T})$, $\psi(0) = 0$, and if $\varepsilon_1 < \varepsilon_2$, then $\psi(\varepsilon_1) < \psi(\varepsilon_2)$. Moreover, if
$\psi(\varepsilon) \to +\infty$ as $\varepsilon \to +\infty$, then $\psi(\varepsilon)$ is said to belong to the class $K_\infty$.

**Definition 7.11.** A continuous function $h_i: \mathfrak{T} \times R^n \to R^{n_i}$ is a member of the
class $K_n$ if there are bounded functions $\eta_{ij}: \mathfrak{T} \times R^n \to R$ such that

$$\|h_i(x, t)\| \leq \sum_{j=1}^{N} \tilde{g}_{ij} \eta_{ij}(x, t) \psi_{3j}(\|x_j\|) \qquad (7.2.46)$$

for all $t$ and $x$, where $\tilde{g}_{ij}$ are elements of $(N \times N)$-dimensional fundamental interaction matrix $\tilde{G}$ and $\psi_{3j} \in K_\varepsilon$ is defined above.

**Definition 7.12.** An $N \times N$ constant "aggregate" matrix $S = (s_{ij})$ is defined
by

$$s_{ij} = -\delta_{ij} + \gamma_i \tilde{g}_{ij} \beta_{ij} \qquad (7.2.47)$$

where $\delta_{ij}$, the Kronecker delta, is one for $i = j$ and zero otherwise; $\gamma_i$ is a positive number; and nonnegative number $\beta_{ij}$ is

$$\beta_{ij} = \max\{0, \text{Sup}(\eta_{ij}(x,t))\} \qquad (7.2.48)$$

The term "aggregate" stems from the theory of vector Lyapunov function $v$; i.e., it can be shown that $\dot{v} \leqslant Sv$, where $v$ is an $N$-dimensional Lyapunov vector function.

One can now state the following theorem to provide the necessary conditions for asymptotic connective stability in the Large.

**Theorem 7.3.** *Let $v(x,t)$ be a continuously differentiable function which is locally Lipschitzian in $x$, $v(0,t) = 0$, and for each subsystem*

$$\psi_{1i}(\|x_i\|) \leqslant v_i(x_i,t) \leqslant \psi_{2i}(\|x_i\|)$$
$$\dot{v}_i(x_i,t) \leqslant \psi_{3i}(\|x_i\|) \qquad (7.2.49)$$

*for all $t$, $x_i$, $\psi_{1i}$, $\psi_{2i} \in K_\infty$, and $\psi_{3i} \in K_\varepsilon$ (Definition 7.10). Furthermore, assume that interconnection functions $h_i(x,t) \in K_n$ (Definition 7.11) for all $i = 1,\ldots,N$. Then the quasi-dominant property\* of the $N \times N$ aggregate matrix $S$ (Definition 7.12) implies that point $x_e = 0$ is asymptotically connectively stable in the Large for the composite system (7.2.38).*

For the complete proof of this theorem, see Šiljak (1978). Here a few comments regarding the properties of the Lyapunov function and the illustration of this theorem for linear systems will be given. The time derivative of the $i$th subsystem Lyapunov function can be shown to satisfy the inequality

$$\dot{v}_i(x_i,t)\big|_{(\text{Lss})} \leqslant \dot{v}_i(x_i,t)\big|_{(\text{Iss})} + L_i\|h_i(x,t)\|, \quad i = 1,\ldots,N \quad (7.2.50)$$

where $L_i$ is a Lipschitz constant, Css and Iss represent composite subsystem (7.2.43) and isolated subsystem (7.2.44), respectively. In view of the condition (7.2.46) on $h_i(x,t)$, (7.2.50) can be rewritten as a differential inequality using the property (7.2.34):

$$\dot{v}(x,t) \leqslant Sp(v(x,t)) \qquad (7.2.51)$$

where $S$ is the $N \times N$ aggregate matrix defined by (7.2.47). In (7.2.51) vector function $p$: $R_+^N \rightarrow R_+^N$ is defined by $p(v) \equiv [\psi_{31}(\psi_{11}(v_1)),\ldots,$ $\psi_{3N}(\psi_{1N}(v_N))]^T$. In sequel, the interpretation of Theorem 7.3 for linear systems along with an illustrative example are presented.

---

\*An $n \times n$ matrix $B$ is said to be quasi-dominant if there is a set of $n$ numbers $c_i > 0$ such that $c_i b_{ii} > \sum_{j \neq i} c_i b_{ij}$, $i = 1,\ldots,n$.

Let the composite subsystem (7.2.43) be linear

$$\dot{x}_i = A_i x_i + \sum_{\substack{j=1 \\ j \neq i}}^{N} G_{ij} x_j, \quad i = 1, \ldots, N \qquad (7.2.52)$$

where $A_i$ and $G_{ij}$ are $n_i \times n_i$ and $n_i \times n_j$ matrices, respectively. The isolated subsystem (7.2.44) will be

$$\dot{x}_i = A_i x_i \qquad (7.2.53)$$

which is assumed to be stable; i.e., for any positive-definite matrix $Q_i$ there is a positive-definite matrix $P_i$ which is the solution of the Lyapunov equation

$$A_i^T P_i + P_i A_i + Q_i = 0 \qquad (7.2.54)$$

The function $v_i(x_i) = (x_i^T P_i x_i)^{1/2}$ is a candidate for a Lyapunov function satisfying the following inequality similar to (7.2.49):

$$\lambda_m^{1/2}(P_i)\|x_i\| \leq v_i(x_i) \leq \lambda_M^{1/2}(P_i)\|x_i\| \qquad (7.2.55)$$

where $\lambda_m$ and $\lambda_M$ are the minimum and maximum eigenvalues of the argument matrix, respectively. The Lyapunov function $v_i(x_i)$ is a Lipschitz function

$$|v_i(x_i) - v_i(y_i)| \leq L_i \|x_i - y_i\| \qquad (7.2.56)$$

where the Lipschitz constant $L_i = \lambda_M(P_i)/\lambda_m^{1/2}(P_i)$ and the interconnection terms satisfy

$$\|G_{ij} x_j\| \leq \zeta_{ij} \|x_j\| \qquad (7.2.57)$$

and $\zeta_{ij} = \lambda_M^{1/2}(G_{ij}^T G_{ij})$. Furthermore, the inequality (7.2.50) becomes

$$\dot{v}_i(x_i)\big|_{(7.2.52)} \leq \dot{v}_i(x_i)\big|_{(7.2.53)} + L_i \sum_{\substack{j=1 \\ j \neq i}}^{N} \zeta_{ij}\|x_j\| \leq -\psi_{3i}(\|x_i\|)$$

$$+ 2L_i \sum_{\substack{j=1 \\ j \neq i}}^{N} \lambda_M^{1/2}(P_j)\lambda_m^{-1}(Q_i) \cdot \zeta_{ij} \psi_{3j}(\|x_j\|) \qquad (7.2.58)$$

where $\psi_{3i}(\|x_i\|) = \frac{1}{2}\lambda_M^{-1/2}(P_i)\lambda_m(Q_i)\|x_i\|$. Finally, the $N \times N$ aggregate matrix $S$ in (7.2.51) has the elements

$$s_{ij} = \begin{cases} -1, & i = j \\ 2L_i \lambda_M^{1/2}(P_j)\lambda_m^{-1}(Q_i)\zeta_{ij}, & i \neq j \end{cases} \qquad (7.2.59)$$

The following example illustrates the application of Theorem 7.3 for the linear case.

**Example 7.2.4.** Let us reconsider the fifth-order system of Example 7.2.1. The $A_i$, $G_{ij}$, $Q_i$, and $P_i$, $i$, $j = 1, 2$, are given in (7.2.16) and (7.2.19). Check whether this system is asymptotically connectively stable in the Large.

SOLUTION: The system consists of two subsystems with a fundamental interconnection matrix $\tilde{G}$:

$$\tilde{G} = \begin{bmatrix} 0 & 1 \\ 1 & 0 \end{bmatrix} \tag{7.2.60}$$

The eigenvalues of $P_i$, $i = 1, 2$, are $\lambda(P_1) = (0.17427, 0.5130)$, $\lambda(P_2) = (0.1876, 0.2724)$. The values of Lipschitz constants $L_i$ using (7.2.56) turn out to be $L_1 = 0.7162$ and $L_2 = 0.522$. The bounds $\zeta_{ij}$ are $\zeta_{12} = 0.484$ and $\zeta_{21} = 1.422$. The aggregate matrix $S$ is obtained from (7.2.59), $s_{11} = s_{22} = -1$, $s_{12} = 0.1808$, and $s_{21} = 1.0634$. The quasi-dominancy condition is to have the leading principle minors of $S$, i.e.,

$$(-1)^k \begin{vmatrix} s_{11} & s_{12} & \cdots & s_{1k} \\ s_{21} & s_{22} & & s_{2k} \\ \cdots & & & \cdots \\ s_{k1} & s_{k2} & & s_{kk} \end{vmatrix} > 0 \tag{7.2.61}$$

for all $k = 1, 2, \ldots, N$. In this case $(-1)^1 |s_{11}| = 1 > 0$ and

$$(-1)^2 \begin{vmatrix} -1 & 0.1808 \\ 1.0634 & -1 \end{vmatrix} = 0.8077 > 0 \tag{7.2.62}$$

Thus, as expected, this system is asymptotically connectively stable in the Large.

## 7.3  Input–Output Stability Methods

The second method of investigating stability of large-scale systems is through the input–output (IO) technique. In this scheme, every subsystem is described by an operator or mathematical relation on a function space, and through the methods of functional analysis the system stability is studied (Moylan and Hill, 1978). The preliminary developments, definitions, motivations, and problem statement are considered in the next section. The input–output stability criterion itself is presented in Section 7.3.2.

### 7.3.1  Problem Development and Statement

As mentioned above, the input–output stability is based on function spaces. Let $U^{(\mu)}$ denote a normed space of $R^\mu$-valued functions $u(t)$ of time; then the "extended normed space" $U_e^{(\mu)}$ is defined as $U_e^{(\mu)} = \{u | u_\tau \in U^{(\mu)} \, \forall \tau \in R\}$, where $u_\tau$ is a "truncated function" defined by

$$u_\tau(t) = \begin{cases} u(t), & t < \tau \\ 0, & \text{otherwise} \end{cases} \tag{7.3.1}$$

Let us define an operator $G: U^{(\mu)} \to U^{(\mu)}$, which is said to be "input–output stable" or simply IO stable if there are two nonnegative constants $\alpha$ and $\beta$ such that

$$\|(Gu)_\tau\| \leqslant \alpha\|u_\tau\| + \beta \quad \text{for all } \tau \in R \qquad (7.3.2)$$

where $\| \, \|$ is the norm in space $U^{(\mu)}$.

The gain of the operator $G$ is defined by

$$\text{gain } G = \max_{u \in U_e^{(\mu)}} \{\|(Gu)_\tau\|/\|u_\tau\|\} \qquad (7.3.3)$$

Let $D$, $F$, $G$, and $H$ be operators from $U^{(\mu)}$ into itself such that $G0 = 0$ and $H0 = 0$ and consider the IO closed-loop system (Zames, 1966)

$$\begin{aligned} e &= Du + \tilde{y}, \quad y = Ge \\ \tilde{e} &= Fu + y, \quad \tilde{y} = H\tilde{e} \end{aligned} \qquad (7.3.4)$$

where $u$ is the input to the system as shown in Figure 7.3. Let $E$, $\tilde{E}$, $Y$, and $\tilde{Y}$ represent operators which map $u \in U^{(\mu)}$ into the solutions $e$, $\tilde{e}$, $y$, and $\tilde{y}$, respectively (Willems, 1970; Desoer and Vidyasagar, 1975). Then the IO system (7.3.4) is said to be IO-stable if the operators $E$, $\tilde{E}$, $Y$, and $\tilde{Y}$ are IO stable. Since in most large-scale systems one would be dealing with decompositions into $N$ subsystems, it is useful to think of $U^{(\mu)}$ as the product of $U^{(\mu_i)}$, $i = 1, 2, \ldots, N$, such that $\mu = \mu_1 + \cdots + \mu_N$ and

$$\|u\| = \left( \sum_{i=1}^{N} \|u_i\|^2 \right)^{1/2}, \quad u = \left( u_1^T, \ldots, u_N^T \right)^T, \quad u_i \in U^{(\mu_i)} \qquad (7.3.5)$$

Let the IO system (7.3.4) be represented by $N$ decoupled subsystems

$$\begin{aligned} e_i &= D_i u + \tilde{y}_i, \quad y_i = G_i e_i \\ \tilde{e}_i &= F_i u + y_i, \quad \tilde{y}_i = H_i \tilde{e}_i + K_i \tilde{e}, \quad i = 1, \ldots, N \end{aligned} \qquad (7.3.6)$$

where $e = (e_1^T, \ldots, e_N^T)^T$, $y = (y_1^T, \ldots, y_N^T)^T$, etc.; $e_i$, $\tilde{e}_i$, $y_i$, and $\tilde{y}_i$ are members of $U_e^{(\mu_i)}$; $G_i$ and $H_i$ are operators from $U_e^{(\mu)}$ into itself; and $D_i$, $F_i$, and $K_i$ are operators from $U_e^{(\mu)}$ into $U_e^{(\mu_i)}$. Araki (1978) has made the assumption that $y_i$ in (7.3.6) depends on $e_i$ as a result of simplification of the criterion to be discussed and its acceptability in most cases. If the operator $K_i$ is removed

**Figure 7.3** A composite input–output system.

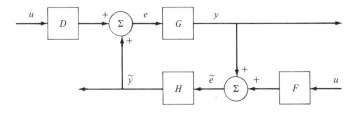

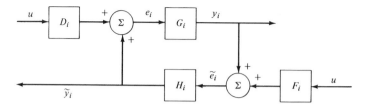

**Figure 7.4** A subsystem for a composite input–output system.

from the second equation in (7.3.6), then the $i$th subsystem becomes isolated, as shown in Figure 7.4, and the operators $K_i$ represent interconnections. In Section 7.7 it will be shown that this interpretation has a correspondence to the Lyapunov methods of Section 7.2.

Let $L_2^{(\mu)}$ denote the $L_2$ space of $R^\mu$-valued function in which the inner product and norm are defined by

$$\langle u, v \rangle = \int_{-\infty}^{\infty} u^T(t) v(t)\, dt$$

$$\|u\|^2 = \langle u, u \rangle = \int_{-\infty}^{\infty} \{u_1^2(t) + u_2^2(t) + \cdots + u_\mu^2(t)\}\, dt \tag{7.3.7}$$

The motivation behind the IO stability of large-scale systems is the work of Zames (1966), who pioneered the IO stability of time-varying nonlinear systems. The following theorem provides the ground rules for it.

**Theorem 7.4.** *Small Gain Theorem. The IO system (7.3.4) is IO stable if*

$$(\text{gain } G) \cdot (\text{gain } H) < 1 \tag{7.3.8}$$

*where the gain $G$ is defined by (7.3.3). The following example illustrates the application of this theorem.*

**Example 7.3.1.** Consider the IO system of Figure 7.5 with the real-valued function $|\psi(\sigma)| \leqslant 0.5\sigma$. Check for its IO stability.

SOLUTION: Let $G$ in Figure 7.5 be represented by $G = \text{diag}(G_1, G_2)$, where $G_i$, $i = 1, 2$, are second-order rational functions of $s$. Since $Gu = (G_1 u_1, G_2 u_2)^T$ and $\|u\|^2 = \|u_1\|^2 + \|u_2\|^2$, the gain $G$ is obtained from

$$\text{gain } G = \max(\text{gain } G_1, \text{gain } G_2) \tag{7.3.9}$$

$$= \max(0.1, 0.5) = 0.5$$

The gain $H = \gamma$ is given by

$$\gamma = \max_{y \neq 0} \left\{ \left( [y_1 + 0.2\psi(y_2)]^2 + [0.2y_2 + 0.5\psi(y_1)]^2 \right) / (y_1^2 + y_2^2) \right\}^{1/2}$$

$$\tag{7.3.10}$$

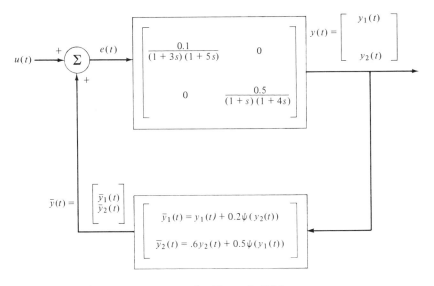

**Figure 7.5** An input–output system for Example 7.3.1.

However, since only an upper bound is available for $\psi$, one can replace $\psi(y_1)$ and $\psi(y_2)$ by $\pm 0.5y_1$ and $\pm 0.5y_2$, respectively, and try to find the maximum in (7.3.10). The gain $G$ would then have an upper bound

$$\text{gain } H \leqslant \sqrt{\lambda_M(H^TH)} \cong 1.2303 \tag{7.3.11}$$

where

$$H = \begin{bmatrix} 1 & 0.2 \\ 0.5 & 0.2 \end{bmatrix}$$

and $\lambda_M$ corresponds to the maximum eigenvalue of its argument. Clearly condition (7.3.8) is satisfied, indicating that system of Figure 7.5 is IO stable. In general if condition (7.3.8) is not satisfied, one may consider a class of norms for $u \in U^{(\mu)}$,

$$\|u\|_D = \{d_1^2\|u_1\|^2 + \cdots + d_N^2\|u_N\|^2\}^{1/2} \tag{7.3.12}$$

and try to find a set of values $D = \text{diag}(d_1, d_2, \ldots, d_N)$ such that (7.3.8) holds. Note that (7.3.5) is a special case of (7.3.12). Under this norm condition, gain condition (7.3.11) becomes

$$\text{gain}_D H \leqslant \sqrt{\lambda_M(DHD^{-1})^T(DHD^{-1})} \tag{7.3.13}$$

Based on the above development the IO stability problem can now be stated as follows: For a large-scale IO system (7.3.4) which can be decomposed into $N$ subsystems (7.3.6), under what conditions on the operators $G_i$,

$H_i$, and $K_i$ is the system IO stable? The IO stability can be conveniently checked by persuing the following algorithm.

**Algorithm 7.2.** Input – Output Stability of Large-Scale Systems

> *Step 1:* Investigate the properties of subsystems operators $G_i$, $H_i$, $i = 1,...,N$.
>
> *Step 2:* Find a functional bounds for interconnection operators $K_i$, $i = 1,...,N$.
>
> *Step 3:* Obtain a set of parameters $d_1,...,d_N$ such that condition (7.3.8) is satisfied.

The next section gives a theorem for IO stability criterion.

## 7.3.2 IO Stability Criterion

The following theorem provides a necessary conditions for IO stability of a large-scale interconnected systems.

**Theorem 7.5.** *The large-scale system* (7.3.4) *decomposed in* (7.3.6) *is IO stable if the following conditions are satisfied*:

1. *Gain* $G_i = \alpha_i < \infty$, $i = 1,...,N$                            (7.3.14)
2. *For a set of* $2N$ *nonnegative constants* $\beta_{ij}$, *the following norm condition holds*:

$$\|(H_i\tilde{e}_i + K_i\tilde{e})_\tau\| \leqslant \sum_{j=1}^{N} \beta_{ij}\|(\tilde{e}_i)_\tau\|, \quad \tilde{e} \in U_e^{(\mu)}, \quad \tau \in R \quad (7.3.15)$$

3. *The* $N \times N$ *matrix* $B = (b_{ij})$ *is an M-matrix*

$$b_{ii} = 1 - \alpha_i\beta_{ii}, \quad b_{ij} = -\alpha_i\beta_{ij}i \neq j \quad (7.3.16)$$

PROOF: By condition 3 there are $d_i > 0$ such that $D^2 - \Omega^T D^2 \Omega$ is positive-definite where $D = \text{diag}(d_1,...,d_N)$, $\Omega = (\omega_{ij})$ and $\omega_{ij} = \alpha_i\beta_{ij}$. This is due to the properties of $M$-matrices as presented by Definitions 7.3 and 7.4. Now define the operator $T$ by $y = Tu$, $y_i = \alpha_i u_i$ and transform the system, as shown in Figure 7.6. By condition 1 one obtains $\text{gain}_D(T^{-1}G) \leqslant 1$. From (7.3.15), one can obtain

$$\sum_{i=1}^{N} d_i^2\|(\tilde{y}_i)_\tau\|^2 \leqslant \sum_{i=1}^{N} d_i^2 \left\{ \sum_{j=1}^{N} \alpha_i\beta_{ij}\|(\hat{e}_j)_\tau\| \right\}^2$$

$$= \sum_{j=1}^{N} \sum_{k=1}^{N} \left( \sum_{i=1}^{N} d_i^2\omega_{ij}\omega_{ik} \right)\|(\hat{e}_j)_\tau\|\cdot\|(\hat{e}_k)_\tau\|$$

$$< \sum_{i=1}^{N} d_i^2\|(\hat{e}_i)_\tau\|^2 \quad (7.3.17)$$

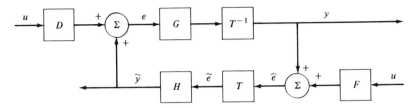

**Figure 7.6** A transformed input–output system.

where $\tilde{y} = KT\hat{e}$, $\hat{e}_\tau \neq 0$ for all $\tau \in R$ and the last inequality is assured by the positive-definiteness of $D^2 - \Omega^T D^2 \Omega$. By (7.3.17) one can obtain gain $_D KT < 1$, and hence (7.3.8) is verified. Thus, system (7.3.4) is IO stable. Q.E.D. ■

The following example illustrates the IO-stability criterion.

**Example 7.3.2.** In this example a fourth-order system block diagram similar to that of Figure 7.5 with the following operators is reconsidered:

$$G_1 = 0.50/\{(s+1)(s+2)\}, \quad G_2 = 6/\{(s+3)(s+4)\}$$
$$H_1 = H_2 = 1, \quad K_1 = 1.5, \quad K_2 = 0.2 \qquad (7.3.18)$$

Check the system's IO stability.

SOLUTION: The first condition of Theorem 7.5 yields gain $G_1 = \alpha_1 = 0.25$ and gain $G_2 = \alpha_2 = 0.5$. The second condition (7.3.15) on interconnections provides $\beta_{11} = \beta_{22} = 1$, $\beta_{12} = 1.5$, and $\beta_{21} = 0.2$. Using the $\alpha_i$ and $\beta_{ij}$ values, the matrix $B$ of the third condition becomes

$$B = \begin{bmatrix} 0.75 & -0.375 \\ -0.10 & 0.50 \end{bmatrix} \qquad (7.3.19)$$

which is clearly an $M$-matrix. Therefore, the system is IO stable.

Araki (1978) has considered the $L_2^{(\mu)}$ space in place of $U^{(\mu)}$ and extended some of Zames's (1966) terminology to give an IO stability criterion based on "inside the sectors" conditions on scalar products of certain operations on $(u)_\tau$ using $G_i$ and $H_i$. The interested reader is encouraged to refer to Araki's (1978) details on other IO stability criteria.

## 7.4 Controllability and Observability of Composite Systems

The earliest known work on this topic is due to Gilbert (1963). Consider a parallel composite system shown in Figure 7.7. The system is composed of two subsystems with the same input $u$, but their respective outputs are added to give the overall system output. Assuming that the eigenvalues of $S_1$ and $S_2$ are distinct (Perkins and Cruz, 1969), it can be deduced that a

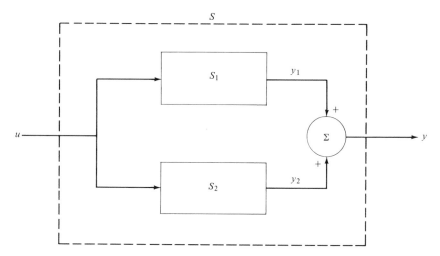

**Figure 7.7** A parallel composite system.

necessary and sufficient condition for system $S$ to be controllable (or observable) is that both $S_1$ and $S_2$ be controllable (or observable). Furthermore, the $n = n_1 + n_2$ eigenvalues of $S$ are the union of $n_1$ eigenvalues of $S_1$ and $n_2$ eigenvalues of $S_2$. Next consider a series composite system shown in Figure 7.8. Here again, assuming that both subsystems have distinct eigenvalues, a necessary condition for the controllability (or observability) of $S$ is that both $S_1$ and $S_2$ are controllable (or observable). Note that the condition is not sufficient, and it is possible for $S_1$ and $S_2$ to be both controllable and observable but for $S$ to be neither. An inspection of Figure 7.8 indicates that under such conditions, the uncontrollable and unobservable modes of $S$ must belong to $S_2$ and $S_1$, respectively. The following example illustrates this situation.

**Figure 7.8** A series composite system.

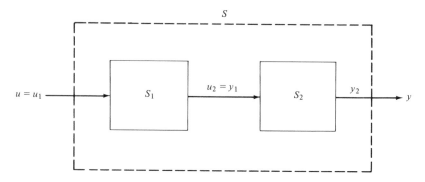

**Example 7.4.1.** Consider a second-order series composite system

$$\dot{x}_1 = -1/3x_1 + u$$
$$\dot{x}_2 = -1/6x_1 - 1/6x_2 + u \qquad (7.4.1)$$

$$y = x_1 - x_2 - 6u \qquad (7.4.2)$$

Check the controllability and observability of the system.

SOLUTION: The two subsystems are clearly both controllable and observable. The composite system's controllability matrix is

$$P = \begin{bmatrix} B & AB \end{bmatrix} = \begin{bmatrix} 1 & -1/3 \\ 1 & -1/3 \end{bmatrix} \qquad (7.4.3)$$

while the observability matrix is

$$Q = \begin{bmatrix} C^T & A^T C^T \end{bmatrix} = \begin{bmatrix} 1 & -1/3 \\ -1 & 1/3 \end{bmatrix} \qquad (7.4.4)$$

Both matrices have rank of 1; hence the system (7.4.1) is neither controllable nor observable.

The next section provides some criteria for checking controllability and observability of parallel–series and feedback composite systems.

## 7.4.1 Frequency Domain Approach

This section is concerned with the application of Rosenbrock's (1970) frequency domain approach to the controllability and observability of parallel–series and feedback composite systems as proposed first by Davison and Wang (1975). However, before that let us define the relatively "prime polynomials" and relatively "prime polynomial matrices."

**Definition 7.13.** Two polynomials $p(s)$ and $q(s)$ are said to be "relatively prime" if their only common divisor is a constant.

If $\phi(s)$ is a third polynomial, then there exist polynomials $v(s)$ and $w(s)$ such that (Rosenbrock, 1968a)

$$w(s)p(s) + v(s)q(s) = \phi(s) \qquad (7.4.5)$$

which may be stated in an alternative form:

$$\begin{vmatrix} p(s) & q(s) \\ -v(s) & w(s) \end{vmatrix} = \phi(s) \qquad (7.4.6a)$$

The so-called "Smith form" of (7.4.6a) is (Gantmacher, 1959)

$$\begin{vmatrix} 1 & 0 \\ 0 & \phi(s) \end{vmatrix} \qquad (7.4.6b)$$

Now let $P(s)$ and $Q(s)$ be $r \times r$ and $r \times m$ polynomial matrices, respectively, with $P(s)$ being nonsingular; then consider the following definition.

**Definition 7.14.** Two polynomial matrices $P(s)$ and $Q(s)$ are said to be "relatively prime" if the Smith form of $[P(s) \quad Q(s)]$ is $[I_r \quad 0]$. In a similar fashion to Equations (7.4.5)–(7.4.6), it can be shown (Rosenbrock, 1968a,b) that for $m \times r$ and $m \times m$ polynomial matrices $V(s)$ and $W(s)$, the matrix

$$\begin{pmatrix} P(s) & Q(s) \\ -V(s) & W(s) \end{pmatrix} \tag{7.4.7a}$$

has Smith form

$$\begin{pmatrix} I_r & 0 \\ 0 & \Phi(s) \end{pmatrix} \tag{7.4.7b}$$

for some nonsingular $m \times m$ diagonal polynomial matrix $\Phi(s)$. Furthermore, note that when $m = r = 1$, Definition 7.14 reduces to Definition 7.13.

## 7.4.1.a Parallel–Series Systems

Consider a parallel–series composite system described by the following two-subsystem state and output equations:

$$\begin{bmatrix} \dot{x}_1 \\ \dot{x}_2 \end{bmatrix} = \begin{bmatrix} A_1 & G \\ 0 & A_2 \end{bmatrix} \begin{bmatrix} x_1 \\ x_2 \end{bmatrix} + \begin{bmatrix} B_1 \\ B_2 \end{bmatrix} u \tag{7.4.8}$$

$$y = (C_1 \quad C_2) \begin{bmatrix} x_1 \\ x_2 \end{bmatrix} + Du \tag{7.4.9}$$

where $x_1$, $x_2$, $u$, and $y$ are $n_1$-, $n_2$-, $m$-, and $r$-dimensional substates and control and output vectors. The subsystems matrices $A_1$ and $A_2$ are $n_1 \times n_1$ and $n_2 \times n_2$, respectively; $G$ is the $n_1 \times n_2$ interaction matrix, while $C_1$ and $C_2$ are $r \times n_1$ and $r \times n_2$ output matrices; and $D$ is an $r \times m$ matrix. Let the eigenvalues of $A_1$ and $A_2$ be

$$\lambda\{A_1\} = \lambda_i^1, \quad i = 1, \ldots, n_1$$
$$\lambda\{A_2\} = \lambda_i^2, \quad i = 1, \ldots, n_2 \tag{7.4.10}$$

The following theorem sets forth the controllability and observability conditions for system (7.4.8)–(7.4.9).

**Theorem 7.6.** *The necessary and sufficient conditions for the controllability of* (7.4.8)–(7.4.9) *are*

C1.     $\operatorname{rank} P_2(\lambda_i^2) = \operatorname{rank}(A_2 - \lambda_i^2 I, B_2) = n_2, \quad i = 1, \ldots, n_2 \quad (7.4.11)$

C2.     $\operatorname{rank} P_1(\lambda_i^1) = \operatorname{rank} \begin{bmatrix} A_1 - \lambda_i^1 I & G & B_1 \\ 0 & A_2 - \lambda_i^1 I & B_2 \end{bmatrix} = n_1 + n_2,$

$$i = 1, \ldots, n_1 \quad (7.4.12)$$

*Moreover, the system* (7.4.8)–(7.4.9) *is observable if and only if*

O1.     $\operatorname{rank} Q_1(\lambda_i^1) = \operatorname{rank} \begin{bmatrix} A_1 - \lambda_i^1 I \\ C_1 \end{bmatrix} = n_1, \quad i = 1, \ldots, n_1 \quad (7.4.13)$

O2.     $\operatorname{rank} Q_2(\lambda_i^2) = \operatorname{rank} \begin{bmatrix} A_1 - \lambda_i^2 I & G \\ 0 & A_2 - \lambda_i^2 I \\ C_1 & C_2 \end{bmatrix} = n_1 + n_2,$

$$i = 1, \ldots, n_2 \quad (7.4.14)$$

PROOF: Consider the controllability part of the theorem. It is therefore desirable to determine when the pair

$$\left\{ \begin{bmatrix} A_1 & G \\ 0 & A_2 \end{bmatrix}, \begin{bmatrix} B_1 \\ B_2 \end{bmatrix} \right\}$$

is controllable. Using Rosenbrock's (1970) result, this pair is controllable if and only if the polynomial matrices

$$\left( sI - \begin{bmatrix} A_1 & G \\ 0 & A_2 \end{bmatrix} \right), \begin{bmatrix} B_1 \\ B_2 \end{bmatrix}$$

are left relatively prime (Definition 7.14), or alternatively the pair is controllable if and only if

$$\operatorname{rank} \left\{ \left( sI - \begin{bmatrix} A_1 & G \\ 0 & A_2 \end{bmatrix} \right), \begin{bmatrix} B_1 \\ B_2 \end{bmatrix} \right\} = n_1 + n_2 \quad (7.4.15)$$

for all complex scalars $s$. The above relation would become (Davison and Wang, 1975)

$$\operatorname{rank} \left\{ \begin{bmatrix} A_1 - sI & G & B_1 \\ 0 & A_2 - sI & B_2 \end{bmatrix} \right\} = n_1 + n_2 \quad (7.4.16)$$

again for all complex scalars $s$. If it is assumed that $(A_2, B_2)$ is controllable, i.e., (7.4.11) holds, or $\operatorname{rank}(A_2 - sI, B_2) = n_2$ for all complex scalars $s$, it would mean that condition (7.4.16) reduces to condition (7.4.12); thus, the sufficiency of the theorem is established. Furthermore, the controllability of

$(A_2, B_2)$ is also a necessary condition which must hold; thus, the results' necessity would follow immediately. The proof of the observability part follows by duality and is left to the reader as an exercise (see Problem 7.8). Q.E.D. ∎

The following example illustrates the method.

**Example 7.4.2.** Consider a fifth-order parallel-series composite system

$$\left[\begin{array}{c} \dot{x}_1 \\ \hline \dot{x}_2 \end{array}\right] = \left[\begin{array}{ccc|cc} -0.1 & 0.5 & 1 & 0.5 & -1 \\ 1 & -1 & 0.2 & 0.1 & 0.4 \\ \hline 0 & 0 & 1 & 0.1 & 0.2 \\ 0 & 0 & 0 & -1 & 0.25 \\ 0 & 0 & 0 & -0.1 & 1 \end{array}\right] \left[\begin{array}{c} x_1 \\ \hline x_2 \end{array}\right] + \left[\begin{array}{c} 1 \\ 0.25 \\ \hline 1 \\ 0.25 \\ 0.5 \end{array}\right] u \tag{7.4.17}$$

$$y = \left[\begin{array}{ccccc} 1 & 0.1 & 1 & 0.5 & 1 \end{array}\right] \left[\begin{array}{c} x_1 \\ \hline x_2 \end{array}\right] + [1]u \tag{7.4.18}$$

Check controllability and observability of this system.

SOLUTION: The eigenvalues of $A_i$, $i = 1, 2$, are $\lambda(A_1) = (0.288, -1.388)$ and $\lambda(A_2) = (1, \pm 0.9874)$. The matrices $P_i(\cdot)$ and $Q_i(\cdot)$ were evaluated using a BASIC program and the following rank conditions were met:

$$\text{rank } P_1\left(\lambda_j^1\right) = 5 = n_1 + n_2, \quad j = 1, 2$$
$$\text{rank } P_2\left(\lambda_k^2\right) = 3 = n_2, \quad k = 1, 2, 3$$
$$\text{rank } Q_1\left(\lambda_j^1\right) = 2 = n_1, \quad j = 1, 2 \tag{7.4.19}$$
$$\text{rank } Q_2\left(\lambda_k^2\right) = 5 = n_1 + n_2, \quad k = 1, 2, 3$$

which indicate that the system is both controllable and observable.

## 7.4.1.b Closed-Loop Composite Systems

Consider a closed-loop composite system

$$\dot{x}_1 = A_1 x_1 + B_1 e, \quad e = u - z$$
$$\dot{x}_2 = A_2 x_2 + B_2 y, \quad z = C_2 x_2 \tag{7.4.20}$$
$$y = C_1 x_1 + D_1 e$$

where $e$ is a measure of system error, $y$ is the overall output, $x_1$ and $x_2$ are subsystems states, and $u$ is the control. In order to check controllability and observability of this system, one can eliminate $e$ and $z$ variables in (7.4.20) and formulate it similarly to system (7.4.8)–(7.4.9), i.e.,

$$
\begin{bmatrix} \dot{x}_1 \\ \dot{x}_2 \end{bmatrix} \begin{bmatrix} A_1 & \vdots & -B_1C_2 \\ \cdots & - & \cdots \\ B_2C_1 & \vdots & A_2 - B_2D_1C_2 \end{bmatrix} \begin{bmatrix} x_1 \\ x_2 \end{bmatrix} + \begin{bmatrix} B_1 \\ \cdots \\ B_2D_1 \end{bmatrix} u
$$

$$
y = \left( C_1 \; \vdots \; -D_1C_2 \right) \begin{bmatrix} x_1 \\ \cdots \\ x_2 \end{bmatrix} + D_1 u \tag{7.4.21}
$$

The following theorem provides a criterion for checking the controllability and observability of (7.4.21).

**Theorem 7.7.** *The necessary and sufficient conditions for the controllability of closed-loop composite system (7.4.21) are*

C3. $\qquad \operatorname{rank} P_1(\lambda_i^1) = \operatorname{rank}\left( A_1 - \lambda_i^1 I, B_1 \right) = n_1, \quad i = 1, \dots, n_1 \quad (7.4.22)$

C4. $\quad \operatorname{rank} P_2(\lambda_i^2) = \operatorname{rank} \begin{bmatrix} A_1 - \lambda_i^2 I & 0 & B_1 \\ B_2C_1 & A_2 - \lambda_i^2 I & B_2D_1 \end{bmatrix} = n_1 + n_2,$

$$i = 1, \dots, n_2$$

*Moreover, the system (7.4.21) is observable if and only if*

O3. $\qquad \operatorname{rank} Q_1(\lambda_i^1) = \operatorname{rank} \begin{bmatrix} A_1 - \lambda_i^1 I \\ C_1 \end{bmatrix} = n_1, \quad i = 1, \dots, n_1 \quad (7.4.24)$

O4. $\quad \operatorname{rank} Q_2(\lambda_i^2) = \operatorname{rank} \begin{bmatrix} A_1 - \lambda_i^2 I & -B_1C_2 \\ 0 & A_2 - \lambda_i^2 I \\ C_1 & -D_1C_2 \end{bmatrix} = n_1 + n_2, \quad i = 1, \dots, n_2$

$$\tag{7.4.25}$$

PROOF: Consider first the controllability part of the theorem. The closed-loop composite system (7.4.21) is controllable if and only if the pair

$$
\left\{ \begin{bmatrix} A_1 & -B_1C_2 \\ B_2C_1 & A_2 - B_2D_1C_2 \end{bmatrix}, \begin{bmatrix} B_1 \\ B_2D_1 \end{bmatrix} \right\}
$$

is controllable, or alternatively if and only if

$$
\left\{ \begin{bmatrix} A_1 & 0 \\ B_2C_1 & A_2 \end{bmatrix}, \begin{bmatrix} B_1 \\ B_2D_1 \end{bmatrix} \right\}
$$

is controllable, or if and only if the pair

$$
\left\{ \begin{bmatrix} A_2 & B_2C_1 \\ 0 & A_1 \end{bmatrix}, \begin{bmatrix} B_2D_1 \\ B_1 \end{bmatrix} \right\}
$$

is controllable. Now by applying Theorem 7.6 for the last pair of matrices, the necessary and sufficient conditions for its controllability resulting in conditions (7.4.22) and (7.4.23) will be determined. By a similar argument, through duality, the observability part can also be proved (see Problem 7.9) Q.E.D. ∎

The following example illustrates this criterion.

**Example 7.4.3.** Let us reconsider the systems of Example 7.4.2 utilizing $A_i$, $B_i$, $C_i$, $i = 1,2$, and $D_1 = [1]$. Check the controllability and observability of the closed-loop form of a system defined by these matrices.

SOLUTION: For this system the following rank conditions were checked:

$$\text{rank } P_1(\lambda_i^1) = 2 = n_1, \quad i = 1,2$$

$$\text{rank } P_2(\lambda_j^2) = 5 = n_1 + n_2, \quad j = 1,2,3$$

$$\text{rank } Q_1(\lambda_i^1) = 2 = n_1, \quad i = 1,2 \qquad (7.4.26)$$

$$\text{rank } Q_2(\lambda_j^2) = 5 = n_1 + n_2, \quad j = 1,2,3$$

which indicates that the system is both controllable and observable.

Some comments are made on the suitability of the above criteria. The usual rank conditions (7.1.3)–(7.1.4) are reduced to those of matrices of much smaller dimensions (7.4.11)–(7.4.14) and (7.4.22)–(7.4.25). However, in the latter case the eigenvalues of two matrices $A_1$ and $A_2$ must be calculated in addition. Davison and Wang (1975) have mentioned that as a result of the finite word length of the computer, the calculations of $A^i B$ and $(A^T)^i C^T$ for $i = 0, 1, 2, \ldots$ give numerical instabilities. The results of Davison and Wang (1975), although of great importance, however, as mentioned by Porter (1976), require the computations of both eigenvalues and rank. Based on the generalized resultant (Rosenbrock, 1968c), Porter (1976) has proposed new criteria for the controllability and observability of composite systems which involve only rank determination.

## 7.4.2 Generalized Resultant Approach

The proposed criteria of Porter (1976) are based on the following results on the "relatively prime" polynomial matrices (see Definition 7.14) which have been established by Rosenbrock (1968a,b,c) in the case of controllability and their extension in the case of observability by duality (Porter, 1976). Considering a system described by the triplet $(C, A, B)$ with $C, A$, and $B$ of $r \times n$, $n \times n$, and $n \times m$ dimensions, the following theorem can be stated.

**Theorem 7.8.** *A system described by a pair* $(B, A)$ *is controllable if and only if any one of the following conditions hold:*

C1. rank $P = \text{rank}\{ B \mid AB \mid \cdots \mid A^{n-1}B \} = n;$

C2. rank $P_s = \text{rank}\{ sI_n - A \mid B \} = n;$

C3. *matrices* $(sI_n - A)$ *and* $B$ *are relatively left prime; and*

C4. rank $P_c = \text{rank}$
$$
\begin{bmatrix}
I_n & 0 & \cdots & & & 0 & B \\
-A & I_n & 0 & \cdots & & 0 & B & 0 \\
0 & -A & I_n & \cdots & & 0 & B & 0 & 0 \\
\vdots & & \ddots & & \vdots & & \ddots & \\
& & & & & & & & \ddots \\
0 & 0 & \cdots & I_n & 0 & B & & \ddots \\
0 & 0 & \cdots & -A & B & 0 & \cdots & 0 & 0
\end{bmatrix} = n^2
$$

$$(7.4.27)$$

A proof of this theorem can be found in Rosenbrock (1968c).

**Theorem 7.9.** *A system described by a pair* $(C, A)$ *is observable if and only if any one of the following conditions hold:*

O1. rank $Q = \text{rank}\{ C^T \mid A^T C^T \mid \ldots (A^T)^{n-1} C^T \} = n;$

O2. rank $Q_s = \text{rank}\{ (sI_n - A)^T \mid C^T)^T = n;$

O3. *matrices* $(sI_n - A)$ *and* $C$ *are relatively right prime; and*

O4. rank $Q_o = \text{rank}$
$$
\begin{bmatrix}
I_n & -A & 0 & \cdots & & 0 \\
0 & I_n & -A & & & \cdot \\
& & & \ddots & & \cdot \\
& & & & & 0 \\
\cdot & & 0 & & -A \\
\cdot & & & & C \\
0 & & & & \\
& C & & & 0 \\
C & 0 & \cdots & & 0
\end{bmatrix} = n^2 \qquad (7.4.28)
$$

The proof of this theorem is the dual of the previous one. Note that the dimensions of $P_c$ and $Q_o$ in (7.4.27) and (7.4.28) are $n^2 \times n(n + m - 1)$ and $n(n + r - 1) \times n^2$, respectively. The following example illustrates the use of conditions (7.4.27) and (7.4.28).

**Example 7.4.4.** Consider a simple second-order system

$$
\dot{x} = \begin{bmatrix} 2 & 0 \\ 1 & -1 \end{bmatrix} x + \begin{bmatrix} 1 & 0.5 \\ 0.2 & 1 \end{bmatrix} u, \quad y = \begin{bmatrix} 1 & 0.5 \\ 0.5 & 1 \end{bmatrix} x \qquad (7.4.29)
$$

It is desired to check the controllability and observability of this system via the conditions C4 and O4.

SOLUTION: The inspection of the system $(C, A, B)$ matrices indicate that the system is both controllable and observable. However, these characteristics are verified using conditions C4 and O4 in (7.4.27) and (7.4.28). The $n^2 \times n(n + m - 1) = (4 \times 6)$-dimensional expanded controllability matrix $P_c$ becomes

$$P_c = \left[\begin{array}{c|c|c} I_2 & 0 & B \\ \hline -A & I_2 & 0 \end{array}\right] = \left[\begin{array}{cc|cc|cc} 1 & 0 & 0 & 0 & 1 & 0.5 \\ 0 & 1 & 0 & 0 & 0.2 & 1 \\ \hline -2 & 0 & 1 & 0 & 0 & 0 \\ -1 & 1 & 0 & 1 & 0 & 0 \end{array}\right] \quad (7.4.30)$$

which has a rank $n^2 = 4$; thus, it is controllable. The $n(n + r - 1) \times n^2 = (6 \times 4)$-dimensional expanded observability matrix $Q_c$ becomes

$$Q_o = \left[\begin{array}{c|c} I_2 & -A \\ \hline 0 & I_2 \\ \hline C & 0 \end{array}\right] = \left[\begin{array}{cc|cc} 1 & 0 & -2 & 0 \\ 0 & 1 & -1 & 1 \\ \hline 0 & 0 & 1 & 0 \\ 0 & 0 & 0 & 1 \\ \hline 1 & 0.5 & 0 & 0 \\ 0.5 & 1 & 0 & 0 \end{array}\right] \quad (7.4.31)$$

which clearly has a rank of $n^2 = 4$, verifying that (7.4.29) is observable as well.

The following theorems treat the general parallel-series and closed-loop composite systems considered in Section 7.4.1 through the resultant approach.

**Theorem 7.10.** *A necessary and sufficient condition for the composite system* (7.4.8)–(7.4.9) *to be controllable is the rank condition*

$$\text{rank } \hat{P}_c = \text{rank} \left[\begin{array}{cccccccccc} I_{n_1} & 0 & & & \cdot & \cdot & \cdot & & 0 & B_1 \\ 0 & I_{n_2} & 0 & & \cdot & \cdot & \cdot & & 0 & B_2 \\ -A_1 & -G & I_{n_1} & 0 & & \cdot & \cdot & 0 & B_1 & 0 \\ 0 & -A_2 & 0 & I_{n_2} & & & & B_2 & 0 \\ & 0 & -A_1 & -G & \cdot & & & 0 & 0 \\ & & 0 & -A_2 & & \cdot & B_1 & 0 & 0 \\ \cdot & \cdot & & & & \cdot & B_2 \\ \cdot & \cdot & & & & & & \cdot & \cdot & \cdot & \cdot \\ & & & & & & & \vdots & \vdots & \vdots & \vdots \\ & & & I_{n_2} & & & & \\ & & & -A_1 & -G & B_1 & 0 & \cdots & & 0 \\ 0 & 0 & & 0 & -A_2 & B_2 & 0 & \cdots & & 0 \end{array}\right] = (n_1 + n_2)^2$$

$$(7.4.32)$$

*and the system is observable if and only if the following condition holds:*

$$
\text{rank } \hat{Q}_o = \text{rank}
\begin{bmatrix}
I_{n_1} & 0 & -A_1 & -G & 0 & \cdot & \cdot & \cdot & 0 \\
0 & I_{n_2} & 0 & -A_2 & 0 & & & & \\
0 & 0 & I_{n_1} & 0 & -A_1 & -G & \cdot & & \vdots \\
& & & I_{n_2} & \cdot & & & & 0 \\
& & & & & & -A_1 & -G & \\
& & & & & I_{n_2} & 0 & -A_2 & \\
& & \mathbf{0} & & & 0 & C_1 & C_2 & \\
& & & & & C_1 & C_2 & 0 & 0 \\
& & C_1 & C_2 & 0 & & & & 0 \\
C_1 & C_2 & 0 & 0 & \vdots & \vdots & \vdots & \vdots & 0
\end{bmatrix}
= (n_1 + n_2)^2
$$

$$(7.4.33)$$

PROOF: In view of system (7.4.8)–(7.4.9) conditions (7.4.32)–(7.4.33) follow from (7.4.27) and (7.4.28), respectively, by allowing $A$, $B$, and $C$ to be represented by

$$
A = \begin{bmatrix} A_1 & G \\ 0 & A_2 \end{bmatrix}, \quad
B = \begin{bmatrix} B_1 \\ B_2 \end{bmatrix}, \quad
C = \begin{bmatrix} C_1 & C_2 \end{bmatrix}
\qquad (7.4.34)
$$

Q.E.D. ∎

The following example illustrates Theorem 7.10.

**Example 7.4.5.** Consider a simple second-order composite system

$$
\dot{x} = \begin{bmatrix} -1 & g \\ 0 & -2 \end{bmatrix} x + \begin{bmatrix} 1 \\ 1 \end{bmatrix} u, \quad y = \begin{bmatrix} 1 & 1 \end{bmatrix} x
\qquad (7.4.35)
$$

where $n_1 = n_2 = m = r = 1$ and interaction element $g$ is unknown. It is desired to find a class of interactions for which the system is both controllable and observable.

SOLUTION: The $\hat{P}_c$ matrix condition (7.4.32) for this system becomes

$$
\hat{P}_c =
\begin{bmatrix}
I_1 & 0 & 0 & B_1 \\
0 & I_1 & 0 & B_2 \\
-A_1 & -G & B_1 & 0 \\
0 & -A_2 & B_2 & 0
\end{bmatrix}
=
\begin{bmatrix}
1 & 0 & 0 & 1 \\
0 & 1 & 0 & 1 \\
1 & -g & 1 & 0 \\
0 & 2 & 1 & 0
\end{bmatrix}
\qquad (7.4.36)
$$

whose determinant is $1 - g$. Thus, for the system to be controllable we must have $g \neq 1$. The observability matrix $\hat{Q}_o$ in (7.4.33) reduces to

$$
\hat{Q}_o = \left[\begin{array}{cccc} I_1 & 0 & -A_1 & -G \\ \hline 0 & I_1 & 0 & -A_2 \\ \hline 0 & 0 & C_1 & C_2 \\ \hline C_1 & C_2 & 0 & 0 \end{array}\right] = \left[\begin{array}{cccc} 1 & 0 & 1 & -g \\ \hline 0 & 1 & 0 & 2 \\ \hline 0 & 0 & 1 & 1 \\ \hline 1 & 1 & 0 & 0 \end{array}\right]  \tag{7.4.37}
$$

whose determinant is $g - 1$. Therefore, for all interaction variables belonging to the class $g \in \{g : g \neq 1\}$, the system is both controllable and observable. Note that the usual rank conditions (7.1.3)–(7.1.4) imply identical results for the system.

The remaining topic left in this section is to find similar conditions for the controllability and observability of closed-loop composite system (7.4.21).

**Theorem 7.11.** *A necessary and sufficient condition for the closed-loop composite system* (7.4.21) *to be controllable is to satisfy the rank condition*

$$
\text{rank } \tilde{P}_c = \text{rank} \left[\begin{array}{ccccccccc}
I_{n_1} & 0 & & \cdots & & & & 0 & B_1 \\
0 & I_{n_2} & 0 & \cdots & & & & 0 & B_2 D_1 \\
-A_1 & 0 & I_{n_1} & 0 & \cdots & & & B_1 & 0 \\
-B_2 C_1 & -A_2 & 0 & & & & 0 & B_2 D_1 & \\
0 & 0 & -A_1 & & & & & 0 & \\
& & -B_2 C_1 & & & 0 & & & \\
& & 0 & & \ddots & & & & \\
\cdot & \cdot & \cdot & & & & & \cdot & \cdot \\
\cdot & \cdot & \cdot & & & & I_{n_2} & & \\
& & & & & -A_1 & 0 & B_1 & \\
0 & 0 & 0 & 0 & \cdots & -B_2 C_1 & -A_2 & B_2 D_1 & 0 & 0
\end{array}\right]
$$
$$
= (n_1 + n_2)^2  \tag{7.4.38}
$$

*and* (7.4.21) *is observable if and only if the following rank condition is satisfied*

$$
\text{rank } \tilde{Q}_o = \text{rank} \left[\begin{array}{ccccccccc}
I_{n_1} & 0 & -A_1 & B_1 C_2 & 0 & \cdots & & 0 \\
0 & I_{n_2} & 0 & -A_2 & 0 & \cdots & & 0 \\
& & 0 & I_{n_1} & & \ddots & \vdots & \\
& & & & \ddots & -A_2 & 0 & 0 \\
& & & & I_{n_1} & 0 & -A_1 & B_1 C_2 \\
& & & & 0 & I_{n_2} & 0 & -A_2 \\
\vdots & \vdots & & & & & C_1 & -D_1 C_2 \\
& & 0 & & & & 0 & 0 \\
0 & 0 & C_1 & -D_1 C_2 & 0 & \cdots & & \cdot \\
C_1 & -D_1 C_2 & 0 & 0 & & \cdots & & 0
\end{array}\right] = (n_1 + n_2)^2  \tag{7.4.39}
$$

PROOF: In view of system (7.4.21), conditions (7.4.38)–(7.4.39) follow from (7.4.27) and (7.4.28), respectively, by allowing $A$, $B$, and $C$ to be represented by

$$A = \begin{bmatrix} A_1 & 0 \\ B_2 C_1 & A_2 \end{bmatrix}, \quad B = \begin{bmatrix} B_1 \\ B_2 D_1 \end{bmatrix} \tag{7.4.40}$$

for controllability and

$$A = \begin{bmatrix} A_1 & -B_1 C_2 \\ 0 & A_2 \end{bmatrix}, \quad C = \begin{bmatrix} C_1 & -D_1 C_2 \end{bmatrix} \tag{7.4.41}$$

for observability in Theorems 7.8 and 7.9, respectively. Q.E.D. ∎

The following example illustrates the criteria (7.4.38) and (7.4.39).

**Example 7.4.6.** Consider a closed-loop composite system

$$\begin{bmatrix} \dot{x}_1 \\ \dot{x}_2 \end{bmatrix} = \begin{bmatrix} -2 & -b \\ 1 & -1-d \end{bmatrix} \begin{bmatrix} x_1 \\ x_2 \end{bmatrix} + \begin{bmatrix} b \\ d \end{bmatrix} u$$

$$y = \begin{pmatrix} 1 & -d \end{pmatrix} \begin{bmatrix} x_1 \\ x_2 \end{bmatrix} + du \tag{7.4.42}$$

where the system matrices, in accordance with closed-loop composite system (7.4.21), are $A_1 = -2$, $A_2 = -1$, $B_2 = C_1 = C_2 = 1$, $B_1 = b$, and $D_1 = d$. The two parameters $b$ and $d$ are forward path gains. Find a region within the $b - d$ plane where the system is neither controllable nor observable.

SOLUTION: The controllability and observability matrices $\tilde{P}_c$ and $\tilde{Q}_o$ for the closed-loop composite system defined by (7.4.38) and (7.4.39) are

$$\tilde{P}_c = \begin{bmatrix} 1 & 0 & 0 & b \\ 0 & 1 & 0 & d \\ 2 & 0 & b & 0 \\ -1 & 1 & d & 0 \end{bmatrix} \quad \text{and} \quad \tilde{Q}_o = \begin{bmatrix} 1 & 0 & 2 & b \\ 0 & 1 & 0 & 1 \\ 0 & 0 & 1 & -d \\ 1 & -d & 0 & 0 \end{bmatrix} \tag{7.4.43}$$

The above matrices would have rank $(n_1 + n_2)^2 = 4$ for all values of $b$ and $d$ except when $b + d = 0$. In other words, the closed-loop composite system (7.4.42) is both controllable and observable everywhere in the $b - d$ plane except on the $b = -d$ line going through the second and fourth quadrant.

Further discussions on these criteria are given in Section 7.7.

## 7.4.3 System Connectability Approach

In this section the notion of connectability is defined and its role in the controllability and observability of composite systems is investigated (Davison, 1977). The approach is based on the application of graph theory

(Deo, 1974). The following definitions and terminologies are needed for the controllability and observability conditions to follow.

### 7.4.3.a  Preliminary Definitions

Consider a denumerable set $x = (x_1,\ldots,x_n)$ and a mapping $\Lambda$ of $x$ into $x$; then a pair $M = (x, \Lambda)$ is said to constitute an "$n$th-order graph." The elements $x_i$, $i = 1,\ldots,n$, are referred to as "vertices" of the graph. The directed line segment from vertex $x_i$ to $x_j$, denoted by $v_i = (x_i, x_j)$, is called an "arc" of the graph. The vertices $x_i$ and $x_j$ are called "initial" and "terminal," respectively. Either the pairs $(x, v)$ or $(x, \Lambda)$ can represent a graph. Any line segment connecting a vertex $x_i$ to a vertex $x_j$ is said to be a "path." A closed path, i.e., one in which the initial and terminal vertices coincide, is said to be a "circuit." Now let us consider the following definitions.

**Definition 7.15.** The "arborescence" of root $x_1 \in x$ of a finite graph $M = (x, v)$ is itself a graph with the following properties:

1. $x_1$ is the terminal vertex of no arc.
2. Each $x_i \neq x_1$ is the terminal vertex of only one arc.
3. There is no circuit contained in the graph $M$.

A "branch arborescence" of root $x_1 \in x$ is a subset of an arborescence resulting from deleting all arcs and vertices of the arborescence except for those vertices and arcs along which are associated with a single arc directed from $x_1$. It must be emphasized that neither arborescence nor a branch of it are unique.

**Definition 7.16.** A "composite system" $\dot{x} = Ax + Bu$, $y = Cx$, denoted by $(C, A, B; N; n_1,\ldots,n_N)$, consists of $N$ subsystems interconnected in an arbitrary fashion with with $x \in R^n$, $u \in R^m$, $y \in R^r$, and $A$ defined by

$$A = \begin{bmatrix} A_1 & G_{12} & \cdots & G_{1N} \\ G_{21} & A_2 & \cdots & G_{2N} \\ \vdots & \vdots & & \vdots \\ G_{N1} & G_{N2} & \cdots & A_N \end{bmatrix} \tag{7.4.44}$$

A "sparse composite system" $(C, A, B; N; n_1,\ldots,n_N)$ is a composite system with the following $A$ matrix:

$$A = \begin{bmatrix} A_1^* & G_{12} & \cdots & G_{1N} \\ G_{21} & A_2^* & \cdots & G_{2N} \\ \vdots & \vdots & & \vdots \\ G_{N1} & G_{N2} & \cdots & A_N^* \end{bmatrix} \tag{7.4.45}$$

where $A_i^* = A_i + B_i K_i C_i$, $i = 1, 2, \ldots, N$, with $(C_i, A_i, B_i)$ being an observable and controllable triplet. Furthermore, all the interconnection matrices $G_{ij}$ are zero except for $G_{ij}$, $i = i_1, i_2, \ldots, i_p$ and $j = j_1, \ldots, j_q$ given by $G_{ij} = k_{ij} \alpha_i \beta_j^T$, $i = i_1, \ldots, j = j_1, \ldots$, where $k_{ij}$ is a nonzero scalar called the "$ij$-interconnection gain," $\alpha_i$ and $\beta_j$ are nonzero $(n_i \times 1)$- and $(n_j \times 1)$-dimensional vectors, respectively. Note that a "general composite system" $(C, A, B; N; n_1, \ldots, n_N)$ has an interconnection matrix $G_{ij} = L_{ij} k_{ij} E_{ij}$, $i = i_1, \ldots, i_p$, $j = j_1, \ldots, j_q$, where $L_{ij}$ and $E_{ij}$ are nonzero matrices of appropriate dimensions and $k_{ij}$ is defined earlier. The $B$ and $C$ matrices are assumed to be nontrivial and given by $B^T \triangleq (B_1^T, \ldots, B_N^T)$ and $C \triangleq (C_1^T, \ldots, C_N^T)$. It is usually possible to represent a general composite system $(C, A, B; N; n_1, \ldots, n_N)$ by a graph consisting of $N + 2$ vertices.

The following examples illustrate some of the above notions.

**Example 7.4.7.** For a graph shown in Figure 7.9, find an arborescence and a branch arborescence of it.

SOLUTION: This graph consists of six vertices and eight arcs. If an arborescence of root $x_4$ is desired, it is required to eliminate the self-loop of $x_4$ and one of the two arcs connecting $x_3$ to $x_5$ (one directly and the other through vertex $x_4$). One possible arborescence of $x_4$ is given in Figure 7.10a. A branch arborescence of root $x_3$ of the graph of Figure 7.9 is shown in Figure 7.10b.

**Example 7.4.8.** Consider a composite system described by

$$\begin{bmatrix} \dot{x}_1 \\ \dot{x}_2 \\ \dot{x}_3 \end{bmatrix} = \begin{bmatrix} A_1^* & G_{12} & G_{13} \\ G_{21} & A_2^* & 0 \\ G_{31} & 0 & A_3^* \end{bmatrix} \begin{bmatrix} x_1 \\ x_2 \\ x_3 \end{bmatrix} + \begin{bmatrix} 0 \\ 0 \\ B_3 \end{bmatrix} u \qquad (7.4.46)$$

$$y = \begin{pmatrix} 0 & C_2 & 0 \end{pmatrix} \begin{bmatrix} x_1 \\ x_2 \\ x_3 \end{bmatrix} \qquad (7.4.47)$$

It is desired to represent this system by a graph $M(C, A, B)$ and find an arborescence of root $u$ for $M(A, B)$ and an arborescence of root $y$ for

**Figure 7.9** A graph for Example 7.4.7.

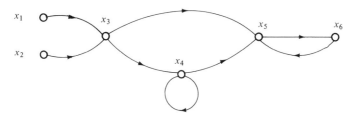

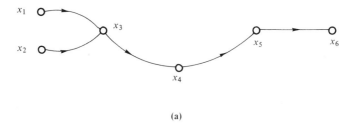

(a)

**Figure 7.10a** An arborescence of root $x_4$ for graph of Example 7.4.7 (Figure 7.9).

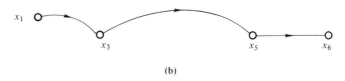

(b)

**Figure 7.10b** A branch arborescence of root $x_3$ for graph of Example 7.4.7 (Figure 7.9).

$M^*(C, A)$. The last notation refers to an "inverse" graph which has all its arrows reversed in direction.

SOLUTION: The graph $M(C, A, B)$ for the system (7.4.46)–(7.4.47) has five $(3 + 2)$ vertices and is shown in Figure 7.11. An arborescence of root $y$ for graph $M(A, B)$ is obtained by first disconnecting all arcs terminating at $y$ and following Definition 7.15. The result is shown in Figure 7.12a. To obtain an arborescence of root $y$ for graph $M^*(C, A)$, it is necessary to reverse the arrows on all arcs, delete all new arcs terminating at $u$, and follow Definition 7.15. The resulting graph is shown in Figure 7.12b. Note

**Figure 7.11** Graph $M(C, A, B)$ for system of Example 7.4.8.

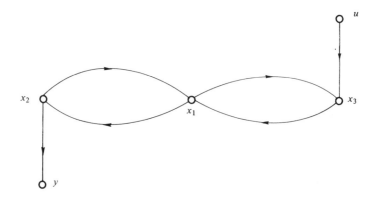

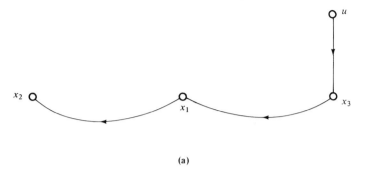

(a)

**Figure 7.12a** An arborescence of root $y$ for graph $M(A, B)$ of Example 7.4.8.

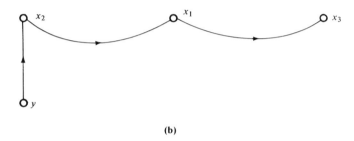

**(b)**

**Figure 7.12b** An arborescence of root $y$ for graph $M^*(C, A)$ of Example 7.4.8.

that in this example, both arborescence graphs turn out to be unique as an exceptional case.

**Definition 7.17.** Let $M(A, B)$ denote the graph of composite system $(A, B; N; n_1,\ldots,n_N)$ and $M(C, A)$ represent the graph of composite system $(C, A; N; n_1,\ldots,n_N)$, where the vertices $y$ and $u$ are eliminated from the two graphs, respectively. Then a composite system $(A, B; N; n_1,\ldots,n_N)$ is called "input connectable" if there exists an arborescence, not necessarily unique, of root $u$ for the graph $M(A, B)$. Furthermore, a composite system $(C, A; N; n_1,\ldots,n_N)$ is called "output connectable" if there exists an arborescence, not necessarily unique, of root $y$ for the inverse graph $M^*(C, A)$. If a composite system is both input and output connectable it is called "connectable."

The system of Example 7.4.8 is both input and output connectable and hence connectable. The notion of connectability, thus introduced, can be used to check the controllability and observability of a composite system.

### 7.4.3.b  Controllability and Observability Conditions

Based on the above preliminaries, the following theorems provide new conditions for the controllability and observability of composite systems.

**Theorem 7.12.** *Consider a sparse composite system* $(C, A, B; N; n_1, \ldots, n_N)$:

1. *If the system is connectable, then it is controllable and observable for almost all output gain matrices $K_i$ and interconnection gains $k_{ij}$.*
2. *If the system is not connectable, then it is never controllable and observable.*

A detailed proof of this theorem can be found in Davison (1977). The following theorem gives conditions for general composite systems.

**Theorem 7.13.** *Consider a general composite system* $(C, A, B; N; n_1, \ldots, n_N)$:

1. *If the system is connectable, then it is controllable and observable for almost all output gain matrices $K_i$ and interconnection gains $K_{ij}$.*
2. *If the system is not connectable, then the general composite system is never controllable and observable.*

In the above theorems, it has been assumed that the composite system's subsystems $(C_i, A_i, B_i)$ are both controllable and observable. Furthermore, a local output feedback is possible for each subsystem. Now let us consider the following example.

**Example 7.4.9.** Consider a system described by a graph shown in Figure 7.13. It is desired to check its controllability and observability.

**Figure 7.13** A graph for system of Example 7.4.9.

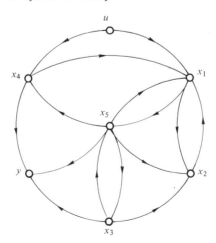

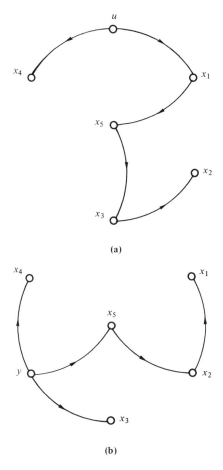

**Figure 7.14** Arborescences of graphs $M(A, B)$ and $M^*(C, A)$ of Example 7.4.9 with respect to (a) root $u$ and (b) root $y$.

SOLUTION: The arborescences of graphs $M(A, B)$ and $M^*(C, A)$ with respect to roots $u$ and $y$ are shown in Figure 7.14. This system is both input and output connectable, thus connectable. Therefore, by Theorem 7.12 this system is both controllable and observable.

The interpretations of Theorem 7.12 are given in Section 7.7.

## 7.5 Structural Controllability and Observability

An important special case of controllability of composite systems is "structural controllability" (Lin, 1974; Glover and Silverman, 1975; Shields and Pearson, 1976; Corfmat and Morse, 1976), where the subsystems of the composite system all have order unity. Some of the important results in structural controllability as reported by Shields and Pearson (1976) are presented first, and then the role of system connectability in structural controllability will be presented.

### 7.5.1 Structure and Rank of a Matrix

The concepts of structure and structural controllability were first introduced by Lin (1974) for single-input linear TIV systems using the graph-theoretic approach. The work of Lin (1974) has been extended by Shields and Pearson (1976).

Consider a linear TIV system

$$\dot{x}(t) = Ax(t) + Bu(t) \qquad (7.5.1)$$

where $x(t) \in R^n$, $u \in R^m$, and $A$ and $B$ are matrices whose elements are either fixed (zero) or indeterminate (arbitrary). The two matrix pairs $(A, B)$ and $(\tilde{A}, \tilde{B})$ are said to have the same "structure" if for every fixed (zero) entry of $(A \ B)$, the corresponding entry of $(\tilde{A} \ \tilde{B})$ is also fixed (zero) and vice versa. A matrix $A$ is said to be a "structural matrix" if it has fixed zeros in certain locations and arbitrary values in all other locations (Shields and Pearson, 1976). A linear system composed of a pair of structured matrices $(A, B)$ is said to be a "structured system."

Two systems $(A, B)$ and $(\tilde{A}, \tilde{B})$ are said to be "structurally equivalent" if there is a one-to-one correspondence between the locations of fixed zero and nonzero entries of their respective matrices. The following definition can now be given.

**Definition 7.18.** A system $(A, B)$ is said to be "structurally controllable" if it has a structurally equivalent system which is controllable in the usual sense, i.e., Equation (7.1.3).

Shields and Pearson (1976) have presented a detailed discussion on the structural properties of matrices which were investigated first by Frobenius (1912) and generalized by König (1931). Two of these properties most useful for the present discussion are "generic rank" and "form" of a matrix $A$ of $n \times m$ $(n \leqslant m)$ dimension.

Let $\Gamma(A, B)$ be a property of the matrices $A$ and $B$ which is assumed to hold for all data points except those which lie on an algebraic hypersurface in $R^K$, where $K$ is the total number of arbitrary entries in $A$ and $B$. More specifically, let $P[\lambda]$ be a polynomial in $K$ variables $\lambda_1, \ldots, \lambda_K$. Let a set of polynomials $\phi_i \in P[\lambda]$; then a "variety" $C \subset R^K$ is the set of common zeros of polynomials $\phi_1, \phi_2, \ldots, \phi_L$, where $L$ is some finite number. A variety $V$ is said to be "proper" if $V \neq R^K$ and "nontrivial" if $V \neq \varnothing$, an empty set. A property $\Gamma$ is "generic" relative to a proper variety $V$ if such a variety exists so that $\ker(\Gamma) \subset V$, where $\ker(\cdot)$ is the kernel of $A$. The kernel of $A$ is also known as the "null-space" of $A$ denoted by $\Pi(A)$, the space of all solutions of $AX = 0$. As an example of the generic property, consider the generic rank of an $n \times m$ matrix $A$ consisting of all arbitrary entries. Let the property $\Gamma(a)$ be defined

$$\Gamma(a) = \begin{cases} 1 & \text{if rank } (A) = n \\ 0 & \text{if rank } (A) < n \end{cases} \tag{7.5.2}$$

where $a \in R^{n \cdot m}$. Moreover, let $\phi$ be a polynomial in $n \cdot m$ arbitrary variables defined as the sum of squares of all possible minors of $A$ of order $n$. Shields and Pearson (1976) state that a structured matrix $A$ has a generic rank denoted by $r(g)$ if there exists a proper variety $V \subset R^K$ such that all points $a \in R^K$ for which rank $A \neq r$ lie on $V$. In terms of the property $\Gamma(a)$ in (7.5.2) and the polynomial $\phi$, this indicates that if $a \in \ker(\Gamma)$, then $\phi(a) = 0$, and, furthermore, the proper variety $V$ is defined by $V = \{a | \phi(a) = 0\}$. It is thus clear that the maximum rank of an $n \times m$ matrix $A$ is the minimum of $n$ and $m$. The following definition gives the form of a matrix.

**Definition 7.19.** An $n \times p$ matrix $A$ is said to be of form $(r)$ for $1 \leqslant r \leqslant n$ if for some $k$, $p - r \leqslant k \leqslant p$, $A$ contains a zero submatrix of dimension $(n + p - k - r + 1) \times k$. The following example illustrates this definition.

**Example 7.5.1.** Consider the matrices

$$A_1 = \begin{bmatrix} x & x & x & x & 0 & x & x & x \\ 0 & x & x & 0 & 0 & x & x & x \\ x & x & 0 & 0 & 0 & 0 & 0 & x \\ x & x & 0 & 0 & 0 & 0 & 0 & x \\ x & x & x & x & x & x & x & x \end{bmatrix}, \quad A_2 = \begin{bmatrix} x & 0 & 0 & 0 & 0 & 0 \\ 0 & x & 0 & 0 & 0 & 0 \\ 0 & 0 & x & 0 & 0 & 0 \\ 0 & 0 & 0 & x & 0 & 0 \\ 0 & 0 & 0 & 0 & x & 0 \\ 0 & 0 & 0 & 0 & 0 & x \end{bmatrix}$$

$$\tag{7.5.3}$$

where $x$ denotes nonzero elements. Find the forms of $A_1$ and $A_2$ matrices.

SOLUTION: For $A_1$ matrix $n = 5$, $p = 8$, and $k = 5$. Then the form of $A_1$ turns out to be $r = 7$, since a zero submatrix of order $(n + p - k - r + 1) \times k = 2 \times 5$ is contained in $A_1$, as shown by dashed lines in (7.5.3). As for matrix $A_2$, there are two zero submatrices of orders $2 \times 4$ and $4 \times 2$, as shown in (7.5.3). For both cases the form turns out to be $r = 7$. In fact, for any diagonal matrix such as $A_2$ of rank $n$, the form is $n + 1$.

The form property of a matrix can be used to find an upper bound on the rank of any matrix.

**Lemma 7.1.** *For every entry* $a \in R^{n \cdot m}$ *in an* $n \times m$ *matrix* $A$, *rank* $A < r$, $1 \leqslant r \leqslant n$, *if and only if* $A$ *has a form* $(r)$.

A simple proof of this lemma has been presented by Shields and Pearson (1976). Now consider two matrices $A$ and $B$ of dimensions $n \times m$ and $n \times m$, respectively. The following definitions will be needed for the conditions on structural controllability set forth in Section 7.5.2.

**Definition 7.20.** For the $n \times (n + m)$ augmented matrix $(A\ B)$, let there be a permutation matrix $P$ satisfying

$$P^T(A\ B) = \begin{bmatrix} P & 0 \\ 0 & I \end{bmatrix} = \begin{bmatrix} A_1 & 0 & 0 \\ A_2 & A_3 & B_2 \end{bmatrix} \qquad (7.5.4)$$

where $\dim(A_1) = r \times r$, $1 \leqslant r \leqslant n$, then the matrix $(A\ B)$ is said to have a "form I." Furthermore, if $(A\ B)$ contains an $((n + m + 1 - k) \times k)$-dimensional zero submatrix for $m < k \leqslant n + m$, i.e., if $(A\ B)$ has a form $(n)$ in the sense of Definition 7.19, then the matrix $(A\ B)$ is said to have a "form II."

### 7.5.2 Conditions for Structural Controllability

The importance of the form of a matrix is in determining whether a system is structurally controllable. One of the initial results along the lines of system controllability under system matrices perturbations is due to Lee and Markus (1967) and states that if a system $\dot{x} = \tilde{A}x + \tilde{B}u$ is controllable, then there is an $\varepsilon > 0$ such that every linear system $\dot{x} = Ax + Bu$ with $\|A - \tilde{A}\| < \varepsilon$ and $\|B - \tilde{B}\| < \varepsilon$ is also controllable. Shields and Pearson (1976) have generalized this result in terms of a proper variety $V \subset R^{N+M}$, where $N$ and $M$ are the number of arbitrary elements of $A$ and $B$, respectively. The above developments do characterize structural controllability but do not give conditions for determining it. The first condition along this line is one of the Lin's (1974) results given below.

**Lemma 7.2.** *The system $(A, b)$ is structurally uncontrollable if and only if the $(n \times (n + 1))$-dimensional matrix $[Ab]$ has either form I or form II.*

The following theorem is the extension of the above result for multi-input system.

**Theorem 7.14.** *The system $(A, B)$ is structurally uncontrollable if and only if the $(n \times (n + m))$-dimensional matrix $[A\ B]$ has either form I or form II.*

A proof of this theorem, based on four lemmas concerning various properties of structured matrices is given by Shields and Pearson (1976).

The application of the above theorem to numerical examples require the recognition of forms I and II. The calculation of form II is simple enough; however, the condition of form I may prove to be a tedious process and sometimes give misleading results.

A generic rank computational algorithm based on combinatorial mathematics (Liu, 1968) due to Prescott and Pearson (1981) is given next. The basic idea is that the generic rank of an $n \times m$ structured matrix $A$ is equivalent to determining the maximum number of "nontaking rooks" that can be placed on an $n \times m$ chessboard, where the zeros of the matrix are interpreted as forbidden positions. A discussion on this theory can be found in Liu (1968).

*Algorithm 7.3.* Generic Rank of a Structured Matrix $r(g)$

*Step 1:* Eliminate any rows or columns of matrix $A$ which contain only zeros. Let the dimension of the resulting matrix be $N \times M$.

*Step 2:* If $\mathrm{Min}(N, M) = 1$, the generic rank of $A$, $\mathrm{gr}(A) = 1(g) = 1$. If $\mathrm{Min}(N, M) = 0$, then $\mathrm{gr}(A) = 0(g)$.

*Step 3:* Identify a nonzero entry in $A$ with the maximum number of zeros in its row and column. This entry is not necessarily unique.

*Step 4:* Compute the generic rank of $A_1$, which is the original matrix $A$ excluding the row and column corresponding to the nonzero entry identified in Step 3. If $\mathrm{gr}(A_1) = \mathrm{Min}(N, M) - 1$, then $\mathrm{gr}(A) = 1 + \mathrm{gr}(A_1)$.

*Step 5:* Compute the generic rank of $A_2$, which is the original matrix $A$ after setting the identified entry of Step 3 to zero. Then $\mathrm{gr}(A) = r(g) = \mathrm{Max}[1 + \mathrm{gr}(A_1), \mathrm{gr}(A_2)]$.

The following example illustrates Algorithm 7.3.

**Example 7.5.2.** Consider a $(6 \times 9)$-dimensional matrix

$$A = \begin{bmatrix} x & x & 0 & 0 & 0 & 0 & x & 0 & x \\ x & x & x & 0 & 0 & 0 & 0 & 0 & 0 \\ 0 & 0 & 0 & 0 & 0 & 0 & 0 & 0 & 0 \\ x & x & 0 & x & x & 0 & x & x & x \\ x & x & x & 0 & x & x & 0 & x & 0 \\ x & x & x & x & x & x & x & x & x \end{bmatrix} \qquad (7.5.5)$$

where $x$ represents nonzero entries. It is desired to find the generic rank of $A$ using Algorithm 7.3.

SOLUTION: After eliminating row 3 and following Step 3 of the algorithm, entry 2, 3 results in the following $A_1$ and $A_2$ matrices:

$$A_1 = \begin{bmatrix} x & x & 0 & 0 & 0 & \textcircled{x} & 0 & x \\ x & x & x & x & 0 & x & x & x \\ x & x & 0 & x & x & 0 & x & 0 \\ x & x & x & x & x & x & x & x \end{bmatrix},$$

$$A_2 = \begin{bmatrix} x & x & 0 & 0 & 0 & 0 & x & 0 & \textcircled{x} \\ x & x & 0 & 0 & 0 & 0 & 0 & 0 & 0 \\ x & x & 0 & x & x & 0 & x & x & x \\ x & x & x & 0 & x & x & 0 & x & 0 \\ x & x & x & x & x & x & x & x & x \end{bmatrix} \qquad (7.5.6)$$

The encircled entries denote those identified at Step 3 of the algorithm. Note also that $n = 6$, $N = 5$, and $m = M = 9$. Repeating Steps 4 and 3 for matrix $A_1$, one obtains the following reduced matrices out of $A_1$:

$$A_1^{(1)} = \begin{bmatrix} x & x & x & x & 0 & x & x \\ x & x & 0 & x & \textcircled{x} & x & 0 \\ x & x & x & x & x & x & x \end{bmatrix}, \quad A_1^{(2)} = \begin{bmatrix} x & x & x & x & x & x \\ x & x & x & x & x & x \end{bmatrix}$$

$$(7.5.7)$$

Similarly, the following three reduced matrices result from repeated application of Steps 4 and 3 to $A_2$:

$$A_2^{(1)} = \begin{bmatrix} x & \textcircled{x} & 0 & 0 & 0 & 0 & 0 & 0 \\ x & x & 0 & x & x & 0 & x & x \\ x & x & x & 0 & x & x & 0 & x \\ x & x & x & x & x & x & x & x \end{bmatrix},$$

$$A_2^{(2)} = \begin{bmatrix} x & 0 & x & x & 0 & x & x \\ x & x & 0 & x & x & 0 & x \\ x & x & x & x & x & x & x \end{bmatrix}, \quad A_2^{(3)} = \begin{bmatrix} x & x & x & 0 & x & x \\ x & x & x & x & x & x \end{bmatrix}$$

$$(7.5.8)$$

Thus,

$$\text{gr}(A_1) = 2 + \text{gr}\left(A_1^{(2)}\right) = 4(g) = 4$$
$$\text{gr}(A_2) = 3 + \text{gr}\left(A_2^{(3)}\right) = 5(g) = 5$$

Since $\text{gr}(A_1) = \text{Min}(N, M) - 1$, by Step 5 of the algorithm, the generic rank of $A$ is given by

$$\text{gr}(A) = \text{Max}\left[1 + \text{gr}(A_1), \text{gr}(A_2)\right] = \text{Max}(1 + 4, 5) = 5(g) = 5 \quad (7.5.9)$$

The above algorithm can be used to determine the structural controllability of a system by utilizing the following definition and a lemma due to Rosenbrock (1970).

**Definition 7.21.** The $n^2 \times n(n + m - 1)$-dimensional "extended controllability matrix" of a system is defined by

$$G_c = \begin{bmatrix} B & I & 0 & 0 & & & & \vdots & & 0 \\ 0 & -A & B & I & 0 & 0 & & & \vdots & 0 \\ 0 & 0 & 0 & -A & B & I & 0 & & \vdots & 0 \\ \vdots & & & & & & \ddots & & & \vdots \\ & & & & & & B & I & 0 \\ 0 & & & \cdots & & & & 0 & -A & B \end{bmatrix} \quad (7.5.10)$$

**Lemma 7.3.** *For a data point $a \in R^{\tilde{N} + \tilde{M}}$ the associated system $(A, B)$ is controllable if and only if*

$$\text{rank}(G_c) = n^2 \quad (7.5.11)$$

*The parameters $\tilde{N}$ and $\tilde{M}$ denote the number of arbitrary elements of $A$ and $B$, respectively.*

Using the above result, one can then state the following theorem for structural controllability of large-scale systems.

**Theorem 7.15.** *The following equivalent conditions hold simultaneously for the system $(A, B)$:*

1. *System $(A, B)$ is structurally uncontrollable.*
2. *The matrix $[A \ B]$ is of form I or form II.*
3. *The matrix $G_c$ is of form $(n^2)$.*

A proof of this theorem can be found in Shields and Pearson (1976). The use of the above lemma and theorem are illustrated by two examples.

**Example 7.5.3.** Consider a system

$$(A, B) = \left( \begin{bmatrix} x & 0 \\ x & x \end{bmatrix}, \begin{bmatrix} x \\ 0 \end{bmatrix} \right) \quad (7.5.12)$$

It is desired to check whether it is structurally controllable.

SOLUTION: The structural controllability of this system can be checked in two different ways using Lemma 7.3 and Theorem 7.15. The extended controllability matrix $G_c$ in 7.5.10 is given by

$$G_c = \begin{bmatrix} B & I & 0 \\ 0 & -A & B \end{bmatrix} = \begin{bmatrix} x & x & 0 & 0 \\ 0 & 0 & x & 0 \\ 0 & x & 0 & x \\ 0 & x & x & 0 \end{bmatrix} \quad (7.5.13)$$

where the unity and negative entries are still shown by an $x$. Using

Algorithm 7.3, the rank of $G_c$ is

$$\text{rank}(G_c) = \text{Max}\left[1 + \text{gr}(G_c)_1, \text{gr}(G_c)_2\right]$$
$$= \text{Max}[1+3,4] = 4 = n^2(g) = n^2 \qquad (7.5.14)$$

which implies that the system is structurally controllable by Lemma 7.3. Alternatively, the form of $G_c$ can be easily found to be 5 and not $n^2 = 4$, which would indicate that the system is structurally controllable by Theorem 7.15. The above results are of course immediate from general condition (7.1.3) as well.

**Example 7.5.4.** Consider a third-order system,

$$(A, B) = \left(\begin{bmatrix} x & 0 & 0 \\ 0 & 0 & 0 \\ 0 & 0 & 0 \end{bmatrix}, \begin{bmatrix} x \\ 0 \\ 0 \end{bmatrix}\right) \qquad (7.5.15)$$

and repeat for structural controllability.

SOLUTION: An inspection of (7.5.15) indicates that the system is not controllable in the general sense. However, this result can be checked through Lemma 7.3 and Theorem 7.15. The extended controllability matrix $G_c$ becomes

$$G_c = \begin{bmatrix} x & x & 0 & 0 & 0 & 0 & 0 & 0 & 0 \\ 0 & 0 & x & 0 & 0 & 0 & 0 & 0 & 0 \\ 0 & 0 & 0 & x & 0 & 0 & 0 & 0 & 0 \\ 0 & x & 0 & 0 & x & x & 0 & 0 & 0 \\ 0 & 0 & 0 & 0 & 0 & 0 & x & 0 & 0 \\ 0 & 0 & 0 & 0 & 0 & 0 & 0 & x & 0 \\ 0 & 0 & 0 & 0 & 0 & x & 0 & 0 & x \\ 0 & 0 & 0 & 0 & 0 & 0 & 0 & 0 & 0 \\ 0 & 0 & 0 & 0 & 0 & 0 & 0 & 0 & 0 \end{bmatrix} \qquad (7.5.16)$$

There is a $5 \times 5$ zero submatrix in $G_c$. The dimension of this zero submatrix is $\{n^2 + n(n+m-1) - k + 1 - r\} \times k$. Since $n = 3$, $m = 1$, and $k = 5$, $r = 9 + 3(3+1-1)+1-5-5 = 9 = n^2$. Thus, $G_c$ has a form $(n^2)$, which indicates that the system is structurally uncontrollable by Theorem 7.15. Alternatively, application of Algorithm 7.3 provides a rank

$$\text{rank } G_c = \text{Max}\left[1 + \text{gr}(G_c)_1, \text{gr}(G_c)_2\right]$$
$$= \text{Max}(1+7,8) = 8 = n^2 - 1(g) = n^2 - 1 \qquad (7.5.17)$$

which determines, by Lemma 7.3, that the system is structurally uncontrollable.

## 7.5.3 *Structural Controllability and Observability via System Connectability*

The notion of system connectability was introduced in Section 7.4.3, where controllability and observability of general composite systems were checked by utilizing this property. In this section, the notion of structural observability is first introduced and then conditions for both structural controllability and observability are given in terms of connectability (Davison, 1977).

**Definition 7.22.** A system $(C, A)$ is said to be "structurally observable" if it has a structurally equivalent system which is observable in the usual sense, i.e., Equation (7.1.4).

Note that this definition is the dual of Definition 7.18. The following theorem and corollary provide conditions for structural controllability and observability.

**Theorem 7.16.** *A system $(A, B)$ is structurally controllable if and only if the following two conditions hold simultaneously:*

1. $\text{rank}(A, B) = n(g).$                                           (7.5.18)
2. $(A, B; n; 1, 1, \ldots, 1)$ *is input-connectable.*

An immediate corollary of this theorem for structural observability is given next.

**Corollary 7.1.** *A system $(C, A)$ is structurally observable if and only if the following two conditions hold simultaneously:*

1. $\text{rank}\begin{bmatrix} A \\ C \end{bmatrix} = n(g).$              (7.5.19)
2. $(C, A; n; 1, 1, \ldots, 1)$ *is output-connectable.*

Note that one can combine the conditions (7.5.18) and (7.5.19) for both properties; i.e., a system $(C, A, B)$ is both structurally controllable and observable if and only if the two generic rank conditions in (7.5.18) and (7.5.19) both hold and the system $(C, A, B; n; 1, 1, \ldots, 1)$ is connectable. This is one of the results obtained by Davison (1977). In the above conditions, the generic rank can be obtained by either Algorithm 7.3 or any other appropriate algorithm. One such algorithm has been suggested by Davison (1977). However, it has been argued (Morari et al., 1978) that the generic rank algorithms, such as those by Davison (1977), are not appropriate because standard rank-finding routines tend to destroy the structure (i.e., lose track of the true zeros) of structured matrices. The following example illustrates the application of Theorem 7.16 and Corollary 7.1.

**Example 7.5.5.** Consider the seventh-order system

$$
(C, A, B) = \left(
\begin{bmatrix}
x & x & 0 & 0 & 0 & 0 & x \\
0 & 0 & x & 0 & x & x & 0
\end{bmatrix},
\begin{bmatrix}
x & x & 0 & 0 & 0 & 0 & 0 \\
0 & x & x & 0 & 0 & 0 & 0 \\
0 & x & 0 & x & 0 & 0 & x \\
x & 0 & 0 & x & 0 & 0 & 0 \\
0 & x & 0 & x & x & 0 & x \\
0 & 0 & x & 0 & 0 & x & x \\
0 & 0 & 0 & 0 & x & x & x
\end{bmatrix},
\begin{bmatrix}
0 & 0 \\
x & 0 \\
x & x \\
0 & 0 \\
x & 0 \\
0 & x \\
x & 0
\end{bmatrix}
\right)
\qquad (7.5.20)
$$

It is desired to check for its structural controllability or observability.

SOLUTION: The system's graph can be seen to have an arborescence with respect to inputs $(u_1, u_2)$ and outputs $(y_1, y_2)$; hence, it is connectable. The remaining conditions are ranks of $(A, B)$ and $\begin{bmatrix} A \\ C \end{bmatrix}$ which can be easily checked by Algorithm 7.3. The results of the two applications are

$$
\mathrm{rank}(A, B) = \mathrm{Max}\big[1 + \mathrm{gr}(AB)_1, \mathrm{gr}(AB)_2\big] = n(g) = n
$$

$$
\mathrm{rank}\begin{bmatrix} A \\ C \end{bmatrix} = \mathrm{Max}\left[1 + \mathrm{gr}\left(\frac{A}{C}\right)_1, \mathrm{gr}\left(\frac{A}{C}\right)_2\right] = n(g) = n \qquad (7.5.21)
$$

which imply that the system (7.5.20) is both structurally controllable and observable.

## 7.6 Controllability of Singularly Perturbed Systems

In Chapter 2, it was seen that through singular perturbation one can find a time-domain model for a large-scale system. Furthermore, in Chapter 6, a near-optimum control for singularly perturbed systems was introduced.

The problem of controllability of a singularly perturbed system in terms of two lower-order subsystems has been considered by many authors. Among them are Kokotović and Haddad (1975), Chow and Kokotović (1976), and Sannuti (1977). In this section, the controllability of singularly perturbed systems is considered. Both linear time-invariant and linear time-varying as well as nonlinear systems are considered.

## 7.6.1 Controllability of Linear TIV Singularly Perturbed Systems

Consider a linear TIV singularly perturbed system

$$\dot{x} = A_1 x + A_{12} z + B_1 u \tag{7.6.1}$$

$$\varepsilon \dot{z} = A_{21} x + A_2 z + B_2 u \tag{7.6.2}$$

where $x$, $z$, and $u$ are $n_s$-, $n_f$-, and $m$-dimensional slow state, fast state, and control vectors, respectively, and constant $A$ and $B$ matrices have compatible dimensions. As it was seen in Section 2.3.2, if perturbation parameter $\varepsilon$ is ignored, (7.6.2) becomes algebraic,

$$0 = A_{21} \hat{x} + A_2 \hat{z} + B_2 \hat{u} \tag{7.6.3}$$

and if $A_2$ is nonsingular, the substitution of $\hat{z}$ from (7.6.3) in (7.6.1) results in the reduced system

$$\dot{\hat{x}} = A_o \hat{x} + B_o \hat{u} \tag{7.6.4}$$

where

$$A_o = A_1 - A_{12} A_2^{-1} A_{21}, \quad B_o = B_1 - A_{12} A_2^{-1} B_2 \tag{7.6.5}$$

As it was seen in Section 2.3.2.a, when the original system's model (7.6.1)–(7.6.2) reduces from $n = n_s + n_f$ dimension to $n_s$ dimension in (7.6.4), the initial transients of fast state $z$, including its initial condition $z(t_o)$, will be lost. A boundary-layer correction similar to (2.3.25) would be needed to compensate for this loss. For the system (7.6.1)–(7.6.2), the boundary-layer correction equation can be derived in a similar way to the development leading to (2.3.25) in Section 2.3.2.a,

$$d\eta(\tau)/d\tau = A_2 \eta(\tau) + B_2 u(\tau) \tag{7.6.6}$$

where $\eta(\tau)$ is the correction for $\hat{z}$ and $\tau = (t - t_o)/\varepsilon$ is the "stretched time scale." Kokotović and Haddad (1975) have used a transformation to find a transformed set of two slow and fast subsystems. However, for the sake of our discussion, it suffices to work with two systems matrix pairs $(A_o, B_o)$ of the reduced system (7.6.4) and $(A_2, B_2)$ of the boundary layer system (7.6.6). The following theorem provide conditions for the controllability of (7.6.1)–(7.6.2):

**Theorem 7.17.** *If $A_2$ is nonsingular and if*

$$\text{rank} \left[ B_o \mid A_o B_o \mid \cdots \mid A_o^{n_s - 1} B_o \right] = n_s \tag{7.6.7}$$

$$\text{rank} \left[ B_2 \mid A_2 B_2 \mid \cdots \mid A_2^{n_f - 1} B_2 \right] = n_f \tag{7.6.8}$$

*then there is an $\varepsilon^* > 0$ such that the singularly perturbed system (7.6.1)–(7.6.2) is controllable for all $0 < \varepsilon \leq \varepsilon^*$.*

Note that if $A_2$ is singular, in view of the discussions made on structural controllability, a matrix $K$ exists such that $A_2 + B_2 K$ is nonsingular, since controllability of (7.6.1)–(7.6.2) is not affected by control $u = Kz + v$ (Kokotović and Haddad, 1975). Therefore, if $A_2$ is singular, one can replace $A_2$ by $A_2 + B_2 K$, use (7.6.5) to evaluate $(A_o, B_o)$, and apply the rank conditions (7.6.7)–(7.6.8). The following example illustrates the above controllability conditions.

**Example 7.6.1.** Consider the singularly perturbed system

$$\dot{x} = \begin{bmatrix} -1.1 & 0 & 0.2 \\ 0.1 & -2 & 0 \\ 0.4 & -0.5 & -3 \end{bmatrix} x + \begin{bmatrix} 0.5 & 0.1 \\ 0.2 & -0.5 \\ 0.1 & 1 \end{bmatrix} z + \begin{bmatrix} 1 & 0.2 \\ 0 & 0.1 \\ 0.5 & 1 \end{bmatrix} u \quad (7.6.9)$$

$$\varepsilon \dot{z} = \begin{bmatrix} 0.75 & 0.2 & 0.8 \\ 0.2 & -0.5 & 0.5 \end{bmatrix} x + \begin{bmatrix} -1 & 0 \\ 0.5 & -1.25 \end{bmatrix} z + \begin{bmatrix} 1 & 0.1 \\ 0 & 0.2 \end{bmatrix} u \quad (7.6.10)$$

It is desired to check its controllability.

SOLUTION: Since matrix $A_2$ is nonsingular, then the reduced system pair $(A_o, B_o)$ is calculated from (7.6.5):

$$(A_o, B_o) = \left( \begin{bmatrix} -0.680 & 0.068 & 0.672 \\ 0.020 & -1.80 & -0.20 \\ 0.935 & -0.80 & -2.20 \end{bmatrix}, \begin{bmatrix} 1.54 & 0.27 \\ 0 & 0.02 \\ 1 & 1.21 \end{bmatrix} \right) \quad (7.6.11)$$

which satisfies the rank condition (7.6.7). The boundary layer system pair

$$(A_2, B_2) = \left( \begin{bmatrix} -1 & 0 \\ 0.5 & -1.25 \end{bmatrix}, \begin{bmatrix} 1 & 0.1 \\ 0 & 0.2 \end{bmatrix} \right) \quad (7.6.12)$$

turns out to satisfy rank condition (7.6.8). Thus, the system (7.6.9)–(7.6.10) is controllable.

### 7.6.2 Controllability of Linear TV Singularly Perturbed Systems

Consider a linear TV singularly perturbed system

$$\dot{x}(t) = A_1(t)x(t) + A_{12}(t)z(t) + B_1(t)u(t) \quad (7.6.13)$$

$$\varepsilon \dot{z}(t) = A_{21}(t)x(t) + A_2(t)z(t) + B_2(t)u(t) \quad (7.6.14)$$

where all matrices are time-varying and are assumed to be twice continuously differentiable over a specified time interval. Assuming that $A_2(t)$ is nonsingular for every time instant $t$, $z$ can be similarly eliminated to give the time-varying reduced system

$$\dot{\hat{x}}(t) = A_o(t)\hat{x}(t) + B_o(t)\hat{u}(t) \quad (7.6.15)$$

where $A_o(t)$ and $B_o(t)$ are the time-varying matrices obtained similarly to

(7.6.5). The boundary-layer system is similarly given by

$$d\eta(\tau)/d\tau = A_2(t)\eta(\tau) + B_2(t)u(\tau) \qquad (7.6.16)$$

where the $A_2(t)$ and $B_2(t)$ matrices can be made constant for a fixed value of $t$. The following definition of complete state controllability, due to Kreindler and Sarachik (1964), is now given.

**Definition 7.23.** A linear time-varying system

$$\dot{y}(t) = F(t)y(t) + G(t)u(t) \qquad (7.6.17)$$

is said to be "completely state" controllable at $t_o$ if every initial state $y(t_o)$ can be transferred to any final state $y(t_f)$ in some final time $t_f > t_o$.

The following lemma, due to Brockett (1970), gives a condition for the controllability of (7.6.17).

**Lemma 7.4.** *The linear TV system* (7.6.17) *is controllable if and only if a symmetric matrix $p(t)$ satisfying*

$$\dot{P}(t) = F(t)P(t) + P(t)F^T(t) + G(t)G^T(t), \ P(t_o) = 0 \quad (7.6.18)$$

*is nonsingular at $t = t_f$ for a finite $t_f > t_o$.*

PROOF: It is known (Kreindler and Sarachik, 1964; Davison and Kunze, 1970) that the system (7.6.17) is controllable if and only if the controllability Grammian matrix $W(t_o, t)$

$$W(t_o, t) = \int_{t_o}^{t} \phi(t_o, t)G(t)G^T(t)\phi^T(t_o, t)\, dt \qquad (7.6.19)$$

is nonsingular at $t = t_1$ for some finite $t_1 > t_o$. In (7.6.19), $\phi(\cdot, \cdot)$ is the state transition matrix of (7.6.17). Now let us define $P(t)$ by

$$W(t_o, t) = \phi(t_o, t)P(t)\phi^T(t_o, t) \qquad (7.6.20)$$

If (7.6.20) is substituted in (7.6.19), differentiating the resulting equation with respect to time, one gets

$$\dot{\phi}(t_o, t)P(t)\phi^T(t_o, t) + \phi(t_o, t)\dot{P}(t)\phi^T(t_o, t) + \phi(t_o, t)P(t)\dot{\phi}^T(t_o, t)$$
$$= \phi(t_o, t)G(t)G^T(t)\phi^T(t_o, t) \quad (7.6.21)$$

Now noting that the state equation for the transition matrix $\phi(t, t_o)$ and its adjoint equation for $\phi^T(t_o, t)$ are

$$\dot{\phi}(t, t_o) = F(t)\phi(t, t_o), \quad \dot{\phi}^T(t_o, t) = -F^T(t)\phi^T(t_o, t) \quad (7.6.22)$$

one can easily see that (7.6.21) is reduced to

$$\phi(t_o, t)\left[-F(t)P(t) + \dot{P}(t) - P(t)F^T(t) - G(t)G^T(t)\right]\phi(t_o, t) = 0$$
$$(7.6.23)$$

which is true if and only if (7.6.18) holds. In view of (7.6.20), nonsingularlity of $W(t_o, t)$ implies that of $P(t)$ and vice versa. This proves the lemma.

Q.E.D. ∎

The above lemma can be used to present the following theorem (Sannuti, 1977) for the controllability of TV singularly perturbed system (7.6.13)–(7.6.14):

**Theorem 7.18.** *The system* (7.6.13)–(7.6.14) *is controllable if*

1. *the reduced system, defined below is controllable*

$$\dot{\hat{x}}(t) = \hat{A}_o(t)\hat{x}(t) + \hat{B}_o(t)v(t) \qquad (7.6.24)$$

*with*

$$\hat{A}_o(t) = A_1(t) - \hat{A}_{12}(t)\hat{A}_2^{-1}(t)A_{21}(t) \qquad (7.6.25)$$

$$\hat{B}_o(t) = B_1(t) - \hat{A}_{12}(t)\hat{A}_2^{-1}(t)B_2(t) \qquad (7.6.26)$$

$$\hat{A}_{12}(t) = A_{12}(t) + B_1(t)K(t) \qquad (7.6.27)$$

$$\hat{A}_2(t) = A_2(t) + B_2(t)K(t) \qquad (7.6.28)$$

$K(t)$ *is an arbitrary matrix such that matrix* $\hat{A}_2(t)$ *is nonsingular for all* $t_o < t \leqslant t_1$ *and* $u(t) = L(t)v(t) + M(t)L(t)x(t)$ *where*

$$L(t) = I_m - K(t)\hat{A}_2^{-1}(t)B_2(t) = \left(I_m + K(t)A_2^{-1}(t)B_2(t)\right)^{-1}$$

(7.6.29)

$$M(t) = -K(t)A_2^{-1}(t)A_{21}(t) \qquad (7.6.30)$$

2. *the boundary-layer system* (7.6.16) *is controllable, i.e.,*

$$\text{rank}\left[ B_2(t) \mid A_2(t)B_2(t) \mid \cdots \mid A_2^{n_f-1}(t)B_2(t)\right] = n_f \quad (7.6.31)$$

*for a fixed* $t$.

Note that for each fixed $t$, the boundary layer system (7.6.16) is time-invariant in the domain of $\tau$, hence justifying the rank condition (7.6.31).

In sequel, a proof for this theorem, due to Sannuti (1977), is given.

PROOF: Condition 2 implies that there exists a matrix $\hat{K}(t)$ such that $\hat{A}_2(t) = A_2(t) + B_2(t)\hat{K}(t)$ is stable, i.e., all eigenvalues of $\hat{A}_2(t)$ have negative real parts for any fixed $t$. Then condition 1 suggests that $A_2(t)$ in (7.6.14) is a stable matrix. Otherwise $A_2(t)$ can be stabilized through a feedback from $z$. In order to prove the theorem, let us transform (7.6.13)–(7.6.14) into a block-diagonal form by letting

$$x = \alpha - \varepsilon W\beta, \quad z = -V\alpha + \beta + \varepsilon VW\beta \qquad (7.6.32)$$

or (7.6.13)–(7.6.14) becomes

$$\dot{\alpha}(t) = F_1(t)\alpha(t) + G_1(t)u(t) \tag{7.6.33a}$$

$$\varepsilon\dot{\beta}(t) = F_2(t)\beta(t) + G_2(t)u(t) \tag{7.6.33b}$$

where

$$F_1 = A_1 - A_{12}V, \quad G_1 = B_1 + WB_2 + \varepsilon WVB_2$$
$$F_2 = A_2 + \varepsilon\dot{V}A_{12}, \quad G_2 = B_2 + \varepsilon VB_1 \tag{7.6.34}$$

Note that the argument $t$ has been dropped for simplicity here. The variables $V$ and $W$ are bounded solutions of the following equations (Chang 1972):

$$\varepsilon\dot{V} = A_2V - \varepsilon V(A_1 - A_{12}V) - A_{21}$$
$$\varepsilon\dot{W} = \varepsilon(A_1 - A_{12}V)W - W(A_2 + \varepsilon VA_{12}) - A_{12} \tag{7.6.35}$$

for all $0 < \varepsilon \leqslant \varepsilon^*$. Furthermore, $V$ and $W$ have the following limits:

$$\lim_{\varepsilon \to 0} V = A_2^{-1}A_{21}, \quad \lim_{\varepsilon \to 0} W = -A_{12}A_2^{-1} \tag{7.6.36}$$

Using the limits in (7.6.36), the limits of the matrices in (7.6.34) are

$$\lim_{\varepsilon \to 0} F_1 = A_1 - A_{12}A_2^{-1}A_{21} = A_o, \quad \lim_{\varepsilon \to 0} F_2 = A_2$$
$$\lim_{\varepsilon \to 0} G_1 = B_1 - A_{12}A_2^{-1}B_2 = B_o, \quad \lim_{\varepsilon \to 0} G_2 = B_2 \tag{7.6.37}$$

Thus, subsystem (7.6.33a) is a regular perturbation of the reduced system (7.6.4) and (7.6.33b) is related to the boundary layer system (7.6.6). Now in view of Lemma 7.4, system (7.6.33) is controllable if

$$P(t) = \begin{bmatrix} P_1(t) & P_{12}(t) \\ P_{12}^T(t) & L_2(t)/\varepsilon \end{bmatrix}$$

is nonsingular at $t = t_1$ for some finite $t_1 > t_o$, where

$$\dot{P}_1 = F_1P_1 + P_1F_1^T + G_1G_1^T, \quad P_1(t_o) = 0 \tag{7.6.38a}$$

$$\varepsilon\dot{P}_{12} = \varepsilon F_1P_{12} + P_{12}F_2^T + G_1G_2^T, \quad P_{12}(t_o) = 0 \tag{7.6.38b}$$

$$\varepsilon\dot{L}_2 = F_2L_2 + L_2F_2^T + G_2G_2^T, \quad L_2(t_o) = 0 \tag{7.6.38c}$$

Now by using relevant singular perturbation methods (O'Malley, 1974; Yackel and Kokotović, 1973), one can assess the nature of the solution of (7.6.38). In fact, since $A_2(t)$ is a stable matrix, for sufficiently small $\varepsilon$ and for all finite $t \geqslant t_o$, one has

$$P_1(t) = \bar{P}_1(t) + 0(\varepsilon)$$
$$P_{12}(t) = \bar{P}_{12}(t) - \bar{P}_{12}(t_o)\xi^T(t) + 0(\varepsilon) \tag{7.6.39}$$
$$L_2(t) = \bar{L}_2(t) - \xi(t)L_2(t_o)\xi^T(t) + 0(\varepsilon)$$

where

$$\dot{\bar{P}}_1 = A_o \bar{P}_1 + \bar{P}_1 A_o^T + B_o B_o^T, \quad \bar{P}_1(t_o) = 0$$

$$\xi(t) = \exp\{A_2(t_o)(t - t_o)/\varepsilon\}, \quad \bar{P}_{12}(t) = -B_o B_2 (A_2^T)^{-1} \quad (7.6.40)$$

$$0 = A_2 \bar{L}_2 + \bar{L}_2 A_2^T + B_2 B_2^T$$

It is noted now that $\xi(t)$ is a boundary layer function; i.e., $\xi(t)$ for all $t > t_o$ can be made small enough by choosing $\varepsilon$ sufficiently small. Now by condition 1, $\bar{P}_1(t)$ is nonsingular for some $t_1$ such that $t - t_1 > t_o$ and by condition 1, $\bar{L}_2(t)$ is nonsingular for all $t \geqslant t_o$ (Brockett, 1970). Moreover, by virtue of (7.6.39), for sufficiently small $\varepsilon$, $P_1(t)$ and $L_2(t)$ are nonsingular at $t = t_1 > t_o$. Finally by rewriting $P(t_1)$ as

$$P(t_1) = \begin{bmatrix} I & 0 \\ P_{12}^T P_1^{-1} & I/\varepsilon \end{bmatrix} \begin{bmatrix} P_1 & P_{12} \\ 0 & L_2 - \varepsilon P_{12}^T P_1^{-1} P_{12} \end{bmatrix}$$

it is seen that $P(t_1)$ is nonsingular, since it is the product of two nonsingular matrices. This completes the proof. Q.E.D. ∎

The following example illustrates the application of the above theorem.

**Example 7.6.2.** Consider the fifth-order linear TV singularly perturbed system

$$\dot{x} = \begin{bmatrix} -t-1.1 & 0 & 0.2 \\ 0.1 & -t-2 & 0 \\ 0.4-0.5t & -0.1t & 0.1t-3 \end{bmatrix} x + \begin{bmatrix} 0 & 0.2 \\ 0 & 0 \\ 0.1 & -0.15 \end{bmatrix} z + \begin{bmatrix} 1 & 0 \\ 0.05 & 0.1 \\ 0 & 1 \end{bmatrix} u$$

$$(7.6.41)$$

$$\varepsilon \dot{z} = \begin{bmatrix} 0.4-0.5t & 0 & 0.2 \\ 0 & 0.2 & 0.1 \end{bmatrix} x + \begin{bmatrix} -t^2-1 & 0.05 \\ -0.15 & -2t \end{bmatrix} z + \begin{bmatrix} 1 & 0.1 \\ 0.05 & 0 \end{bmatrix} u$$

$$(7.6.42)$$

It is desired to check whether the system is controllable for time interval $0 < t \leqslant 1.0$.

SOLUTION: The controllability of the reduced system can be checked by applying Lemma 7.4 for $\hat{A}_o(t)$ and $\hat{B}_o(t)$ defined in (7.6.25)–(7.6.26). Since $A_2(t)$ is stable over the time interval of interest, the matrix $K(t)$ in (7.6.28) is chosen to be zero. The Lyapunov differential equation

$$\dot{P}_o(t) = \hat{A}_o(t) P_o(t) + P_o(t) \hat{A}_o^T(t) + \hat{B}_o^T(t) \hat{B}_o(t), \quad P_o(0) = 0$$

$$(7.6.43)$$

was solved using a fourth-order Runge–Kutta method and a step size $\Delta t = 0.05$. The value of $P_o(1)$ turned out to be

$$P_o(1) = \begin{bmatrix} -10.02 & 2.27 & 45.26 \\ 2.27 & -0.71 & -11.95 \\ 45.26 & -11.95 & -226.7 \end{bmatrix}$$

$$(7.6.44)$$

which is nonsingular with a determinant of $-14.92$. The boundary layer system

$$(A_2, B_2) = \left( \begin{bmatrix} -t^2 - 1 & 0.05 \\ -0.15 & -2t \end{bmatrix}, \begin{bmatrix} 1 & 0.1 \\ 0.5 & 0 \end{bmatrix} \right) \qquad (7.6.45)$$

turned out to be controllable for all $0 < t \leqslant 1.0$. Thus, by Theorem 7.18 the system (7.6.41)–(7.6.42) is controllable.

## 7.6.3 Controllability of Quasilinear Systems

In this section the controllability of nonlinear systems is extended to singularly perturbed systems. Several authors (Davison and Kunze, 1970; Mirza and Womack, 1979; Klamka, 1975a, b) have considered the former problem, while Sannuti (1977) has extended the controllability of quasilinear system (Davison and Kunze, 1970) to the singularly perturbed case. Consider the system

$$\dot{x} = A_1(x, t)x + A_{12}(x, t)z + B_1(x, t)u \qquad (7.6.46)$$

$$\varepsilon \dot{z} = A_{21}(x, t)x + A_2(x, t)z + B_2(x, t)u \qquad (7.6.47)$$

where the matrices $A_i$, $A_{ij}$, and $B_i$ are assumed twice continuously differentiable and bounded with respect to $x$ and $t$ (Sannuti, 1977). Moreover, $A_2(x, t)$ is assumed to be nonsingular. The reduced and boundary layer systems are similarly defined by

$$\dot{x} = A_o(x, t)x + B_o(x, t)u \qquad (7.6.48)$$

$$d\eta/d\tau = A_2(x, t)\eta + B_2(x, t)u \qquad (7.6.49)$$

Note that once again in the $\tau$-domain, $x(t)$ and $t$ in (7.6.49) are held fixed, implying that the boundary layer system is considered to be time-invariant. If the argument $x$ of matrices in (7.6.46)–(7.6.47) is replaced by a specified vector function $v(t)$, then (7.6.48) becomes linear time-varying similar to (7.6.17) hence, the result of Lemma 7.4 can be used. If the $n$-dimensional vector function $v(t)$ is assumed to be continuous over an interval $[t_o, t_f]$, i.e., $v(t) \in \mathcal{C}_n[t_o, t_f]$, then the following lemma, due to Davison and Kunze (1970), gives conditions for the controllability of (7.6.48).

**Lemma 7.5.** *If for some $t_f > t_o$ a constant $d > 0$ exists such that*

$$\inf_{v(t) \in \mathcal{C}_n[t_o, t_f]} \det D(t_o, t_f; v) \geqslant d \qquad (7.6.50)$$

*where*

$$D(t_o, t_f; v) = \Phi(t_o, t)P(t_o, t; v)\Phi^T(t_o, t) \qquad (7.6.51)$$

*$\Phi(t_o, t)$ is the transition matrix of*

$$\dot{\Phi}(t_o, t) = A_o(v, t)\Phi(t_o, t) \qquad (7.6.52)$$

*and $P(\cdot,\cdot)$ is the solution of*

$$\dot{P}(t_o,t;v) = A_o(v,t)P(t_o,t;v) + P(t_o,t;v)A_o^T(v,t)$$
$$+ B_o(x,t)B_o^T(x,t), \quad P(t_o,\cdot) = 0 \qquad (7.6.53)$$

*then the quasilinear system is controllable.*

A proof of this result has been presented by Davison and Kunze (1970). The controllability conditions of singularly perturbed quasilinear system (7.6.46)–(7.6.47) are given by the following theorem.

**Theorem 7.19.** *For a small $\varepsilon > 0$, the system (7.6.46)–(7.6.47) is completely state controllable if the following conditions hold:*

1. *the reduced system (7.6.48) satisfies condition (7.6.50), and*
2. *the boundary layer system (7.6.49) is controllable, i.e.,*

$$\text{rank}\, G\big(B_2(\cdot), A_2(\cdot)\big)$$
$$= \text{rank}\Big[ B_2(v,t) \,\Big|\, A_2(v,t)B_2(v,t) \,\Big|\, \cdots \,\Big|\, A_2^{n_f-1}(v,t)B_2(v,t)\Big]$$
$$= n_f \qquad (7.6.54)$$

PROOF: It is clear from the proof of Theorem 7.18 that the linear system resulting from substituting each prescribed $v(t)$ for the argument $x(t)$ of the matrices in (7.6.46)–(7.6.47) will satisfy the condition (7.6.50) of Davison and Kunze (1970). Thus, Lemma 7.5 proves this theorem. Q.E.D. ∎

The above development is illustrated by an example.

**Example 7.6.3.** Consider the quasilinear singularly perturbed system

$$\dot{x} = \begin{bmatrix} x_1 & x_2 \\ x_1 x_2 & x_1 \end{bmatrix} x + \begin{bmatrix} x_1 & -1 & 0.1 \\ -0.2 & 0.5 & -x_2 \end{bmatrix} z + \begin{bmatrix} x_1 \\ 0.1 \end{bmatrix} u \quad (7.6.55a)$$

$$\varepsilon \dot{z} = \begin{bmatrix} x_1^2 & -x_2 \\ -x_1 & x_2^2 \\ -x_2^2 & 3x_1 \end{bmatrix} x + \begin{bmatrix} -x_1^2 & 0.1 & 1 \\ -0.2 & -x_1 x_2 & 0.65 \\ -1 & 0 & -x_2^2 \end{bmatrix} z + \begin{bmatrix} 1 \\ x_2 \\ 0 \end{bmatrix} u \quad (7.6.55b)$$

It is desired to check the controllability of this system over $t \in [0, 0.75]$ and the class of specified second-order vector functions $v(t) = [t\exp(-at)\ 1 - \exp(-at)]$ where $1 \leqslant a \leqslant 3$.

SOLUTION: This problem was solved by specifying the $A_i$, $A_{ij}$ and $B_i$, $i,j = 1,2$, matrices using the vector $v(t)$ and integrating the Lyapunov differential equation (7.6.53). For the desired range of parameter $a$, the condition (7.6.51) was proportionally found to vary in the manner shown in Figure 7.15. The condition is seen to be violated at $a = 2.737395$. The determinant

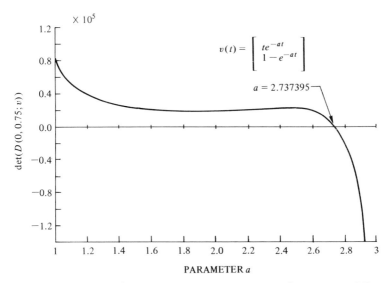

$$v(t) = \begin{bmatrix} te^{-at} \\ 1 - e^{-at} \end{bmatrix}$$

$a = 2.737395$

PARAMETER $a$

**Figure 7.15** Variation of $\det(D(\cdot,\cdot))$ versus parameter $a$ for system of Example 7.6.3.

of the $D(\cdot)$ matrix has a minimum of about $d = 18007.16$ at $a = 1.8$, which indicates that for the class of vectors

$$v(t) \in \mathcal{C}_2[0,0.75] = \left\{ 1.0 \leqslant a < 2.5 : v(t) = \begin{bmatrix} te^{-at} \\ 1 - 3^{-at} \end{bmatrix} \right\} \quad (7.6.56)$$

the reduced system is controllable. For this class of values, the condition (7.6.54) for the boundary layer system shown in Figure 7.16 was satisfied for

**Figure 7.16** Variation of $\det(G(\cdot))$ versus time for Example 7.6.3.

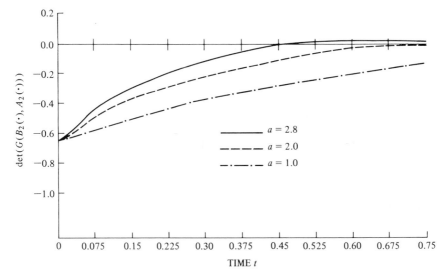

$a = 2.8$

$a = 2.0$

$a = 1.0$

TIME $t$

most members. To be exact, this condition was violated for all values of $a > 2.15$, which indicates that the two conditions hold simultaneously for $1.0 \leqslant a \leqslant 2.15$ with a value of $d \cong 20000$.


## 7.7 Discussion and Conclusions

In this chapter three of the most fundamental issues of large-scale systems, i.e. stability, controllability, and observability, have been briefly discussed. In this section a comparison between the two main techniques of large-scale systems stability—Lyapunov and input–output—is made first, followed by a brief run-down on researchers' efforts since 1966. The second part of the discussion is devoted to the controllability and observability of large-scale systems. In the final segment of this section, attention is focused on controllability based on decentralized structure.


### 7.7.1 Discussion of the Stability of Large-Scale Systems

The discussion on the stability of large-scale systems begins by pointing out that Lyapunov and IO stability methods imply each other (Araki, 1978). In order to facilitate this discussion, consider a large-scale interconnected system represented by

$$\dot{x}_i(t) = A_i x_i(t) + b_i \{ - \psi_i(y_i(t), t) + \tilde{h}_i(y_1(t), \ldots, y_N(t), t) + z_i(t) \}$$
$$(7.7.1)$$

$$y_i(t) = c_i^T x_i(t), \quad i = 1, \ldots, N \tag{7.7.2}$$

where $x_i$ is $n_i \times 1$ state vector of $i$th subsystem, $A_i$, $b_i$, and $c_i$ are a constant matrix and vectors with the triplet $(b_i, A_i, c_i^T)$ being both controllable and observable, and real-valued functions $\psi_i(\cdot, t)$ and $\tilde{h}_i(\cdot, \cdot, \ldots, t)$ are assumed to satisfy

$$\gamma_i \tau^2 \leqslant \psi_i(\tau, t)\tau \leqslant \delta_i \tau^2, \quad t, \tau \in R \tag{7.7.3}$$

$$|\tilde{h}_i(\tau_1, \ldots, \tau_N, t)| \leqslant \sum_{j=1}^{N} b_{ij} |\tau_j|, \quad t, \tau_j \in R \tag{7.7.4}$$

where $\gamma_i$, $\delta_i$, and $b_{ij}$ are nonnegative constants with $\delta_i \geqslant \gamma_i$. It is noted that this system is a special case of composite input-output system (7.3.4) with $D = I$, $F = 0$, $\mu = N$, and $\mu_i = 1, \ldots, N$.

Araki (1978) has stated a corollary, given below, which provides conditions for the stability of system (7.7.1)–(7.7.4) via the Nyquist criterion.

**Corollary 7.2.** *Let* $a_i$, $i = 1, \ldots, N$, *be positive constants and* $E = (e_{ij})$ *defined by (7.2.13) be an M-matrix where* $e_{ii} = a_i - b_{ii}$ *and* $e_{ij} = -b_{ij}$, $i \neq j$ *and* $b_{ij}$ *are given in (7.7.4), when* $\delta_i = \infty$ *for* $j = 1, \ldots, N$; *then the system of*

(7.7.1)–(7.7.2) *is $L_2$-stable if the Nyquist diagram of each transfer function $\bar{g}_i(s)$*

1. *does not intersect or encircle a disk with center at $c_i = \{\frac{1}{2}[-(\gamma_i - a_i)^{-1} + \varepsilon_i], j0\}$ and radius of $r_i = \frac{1}{2}((\gamma_i - a_i)^{-1} + \varepsilon_i)$ for some $\varepsilon_i > 0$ and if $\gamma_i < a_i$. Note that $j0$ represents a zero imaginary quantity on the s-plane and is not be be confused with the index $j$ above;*
2. *lies inside the disk with center at $c_i$ and radius $r_i = \frac{1}{2}((\gamma_i - a_i)^{-1} - \varepsilon_i)$ for some $\varepsilon_i$ satisfying $|(\gamma_i - a_i)^{-1}| > \varepsilon_i > 0$ and if $\gamma_i < a_i$;*
3. *and lies to the right of a line $s = \varepsilon_i$ parallel to the imaginary axis for some $\varepsilon_i > 0$ and if $\gamma_i = a_i$.*

Typical transfer function $\bar{g}_i(s)$ is given by

$$\bar{g}_i(s) = c_i^T (sI - A_i)^{-1} b_i \tag{7.7.5}$$

Furthermore, let the disturbance inputs $u_i(t) = 0$ for $i = 1, \ldots, N$. The system would thus become a special case of (7.2.2) where

$$f_i(x_i, t) = A_i x_i - b_i \psi_i (c_i^T x_i) \tag{7.7.6}$$

$$g_i(x, t) = b_i \tilde{h}_i (c_1^T x_1, \ldots, c_N^T x_N, t) \tag{7.7.7}$$

For the sake of simplicity assume that condition 3 of Corollary 7.2 is the only one holding for this unforced system. In other words, every $\bar{g}_i(s)$ satisfies condition 3. Then by utilizing Lefschetz's form of the Kalman–Yakubovich Lemma (Lefschetz, 1965), there are positive-definite matrices $P_i$ and $Q_i$ satisfying

$$A_i^T P_i + P_i A_i + Q_i = 0 \tag{7.7.8}$$

$$P_i b_i - c_i = 0 \tag{7.7.9}$$

If one would let $v_i(x_i, t) = x_i^T P_i x_i$, then through (7.7.3), (7.7.6), (7.7.8), (7.7.9) the time derivative of $v_i$ would be (Araki, 1978)

$$\dot{v}_i(x_i, t)|_{(Iss)} = x_i^T (A_i^T P_i + P_i A_i) x_i - 2 x_i^T P_i b_i \psi_i (c_i^T x_i, t)$$

$$\leqslant - x_i^T Q_i x_i - x_i^T (-2 P_i b_i + 2 c_i) \psi_i (c_i^T x_i, t) - 2 \gamma_i (c_i^T x_i)^2 \tag{7.7.10}$$

$$= - x_i^T Q_i x_i - 2 \gamma_i (c_i^T x_i)^2 \tag{7.7.11}$$

Moreover, from (7.7.4), (7.7.7), and (7.7.9), one would get

$$(\partial v_i(x_i, t)/\partial x_i)^T g_i(x, t) \leqslant 2 x_i^T P_i b_i \tilde{h}_i (c_1^T x_1, \ldots, c_N^T x_N, t)$$

$$\leqslant \sqrt{2} |c_i^T x_i| \sum_{j=1}^{N} b_{ij} \sqrt{2} |c_j^T x_j| \tag{7.7.12}$$

Now by choosing $\omega_i(x_i) = \sqrt{2} |c_i^T x_i|$, $a_i = \gamma_i$ and $z_i(x_i) = x_i^T Q_i x_i$, it becomes clear that relations (7.7.11) and (7.7.12) are identical to conditions (7.2.22) and (7.2.23) of Theorem 7.2, respectively. Therefore it has been shown that condition 3 of Corollary 7.2 (IO stability) implies conditions 1 and 2 of Theorem 7.2 (Lyapunov stability).

The converse of the above can also be easily shown to hold. Let $A_i$ be a Hurwitz matrix and that conditions of Theorem 7.2 hold where

$$v_i(x_j, t) = x_i^T P_i x_i; \quad \omega_i(x_i) = \alpha_i |c_i^T x_i|, \quad \alpha_i > 0 \qquad (7.7.13)$$

where $P_i$ is the positive-definite solution of (7.7.8). The condition (7.7.3) implies (7.7.10). Now by assuming that

$$a_i = \gamma_i, \quad \alpha_i = \sqrt{2}, \quad z_i(x_i) = x_i^T Q_i x_i \qquad (7.7.14)$$

the right-hand side of (7.7.10) can be bounded similar to (7.2.22) of Theorem 7.2 and that (7.7.9) is required. Then again by the Kalman–Yakubovich Lemma (Lefschetz, 1965), condition 3 of Corollary 7.2 is satisfied. Thus, in a limited case, it has been shown that conditions of Corollary 7.2 and Theorem 7.2 imply each other. Table 7.1 provides a comparison between IO and Lyapunov stability.

The notion of connective stability, introduced by Šiljak (1972b, 1978), takes into account the structural perturbations of a large-scale composite system on the overall stability. The scheme is applicable to both linear and nonlinear systems, and a simple algebraic test would normally be sufficient for the required criterion. There are two conceptually important conclusions on connective stability. One is that this stability notion establishes an ability for the system to withstand sudden perturbations, hence a dynamic reliability property. The second is that the stability of the system (7.2.27) would still hold even for nonlinear interconnection functions $g_{ij}(t, x)$ whose actual shapes are not necessary as long as they are continuous and bounded between zero and one. The latter point would indicate that connective stability implies that the system would remain stable in spite of perturbations such as inaccurate measurements, parameter settings, computations, nonlinear characteristics, etc.

In spite of the treatments in this chapter, the fact remains that it is very improbable that a practical large-scale system is asymptotically stable in the large. Therefore, one would have to rely on local analysis using Lyapunov functions in most practical considerations. Even so, the construction of Lyapunov functions for subsystems with the "best" set of parameters is a rather laborious task. The following steps, suggested by Araki (1978), offer a workable procedure: (1) Consider a nominal (equilibrium) point and extrapolate a system equation around it; (2) continue with an IO stability which is normally somewhat simpler than constructing Lyapunov functions; and (3) interpret the results of IO stability to form Lyapunov functions

**Table 7.1** A Comparison of IO and Lyapunov Stability Methods

| Basic Requirements | Inputs–Output Stability | Lyapunov Stability |
|---|---|---|
| main approach | small gain theorem (and circle criteria in $L_2$ case) | second method of Lyapunov |
| subsystems knowledge | gains (and sector conditions in $L_2$ case) | Lyapunov functions (stable) or positive-definite decrescent, radially unbounded functions (unstable) |
| interconnections knowledge | (functional) bounds | (instantaneous) bounds |
| derivation of composite system stability conditions | determination of weights $c_i$ which guarantees small gain condition with respect to the norm $$\left\{ \sum_{i=1}^{N} \left( c_i \|u_i\|^2 \right) \right\}^{1/2} \quad \text{or}$$ circle condition with respect to the inner product $$\sum_{i=1}^{N} \{ c_i^2 \langle u_i, y_i \rangle \}$$ | determination of weights $c_i$ which guarantees negative-definitness of $$\sum_{i=1}^{N} c_i v_i(x_i, t)$$ |
| test | | Metzler matrix test |

similar to the development following Equations (7.7.1)–(7.7.13) for a particular system. It should, however, be mentioned that this development is not
complete, and further work on the derivations of Lyapunov functions from
frequency domain conditions are necessary.

Finally a few comments regarding a historical viewpoint on the major
contributions of large-scale composite systems stability is due. In order to
facilitate this, Table 7.2 summarizes the development on the application of
Lyapunov method to composite systems. As shown, the method was first
considered by Bailey (1966). The basic assumptions made here were
quadratic order Lyapunov functions for subsystems, linear interconnections,
and vector Lyapunov functions. Following the initial attempt by Bailey
(1966), several authors have extended and improved it by altering the above
three points as shown in Table 7.2.

**Table 7.2** A Summary of Eight Approaches in Lyapunov Stability of Large-scale Composite Systems

| Contributors | Subsystems Lyapunov Functions | Assumptions on Interactions | Stability Criterion Technique | Required Tests | Test Involving Arbitrary Parameters |
|---|---|---|---|---|---|
| Bailey (1966) | quadratic | linear | vector Lyapunov | stability of linear time-invariant comparison system | no |
| Thompson (1970) | quadratic | linear | scalar Lyapunov | positive-definitness of a matrix or other conditions | yes |
| Michel and Porter (1972) | quadratic | linear bounds | scalar Lyapunov | positive-definitness of a matrix | yes |
| Araki and Kondo (1972) Araki (1978) | quadratic | linear bounds | scalar Lyapunov | Metzler matrix | no |
| Šiljak (1972b, 1978) (connective stability) | linear | linear bounds | vector Lyapunov | Metzler matrix | no |
| Grujic and Šiljak (1973b) | linear | linear bounds | scalar Lyapunov | Metzler matrix | no |
| Suda (1973) | quadratic | mean-square bounds | scalar Lyapunov | Metzler matrix | no |
| Moylan and Hill (1978) (dissipative systems) | quadratic | linear | scalar Lyapunov | quasi-dominancy of a matrix | no |

Another line of research on the stability of large-scale systems has been that of the so-called dissipative systems. A system with $m$ inputs and $r$ outputs is said to be $(C, Q, P)$-dissipative if the truncated inner product relation

$$\langle u, Pu \rangle_\tau + 2\langle y, Qu \rangle_\tau + \langle y, Cy \rangle_\tau \geqslant 0 \qquad (7.7.15)$$

for all $\tau \varepsilon R$ and $C, Q$, and $P$ are $r \times r$, $r \times m$ and $m \times m$ matrices, with $C$ and $Q$ being symmetric as well. Moylan and Hill (1978) have assumed linear interconnections for dissipative systems and have presented a criterion based on the quasidominancy condition of a single matrix within the context of both Lyapunov and IO stability. The main characteristics of this is summarized in Table 7.2.

## 7.7.2 Discussion of the Controllability and Observability of Large-Scale Systems

The controllability and observability of composite systems were considered in Section 7.4. The frequency domain approach dealing with series–parallel and closed-loop composite systems was taken up in Section 7.4.1. The necessary and sufficient conditions (Theorems 7.6 and 7.7) have been presented which depend on the parameters of system state equations and subsystems interconnections (Davison and Wang, 1975). The conditions to be checked, although computationally simple, involve both rank and eigenvalue determinations. This may very well pose severe problems for large-scale systems. This approach has been extended, in turn, by Porter (1976) within the context of general series–parallel composite systems in Section 7.4.2 and by Davison (1976, 1977) within the context of connectability in Section 7.4.3. The necessary and sufficient conditions for controllability and observability of general composite systems (Theorems 7.8 and 7.9) do not require computation of any eigenvalues, unlike the earlier results of Davison and Wang (1975). It is generally agreed that the evaluation of a matrix rank is much less time consuming than its eigenvalues. The notion of connectability was introduced in Section 7.4.3, and the large-scale composite systems controllability and observability have been derived from it (Theorems 7.12 and 7.13). The graph-theoretic approach utilized here is rather simple. However, the generation of large graphs for realistic applications with the aid of digital computers must be utilized. It has been shown that a composite system with arbitrary interconnection and any number of inputs and outputs is controllable and observable for almost all interconnection gains between subsystems, provided that the system is connectable. The application of this result to structural controllability was given in Section 7.5.3.

The structural controllability and observability of large-scale systems was discussed in Section 7.5. The original proposal of the structural controllability was due to Lin (1974) and used a graph-theoretic scheme for SISO systems. The results of Lin (1974) were extended to MIMO systems through an algebraic approach which is more tractable and simpler to use. The generic rank determination through Algorithm 7.3 is a useful computational tool in evaluating the rank of a matrix. This algorithm cannot only be used in checking structural controllability, as demonstrated in Section 7.5.2 but also in composite systems considered earlier: Theorem 7.15 due to Shields and Pearson (1976) with the aid of Algorithm 7.3 provides a simple scheme for checking the structural controllability of large-scale systems. The rank determination of usual controllability and observability matrices along with input–output connectability (Definition 7.18) are used by Davison (1976) to set up ground rules for structural controllability and observability in Section 7.5.3. The numerical Example 7.5.5 demonstrated that these criteria (Theorem 7.16 and Corollary 7.1) are fairly simple to use. Either Algorithm 7.3 or a generic rank determination scheme by Davison (1977) can be used for satisfying one of the two conditions in the proposed criteria.

Another relevant area of research is controllability under decentralized structure. Kobayashi et al. (1978) have presented necessary and sufficient conditions for the controllability under decentralized structure. A system is said to be controllable under decentralized information structure if there is a finite number $t_f > 0$ and a decentralized control law such that the final state $x(t_f) = 0$ for any initial state $x(t_o)$. Consider a decentralized control system with $N$ stations

$$\dot{x}(t) = Ax(t) + \sum_{i=1}^{N} B_i u_i(t) \qquad (7.7.16a)$$

$$y_i(t) = C_i x(t) \qquad (7.7.16b)$$

where $x(t)$, $y_i(t)$, and $u_i(t)$ are $n \times 1$, $r_i \times 1$ and $m_i \times 1$ vectors representing the system state and the $i$th station's output and control. Under a decentralized control $u_i(t) = K_i y_i(t)$, system (7.7.16) is controllable if the set of all fixed modes (Section 5.3.1)

$$\Lambda^*(C, A, B, K) = \phi \qquad (7.7.17)$$

where $\phi$ denotes an empty set. It is noted that this result is essentially that of Theorem 5.1 when dealing with decentralized stabilization. This result leads to a necessary condition for pole assignability. The interested reader is encouraged to refer to the work of Kobayashi et al. (1978).

In summary, in Sections 7.4 and 7.5 we have attempted to present an up-to-date overview on two important and fundamental issues for any systems, large or small, i.e., controllability and observability. Although the main topics, such as general composite systems, controllability and observability, and structural controllability and observability, are overviewed in some detail, the state of the art still lacks powerful computational techniques to handle very large problems.

## Problems

**7.1.** Consider a third-order system decomposed into second- and first-order subsystems:

$$\dot{x} = \begin{bmatrix} \dot{x}_1 \\ \hline \dot{x}_2 \end{bmatrix} = \begin{bmatrix} -1 & 0.1 & 0.1 \\ 0.2 & -1 & 0.5 \\ \hline 1 & 0.8 & -2 \end{bmatrix} \begin{bmatrix} x_1 \\ \hline x_2 \end{bmatrix}$$

Check whether this system is asymptotically stable in the sense of Lyapunov using Theorem 7.1.

**7.2.** Repeat Example 7.2.2. for the following nonlinear system:

$$\dot{x}_1 = -\tfrac{4}{5}x_1^5 + g_1(x,t)$$
$$\dot{x}_2 = -\tfrac{1}{5}x_2^5 + g_2(x,t)$$

where $g_i(x,t)$, $i = 1,2$, should be defined in the process.

**7.3.** For the nonlinear interconnected system

$$\dot{x}_1 = 0.2x_1 - x_2\cos x_1 + 0.1x_1\sin x_1x_2$$
$$\dot{x}_2 = x_2 - x_2\cos x_1 + 0.25x_2\cos x_1x_2$$
$$\dot{x}_3 = x_3 - x_2\sin x_1 + 0.125x_1\cos x_1x_2$$

check its stability in the sense of Lyapunov.

**7.4.** Consider the system of Figure 7.3 and let the forward path's diagonal transfer functions $G_i(x)$, $i = 1,2$, be

$$G_1(s) = 0.5/((1+2s)(1+3s)), \quad G_2(s) = 1/((1+s)(1+6s))$$

and the output functions be

$$\tilde{y}_1(t) = y_1(t) + 0.5\psi(y_2(t))$$
$$\tilde{y}_2(t) = 0.4y_2(t) + 0.8\psi(y_1(t))$$

Check for the IO stability of this system.

**7.5.** Repeat Example 7.3.2 for

$$G_1(s) = 1/((s+3)(s+5)), \quad G_2(s) = 5/((s+2)(s+4))$$
$$H_1 = 1, \quad H_2 = K_1 = 2, \quad K_2 = 0.5$$

**7.6.** Consider a system

$$\dot{x}_1 = -x_1 + 0.08x_2$$
$$\dot{x}_2 = 0.5x_1 - x_2$$

Check the stability of this system i.s.L.

**7.7.** Using the development in the proof of Theorem 7.1, prove Theorem 7.2.

**7.8.** By duality to the proof of Theorem 7.6, prove the observability part of that theorem.

**7.9.** Repeat Problem 7.8 for Theorem 7.7.

**7.10.** Consider a sixth-order system

$$
\begin{bmatrix} \dot{x}_1 \\ \dot{x}_2 \end{bmatrix} =
\left[
\begin{array}{ccc:ccc}
-1.5 & 0.2 & 0.1 & 0.2 & 0.1 & 0.1 \\
0.1 & -3 & 0.3 & 0.1 & 0.1 & 0.2 \\
0.2 & -1 & -2 & 0.2 & 0.3 & 0.4 \\
\hdashline
1 & 0 & 1 & -4 & 1 & 0 \\
0 & 1 & 0 & 0 & -2 & 0.2 \\
0.5 & 0 & 1 & -0.5 & 0.2 & -5
\end{array}
\right]
\begin{bmatrix} x_1 \\ x_2 \end{bmatrix}
$$

Is the system asymptotically connectively stable?

**C7.11.** Consider a fifth-order parallel-series composite system

$$
\begin{bmatrix} \dot{x}_1 \\ \dot{x}_2 \end{bmatrix} =
\left[ \begin{array}{ccc|cc}
-1 & 0.1 & 0.5 & 0 & 0 \\
0 & -0.5 & 0.1 & 0 & 0 \\
0.1 & 0 & -0.1 & 0 & 0 \\ \hline
0.1 & 0 & 0.1 & 0.1 & -0.2 \\
0 & 0.2 & 0 & -0.1 & -0.25
\end{array} \right]
\begin{bmatrix} x_1 \\ \hline x_2 \end{bmatrix} +
\begin{bmatrix} 1 \\ 0.2 \\ 0.4 \\ 0 \\ 1 \end{bmatrix} u
$$

$$
y = \begin{bmatrix} 1 & 0.5 & 1 & 1 & 1 \end{bmatrix} \begin{bmatrix} x_1 \\ x_2 \end{bmatrix} + [1] u
$$

Determine whether this system is controllable and/or observable.

**C7.12.** For the system of Problem C7.11, determine the controllability and observability of its closed-loop form.

**7.13.** For a system

$$
\dot{x} = \begin{bmatrix} 1 & -1 \\ 2 & 0 \end{bmatrix} x + \begin{bmatrix} 0.5 & 0.2 \\ 1 & 1 \end{bmatrix} u, \quad y = \begin{bmatrix} 0.5 & 1 \\ 1 & 0.5 \end{bmatrix} x
$$

determine its controllability and observability via Theorems 7.8 and 7.9.

**7.14.** A second-order composite system is given by

$$
\dot{x} = \begin{bmatrix} -2 & b \\ a & -1 \end{bmatrix} x + \begin{bmatrix} 1 \\ 1 \end{bmatrix} u, \quad y = \begin{bmatrix} 1 & 1 \end{bmatrix} x
$$

with unknown interconnections $a$ and $b$. Determine a region in the $(a - b)$-plane where the system is both controllable and observable.

**7.15.** A closed-loop composite system is given by

$$
\begin{bmatrix} \dot{x}_1 \\ \dot{x}_2 \end{bmatrix} =
\left[ \begin{array}{c|c} -d & -2 \\ \hline -1 & 1 \end{array} \right]
\begin{bmatrix} x_1 \\ x_2 \end{bmatrix} +
\begin{bmatrix} c \\ d \end{bmatrix} u
$$

$$
y = (d \quad -1) \begin{bmatrix} x_1 \\ x_2 \end{bmatrix} + u
$$

Determine whether the system is controllable or observable for $d \geqslant 2$ and $c \leqslant 3$.

**7.16.** Find the generic rank of the following matrix by Algorithm 7.3.

$$
A = \begin{bmatrix}
0 & x & 0 & x & x & x & 0 \\
x & x & x & 0 & 0 & 0 & 0 \\
x & x & x & 0 & 0 & 0 & 0 \\
0 & x & x & 0 & 0 & 0 & x \\
x & x & x & 0 & 0 & 0 & x \\
x & x & 0 & 0 & x & x & x \\
x & x & x & x & x & x & x
\end{bmatrix}
$$

where an $x$ represents a nonzero entry.

**7.17.** Check whether a system described by the matrices

$$(A,B) = \left( \begin{bmatrix} x & x & 0 \\ 0 & x & x \\ x & 0 & x \end{bmatrix}, \begin{bmatrix} 0 \\ x \end{bmatrix} \right)$$

is structurally controllable.

**7.18.** Determine the structural controllability and observability of the system

$$(C,A,B) = \left( \begin{bmatrix} x & 0 & x & 0 & x \\ x & x & 0 & 0 & x \end{bmatrix}, \begin{bmatrix} x & 0 & 0 & x & x \\ 0 & x & x & x & x \\ 0 & 0 & 0 & 0 & x \\ x & x & 0 & 0 & x \\ x & x & x & x & x \end{bmatrix}, \begin{bmatrix} 0 & x \\ x & x \\ 0 & 0 \\ x & x \\ x & 0 \end{bmatrix} \right)$$

by using Theorem 7.16 and Corollary 7.1.

**C7-19.** A singularly perturbed system is given by

$$\dot{x} = \begin{bmatrix} -1 & -2 \\ 0.1 & -1 \end{bmatrix} x + \begin{bmatrix} 0.2 & 0.5 & 0.2 \\ -0.5 & 1 & 0.1 \end{bmatrix} z + \begin{bmatrix} 1 & 0.5 \\ 0.2 & 1 \end{bmatrix} u$$

$$\epsilon \dot{z} = \begin{bmatrix} 0.8 & 0.5 \\ 0 & 0.2 \\ -1 & 0 \end{bmatrix} x + \begin{bmatrix} -0.8 & 0 & 0.2 \\ 0 & -2 & 0.2 \\ -1 & 0.1 & -1 \end{bmatrix} z + \begin{bmatrix} 1 & 0 \\ 0 & 1 \\ 1 & 0 \end{bmatrix} u$$

Determine its controllability.

# References

Araki, M. 1976. Input-Output stability of composite feedback systems. *IEEE Trans. Aut. Cont.* AC-21:254–259.

Araki, M. 1978. Stability of large-scale nonlinear systems—Quadratic-order theory of composite-system method using M-matrices. *IEEE Trans. Aut. Cont.* AC-23:129–142.

Araki, M., and Kondo, B. 1972. Stability and transient behavior of composite nonlinear systems. *IEEE Trans. Aut. Cont.* AC-17:537–541.

Bailey, F. N. 1966. The application of Lyapunov's second method to interconnected systems. *SIAM J. Contr.* 3:443–462.

Bhandarkar, M. V., and Fahmy, M. M. 1972. Controllability of tandem connected systems. *IEEE Trans. Aut. Cont.* AC-17:150–151.

Birkhoff, G., and Rota, G. C. 1962. *Ordinary Differential Equations.* Blaisdell, Waltham, MA.

Brasch, F. M.; Howze, J. W.; and Pearson, J. B. 1971. On the controllability of composite systems. *IEEE Trans. Aut. Cont.* AC-16:205–206.

Brockett, R. W. 1970. *Finite Dimensional Linear Systems.* Wiley, New York.

Chang, K. W. 1972. Singular perturbation of a general boundary value problem. *SIAM J. Math. Anal.* 3:520–526.

Chen, C. T., and Desoer, C. A. 1967. Controllability and observability of composite systems. *IEEE Trans. Aut. Cont.* AC-12:402–409.

Chow, J. H., and Kokotović, P. V. 1976. A decomposition of near-optimum regulars for systems with slow and fast modes. *IEEE Trans. Aut. Cont.* AC-21:701–705.

Cook, P. A. 1974. On the stability of interconnected systems. *Int. J. Contr.* 20:407–416.

Corfmat, J. P., and Morse, A. S. 1975. Structurally controllable and structurally canonical systems. Internal Report, Dept. Engr. and Appl. Sci., Yale University, New Haven, CT.

Corfmat, J. P.,and Morse, A. S. 1976. Control of linear system through specified input channels. *SIAM J. Contr.* 14.

Cuk, S. M., and Šiljak, D. D. 1973. Decomposition-aggregation stability analysis of the spinning skylab. *Proc. 7th Asilomar Conf. on Circuits, Systems and Computers* (Pacific Grove, CA).

Davison, E. J. 1976. Connectability and structural controllability of composite systems. *Proc. IFAC Symposium on Large Scale Systems* (Udine, Italy) pp. 241–245.

Davison, E. J. 1977. Connectability and structural controllability of composite systems. *IFAC J. Automatica* 13:109–123.

Davison, E. J., and Kunze, E. G. 1970. Some sufficient conditions for the global and local controllability of nonlinear time-varying systems. *SIAM J. Contr.* 8:489–498.

Davison, E. J., and Wang, S. H. 1975. New results on the controllability and observability of composite systems. *IEEE Trans. Aut. Cont.* AC-20:123–128.

Deo, N. 1974. *Graphy Theory with Applications to Engineering and Computer Science*, pp. 206–226. Prentice-Hall, Englewood Cliffs, NJ.

Desoer, C. A., and Vidyasagar, M. 1975. *Feedback Systems: Input-Output Properties*. Academic Press, New York.

Frobenius, G. 1912. Uber matrizen mit nicht negativen elementen. *Berlin Akad.* 23:456–477.

Gantmacher, F. R. 1959. *The Theory of Matrices*. Chealsea, London, England.

Gilbert, E. G. 1963. Controllability and Observability in multivariable control systems. *SIAM J. Contr.* 2:128–151.

Glover, K., and Silverman, L. M. 1975. Characterization of structural controllability. Internal Report, Dept. Elec. Engr., Univ. S. California, Los Angeles, CA.

Grasselli, O. M. 1972. Controllability and observability of series connections of systems. *Ricerche di Automatica* 3:44–53.

Grujić, L. T. and Šiljak, D. D. 1973a. On the stability of discrete composite systems. *IEEE Trans. Aut. Cont.* AC-18:522–524.

Grujić, L. T., and Šiljak, D. D. 1973b. Asymptotic stability and unstability of large-scale system. *IEEE Trans. Aut. Cont.* AC-18:636–645.

Hautus, M. L. J. 1975. Input regularity of cascaded systems. *IEEE Trans. Aut. Cont.* AC-20:120–123.

Kalman, R. E. 1961. Contribution to the theory of optimal control. *Bol. Soc. Math. Mexicana* 5:102–119.

Klamka, J. 1972. Uncontrollability and unobservability of multivariable systems. *IEEE Trans. Aut. Cont.* AC-17:725–726.

Klamka, J. 1974. Uncontrollability of composite systems. *IEEE Trans. Aut. Cont.* AC-19:280–281.

Klamka, J. 1975a. On the global controllability of perturbed nonlinear systems. *IEEE Trans. Aut. Cont.* AC-20:170–172.

Klamka, J. 1975b. Controllability of nonlinear systems with delay in control. *IEEE Trans. Aut. Cont.* AC-20:702–704.

Kobayashi, H.; Hanafusa, H.; and Yoshikawa, T. 1978. Controllability under decentralized information structure. *IEEE Trans. Aut. Cont.* AC-23:182–188.

Kokotović, P. V., and Haddad, A. H. 1975. Controllability and time-optimal control of systems with slow and fast modes. *IEEE Trans. Aut. Cont.* AC-20:111–113.

König, D. 1931. Graphak es matrixok. *Mater Fiziol Lapok.* 38:116–119.

Kriendler, E., and Sarachik, P. E. 1964. On the concepts of controllability and observability of linear systems. *IEEE Trans. Aut. Cont.* AC-9:129–136.

Lasley, E. L., and Michel, A. N. 1976a. Input-Output stability of interconnected systems. *IEEE Trans. Aut. Cont.* AC-21:84–89.

Lasley, E. L., and Michel, A. N. 1976b. $L_\infty^-$ and $\ell_\infty^-$ stability of interconnected systems. *IEEE Trans. Cir. Syst.* CAS-23:261–270.

Lee, E. B., and Markus, L. 1967. *Foundations of Optimal Control Theory*. Wiley, New York.

Lefschetz, S. 1965. *Stability of Nonlinear Control Systems*. Academic Press, New York.

Lin, C. T. 1974. Structural controllability. *IEEE Trans. Aut. Cont.* AC-19:201–208.

Liu, C. L. 1968. *Introduction to Combinatorial Mathematics*, chapter 11. McGraw-Hill, New York.

Matrosov, V. M. 1972. Method of Lyapunov vector functions in feedback systems. *Aut. Remote Contr.* 33:1458–1469.

Michel, A. N. 1975a. Stability and trajectory behavior of composite systems. *IEEE Trans. Cir. Syst.* CAS-22:305–312.

Michel, A. N. 1975b. Stability analysis of stochastic large-scale systems. *Z. Angew. Math. Mech.* 55:93–105.

Michel, A. N., and Porter, D. W. 1972. Stability analysis of composite systems. *IEEE Trans. Aut. Cont.* AC-17:111–116.

Mirza, K., and Womack, B. F. 1979. On the controllability of a class of nonlinear systems. *IEEE Trans. Aut. Cont.* AC-17:531–534. (For modifications see *IEEE Trans. Aut. Cont.* AC-19:459–460).

Morari, M.; Stephanopoulos, G.; Shields, R. W.; and Pearson, J. B. 1978. Comments on finding the generic rank of a structured matrix, and authors' response. *IEEE Trans. Aut. Cont.* AC-23:509–510.

Moylan, P. J. and Hill, D. J. 1978. Stability criteria for large-scale systems. *IEEE Trans. Aut. Cont.* AC-23:143–149.

O'Malley, R. E. 1974. *Introduction to Singular Perturbations*. Academic Press, New York.

Perkins, W. R. and Cruz, J. B., Jr. 1969. Engineering of Dynamic Systems, pp. 418–421. Wiley, New York.

Piontkovskii, A. A., and Rutkovskaya, L. D. 1967. Investigation of certain stability-theory problems by the vector Lyapunov function method. *Aut. Remote Contr.* 28:1422–1429.

Porter, B. 1976. Necessary and sufficient conditions for the controllability and observability of general composite systems. *Proc. IFAC Symposium on Large Scale Systems* (Udine, Italy), pp. 265–269.

Porter, D. W., and Michel, A. N. 1974. Input-output stability of time-varying non-linear multiloop feedback systems. *IEEE Trans. Aut. Cont.* AC-19:422–427.

Prescott, R., and Pearson, J. B. 1981. Private communication, Rice University, Houston, TX.

Rasmussen, R. D., and Michel, A. N. 1976a. On vector Lyapunov function for stochastic dynamical systems. *IEEE Trans. Aut. Cont.* AC-21:250–254.

Rasmussen, R. D., and Michel, A. N. 1976b. Stability of interconnected dynamical systems described on Banach spaces. *IEEE Trans. Aut. Cont.* AC-21:464–471.

Rosenbrock, H. H. 1960. An automatic method for finding the greatest or least value of a function. *Computer J.* 3:175–184.

Rosenbrock, H. H. 1968a. Relatively prime polynomial matrices. *Electronics Letters* 4:227–228.

Rosenbrock, H. H. 1968b. Some properties of relatively prime polynomial matrices. *Electronics Letters.* 4:374–375.

Rosenbrock, H. H. 1968c. Generalized resultant. *Electronics Letters.* 4:250–251.

Rosenbrock, H. H. 1970. *State Space and Multivariable Theory.* Nelson and Sons, London.

Sandell, N. R.; Varaiya, P.; Athans, M. and Safonov, M. G. 1978. Survey of decentralized control methods for large scale systems. *IEEE Trans. Aut. Cont.* AC-23:108–128.

Sannuti, P. 1977. On the controllability of singularly perturbed systems. *IEEE Trans. Aut. Cont.* AC-22:622–624.

Sezer, E., and Hüseyin, Ö. 1977. A counter-example on "On the controllability of composite systems." *IEEE Trans. Aut. Cont.* AC-22:683–684.

Sezer, E., and Hüseyin, Ö. 1979. On the controllability of composite systems. *IEEE Trans. Aut. Cont.* AC-24:327–329.

Shields, R. W., and Pearson, J. B. 1976. Structural controllability of multiinput linear systems. *IEEE Trans. Aut. Cont.* AC-21:203–212.

Šiljak, D. D. 1972a. Stability of large-scale systems. *Proc. 5th IFAC World Congress* (Paris, France).

Šiljak, D. D. 1972b. Stability of large-scale systems under structural perturbations. *IEEE Trans. Syst. Man. Cyber.* SMC-2:657–663.

Šiljak, D. D. 1974a. Large-scale systems: Complexity, stability, reliability. *Proc. Utah St. Univ.* (Ames Research Ctr. Seminar Workshop on Large Scale Dynamic Systems, Utah State Univ., Logan, Utah).

Šiljak, D. D. 1974b. On the connective stability and instability of competitive equilibrium *Proc. 1974 JACC* (Austin, TX.)

Šiljak, D. D. 1975. When is a complex system stable? Math. *Biosci.* 25:25–50.

Šiljak, D. D. 1976. Large-scale systems: Complexity, stability, reliability. *J. Franklin Inst.* 30:49–69.

Šiljak, D. D. 1978. *Large-Scale Dynamic Systems: Stability and Structure*, pp. 68–74. Elsevier North Holland, New York.

Suda, N. 1973. Analysis of large-scale systems by decomposition. *Aut. Cont. Technique* 15:3–18 (in Japanese).

Sundareshan, M. K., and Vidyasagar, M. 1975. $L_2$-stability of large-scale dynamical systems criteria via positive operator theory. Technical Report, Faculty of Engr., Concordia Univ., Canada.

Thompson, W. E. 1970. Exponential stability of interconnected systems. *IEEE Trans. Aut. Cont.* AC-15:504–506.

Wang, S. H., and Davison, E. J. 1973a. On the controllability and observability of composite systems. *IEEE Trans. Aut. Cont.* AC-18:74–75.

Wang, S. H., and Davison, E. J. 1973b. On the stabilization of decentralized control systems. *IEEE Trans. Aut. Cont.* AC-18:473–478.

Willems, J. C. 1970. Stability Theory of Dynamical Systems. Nelson, London.

Wolovich, W. A., and Huang, H. L. 1974. Composite system controllability and observability. *IFAC J. Automatica* 10:209–212.

Yackel, R. A., and Kokotović, P. V. 1973. A boundary layer method for the matrix Riccati equation. *IEEE Trans. Aut. Cont.* AC-18:17–24.

Yonemura, Y., and Ito, M. 1972. Controllability of composite systems in tandem connection. *IEEE Trans. Aut. Cont.* AC-17:722–724.

Zames, G. 1966. On input-output stability of time-varying nonlinear systems. Parts I and II. *IEEE Trans. Aut. Cont.* AC-11:228–238, 465–476.

# Solutions and Answers
# to Selected Problems

## Chapter 1

**1.2** The concept of centrality holds for (**a**) and (**d**).

**1.3** The water resources allocation of the state can be considered as a hierarchical structure, Figure P1.3.

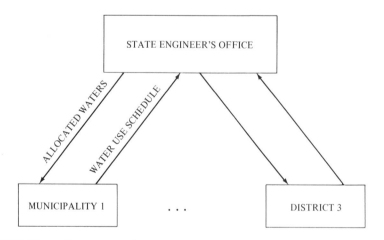

**Figure P1.3** Hierarchical structure of water resources problem.

## Chapter 2

**2.2** $\lambda\{A\} = \{-1.208, 0.622, -0.843\}$ Modal matrix is

$$M = \begin{bmatrix} -0.04 & 0.34 & -0.008 \\ -0.81 & 0.71 & -0.808 \\ -0.58 & 0.61 & 0.588 \end{bmatrix}$$

A first-order aggregated model is $\dot{z} = 0.622z - 0.089u$. This reduced model is not dynamically exact.

**2.4** An aggregation matrix $C = [1 \quad 0]$ will provide a reduced model $\dot{z} = -z + u$, and $C = [-1/8 \quad 9/8]$ will give $\dot{z} = -10z + u$. Both models are aggregated exactly, i.e., $FC = CA$, and $G = CB$.

**2.6** The modal matrix $M$ is

$$M_l = M_3$$

$$M = \begin{bmatrix} v_1 & | & w_1 & | & \xi_1 & | & \nu_1 \end{bmatrix} = \begin{bmatrix} v_{11} & w_{11} & \xi_{11} & \nu_{11} \\ v_{12} & w_{12} & \xi_{12} & \nu_{12} \\ v_{13} & w_{13} & \xi_{13} & \nu_{13} \\ v_{14} & w_{14} & \xi_{14} & \nu_{14} \end{bmatrix}$$

where a $2 \times 2$ or a $3 \times 3$ aggregated model can be obtained using $F = M_l P \Lambda P^T M_l^{-1}$, $G = M_l PM^{-1}B$, $C = M_l PM^{-1}$, where

$$P = \begin{bmatrix} 1 & 0 & 0 & 0 \\ 0 & 1 & 0 & 0 \\ 0 & 0 & 1 & 0 \end{bmatrix}, \quad \Lambda = \begin{bmatrix} b & c & 0 & 0 \\ -c & b & 0 & 0 \\ 0 & 0 & a & 1 \\ 0 & 0 & 0 & a \end{bmatrix}$$

**2.9** $\lambda\{A\} = \{-1 \pm j, -10\}$, the modal matrix is

$$M = \begin{bmatrix} 0 & -0.5 & -0.0099499 \\ -0.5 & 0.5 & 0.099499 \\ 1 & 0 & -0.99499 \end{bmatrix}$$

and a second-order aggregated model can be obtained:

$$\dot{z} = \begin{bmatrix} 0 & 1 \\ -2 & -2 \end{bmatrix} z + \begin{bmatrix} 1 \\ 1.5 \end{bmatrix} u$$

**2.11** The transformation matrix $P$ is given by

$$P = \begin{bmatrix} 0.5 & 9 & 2 & 1 \\ 0 & 8.94 & 2 & 1 \\ 0 & 0 & -7.43 & 1 \\ 0 & 0 & 0 & 1 \end{bmatrix}$$

with an $R = [I_2 \mid 0_{2\times2}]$, the aggregation matrices are

$$F = \begin{bmatrix} -1 & 0.95 \\ -1 & 0.89 \end{bmatrix}, \quad G = \begin{bmatrix} 1 \\ 1 \end{bmatrix}$$

$$C = \begin{bmatrix} 0.5 & 9 & 2 & 1 \\ 0 & 0.89 & 2 & 1 \end{bmatrix}, \quad C_l^T = \begin{bmatrix} 0.167 \\ 0.624 \end{bmatrix}$$

**2.15**  Consider a $2 \times 1$ partition,

$$
A = \left[ \begin{array}{cc|c}
0 & 1 & 0 \\
0 & 0 & 1 \\
\hline
-1 & -a & -b
\end{array} \right]
$$

Then $r = 0$ and $R = b$; hence, $r/R = 0/b \ll 1$. $(n_1 \varepsilon_{12} \varepsilon_{21})/R^2 = 2a/b^2 \ll 1$ implies that for weak coupling we need to have $2a \ll b^2$. To ensure this one can let $2a \leqslant b^2/10$ or one can have a region as shown in Figure P2.15.

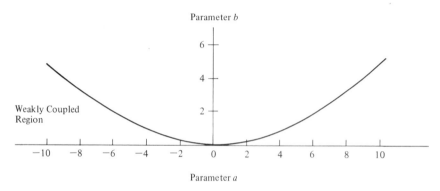

Figure P2.15 Desired regions for weak coupling.

**C2.16**  The eigenvalues of matrix $A$ are $\lambda\{A\} = \{30, -20, -15.4, -1.1 \pm j1.2, 0.0313 \pm j0.43, -1.9\}$. A three fast and five slow modes separation can be sought. After ten iterations, the $E$ interconnection matrices turn out to be

$$
C_{ij} = 10^{-4} \left[ \begin{array}{ccccc}
-0.0194 & 0.0 & 0.0625 & -0.047 & 0.0 \\
-0.0316 & 0.0 & -0.17 & -0.083 & 0.0 \\
-0.189 & 0.0474 & 5.25 & -0.35 & 0.0231
\end{array} \right]
$$

$$
E_{ij} = \left[ \begin{array}{ccc}
0.0 & 0.0 & 0.0 \\
-0.029 & 0.016 & 0.0 \\
0.87 & -0.48 & -0.00312 \\
-24.7 & 13.7 & 0.089 \\
-10.9 & 6.05 & 0.039
\end{array} \right]
$$

which indicates that the interactions have been weakened in the most part. The slow and fast subsystems are

$$
\text{Slow:} \quad \dot{\xi}_{10} = \left[ \begin{array}{ccccc}
-20 & -1 & -0.007 & 0 & 0 \\
1 & 30 & 1.13 & 0 & -0.001 \\
-0.22 & -0.29 & -3.34 & -0.13 & 0.023 \\
7.4 & -2.15 & 40.7 & -0.16 & -0.61 \\
1.36 & -50.5 & 13.1 & 6.74 & -15.6
\end{array} \right] \xi_{10}
$$

$$
\text{Fast:} \quad \varepsilon \dot{\eta}_{10} = \begin{bmatrix} 1.51 & -1.07 & 0.0458 \\ 2.7 & -1.77 & 0.1018 \\ 10.9 & -10.04 & -0.0107 \end{bmatrix} \eta_{10}
$$

**C2.17** $\lambda\{A\} = \{-0.123 \pm j0.312, -2.5 \pm j24.5, -6.25 \pm j62.20\}$ for a $2 \times 4$ partition, $r = 0.336$, $R = 24.6$, $\varepsilon_{12} = 0.0706$, $\varepsilon_{21} = 0$, $n_1 = 2$, then $(r/R) = 0.014 \ll 1$, $n_1 \varepsilon_{12} \varepsilon_{21} / R^2 = 0 \ll 1$. Hence the system is weakly coupled.

**2.18** $\hat{z} = \hat{x}/5$, $\dot{\hat{x}} = -4/5\hat{x}$ leading to $\hat{x}(t) = -\exp(-4/5t)$, $\hat{z}(t) = -1/5 \exp(-4/5t)$. Boundary layer $\eta = z - \hat{z} = z - \hat{x}/5$, $d\eta(\tau)/d\tau = -5\eta(\tau)$, $\eta(\tau) = 6/5\exp(-5\tau)$ where $\tau = t/\varepsilon$. Thus $z(t) = -1/5 \exp(-4/5t) + 6/5\exp(-5/\varepsilon t)$.

**2.19**

$$
P(0,2) = \begin{bmatrix} -A_0 & E_1 & 0 \\ 0 & -A_1 & E_2 \end{bmatrix}
$$

$$
= \begin{bmatrix} -1 & 0 & 0 & k & 0 & 0 \\ -1 & -1 & -k & 0 & 0 & 0 \\ 0 & 0 & -k & -1 & 0 & 1 \\ 0 & 0 & -1 & -1 & 1 & 0 \end{bmatrix}
$$

If rank $(P(0,2)) = 4$, the system is solvable. This implies that $k \neq 1$. For conditionability rank $(Q(0,2)) = 2$, where

$$
Q(0,2) = \begin{bmatrix} 0 & k \\ -k & 0 \\ -k & -1 \\ -1 & -1 \end{bmatrix}
$$

here for all values of $k$, the system is conditionable.

## Chapter 3

**3.1** The time moments are $c_o = 1$, $c_1 = 1$, $c_2 = -1$, $c_3 = -3,\ldots$, $\hat{a}_1$ and $\hat{a}_2$ coefficient vectors are

$$
\hat{a}_1 = C_{21}^{-1}\hat{c}_2 = \begin{bmatrix} -1 & -1 \\ 1 & -1 \end{bmatrix}^{-1}\begin{bmatrix} -1 \\ -3 \end{bmatrix} = \begin{bmatrix} a_{12} \\ a_{13} \end{bmatrix} = \begin{bmatrix} -1 \\ 2 \end{bmatrix}
$$

$$
\hat{a}_2 = \hat{c}_1 - C_{11}\hat{a}_1 = \begin{bmatrix} 1 \\ 1 \end{bmatrix} - \begin{bmatrix} 0 & 0 \\ -1 & 0 \end{bmatrix}\begin{bmatrix} -1 \\ 2 \end{bmatrix} = \begin{bmatrix} a_{21} \\ a_{22} \end{bmatrix} = \begin{bmatrix} 1 \\ 0 \end{bmatrix}
$$

Hence

$$
R_2(s) = 1/(1 - s + 2s^2)
$$

**3.2**  The moments are $c_o = 2$, $c_1 = \frac{3}{2}$, $c_2 = \frac{5}{12}$, $c_3 = -\frac{5}{12}$, $c_4 = -\frac{11}{18}$, $c_5 = -\frac{23}{144}$, etc. A second-order and a third-order reduced model are obtained,

$$R_2(s) = (3.55 - 0.99s)/(1.774 - 1.82s + s^2)$$

$$R_3(s) = (-0.208 + 3.885s - 0.86s^2)$$
$$/(-0.104 + 2.02s - 1.924s^2 + s^3)$$

In this case the full model and both reduced models are unstable.

**C3.4**

$$\hat{G}(s) = (220s^3 + 80s^2 + s + 1)/(210s^4 + 80s^3 + 35s^2 + 4s + 1)$$

| $\hat{\alpha}$-table | | | $\hat{\beta}$-table | |
|---|---|---|---|---|
| 210 | 35 | 1 | 220 | 1 |
| 80 | 4 | 0 | 80 | 1 |
| $\hat{\alpha}_1 = 2.625$ | 24.5 | 1 | $\hat{\beta}_1 = 2.75$     $-10$ | 0 |
| $\hat{\alpha}_2 = 3.2653$ | 0.7347 | 0 | $\hat{\beta}_2 = 3.2653$     $-2.2653$ | 0 |
| $\hat{\alpha}_3 = 33.3472$ | 1 | | $\hat{\beta}_3 = 13.611$     0 | |
| $\hat{\alpha}_4 = 0.7347$ | | | $\hat{\beta}_4 = -2.2653$ | |

using the relations (3.4.14)–(3.4.16),

$$\hat{R}_2(s) = (8.9796s + 3.2653)/(8.5714s^2 + 3.2653s + 1)$$

$$\hat{R}_3(s) = \frac{299.4445s^2 + 108.8886s - 10.861}{285.8322s^3 + 108.8886s^2 + 35.9722s + 1}$$

hence

$$R_2(s) = (8.9796 + 3.2653s)/(s^2 + 3.2653s + 8.5714)$$

$$R_3(s) = \frac{-10.861s^2 + 108.886s + 299.4445}{s^3 + 35.9722s^2 + 108.8886s + 285.8322}$$

**3.5**  The system is unstable with closed-loop poles at $1, -1 \pm j$.

(i) *Padé.*  $c_o = -3, c_1 = -2.5, c_3 = -2.75, \ldots$. A second-order reduced model is $R_2(s) = (0.2609 + 3.609s)/(-0.087 - 1.13s + s^2)$ with poles at $-0.0723$ and $1.203$.

(ii) *Routh.*  Let $\tilde{G}(s) = G(s+2) = (s^2 + 9s + 15)/(s^3 + 7s^2 + 16s + 10)$ and apply Routh's $\alpha - \beta$ approach. From $\hat{\alpha}$-table $\hat{\alpha}_1 = 0.625$, $\hat{\alpha}_2 = 2.51, \ldots$, and from $\hat{\beta}$-table $\hat{\beta}_1 = 0.9375$, $\hat{\beta}_2 = 1.412, \ldots$. Then $\tilde{R}_2(s) = (2.35 + 1.412s)/(1.57 + 2.51s + s^2)$ and

$R_2(s) = \tilde{R}_2(s - 2) = (1.412s - 0.474)/(s^2 - 1.49s + 0.55)$, which leads to poles at 0.816 and 0.6741.

(iii) *Modal-Continued Fraction.* To preserve $s = 1$, $R_1(s) = 3.6/(s - 1)$ by first Cauer's method and $R_1(s) = 1/(s - 1)$ by second Cauer's method. A second-order reduced model is not possible, since the pair of complex poles are on the left-half plane, and one cannot split a pair of complex conjugate poles.

**3.7** Let $R_2(s) = (1 + c_1 s)/(1 + d_1 s + d_2 s^2)$ with $d_1 = 18$. For the polynomial $1 + 18s + d_2 s^2 = 0$ to have a root $s_1 = -2$, $d_2 = 35/4 = 8.75$. To find $c_1$, $P_2 = Q_2$ equation must be set up, i.e., $1171 = 489.2 + 4c_1^2$ or $c_1 = 13.056$. Hence, $R_2(s) = (1 + 13.056s)/(1 + 18s + 8.75s^2)$.

**3.9** Roots of the characteristic equation are $-1 \pm j2, -10$. Thus a second-order reduced model is sought.

(i) *Padé – Modal.* The new characteristic polynomial is $(s + 1 + j2)(s + 1 - j2) = s^2 + 2s + 5$, i.e., $b_o = 5$ and $b_1 = 2$. The time moments of the systems are $c_o = \frac{1}{25}$, $c_1 = \frac{1}{50}$, $c_2 = \frac{1}{2500}$, etc. Hence the coefficients of the reduced model's numerator are obtained from

$$\begin{bmatrix} a_o \\ a_1 \end{bmatrix} = \begin{bmatrix} \frac{1}{25} & 0 \\ \frac{1}{50} & \frac{1}{25} \end{bmatrix} \begin{bmatrix} 5 \\ 2 \end{bmatrix} = \begin{bmatrix} 0.2 \\ 0.18 \end{bmatrix}$$

thus

$$R_2(s) = (0.2 + 0.18s)/(s^2 + 2s + 5)$$

(ii) *Padé-Routh.* Using $\hat{G}(s) = (1 + 2s + 2s^2)/(1 + 12s + 25s^2 + 50s^3)$, $\alpha_1 = 2$, $\alpha_2 = 2.5$ and hence $Q_2(s) = s^2 + \alpha_2 s + \alpha_1 \alpha_2 = s^2 + 2.5s + 5$. The coefficients of the numerator are obtained from, $a_o = b_o c_o = 5(0.04) = 0.2$ and $a_1 = b_o c_1 + b_1 c_o = 5(0.02) + 2.5(0.04) = 0.2$. Thus,

$$R_2(s) = (0.2 + 0.2s)/(s^2 + 2.5s + 5)$$

**C3.10**

$$H(s) = \left( A_{21} + A_{22}s + A_{23}s^3 \right)/\left( a_1 + a_2 s + a_3 s^2 + a_4 s^3 \right)$$

$$H_1 = A_{11} A_{21}^{-1} = \begin{bmatrix} -3 & 5 \\ 4.2 & -24 \end{bmatrix}, \quad A_{31} = \begin{bmatrix} 660 & 0 \\ -516 & 272 \end{bmatrix}$$

$$H_2 = A_{21} A_{31}^{-1} = \begin{bmatrix} 0.9385 & 0.73529 \\ 1.49866 & 1.10294 \end{bmatrix}$$

Then,

$$M_2(s) = H_2(sI + H_1H_2)^{-1}$$
$$= \frac{\begin{bmatrix} 0.9385s + 0.16041 & 0.73529s + 0.13369 \\ 1.49866s + 0.28072 & 1.10294s + 0.20054 \end{bmatrix}}{s^2 + 0.623s + 0.0802}$$

## Chapter 4

**C4.1** The goal coordination with Riccati formulation at the first level and a conjugate gradient iteration at the second level can be used. The initial variables were chosen:

$$x_1(0) = \begin{bmatrix} 1 \\ 0 \end{bmatrix}, \quad \alpha_1(0) = \begin{bmatrix} 1 \\ 1 \end{bmatrix}, \quad z_1(0) = \begin{bmatrix} 0 \\ 0 \end{bmatrix}, \quad S_1 = \text{diag}(2,4)$$

$$x_2(0) = \begin{bmatrix} 1 \\ 0 \end{bmatrix}, \quad \alpha_2(0) = \begin{bmatrix} 1 \\ 1 \end{bmatrix}, \quad z_2(0) = \begin{bmatrix} 0.5 \\ 0 \end{bmatrix}, \quad S_2 = \text{diag}(4,2)$$

The Riccati matrices were solved using a forth-order Runge-Kutta method and then were fitted into third-order polynomials using

**Figure PC4.1** Normalized interaction error versus iteration.

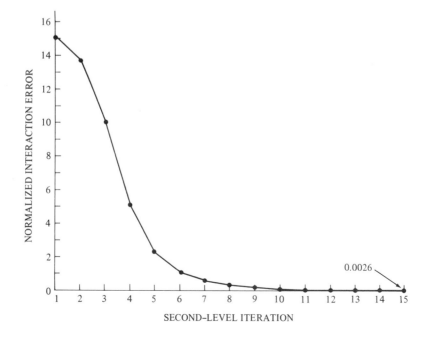

Chebyschev method:

$$K_1(t) = \begin{bmatrix} 0.36 + 0.107t - 0.034t^2 & -0.18 - 0.045t + 0.016t^2 \\ -0.18 - 0.045t + 0.016t^2 & 0.89 + 0.273t - 0.086t^2 \end{bmatrix}$$

$$K_2(t) = \begin{bmatrix} 0.62 + 0.2t - 0.061t^2 & -0.092 - 0.023t + 0.008t^2 \\ -0.092 - 0.023t + 0.008t^2 & 0.445 + 0.137t - 0.043t^2 \end{bmatrix}$$

The normalized interaction error reduced from 15.12 to 0.0026 in 15 iterations as shown in Figure PC4.1.

**C4.4** For initial conditions $x_1^T(0) = [1 \quad 0]$, $x_2^T(0) = [0.5 \quad -1 \quad 0]$, initial Lagrange multipliers $\alpha_1^T(0) = [0.5 \quad 0.5]$ and $\alpha_2^T(0) =$

**Figure PC4.4** Normalized interaction error versus iteration.

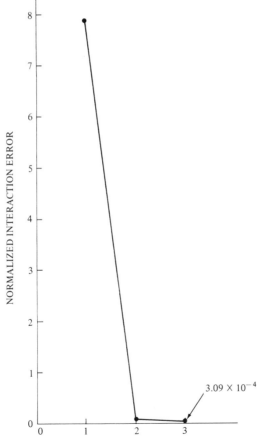

INTERACTION PREDICTION ITERATIONS

$[0.2 \quad 0 \quad 0.1]$ and initial interaction vectors $z_1^T(0) =$ $[-0.45 \quad -0.45]$ and $z_2^T(0) = [0.2 \quad 0.1 \quad 0]$, the interaction prediction resulted an interaction error of $3.09 \times 10^{-4}$ in three iterations as shown in Figure PC4.4.

**4.6** Noninteracting AMREs lead to $k_1 = 2.73$ and $k_2 = 4.24$, $J^* = 3.4841$. Neutral interaction for $g_{11} = g_{22} = 0$, $g_{12} = -1.55g_{21}$. For an interaction

$$G = \begin{bmatrix} 4 & 5 \\ 4 & 8 \end{bmatrix}, \quad S = \begin{bmatrix} 0 & -1.35 \\ 1.35 & 0 \end{bmatrix}$$

$$K + \hat{K} = \begin{bmatrix} 1.09 & -0.68 \\ -0.67 & 1.18 \end{bmatrix}$$

which lead to $\hat{J} = 0.4613$, hence a beneficial $G$ with $\rho = -0.8676$. The corrector component of control is

$$u^c = -B^p P x = -\begin{bmatrix} 2.875 & 3.5 \\ 2.2 & 4.54 \end{bmatrix}\begin{bmatrix} 2.73 & 0 \\ 0 & 4.24 \end{bmatrix}x$$

$$= -\begin{bmatrix} 7.85 & 14.6 \\ 6 & 19.24 \end{bmatrix}x$$

For a nonbeneficial interaction, try

$$G = \begin{bmatrix} 0 & -10 \\ 1 & 0 \end{bmatrix}$$

which leads to

$$S = \begin{bmatrix} 0 & -11.93 \\ 11.93 & 0 \end{bmatrix}, \quad K + \hat{K} = \begin{bmatrix} 1.45 & 1.28 \\ 1.28 & 10.65 \end{bmatrix}$$

and $\hat{J} = 7.3316 > J^* = 3.4841$. The upper value $\rho \leqslant 2.42$ and $\rho = 1.1043$. The $u^c$ control is

$$u^c = \begin{bmatrix} -3.03 & 1.67 \\ 0.69 & 2.35 \end{bmatrix}x \text{ and } u = u^c + u^l = \begin{bmatrix} -5.76 & 1.67 \\ 0.69 & -1.89 \end{bmatrix}x.$$

**4.7** For noninteraction case, $K = \text{diag}(2.414, 2.414)$ then $J^* = 1.207$. For $b = -a$, the interconnection is neutral. For other cases, the solution of (4.4.41) leads to

$$S = \begin{bmatrix} 0 & 1.207(a-b) \\ -1.207(a-b) & 0 \end{bmatrix}$$

then

$$\hat{K} = (S - KG)(A + G)^{-1} = \frac{1.207(a+b)}{1-ab}\begin{bmatrix} b & -1 \\ -1 & a \end{bmatrix}$$

hence,

$$\hat{J} = 1/2 x^T(0)(K + \hat{K})x(0) = 1.207 + 1.207(ab + b^2)/(1-ab)$$

Hence, for $\hat{J} - J^* > 0$, $G$ would be nonbeneficial, and for $\hat{J} - J^* < 0$, $G$ would be beneficial. This indicates that the quantity $1.207b^2 + 2.207ab - 1$ would be positive or negative, respectively. The regions of the $(b - a)$ plane are shown in Figure P4.7.

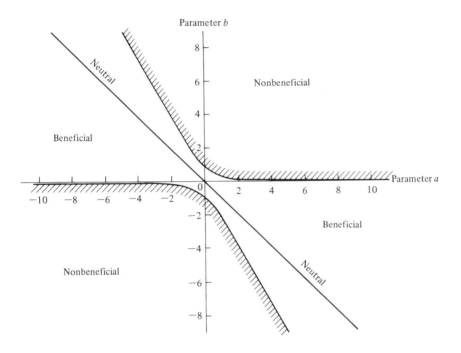

**Figure P4.7** Desired regions for different interactions.

**C4.10** For a $2 \times 3$ decomposition,

$$K = \text{Block-Diag}\left\{\begin{bmatrix} 0.099 & 0.0028 \\ 0.0028 & 0.2503 \end{bmatrix}, \begin{bmatrix} 0.9167 & 0 & 0.167 \\ 0 & 1.0 & 0 \\ 0.167 & 0 & 1.167 \end{bmatrix}\right\}$$

$$\hat{K} = \begin{bmatrix} 0.0374 & -0.00106 & 0.0293 & 0.008 & -0.1818 \\ -0.00106 & 0.2 & 0.0421 & -0.4 & 0.01407 \\ 0.0293 & 0.0421 & 0.034 & -0.036 & -0.0216 \\ 0.008 & -0.4 & -0.036 & 0.0016 & -0.036 \\ -0.1818 & 0.01407 & -0.0216 & -0.036 & -0.0216 \end{bmatrix}$$

$\hat{J}$ for $x_o^T = (1 \quad 1 \quad 1 \quad 1 \quad 1)$ is $\hat{J} = 1.42727$. $J^* = J_1^* + J_2^* = 0.17743793 + 1.708333 = 1.885771$ and $\rho = -0.243137$. The optimum (centralized) Riccati matrix is

$$K_f = \begin{bmatrix} 0.13434 & 0.00382 & 0.0275 & 0.0037 & -0.1766 \\ 0.00382 & 0.3727 & 0.03125 & -0.2855 & 0.002257 \\ 0.0275 & 0.03125 & 0.9454 & -0.0182 & 0.1481 \\ 0.0037 & -0.2855 & -0.0182 & 1.0 & -0.014 \\ -0.1766 & 0.002257 & 0.1481 & -0.014 & 1.1325 \end{bmatrix}$$

then $J^o = 1.515431$. Since $J^* > J^o$, the interaction $G$ matrix is beneficial. The closed-loop hierarchically controlled system state equation is

$$\dot{x} = \left[A - (B + B^p)P\right]x$$

$$= \begin{bmatrix} -5.094 & 0.19736 & 0 & 0.08137 & 0 \\ 0.00011 & -2 & 0 & -1.376 & 0 \\ 0.00528 & 0.00015 & -1 & 0.001886 & 1 \\ 0.000418 & 0.000012 & 0 & -2.05 & 0 \\ -0.0155 & -0.00044 & -0.5 & -0.0198 & -1 \end{bmatrix} x$$

with

$$P = R^{-1}B^T K = \begin{bmatrix} 0.099 & 0.00279 & 0 & 0 & 0 \\ 0 & 0 & 0 & 1 & 0 \end{bmatrix}$$

**4.11** The $K_i(k)$ and $P_i(k)$, $i = 1, 2$, $0 \leqslant k \leqslant 5$ sequences are

$$K_1(k) = K_2(k) = \{1.366, 1.366, 1.364, 1.333, 1.00\}$$
$$P_1(k) = P_2(k) = \{0.366, 0.366, 0.364, 0.333, 0.0\}$$

The controls $u_i(k) = u_i^l(k) + u_i^g(k)$, $i = 1, 2$ converge in 5 interactions to

$$u_1(k) = \{-0.866, 1.183, -1.611, 2.120, -1.696\}$$
$$u_2(k) = \{-1.366, 1.866, -2.544, 3.392, -3.392\}$$

## Chapter 5

**5.1** No fixed modes. System is stabilizable through decentralized control.

**5.2** System has no fixed modes, hence a decentralized control is possible. $\lambda\{A\} = (1, -1)$. $\eta = \min(n_c, n_o) = \min(1, 1) = 1$. The unknown augmented system's gain matrix is given by

$$K_\eta = K_1 = \begin{bmatrix} k_1 & 0 & h_1 \\ 0 & k_2 & 0 \\ \hline s_1 & 0 & f_1 \end{bmatrix}$$

with

$$A_1 + B_1 K_1 C_1 = \begin{bmatrix} 1+k_1 & 0 & | & h_1 \\ 0.5 & -1+k_2 & | & 0 \\ - - - - & - - - - & -|- - \\ s_1 & 0 & | & f_1 \end{bmatrix}$$

where

$$A_1 = \begin{bmatrix} 1 & 0 & 0 \\ 0.5 & -1 & 0 \\ 0 & 0 & 0 \end{bmatrix} \quad \text{and} \quad B_1 = C_1 = I_3$$

Let the desired poles of the closed-loop system be at $-3$, $-2$, and $-1$. For the first two poles $k_1 = -4$ and $k_2 = -1$. To find the other missing parameters the development of (5.3.31) of Example 5.3.4 can be repeated, i.e., use

$$\det\left\{ (\lambda - f_1) - (s_1 \quad 0)(\lambda I - A - BKC)^{-1}\binom{h_1}{0} \right\} = 0$$

to find $(\lambda - f_1 - s_1 h_1/2)|_{\lambda = -1} = 0$. Let $s_1 = h_1 = 2$ hence $f_1 = -2$. In summary the two decentralized control laws are

$$u_1 = 2z_1 - 4y_1, \quad \dot{z}_1 = -2z_1 + 2y_1, \quad z_1(0) = 0$$
$$u_2 = -y_2$$

**5.4** All three subsystems are completely controllable and $\lambda\{A_1\} = 0, 0.5,$ $\lambda\{A_2\} = -0.5$, and $\lambda\{A_3\} = \pm 0.894$, indicating that two of the three subsystems are unstable. The solutions of three subsystems' AMREs with $\delta = 0$ are

$$K_1 = \begin{bmatrix} 2.014 & 1.82 \\ 1.82 & 3.534 \end{bmatrix}, \quad K_2 = 0.6083$$

$$K_3 = \begin{bmatrix} 2.68 & -0.445 \\ -0.445 & 0.54 \end{bmatrix}$$

As the first trial, let $f_{11} = 0.1$, $f_{12} = -0.25$, $f_{13} = 0.3$, $f_{21} = -0.16$, $f_{22} = 0.5$, $f_{23} = 0.61$, $f_{31} = 0.2$, $f_{32} = 0.95$, and $f_{33} = -0.45$. These values lead to the following parameters $\eta_i$, $i = 1, 2, 3$ as defined by (5.3.161), i.e., $\eta_1 = 1.04$, $\eta_2 = 1.617$, and $\eta_3 = 1.98$. These values lead to the following closed-loop matrix:

$$A_c = \begin{bmatrix} -0.944 & -0.943 & -0.25 & 0.3 & 0.3 \\ 1 & 0.5 & 0 & 0 & 0 \\ -0.16 & 0 & -0.492 & 0.61 & 0.61 \\ 0.2 & 0 & 0.95 & -1.67 & -0.74 \\ 0.2 & 0 & 0.95 & -1.67 & -1.54 \end{bmatrix}$$

with $\lambda\{A_c\} = (-3.23, -0.1932 \pm j0.67, -0.3462, -0.1816)$. For a

$\delta = 0.1$

$$K_1 = \begin{bmatrix} 1.8033 & 1.3956 \\ 1.3956 & 1.54 \end{bmatrix}, \quad K_2 = 0.11$$

$$K_3 = \begin{bmatrix} 2.582 & -0.3106 \\ -0.3106 & 0.10 \end{bmatrix}$$

For this case $f_{11} = -0.4$, $f_{12} = -0.24$, $f_{13} = 0.351$, $f_{21} = -0.147$, $f_{22} = -0.324$, $f_{23} = 0.25$, $f_{31} = 0.28$, $f_{32} = -0.452$, and $f_{33} = -0.165$. The values of $\eta_i$ parameters are $\eta_1 = 1.0896$, $\eta_2 = 1.0271$, and $\eta_3 = 1.05085$. The closed-loop matrix is given by

$$A_c = \begin{bmatrix} -1.282 & -0.76035 & -0.24 & 0.351 & 0.351 \\ 1 & 0.6 & 0 & 0 & 0 \\ -0.147 & 0 & -0.7804 & 0.25 & 0.25 \\ 0.28 & 0 & -0.452 & -0.258 & -0.254 \\ 0.28 & 0 & -0.452 & -0.358 & -0.954 \end{bmatrix}$$

with $\lambda\{A_c\} = (-0.0908 \pm j0.263, -1.073 \pm j0.1387, -0.347)$. The results of these and a third trial are summarized below:

| No. | $\delta$ | $f_{ij}, j = 1,2,3$ and $i = 1,2,3$ | $\eta_1, \eta_2, \eta_3$ | Closed-Loop Poles |
|-----|----------|-------------------------------------|--------------------------|-------------------|
| 1 | 0 | $f_{11} = 0.1, f_{12} = -0.25, f_{13} = 0.3$ <br> $f_{21} = -0.16, f_{22} = 0.5, f_{23} = 0.61$ <br> $f_{31} = 0.2, f_{32} = 0.95, f_{33} = -0.45$ | 1.04 <br> 1.617 <br> 1.98 | $-3.23, -0.1932 \pm j0.67$ <br> $-0.3462,$ <br> $-0.1816$ |
| 2 | 0 | $-2.0, -0.5, 0.1$ <br> $0.63, 0.25, -0.1$ <br> $-0.45, 0.353, 0.9$ | 17.063 <br> 1.1618 <br> 3.681 | $-18.3, -0.282,$ <br> $-1.26 \pm j0.55,$ <br> $-0.639$ |
| 3 | 0.1 | $-0.4, -0.24, 0.351$ <br> $-0.147, -0.324, 0.25$ <br> $0.28, -0.452, -0.165$ | 1.0896 <br> 1.0271 <br> 1.05085 | $-0.0908 \pm j0.263,$ <br> $-1.073 \pm j0.1387$ <br> $-0.347$ |

**C5.8**  The two AMRE's (5.3.112) result in

$$K_1 = \begin{bmatrix} 95.2 & 14 \\ 14 & 7 \end{bmatrix}, \quad K_2 = \begin{bmatrix} 239.4 & 27 \\ 27 & 9 \end{bmatrix}$$

$\lambda\{K_1\} = (4.83, 97.37)$ and $\lambda\{K_2\} = (5.88, 242.5)$ with

$$P_i = Q_i + K_i S_i K_i, \quad i = 1,2$$

$$P_1 = \begin{bmatrix} 198 & 98 \\ 98 & 51 \end{bmatrix}, \quad P_2 = \begin{bmatrix} 731 & 243 \\ 243 & 83 \end{bmatrix}$$

and $\lambda\{P_1\} = (2, 247)$, $\lambda\{P_2\} = (2, 812)$. To check the condition (5.3.123) one has

$$\min_i \lambda_m(P_i) = 2, \quad \max_i \lambda_M(K_i) = 242.5,$$

$$\gamma = \lambda_M^{1/2}(G^T G) = \sqrt{0.29} = 0.539$$

thus since $\min_i \lambda_m(P_i) < 2\gamma \lambda_M(K_i)$ the required conditions are not satisfied. Although the eigenvalues of the closed-loop system

$$\lambda \begin{bmatrix} A_1 - S_1 K_1 & G_{12} \\ G_{21} & A_2 - S_2 K_2 \end{bmatrix}$$

$$= (-6.63, \ -1.1396, \ -3.2409, \ -4.988)$$

indicating that the system has been stabilized, but it is not exponentially so. Under this condition a new value of $\alpha$ can be assumed and the process be repeated.

**5.10** The proof is essentially the same as that of Theorem 5.6 except for replacing $\dot{K}_i$ in (5.3.155) by 0 which would, in turn, be replaced by the left-hand side of Equation (5.3.159). This is a limiting case for Theorem 5.6.

**C5.11** The eigenvalues of $A$ are $\lambda\{A\} = (-3.81, \ -0.83, \ -0.26, \ 0, \ 2.38)$. A $2 \times 3$ decomposition of the system is suggested, where the submatrices are already in controllable canonical forms. The eigenvalues $\lambda\{A_1\} = (2, \ -1)$ and $\lambda\{A_2\} = (0.31 \pm j0.42, \ -3.62)$. For the desired eigenvalues of $A_i$, $i = 1,2$ the gains vectors are $k_1^T = [-4 \quad -4]$ and $k_2^T = [-259 \quad -128 \quad -17]$. The two closed-loop matrices are

$$\hat{A}_1 = \begin{bmatrix} 0 & 1 \\ -2 & -3 \end{bmatrix}, \quad \hat{A}_2 = \begin{bmatrix} 0 & 1 & 0 \\ 0 & 0 & 1 \\ -260 & -126 & -20 \end{bmatrix}$$

The $M_i$ modal matrices are

$$M_1 = \begin{bmatrix} 0.44721 & -0.70711 \\ -0.89443 & -0.70711 \end{bmatrix}$$

$$M_2 = \begin{bmatrix} 0.035503 & 0.014793 & -0.00995 \\ -0.19231 & -0.038462 & -0.0995 \\ 1 & 0 & -0.995 \end{bmatrix}$$

Then the interconnected subsystem is

$$\begin{bmatrix} \dot{\hat{x}}_1 \\ \hline \dot{\hat{x}}_2 \end{bmatrix}$$

$$= \begin{bmatrix} -2 & 0 & | & -0.123 & -0.0246 & -0.064 \\ 0 & -1 & | & -0.1943 & -0.039 & -0.10 \\ \hline -12.3 & -9.7 & | & -5 & 1 & 25.07 \\ -11.9 & -9.4 & | & -1 & -5 & -73.6 \\ 28.35 & 22.42 & | & 0 & 0 & -10 \end{bmatrix} \begin{bmatrix} \hat{x}_1 \\ \hline \hat{x}_2 \end{bmatrix}$$

which provide eigenvalues $-11.97$, $-4.7 \pm j4.32$, $-1.61$, and $0.003067$ indicating that the system has not been stabilized yet. To check the Sevastyanov–Kotelyanski condition it is noted that

$$\alpha_1 = \min\{|-1|, |-2|\} = 1, \quad \alpha_2 = 5$$

$$\hat{\gamma}_{12} = \lambda_M^{1/2}\left\{ \hat{G}_{12}^T\left( I_1 - \hat{b}_1\left(\hat{b}_1^T\hat{b}_1\right)^{-1}\hat{b}_1^T \right) \right.$$

$$\left. \left( I_1 - \hat{b}_1\left(\hat{b}_1\left(\hat{b}_1^T\hat{b}_1\right)^{-1}\hat{b}_1^T\right)\hat{G}_{12} \right\} = \sqrt{0.0691} = 0.2629$$

and

$$\hat{\gamma}_{21} = \sqrt{1781.7} = 42.2107$$

Hence,

$$\hat{S} = \begin{bmatrix} -1 & 0.2629 \\ 42.2107 & -5 \end{bmatrix}$$

which violates the condition (5.3.93). At this point the algorithm can be repeated by choosing a different set of eigenvalues for $\hat{A}_1$, say $\lambda\{\hat{A}_1\} = (-3, -2)$. The new final form of the closed-loop system will be

$$\dot{x} = \begin{bmatrix} -2 & 0 & -0.0165 & -0.0033 & -0.0086 \\ 0 & -3 & 0.0827 & 0.0165 & 0.0428 \\ -12.3 & -9.7 & -5 & 1 & 25.07 \\ -11.9 & -9.4 & -1 & -5 & -73.6 \\ 28.35 & 22.42 & 0 & 0 & -10 \end{bmatrix} \hat{x}$$

Its eigenvalues are $-8.64 \pm j1.129$, $-1.853$ and $-2.936 \pm j1.78$ which has resulted a stable closed-loop system. The new $\hat{S}$ matrix is

$$\hat{S} = \begin{bmatrix} -2 & 0.0964 \\ 42.120 & -5 \end{bmatrix}$$

which result in (a) $(-1)^1(-2) = 2 > 0$ and $(-1)^2|\hat{S}| = 5.94 > 0$ hence satisfying the conditions (5.3.93).

**5.12** Using Equations (5.4.3), $T_1(1,1) = 2$, $T_1(1,2) = 0.5$, $T_1(2,1) = 0$, and $T_2(2,2) = 1.5$. By Algorithm 5.5, $y^1 = [2 \quad 0.5]$, $y^2 = [0 \quad 1.5]$.

**5.15** Let $\lambda_1 = 0$ and since $K_i = I_{ri}$, (5.4.3) can be used instead of (5.4.4) to find the steady-state tracking parameters. $T_1(1,1; 1) = 3$, $T_1(1,2; 1) = -2$, $T_1(2,1; 1) = 4$ and $T_1(2,2; 1) = 2$. The rank conditions of Theorem 5.9 are satisfied and hence a decentralized robust controller can be used for the system.

**C5.16** The tracking parameters are $T_1(1,1) = 1.5$, $T_1(1,2) = 0.5$, $T_1(2,1) = 0.525$, and $T_1(2,2) = 0.525$. Let $u_1 = -\alpha_1[T_1(1,1)]^{-1}\eta_1 = -0.667\alpha_1\eta_1$

with $\dot{\eta}_1 = e_1 = x_1 + x_2 + u_1 - 1$. The closed-loop system after tuning the first regulator is

$$
\begin{bmatrix} \dot{x}_1 \\ \dot{x}_2 \\ \dot{\eta}_1 \end{bmatrix} = \begin{bmatrix} -1 & 0.1 & -0.667\alpha_1 \\ 0 & -1 & 0 \\ 1 & 1 & -0.667\alpha_1 \end{bmatrix} \begin{bmatrix} x_1 \\ x_2 \\ \eta_1 \end{bmatrix} + \begin{bmatrix} 0 \\ 0 \\ -1 \end{bmatrix}
$$

A one-dimensional search on $\lambda\{A_c\}$ for $\alpha_1$ provides an $\alpha_1^* = 10$ with $\lambda\{A_c\} = (-5, -2.66, -1)$. Then tuning the second controller $u_2 = -1.9\alpha_2\eta_2 = x_1 + x_2 - 1$ would provide

$$
\begin{bmatrix} \dot{x}_1 \\ \dot{x}_2 \\ \dot{\eta}_1 \\ \dot{\eta}_2 \end{bmatrix} = \begin{bmatrix} -1 & 0.1 & -6.67 & 0 \\ 0 & -1 & 0 & -1.9\alpha_2 \\ 1 & 1 & -6.67 & 0 \\ 1 & 1 & 0 & 0 \end{bmatrix} \begin{bmatrix} x_1 \\ x_2 \\ \eta_1 \\ \eta_2 \end{bmatrix} + \begin{bmatrix} 0 \\ 0 \\ -1 \\ -1 \end{bmatrix}
$$

once again after a one-dimensional search a set of $\alpha_2$ values are obtained by

| $\alpha_2$ | $\lambda\{A_c\}$ |
|---|---|
| 0.1 | $-5.03, -2.55, -1.11, -0.9806$ |
| 0.5 | $-5.12, -0.775 \pm j0.2827, -2.0015$ |
| 1 | $-5.209, -1.09 \pm j0.95, -1.2817$ |
| 10 | $-0.862 \pm j4.564, -5.84, -1.107$ |

where a good choice would be $\alpha_2^* = 0.5$ where a pair of complex conjugate dominant closed-loop poles can be realized for a reasonable time response speed and regulation.

# Chapter 6

## C6.1

$$\lambda\{A\} = \{-0.1 \pm j, -2, -5\}, \quad l = 2.$$

$$
M_l = \begin{bmatrix} 0.2902 & 0.9415 \\ -0.9705 & 0.1961 \end{bmatrix}, \quad P = \begin{bmatrix} I_2 & \vdots & 0_2 \end{bmatrix}
$$

$$
C = M_l P M^{-1} = \begin{bmatrix} 0.66 & -0.126 & -0.347 & -0.06 \\ 0.6 & 1.2 & 0.605 & 0.08 \end{bmatrix}
$$

The aggregated model is given by

$$
(F, G) = \left( \begin{bmatrix} 0 & 1 \\ -1.01 & -0.2 \end{bmatrix}, \begin{bmatrix} 0 \\ 0.1 \end{bmatrix} \right)
$$

$$
Q_a = \begin{bmatrix} 2.532 & -0.526 \\ 0.46 & 0.944 \end{bmatrix}, \quad K_a = \begin{bmatrix} 8.207 & 1.246 \\ 1.246 & 7.27 \end{bmatrix}
$$

aggregated (near-optimum) control is given by

$$u^a = - R^{-1}G^T K_a Cx = -[\,0.515 \quad 0.854 \quad 0.4 \quad 0.05\,]x$$

The optimum control resulted from the solution of a $4 \times 4$ AMRE is given by,

$$u^* = - R^{-1}B^T Kx = -[\,0.05 \quad 1.51 \quad 1.305 \quad 0.445\,]x$$

which is somewhat different from $u^a(t)$.

**6.2**  Degenerate system equations are

$$\dot{K} = -2K - K^2 + 1, \quad \hat{P} = K\hat{x}$$
$$\dot{\hat{x}} = -\hat{x} + \hat{z} + \hat{p} + \hat{q}, \quad \hat{z} = \hat{p} + \hat{q}$$
$$\hat{q} = \hat{p} - \hat{z}.$$

Zeroth-order left-hand boundary layer terms are

$$L_o x(\tau) = L_o z(\tau) = (1 - \hat{z}(0))e^{-\tau} \quad \text{and} \quad L_o p(\tau) = L_o q(\tau) = 0$$

For the case of time-invariant system, $K = 0.414$, $\hat{x}(t) = e^{-0.172t}$, $\hat{u}(t) = 0.414\, e^{-0.172t}$.

**C6.3**  The results of Algorithm 6.1 are given step by step.

Step 0: $K_1^0 = \begin{bmatrix} 0.1961 & 0.0031 \\ 0.0031 & 1.000 \end{bmatrix}$, $K_2^0 = \begin{bmatrix} 0.9956 & 0.0658 \\ 0.0658 & 0.9115 \end{bmatrix}$

Step 1: $G_1 = \begin{bmatrix} -5.2 & 0.097 \\ 0 & -1 \end{bmatrix}$, $G_2 = \begin{bmatrix} -0.5 & 0.1 \\ -0.066 & -1.011 \end{bmatrix}$

let $\varepsilon = 0.01$

$$F_{12}^0 = \begin{bmatrix} 0 & -0.196 \\ 0.33 & 4.554 \end{bmatrix}, \quad \text{then}$$

$$K_{12}^1 = \begin{bmatrix} 0.000365 & -0.031592 \\ 0.119971 & 2.26862 \end{bmatrix}$$

Step 2: Using Algorithm 6.2 to solve the Lyapunov equations (6.2.46) leads to

$$K_1^2 = \begin{bmatrix} -1.921 \times 10^{-4} & -2.786 \times 10^{-2} \\ -2.786 \times 10^{-2} & 17.5372 \end{bmatrix}$$

with

$$F_1^1 = \begin{bmatrix} -0.002 & -0.172 \\ -0.172 & 35.08 \end{bmatrix}$$

$$K_2^2 = \begin{bmatrix} 4.0905 \times 10^{-4} & -3.10692 \times 10^{-3} \\ -3.107 \times 10^{-3} & 6.1176 \times 10^{-2} \end{bmatrix}$$

with

$$F_2^1 = \begin{bmatrix} -2.67 \times 10^{-7} & -7.076 \times 10^{-4} \\ -7.076 \times 10^{-4} & 0.12437 \end{bmatrix}$$

Step 3: $F_{12}^2 = \begin{bmatrix} 0 & -1.9209 \times 10^{-4} \\ -0.01553 & 0.3337 \end{bmatrix}$

and

$$K_{12}^3 = \begin{bmatrix} 3.57785 \times 10^{-7} & -3.09388 \times 10^{-5} \\ -3.0636 \times 10^{-3} & -1.66067 \times 10^{-1} \end{bmatrix}$$

Step 4: Solutions of Lyapunov equations for $K_i^4$, $i = 1, 2$ are

$$K_1^4 = \begin{bmatrix} -1.842 \times 10^{-10} & -5.16 \times 10^{-5} \\ -5.16 \times 10^{-5} & -1.688 \end{bmatrix}$$

with

$$F_1^3 = \begin{bmatrix} -1.914 \times 10^{-9} & -3.19 \times 10^{-4} \\ -3.19 \times 10^{-4} & -3.376 \end{bmatrix}$$

$$K_2^4 = \begin{bmatrix} 4.0826 \times 10^{-7} & -3.099 \times 10^{-6} \\ -3.099 \times 10^{-6} & 6.087 \times 10^{-5} \end{bmatrix}$$

with

$$F_2^3 = \begin{bmatrix} -2.56 \times 10^{-3} & -7.155 \times 10^{-7} \\ -7.155 \times 10^{-7} & -1.24 \times 10^{-4} \end{bmatrix}$$

Then

$$P = K^0 + \varepsilon K^1 + \varepsilon^2 K^2/2! + \varepsilon^3 K^3/3! + \varepsilon^4 K^4/4!$$

$$= \begin{bmatrix} 0.19615 & 0.00316 & 3.653 \times 10^{-6} & -3.1592 \times 10^{-4} \\ 0.00316 & 1.00119 & 1.1997 \times 10^{-3} & 0.022686 \\ 3.653 \times 10^{-6} & 1.1997 \times 10^{-3} & 0.995661 & 0.06587 \\ -3.1592 \times 10^{-4} & 0.022686 & 0.06587 & 0.91152 \end{bmatrix}$$

and

$$u^a(t) = -R^{-1}B^T P x$$

$$= -\begin{bmatrix} 0.19615 & 0.003164 & 3.653 \times 10^{-6} & -3.1592 \times 10^{-4} \\ -3.1592 \times 10^{-4} & 0.022686 & 0.06587 & 0.91152 \end{bmatrix} x$$

Next, the optimum control was obtained using a fourth-order AMRE; the exact Riccati matrix turned out to be

$$K = \begin{bmatrix} 0.19615 & 0.00316 & 3.65 \times 10^{-6} & -3.16 \times 10^{-4} \\ 0.00316 & 1.001 & 0.001199 & 0.02268 \\ 3.65 \times 10^{-6} & 0.001199 & 0.996 & 0.0659 \\ -3.16 \times 10^{-4} & 0.02268 & 0.0659 & 0.911528 \end{bmatrix}$$

which is essentially identical to $P$. The optimum control $u^*(t)$ turns out to be almost exactly as $u^a(t)$. Note that as it was mentioned in Section 6.2.2.a, the near-optimum cost $J^a = \frac{1}{2}x_o^T P x_o$ approximates $J^* = \frac{1}{2}x_o^T K x_o$ up to $2m + 1 = 9$ terms.

**C6.7** Rewrite the state equations

$$\dot{x} = -x + u + \varepsilon(y - x(t - 0.1))$$
$$\dot{y} = -0.5y + v + \varepsilon(-10x - 10y(t - 0.1))$$

$\varepsilon = 0.1$, $x(a) = y(a) = -1$, $-0.1 \leqslant a \leqslant 0$. The decoupled systems zeroth-order Riccati matrices are $K^o = 0.414213562$, $P^o = 0.618033989$ leading to $u^o = -0.414213562x$, $v^o = -0.618033989y$, $x^o(t) = -e^{-1.414t}$, $y^o(t) = -e^{-1.118t}$, $p^o(t) = 0.414214e^{-1.414t}$, $q^o(t) = 0.618034e^{-1.118t}$. The first-order adjoint vectors are

$$g_x^1(t) = 0.6525e^{1.414t} + 0.5229e^{-1.414t} - 7.9130e^{-1.118t} \cdots 0 \leqslant t < 0.9$$

$$= -0.6024e^{-1.414t} + 0.0346e^{1.414t} \cdots 0.9 \leqslant t \leqslant 1$$

$$g_y^1(t) = 8.042e^{-1.414t} + 0.756e^{-1.118t} - 1.1509e^{1.118t} \cdots 0 \leqslant t < 0.9$$

$$= 0.90362e^{1.118t} - 8.454e^{-1.118t} \cdots 0.9 \leqslant t \leqslant 1$$

Thus,

$$u \approx -0.414x - 0.414g_x^1$$
$$v \approx -0.618y - 0.618g_y^1$$

**6.8** Full model's Riccati matrix is

$$K_f = \begin{bmatrix} 0.0826 & 0.0190 & 0.0014 & 0.00320 & 0.0086 \\ 0.0190 & 0.0074 & 0.00055 & 0.0013 & 0.0036 \\ 0.0014 & 0.00055 & 0.00035 & 0.00067 & 0.00134 \\ 0.00320 & 0.0013 & 0.00067 & 0.00134 & 0.0048 \\ 0.0086 & 0.0036 & 0.00134 & 0.0048 & 0.0197 \end{bmatrix}$$

Aggregated model's Riccati matrix is

$$K_a = \begin{bmatrix} 0.0407 & 0.0072 \\ 0.0072 & 0.0016 \end{bmatrix}$$

with aggregation matrix

$$C = \begin{bmatrix} 1 & 0 & -0.004 & -0.00224 & -0.336 \\ 0 & 1 & 0.115 & 0.404 & 3.22 \end{bmatrix}$$

using $x_o^T = (0.5 \quad 0 \quad 0 \quad 0 \quad 0)$, one has $0.00508707 \leqslant J \leqslant 0.0102014668$.

# Chapter 7

**7.2** $v_1(x) = -\frac{2}{15}x_1^6$, $w_1(x) = \frac{4}{5}x_1^2$, $v_2(x) = -\frac{1}{30}x_2^6$, $w_1(x) = \frac{1}{5}x_1^5$. Let $a_1 = a_2 = 1$, $g_1(x, t) = \frac{1}{4}\psi_1(x_1) + \hat{g}_1(x, t) = -\frac{1}{5}x_1^5 - \frac{1}{10}x_2^5$, $g_2(x, t) = \frac{1}{4}\psi_2(x_2) + \hat{g}_2(x, t) = -\frac{1}{20}x_2^5 + \frac{2}{5}x_1^5$, $b_{11} = b_{22} = 0.25$ and $b_{12} = b_{21} = 0.5$. The resulting $E$ matrix is

$$E = \begin{bmatrix} 0.75 & -0.5 \\ -0.5 & 0.75 \end{bmatrix}$$

which is an $M$-matrix. All three conditions of Theorem 7.1 hold and the system is uniformly asymptotically stable i.s.L.

**7.4** The first condition of Theorem 7.5 would give gain $(G_1) = \alpha_1 = 0.5 < \infty$ and gain $(G_2) = \alpha_2 = 1 < \infty$. The second condition is satisfied by noting that $\beta_{11} = 1$, $\beta_{12} = 0.5$, $\beta_{21} = 0.8$, and $\beta_{22} = 0.4$. The final condition leads to a $2 \times 2$ matrix $B$,

$$B = \begin{bmatrix} 0.5 & -0.25 \\ -0.8 & 0.6 \end{bmatrix}$$

which is an $M$-matrix. Hence by Theorem 7.5, the system is I/O stable.

**7.7** Proof is very similar to that of Theorem 7.1

**7.8** The proof follows that of Theorem 7.6 identically.

**7.10** Using $Q_1 = I_3$ and $Q_2 = 2I_3$ the solutions of the Lyapunov equations (7.2.54) are

$$P_1 = \begin{bmatrix} 0.337 & 0.0121 & 0.0236 \\ 0.0121 & 0.180 & -0.037 \\ 0.0236 & -0.037 & 0.2456 \end{bmatrix}$$

$$P_2 = \begin{bmatrix} 0.2513 & 0.04 & -0.0102 \\ 0.040 & 0.522 & 0.02 \\ -0.0102 & 0.02 & 0.2008 \end{bmatrix}$$

then

$$\lambda\{P_1\} = (0.3431, 0.1606, 0.259)$$
$$\lambda\{P_2\} = (0.249, 0.196, 0.528)$$
$$L_1 = 0.856, \quad L_2 = 1.193$$

$$G_{12}^T G_{12} = \begin{bmatrix} 0.09 & 0.09 & 0.12 \\ 0.09 & 0.11 & 0.15 \\ 0.12 & 0.15 & 0.21 \end{bmatrix}, \quad G_{21}^T G_{21} = \begin{bmatrix} 1.25 & 0 & 1.5 \\ 0 & 1 & 0 \\ 1.5 & 0 & 2 \end{bmatrix}$$

the $\xi_{12} = 0.626$, $\xi_{21} = 1.78$, $s_{11} = s_{22} = -1$,
$s_{12} = 2L_1 \lambda_M^{1/2}(P_2)\lambda_m^{-1}(Q_2)\xi_{12} = 0.390$,
$s_{21} = 2L_2 \lambda_M^{1/2}(P_1)\lambda_m^{-1}(Q_1)\xi_{21} = 2.475$; then

$$(-1)^2 \begin{vmatrix} -1 & 0.39 \\ 2.475 & -1 \end{vmatrix} > 0$$

Thus the system is asymptotically connectively stable.

**C7.11** $\lambda(A_1) = (-1.0507, -0.504, -0.00453)$ and $\lambda(A_2) = (-0.3, 0.15)$ with rank $(P_2(\lambda_1^2)) = n_2 = 2$, rank $(P_2(\lambda_2^2)) = n_1 = 3$. The system is controllable with

$$\text{rank}\left(P_1(\lambda_2^1)\right)$$

$$= \text{rank} \begin{bmatrix} -0.496 & 0.1 & 0.5 & 0 & 0 & 1 \\ 0 & 0.004 & 0.1 & 0 & 0 & 0.2 \\ 0.1 & 0 & 0.404 & 0 & 0 & 0.4 \\ 0.1 & 0 & 0.1 & 0.604 & -0.2 & 0 \\ 0 & 0.2 & 0 & -0.1 & 0.254 & 1 \end{bmatrix}$$

$$= 5 = n_1 + n_2$$

similarly rank $(P_1(\lambda_3^1)) = 5$. Also for observability rank $(Q_1(\lambda_i^1))$ $= n_1 = 3$ for $i = 1,2,3$ and rank $(Q_2(\lambda_i^2)) = 5$. Thus the system is also observable.

**C7.12** System is both controllable and observable.

**7.14** $\begin{vmatrix} B & AB \end{vmatrix} = a - b + 1$ and $\begin{vmatrix} C^T & A^T C^T \end{vmatrix} = -a + b + 1$; hence the system is both controllable and observable everywhere on the $b - a$ plane except on the lines shown in Figure P7.14.

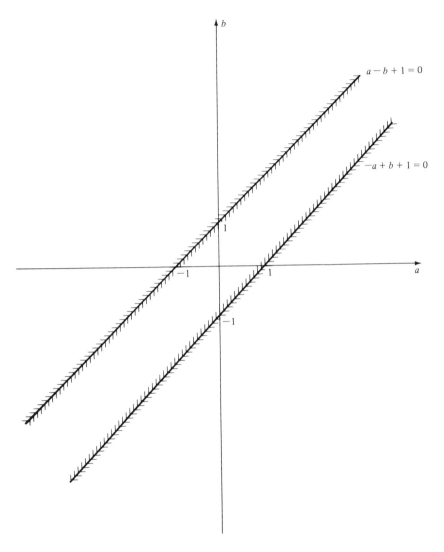

**Figure P7.14**

**7.16** $N = M = 7$. The $A_i$, $i = 1, 2$ matrices are

$$
A_1 = \begin{bmatrix}
x & x & x & 0 & 0 & 0 \\
x & x & x & 0 & 0 & 0 \\
0 & x & x & 0 & 0 & x \\
x & x & x & 0 & 0 & x \\
x & x & 0 & \circledx & x & x \\
x & x & x & x & x & x
\end{bmatrix}
$$

$$A_2 = \begin{bmatrix} 0 & x & 0 & 0 & \textcircled{x} & x & 0 \\ x & x & x & 0 & 0 & 0 & 0 \\ x & x & x & 0 & 0 & 0 & 0 \\ 0 & x & x & 0 & 0 & 0 & x \\ x & x & x & 0 & 0 & 0 & x \\ x & x & 0 & 0 & x & x & x \\ x & x & x & x & x & x & x \end{bmatrix}$$

and

$$A_1^{(2)} = \begin{bmatrix} x & x & x & 0 \\ x & x & x & 0 \\ 0 & x & x & \textcircled{x} \\ x & x & x & x \end{bmatrix}, \quad A_2^{(3)} = \begin{bmatrix} x & x & x \\ x & x & x \\ x & x & x \end{bmatrix}$$

where pivot elements for $A_1^{(1)}$, $A_2^{(2)}$, and $A_2^{(2)}$ were chosen at locations (5,4), (5,5), and (5,4), respectively. The generic rank is given by $gr(A) = \text{Max}(1 + gr(A_1), gr(A_2)) = \text{Max}(7,7) = 7(g) = 7$.

**7.17** $gr(A_1) = 8(g)$, $gr(A_2) = 9(g)$, $gr(A) = \text{Max}[1 + gr(A_1), gr(A_2)] = 9$.

**7.18** The generic ranks are $gr(A, B) = 5 = n$, $gr(\frac{A}{C}) = 5$. The graph of the system has nine vertices and the system is both input and output connectable. Thus both sets of conditions of Theorem 7.16 and Corollary 7.1 are satisfied leading to the conclusion that the system is structurally controllable as well as observable.

**C7.19** Choose an arbitrary gain matrix

$$K(t) = \begin{bmatrix} 1 & 0 & 1 \\ 0 & 1 & 1 \end{bmatrix}$$

then

$$\hat{A}_2(t) = A_2 + B_2 K(t) = \begin{bmatrix} 0.2 & 0 & 1.2 \\ 0 & -1 & 1.2 \\ 0 & 0.1 & 0 \end{bmatrix}$$

$$\hat{A}_{12}(t) = \begin{bmatrix} 1.2 & 1 & 1.7 \\ -0.3 & 2 & 1.3 \end{bmatrix}$$

$$\hat{A}_o(t) \begin{bmatrix} -1.284 & -1.974 \\ -0.521 & -1.25 \end{bmatrix}, \quad \hat{B}_o(t) = \begin{bmatrix} 1.19 & 0.762 \\ -0.44 & 1.5 \end{bmatrix}$$

then $(\hat{A}_o, \hat{B}_o)$ is controllable. The boundary layer system is controllable since rank $\left( B_2 \mid A_2 B_2 \mid A_2^2 B_2 \right) = 3$ by Theorem 7.18.

# Author Index

# Subject Index